The Customary of

Our Lady of Walsingham

© The Personal Ordinariate of Our Lady of Walsingham 2012

Imprimatur: Keith Newton,
Ordinary of the Personal Ordinariate
of Our Lady of Walsingham.
The Solemnity of SS Peter and Paul,
29th June 2012.

First published in 2012 by the Canterbury Press Norwich
Editorial office
Invicta House
108–114 Golden Lane,
London, EC1Y 0TG

Canterbury Press is an imprint of Hymns Ancient and Modern Ltd
(a registered charity)
13a Hellesdon Park Road,
Norwich, NR6 5DR

www.canterburypress.co.uk

Acknowledgements to copyright holders of published texts are
on the last pages of this volume.

978 1 84825 122 9

Printed in Great Britain by
CPI Group (UK) Ltd, Croydon

CONTENTS

INTRODUCTION

THE APOSTOLIC CONSTITUTION, *Anglicanorum cœtibus*, published on 4th November 2009, led to the erection, on 15th January 2011, of the first of the Personal Ordinariates, the Ordinariate of Our Lady of Walsingham, established for England and Wales, but making provision, at least for the time being, for groups in Scotland too. Since then, whilst this *Customary* has been in preparation, two further Ordinariates have been announced. On 1st January 2012, the Personal Ordinariate of the Chair of St Peter was erected. Established for the United States of America, provision was made too for Ordinariate groups emerging in Canada. On 15th June 2012, the Personal Ordinariate of Our Lady of the Southern Cross was established for Australia. The inspiration is the parable of the mustard seed (Mt 13:31). May this smallest of seeds, a new strategy for ecumenism, become a fruitful and mighty tree.

Those entering the full communion of the Catholic Church by means of the Ordinariates bring with them many riches, as the Holy Father, Pope Benedict XVI, has frequently said. As Western Catholics they share in the fullness of the Roman Rite. They discover afresh that much of the liturgical patrimony of Anglicanism derives from earlier ages, when those in communion with the See of Canterbury were also in communion with the See of Rome. They discover, furthermore, in the *Book of Divine Worship*, in use in parts of North America, much that derives from the last 500 years, that is, since the Reformation and the break in communion with the Holy See. Chief amidst the treasures of this tradition, the fragments of a broken vase, as it were, is a rich and deeply resonant liturgical language, a residual sacral dialect and not a new one. It is the language of Thomas Cranmer and of the King James Bible, but it is also the language of Bishop Challoner's *The Garden of the Soul*, and his mid-eighteenth century revision of the Douai-Rheims Bible.

The Customary of Our Lady of Walsingham

The liturgical books which will replace the *Book of Divine Worship* will take several years to emerge if they are to serve the developing Ordinariates worthily. *The Customary of Our Lady of Walsingham* is a first step, as the Ordinariates are established, to bring into the discussion and exchange something of the experience of England and Wales, which is, after all, the motherland of the Prayer Book tradition. Though some of the insights and reflections of those who have been using the *Book of Divine Worship* are also reflected here, the main task for British Ordinariate Catholics is surely now to catch up with the pioneers of earlier years. In so doing, we hope that this collection, permitted by a simple *Imprimatur* for daily devotion and worship in the Personal Ordinariate of Our Lady of Walsingham, will commend itself, and be of interest and use, as appropriate, and however temporarily, throughout the English-speaking world. It is right and just – indeed meet and right, in the words of the Prayer Book - that this Customary is published in the 350th anniversary year of the Book of Common Prayer (1662).

Liturgical Developments since 1970

The *Book of Divine Worship* (published in 2003) contained the liturgical resources of American former Anglicans, who, since 1980, have come corporately into the Catholic Church as part of the Pastoral Provision. Since it had its origin in the United States of America, its Anglican resources were drawn from the Episcopalian Prayer Books of 1928 and 1979. These Prayer Books belong to the Book of Common Prayer family, and have their origin in the work of Thomas Cranmer in the sixteenth century. Nevertheless, from the seventeenth century onwards, there has been a history of divergence between the English Prayer Book tradition, and the Scottish and American Prayer Book tradition. Accordingly, the English Book of Common Prayer, proposed in 1928, but not accepted by the British Parliament, and the *Alternative Service Book* of 1980, two landmarks of liturgical reform in the Church of England, read somewhat differently from their American counterparts of a similar period (1928 and 1979). Australian liturgical reform has its own history. Known until half a century ago as 'the Church of England in Australia and Tasmania', the Anglican Church of Australia retained the English Book of Common Prayer. *An Australian Prayer Book* (1978), was a conservative revision, an example, on another continent, of continuing liturgical ferment. Some of this ferment can be attributed to an over-optimistic view regarding ecumenical convergence in liturgical theology, reflected in consensual ecumenical English liturgical texts,[1] and some to the continuing reverberations of the Catholic liturgical revolution following the Second Vatican Council.

A further consideration is that many of those who remained in communion with the See of Canterbury until the beginning of the second decade of the

---

[1] The texts of the English Language Liturgical Consultation, *Praying Together* (1998), were in wide use ecumenically. The Church of England was not able to use them without alteration. They were discarded by the International Commission on English in the Liturgy: the Roman Missal (2010) uses a different principle of translation, as we go on to describe.

third millennium, a generation later than the pioneers of the Pastoral Provision in the United States, have benefited from a third landmark of liturgical reform in the Church of England, and equivalent work throughout the Anglican Communion,[2] the *Common Worship* anthology, which began to appear at the turn of the millennium. The importance of the English collection is not only in what it contains but also in its policy, very different from liturgical revision in England in the 1970s, though preserved in the Episcopalian Book of Common Prayer of 1979, of giving old and new something approaching an equal voice. This is one part of a much wider cultural shift, as evidenced by the replacement of the dynamic equivalent translations of the Roman Liturgy of forty years ago by a new English translation which is more faithful to the Latin, and more self-consciously sacral in style. In a word, the policy of wholesale modernisation, one interpretation of *aggiornamento*, has now been replaced by bringing out of the treasure-house 'what is new and what is old' (Mt 10:52).

Issues of Language and Translation

Nevertheless there is a desire not to create a needless pluriformity of liturgical use and, because a new English translation of the Roman Missal had only just emerged, using a form of English which is once contemporary and sacral, the decision has been taken not to encourage the cacophony of another contemporary dialect. Though the *Book of Divine Worship* had included both traditional and contemporary language orders, this *Customary* is mainly in traditional language. There are some exceptions to this, as there always will be with liturgy as a living expression of worship, but the occasional use of modern texts and translations is set within the framework of traditional liturgies.

On 8th March, 2001, the Congregation for Divine Worship and the Discipline of the Sacraments issued *Liturgiam authenticam*.[3] It concerned the use of vernacular languages in the publication of the books of the Roman Liturgy and has been the controlling document, for a decade, for all that has been produced in English. It is in the spirit of *Liturgiam authenticam* that the version of Holy Scripture on which this *Customary* relies is the *Revised Standard Version* (RSV), a version which is firmly within the English tradition of Bible translation – justly commemorated 400 years after the *Authorised Version* of 1611 – and which, through the good offices of the Catholic Biblical Association of Great Britain, was published as an ecumenical text

---

[2] for example, *A Prayer Book for Australia* (1995)
[3] The Fifth Instruction 'for the right implementation of the Constitution on the Sacred Liturgy of the Second Vatican Council' (*Sacrosanctum Concilium*, art. 36) *Liturgiam authenticam*.

in the mid-1960s. This text received recognition in the United States of America, the country which had produced, in the *American Standard Version* of 1901, itself a revision of the King James Bible. In essence, there is a tradition of biblical expression – a common memory – from which some other versions, however excellent they be as regards dynamic equivalent accuracy and narrative power, diverge. More recently, in the 1990s, the same tradition has produced the *New Revised Standard Version* (NRSV), also available as a Catholic edition. This version has received high acclaim but there remain some unresolved issues in areas in which *Liturgiam authenticam* prescribes a different, and more literal, translation policy. A specific concern has been the use of 'inclusive language' in English, where, strictly speaking, this interprets in a particular way, rather than translates, what is found in the Hebrew and Greek originals. Whilst these issues continue to be addressed, the Congregation for Divine Worship and the Discipline of the Sacraments has issued a decree permitting the use of the RSV Lectionary, Second Catholic Edition,[4] copies of which were generously donated to the Personal Ordinariate of Our Lady of Walsingham by private benefactors from all over the world.[5]

The proclamation of Scripture needs to be urgent and contemporary, as well as resonant of the tradition. The RSV, Second Catholic Edition, like the NRSV, adopts the well-established usage in liturgical English of addressing God in the modern second person.[6] The prayers for the liturgy in the *Customary*, however, for the most part do not follow that usage, but, in practice, as in hymns and prayers generally, not to mention the whole corpus of English poetry, little is lost and much is gained by occasional differences in language register.

Psalmody
An area in which there will be inevitable pluriformity is the psalter. The fundamental psalter for this *Customary* is the Miles Coverdale version of 1535 which, partly through accident and partly through decision, has remained the psalter of the Book of Common Prayer tradition to the present day and which

---

[4] 15th February 2012. The Lectionary is as published by Ignatius Press, San Francisco, 2006. Permission to use the 1970 RSV Lectionary (First Catholic Edition) has never been revoked.

[5] The facilitator of this imaginative, practical, and helpful gesture was Fr Christopher G. Phillips, the pastor of Our Lady of the Atonement Catholic Church in San Antonio, Texas.

[6] The RSV, First Catholic Edition, was modified by the use of the modern second person singular in *The Divine Office*.

was accepted for use in the Catholic Church as part of the *Book of Divine Worship*. None of the recent attempts to replace it have commended themselves sufficiently widely. A scholarly revision, *The Revised Psalter*, was approved by the Convocation of Canterbury and York of the Church of England in October 1963, and numbered among its consultants not only C S Lewis but also the poet T S Eliot. In the end the churchmen were enthusiastic but the musicians were not and this was a bird that never flew. More recent psalters have been constructed, for the *Alternative Service Book 1980* and for *Common Worship* (2000), but an accepting consensus has not emerged, and perhaps never could in a fragmenting culture. Meanwhile, the contemporary psalter of the 1979 Book of Common Prayer (USA), available without copyright restriction, commended itself for use not only for the *Book of Divine Worship* but also for the immensely successful English experimental Office Book, *Celebrating Common Prayer* (1992), a joint venture of the Church of England Liturgical Commission and the Anglican Society of Saint Francis. It has to be said, however, that neither this American psalter nor the fine and resonant one produced for *Common Worship* conforms fully to the instruction *Liturgiam authenticam*. It seems safest, then, to remain with the Coverdale version which will inevitably, and profitably, complement the *Revised Grail Psalter* (2010) which is the version of psalmody authorised for the celebration of the Roman Rite in English. This revision, recovering a stronger sacral register than had its predecessor, the *Grail Psalter* (1963). Those who regret that the Catholic Church and the Church of England had not gathered round and adopted the Revised Psalter as commended by C S Lewis and T S Eliot in 1963 may take comfort, and find refuge in, the psalter of the Second Catholic Edition of the *Revised Standard Version*, available within Mass lectionary publications. The use of this psalmody, spoken on ferias, would complement the psalmody of the Revised Grail Psalter, sung at Mass on Sundays and feasts.

The Calendar

The Proper Liturgical Calendar of the Personal Ordinariate of Our Lady of Walsingham was approved and confirmed by the Congregation of Divine Worship on 15th February 2012.[7] Every Particular Church – usually a diocese – has its own Calendar, and it is here that an Ordinariate Calendar is most distinctive. There are very few modifications to the General Roman Calendar or to the National Calendars. The one modification to the General Roman Calendar in England and Wales is that St Bonaventure, an obligatory memorial

---

[7] that is, on the same day as the decree permitting use of the RSV Lectionary, Second Catholic Edition.

in the Roman Calendar, becomes an optional memorial, permitting the celebration of St Swithun's Day (15th July), where this is desirable. As in diocesan Calendars, the Ordinariate Calendar has a number of distinct observances. Thus, in the Ordinariate Calendar of Our Lady of Walsingham, two observances which are in the National Calendar of England are enhanced: Our Lady of Walsingham becomes a titular solemnity and Blessed John Henry Newman, Patron of the Ordinariate, becomes a feast.

Similar Calendars have been approved for the Personal Ordinariate of the Chair of St Peter and for the Personal Ordinariate of Our Lady of the Southern Cross. So that this *Customary* is not only of interest but also as useful as possible, the Calendar provided in this *Customary* includes the distinctive celebrations of all three Ordinariates. The Ordinariate Calendars are a very slight modification of the Roman Calendar, in that certain Sunday titles, which have been a traditional part of Anglican patrimony, are retained. The Sundays *per annum* are called 'after Epiphany' and 'after Trinity' and the ancient description of the Sundays before Lent as *Septuagesima, Sexagesima, and Quinquagesima* is also retained. There is an allusion to the old Pentecost Octave and how the themes of Pentecost may be sustained in the days between Pentecost and Trinity Sunday. Nevertheless, the shape of the General Roman Calendar, its logic and, indeed, the readings appointed for use during the year, are all preserved. It should be stressed too that the Ordinariate Calendar is subject to exactly the same canons, conventions, and regulations as the other Calendars of the Latin Rite of the Catholic Church.

The Mass and the Sacraments

Anglicans who have looked towards unity with Rome in the last 150 years have often used noble, yet unauthorised translations of the pre-conciliar *Missale Romanum*. Chief among these translations have been the *Anglican Missal*, first produced in England in 1921 by the Society of Saints Peter and Paul, and widely adopted subsequently in North America, and the *English Missal*, the fifth edition of which was published in 1958 and reissued in 2001.[8] Closer to the *Missale Romanum* than the *Anglican Missal*, the *English Missal* continues to sell well but has not been in widespread use in England since the 1970s, when Anglo-Catholics, in a rare moment of near unanimity, seemed to decide that the *Novus Ordo* in English provided the one thing hitherto lacking in Catholic liturgy, the use of the vernacular. Meanwhile, as the *Book of Divine Worship* has

---

[8] Canterbury Press, Norwich, a publishing imprint of Hymns Ancient & Modern Ltd.

shown, there is an abiding affection, especially elsewhere in the English-speaking world, for using Prayer Book texts in the celebration of Mass. Quite how this should be done, and what distinctive provision should be made generally for sacraments and non-eucharistic pastoral services, are matters in hand.

Conclusion

The underlying questions demand a full and deep exploration and there is much work to be done before the Ordinariates have their own sacramental and other rites. Meanwhile the texts set out in this *Customary* - the Divine Office and supporting material – provide for those who will use them a rich treasury of devotion. Those canonically bound to recite the Office will be guided by the appropriate authority as regards the extent to which these texts may be used.

It is not possible publically to thank all those who have assisted to date in this enterprise. Jane Goodenough has done invaluable work, seeking out copyright permission on our behalf. Christine Smith, and the Canterbury Press, have given us advice, encouragement, and practical help at every turn. Particular mention must be made too of the encouragement and enthusiasm for the project of Professor Eamon Duffy in Cambridge, and of the diligent contribution of Fr Daniel Lloyd, curate of the Oxford Ordinariate Group. Fr Lloyd was given the modest task of preparing the final text for the presses. In the course of this work, he inserted hymns and other musical material, which have greatly enhanced the *Customary*: a typesetter became a fellow contributor and editor and we are truly grateful for this enrichment.

Monsignor Andrew Burnham
Fr Aidan Nichols OP

22nd June 2012
St John Fisher and St Thomas More

I. Calendar

LITURGICAL CALENDAR
FOR THE CUSTOMARY

The Seasons: Temporale

The date of Easter being moveable, Sundays marked ***** *are not needed in every annual cycle.*

Advent

First Sunday of Advent
Second Sunday of Advent
Third Sunday of Advent
*From 17 December (***O Sapientia***) begin the eight days of prayer before Christmas Day*
Fourth Sunday of Advent
Christmas Eve

Christmas

THE NATIVITY OF THE LORD (Christmas)
Sunday within the Octave of the Nativity: The Holy Family of Jesus,
Mary and Joseph *(if there is no Sunday, 30 December)*
*Second Sunday after Christmas

Epiphany

**EPIPHANY OF THE LORD (Manifestation of Christ to the Gentiles
(6 January)** *(or, as permitted or required by authority, the Sunday between 2 and
8 January)*
Baptism of the Lord - *Sunday after Epiphany (or, if the Epiphany is celebrated on
Sunday 7 or 8 January, on Monday 8 or 9 January)*

3

Time after Epiphany

Time after Epiphany begins usually with Monday of Week 1 on the day following the Baptism of the Lord. For the weekdays following the Baptism of the Lord, the propers for the Week after Epiphany (Week 1) are used. Even when the Baptism of the Lord is transferred to the Monday, the Sunday after the Baptism of the Lord is observed as the Second Sunday after Epiphany. For the purposes of the lectionary, this is Sunday 2 in Ordinary Time and the Sundays thereafter Sundays 3, 4, 5 &c. until Lent begins.

Second Sunday after Epiphany
* Third Sunday after Epiphany
* Fourth Sunday after Epiphany
* Fifth Sunday after Epiphany
* Sixth Sunday after Epiphany

_____

Feast of the Lord

Presentation of the Lord (Candlemas) - *2 February*

_____

Third Sunday before Lent *(Septuagesima)*
Second Sunday before Lent *(Sexagesima)*
Sunday next before Lent *(Quinquagesima)*

Lent

Ash Wednesday
First Sunday in Lent
Second Sunday in Lent
Third Sunday in Lent
Fourth Sunday in Lent (Mothering Sunday)
Fifth Sunday in Lent (Passion Sunday)
Palm Sunday
Monday of Holy Week
Tuesday of Holy Week
Wednesday of Holy Week
Maundy Thursday
Good Friday
Holy Saturday (Easter Eve)

Easter

Easter Sunday
Monday of Easter Week
Tuesday of Easter Week
Wednesday of Easter Week
Thursday of Easter Week
Friday of Easter Week
Saturday of Easter Week
Second Sunday of Easter (Divine Mercy Sunday)
Third Sunday of Easter
Fourth Sunday of Easter
Fifth Sunday of Easter
Sixth Sunday of Easter

Scheme A

Ascension Day *(Thursday of Week 6 of Eastertide)*
From Friday after Ascension Day begin the nine days of prayer before Pentecost
Seventh Sunday of Easter *(Sunday after Ascension)*
Pentecost (Whit Sunday)

Scheme B

Ascension of the Lord *(Sunday 7 of Eastertide)*
Pentecost (Whit Sunday)

Pentecost Octave

The ancient Octave of Pentecost began with Whit Sunday and continued until Trinity Sunday. For the midweek ferias following Pentecost the weekday lectionary is used, as prescribed for Time after Pentecost, but the Mass propers and red as the liturgical colour may sustain the themes of Pentecost.

SOLEMNITY OF THE MOST HOLY TRINITY (Trinity Sunday)
(Sunday after Pentecost)

Time after Trinity

For the purposes of the Roman Lectionary, Ordinary Time resumes on the Monday of the week following Pentecost. The numbering of Sundays (Sunday 8, 9, 10, 11, 12) resumes either on the First Sunday after Trinity, or on the first Sunday thereafter on which a solemnity is not celebrated. Sunday numbers for the purposes of the Roman Lectionary remain in sequence until Sunday 33. Sunday 34 is Christ the King and Week 34 the final six days of the liturgical year.

Solemnities after Trinity (i)

SOLEMNITY OF THE MOST HOLY BODY AND BLOOD OF CHRIST (Corpus Christi)
(Thursday after Trinity Sunday or, as permitted or required by authority, on the First Sunday after Trinity) *

SOLEMNITY OF THE MOST SACRED HEART OF JESUS
(Friday after the First Sunday after Trinity or, as permitted or required by authority, on the Second Sunday after Trinity)

Trinity Sunday and the Sundays after Trinity:

Trinity Sunday
First Sunday after Trinity *(if not kept as the Solemnity of Corpus Christi)*
Second Sunday after Trinity
Third Sunday after Trinity
Fourth Sunday after Trinity
Fifth Sunday after Trinity
Sixth Sunday after Trinity
Seventh Sunday after Trinity
Eighth Sunday after Trinity
Ninth Sunday after Trinity
Tenth Sunday after Trinity
Eleventh Sunday after Trinity
Twelfth Sunday after Trinity

---

* For Corpus Christi and the Sacred Heart, see the note on external solemnities below.

Thirteenth Sunday after Trinity
Fourteenth Sunday after Trinity
Fifteenth Sunday after Trinity
Sixteenth Sunday after Trinity
Seventeenth Sunday after Trinity
* Eighteenth Sunday after Trinity
* Nineteenth Sunday after Trinity
* Twentieth Sunday after Trinity
* Twenty-first Sunday after Trinity
* Twenty-second Sunday after Trinity
* Twenty-third Sunday after Trinity
* Twenty-fourth Sunday after Trinity

Solemnities after Trinity (ii)

Last Sunday of the Year: SOLEMNITY OF OUR LORD JESUS
CHRIST, KING OF THE UNIVERSE - *The propers of the Sunday next before
Advent are used during the final week of the liturgical year, Week 34.*

Dedication Festival - *The First Sunday in October as permitted or required by
authority, may be kept locally as the Dedication Festival if the date of consecration or
dedication is not known.*

Rogation Days

The Rogation Days are the three days following Rogation Sunday (Sixth Sunday of Easter)

Ember Days

The Ember Days at the four seasons are the Wednesday, Friday, and Saturday after
> *First Sunday in Lent*
> *Pentecost*
> *14 September*
> *13 December*

7

Holy Days: Sanctorale

The version of the Sanctorale is that of the Personal Ordinariate of Our Lady of Walsingham under the Patronage of Blessed John Henry Newman. It conforms to the General Calendar of the Roman Church and to the National Calendar for England. Since the Personal Ordinariate has the privileges of a local Church, the Ordinariate Calendar, like diocesan calendars, has local characteristics.

*Different degrees of celebration are distinguished by typography. Observances peculiar to the Ordinariate Calendar are inset and **printed in bold italics**. With the exception of the feast of All Saints of England or All Saints of Wales on the octave day of All Saints, they are all optional memorias. Where necessary, the names of the Ordinariates are abbreviated as follows: The Personal Ordinariate of Our Lady of Walsingham – OLW; of the Chair of St Peter – CSP; of Our Lady of the Southern Cross – OLSC.*

- **SOLEMNITIES**

On solemnities (**BOLD CAPITALS**) the *Gloria in excelsis* and Creed are used at Mass. The Mass propers and the readings (of which there are three) are as appointed for the day.

- **External solemnity**

The external solemnity of any feast means the celebration of the feast without an office, for the good of the faithful, either on the day on which the feast is impeded, or on a Sunday when the feast occurs during the week, or on some other established day.

This convention is sometimes applied to the celebration of Epiphany, the Ascension, Corpus Christi, and the Sacred Heart (as indicated above). It may also be applied to the feast of a duly constituted principal patron, the anniversary of the dedication of the church in which the Mass is said, the titular feast of the church itself, the titular feast of the order or congregation, the feast of the holy founder of the order or congregation, and solemnities which are celebrated with an especially large attendance by the faithful (of this matter the local ordinary is the judge).

- **Feasts**

On feasts (**Bold Type**), the *Gloria in excelsis* is used.

The Mass propers and the readings (of which there are two) are as appointed for the day.

- Obligatory memorias

On obligatory memorias (Ordinary Type), the *Gloria in excelsis* is not used. The Mass propers of the day are used but the readings are often the normal weekday ones. In Lent the collect of the memoria replaces the collect of the Lent weekday but the remainder of the Mass is as for the Lent weekday.

- *Optional memorias*

Optional memorias (*Italics*), where observed, are observed like obligatory ones. Observance of the Optional memorias of the General Calendar remains available to those following the Calendar of the Ordinariate but these memorias are not included in this version of the Calendar.

1	The Octave Day of the Nativity of the Lord
	SOLEMNITY OF MARY, MOTHER OF GOD
2	SS Basil the Great and Gregory Nazianzen,
	Bishops and Doctors of the Church
3	*Most Holy Name of Jesus*
6	**THE EPIPHANY OF THE LORD**
	(The Manifestation of Christ to the Gentiles)
7	*St Raymond of Penyafort, Priest*
12	In England: *St Ælred of Rievaulx, Abbot*
	St Benedict Biscop, Abbot
	Optional Memorial OLW and CSP
13	*St Hilary, Bishop and Doctor of the Church*
	St Kentigern (Mungo), Bishop
17	St Antony of Egypt, Abbot
19	In England: *St Wulstan, Bishop*
20	*St Fabian, Pope, Martyr*
	St Sebastian, Martyr
21	St Agnes, Virgin, Martyr
22	*St Vincent, Deacon, Martyr*
24	St Francis de Sales, Bishop and Doctor of the Church
25	**The Conversion of St Paul the Apostle**
	In Australia: Australia Day, *Day of Prayer*
26	SS Timothy and Titus, Bishops
27	*St Angela Merici, Virgin*
28	St Thomas Aquinas, Priest and Doctor of the Church
31	St John Bosco, Priest

Sunday after 6 January: **The Baptism of the Lord**

When the Solemnity of the Epiphany is transferred to the Sunday that occurs on 7 or 8 January, the Feast of the Baptism of the Lord is celebrated on the following Monday.

1	***St Brigid of Kildare, Abbess***
2	**The Presentation of the Lord (Candlemas)**
3	*St Ansgar, Bishop*
4	***St Gilbert of Sempringham, Religious***
	Optional Memorial OLW and CSP
5	St Agatha, Virgin and Martyr
6	St Paul Miki and Companions, Martyrs
8	*St Jerome Emiliani, Priest*
	St Josephine Bakhita, Virgin
9	In Wales: *St Teilo, Bishop*
10	St Scholastica, Virgin
11	*Our Lady of Lourdes*
14	**SS Cyril, Monk, and Methodius, Bishop,**
	Patrons of Europe
17	*The Seven Holy Founders of the Servite Order*
21	*St Peter Damian, Bishop and Doctor of the Church*
22	**The Chair of St Peter the Apostle**
	TITULAR SOLEMNITY *CSP*
23	St Polycarp, Bishop and Martyr

March

1	**St David, Bishop, Patron of Wales** (In Wales: **SOLEMNITY**)
	Optional Memorial CSP
4	*St Casimir*
5	***St Piran, Abbot***
7	SS Perpetua and Felicity and their Companions, Martyrs
8	*St John of God, Religious*
9	*St Frances of Rome, Religious*
17	*St Patrick, Bishop, Patron of Ireland* (In England: **Feast**)
18	*St Cyril of Jerusalem, Bishop and Doctor of the Church*
19	**ST JOSEPH, SPOUSE OF THE BLESSED VIRGIN MARY**
23	*St Turibius of Mongrovejo, Bishop*
25	**THE ANNUNCIATION OF THE LORD (Lady Day)**

April

2	*St Francis of Paola, Hermit*
4	*St Isidore, Bishop and Doctor of the Church*
5	*St Vincent Ferrer, Priest*
7	St John Baptist de la Salle, Priest
11	St Stanislaus, Bishop and Martyr
16	***St Magnus of Orkney, Martyr***
19	***St Alphege, Bishop, Martyr***
20	In Wales: *St Beuno, Abbot*
21	*St Anselm, Bishop, Doctor of the Church*
23	*St George, Martyr*
	In England: **ST GEORGE, MARTYR,**
	PATRON OF ENGLAND
24	***St Mellitus, Bishop***
	In England: *St Adalbert, Bishop and Martyr*
	St Fidelis of Sigmaringen, Priest and Martyr
25	**St Mark, Evangelist**
	In Australia: **ANZAC Day,** *Day of Prayer for War Dead*
28	*St Peter Chanel, Priest, Martyr*
	St Louis Grignon de Montfort, Priest
29	**St Catherine of Siena, Virgin, Doctor of the Church, Patron of Europe**
30	*St Pius V, Pope*

1	*St Joseph the Worker*
2	St Athanasius, Bishop and Doctor of the Church
3	**SS Philip and James, Apostles**
4	In England: **The English Martyrs**
	Memorial CSP
5	In Wales: *St Asaph, Bishop*
6	***St John the Apostle in Eastertide***
	(formerly* St John *ante portam Latinam)
12	*SS Nereus and Achilles, Martyrs*
	St Pancras, Martyr
13	*Our Lady of Fatima*
14	**St Matthias, Apostle**
18	*St John I, Pope, Martyr*
19	In England: *St Dunstan, Bishop*
	Sts Dunstan, Ethelwold and Oswald, Bishops
	Optional Memorial CSP
20	*St Bernardine of Siena, Priest*
21	***St Helena***
	St Godric of Finchale, Religious
	St Christopher Magallanes, Priest, and Companions, Martyrs
22	*St Rita of Cascia, Religious*
23	***St Petroc, Abbot***
24	***St Aldhelm, Bishop***
	In Australia: **OUR LADY OF THE SOUTHERN CROSS**
	TITULAR SOLEMNITY *OLSC*
25	*St Bede the Venerable, Priest and Doctor of the Church*
	(In England: Obligatory Memorial)
	St Gregory VII, Pope
	St Mary Magdalene de'Pazzi, Virgin
26	St Philip Neri, Priest
27	*St Augustine of Canterbury, Bishop*
	(In England: **Feast**)
	Patron, OLSC
31	**The Visitation of the Blessed Virgin Mary**

First Sunday after Pentecost:	**TRINITY SUNDAY**
Thursday or Sunday after Trinity Sunday:	**THE MOST HOLY BODY AND BLOOD OF CHRIST (CORPUS CHRISTI)**

1	St Justin, Martyr
2	*SS Marcellinus and Peter, Martyrs*
3	St Charles Lwanga and his Companions, Martyrs
5	St Boniface, Bishop and Martyr
6	*St Norbert, Bishop*
9	In England: *St Columba, Abbot*

Optional Memorial CSP

St Ephrem, Deacon, Doctor of the Church

11	St Barnabas, Apostle
13	St Anthony of Padua, Priest and Doctor of the Church
16	In England: *St Richard of Chichester, Bishop*

Optional Memorial CSP

19	*St Romuald, Abbot*
20	In England: *St Alban, Martyr*

as *St Alban, Protomartyr of England,*

Optional Memorial CSP

In Wales: *SS Alban, Julius and Aaron, Protomartyrs of Britain*

21	St Aloysius Gonzaga, Religious
22	*SS John Fisher, Bishop, and Thomas More, Martyrs* (In England: **Feast**)

Memorial CSP

23	In England: *St Etheldreda (Audrey), Abbess*

Sts Hilda, Etheldreda, Mildred and All Holy Nuns

or: **St Paulinus of Nola, Bishop**

Optional Memorials CSP

24	THE NATIVITY OF ST JOHN THE BAPTIST
27	*St Cyril of Alexandria, Bishop and Doctor of the Church*
28	St Irenæus, Bishop and Martyr
29	SS PETER AND PAUL, APOSTLES
30	*The First Martyrs of the Holy Roman Church*

Friday after the Second Sunday after Pentecost:

THE MOST SACRED HEART OF JESUS

Saturday after the Second Sunday after Pentecost:

The Immaculate Heart of the Blessed Virgin Mary

JULY

1	In England: *St Oliver Plunket, Bishop and Martyr*
3	**St Thomas, Apostle**
4	*St Elizabeth of Portugal*
5	*St Anthony Zaccaria, Priest*
6	*St Maria Goretti, Virgin and Martyr*
9	*St Augustine Zhao Rong, Priest, and Companions, Martyrs*
	Our Lady of the Atonement
	Optional Memorial CSP
11	**St Benedict, Abbot, Patron of Europe**
12	In England: *St John Jones, Martyr*
13	*St Henry*
14	*St Camillus de Lellis, Priest*
15	St Bonaventure, Bishop and Doctor of the Church
	Optional Memorial OLW
	St Swithun, Bishop
16	**St Osmund, Bishop**
	Our Lady of Mount Carmel
20	**St Margaret of Antioch, Martyr**
	St Apollinaris, Bishop, Martyr
21	*St Lawrence of Brindisi, Priest and Doctor of the Church*
22	St Mary Magdalen
23	**St Bridget of Sweden, Religious, Patron of Europe**
	In Wales: *SS Philip Evans and John Lloyd, Martyrs*
24	*St Sharbel Makhluf, Priest*
25	**St James, Apostle**
26	SS Joachim and Anne, Parents of the Blessed Virgin Mary
29	St Martha
30	*St Peter Chrysologus, Bishop and Doctor of the Church*
31	St Ignatius of Loyola, Priest

1	St Alphonsus Mary de Liguori, Bishop and Doctor of the Church
2	*St Eusebius of Vercelli, Bishop*
	St Peter Julian Eymard, Priest
	In Wales: *St Germanus of Auxerre, Bishop*
4	St John Mary Vianney, Priest
5	**St Oswald, Martyr**
	The Dedication of the Basilica of St Mary Major
6	**The Transfiguration of the Lord**
7	*St Sixtus II, Pope, and Companions, Martyrs*
	St Cajetan, Priest
8	St Dominic, Priest
	In Australia: **ST MARY OF THE CROSS**
9	**St Teresa Benedicta of the Cross, Virgin and Martyr, Patron of Europe**
10	**St Laurence, Deacon and Martyr**
11	St Clare, Virgin
12	*St Jane Frances de Chantal, Religious*
13	*SS Pontian, Pope, and Hippolytus, Priest, Martyrs*
14	St Maximilian Mary Kolbe, Priest and Martyr
15	**THE ASSUMPTION OF THE BLESSED VIRGIN MARY**
16	*St Stephen of Hungary*
19	*St John Eudes, Priest*
20	St Bernard, Abbot and Doctor of the Church
21	St Pius X, Pope
22	The Queenship of the Blessed Virgin Mary
23	*St Rose of Lima, Virgin*
24	**St Bartholomew, Apostle**
25	*St Louis*
	St Joseph Calasanz, Priest
26	In England: *Blessed Dominic of the Mother of God, Priest*
	In Wales: *St David Lewis, Martyr*
27	St Monica
28	St Augustine of Hippo, Bishop and Doctor of the Church
29	The Beheading of St John the Baptist
30	In England:*SS Margaret Clitherow, Anne Line, and Margaret Ward, Virgin, Martyrs*
	Optional Memorial CSP
31	In England: *St Aidan, Bishop, and Saints of Lindisfarne*
	Optional Memorial CSP

3   *St Gregory the Great, Pope and Doctor of the Church* (In England: **Feast**)

4   In England: *St Cuthbert, Bishop*
          Optional Memorial CSP

8   **The Nativity of the Blessed Virgin Mary**

9   *St Peter Claver, Priest*

11   In Wales: *St Deiniol, Bishop*

12   *The Most Holy Name of Mary*

13   St John Chrysostom, Bishop and Doctor of the Church

14   **The Exaltation of the Holy Cross (Holy Cross Day)**

15   Our Lady of Sorrows

16   St Cornelius, Pope, and Cyprian, Bishop, Martyrs

17   ***St Ninian, Bishop***
          St Edith of Wilton, Religious
     St Robert Bellarmine, Bishop and Doctor of the Church

19   In England: *St Theodore of Canterbury, Bishop*
          St Theodore of Canterbury, Bishop
          St Adrian, Abbot
          Optional Memorials CSP
     St Januarius, Bishop and Martyr

20   St Andrew Kim Taegŏn, Priest, and Paul Chŏng Ha-sang, and Companions, Martyrs

21   **St Matthew, Apostle, Evangelist**

23   *St Pius of Pietrelcina, Religious*

24   **OUR LADY OF WALSINGHAM**
         TITULAR SOLEMNITY *OLW*
         Feast *CSP*

26   *SS Cosmas and Damian, Martyrs*

27   St Vincent de Paul, Priest

28   *St Wenceslaus, Martyr*
     St Lawrence Ruiz and Companions, Martyrs

29   **SS Michael, Gabriel, and Raphael, Archangels**

30   St Jerome, Priest and Doctor of the Church

1	St Thérèse of the Child Jesus, Virgin and Doctor of the Church
2	The Holy Guardian Angels
3	*St Thomas of Hereford, Bishop*
4	St Francis of Assisi
6	*St Bruno, Priest*
7	Our Lady of the Rosary
9	In England: Blessed John Henry Newman, Priest
	Feast *OLW*
	Optional Memorial CSP
10	In England: *St Paulinus of York, Bishop*
11	*St Ethelburga, Abbess*
12	In England: *St Wilfrid, Bishop*
	Optional Memorial CSP
13	In England: *St Edward the Confessor*
	Optional Memorial CSP
14	*St Callistus I, Pope and Martyr*
15	St Teresa of Jesus, Virgin and Doctor of the Church
	In Wales: *St Richard Gwyn, Martyr*
16	*St Hedwig, Religious*
	St Margaret Mary Alacoque, Virgin
17	St Ignatius, Bishop and Martyr
18	**St Luke, Evangelist**
19	*St Frideswide, Abbess*
	SS John de Brébeuf and Isaac Jogues, Priests, and Companions, Martyrs
	St Paul of the Cross, Priest
23	*St John of Capistrano, Priest*
24	*St Anthony Mary Claret, Bishop*
25	In Wales: **Six Welsh Martyrs and their Companions**
26	*SS Chad and Cedd, Bishops*
28	**SS Simon and Jude, Apostles**

NOVEMBER

1	**ALL SAINTS**
2	**THE COMMEMORATION OF ALL THE FAITHFUL DEPARTED (All Souls' Day)**
3	In England and Wales: *St Winefride, Virgin* *St Martin de Porres, Religious*
3	St Charles Borromeo, Bishop
6	In Wales: *St Illtud, Abbot*
7	In England: *St Willibrord, Bishop*
8	***All Saints and Martyrs of England*** *or **All Saints of Wales*** ***Feast OLW***
9	The Dedication of the Lateran Basilica
10	St Leo the Great, Pope, Doctor of the Church
11	St Martin of Tours, Bishop
12	St Josaphat, Bishop and Martyr In Wales: *St Dyfrig, Bishop*
15	*St Albert the Great, Bishop and Doctor of the Church*
16	*St Margaret of Scotland* *St Gertrude, Virgin* In England: *St Edmund of Abingdon, Bishop*
17	*St Elizabeth of Hungary, Religious* (In Wales: Obligatory Memorial) In England: *St Hugh of Lincoln, Bishop* In England: *St Hilda, Abbess*
18	*The Dedication of the Basilicas of SS Peter and Paul, Apostles*
20	***St Edmund, Martyr*** ***Optional Memorial OLW and CSP***
21	The Presentation of the Blessed Virgin Mary
22	St Cecilia, Virgin, Martyr
23	*St Clement, Pope, Martyr* *St Columban, Abbot*
24	St Andrew Dung-Lac, Priest, and Companions, Martyrs
25	*St Catherine of Alexandria, Virgin and Martyr*
30	St Andrew, Apostle

Last Sunday of the Church's Year: **OUR LORD JESUS CHRIST, KING OF THE UNIVERSE**

19

DECEMBER

1	***St Edmund, Campion, Priest and Martyr,*** *Memorial OLW*
3	St Francis Xavier, Priest
4	*St John Damascene, Priest and Doctor of the Church*
6	*St Nicholas, Bishop*
7	St Ambrose, Bishop and Doctor of the Church
8	**THE IMMACULATE CONCEPTION OF THE BLESSED VIRGIN MARY**
9	*St Juan Diego Cuahtlatoatzin*
10	In Wales: *St John Roberts, Priest and Martyr*
11	*St Damasus I, Pope*
12	*Our Lady of Guadaloupe*
13	St Lucy, Virgin and Martyr
14	St John of the Cross, Priest and Doctor of the Church
17	***O Sapientia***
21	*St Peter Canisius, Priest and Doctor of the Church*
23	*St John of Kanty, Priest*
25	**THE NATIVITY OF THE LORD (CHRISTMAS)**
26	**St Stephen, The First Martyr**
27	**St John, Apostle and Evangelist**
28	**The Holy Innocents, Martyrs**
29	*St Thomas of Canterbury, Bishop and Martyr* (In England: **Feast**)
31	St Sylvester I, Pope

Sunday within the Christmas Octave or, if no Sunday available, 30 December: **The Holy Family of Jesus, Mary, and Joseph**

TABLE OF MOVEABLE FEASTS

Year	Ash Weds.	Easter	Ascension	Pentecost	Monday after Pentecost
2012	22 Feb.	8 Apr.	17 May	27 May	28 May: Week 8
2013	13 Feb.	31 Mar.	9 May	19 May	20 May: Week 7
2014	5 Mar.	20 Apr.	29 May	8 June	9 June: Week 10
2015	18 Feb.	5 Apr.	14 May	24 May	25 May: Week 8
2016	10 Feb.	27 Mar.	5 May	15 May	16 May: Week 7
2017	1 Mar.	16 Apr.	25 May	4 Jun.	5 June: Week 9
2018	14 Feb.	1 Apr.	10 May	20 May	21 May: Week 7
2019	6 March	21 Apr.	30 May	9 June	10 June: Week 10
2020	26 Feb.	12 Apr.	21 May	31 May	1 June: Week 9
2021	17 Feb.	4 Apr.	13 May	23 May	24 May: Week 8
2022	2 Mar.	17 Apr.	26 May	5 June	6 June: Week 10
2023	22 Feb.	9 Apr.	18 May	28 May	29 May: Week 8
2024	14 Feb.	31 Mar.	9 May	19 May	20 May: Week 7
2025	5 Mar.	20 Apr.	29 May	8 Jun.	9 June: Week 10

II. Divine Office

GENERAL NOTES

The Daily Office

Recitation of Morning and Evening Prayer, with the prescribed psalms and readings, as set out in this *Customary*, is a complete celebration of the daily cycle of the Office. Prayer During the Day and Compline are provided for additional use, as required. Any of the offices may be replaced by the corresponding office or offices from the Liturgy of the Hours, though care should be taken over maintaining continuity of cycles of psalmody and reading.

When traditional musical settings are used, Evensong may begin with the singing of the versicle and response 'O Lord open thou our lips &c.' as at Morning Prayer, and, especially in Lent, when 'alleluia' is omitted, this versicle and response may be used:

Praise ye the Lord.

The Lord's Name be praised

The words 'Holy Ghost' may always be substituted for 'Holy Spirit'. Similarly, in the Lord's Prayer, 'which art' may be substituted for 'who art', 'in earth' for 'on earth', and 'them that' for 'those who'.

The salutation and response are omitted, even in sung settings, when the minister is a lay person.

At Morning Prayer, when the first reading is taken from the *Liturgy of the Hours*, and the second reading is taken either from the *Liturgy of the Hours* or from the *Customary*, the first responsory may replace the Ferial Canticle at Morning Prayer. The *Te Deum*, when appointed, and the *Benedictus* are never omitted.

At Morning and Evening Prayer on Trinity Sunday and on major feasts, the Apostles' Creed may be replaced by *Quicunque vult*.

If Mass is to be celebrated immediately following Morning Prayer, the Office may end with the *Benedictus*. The Creed may also be omitted at the Office if it is to be used at Mass later that morning.

In Republican Administrations 'O Lord, save the President' may replace 'O Lord, save the Queen'.

23

The Choice of Readings for the Customary

Biblical Readings

The text of lessons, except where otherwise noted, follows the Revised Standard Version, Second Catholic Edition (2002). The scheme of biblical readings, as given in the Lectionary (see pages 839ff.), is drawn from the Roman Lectionary. A short lectionary is also provided for travellers (see pages 920ff).

Post-Biblical Readings

These readings are of two kinds: 'alternative' and 'supplementary'. What they have in common is that they derive from English and Welsh sources – with two exceptions for Irish and Scottish saints.

A. The larger set are **alternative** readings to those already given for the second, post-biblical, reading in the *Officium Lectionum* of the Roman Rite *Liturgy of the Hours*. These alternative readings, whether for the privileged seasons (Advent and Christmastide, Lent and Eastertide), for time after Epiphany or after Trinity, or for festivals (whether of the Lord, the Blessed Virgin Mary, the saints, or the Dedication of a Church), derive from both pre-Reformation and post-Reformation sources.

> 1. The pre-Reformation sources, whether late patristic or mediæval, are the work of writers who were in full communion with the Apostolic See.

> 2. The post-Reformation sources derive from both Catholic and Anglican writers: in the Catholic case, from either canonized saints (Fisher, More, Campion) or *beati* (Newman), and in the Anglican case, from writers who have been generally judged by competent commentators as representing a Catholic-minded stream in Anglican theology and spirituality.

These latter themselves fall into three groups:

> I. seventeenth century or early eighteenth century divines whose works were collected into the mid-nineteenth century 'Library of Anglo-Catholic Theology' (Andrewes, Laud, Frank, Pearson, Beveridge, Wilson), to whom have been added the related figures of Traherne and Ken;

> II. the Tractarians (Keble, Pusey, Newman in his Anglican phase, [Robert] Wilberforce, Manning in his Anglican phase) and their immediate successors (Liddon, Neale);

III. twentieth century Anglo-Catholic writers (Dix, Eliot, Ramsey, Farrer, Mascall).

In every case the extracts drawn from these writers have been selected not only for the quality of the passages but also for their thorough congruence with a (Roman) Catholic doctrinal understanding.

B. The smaller set are **supplementary** readings to those found in the Roman rite *Liturgy of the Hours*. That is to say, they provide readings for saints or seasons which do not occur in the General Calendar of the Roman Liturgy or in the National Proper for England and Wales. That set of supplementary readings itself consists of two sub-sets:

> 1. Readings for the *Sanctorale*. These have been selected in accordance with the principles invoked by the Congregation for Divine Worship – namely, they are:
>> (a) by writers of the patristic period; or
>> (b) by writers of the mediæval period; or
>> (c) by canonized saints or *beati* (specifically, in this case, Blessed John Henry Newman).

> 2. Readings for the *Temporale* – specifically the Week after Pentecost, which is a constant in Anglican liturgical patrimony. These have been drawn from both Catholic (Newman) and Anglican writers: the Anglicans selected on the same basis as with the Alternative readings (Andrewes, Traherne, Dix).

In the total body of readings, the single author most generously represented is Blessed John Henry Newman, under whose special patronage the Ordinariate of Our Lady of Walsingham has been placed by Pope Benedict XVI.

The overall aim in making this collection has been twofold:

1. to assist a movement of *ressourcement* whereby the Catholic Church, through the form of the Ordinariate of Our Lady of Walsingham, can appropriate more fully the saints and spiritual writers of the British Isles in its Liturgy; and
2. to identify a body of writing which is fully in harmony with the doctrine taught by the Magisterium of the Catholic Church yet derives from the Anglican patrimony, in accordance with the Apostolic Constitution *Anglicanorum cœtibus*, III, which speaks of the maintenance of not only the 'liturgical' but also the 'spiritual', as well as 'pastoral', traditions of the Anglican Communion as a 'precious gift'.

25

Use of the Post-Biblical Readings

Certain readings by writers of the patristic period, or of the mediæval period, or by canonized saints or *beati* (especially those in this collection by Blessed John Henry Newman), as set out in this Customary, may be used, within the Ordinariates, as the second reading at the Office of Readings in the Liturgy of the Hours. They may also be read as the second lesson at either Morning or Evening Prayer in the Divine Office set out in this Customary. Other readings, though they may be read as the second lesson at either Morning or Evening Prayer in the Divine Office set out in this Customary, should not be used in place of the appointed readings in the Office of Readings in the Liturgy of the Hours.

Many post-biblical readings, having the character of a homily, or drawn from a homily, may commend themselves for use in addition to two Biblical readings. Suitable points for this third reading would be following the *Benedictus* at Morning Prayer, or after the *Nunc Dimittis*, or other Second Canticle at the end of Evening Prayer, in place of a sermon. The congregation would sit for such a reading.

The Choice of Hymns for the Customary

Rather than make an inevitably subjective selection of hymns for inclusion in the Customary, the decision was taken to include what are mainly traditional Office Hymns. Most of these are, in one sense, extremely old – some dating from the first millennium – and, in another sense, part of the search for the recovery of Catholicity which characterised the Oxford Movement. As in the *English Hymnal*, what are presented here are the plainsong tunes associated with the hymns, some of them belonging to the Sarum Use. As with the *English Hymnal*, many of these tunes will be seldom used. They occur infrequently and cannot be mastered except by trained musicians. Nevertheless the tunes are in the Customary and, since most Office Hymns are in long metre (8.8.8.8), here are listed a few easy, general purpose tunes for the convenience of those who wish to sing the words without grappling with undue musical complexity. In most cases the words associated with the tune are suitable and may be sung instead of the words of the Office Hymn. At the foot of the list are two robust tunes in 11.11.11.5 metre, for which there is an occasional need. Numbers refer to hymn numbers in the *English Hymnal* but names of tunes are usually common to various hymn books. The seasons are suggestions: most hymns are specific to seasons but most tunes are suitable for any time of year. *O salutaris* at Benediction may be sung to any long metre tune. A selection of hymns for the Offices in time *per annum* is found from page 388 onwards.

LM (8.8.8.8)

Morning	61/2	*Illsley*
	257	*Morning Hymn*
	259	*Angel's Song (Song 34)*
	260	*Melcombe*
Evening	51	*Lucis Creator* (Modern Tune)
	267	*Tallis's Canon*
Advent	2	*Verbum supernum* (Mechlin Melody)
	9	*Winchester New*
Christmas	14	*Puer nobis nascitur* (Modern Tune)
	17	*Vom Himmel Hoch*
Epiphany	38	*St Venantius*
Lent	65	*Jesu Corona*
Passiontide	484	*Breslau*
	597	*Herongate*
Easter	181	*Deus tuorum militum* (Modern Tune)
Ascension	141/2	*Gonfalon Royal*
Pentecost	154	*Veni Creator* (Mechlin Version)
General	167	*Duke Street*
	365	*Old Hundredth*
	420	*Truro*
	459	*Eisenach*
	475	*Wareham*
Our Lady	266	*Angelus*
Saints & Martyrs	249	*Deo gracias* (Modern Tune)

11.11.11.5

208	*Diva servatrix*
435	*Iste Confessor*
	Lobet den Herren

MORNING PRAYER

Musical settings of the Offices are found on page 124.

☩   O Lord, open thou our lips.

People   **And our mouth shall shew forth thy praise.**

☩   O God, make speed to save us.

People   **O Lord, make haste to help us.**

> **Glory be to the Father, and to the Son: and to the Holy Spirit;**
> **as it was in the beginning, is now and ever shall be: world without end. Amen. [Alleluia]**

Invitatory

Through the Year
Let us come before God's presence with thanksgiving:

People   **O come, let us adore him.**

or

The earth is the Lord's for he made it:

People   **O come, let us adore him.**

or

O worship the Lord in the beauty of holiness:

People   **O come, let us adore him.**

or

The mercy of the Lord is everlasting:

People   **O come, let us adore him.**

In Advent
Our King and Saviour draws nigh:

People   **O come, let us adore him.**

From Christmas until the Epiphany
Alleluia. Unto us a child is born:

People   **O come, let us adore him. Alleluia.**

At the Epiphany and on the Baptism of the Lord,
and on the Feasts of the Transfiguration and the Holy Cross
The Lord has made manifest his glory:

People **O come, let us adore him.**

In Lent
The Lord is full of compassion and mercy:

People **O come, let us adore him.**

From Easter Day until the Ascension
Alleluia. The Lord is risen indeed:

People **O come, let us adore him.**

From Ascension Day until the Day of Pentecost
Alleluia. Christ the Lord has ascended into heaven:

People **O come, let us adore him. Alleluia.**

On the Day of Pentecost
Alleluia. The Spirit of the Lord has filled the whole world:

People **O come, let us adore him. Alleluia.**

On Trinity Sunday
Father, Son, and Holy Spirit, one God:

People **O come, let us adore him.**

The Alleluias in the following Antiphons are used only in Eastertide.

On Feasts of the Incarnation and of the Blessed Virgin Mary
[Alleluia.] The Word was made flesh and dwelt among us:

People **O come, let us adore him. [Alleluia.]**

On All Saints and other Saints' Days
[Alleluia.] The Lord is glorious in his saints:

People **O come, let us adore him. [Alleluia.]**

One of the following is used:

Psalm 95

Venite, exultemus Domino

1   O COME, let us sing unto the Lord :
let us heartily rejoice in the strength of our salvation.

2   Let us come before his presence with thanksgiving :
and shew ourselves glad in him with psalms.

3   For the Lord is a great God :
and a great King above all gods.

4   In his hand are all the corners of the earth :
and the strength of the hills is his also.

5   The sea is his, and he made it :
and his hands prepared the dry land.

6   O come, let us worship, and fall down :
and kneel before the Lord our Maker.

7   For he is the Lord our God :
and we are the people of his pasture, and the sheep of his
hand.

[8   Today if ye will hear his voice, harden not your hearts :
as in the provocation,
and as in the day of temptation in the wilderness;

9   When your fathers tempted me :
proved me, and saw my works.

10   Forty years long was I grieved with this generation, and said :
It is a people that do err in their hearts,
for they have not known my ways.

11   Unto whom I sware in my wrath :
that they should not enter into my rest.]

Glory be to the Father, and to the Son :
and to the Holy Spirit;
as it was in the beginning, is now, and ever shall be :
world without end. Amen.

Psalm 24

Domini est terra

1   THE earth is the Lord's, and all that therein is :
the compass of the world, and they that dwell therein.

2   For he hath founded it upon the seas :
and prepared it upon the floods.

3   Who shall ascend into the hill of the Lord :
or who shall rise up in his holy place?

4   Even he that hath clean hands, and a pure heart :
and that hath not lift up his mind unto vanity,
  nor sworn to deceive his neighbour.

5   He shall receive the blessing from the Lord :
and righteousness from the God of his salvation.

6   This is the generation of them that seek him :
even of them that seek thy face, O Jacob.

7   Lift up your heads, O ye gates,
  and be ye lift up, ye everlasting doors :
and the King of glory shall come in.

8   Who is the King of glory :
it is the Lord strong and mighty,
  even the Lord mighty in battle.

9   Lift up your heads, O ye gates,
  and be ye lift up, ye everlasting doors :
and the King of glory shall come in.

10   Who is the King of glory :
even the Lord of hosts, he is the King of glory.

Glory be to the Father, and to the Son :
and to the Holy Spirit;
as it was in the beginning, is now, and ever shall be :
world without end. Amen.

Psalm 67

Deus misereatur

1   GOD be merciful unto us, and bless us :
and shew us the light of his countenance, and be merciful
    unto us :

2   That thy way may be known upon earth :
thy saving health among all nations.

3   Let the people praise thee, O God :
yea, let all the people praise thee.

4   O let the nations rejoice and be glad :
for thou shalt judge the folk righteously,
    and govern the nations upon earth.

5   Let the people praise thee, O God :
let all the people praise thee.

6   Then shall the earth bring forth her increase :
and God, even our own God, shall give us his blessing.

7   God shall bless us :
and all the ends of the world shall fear him.

Glory be to the Father, and to the Son :
and to the Holy Spirit;
As it was in the beginning, is now, and ever shall be :
world without end. Amen.

Or, in Easter week,

Easter Anthems

Pascha nostrum

[*Alleluia.*]
1   CHRIST our Passover is sacrificed for us,
       therefore let us keep the feast;
2   Not with the old leaven, nor with the leaven of malice and
         wickedness :
       but with the unleavened bread of sincerity and truth.
       [*Alleluia.*]
3   Christ being raised from the dead dieth no more :
       death hath no more dominion over him.
4   For in that he died, he died unto sin once :
       but in that he liveth, he liveth unto God.
5   Likewise reckon ye also yourselves
         to be dead indeed unto sin :
       but alive unto God through Jesus Christ our Lord. [*Alleluia.*]
6   Christ is risen from the dead :
       and become the first fruits of them that slept.
7   For since by man came death :
       by man came also the resurrection of the dead.
8   For as in Adam all die :
       even so in Christ shall all be made alive. [*Alleluia.*]

1 Cor 5:7–8; Rom 6:9–11; 1 Cor 15:20–22

Glory be to the Father, and to the Son :
and to the Holy Spirit;
as it was in the beginning, is now, and ever shall be :
world without end. Amen.

Or, especially in Eastertide and on Saints' Days

Psalm 100

Jubilate Deo

1   O BE joyful in the Lord, all ye lands :
     serve the Lord with gladness,
        and come before his presence with a song.
2   Be ye sure that the Lord he is God :
     it is he that hath made us, and not we ourselves;
        we are his people, and the sheep of his pasture.
3   O go your way into his gates with thanksgiving,
        and into his courts with praise :
     be thankful unto him, and speak good of his Name.
4   For the Lord is gracious, his mercy is everlasting :
     and his truth endureth from generation to generation.

     Glory be to the Father, and to the Son :
     and to the Holy Spirit;
     as it was in the beginning, is now, and ever shall be :
     world without end. Amen.

Office Hymn

A hymn may be sung.

Psalmody

The psalmody is as appointed for the morning of the month or as in the lectionary.

At the end of each psalm these words are said or sung:

     Glory be to the Father, and to the Son :
     and to the Holy Spirit;
     as it was in the beginning, is now, and ever shall be :
     world without end. Amen.

First Lesson

The reading is as prescribed in the lectionary or the first reading appointed for the Office of Readings.

At the end of each the reader may say

The Word of the Lord.

People   **Thanks be to God.**

Ferial Canticle

One of the following is normally used:

Benedicite, omnia opera*

1   O ALL ye Works of the Lord, bless ye the Lord :
    praise him, and magnify him for ever.
2   O ye Angels of the Lord, bless ye the Lord :
    praise him, and magnify him for ever.
3   O ye Heavens, bless ye the Lord :
    [*praise him, and magnify him for ever.*]
4   O ye Waters that be above the Firmament,
        bless ye the Lord :
    [*praise him, and magnify him for ever.*]
5   O all ye Powers of the Lord, bless ye the Lord :
    [*praise him, and magnify him for ever.*]
6   O ye Sun and Moon, bless ye the Lord :
    [*praise him, and magnify him for ever.*]
7   O ye Stars of Heaven, bless ye the Lord :
    [*praise him, and magnify him for ever.*]
8   O ye Showers and Dew, bless ye the Lord :
    [*praise him, and magnify him for ever.*]
9   O ye Winds of God, bless ye the Lord :
    [*praise him, and magnify him for ever.*]

---

* especially Weeks 1 and 3

10	O ye Fire and Heat, bless ye the Lord :
	[praise him, and magnify him for ever.]
11	O ye Winter and Summer, bless ye the Lord :
	[praise him, and magnify him for ever.]
12	O ye Dews and Frosts, bless ye the Lord :
	[praise him, and magnify him for ever.]
13	O ye Frost and Cold, bless ye the Lord :
	[praise him, and magnify him for ever.]
14	O ye Ice and Snow, bless ye the Lord :
	[praise him, and magnify him for ever.]
15	O ye Nights and Days, bless ye the Lord :
	[praise him, and magnify him for ever.]
16	O ye Light and Darkness, bless ye the Lord :
	[praise him, and magnify him for ever.]
17	O ye Lightnings and Clouds, bless ye the Lord :
	praise him, and magnify him for ever.
18	O let the Earth bless the Lord :
	yea, let it praise him, and magnify him for ever.
19	O ye Mountains and Hills, bless ye the Lord :
	[praise him, and magnify him for ever.]
20	O all ye Green Things upon the Earth, bless ye the Lord :
	[praise him, and magnify him for ever.]
21	O ye Wells, bless ye the Lord :
	[praise him, and magnify him for ever.]
22	O ye Seas and Floods, bless ye the Lord :
	[praise him, and magnify him for ever.]
23	O ye Whales, and all that move in the Waters, bless ye the Lord :
	[praise him, and magnify him for ever.]
24	O all ye Fowls of the Air, bless ye the Lord :
	[praise him, and magnify him for ever.]
25	O all ye Beasts and Cattle, bless ye the Lord :
	praise him, and magnify him for ever.
26	O ye Children of Men, bless ye the Lord :
	[praise him, and magnify him for ever.]
27	O let Israel bless the Lord :
	[praise him, and magnify him for ever.]
28	O ye Priests of the Lord, bless ye the Lord :
	[praise him, and magnify him for ever.]

29	O ye Servants of the Lord, bless ye the Lord :
	[praise him, and magnify him for ever.]
30	O ye Spirits and Souls of the Righteous, bless ye the Lord :
	[praise him, and magnify him for ever.]
31	O ye holy and humble Men of heart, bless ye the Lord :
	[praise him, and magnify him for ever.
32	*O Ananias, Azarias and Misael, bless ye the Lord :]*
	praise him, and magnify him for ever.

Song of the Three Holy Children 35-66

Let us bless the Father, the Son, and the Holy Spirit :
praise him and magnify him for ever.

or[+]

Benedictus es Domine

1	BLESSED art thou, O Lord, God of our fathers :
	praised and exalted above all for ever.
2	And blessed is thy glorious, holy name :
	praised and exalted above all for ever.
3	Blessed art thou in the temple of thy holiness :
	praised and exalted above all for ever.
4	Blessed art thou that beholdest the depths,
	and dwellest between the Cherubim :
	praised and exalted above all for ever.
5	Blessed art thou on the glorious throne of thy kingdom :
	praised and exalted above all for ever.
6	Blessed art thou in the firmament of heaven :
	praised and exalted above all for ever.

Song of the Three Holy Children 29-34

Blessed art thou, O Father, Son, and Holy Spirit;
praised and exalted above all for ever.

[+] especially Weeks 2 and 4

On *Ash Wednesday* the canticle **Deducant oculi mei lacrimam** *(Jer 14:17-21) may be used here.*

On *Good Friday*, *the canticle* **Domine, audivi auditionem tuam** *(Hab 3:2-4, 13a, 15-19) may be used here.*

On *Holy Saturday, All Souls' Day and at the Office for the Dead, the canticle* **Ego dixi: in dimidio dierum meorum** *(Is 38:10-14, 17-20) may be used.*

For these canticles, see page 51 onwards.

Festal Canticle

On days when it is appointed to be used:

Te Deum laudamus

WE praise thee, O God :
we acknowledge thee to be the Lord.
All the earth doth worship thee :
the Father everlasting.
To thee all angels cry aloud :
the heavens and all the powers therein.
To thee Cherubin and Seraphin :
continually do cry,
Holy, Holy, Holy : Lord God of Sabaoth;
heaven and earth are full of the majesty : of thy glory.
The glorious company of the apostles : praise thee.
The goodly fellowship of the prophets : praise thee.
The noble army of martyrs : praise thee.
The holy Church throughout all the world :
doth acknowledge thee;
The Father : of an infinite majesty;
Thine honourable, true : and only Son;
Also the Holy Spirit : the Comforter.

Thou art the King of glory : O Christ.
Thou art the everlasting Son : of the Father.
When thou tookest upon thee to deliver man :
thou didst not abhor the Virgin's womb.
When thou hadst overcome the sharpness of death :
thou didst open the kingdom of heaven to all believers.
Thou sittest at the right hand of God :
in the glory of the Father.
We believe that thou shalt come : to be our judge.
We therefore pray thee, help thy servants :
whom thou hast redeemed with thy precious blood.
Make them to be numbered with thy Saints :
in glory everlasting.

The canticle may end at this point and **O Lord, save thy people** *&c., may be used as a set of suffrages after the Lord's Prayer. See page 45.*

O Lord, save thy people :
and bless thine heritage.
Govern them :
and lift them up for ever.
Day by day :
we magnify thee;
and we worship thy Name :
ever world without end.
Vouchsafe, O Lord :
to keep us this day without sin.
O Lord, have mercy upon us :
have mercy upon us.
O Lord, let thy mercy lighten upon us :
as our trust is in thee.
O Lord, in thee have I trusted :
let me never be confounded.

Second Lesson

The reading is as prescribed in the lectionary or the second reading appointed for the Office of Readings. See also Times and Seasons.

At the end of each the reader may say

The Word of the Lord.

People   **Thanks be to God.**

Benedictus

✠ BLESSED be the Lord God of Israel :
for he hath visited, and redeemed his people;

2 And hath raised up a mighty salvation for us :
in the house of his servant David;

3 As he spake by the mouth of his holy Prophets :
which have been since the world began;

4 That we should be saved from our enemies :
and from the hands of all that hate us;

5 To perform the mercy promised to our forefathers :
and to remember his holy covenant;

6 To perform the oath which he sware to our forefather
Abraham :
that he would give us,

7 That we being delivered out of the hands of our enemies :
might serve him without fear,

8 In holiness and righteousness before him :
all the days of our life.

9 And thou, child, shalt be called the Prophet of the Highest :
for thou shalt go before the face of the Lord to prepare his
ways;

10 To give knowledge of salvation unto his people :
for the remission of their sins;

11 Through the tender mercy of our God :
whereby the day-spring from on high hath visited us;

12 To give light to them that sit in darkness,
and in the shadow of death :
and to guide our feet into the way of peace.

Lk1:68-79

Glory be to the Father, and to the Son :
and to the Holy Spirit;
as it was in the beginning, is now, and ever shall be:
world without end. Amen.

Apostles' Creed

People

**I BELIEVE in God the Father almighty,
maker of heaven and earth:
and in Jesus Christ his only Son our Lord,
who was conceived by the Holy Spirit,
born of the Virgin Mary,
suffered under Pontius Pilate,
was crucified, dead, and buried.
He descended into hell;
the third day he rose again from the dead;
he ascended into heaven,
and sitteth on the right hand of God the Father
   almighty;
from thence he shall come to judge the quick
   and the dead.
I believe in the Holy Spirit;
the holy Catholic Church;
the Communion of Saints;
the Forgiveness of sins;
the Resurrection of the body,
and the Life everlasting. Amen.**

[The Lord be with you:

People   **and with thy spirit.]**

Let us pray.

Lord, have mercy upon us.

People   **Christ, have mercy upon us.**
Lord, have mercy upon us.

People	**OUR** Father, who art in heaven, hallowed be thy name; thy kingdom come; thy will be done; on earth as it is in heaven. Give us this day our daily bread. And forgive us our trespasses, as we forgive those who trespass against us. And lead us not into temptation; but deliver us from evil. Amen.

Suffrages

Then follows one of these sets of suffrages:

A1

O Lord, shew thy mercy upon us:

People   **and grant us thy salvation.**

O Lord, save the *Queen*:

People   **and mercifully hear us when we call upon thee.**

Endue thy ministers with righteousness:

People   **and make thy chosen people joyful.**

O Lord, save thy people:

People   **and bless thine inheritance.**

Give peace in our time, O Lord:

People   **because there is none other that fighteth for us, but only thou, O God.**

O God, make clean our hearts within us:

People   **and take not thy Holy Spirit from us.**

A2

O Lord, shew thy mercy upon us:
People   **and grant us thy salvation.**

Endue thy ministers with righteousness:
People   **and make thy chosen people joyful.**

Give peace in our time, O Lord:
People   **for only in thee can we live in safety.**

Lord, keep this nation under thy care:
People   **and guide us in the way of justice and truth.**

Let thy way be known upon earth:
People   **thy saving health among all nations.**

Let not the needy, O Lord, be forgotten:
People   **nor the hope of the poor be taken away.**

Create in us clean hearts, O God:
People   **and sustain us with thy Holy Spirit.**

B

Not for use when the longer form of the Te Deum *has been used.*

O Lord, save thy people, and bless thine heritage:

People **govern them and lift them up for ever.**

Day by day we magnify thee:

People **and we worship thy Name ever world without end.**

Vouchsafe, O Lord, to keep us this day without sin:

People **O Lord, have mercy upon us, have mercy upon us.**

O Lord, let thy mercy lighten upon us:

People **as our trust is in thee.**

O Lord, in thee have I trusted:

People **let me never be confounded.**

45

Collects

Collect of the Day

Collect for Peace

> O GOD, who art the author of peace and lover of concord, in knowledge of whom standeth our eternal life, whose service is perfect freedom: defend us thy humble servants in all assaults of our enemies; that we, surely trusting in thy defence, may not fear the power of any adversaries; through the might of Jesus Christ our Lord. **Amen.**

Collect for Grace

> O LORD, our heavenly Father, almighty and everlasting God, who hast safely brought us to the beginning of this day: defend us in the same with thy mighty power; and grant that this day we fall into no sin, neither run into any kind of danger, but that all our doings may be ordered by thy governance, to do always that is righteous in thy sight; through Jesus Christ our Lord. **Amen.**

Conclusion

The order for the end of the service may include:

a. Hymns or anthems
b. A sermon
c. Further Prayers (including the Prayers below)

The General Thanksgiving

People **ALMIGHTY God, Father of all mercies,**
we thine unworthy servants
do give thee most humble and hearty thanks
for all thy goodness and loving-kindness
to us and to all men. We bless
thee for our creation, preservation,
and all the blessings of this life;
but above all for thine inestimable love
in the redemption of the world by our Lord Jesus
** Christ,**
for the means of grace, and for the hope of glory.
And, we beseech thee,
give us that due sense of all thy mercies,
that our hearts may be unfeignedly thankful;
and that we shew forth thy praise,
not only with our lips, but in our lives,
by giving up our selves to thy service,
and by walking before thee
in holiness and righteousness all our days;
through Jesus Christ our Lord,
to whom, with thee and the Holy Spirit,
be all honour and glory, world without end. Amen.

A Prayer for the Pope

O GOD, the pastor and ruler of all the faithful, mercifully look upon thy servant Benedict whom thou hast been pleased to set as pastor over thy Church: grant him, we beseech thee, to be in word and conversation a wholesome example to the people committed to his charge; that he with them may attain unto everlasting life; through Jesus Christ our Lord. **Amen.**

A Prayer for the Clergy and People

ALMIGHTY and everlasting God, who alone workest great marvels: send down upon our bishops and clergy, and all congregations committed to their charge, the healthful spirit of thy grace; and that they may truly please thee, pour upon them the continual dew of thy blessing. Grant this, O Lord, for the honour of our advocate and mediator, Jesus Christ. **Amen.**

For British Subjects

A Prayer for the Queen and Royal Family

Let us pray.

ALMIGHTY God we pray for thy servant *Elizabeth* our *Queen*, now by thy mercy reigning over us. Adorn *her* yet more with every virtue, remove all evil from *her* path, that with *her consort*, and all the royal family, *she* may come at last in grace to thee, the way, the truth, and the life, who livest and reignest with the Father in the unity of the Holy Spirit, one God, for ever and ever. **Amen.**

For the Nation

ALMIGHTY God, we commend the people of this land to thy care and protection. Give to our rulers [especially...], the government and all in authority, wisdom and strength to work for the welfare of all in the community, so that we may live in security and peace, through Jesus Christ our Lord. **Amen.**

A Prayer of Saint Chrysostom

ALMIGHTY God, who hast given us grace at this time with one accord to make our common supplications unto thee; and dost promise that when two or three are gathered together in thy Name thou wilt grant their requests: fulfil now, O Lord, the desires and petitions of thy servants, as may be most expedient for them; granting us in this world knowledge of thy truth, and in the world to come life everlasting. **Amen.**

The Office concludes as follows:

The grace of our Lord Jesus Christ,
and the love of God,
and the fellowship of the Holy Spirit,
be with us all evermore.

People   **Amen.**

or

[The Lord be with you:

People   **and with thy spirit.]**

Let us bless the Lord.

People   **Thanks be to God.**

✠   The Lord bless us, and keep us from all evil,
and bring us to everlasting life.

People   **Amen.**

Old Testament Canticles

for use after the Old Testament Lesson at Morning Prayer on certain occasions.
Glory be &c. is not said after these canticles.

Ash Wednesday

Deducant oculi mei lacrimam

1   Let my eyes run down with tears night and day :
     and let them not cease,
2   For the virgin daughter of my people is smitten with a great
          wound :
     with a very grievous blow.
3   If I go out into the field :
     behold, those slain by the sword!
4   And if I enter the city :
     behold, the diseases of famine!
5   For both prophet and priest ply their trade through the land :
     and have no knowledge.
6   Have you utterly rejected Judah? :
     Does your soul loathe Zion?
7   Why have you smitten us :
     so that there is no healing for us?
8   We looked for peace, but no good came :
     for a time of healing, but behold, terror.
9   We acknowledge our wickedness, O Lord,
          and the iniquity of our fathers :
     for we have sinned against you.
10   Do not spurn us, for your name's sake;
     do not dishonour your glorious throne :
          remember and do not break your covenant with us.

Jer 14:17-21

Good Friday

Domine, audivi auditionem tuam

1   Lord, I have heard of your renown :
and I stand in awe, O Lord, of your work.

2   In the midst of the years renew it;
  in the midst of the years make it known :
in wrath remember mercy.

3   God came from Teman, and the Holy One from
  Mount Paran :
his glory covered the heavens, and the earth was full of
  his praise.

4   His brightness was like the sun :
rays flashed from his hand; there he veiled his power.

5   You came forth to save your people :
to save your anointed.

6   You trampled the sea with your horses :
churning the mighty waters.

7   I hear, and my belly trembles :
my lips quiver at the sound;

8   Rottenness enters into my bones :
and my steps totter beneath me.

9   I will quietly wait for the day of trouble :
to come upon the people that invade us.

10   Though the fig tree does not blossom,
  nor fruit appear on the vines :
the produce of the olive fail, and the fields yield no food,

11   Though the flock be cut off from the fold :
and there be no herd in the stalls,

12   Yet will I rejoice in the Lord :
I will exult in the God of my salvation.

13   God, the Lord, is my strength :
he makes my feet like hinds' feet,
  and makes me tread upon the high places.

Hab 3:2-4, 13a, 15-19

Ego dixi: in dimidio dierum meorum

1   I said, In the noontide of my days I must depart;
      I am consigned to the gates of Sheol :
       for the rest of my years.

2   I said, I shall not see the Lord :
      in the land of the living;

3   I shall look upon man no more :
      among the inhabitants of the world.

4   My dwelling is plucked up and removed from me :
      like a shepherd's tent;

5   Like a weaver I have rolled up my life :
      he cuts me off from the loom;

6   From day to night you bring me to an end :
      I cry for help until morning;

7   Like a lion he breaks all my bones :
      from day to night you bring me to an end.

8   Like a swallow or a crane I clamour :
      I moan like a dove.

9   My eyes are weary with looking upward :
      O Lord, I am oppressed; be my security!

10   Behold, it was for my welfare :
      that I had great bitterness;

11   But you have held back my life :
      from the pit of destruction,

12   For you have cast all my sins :
      behind your back.

13   For Sheol cannot thank you :
      death cannot praise you;

14   Those who go down to the pit :
      cannot hope for your faithfulness.

15   The living, the living, he thanks you, as I do this day :
      the father makes known to the children your faithfulness.

16   The Lord will save me, and we will sing to stringed
       instruments :
      all the days of our life, at the house of the Lord.

Is 38:10-14, 17-20

PRAYER DURING THE DAY

✠ O God, make speed to save us.

People **O Lord, make haste to help us.**

Glory be to the Father, and to the Son:
and to the Holy Spirit;
as it was in the beginning, is now and ever shall be:
world without end. Amen. [Alleluia]

Office Hymn

One of the following or another suitable hymn is used.

(Terce)

Nunc, Sancte, nobis, Spiritus

1.Come, Holy Spirit, live in us
   with God the Father and the Son,
and grant us your abundant grace
   to sanctify and make us one.

2.May mind and tongue made strong in love,
   your praise throughout the world proclaim,
and may that love within our hearts
   set fire to others with its flame.

3.Most blessed Trinity of love
   for whom the heart of man was made,
to you be praise in timeless song,
   and everlasting homage paid. Amen.

St Ambrose? Tr. Stanbrook Abbey

(Sext)

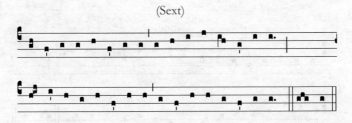

Rector potens, verax Deus

1.O God of truth and Lord of power,
   with order ruling time and change,
whose splendour shines in morning light,
   whose glory burns in midday fire:

2.Extinguish every flame of strife
   and banish every wrong desire;
grant health of body and of mind,
   create in us true peace of heart.

3.To God the Father glory be,
   all glory to his only Son
and to the Spirit, Paraclete,
   in time and in eternity. Amen.

St Ambrose? Tr. St Mary's Abbey, West Malling

(None)

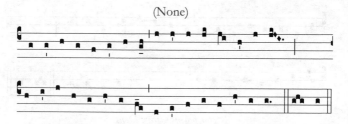

Rerum, Deus, tenax vigor

1. Eternal Father, loving God,
   Who made us from the dust of earth,
   transform us by the Spirit's grace,
   give value to our little worth.

2. Prepare us for that day of days
   when Christ from heaven will come with might
   to call us out of dust again,
   our bodies, glorified in light.

3. O Godhead, here untouched, unseen,
   all things created bear your trace;
   the seed of glory sown in man
   will flower when we see your face. Amen.

St Ambrose? Tr. Stanbrook Abbey

The Psalmody is as below or as prescribed by the Ordinary.

At the end of the psalmody these words are said or sung:

Glory be to the Father, and to the Son :
and to the Holy Spirit;
as it was in the beginning, is now, and ever shall be :
world without end. Amen.

Psalmody

[A] Psalm 119*

Sunday [A]

(Terce)

Beati immaculati

1   BLESSED are those that are undefiled in the way :
and walk in the law of the Lord.

2   Blessed are they that keep his testimonies :
and seek him with their whole heart.

3   For they who do no wickedness :
walk in his ways.

4   Thou hast charged :
that we shall diligently keep thy commandments.

5   O that my ways were made so direct :
that I might keep thy statutes!

6   So shall I not be confounded :
while I have respect unto all thy commandments.

7   I will thank thee with an unfeigned heart :
when I shall have learned the judgments of thy
righteousness.

8   I will keep thy ceremonies :
O forsake me not utterly.

In quo corriget?

9   Wherewithal shall a young man cleanse his way :
even by ruling himself after thy word.

10   With my whole heart have I sought thee :
O let me not go wrong out of thy commandments.

11   Thy words have I hid within my heart :
that I should not sin against thee.

12   Blessed art thou, O Lord :
O teach me thy statutes.

---

* especially Weeks 1 and 3. When the Psalter in course is used for Morning and
Evening Prayer, the Songs of the Ascent (B) are used on the twenty-fourth to
twenty-sixth days of the month at Prayer during the Day.

13	With my lips have I been telling :
	of all the judgments of thy mouth.
14	I have had as great delight in the way of thy testimonies :
	as in all manner of riches.
15	I will talk of thy commandments :
	and have respect unto thy ways.
16	My delight shall be in thy statutes :
	and I will not forget thy word.

(Sext)

Retribue servo tuo

17	O do well unto thy servant :
	that I may live, and keep thy word.
18	Open thou mine eyes :
	that I may see the wondrous things of thy law.
19	I am a stranger upon earth :
	O hide not thy commandments from me.
20	My soul breaketh out for the very fervent desire :
	that it hath alway unto thy judgments.
21	Thou hast rebuked the proud :
	and cursed are they that do err from thy commandments.
22	O turn from me shame and rebuke :
	for I have kept thy testimonies.
23	Princes also did sit and speak against me :
	but thy servant is occupied in thy statutes.
24	For thy testimonies are my delight :
	and my counsellors.

(None)

Adhæsit pavimento

25	My soul cleaveth to the dust :
	O quicken thou me, according to thy word.
26	I have acknowledged my ways, and thou heardest me :
	O teach me thy statutes.
27	Make me to understand the way of thy commandments :
	and so shall I talk of thy wondrous works.
28	My soul melteth away for very heaviness :
	comfort thou me according unto thy word.

29 Take from me the way of lying :
and cause thou me to make much of thy law.
30 I have chosen the way of truth :
and thy judgments have I laid before me.
31 I have stuck unto thy testimonies :
O Lord, confound me not.
32 I will run the way of thy commandments :
when thou hast set my heart at liberty.

Monday [A]

(Terce)

Legem pone

33   Teach me, O Lord, the way of thy statutes :
and I shall keep it unto the end.

34   Give me understanding, and I shall keep thy law :
yea, I shall keep it with my whole heart.

35   Make me to go in the path of thy commandments :
for therein is my desire.

36   Incline my heart unto thy testimonies :
and not to covetousness.

37   O turn away mine eyes, lest they behold vanity :
and quicken thou me in thy way.

38   O stablish thy word in thy servant :
that I may fear thee.

39   Take away the rebuke that I am afraid of :
for thy judgments are good.

40   Behold, my delight is in thy commandments :
O quicken me in thy righteousness.

(Sext)

Et veniat super me

41   Let thy loving mercy come also unto me, O Lord :
even thy salvation, according unto thy word.

42   So shall I make answer unto my blasphemers :
for my trust is in thy word.

43   O take not the word of thy truth utterly out of my mouth :
for my hope is in thy judgments.

44   So shall I alway keep thy law :
yea, for ever and ever.

45   And I will walk at liberty :
for I seek thy commandments.

46   I will speak of thy testimonies also, even before kings :
and will not be ashamed.

47   And my delight shall be in thy commandments :
which I have loved.

48   My hands also will I lift up unto thy commandments,
which I have loved :
and my study shall be in thy statutes.

(None)

Memor esto servi tui

49   O think upon thy servant, as concerning thy word :
wherein thou hast caused me to put my trust.

50   The same is my comfort in my trouble :
for thy word hath quickened me.

51   The proud have had me exceedingly in derision :
yet have I not shrinked from thy law.

52   For I remembered thine everlasting judgments, O Lord :
and received comfort.

53   I am horribly afraid :
for the ungodly that forsake thy law.

54   Thy statutes have been my songs :
in the house of my pilgrimage.

55   I have thought upon thy Name, O Lord, in the
night-season :
and have kept thy law.

56   This I had :
because I kept thy commandments.

(Terce)

Portio mea, Domine

57 Thou art my portion, O Lord :
    I have promised to keep thy law.

58 I made my humble petition in thy presence with my
        whole heart :
    O be merciful unto me, according to thy word.

59 I called mine own ways to remembrance :
    and turned my feet unto thy testimonies.

60 I made haste, and prolonged not the time :
    to keep thy commandments.

61 The congregations of the ungodly have robbed me :
    but I have not forgotten thy law.

62 At midnight I will rise to give thanks unto thee :
    because of thy righteous judgments.

63 I am a companion of all them that fear thee :
    and keep thy commandments.

64 The earth, O Lord, is full of thy mercy :
    O teach me thy statutes.

(Sext)

Bonitatem fecisti

65 O Lord, thou hast dealt graciously with thy servant :
    according unto thy word.

66 O learn me true understanding and knowledge :
    for I have believed thy commandments.

67 Before I was troubled, I went wrong :
    but now have I kept thy word.

68 Thou art good and gracious :
    O teach me thy statutes.

69 The proud have imagined a lie against me :
    but I will keep thy commandments with my whole heart.

70 Their heart is as fat as brawn :
    but my delight hath been in thy law.

71 It is good for me that I have been in trouble :
    that I may learn thy statutes.

72 The law of thy mouth is dearer unto me :
    than thousands of gold and silver.

Manus tuæ fecerunt me

73   Thy hands have made me and fashioned me:
      O give me understanding, that I may learn thy
        commandments.

74   They that fear thee will be glad when they see me :
      because I have put my trust in thy word.

75   I know, O Lord, that thy judgments are right :
      and that thou of very faithfulness hast caused me to be
        troubled.

76   O let thy merciful kindness be my comfort :
      according to thy word unto thy servant.

77   O let thy loving mercies come unto me, that I may live :
      for thy law is my delight.

78   Let the proud be confounded, for they go wickedly about to
       destroy me :
      but I will be occupied in thy commandments.

79   Let such as fear thee, and have known thy testimonies :
      be turned unto me.

80   O let my heart be sound in thy statutes :
      that I be not ashamed.

(Terce)

Defecit anima mea

81 My soul hath longed for thy salvation :
and I have a good hope because of thy word.

82 Mine eyes long sore for thy word :
saying, O when wilt thou comfort me?

83 For I am become like a bottle in the smoke :
yet do I not forget thy statutes.

84 How many are the days of thy servant :
when wilt thou be avenged of them that persecute me?

85 The proud have digged pits for me :
which are not after thy law.

86 All thy commandments are true :
they persecute me falsely; O be thou my help.

87 They had almost made an end of me upon earth :
but I forsook not thy commandments.

88 O quicken me after thy loving-kindness :
and so shall I keep the testimonies of thy mouth.

(Sext)

In æternum, Domine

89 O Lord, thy word :
endureth for ever in heaven.

90 Thy truth also remaineth from one generation to another :
thou hast laid the foundation of the earth, and it abideth.

91 They continue this day according to thine ordinance :
for all things serve thee.

92 If my delight had not been in thy law :
I should have perished in my trouble.

93 I will never forget thy commandments :
for with them thou hast quickened me.

94 I am thine, O save me :
for I have sought thy commandments.

95 The ungodly laid wait for me to destroy me :
but I will consider thy testimonies.

96 I see that all things come to an end :
but thy commandment is exceeding broad.

(None)

Quomodo dilexi!

97   Lord, what love have I unto thy law :
all the day long is my study in it.

98   Thou through thy commandments hast made me wiser
    than mine enemies :
for they are ever with me.

99   I have more understanding than my teachers :
for thy testimonies are my study.

100   I am wiser than the aged :
because I keep thy commandments.

101   I have refrained my feet from every evil way :
that I may keep thy word.

102   I have not shrunk from thy judgments :
for thou teachest me.

103   O how sweet are thy words unto my throat :
yea, sweeter than honey unto my mouth.

104   Through thy commandments I get understanding :
therefore I hate all evil ways.

Thursday [A]

Lucerna pedibus meis

105   Thy word is a lantern unto my feet :
and a light unto my paths.

106   I have sworn, and am stedfastly purposed :
to keep thy righteous judgments.

107   I am troubled above measure :
quicken me, O Lord, according to thy word.

108   Let the free-will offerings of my mouth please thee, O Lord :
and teach me thy judgments.

109   My soul is alway in my hand :
yet do I not forget thy law.

110   The ungodly have laid a snare for me :
but yet I swerved not from thy commandments.

111   Thy testimonies have I claimed as mine heritage for ever :
and why? they are the very joy of my heart.

112   I have applied my heart to fulfil thy statutes alway :
even unto the end.

(Sext)

Iniquos odio habui

113   I hate them that imagine evil things :
but thy law do I love.

114   Thou art my defence and shield :
and my trust is in thy word.

115   Away from me, ye wicked :
I will keep the commandments of my God.

116   O stablish me according to thy word, that I may live :
and let me not be disappointed of my hope.

117   Hold thou me up, and I shall be safe :
yea, my delight shall be ever in thy statutes.

118   Thou hast trodden down all them that depart from thy
statutes :
for they imagine but deceit.

119   Thou puttest away all the ungodly of the earth like dross :
therefore I love thy testimonies.

120   My flesh trembleth for fear of thee :
and I am afraid of thy judgments.

Feci judicium

121 I deal with the thing that is lawful and right :
O give me not over unto mine oppressors.

122 Make thou thy servant to delight in that which is good :
that the proud do me no wrong.

123 Mine eyes are wasted away with looking for thy health :
and for the word of thy righteousness.

124 O deal with thy servant according unto thy loving mercy :
and teach me thy statutes.

125 I am thy servant, O grant me understanding :
that I may know thy testimonies.

126 It is time for thee, Lord, to lay to thine hand :
for they have destroyed thy law.

127 For I love thy commandments :
above gold and precious stone.

128 Therefore hold I straight all thy commandments :
and all false ways I utterly abhor.

Friday [A]

(Terce)

Mirabilia

129   Thy testimonies are wonderful :
therefore doth my soul keep them.

130   When thy word goeth forth :
it giveth light and understanding unto the simple.

131   I opened my mouth, and drew in my breath :
for my delight was in thy commandments.

132   O look thou upon me, and be merciful unto me :
as thou usest to do unto those that love thy Name.

133   Order my steps in thy word :
and so shall no wickedness have dominion over me.

134   O deliver me from the wrongful dealings of men :
and so shall I keep thy commandments.

135   Shew the light of thy countenance upon thy servant :
and teach me thy statutes.

136   Mine eyes gush out with water :
because men keep not thy law.

(Sext)

Justus es, Domine

137   Righteous art thou, O Lord :
and true is thy judgment.

138   The testimonies that thou hast commanded :
are exceeding righteous and true.

139   My zeal hath even consumed me :
because mine enemies have forgotten thy words.

140   Thy word is tried to the uttermost :
and thy servant loveth it.

141   I am small, and of no reputation :
yet do I not forget thy commandments.

142   Thy righteousness is an everlasting righteousness :
and thy law is the truth.

143   Trouble and heaviness have taken hold upon me :
yet is my delight in thy commandments.

144   The righteousness of thy testimonies is everlasting :
O grant me understanding, and I shall live.

Clamavi in toto corde meo

145   I call with my whole heart :
hear me, O Lord, I will keep thy statutes.

146   Yea, even unto thee do I call :
help me, and I shall keep thy testimonies.

147   Early in the morning do I cry unto thee :
for in thy word is my trust.

148   Mine eyes prevent the night-watches :
that I might be occupied in thy words.

149   Hear my voice, O Lord, according unto thy loving-kindness :
quicken me, according as thou art wont.

150   They draw nigh that of malice persecute me :
and are far from thy law.

151   Be thou nigh at hand, O Lord :
for all thy commandments are true.

152   As concerning thy testimonies, I have known long since :
that thou hast grounded them for ever.

Saturday [A]

Vide humilitatem

153 O consider mine adversity, and deliver me :
for I do not forget thy law.

154 Avenge thou my cause, and deliver me :
quicken me, according to thy word.

155 Health is far from the ungodly :
for they regard not thy statutes.

156 Great is thy mercy, O Lord :
quicken me, as thou art wont.

157 Many there are that trouble me, and persecute me :
yet do I not swerve from thy testimonies.

158 It grieveth me when I see the transgressors :
because they keep not thy law.

159 Consider, O Lord, how I love thy commandments :
O quicken me, according to thy loving-kindness.

160 Thy word is true from everlasting :
all the judgments of thy righteousness endure for evermore.

(Sext)

Principes persecuti sunt

161 Princes have persecuted me without a cause :
but my heart standeth in awe of thy word.

162 I am as glad of thy word :
as one that findeth great spoils.

163 As for lies, I hate and abhor them :
but thy law do I love.

164 Seven times a day do I praise thee :
because of thy righteous judgments.

165 Great is the peace that they have who love thy law :
and they are not offended at it.

166 Lord, I have looked for thy saving health :
and done after thy commandments.

167 My soul hath kept thy testimonies :
and loved them exceedingly.

168 I have kept thy commandments and testimonies :
for all my ways are before thee.

Appropinquet deprecatio

169   Let my complaint come before thee, O Lord :
give me understanding, according to thy word.

170   Let my supplication come before thee :
deliver me, according to thy word.

171   My lips shall speak of thy praise :
when thou hast taught me thy statutes.

172   Yea, my tongue shall sing of thy word :
for all thy commandments are righteous.

173   Let thine hand help me :
for I have chosen thy commandments.

174   I have longed for thy saving health, O Lord :
and in thy law is my delight.

175   O let my soul live, and it shall praise thee :
and thy judgments shall help me.

176   I have gone astray like a sheep that is lost :
O seek thy servant, for I do not forget thy
commandments.

[B] Songs of Ascent[*]

Series I
(Terce, or Prayer during the Day on Sundays, Mondays and Thursdays)

Psalm 120

Ad Dominum

1   WHEN I was in trouble I called upon the Lord :
      and he heard me.

2   Deliver my soul, O Lord, from lying lips :
      and from a deceitful tongue.

3   What reward shall be given or done unto thee,
        thou false tongue :
      even mighty and sharp arrows, with hot burning coals.

4   Woe is me, that I am constrained to dwell with Mesech :
      and to have my habitation among the tents of Kedar.

5   My soul hath long dwelt among them :
      that are enemies unto peace.

6   I labour for peace, but when I speak unto them thereof :
      they make them ready to battle.

Psalm 121

Levavi oculus

1   I WILL lift up mine eyes unto the hills :
      from whence cometh my help.

2   My help cometh even from the Lord :
      who hath made heaven and earth.

3   He will not suffer thy foot to be moved :
      and he that keepeth thee will not sleep.

4   Behold, he that keepeth Israel :
      shall neither slumber nor sleep.

5   The Lord himself is thy keeper :
      the Lord is thy defence upon thy right hand;

---

[*] especially Weeks 2 and 4. When the Psalter in course is used for Morning and Evening Prayer, portions of Psalm 119 (A) are used on the twenty-seventh day of the month at Prayer during the Day.

6   so that the sun shall not burn thee by day :
         neither the moon by night.

7   The Lord shall preserve thee from all evil :
         yea, it is even he that shall keep thy soul.

8   The Lord shall preserve thy going out, and thy coming in :
         from this time forth for evermore.

Psalm 122

Lætatus sum

1   I WAS glad when they said unto me :
         We will go into the house of the Lord.

2   Our feet shall stand in thy gates :
         O Jerusalem.

3   Jerusalem is built as a city :
         that is at unity in itself.

4   For thither the tribes go up, even the tribes of the Lord :
         to testify unto Israel, to give thanks unto the Name of
           the Lord.

5   For there is the seat of judgment :
         even the seat of the house of David.

6   O pray for the peace of Jerusalem :
         they shall prosper that love thee.

7   Peace be within thy walls :
         and plenteousness within thy palaces.

8   For my brethren and companions' sakes :
         I will wish thee prosperity.

9   Yea, because of the house of the Lord our God :
         I will seek to do thee good.

Series II
(Sext, or Prayer during the Day on Sundays, Tuesdays and Fridays)

Psalm 123

Ad te levavi oculos meos

1 UNTO thee lift I up mine eyes :
O thou that dwellest in the heavens.

2 Behold, even as the eyes of servants look unto the hand of
their masters, and as the eyes of a maiden unto the hand of
her mistress :
even so our eyes wait upon the Lord our God,
until he have mercy upon us.

3 Have mercy upon us, O Lord, have mercy upon us :
for we are utterly despised.

4 Our soul is filled with the scornful reproof of the wealthy :
and with the despitefulness of the proud.

Psalm 124

Nisi quia Dominus

1 IF THE Lord himself had not been on our side, now may
Israel say :
if the Lord himself had not been on our side, when men rose
up against us;

2 They had swallowed us up quick :
when they were so wrathfully displeased at us.

3 Yea, the waters had drowned us :
and the stream had gone over our soul.

4 The deep waters of the proud :
had gone even over our soul.

5 But praised be the Lord :
who hath not given us over for a prey unto their teeth.

6 Our soul is escaped even as a bird out of the snare of the
fowler :
the snare is broken, and we are delivered.

7 Our help standeth in the Name of the Lord :
who hath made heaven and earth.

Psalm 125

1   THEY that put their trust in the Lord shall be even as the
        mount Sion :
    which may not be removed, but standeth fast for ever.

2   The hills stand about Jerusalem :
    even so standeth the Lord round about his people,
        from this time forth for evermore.

3   For the rod of the ungodly cometh not into the lot of
        the righteous :
    lest the righteous put their hand unto wickedness.

4   Do well, O Lord :
    unto those that are good and true of heart.

5   As for such as turn back unto their own wickedness :
    the Lord shall lead them forth with the evil-doers;
        but peace shall be upon Israel.

Psalm 126

In convertendo

1   WHEN the Lord turned again the captivity of Sion :
     then were we like unto them that dream.
2   Then was our mouth filled with laughter :
     and our tongue with joy.
3   Then said they among the heathen :
     The Lord hath done great things for them.
4   Yea, the Lord hath done great things for us already :
     whereof we rejoice.
5   Turn our captivity, O Lord :
     as the rivers in the south.
6   They that sow in tears :
     shall reap in joy.
7   He that now goeth on his way weeping, and beareth forth
         good seed :
     shall doubtless come again with joy,
         and bring his sheaves with him.

Psalm 127

Nisi Dominus

1   EXCEPT the Lord build the house :
     their labour is but lost that build it.
2   Except the Lord keep the city :
     the watchman waketh but in vain.
3   It is but lost labour that ye haste to rise up early, and so late
         take rest, and eat the bread of carefulness :
     for so he giveth his beloved sleep.
4   Lo, children and the fruit of the womb :
     are an heritage and gift that cometh of the Lord.
5   Like as the arrows in the hand of the giant :
     even so are the young children.
6   Happy is the man that hath his quiver full of them :
     they shall not be ashamed when they speak with their
         enemies in the gate.

Psalm 128

Beati omnes

1 BLESSED are all they that fear the Lord :
and walk in his ways.
2 For thou shalt eat the labours of thine hands :
O well is thee, and happy shalt thou be.
3 Thy wife shall be as the fruitful vine :
upon the walls of thine house.
4 Thy children like the olive-branches :
round about thy table.
5 Lo, thus shall the man be blessed :
that feareth the Lord.
6 The Lord from out of Sion shall so bless thee :
that thou shalt see Jerusalem in prosperity all thy life long.
7 Yea, that thou shalt see thy children's children :
and peace upon Israel.

At the end of the psalmody these words are said or sung:

Glory be to the Father, and to the Son :
and to the Holy Spirit;
as it was in the beginning, is now, and ever shall be :
world without end. Amen.

Short Readings

A short reading from Scripture and a collect or prayer follow. See also Times and Seasons.

Through the Year

Sunday (1)

(Terce)   *1 Jn 4:16*

So we know and believe the love God has for us. God is love, and he who abides in love abides in God, and God abides in him.

(Sext)   *Gal 6:8*

For he who sows to his own flesh will from the flesh reap corruption; but he who sows to the Spirit will from the Spirit reap eternal life.

(None)   *Gal 6:9-10*

And let us not grow weary in well-doing, for in due season we shall reap, if we do not lose heart. So then, as we have opportunity, let us do good to all men, and especially to those who are of the household of faith.

Sunday (2)

(Terce)   *Rom 5:1-2, 5*

Since we are justified by faith, we have peace with God through our Lord Jesus Christ. Through him we have obtained access to this grace in which we stand, and we rejoice in our hope of sharing the glory of God. Hope does not disappoint us, because God's love has been poured into our hearts through the Holy Spirit which has been given to us.

(Sext)   *Rom 8:26*

The Spirit helps us in our weakness; for we do not know how to pray as we ought, but the Spirit himself intercedes for us with sighs too deep for words.

(None)   *2 Cor 1:21-22*

It is God who establishes us with you in Christ, and has commissioned us; he has put his seal upon us and given us his Spirit in our hearts as a guarantee.

Sunday (3)

(Terce)   *Rom 8:15-16*

For you did not receive the spirit of slavery to fall back into fear, but you have received the spirit of sonship. When we cry, 'Abba! Father!' it is the Spirit himself bearing witness with our spirit that we are children of God.

(Sext)   *Rom 8:22-23*

We know that the whole creation has been groaning in travail together until now; and not only the creation, but we ourselves, who have the first fruits of the Spirit, groan inwardly as we wait for adoption as sons, the redemption of our bodies.

(None)   *2 Tim 1:9*

God, saved us and called us with a holy calling, not in virtue of our works but in virtue of his own purpose and the grace which he gave us in Christ Jesus ages ago.

Sunday (4)

(Terce) *1 Cor 6:19-20*

Do you not know that your body is a temple of the Holy Spirit within you, which you have from God? You are not your own; you were bought with a price. So glorify God in your body.

(Scxt) *Deut 10:12*

And now, Israel, what does the Lord your God require of you, but to fear the Lord your God, to walk in all his ways, to love him, to serve the Lord your God with all your heart and with all your soul,

(None) *Song 8:6b-7*

Love is strong as death, jealousy is cruel as the grave. Its flashes are flashes of fire, a most vehement flame. Many waters cannot quench love, neither can floods drown it. If a man offered for love all the wealth of his house, it would be utterly scorned.

The Collect of the day or the following prayer is said:

> Christ be with me, Christ within me,
> Christ behind me, Christ before me,
> Christ beside me, Christ to win me,
> Christ to comfort and restore me.
> Christ beneath me, Christ above me,
> Christ in quiet, Christ in danger,
> Christ in hearts of all that love me,
> Christ in mouth of friend and stranger.

from St Patrick's Breastplate

Monday (1)

(Terce)   *Rom 13:8, 10*
Owe no one anything, except to love one another; for he who loves
his neighbour has fulfilled the law. Love does no wrong to a
neighbour; therefore love is the fulfilling of the law.

(Sext)   *Jas 1:19-20, 26*
Know this, my beloved brethren. Let every man be quick to hear,
slow to speak, slow to anger, for the anger of man does not work the
righteousness of God. If any one thinks he is religious, and does not
bridle his tongue but deceives his heart, this man's religion is vain.

(None)   *1 Pet 1:17-19*
If you invoke as Father him who judges each one impartially
according to his deeds, conduct yourselves with fear throughout the
time of your exile. You know that you were ransomed from the futile
ways inherited from your fathers, not with perishable things such as
silver or gold, but with the precious blood of Christ, like that of a
lamb without blemish or spot

Monday (2)

(Terce)   *Jer 31:33*
This is the covenant which I will make with the house of Israel after
those days, says the Lord: I will put my law within them, and I will
write it upon their hearts; and I will be their God, and they shall be my
people.

(Sext)   *Jer 32:40*
I will make with them an everlasting covenant, that I will not turn
away from doing good to them; and I will put the fear of me in their
hearts, that they may not turn from me.

(None)   *Ezek 34:31*
You are my sheep, the sheep of my pasture, and I am your God, says
the Lord God.

Monday (3)

(Terce) *2 Cor 13:11*

Finally, brethren, farewell. Mend your ways, heed my appeal, agree with one another, live in peace, and the God of love and peace will be with you.

(Sext) *Rom 6:22*

But now that you have been set free from sin and have become slaves of God, the return you get is sanctification and its end, eternal life.

(None) *Col 1:21-22*

And you, who once were estranged and hostile in mind, doing evil deeds, he has now reconciled in his body of flesh by his death, in order to present you holy and blameless and irreproachable before him.

Monday (4)

(Terce) *Lev 20:26*

You shall be holy to me; for I the Lord am holy, and have separated you from the peoples, that you should be mine.

(Sext) *Wis 15:1, 3*

But you, our God, are kind and true, patient, and ruling all things in mercy. For to know you is complete righteousness, and to know your power is the root of immortality.

(None) *Bar 4:21-22*

Take courage, my children, cry to God, and he will deliver you from the power and hand of the enemy. For I have put my hope in the Everlasting to save you, and joy has come to me from the Holy One, because of the mercy which soon will come to you from your everlasting Saviour.

Eternal Light, shine into our hearts.
Eternal Goodness, deliver us from evil.
Eternal Power, be our support
Eternal Wisdom, scatter the darkness of our ignorance.
Eternal Pity, have mercy upon us;
that with all our heart and mind and soul and strength
we may seek thy face and be brought by thine infinite mercy
into thy holy presence;
through Jesus Christ our Lord.

Alcuin of York (804)

Tuesday(1)

(Terce) *Jer 17:7-8*

'Blessed is the man who trusts in the Lord, whose trust is the Lord. He is like a tree planted by water, that sends out its roots by the stream, and does not fear when heat comes, for its leaves remain green, and is not anxious in the year of drought, for it does not cease to bear fruit.'

(Sext) *Prov 3:13-15*

Happy is the man who finds Wisdom, and the man who gets understanding, for the gain from it is better than gain from silver and its profit better than gold. She is more precious than jewels, and nothing you desire can compare with her.

(None) *Job 5:17-18*

Behold, happy is the man whom God reproves; therefore despise not the chastening of the Almighty. For he wounds, but he binds up; he smites, but his hands heal.

Tuesday (2)

(Terce) *1 Cor 12:4-6*

Now there are varieties of gifts, but the same Spirit; and there are varieties of service, but the same Lord; and there are varieties of working, but it is the same God who inspires them all in every one.

(Sext) *1 Cor 12:12-13*

Just as the body is one and has many members, and all the members of the body, though many, are one body, so it is with Christ. For by one Spirit we were all baptized into one body - Jews or Greeks, slaves or free - and all were made to drink of one Spirit.

(None) *1 Cor 12:24b, 25-26*

God has so composed the body, giving the greater honour to the inferior part, that there may be no discord in the body, but that the members may have the same care for one another. If one member suffers, all suffer together; if one member is honoured, all rejoice together.

Tuesday (3)

(Terce) *Jer 22:3*

Thus says the Lord: Do justice and righteousness, and deliver from the hand of the oppressor him who has been robbed. And do no wrong or violence to the alien, the fatherless, and the widow, nor shed innocent blood in this place.

(Sext) *Deut 15:7-8*

If there is among you a poor man, one of your brethren, in any of your towns within your land which the Lord your God gives you, you shall not harden your heart or shut your hand against your poor brother, but you shall open your hand to him, and lend him sufficient for his need, whatever it may be.

(None) *Prov 22:22-23*

Do not rob the poor, because he is poor, or crush the afflicted at the gate; for the Lord will plead their cause and despoil of life those who despoil them.

Tuesday (4)

(Terce) *1 Jn 3:17-18*

If any one has the world's goods and sees his brother in need, yet closes his heart against him, how does God's love abide in him? Little children, let us not love in word or speech but in deed and in truth.

(Sext) *Deut 30:11, 14*

For this commandment which I command you this day is not too hard for you, neither is it far off. But the word is very near you; it is in your mouth and in your heart, so that you can do it.

(None) *Is 55:10-11*

For as the rain and the snow come down from heaven, and return not thither but water the earth, making it bring forth and sprout, giving seed to the sower and bread to the eater, so shall my word be that goes forth from my mouth; it shall not return to me empty, but it shall accomplish that which I purpose, and prosper in the thing for which I sent it.

The Collect of the day or the following prayer is said:

O Eternal God,
the light of the minds that know thee,
the joy of the hearts that love thee,
and the strength of the wills that serve thee:
grant us so to know thee
that we may truly love thee,
and so to love thee
that we may truly serve thee,
thou whose service is perfect freedom;
through Jesus Christ our Lord.

after St Augustine of Hippo (430)

Wednesday (1)

(Terce)   *1 Pet 1:13-14*
Therefore gird up your minds, be sober, set your hope fully upon the grace that is coming to you at the revelation of Jesus Christ. As obedient children, do not be conformed to the passions of your former ignorance.

(Sext)   *1 Pet 1:15-16*
As he who called you is holy, be holy yourselves in all your conduct; since it is written, 'You shall be holy, for I am holy.'

(None)   *Jas 4:7-8a, 10*
Submit yourselves therefore to God. Resist the devil and he will flee from you. Draw near to God and he will draw near to you. Humble yourselves before the Lord and he will exalt you.

Wednesday (2)

(Terce)   *Deut 1:16-17a*
And I charged your judges at that time, 'Hear the cases between your brethren, and judge righteously between a man and his brother or the alien that is with him. You shall not be partial in judgment; you shall hear the small and the great alike; you shall not be afraid of the face of man, for the judgment is God's; and the case that is too hard for you, you shall bring to me, and I will hear it.'

(Sext)   *Is 55:8-9*
For my thoughts are not your thoughts, neither are your ways my ways, says the Lord. For as the heavens are higher than the earth, so are my ways higher than your ways and my thoughts than your thoughts.

(None)   *1 Sam 16:7b*
The Lord sees not as man sees; man looks on the outward appearance, but the Lord looks on the heart.

Wednesday (3)

(Terce)   *1 Cor 13:4-7*

Love is patient and kind; love is not jealous or boastful; it is not arrogant or rude. Love does not insist on its own way; it is not irritable or resentful; it does not rejoice at wrong, but rejoices in the right. Love bears all things, believes all things, hopes all things, endures all things.

(Sext)   *1 Cor 13:8-9, 13*

Love never ends; as for prophecies, they will pass away; as for tongues, they will cease; as for knowledge, it will pass away. For our knowledge is imperfect and our prophecy is imperfect. So faith, hope, love abide, these three; but the greatest of these is love.

(None)   *Col 3:14-15*

And above all these put on love, which binds everything together in perfect harmony. And let the peace of Christ rule in your hearts, to which indeed you were called in the one body. And be thankful.

Wednesday (4)

(Terce)   *1 Cor 10:24, 31*

Let no one seek his own good, but the good of his neighbour: whether you eat or drink, or whatever you do, do all to the glory of God.

(Sext)   *Col 3:17*

And whatever you do, in word or deed, do everything in the name of the Lord Jesus, giving thanks to God the Father through him.

(None)   *Col 3:23-24*

Whatever your task, work heartily, as serving the Lord and not men, knowing that from the Lord you will receive the inheritance as your reward; you are serving the Lord Christ.

The Collect of the day or the following prayer is said:

O Lord our God,
grant us grace to desire thee with our whole heart;
that so desiring, we may seek and find thee;
and so finding, may love thee;
and so loving, may hate those sins
   from which thou hast delivered us;
through Jesus Christ our Lord.

St Anselm

Thursday (1)

(Terce) *Amos 4:13*

For behold, he who forms the mountains, and creates the wind, and declares to man what is his thought; who makes the morning darkness, and treads on the heights of the earth - the Lord, the God of hosts, is his name!

(Sext) *Amos 5:8*

He who made the Pleiades and Orion, and turns deep darkness into the morning, and darkens the day into night, who calls for the waters of the sea, and pours them out upon the surface of the earth, the Lord is his name,

(None) *Amos 9:6*

He who builds his upper chambers in the heavens, and founds his vault upon the earth; who calls for the waters of the sea, and pours them out upon the surface of the earth - the Lord is his name.

Thursday (2)

(Terce) *Gal 5:13-14*

For you were called to freedom, brethren; only do not use your freedom as an opportunity for the flesh, but through love be servants of one another. For the whole law is fulfilled in one word, 'You shall love your neighbour as yourself.'

(Sext) *Gal 5:16-17*

Walk by the Spirit, and do not gratify the desires of the flesh. For the desires of the flesh are against the Spirit, and the desires of the Spirit are against the flesh; for these are opposed to each other, to prevent you from doing what you would.

(None) *Gal 5:22, 23a, 25*

The fruit of the Spirit is love, joy, peace, patience, kindness, goodness, faithfulness, gentleness, self-control. If we live by the Spirit, let us also walk by the Spirit.

Thursday (3)

(Terce)   *Wis 19:22*

In everything, O Lord, you have exalted and glorified your people; and you have not neglected to help them at all times and in all places.

(Sext)   *Deut 4:7*

For what great nation is there that has a god so near to it as the Lord our God is to us, whenever we call upon him?

(None)   *Esther 10:9*

And my nation, this is Israel, who cried out to God and were saved. The Lord has saved his people; the Lord has delivered us from all these evils; God has done great signs and wonders, which have not occurred among the nations.

Thursday (4)

(Terce)   *1 Jn 3:23-24*

This is his commandment, that we should believe in the name of his Son Jesus Christ and love one another, just as he has commanded us. All who keep his commandments abide in him, and he in them. And by this we know that he abides in us, by the Spirit which he has given us.

(Sext)   *Wis 1:1-2*

Love righteousness, you rulers of the earth, think of the Lord with uprightness, and seek him with sincerity of heart; because he is found by those who do not put him to the test, and manifests himself to those who do not distrust him.

(None)   *Heb 12:1-2*

Since we are surrounded by so great a cloud of witnesses, let us also lay aside every weight, and sin which clings so closely, and let us run with perseverance the race that is set before us, looking to Jesus the pioneer and perfecter of our faith, who for the joy that was set before him endured the cross, despising the shame, and is seated at the right hand of the throne of God.

O gracious and holy Father,
give us Wisdom to perceive thee,
intelligence to understand thee,
diligence to seek thee,
patience to wait for thee,
eyes to behold thee,
a heart to meditate upon thee,
and a life to proclaim thee,
through the power of the Spirit
of Jesus Christ our Lord.

St Benedict of Nursia (c550)

Friday (1)

(Terce) *Phil 2:2b-4*

Be of the same mind, having the same love, being in full accord and of one mind. Do nothing from selfishness or conceit, but in humility count others better than yourselves. Let each of you look not only to his own interests, but also to the interests of others.

(Sext) *2 Cor 13:4*

For Christ was crucified in weakness, but lives by the power of God. For we are weak in him, but in dealing with you we shall live with him by the power of God.

(None) *Col 3:12-13*

Put on then, as God's chosen ones, holy and beloved, compassion, kindness, lowliness, meekness, and patience, forbearing one another and, if one has a complaint against another, forgiving each other; as the Lord has forgiven you, so you also must forgive.

Friday (2)

(Terce) *Deut 1:31b*

You have seen how the Lord your God bore you, as a man bears his son, in all the way that you went until you came to this place.

(Sext) *Bar 4:28-29*

For just as you purposed to go astray from God, return with tenfold zeal to seek him. For he who brought these calamities upon you will bring you everlasting joy with your salvation.

(None) *Wis 1:13-15*

God did not make death, and he does not delight in the death of the living. For he created all things that they might exist, and the generative forces of the world are wholesome, and there is no destructive poison in them; and the dominion of Hades is not on earth. For righteousness is immortal.

Friday (3)

(Terce) *Rom 1:16b-17*

The gospel is the power of God for salvation to every one who has faith, to the Jew first and also to the Greek. For in it the righteousness of God is revealed through faith for faith; as it is written, 'He who through faith is righteous shall live'.

(Sext) *Rom 3:21-22a*

But now the righteousness of God has been manifested apart from law, although the law and the prophets bear witness to it, the righteousness of God through faith in Jesus Christ for all who believe.

(None) *Eph 2:8-9*

For by grace you have been saved through faith; and this is not your own doing, it is the gift of God - not because of works, lest any man should boast.

Friday (4)

(Terce) *Rom 12:17a, 19b-21*

Repay no one evil for evil but leave it to the wrath of God; for it is written, 'Vengeance is mine, I will repay, says the Lord'. Do not be overcome by evil, but overcome evil with good.

(Sext) *1 Jn 3:16*

By this we know love, that he laid down his life for us; and we ought to lay down our lives for the brethren.

(None) *1 Jn 4:9-11*

In this the love of God was made manifest among us, that God sent his only Son into the world, so that we might live through him. In this is love, not that we loved God but that he loved us and sent his Son to be the expiation for our sins. Beloved, if God so loved us, we also ought to love one another.

The Collect of the day or the following prayer is said:

Thanks be to thee, Lord Jesus Christ
for all the benefits thou hast given us,
for all the pains and insults thou hast borne for us.
O most merciful Redeemer, friend and brother,
may we know thee more clearly,
love thee more dearly,
and follow thee more nearly,
day by day.

after St Richard of Chichester (1253)

Saturday (1)

(Terce) *1 Kings 8:60-61*
That all the peoples of the earth may know that the Lord is God; there is no other, let your heart therefore be wholly true to the Lord our God, walking in his statutes and keeping his commandments, as at this day.

(Sext) *Jer 17:9-10*
The heart is deceitful above all things, and desperately corrupt; who can understand it? 'I the Lord search the mind and try the heart, to give to every man according to his ways, according to the fruit of his doings'.

(None) *Wis 7:27a, 8:1*
Though Wisdom is but one, she can do all things, and while remaining in herself, she renews all things. She reaches mightily from one end of the earth to the other, and she orders all things well.

Saturday (2)

(Terce) *Deut 8:5b-6*
 As a man disciplines his son, the Lord your God disciplines you. So you shall keep the commandments of the Lord your God, by walking in his ways and by fearing him.

(Sext) *1 Kings 2:2b-3*
Be strong and keep the charge of the Lord your God, walking in his ways and keeping his statutes, his commandments, his ordinances, and his testimonies, as it is written in the law of Moses, that you may prosper in all that you do and wherever you turn.

(None) *Jer 6:16*
Thus says the Lord: Stand by the roads, and look, and ask for the ancient paths, where the good way is; and walk in it, and find rest for your souls. But they said, 'We will not walk in it.'

Saturday (3)

(Terce)   *1 Sam 15:22*
Has the Lord as great delight in burnt offerings and sacrifices, as in obeying the voice of the Lord? Behold, to obey is better than sacrifice, and to hearken than the fat of rams.

(Sext)   *Gal 5:26; 6:2*
Let us have no self-conceit, no provoking of one another, no envy of one another. Bear one another's burdens, and so fulfil the law of Christ.

(None)   *Mic 6:8*
He has showed you, O man, what is good; and what does the Lord require of you but to do justice, and to love kindness, and to walk humbly with your God?

Saturday (4)

(Terce)   *Dan 6:26b-27a*
He is the living God, enduring for ever; his kingdom shall never be destroyed, and his dominion shall be to the end. He delivers and rescues, he works signs and wonders in heaven and on earth.

(Sext)   *Rom 15:5-7*
May the God of steadfastness and encouragement grant you to live in such harmony with one another, in accord with Christ Jesus, that together you may with one voice glorify the God and Father of our Lord Jesus Christ. Welcome one another, therefore, as Christ has welcomed you, for the glory of God.

(None)   *Phil 4:8, 9b*
Finally, brethren, whatever is true, whatever is honourable, whatever is just, whatever is pure, whatever is lovely, whatever is gracious, if there is any excellence, if there is anything worthy of praise, think about these things and the God of peace will be with you.

The Collect of the day or the following prayer is said:

God be in my head, and in my understanding;
God be in my eyes, and in my looking;
God be in my mouth, and in my speaking;
God be in my heart, and in my thinking;
God be at mine end, and at my departing.

Sarum Primer

Conclusion

	[The Lord be with you:
People	**and with thy spirit.]**

	Let us bless the Lord.
People	**Thanks be to God.**

✠	May the divine assistance remain with us always.
People	**Amen.**

EVENING PRAYER

The service may begin with a seasonal sentence of Scripture and the Penitential Rite or with the versicle O God, make speed to save us.

Penitential Rite

Minister Dearly beloved, we have come together in the presence of almighty God our heavenly Father, to render thanks for the great benefits that we have received at his hands, to set forth his most worthy praise, to hear his holy Word, and to ask, for ourselves and on behalf of others, those things that are necessary for our life and our salvation. And so that we may prepare ourselves in heart and mind to worship him, let us kneel in silence, and with penitent and obedient hearts confess our sins, that we may obtain forgiveness by his infinite goodness and mercy.

or

Let us humbly confess our sins unto Almighty God.

Silence may be kept.

People **Almighty and most merciful Father,
we have erred and strayed from thy ways
    like lost sheep,
we have followed too much the devices and desires
    of our own hearts,
we have offended against thy holy laws,
we have left undone those things
    which we ought to have done,
and we have done those things
    which we ought not to have done.**

But thou, O Lord, have mercy upon us,
spare thou those who confess their faults,
restore thou those who are penitent,
according to thy promises declared unto mankind
in Christ Jesus our Lord;
and grant, O most merciful Father, for his sake,
that we may hereafter live a godly, righteous,
  and sober life,
to the glory of thy holy Name. Amen.

Minister May the Almighty and merciful Lord grant us absolution and
remission of all our sins, true repentance, amendment of life,
and the grace and consolation of his Holy Spirit. **Amen**.

✠ O God, make speed to save us.

People **O Lord, make haste to help us.**

**Glory be to the Father, and to the Son:
and to the Holy Spirit;
as it was in the beginning, is now and ever shall be:
world without end. Amen. [Alleluia]**

*The following or other suitable anthem may be sung during the lighting of candles.
Ps 141:1-4b, 8 and Ps 134 are also suitable. Incense may be burned.*

Lucernarium

Phos hilaron

Either

Hail, gladdening Light, of his pure glory poured,
who is immortal Father, heavenly blest;
holiest of holies, Jesus Christ our Lord.

Now are we come to the sun's hour of rest;
the lights of evening round us shine,
we hymn the Father, Son, and Holy Spirit divine.

Worthiest art thou at all times to be sung,
with undefilèd tongue,
Son of our God, giver of life, alone!
therefore in all the world thy glories, Lord, they own.

Trans. John Keble (1792-1866)

Or

O gladsome light, O grace
  of God the Father's face,
the eternal splendour wearing;
  celestial, holy, blest,
our Saviour Jesus Christ,
  joyful in thine appearing!

Now, ere day fadeth quite,
  we see the evening light,
our wonted hymn outpouring;
  Father of might unknown,
thee, his incarnate Son,
  and Holy Spirit adoring.

To thee of right belongs
  all praise of holy songs,
O Son of God, life giver;
  thee, therefore, O Most High,
the world doth glorify,
  and shall exalt forever.

Trans. Robert Bridges (1844-1930)

For musical settings of these texts, see page 125 onwards.

Psalmody

The psalmody is as appointed for the morning of the month or as in the lectionary.

At the end of each psalm these words are said or sung:

> Glory be to the Father, and to the Son :
> and to the Holy Spirit;
> as it was in the beginning, is now, and ever shall be :
> world without end. Amen.

First Lesson

The reading is as prescribed in the lectionary.

At the end of each the reader may say

The Word of the Lord.

People **Thanks be to God.**

Office Hymn

A hymn may be sung.

Gospel Canticle

Magnificat

✠ MY soul doth magnify the Lord :
and my spirit hath rejoiced in God my Saviour.

2   For he hath regarded :
the lowliness of his hand-maiden.

3   For behold, from henceforth :
all generations shall call me blessed.

4   For he that is mighty hath magnified me :
and holy is his Name.

5   And his mercy is on them that fear him :
throughout all generations.

6   He hath shewed strength with his arm :
he hath scattered the proud in the imagination of their
    hearts.

7   He hath put down the mighty from their seat :
and hath exalted the humble and meek.

8   He hath filled the hungry with good things :
and the rich he hath sent empty away.

9   He remembering his mercy hath holpen his servant Israel :
as he promised to our forefathers, Abraham and his seed for
    ever.

Lk 1:46-55

Glory be to the Father, and to the Son :
and to the Holy Spirit;
As it was in the beginning, is now, and ever shall be :
world without end. Amen.

Second Lesson

The reading is as prescribed in the lectionary.

At the end of each the reader may say

The Word of the Lord.

People   **Thanks be to God.**

Second Canticle

Either

Nunc dimittis

1   Lord, now lettest thou thy servant depart in peace :
      according to thy word.
2   For mine eyes have seen :
      thy salvation;
3   Which thou hast prepared :
      before the face of all people;
4   To be a light to lighten the Gentiles :
      and to be the glory of thy people Israel.

Lk 2:29-32

      Glory be to the Father, and to the Son :
      and to the Holy Spirit;
      as it was in the beginning, is now, and ever shall be :
      world without end. Amen.

Or, when Compline is to follow later, another New Testament canticle is used (see below, page 116 onwards)

Apostles' Creed

People   **I BELIEVE in God the Father almighty,
maker of heaven and earth:
and in Jesus Christ his only Son our Lord,
who was conceived by the Holy Spirit,
born of the Virgin Mary,
suffered under Pontius Pilate,
was crucified, dead, and buried.
He descended into hell;
the third day he rose again from the dead;
he ascended into heaven,
and sitteth on the right hand of God the Father
   almighty;
from thence he shall come to judge the quick
   and the dead.
I believe in the Holy Spirit;
the holy Catholic Church;
the Communion of Saints;
the Forgiveness of sins;
the Resurrection of the body,
and the Life everlasting. Amen.**

[The Lord be with you:

People   **and with thy spirit.]**

Let us pray.

Lord, have mercy upon us.

People   **Christ, have mercy upon us.**

Lord, have mercy upon us.

People   **OUR Father, who art in heaven, hallowed be thy name;
thy kingdom come; thy will be done; on earth as it is in
heaven. Give us this day our daily bread. And forgive us
our trespasses, as we forgive those who trespass against
us. And lead us not into temptation; but deliver us from
evil. Amen.**

Suffrages

Then follows one of these sets of suffrages:

A1

O Lord, shew thy mercy upon us:
People   **and grant us thy salvation.**

O Lord, save the *Queen*:
People   **and mercifully hear us when we call upon thee.**

Endue thy ministers with righteousness:
People   **and make thy chosen people joyful.**

O Lord, save thy people:
People   **and bless thine inheritance.**

Give peace in our time, O Lord:
People   **because there is none other that fighteth for us,
but only thou, O God.**

O God, make clean our hearts within us:
People   **and take not thy Holy Spirit from us.**

/

A2

O Lord, shew thy mercy upon us:

People **and grant us thy salvation.**

Endue thy ministers with righteousness:

People **and make thy chosen people joyful.**

Give peace in our time, O Lord:

People **for only in thee can we live in safety.**

Lord, keep this nation under thy care:

People **and guide us in the way of justice and truth.**

Let thy way be known upon earth:

People **thy saving health among all nations.**

Let not the needy, O Lord, be forgotten:

People **nor the hope of the poor be taken away.**

Create in us clean hearts, O God:

People **and sustain us with thy Holy Spirit.**

B

That this evening may be holy, good, and peaceful:

People   **we pray to thee, O Lord.**

That thy holy angels may lead us in paths of peace
and goodwill:

People   **we pray to thee, O Lord.**

That we may be pardoned and forgiven for our sins
and offences:

People   **we pray to thee, O Lord.**

That there may be peace to thy Church and to the
whole world:

People   **we pray to thee, O Lord.**

That we may depart this life in thy faith and fear,
and not be condemned before the great judgment seat
of Christ:

People   **we pray to thee, O Lord.**

That we may be bound together by the Holy Spirit in the
communion of Blessed Mary ever-Virgin, (of Saint *N.*)
and of all thy Saints,
entrusting one another and all our life to Christ:

People   **we pray to thee, O Lord.**

Collects

Collect of the Day

Collect for Peace

O GOD, from whom all holy desires, all good counsels, and all just works do proceed: give unto thy servants that peace which the world cannot give; that both our hearts may be set to obey thy commandments, and also that by thee we being defended from the fear of our enemies may pass our time in rest and quietness; through the merits of Jesus Christ our Saviour. **Amen.**

Collect against all Perils

LIGHTEN our darkness, we beseech thee, O Lord: and by thy great mercy defend us from all perils and dangers of this night; for the love of thy only Son, our Saviour Jesus Christ. **Amen.**

Conclusion

The order for the end of the service may include:

a. Hymns or anthems
b. A sermon
c. Benediction of the Blessed Sacrament
d. Further Prayers (including the Prayers below)

The General Thanksgiving

People **ALMIGHTY God, Father of all mercies,
we thine unworthy servants
do give thee most humble and hearty thanks
for all thy goodness and loving-kindness
to us and to all men. We bless
thee for our creation, preservation,
and all the blessings of this life;
but above all for thine inestimable love
in the redemption of the world by our Lord Jesus
  Christ,
for the means of grace, and for the hope of glory.
And, we beseech thee,
give us that due sense of all thy mercies,
that our hearts may be unfeignedly thankful;
and that we shew forth thy praise,
not only with our lips, but in our lives,
by giving up our selves to thy service,
and by walking before thee
in holiness and righteousness all our days;
through Jesus Christ our Lord,
to whom, with thee and the Holy Spirit,
be all honour and glory, world without end. Amen.**

A Prayer for the Pope

O GOD, the pastor and ruler of all the faithful, mercifully look upon thy servant Benedict whom thou hast been pleased to set as pastor over thy Church: grant him, we beseech thee, to be in word and conversation a wholesome example to the people committed to his charge; that he with them may attain unto everlasting life; through Jesus Christ our Lord. **Amen.**

A Prayer for the Clergy and People

> ALMIGHTY and everlasting God, who alone workest great marvels, send down upon our bishops and clergy, and all congregations committed to their charge, the healthful spirit of thy grace; and that they may truly please thee, pour upon them the continual dew of thy blessing. Grant this, O Lord, for the honour of our advocate and mediator, Jesus Christ. **Amen.**

For British Subjects

A Prayer for the Queen and Royal Family

> Let us pray.

> ALMIGHTY God we pray for thy servant *Elizabeth* our *Queen*, now by thy mercy reigning over us. Adorn *her* yet more with every virtue, remove all evil from *her* path, that with *her consort*, and all the royal family, *she* may come at last in grace to thee, the way, the truth, and the life, who livest and reignest with the Father in the unity of the Holy Spirit, one God, for ever and ever.
> **Amen.**

For the Nation

ALMIGHTY God, we commend the people of this land to thy care and protection. Give to our rulers [especially...), the government and all in authority, Wisdom and strength to work for the welfare of all in the community, so that we may live in security and peace, through Jesus Christ our Lord. **Amen.**

A Prayer of Saint Chrysostom

ALMIGHTY God, who hast given us grace at this time with one accord to make our common supplications unto thee; and dost promise that when two or three are gathered together in thy Name thou wilt grant their requests: fulfil now, O Lord, the desires and petitions of thy servants, as may be most expedient for them; granting us in this world knowledge of thy truth, and in the world to come life everlasting. **Amen.**

The Office concludes as follows:

The grace of our Lord Jesus Christ,
and the love of God,
and the fellowship of the Holy Spirit,
be with us all evermore.

People   **Amen.**

or

[The Lord be with you:

People   **and with thy spirit.]**

Let us bless the Lord.

People   **Thanks be to God.**

✠   May the souls of the faithful, through the mercy of God
rest in peace.

People   **Amen.**

The Anthem to the Blessed Virgin Mary follows the final office of the day (see pages 151 and 928).

New Testament Canticles

for use after the New Testament Lesson at Evening Prayer in the place of Nunc Dimittis when Compline is to follow later. The Canticle is set for the day of the week, as below, except where the Lectionary prescribes differently.

Sunday I

Christus Iesus

1   Though he was in the form of God :
Jesus did not count equality with God a thing to be grasped.

2   He emptied himself, taking the form of a servant :
being born in the likeness of men.

3   And being found in human form :
he humbled himself and became obedient unto death,
    even death on a cross.

4   Therefore God has highly exalted him :
and bestowed on him the name which is above every name,

5   That at the name of Jesus every knee should bow :
in heaven and on earth and under the earth,

6   And every tongue confess that Jesus Christ is Lord :
to the glory of God the Father.

Phil 2:6-11

Glory be to the Father, and to the Son :
and to the Holy Spirit;
As it was in the beginning, is now, and ever shall be :
world without end. Amen.

Salus et gloria

Alleluia.
Salvation and glory and power belong to our God,
[Alleluia.]
His judgments are true and just.
Alleluia [Alleluia.]

Alleluia.
Praise our God, all you his servants,
[Alleluia.]
You who fear him, small and great.
Alleluia [Alleluia.]

Alleluia.
The Lord our God, the almighty, reigns,
[Alleluia.]
Let us rejoice and exult and give him the glory.
Alleluia [Alleluia.]

Alleluia.
The marriage of the Lamb has come,
[Alleluia.]
and his Bride has made herself ready.
Alleluia [Alleluia.]

Rev 19:1, 2, 5-7

Glory be to the Father, and to the Son :
and to the Holy Spirit;
As it was in the beginning, is now, and ever shall be :
world without end. Amen.

Christus passus est

1   Christ suffered for you :
leaving you an example, that you should follow in his steps.

2   He committed no sin :
no guile was found on his lips.

3   When he was reviled :
he did not revile in return.

4   When he suffered, he did not threaten :
but he trusted to him who judges justly.

5   He himself bore our sins :
in his body on the tree,

6   That we might die to sin :
and live to righteousness.

1 Pet 2:21-24

Glory be to the Father, and to the Son :
and to the Holy Spirit;
As it was in the beginning, is now, and ever shall be :
world without end. Amen.

Monday

Benedictus Deus et Pater

1   Blessed be the God and Father of our Lord Jesus Christ :
who has blessed us in Christ with every spiritual blessing in
  the heavenly places.

2   He chose us in him before the foundation of the world :
that we should be holy and blameless before him.

3   He destined us in love to be his sons through Jesus Christ :
according to the purpose of his will,

4   To the praise of his glorious grace :
which he freely bestowed on us in the Beloved.

5   In him we have redemption through his blood :
the forgiveness of our trespasses,
  according to the riches of his grace
which he lavished upon us.

6   He has made known to us in all Wisdom and insight the
  mystery of his will :
according to his purpose which he set forth in Christ.

7   His purpose he set forth in Christ :
as a plan for the fullness of time,

8   To unite all things in him :
things in heaven and things on earth.

Eph 1:3-10

Glory be to the Father, and to the Son :
and to the Holy Spirit;
As it was in the beginning, is now, and ever shall be :
world without end. Amen.

Tuesday

Dignus es, Domine

1   Worthy are you, our Lord and God :
to receive glory and honour and power,

2   For you created all things :
and by your will they existed and were created.

3   Worthy are you, O Lord :
to take the scroll and to open its seals,

4   For you were slain and by your blood you ransomed men
for God :
from every tribe and tongue and people and nation.

5   You have made us a kingdom and priests to our God :
and we shall reign on earth.

6   Worthy is the Lamb who was slain,
to receive power and wealth and Wisdom :
and might and honour and glory and blessing!

Rev 4:11; 5:9, 10, 12

Glory be to the Father, and to the Son :
and to the Holy Spirit;
As it was in the beginning, is now, and ever shall be :
world without end. Amen.

Wednesday

Gratias agamus Deo Patri

1   Let us give thanks to the Father :
     who has qualified us to share in the inheritance of the saints
        in light.
2   He has delivered us from the dominion of darkness
        and transferred us to the kingdom of his beloved Son :
     in whom we have redemption, the forgiveness of sins.
3   He is the image of the invisible God,
        the first-born of all creation :
     for in him all things were created, in heaven and on earth,
        visible and invisible.
4   All things were created through him and for him :
     he is before all things, and in him all things hold together.
5   He is the head of the body, the church :
     he is the beginning, the first-born from the dead,
        that in everything he might be pre-eminent.
6   For in him all the fullness of God was pleased to dwell :
     and through him to reconcile to himself all things,
7   Whether on earth or in heaven :
     making peace by the blood of his cross.

Col 1:12-20

Glory be to the Father, and to the Son :
and to the Holy Spirit;
As it was in the beginning, is now, and ever shall be :
world without end. Amen.

Thursday

Gratias agimus tibi

1   We give thanks to you, Lord God almighty :
who are and who were,
   that you have taken your great power and begun to reign.

2   The nations raged, but your wrath came :
and the time for the dead to be judged,

3   For rewarding your servants, the prophets and saints :
and those who fear your name, both small and great,

4   Now the salvation and the power and the kingdom of our
   God and the authority of his Christ have come :
for the accuser of our brethren has been thrown down,
   who accuses them day and night before our God.

5   And they have conquered him by the blood of the Lamb
   and by the word of their testimony :
for they loved not their lives even unto death.

6   Rejoice then, O heaven :
and you that dwell therein.

Rev 11:17-18; 12:10b-12a

Glory be to the Father, and to the Son :
and to the Holy Spirit;
As it was in the beginning, is now, and ever shall be :
world without end. Amen.

Friday

Magna et mirabilia

1   Great and wonderful are your deeds, O Lord God the
     almighty :
    just and true are your ways, O King of the ages!

2   Who shall not fear and glorify your name, O Lord? :
    for you alone are holy.

3   All nations shall come and worship you :
    for your judgments have been revealed.

Rev 15:3-4

Glory be to the Father, and to the Son :
and to the Holy Spirit;
As it was in the beginning, is now, and ever shall be :
world without end. Amen.

Saturday
(see Sunday I)

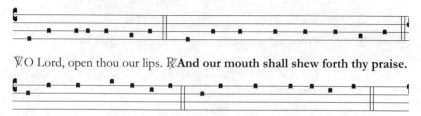

℣.O Lord, open thou our lips. ℟.**And our mouth shall shew forth thy praise.**

℣.O God, make speed to save us. ℟.**O Lord, make haste to help us.**

℣.Glory be to the Father, and to the Son: and to the Ho-ly Spir-it;

℟.**As it was in the beginning, is now and ever shall be: world without end.**

A-men. Al-le- lu- ia.*

*in Lent:

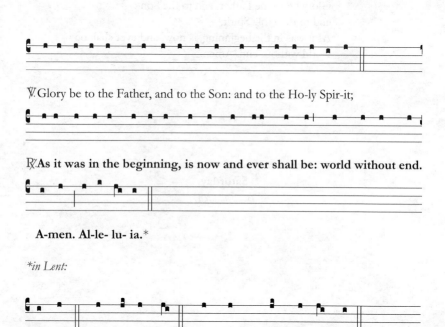

A-men. ℣.Praise ye the Lord. ℟.**The Lord's Name be prais-ed.**

Phos Hilaron

1.O gladsome light, O grace
 of God the Father's face,
the eternal splendour wearing;
 celestial, holy, blest,
our Saviour Jesus Christ,
 joyful in thine appearing!

2.Now, ere day fadeth quite,
 we see the evening light,
our wonted hymn outpouring;
 Father of might unknown,
thee, his incarnate Son,
 and Holy Spirit adoring.

3.To thee of right belongs
 all praise of holy songs,
O Son of God, life giver;
 thee, therefore, O Most High,
the world doth glorify,
 and shall exalt forever.

Trans. Robert Bridges (1844-1930)
Tune: Melody for Nunc dimittis *in the* Genevan Psalter *1549*
supplied by Louis Bourgeois (c. 1510-61)

Or:

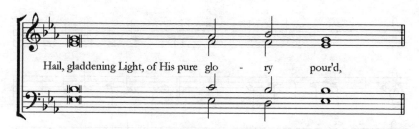

Hail, gladdening Light, of His pure glo - ry pour'd,

who is the Immortal Fa - ther, heaven - ly, blest,

ho - li -est of ho - lies, Je - sus Christ, our Lord.

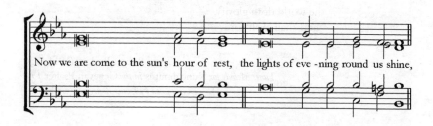

Now we are come to the sun's hour of rest, the lights of eve -ning round us shine,

we hymn the Fa - ther, Son, and Ho - ly Spir - it di - vine.

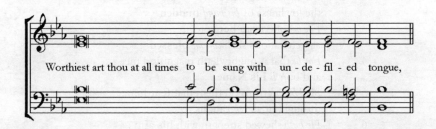

Worthiest art thou at all times to be sung with un - de - fil - ed tongue,

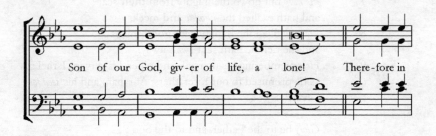

Son of our God, giv - er of life, a - lone! There - fore in

all the world thy glo - ries, Lord, they own. A - men.

Words: John Keble
Tune: Sebaste, John Stainer

Magnificat

Simple Tone (I.i)

MY soul doth magnify **the** Lord: and my spirit hath rejoiced in *God my* **Sa**viour.

2   *For he* hath re**gar**ded :
the lowliness of *his hand*-**maid**en.

3   *For be*hold, from **hence**forth :
all generations shall *call me* **bless**ed.

4   *For he* that is mighty hath magni**fied** me:
and ho*ly is* **his** Name.

5   *And his* mercy is on them that **fear** him :
throughout all *gene*rations.

6   *He hath* shewed strength with **his** arm :
he hath scattered the proud in the imagina*tion of* **their** hearts.

7   *He hath* put down the mighty from **their** seat :
and hath exalted the *humble* **and** meek.

8   *He hath* filled the hungry with **good** things :
and the rich he hath sent *empty* **a**way.

9   *He re*membering his mercy hath holpen his servant Is**ra**el :
as he promised to our forefathers, Abraham and his *seed for*
ever.

     Glory be to the Father, and to **the** Son :
and to the *Holy* **Spir**it;
As it was in the beginning, is now, and ever **shall** be :
world with*out end.* **A**men.

Solemn Tone (VIII.1)

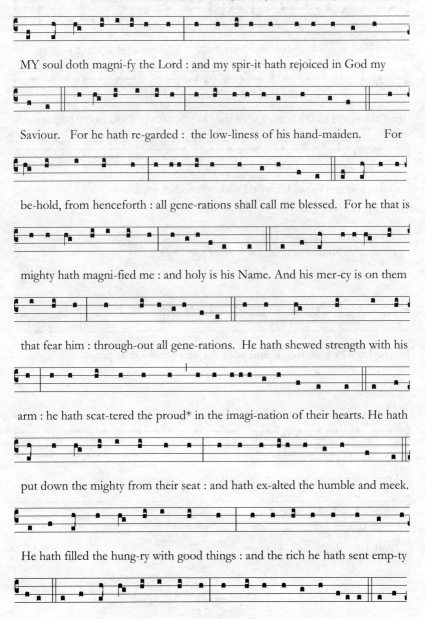

MY soul doth magni-fy the Lord : and my spir-it hath rejoiced in God my

Saviour.   For he hath re-garded :   the low-liness of his hand-maiden.   For

be-hold, from henceforth : all gene-rations shall call me blessed.   For he that is

mighty hath magni-fied me : and holy is his Name.   And his mer-cy is on them

that fear him : through-out all gene-rations.   He hath shewed strength with his

arm : he hath scat-tered the proud* in the imagi-nation of their hearts. He hath

put down the mighty from their seat : and hath ex-alted the humble and meek.

He hath filled the hung-ry with good things : and the rich he hath sent emp-ty

away.   He re-member-ing his mer-cy : hath holpen his servant Isra-el.   As he

129

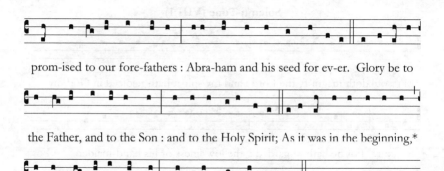

prom-ised to our fore-fathers : Abra-ham and his seed for ev-er. Glory be to

the Father, and to the Son : and to the Holy Spirit; As it was in the beginning,*

is now, and ev-er shall be: world with-out end. A-men.

A setting of the Nunc Dimittis *may be found on page 145.*

[℣. The Lord be with you: ℟. **and with thy spir-it.**] ℣. Let us pray.

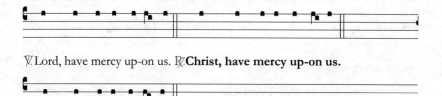

℣. Lord, have mercy up-on us. ℟. **Christ, have mercy up-on us.**

℣. Lord, have mercy up-on us.

A1

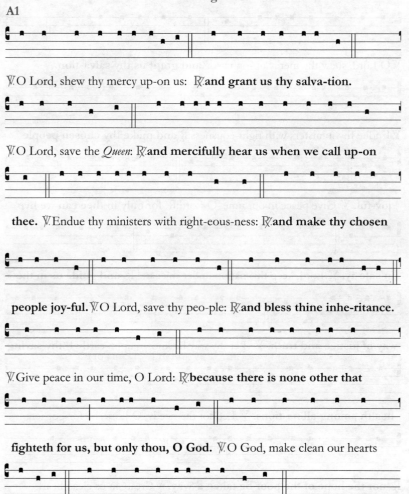

℣.O Lord, shew thy mercy up-on us: ℟.**and grant us thy salva-tion.**

℣.O Lord, save the *Queen*: ℟.**and mercifully hear us when we call up-on**

thee. ℣.Endue thy ministers with right-eous-ness: ℟.**and make thy chosen**

people joy-ful. ℣.O Lord, save thy peo-ple: ℟.**and bless thine inhe-ritance.**

℣.Give peace in our time, O Lord: ℟.**because there is none other that**

fighteth for us, but only thou, O God. ℣.O God, make clean our hearts

with-in us: ℟.**and take not thy Holy Spirit from us.**

℣. O Lord, shew thy mercy up-on us: ℟. and grant us thy salva-tion.

℣. Endue thy ministers with right-eousness:℟. and make thy chosen people

joy-ful. ℣. Give peace in our time, O Lord:℟. for only in thee can we live

in safe-ty. ℣. Lord, keep this nation under thy care: ℟. and guide us in the

way of justice and truth. ℣. Let thy way be known upon earth: ℟. thy saving

health among all na-tions. ℣. Let not the needy, O Lord, be for-got-ten:

℟. nor the hope of the poor be taken a-way. ℣. Create in us clean hearts,

O God: ℟. and sustain us with thy Holy Spir-it.

B (Morning Prayer)

℣. O Lord, save thy people, and bless thine her-itage: ℞. **govern them and lift**

them up for ev-er. ℣. Day by day we magni-fy thee: ℞. **and we worship thy**

Name ever world with-out end. ℣. Vouchsafe, O Lord, to keep us this day

with-out sin: ℞. **O Lord, have mercy upon us, have mercy up-on us.**

℣. O Lord, let thy mercy lighten up-on us: ℞. **as our trust is in thee.** ℣. O Lord,

in thee have I trust-ed: ℞. **let me never be confound-ed.**

B (Evening Prayer)

℣. That this evening may be holy,   ℟. **we pray to thee, O Lord.**
good, and peace-ful:

℣. That thy holy angels may lead us
in paths of peace and good-will: ℟.

℣. That we may be pardoned and forgiven
for our sins and of-fen-ces: ℟.

℣. That there may be peace
to thy Church and to the whole world: ℟.

℣. That we may depart this life in thy faith and fear,
and not be condemned before the great judgment seat of Christ: ℟.

℣. That we may be bound together by the Holy Spirit
in the communion of Blessed Mary ever-Virgin,
(of Saint N.) and of all thy Saints,
entrusting one another and all our life to Christ: ℟.

Collects

Almighty God…   now and ev- er. ℟. A-men.
                  world with-out end.
                  Christ our Lord.

Other Collects are inflected similarly; or the following inflections may be used, with Amen as above:

Jesus Christ our Lord.   Jesus Christ, our Sa-viour.
Saviour, Je- sus Christ.

Conclusion

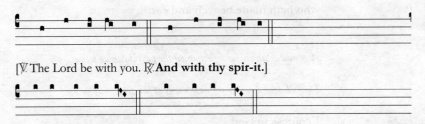

[℣. The Lord be with you. ℟. **And with thy spir-it.**]

℣. Let us bless the Lord. ℟. **Thanks be to God.**

May the souls… *may be sung on a low monotone.*

NIGHT PRAYER
(COMPLINE)

Preparation

✠	The Lord almighty grant us a quiet night and a perfect end.
People	**Amen.**

Brethren, be sober, be vigilant; because your adversary the devil, as a roaring lion, walks about, seeking whom he may devour: whom resist, steadfast in the faith.

1 Pet 5:8, 9

	But thou, O Lord, have mercy upon us.
People	**Thanks be to God.**

✠	Our help is in the name of the Lord:
People	**who hath made heaven and earth.**

A period of silence for reflection on the past day may follow.

The following or other suitable words of penitence may be used.

People	**I confess to God,**
	to blessed Mary,
	and to all the Saints,
	that I have sinned exceedingly
	in thought, word, and deed,

And, striking their breasts, they say

through my own fault;

and they continue

I ask holy Mary,
and all the Saints of God,
to pray for me.

The minister says

May almighty God have mercy upon us,
forgive us all our sins;
deliver us from every evil;
confirm and strengthen us in goodness;,
and bring us to everlasting life.

People   **Amen.**

℣.O God, make speed to save us. ℟.**O Lord, make haste to help us.**

℣.Glory be to the Father, and to the Son: and to the Ho-ly Spir-it;

℟.**As it was in the beginning, is now and ever shall be: world without end.**

  A-men. Al-le- lu- ia.*

*in Lent:

  A-men. ℣.Praise ye the Lord. ℟.**The Lord's Name be prais-ed.**

The following or another suitable hymn may be sung

Tune I (Sundays and Feasts)

Tune II (Ferias)

1.Before the ending of the day,
 Creator of the world we pray,
that with thy wonted favour thou
 wouldst be our guard and keeper now.

2.From all ill dreams defend our eyes,
 from nightly fears and fantasies;
tread underfoot our ghostly foe,
 that no pollution we may know.

3.O Father, that we ask be done,
 through Jesus Christ, thine only Son;
who, with the Holy Ghost and thee,
 doth live and reign eternally. Amen.

Before 8th cent. Tr. J. M. Neale (1818-1866)

One or more of the following psalms may be used. They may be sung to this tone:

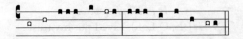

Psalm 4

Cum invocarem

1   *HEAR me* when I call, O God of my **right**eousness :
thou hast set me at liberty when I was in trouble;
have mercy upon me, and hearken *unto* **my** prayer.

2   O ye sons of men,
how long will ye blaspheme mine **hon**our :
and have such pleasure in vanity, and seek *after* **leas**ing?

3   Know this also, that the Lord hath chosen to himself the
man that is **god**ly :
when I call upon the Lord, *he will* **hear** me.

4   Stand in awe, and **sin** not :
commune with your own heart, and in your *chamber,*
and be still.

5   Offer the sacrifice of **right**eousness :
and put your *trust in* **the** Lord.

6   There be many **that** say :
Who will *shew us* **an**y good?

7   Lord, lift **thou** up :
the light of thy counte*nance up***on** us.

8   Thou hast put gladness in **my** heart :
since the time that their corn, and *wine, and* **oil** increased.

9   I will lay me down in peace, and take **my** rest :
for it is thou, Lord, only, that makest me *dwell in* **safe**ty.

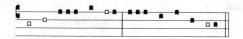

Psalm 31:1-6

In te, Domine, speravi

1   *IN THEE*, O Lord, have I put **my** trust :
      let me never be put to confusion, deliver me *in thy*
         righteousness.

2   Bow down thine ear **to** me :
      make haste *to de*liver me.

3   And be thou my strong rock, and house of **de**fence :
      that thou *mayest* **save** me.

4   For thou art my strong rock, and my **cas**tle :
      be thou also my guide, and lead me *for thy* **name's** sake.

5   Draw me out of the net, that they have laid privily **for** me :
      for *thou art* **my** strength.

6   Into thy hands I commend my **spir**it :
      for thou hast redeemed me, O *Lord, thou* **God** of truth.

Psalm 91

Qui habitat

1   *WHOSO* dwelleth under the defence of the **Most** High :
      shall abide under the shadow of *the al***might**y.

2   I will say unto the Lord, Thou art my hope, and my
         stronghold :
      my God, in *him will* **I** trust.

3   For he shall deliver thee from the snare of the **hunt**er :
      and from the *noisome* **pest**ilence.

4   He shall defend thee under his wings, and thou shalt be safe
         under his **feath**ers :
      his faithfulness and truth shall be thy *shield and* **buck**ler.

5   Thou shalt not be afraid for any terror **by** night :
      nor for the arrow that *flieth* **by** day;

6   For the pestilence that walketh in **dark**ness :
      nor for the sickness that destroyeth *in the* **noon**day.

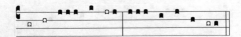

7 A thousand shall fall beside thee, and ten thousand at thy
  right hand :
  but it shall *not come* **nigh** thee.

8 Yea, with thine eyes shalt thou **be**hold :
  and see the reward of *the un*godly.

9 For thou, Lord, art **my** hope :
  thou hast set thine house of de*fence ve***ry** high.

10 There shall no evil happen un**to** thee :
  neither shall any plague come *nigh thy* **dwell**ing.

11 For he shall give his angels charge ov**er** thee :
  to keep *thee in* **all** thy ways.

12 They shall bear thee in **their** hands :
  that thou hurt not thy *foot a***gainst** a stone.

13 Thou shalt go upon the lion and **ad**der :
  the young lion and the dragon shalt thou tread *under* **thy**
  feet.

14 Because he hath set his love upon me, therefore will I deli**ver**
  him :
  I will set him up, because *he hath* **known** my name.

15 He shall call upon me, and I will **hear** him :
  yea, I am with him in trouble; I will deliver him, and bring
  him to **hon**our.

16 With long life will I satis**fy** him :
  and shew him *my sal***va**tion.

Psalm 134

Ecce nunc

1 *BEHOLD* now, praise **the** Lord :
  all ye *servants* **of** the Lord;

2 Ye that by night stand in the house of **the** Lord :
  even in the courts of the *house of* **our** God.

3 Lift up your hands in the **sanc**tuary :
  and praise **the** Lord.

4 The Lord that made heaven **and** earth :
  give thee blessing *out of* **Si**on.

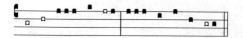

At the end of the psalmody these words are said or sung:

Glory be to the Father, and to **the** Son :
and to the *Holy* **Spir**it;
as it was in the beginning, is now, and ever **shall** be :
world with*out end.* **A**men.

Scripture Reading

One of the following short lessons or another suitable passage is read

Thou, O Lord, art in the midst of us, and we are called by thy name; leave us not, O Lord our God.

Jer 14:9

or

Now the God of peace, that brought again from the dead our Lord Jesus, that great shepherd of the sheep, through the blood of the everlasting covenant, make you perfect in every good work to do his will, working in you that which is well-pleasing in his sight; through Jesus Christ, to whom be glory for ever and ever. Amen.

Heb 13:20, 21

At the end the following may be said

People **Thanks be to God.**

The following responsory may be said or sung:

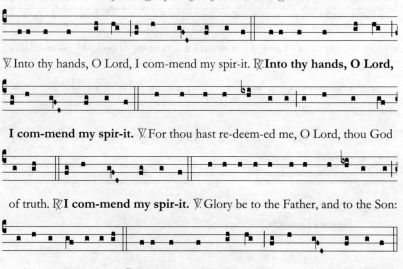

℣. Into thy hands, O Lord, I com-mend my spir-it. ℟. **Into thy hands, O Lord,**

I com-mend my spir-it. ℣. For thou hast re-deem-ed me, O Lord, thou God

of truth. ℟. **I com-mend my spir-it.** ℣. Glory be to the Father, and to the Son:

and to the Ho-ly Spirit. ℟. **Into thy hands, O Lord, I com-mend my spirit.**

or, in Eastertide

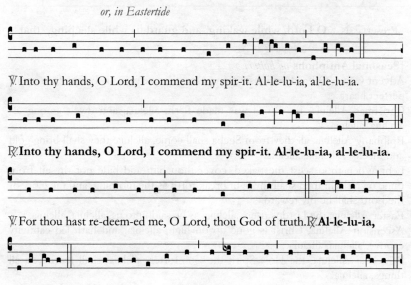

℣. Into thy hands, O Lord, I commend my spir-it. Al-le-lu-ia, al-le-lu-ia.

℟. **Into thy hands, O Lord, I commend my spir-it. Al-le-lu-ia, al-le-lu-ia.**

℣. For thou hast re-deem-ed me, O Lord, thou God of truth. ℟. **Al-le-lu-ia,**

al-le-lu-ia. ℣. Glory be to the Fa-ther, and to the Son: and to the Holy Spirit.

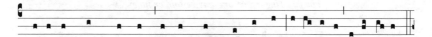

℞. Into thy hands, O Lord, I commend my spir-it. Al-le-lu-ia, al-le-lu-ia.

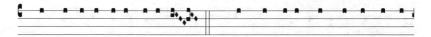

℣. Keep me as the apple of an eye.　　℞. Hide me under the shadow of thy

wings.

Gospel Canticle

Nunc dimittis

Antiphon†

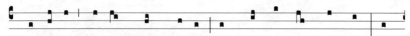

Preserve us, * **O Lord, while waking, and guard us while sleeping,　that**

---

†**Seasonal Antiphons** *ad libitum*

Advent Come, O Lord, and visit us in peace: that we may joy before thee with a perfect heart.

Christmas Alleluia, the Word was made flesh, alleluia: and dwelt among us, alleluia, alleluia.

Epiphany Alleluia, all they from Sheba shall come, alleluia: they shall bring gold and incense, alleluia, alleluia.

Lent When thou seest the naked, cover thou him and hide not thyself from thine own flesh: then shall thy light break forth as the morning, and the glory of the Lord shall be thy reward.

Easter Alleluia, the Lord is risen, alleluia: as he said unto us, alleluia, alleluia.

Ascension Alleluia, Christ is gone up on high, alleluia: and hath led captivity captive, alleluia, alleluia.

Pentecost Alleluia, the Holy Spirit the Comforter, alleluia: shall teach you all things, alleluia.

Trinity, All Saints, Feast Days Grant us thy light, O Lord: that the darkness of our hearts being wholly passed away, we may attain at length to the light, which is Christ.

awake we may watch with Christ, and asleep we may rest in peace.

✠   *LORD, now* lettest thou thy *servant* depart **in** peace :
according *to* **thy** word.

2   For mine *eyes* have seen thy *sal*vation :
Which thou hast prepared before the face of *all* **peo**ple;

3   To be a light to *lighten* the **Gent**iles :
and to be the glory of thy peo*ple* **Is**rael.

Lk 2:29-32

Glory be to the *Father,* and to **the** Son :
and to the Ho*ly* **Spir**it;
as it was in the beginning, is now, and *ever* **shall** be :
world without *end.* **A**men.

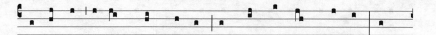

Preserve us, O Lord, while waking, and guard us while sleeping, that

awake we may watch with Christ, and asleep we may rest in peace.

Prayers

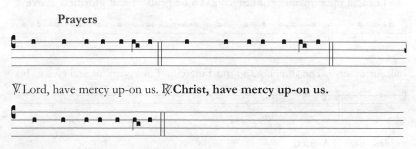

℣. Lord, have mercy up-on us. ℟. **Christ, have mercy up-on us.**

℣. Lord, have mercy up-on us.

People   **Our Father, who art in heaven,**
hallowed be thy name;
thy kingdom come;
thy will be done,
on earth as it is in heaven.
Give us this day our daily bread.
And forgive us our trespasses,
as we forgive those who trespass against us.
And lead us not into temptation;
but deliver us from evil. Amen.

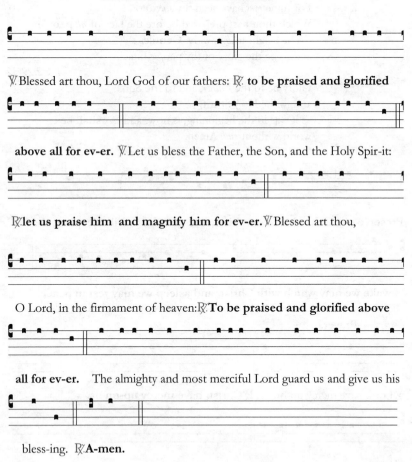

℣. Blessed art thou, Lord God of our fathers: ℟. **to be praised and glorified**

above all for ev-er. ℣. Let us bless the Father, the Son, and the Holy Spir-it:

℟. **let us praise him and magnify him for ev-er.** ℣. Blessed art thou,

O Lord, in the firmament of heaven: ℟. **To be praised and glorified above**

all for ev-er.   The almighty and most merciful Lord guard us and give us his

bless-ing. ℟. **A-men.**

146

[The following may be omitted:

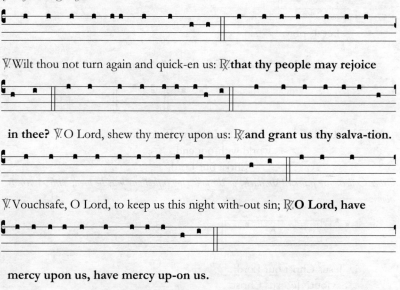

℣. Wilt thou not turn again and quick-en us: ℟. **that thy people may rejoice**

in thee? ℣. O Lord, shew thy mercy upon us: ℟. **and grant us thy salva-tion.**

℣. Vouchsafe, O Lord, to keep us this night with-out sin; ℟. **O Lord, have**

mercy upon us, have mercy up-on us.

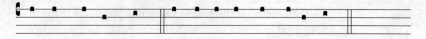

℣. O Lord, hear our prayer; ℟. **And let our cry come un-to thee.**]

Let us pray.

One or more of the following Collects is said

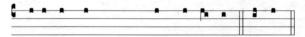

Almighty God...   now and ev- er. ℟. **A-men.**
                              world with-out end.
                              Christ our Lord.

Other Collects are inflected similarly; or the following inflections may be used, with Amen as above:

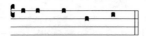

Jesus Christ our Lord.
Saviour, Je- sus Christ.

VISIT, we beseech thee, O Lord, this place, and drive from it all the snares of the enemy: let thy holy angels dwell herein to preserve us in peace; and may thy blessing be upon us evermore; through Jesus Christ our Lord. **Amen.**

LIGHTEN our darkness, we beseech thee, O Lord: and by thy great mercy defend us from all perils and dangers of this night; for the love of thy only Son, our Saviour, Jesus Christ. **Amen.**

O LORD Jesus Christ, son of the living God, who at this evening hour didst rest in the sepulchre, and didst thereby sanctify the grave to be a bed of hope to thy people: make us so to abound in sorrow for our sins, which were the cause of thy passion, that when our bodies lie in the dust, our souls may live with thee; who livest and reignest with the Father and the Holy Spirit, one God, world without end. **Amen.**

LOOK down, O Lord, from thy heavenly throne, illuminate the darkness of this night with thy celestial brightness, and from the sons of light banish the deeds of darkness; through Jesus Christ our Lord. **Amen.**

BE PRESENT, O merciful God, and protect us through the silent hours of this night, so that we who are wearied by the changes and chances of this fleeting world, may repose upon thy eternal changelessness; through Jesus Christ our Lord. **Amen.**

Conclusion

℣. We will lay us down in peace and take our rest. ℟. **For it is thou, Lord, only**

that makest us dwell in safe-ty.

or

℣. We will lay us down in peace and take our rest. ℟. **For it is thou, Lord,**

on-ly that mak-est us dwell in safe- ty.

℣. Abide with us, O Lord:

℟. **for it is toward evening and the day is far spent.**

149

℣. As the watchmen look for the morn-ing:

℟. so do we look for thee, O Christ.

* **[℣. Come with the dawning of the day:**

℟. and make thyself known in the breaking of bread.]

[℣. The Lord be with you. ℟. **And with thy spir-it.**]

℣. Let us bless the Lord. ℟. **Thanks be to God.**

☩   The almighty and merciful Lord,
                the Father, the Son and the Holy Spirit,
                bless us and preserve us.
People   **Amen.**

The Anthem to the Blessed Virgin Mary follows the final office of the day (see page 151 onwards). Plainsong settings are found on page 928.

---

* The response in square brackets **[ ]** is normally used only if Mass is to be celebrated the following morning.

ANTHEMS TO THE BLESSED VIRGIN MARY
FOLLOWING THE FINAL OFFICE OF THE DAY

The versicles, responses and prayers may be omitted.

I   **From Advent Sunday until Candlemas**

Alma Redemptoris Mater
Mother of Christ! hear thou thy people's cry,
Star of the deep, and portal of the sky!
Mother of him who thee from nothing made,
Sinking we strive, and call to thee for aid;
Oh, by that joy which Gabriel brought to thee,
Thou Virgin first and last, let us thy mercy see.

Divine Office (14)

From Advent Sunday until Christmas Eve

℣. The angel of the Lord declared unto Mary:
℟. **and she conceived by the Holy Spirit.**

Let us pray.

WE BESEECH thee, O Lord, pour thy grace into our
hearts: that, as we have known the incarnation of thy Son
Jesus Christ by the message of an angel, so by his cross and
passion we may be brought unto the glory of his
resurrection; through the same Jesus Christ our Lord.

From Christmas until Candlemas

℣. After childbirth thou didst remained a pure virgin:
℟. **Mother of God intercede for us.**

Let us pray.

O GOD, who, by the fruitful virginity of blessed Mary, hast bestowed upon mankind the reward of eternal salvation: grant, we beseech thee, that we may experience her intercession, through whom we have been made worthy to receive the author of life; our Lord Jesus Christ, thy Son.

✠   May the divine assistance remain with us always.

People   **Amen.**

II   **From Candlemas until Wednesday in Holy Week**

Ave regina cælorum
Hail, Queen of Heaven, beyond compare,
to whom the angels homage pay;
hail, Root of Jesse, Gate of Light,
that opened for the world's new Day.

Rejoice, O Virgin unsurpassed,
in whom our ransom was begun,
for all thy loving children pray
to Christ, our Saviour, and thy Son.

or

Hail, O Queen of Heaven enthroned!
Hail, by angels Mistress owned!
Root of Jesse, Gate of Morn,
whence the world's true Light was born.

Glorious Virgin, joy to thee,
loveliest whom in heaven they see.
Fairest thou, where all are fair:
plead with Christ our sins to spare.

℣.   Grant that I may praise thee, sacred Virgin:
℟.   **give me strength against thine enemies.**

Let us pray.

GRANT us protection in our weakness, O merciful God, that we who commemorate the holy Mother of God may triumph over our iniquities with the help of her intercession; through Christ our Lord.

✠

People May the divine assistance remain with us always.
Amen.

III **During Eastertide**

Regina cæli, lætare
Joy to thee, O Queen of heaven, alleluia.
he whom thou wast meet to bear, alleluia.
as he promised hath arisen, alleluia.
pour for us to God thy prayer, alleluia.

℣. Rejoice and be glad, O Virgin Mary, alleluia:
℟. **for the Lord has risen indeed, alleluia.**

Let us pray.

O GOD, who by the resurrection of thy Son, our Lord Jesus Christ, hast brought joy to the whole world: grant, we beseech thee, that, through his mother the Virgin Mary, we may obtain the joys of everlasting life; through the same Christ our Lord.

✠

People May the divine assistance remain with us always.
Amen.

153

Salve, Regina

Hail, holy Queen, mother of mercy,
hail our life, our sweetness, and our hope.
To thee do we cry,
poor banished children of Eve.
To thee do we send up our sighs,
mourning and weeping in this vale of tears.
Turn then, most gracious advocate,
thine eyes of mercy towards us,
and after this our exile
shew to us the blessed fruit of thy womb, Jesus.
O clement, O loving,
O sweet Virgin Mary.

℣.   Pray for us, O holy Mother of God,
℞.   **that we may be made worthy of the promises of Christ.**

Let us pray.

ALMIGHTY, everlasting God, who by the cooperation of the Holy Spirit, didst prepare the body and soul of the glorious Virgin-Mother Mary to become a worthy dwelling for thy Son; grant that we who rejoice in her commemoration may, by her loving intercession, be delivered from present evils and from eternal death; through the same Christ our Lord.

✠

People   May the divine assistance remain with us always.
Amen.

III. The Litany

The Litany

To be said or sung, kneeling, standing, or in procession before Mass or after the Collects of Morning or Evening Prayer; or separately, especially in Lent and on Rogation days.

Cantor   O God the Father of heaven:
have mercy upon us miserable sinners.

People   **O God the Father of heaven:
have mercy upon us miserable sinners.**

O God the Son, Redeemer of the world:
have mercy upon us miserable sinners.

People   **O God the Son, Redeemer of the world:
have mercy upon us miserable sinners.**

O God the Holy Spirit,
proceeding from the Father and the Son:
have mercy upon us miserable sinners.

People   **O God the Holy Spirit,
proceeding from the Father and the Son:
have mercy upon us miserable sinners.**

O holy, blessed, and glorious Trinity,
three Persons and one God:
have mercy upon us miserable sinners.

People   **O holy, blessed, and glorious Trinity,
three Persons and one God:
have mercy upon us miserable sinners.**

Saint Mary, Mother of God, our Saviour Jesus Christ,

People   **pray for us.**

All holy angels and archangels,
and all holy orders of blessed spirits,

People   **pray for us.**

All holy patriarchs and prophets,
apostles, martyrs, confessors and virgins;
and the blessed company of heaven,

People   **pray for us.**

Remember not, Lord, our offences,
  nor the offences of our forefathers;
neither take thou vengeance of our sins:
spare us, good Lord, spare thy people,
  whom thou hast redeemed with thy most precious blood,
and be not angry with us for ever.

People   **Spare us, good Lord.**

From all evil and mischief;
from sin, from the crafts and assaults of the devil;
from thy wrath, and from everlasting damnation,

People   **good Lord, deliver us.**

From all blindness of heart;
from pride, vain-glory, and hypocrisy;
from envy, hatred, and malice, and all uncharitableness,

People   **good Lord, deliver us.**

From fornication, and all other deadly sin;
and from all the deceits of the world, the flesh, and the devil,

People   **good Lord, deliver us.**

From lightning and tempest;
from plague, pestilence, and famine;
from battle and murder, and from sudden death,

People   **good Lord, deliver us.**

From all sedition, privy conspiracy, and rebellion;
from all false doctrine, heresy, and schism;
from hardness of heart,
  and contempt of thy Word and Commandment,

People   **good Lord, deliver us.**

By the mystery of thy holy Incarnation;
by thy holy Nativity and Circumcision;
by thy Baptism, Fasting, and Temptation,

People   **good Lord, deliver us.**

By thine Agony and bloody Sweat;
by thy Cross and Passion;
by thy precious Death and Burial;
by thy glorious Resurrection and Ascension;
and by the coming of the Holy Spirit,

People　**good Lord, deliver us.**

In all time of our tribulation; in all time of our wealth;
in the hour of death, and in the day of judgment,

People　**good Lord, deliver us.**

We sinners do beseech thee to hear us, O Lord God;
and that it may please thee to rule and govern
　thy holy Church universal in the right way,

People　**we beseech thee to hear us, good Lord.**

That it may please thee to bless *N.*, our Pope,
　and *N.*, our Ordinary,

People　**we beseech thee to hear us, good Lord.**

That it may please thee to illuminate
　all Bishops, Priests, and Deacons,
with true knowledge and understanding of thy Word;
and that both by their preaching and living
　they may set it forth and shew it accordingly,

People　**we beseech thee to hear us, good Lord.**

(I)　　*For British Subjects*

That it may please thee so to rule the hearts of thy
　servant, *Elizabeth* our *Queen*, and all set in authority
　under *her*, that they may above all things seek thy
　honour and glory,

People　**we beseech thee to hear us, good Lord.**

That it may please thee so to rule the hearts of thy
   servant, *N.*, the President (of *N.*), and all others in
   authority,
that they may above all things seek thy honour and
   glory,

People   **we beseech thee to hear us, good Lord**.

That it may please thee to guide all Judges and Magistrates,
   giving them grace to execute justice, and to maintain truth,

People   **we beseech thee to hear us, good Lord.**

That it may please thee to bless and keep all thy people,

People   **we beseech thee to hear us, good Lord.**

That it may please thee to give to all nations
   unity, peace, and concord,

People   **we beseech thee to hear us, good Lord.**

That it may please thee to give us an heart to love and dread
   thee,
and diligently to live after thy commandments,

People   **we beseech thee to hear us, good Lord.**

 That it may please thee to give to all thy people increase of
   grace,
to hear meekly thy Word, and to receive it with pure
   affection,
and to bring forth the fruits of the Spirit,

People   **we beseech thee to hear us, good Lord.**

That it may please thee to bring into the way of truth
   all such as have erred, and are deceived,

People   **we beseech thee to hear us, good Lord.**

That it may please thee to strengthen such as do stand;
and to comfort and help the weak-hearted;
and to raise up them that fall;
and finally to beat down Satan under our feet,

People **we beseech thee to hear us, good Lord.**

That it may please thee to succour, help, and comfort
all that are in danger, necessity, and tribulation,

People **we beseech thee to hear us, good Lord.**

That it may please thee to preserve all that travel
   by land or air or water,
all women labouring of child, all sick persons, and young
   children;
and to shew thy pity upon all prisoners and captives,

People **we beseech thee to hear us, good Lord.**

That it may please thee to defend, and provide for,
   the fatherless children, and widows,
and all that are desolate and oppressed,

People **we beseech thee to hear us, good Lord.**

That it may please thee to have mercy upon all men,

People **we beseech thee to hear us, good Lord.**

That it may please thee to forgive our enemies,
   persecutors, and slanderers,
   and to turn their hearts,

People **we beseech thee to hear us, good Lord.**

That it may please thee to give and preserve to our use
   the kindly fruits of the earth,
so as in due time we may enjoy them,

People **we beseech thee to hear us, good Lord.**

That it may please thee to give us true repentance;
to forgive us all our sins, negligences, and ignorances;
and to endue us with the grace of thy Holy Spirit,
to amend our lives according to thy holy Word,

People **we beseech thee to hear us, good Lord.**

	Son of God: we beseech thee to hear us.
People	**we beseech thee to hear us, good Lord.**

	That it may please thee to grant that, by the intercession of (*N.* and of) all thy Saints, we may finally attain to thy heavenly kingdom,
People	**we beseech thee to hear us, good Lord.**

	That it may please thee to grant to all the faithful departed eternal rest and perpetual light,
People	**we beseech thee to hear us, good Lord.**

	O Lamb of God: that takest away the sins of the world,
People	**grant us thy peace.**

	O Lamb of God: that takest away the sins of the world,
People	**have mercy upon us.**

	O Christ, hear us.
People	**O Christ, hear us.**

	Lord, have mercy upon us.
People	**Lord, have mercy upon us.**

	Christ, have mercy upon us.
People	**Christ, have mercy upon us.**

	Lord, have mercy upon us.
People	**Lord, have mercy upon us.**

Our Father, who art in heaven, hallowed be thy name; thy kingdom come; thy will be done, on earth as it is in heaven. Give us this day our daily bread. And forgive us our trespasses, as we forgive those who trespass against us. And lead us not into temptation; but deliver us from evil. Amen.

	O Lord, deal not with us after our sins:
People	**neither reward us after our iniquities.**

Let us pray.

O God, merciful Father, that despisest not the sighing of a
contrite heart, nor the desire of such as be sorrowful:
mercifully assist our prayers that we make before thee in all
our troubles and adversities, whensoever they oppress us;
and graciously hear us, that those evils, which the craft and
subtilty of the devil or man worketh against us, be brought
to nought, and by the providence of thy goodness they may
be dispersed; that we thy servants, being hurt by no
persecutions, may evermore give thanks unto thee in thy
holy Church; through Jesus Christ our Lord.

People   **O Lord, arise, help us, and deliver us
for thy Name's sake.**

O God, we have heard with our ears,
and our fathers have declared unto us,
the noble works that thou didst in their days,
and in the old time before them.

People   **O Lord, arise, help us, and deliver us
for thine honour.**

Glory be to the Father, and to the Son
and to the Holy Spirit;

People   **as it was in the beginning,
is now, and ever shall be
world without end. Amen.**

From our enemies defend us, O Christ:

People   **graciously look upon our afflictions.**

Pitifully behold the sorrows of our hearts:

People   **mercifully forgive the sins of thy people.**

Favourably with mercy hear our prayers:

People   **O Son of David, have mercy upon us.**

Both now and ever vouchsafe to hear us, O Christ:

People **graciously hear us, O Christ;**
graciously hear us, O Lord Christ.

O Lord, let thy mercy be shewed upon us:

People **as we do put our trust in thee.**

Let us pray.

We humbly beseech thee, O Father, mercifully to look upon our infirmities; and for the glory of thy Name turn from us all those evils that we most righteously have deserved; and grant that in all our troubles we may put our whole trust and confidence in thy mercy, and evermore serve thee in holiness and pureness of living, to thy honour and glory; through our only Mediator and Advocate, Jesus Christ our Lord. **Amen.**

Almighty God, who hast given us grace at this time with one accord to make our common supplications unto thee; and dost promise that when two or three are gathered together in thy Name thou wilt grant their requests: fulfil now, O Lord, the desires and petitions of thy servants, as may be most expedient for them; granting us in this world knowledge of thy truth, and in the world to come life everlasting. **Amen.**

✠ The grace of our Lord Jesus Christ,
and the love of God,
and the fellowship of the Holy Spirit,
be with us all evermore.
Amen.

2 Corinthians 13:13

163

IV. Times and Seasons

Part I Temporale:

Advent to the
Baptism of the Lord
and
Candlemas

TIMES AND SEASONS

From the First Sunday of Advent until Christmas Eve

Office

Opening Sentence
The night is far spent, and the day is at hand: let us therefore cast off the works of darkness, and let us put on the armour of light.

Rom 13:12

Hymns

Evening Prayer *Until 16 December*   *Vespers*

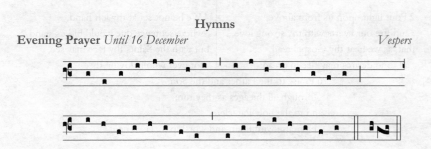

Conditor alme siderum

1. Creator of the stars of night,
   thy people's everlasting light,
Jesu, Redeemer, save us all,
   and hear thy servants when they call.

2. Thou, grieving that the ancient curse
   should doom to death a universe,
hast found the medicine, full of grace,
   to save and heal a ruined race.

3. Thou cam'st, the Bridegroom of the bride,
   as drew the world to evening-tide;
proceeding from a virgin shrine,
   the spotless Victim all divine:

4. At whose dread name, majestic now,
   all knees must bend, all hearts must bow;
and things celestial thee shall own,
   and things terrestrial, Lord alone.

5. O thou whose coming is with dread
   to judge and doom the quick and dead:
preserve us, while we dwell below,
   from every insult of the foe.

6. To God the Father, God the Son,
   and God the Spirit, Three in One,
laud, honour, might and glory be
   from age to age eternally. Amen.

7th cent. Tr. J.M. Neale

165

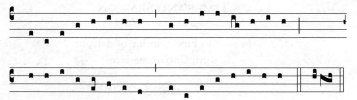

Verbum supernum

1.High Word of God, who once did come,
  leaving thy father and thy home,
to succour by thy birth our kind,
  when, towards thy advent, time declined.

2.Pour light upon us from above,
  and fire our hearts with thy strong love,
that, as we hear thy Gospel read,
  all fond desires may flee in dread;

3.That when thou comest from the skies,
  Great Judge, to open thine assize,
to give each hidden sin its smart,
  and crown as kings the pure in heart,

4.We be not set at thy left hand,
  where sentence due would bid us stand,
but with the Saints thy face may see,
  for ever wholly loving thee.

6.Praise to the Father and the Son,
  through all the ages as they run;
and to the holy Paraclete
  be praise with them and worship meet. Amen.

c.10th cent. Tr. Charles Bigg (1840-1908)

See also Vox clara ecce intonat *(Lauds), found as* Hark! a herald voice is calling, *at EH 5.*

Veni, Redemptor Gentium

1.Come, thou Redeemer of the earth,
   and manifest thy virgin birth:
let every age adoring fall;
   such birth befits the God of all.

2.Begotten of no human will,
   but of the Spirit, thou art still
the Word of God in flesh arrayed,
   the promised fruit to man displayed.

3.The virgin womb that burden gained
   with virgin honour all unstained;
the banners there of virtue glow;
   God in his temple dwells below.

4.Forth from his chamber goeth he,
   that royal home of purity,
a giant in twofold substance one,
   rejoicing now his course to run.

5.From God the Father he proceeds,
   to God the Father back he speeds;
his course he runs to death and hell,
   returning on God's throne to dwell.

6.O equal to thy Father, thou!
   Gird on thy fleshly mantle now;
the weakness of our mortal state
   with deathless might invigorate.

7.Thy cradle here shall glitter bright,
   and darkness breathe a newer light,
where endless faith shall shine serene,
   and twilight never intervene.

8.All laud to God the Father be,
   all praise, eternal Son, to thee;
all glory, as is ever meet,
   to God the Holy Paraclete. Amen.

St Ambrose. *Tr.* J. M. Neale *and others*

See also EH 14 (modern tune), Puer nobis nascitur.

Veni, Veni, Emmanual

1. O come, O come, Emmanuel!
   redeem thy captive Israel
   that into exile drear is gone,
   far from the face of God's dear Son.
   Rejoice! Rejoice! Emmanuel
   Shall come to thee, O Israel.

2. O come, thou Branch of Jesse! draw
   the quarry from the lion's claw;
   from the dread caverns of the grave,
   from nether hell, thy people save.

3. O come, O come, thou Dayspring
   bright!
   pour on our souls thy healing light;
   dispel the long night's lingering gloom,
   and pierce the shadows of the tomb.

4. O Come, thou Lord of David's Key!
   the royal door fling wide and free;
   safeguard for us the heavenward road,
   and bar the way to death's abode.

5. O come, O come, Adonai,
   who in thy glorious majesty
   from that high mountain clothed in awe,
   gavest thy folk the elder Law.

18th cent. Tr. T. A. Lacey (1853-1931)

168

First Sunday of Advent

A reading from the sermons of Blessed John Henry Newman

One year goes and then another, but the same warnings recur. The frost or the rain comes again; the earth is stripped of its brightness; there is nothing to rejoice in. And then, amid this unprofitableness of earth and sky, the well-known words return; the Prophet Isaiah is read; the same Epistle and Gospel, bidding us 'awake out of sleep', (Rom 13:11) and welcome him 'that cometh in the Name of the Lord' (Mt 21:9); the same Collects, beseeching him to prepare us for judgment. O blessed they who obey these warning voices, and look out for him whom they have not seen, because they 'love his appearing' (2 Tim 4:8)!

We cannot have fitter reflections at this Season than those which I have entered upon. What may be the destiny of other orders of beings we know not – but this we know to be our fearful lot, that before us lies a time when we must have the sight of our Maker and Lord face to face. We know not what is reserved for other beings; there may be some, which, knowing nothing of their Maker, are never to be brought before him. For what we can tell, this may the case with the brute creation. It may be the law of their nature that they should live or die, or live on an indefinite period, upon the very outskirts of his government, sustained by him, but never permitted to know or approach him. But this is not our case. We are destined to come before him; nay, and to come before him in judgment; and that on our first meeting; and that suddenly. We are not merely to be rewarded or punished, we are to be judged. Recompense is to come upon our actions, not by a mere general provision or course of nature, as it does at present, but from the Lawgiver himself in person. We have to stand before his righteous Presence, and that one by one. One by one we shall have to endure his holy and searching eye. At present we are in a world of shadows. What we see is not substantial. Suddenly it will be rent in twain and vanish away, and our Maker will appear. And then, I say, that first appearance will be nothing less than a personal intercourse between the Creator and every creature. he will look on us, while we look on him. [...]

And in the worship and service of Almighty God, which Christ and his Apostles have left to us, we are vouchsafed means, both moral and mystical, of

---

Bl. John Henry Newman, 'Worship, a Preparation for Christ's Coming', in J. H. Newman, *Parochial and Plain Sermons* V (London: Rivingtons, 1882), pp. 3-4, 7-8, 9-10.

approaching God, and gradually learning to bear the sight of him. This indeed is the most momentous reason for religious worship, as far as we have grounds for considering it a true one. Men sometimes ask, Why need they *profess* religion: Why need they go to church? Why need they observe certain rites and ceremonies: Why need they watch, pray, fast, and meditate? Why is it not enough to be just, honest, sober, benevolent, and otherwise virtuous? Is not this the true and real worship of God? Is not activity in mind and conduct the most acceptable way of approaching him? How can they please him by submitting to certain religious forms, and taking part in certain religious acts? Or if they must do so, why may they not choose their own? Why must they come to church for them? Why must they be partakers in what the Church calls Sacraments? I answer, they must do so, first of all and especially, because God tells them so to do. But besides this, I observe that we see this plain reason why, that they are one day to change their state of being. They are not to be here for ever. Direct intercourse with God on their part now, prayer and the like, may be necessary to their meeting him suitably hereafter: and direct intercourse on his part with them, or what we call sacramental communion, may be necessary in some incomprehensible way, even for preparing their very nature to bear the sight of him.

Let us then take this view of religious service: it is 'going out to meet the Bridegroom' (Mt 25:1), who, if not seen 'in his beauty' (Is 33:17), will appear in consuming fire. [...]

[W]hen we come to church, then let us say: – The day will be when I shall see Christ surrounded by his Holy Angels. I shall be brought into that blessed company, in which all will be pure, all bright. I come then to learn to endure the sight of the Holy One and his Servants; to nerve myself for a vision which is fearful before it is ecstatic, and which they only enjoy whom it does not consume. When men in this world have to undergo any great thing, they prepare themselves beforehand, by thinking often of it, and they call this making up their mind. Any unusual trial they thus make familiar to them. Courage is a necessary step in gaining certain goods, and courage is gained by steady thought. Children are scared, and close their eyes, at the vision of some mighty warrior or glorious king. And when Daniel saw the Angel, like St John, 'his comeliness was turned in him into corruption, and he retained no strength' (Dan 10: 8). I come then to church, because I am an heir of heaven. It is my desire and hope one day to take possession of my inheritance: and I come to make myself ready for it, and I would not see heaven yet, for I could not bear to see it. I am allowed to be in it without seeing it, that I may learn to see it. And by psalm and sacred song, by confession and by praise, I learn my part.

Second Sunday of Advent

A reading from John Pearson, *Exposition of the Creed*

That the Messias was to come again, was not only certainly but copiously foretold: the Scriptures did often assure us of a second advent. As often we read of his griefs and humility, so often we are admonished of his coming to suffer; as often as we hear of his power and glory, so often we are assured of his coming to judge. We must not fancy with the Jews, a double Messias, one the son of Joseph, the other of David; one of the tribe of Ephraim, the other of Judah: but we must take that for a certain truth which they have made an occasion of their error: that the Messias is twice to come, once in all humility, to suffer and die, as they conceived of their son of Joseph; and again in glory, to govern and judge, as they expect the son of David. [...] From whence it followeth, that, being Christ is already come, lowly and sitting upon an ass, therefore he shall come gloriously with the clouds of heaven. For if both these descriptions cannot belong to one and the same advent, as the Jews acknowledge, and both of them must be true, because equally prophetical: then there must be a double advent of the same Messias, and so his second coming was foretold. [...]

He humbled himself so far as to take upon him our nature: in that nature so taken, he humbled himself to all the infirmities which that was capable of, to all the miseries which this life could bring, to all the pains and sorrows which the sins of all the world could cause: and therefore in regard of his humiliation did God exalt him, and part of the exaltation due unto him was this power of judging. The Father therefore, who is only God, and never took upon him the nature of men or angels, 'judgeth no man' (and the same reason reacheth also the Holy Ghost); but 'hath committed all judgment to the Son' (Jn 5: 22, 25);

John Pearson, *An Exposition of the Creed*, VII. 292-293, 298, in *An Exposition of the Creed, by John Pearson. Revised and corrected by the Rev. Temple Chevallier* (Cambridge, Cambridge University Press, 1859, 2nd edition), pp. 545-547, 555-556.

and the reason why he hath committed it to him, is, because he is not only the Son of God, and so truly God, but also the Son of man, and so truly man; because he is that Son of man, who suffered so much for the sons of men.

From whence at last it clearly appeareth, not only that it is a certain truth that Christ shall judge the world; but also the reasons are declared and manifested unto us why he hath that power committed unto him, why he shall come to judge the quick and the dead. For certainly it is a great demonstration of the justice of God, so highly to reward that Son of man, as to make him judge of all the world, who came into the world, and was judged here; to give him absolute power of absolution and condemnation, who was by us condemned to die, and died that he might absolve us; to cause all the sons of men to bow before his throne, who did not disdain for their sakes to stand before the tribunal, and receive that sentence 'Let him be crucified' (Mt 27: 23), which event as infallible, and reason as irrefragable, Christ himself did shew at the same time when he stood before the judgment-seat, saying, 'Nevertheless I say unto you, Hereafter shall ye see the Son of man sitting on the right hand of power, and coming in the clouds of heaven' (Mt 26:64).

Third Sunday of Advent

A reading from Richard of St Victor, *The Mystical Ark*

The holy soul and friend of the true Bridegroom ought always to thirst with great longing for the coming of her Beloved, being always prepared to run to the One who calls and to open to the One who knocks. I say, the soul ought always to be anxious about this matter and to be found prepared, lest the One who comes suddenly and unexpectedly finds her less adorned and less splendidly dressed and lest he endure any of the trouble of a long period of waiting when shut out for a long time. Troublesome and very burdensome to one burning with desire are these words, 'Command, command again; command, command again; wait, wait again; wait, wait again; a little here, a little there' (Is 28: 10, 13). These surely are words of a lazy soul, a soul that is tepid, less careful and excessively ungrateful. For what can such a soul say when she is

---

Richard of St Victor, *The Mystical Ark* IV. xiii, in Richard of St Victor, *The Twelve Patriarchs. The Mystical Ark. Book Three of The Trinity*. Translation and introduction by Grover A. Zinn (London: Society for the Promotion of Christian Knowledge, 1979), pp. 279-281.

found in her sordidness, when she grieves that she has been caught off-guard by an unexpected coming of the lover and is ashamed to be found less adorned and less splendidly dressed? She says, 'I certainly ought to have known beforehand about your coming so that I could receive you solemnly and run to meet you with all due swiftness in the way in which I ought. In the future, therefore, announce your coming to me in advance and inform me beforehand of the hour of your coming by means of a messenger who comes in advance. And so, let a messenger run between, to teach me what you wish me to do. I say, let an intermediary messenger run between us, to instruct me concerning individual things and teach me not only about my condition but even about your condition. Let him teach me how it is with you and what from me will be pleasing to you. And so: Command and command again; announce and announce again. It is not fitting for lovers not to know mutual pursuits and mutual longings for one another; nor does it suffice for a soul that is seething with burning desire to hear only once. Therefore I beg you: Command and command again; command and command again'.

Perhaps he greatly loves and burns greatly with desire for those things which he pursues so and seeks so urgently by an intermediary. Let us see, therefore, what he must do. Behold, according to his word, after messengers have been sent often and have been sent again, finally at last he follows after his messengers so that the soul may enjoy fully the desired embraces and may be caressed with mutual love. Behold now he stands before the door; behold now he knocks at the door. Behold the voice of your Beloved as he knocks: 'Open to me, my sister, my friend, my dove, my unstained one, for my head is full of dew, and the curls of my hair are full of the drops of the night' (Song 5:2). What, I beg you; what, I say, does it profit that he sent messengers in advance, if he finds a closed door? But at the very least, why at the voice of the Beloved do you not spring up, open, bring in and fall into an embrace? [...]

He stands behind the wall, looking through the windows, gazing through the lattices. Hear him calling; receive as you wish the One who knocks. Lo, your Beloved is speaking to you: 'Arise, my friend, my love, my beautiful one; be quick and come' (Song 2:10).

Fourth Sunday of Advent

A reading from the sermons of John Keble

The very time and season of the year – the time of winter, the time of Advent, teaches us how long-suffering God is; he has spared us now once more through all the four seasons of the year. Others have died and been buried around us: we have heard the Church bell go for the departure of many a friend and neighbour, and we are still here. Again we see the leaves fallen from the trees, the sun low, the darkness long; but as yet our leaves abide, our sun is not set, the long darkness of the grave has not come upon us. Why, but because God is long-suffering? he had borne with us so many years before, and now it has pleased him to bear with us one year longer.

We are come to Advent again. The holy season, the time of preparation and penitence, has come upon us, before we have been taken into those regions, where preparation and penitence cannot be; it will be for the careless ones, only remorse and regret; and these will come too late. Advent has come upon us once again, while we are yet on our trial. We have been permitted to wake up this morning in this world, and not in Eternity. We are not as yet where it will be too late to pray. God has allowed us once more to hear the voice of his Church, warning us of the Great Day of wrath, before it is actually come upon us. The horror, the confusion, the despair of the Resurrection Day, such as it will appear to the wicked, has not yet surprised us. Our night has not come; it is yet day; we are still enabled to work the work of him that sent us, if we will. Whose doing is it, that things are yet so well with us? As for ourselves, we know very well that we are not able to keep ourselves in being, a single hour, nor to raise ourselves out of sleep. Which of us can say, that he has lived so as truly to deserve any such favour of God? No. It is all his patience and long-suffering: and while it shames and humbles us to think that we should hitherto have walked so unworthy of it, yet will may it encourage and hearten us to make much of the time to come, be it long or short, for which he has so graciously spared us.

John Keble, 'Sermon XIX. God's Longsuffering a Call to Repentance, I. his Longsuffering with the World, and the Church', in *Sermons for Advent to Christmas Eve, by the late Rev. John Keble* (Oxford and London: Parker, 1875), pp. 203-8.

[...] It is now near 1850 years, since the most High God himself, God the Son, took to himself our nature, and became Man, to redeem and save this fallen, unworthy world of ours. And having sacrificed himself for us, and risen again from the dead to give us new life, he went up into Heaven with our human nature, exalting it even to the Right Hand of the Father: there he pleads for us night and day, and from thence he Sent, and evermore sends his own Co-equal, Co-eternal Spirit, to regenerate us one by one, to unite us to himself, to dwell in our hearts and bodies, and make us partakers of the Divine Nature, truly good, and truly fit for Heaven. All this, I said, Jesus Christ did for his Church 1850 years ago, and has been continually repeating it all, in virtue and effect, to each person, whom by his Sacraments he has made and continued a member of that Church. What a world of mercy and goodness is here! And what a world of sin, obstinate sin, in men's hearts, to slight and abuse it, as we see and know they do! What a world again of patient forbearance and long-suffering in him, who bears so long with all this sad ingratitude, and still continues to us not only the rain from heaven and fruitful seasons, but also the high and precious treasures of his Church!

[...] If there be any wrong way, in which we are going on, and will not amend it, we know that after a few more preparatory Advents, the real Coming, the last Advent, will dawn upon us, and the time of God's long-suffering will be gone for ever. But what a day of joy will that be, to those who have allowed their hearts to be touched by his goodness! Think it well over, my brethren, and choose the better part, while yet there is time.

Sunday   *Rev 22:17, 20*
The Spirit and the Bride say, 'Come.' And let him who hears say,
'Come.' And let him who is thirsty come, let him who desires take the
water of life without price. he who testifies to these things says,
'Surely I am coming soon.' Amen. Come, Lord Jesus!

Monday   *Is 11:1-4*
There shall come forth a shoot from the stump of Jesse, and a branch
shall grow out of his roots. And the Spirit of the Lord shall rest upon
him, the spirit of wisdom and understanding, the spirit of counsel and
might, the spirit of knowledge and the fear of the Lord. And his
delight shall be in the fear of the Lord. He shall not judge by what his
eyes see, or decide by what his ears hear; but with righteousness he
shall judge the poor, and decide with equity for the meek of the earth;
and he shall strike the earth with the rod of his mouth, and with the
breath of his lips he shall slay the wicked.

Tuesday   *Jer 23:5-6*
Behold, the days are coming, says the Lord, when I will raise up for
David a righteous Branch, and he shall reign as king and deal wisely,
and shall execute justice and righteousness in the land. In his days
Judah will be saved, and Israel will dwell securely. And this is the
name by which he will be called: 'The Lord is our righteousness.'

Wednesday   *Is 12:2*
Behold, God is my salvation; I will trust, and will not be afraid; for the
Lord God is my strength and my song, and he has become my
salvation.

Thursday   *Hag 2:6, 9*
Thus says the Lord of hosts: 'Once again, in a little while, I will shake
the heavens and the earth and the sea and the dry land. The latter
splendour of this house shall be greater than the former', says the
Lord of hosts; 'and in this place I will give prosperity', says the Lord
of hosts.

Friday   *Rom 13:11-14*

You know what hour it is, how it is full time now for you to wake
from sleep. For salvation is nearer to us now than when we first
believed; the night is far gone, the day is at hand. Let us then cast off
the works of darkness and put on the armour of light; let us conduct
ourselves becomingly as in the day, not in revelling and drunkenness,
not in debauchery and licentiousness, not in quarrelling and jealousy.
But put on the Lord Jesus Christ, and make no provision for the flesh,
to gratify its desires.

Saturday   *Is 4:2, 3*

In that day the branch of the Lord shall be beautiful and glorious, and
the fruit of the land shall be the pride and glory of the survivors of
Israel. And he who is left in Zion and remains in Jerusalem will be
called holy, every one who has been recorded for life in Jerusalem.

Advent Prayer during the Day

Keep us, O Lord,
while we tarry on this earth,
in a serious seeking after thee,
and in an affectionate walking with thee,
every day of our lives;
that when thou comest,
we may be found not hiding our talent,
nor serving the flesh,
nor yet asleep with our lamp unfurnished,
but waiting and longing for our Lord,
our glorious God for ever.

Richard Baxter

Collects

First Sunday of Advent
ALMIGHTY God, give us grace that we may cast away the works of darkness, and put upon us the armour of light, now in the time of this mortal life in which thy Son Jesus Christ came to visit us in great humility: that in the last day, when he shall come again in his glorious majesty to judge both the quick and the dead, we may rise to the life immortal; through him who liveth and reigneth with thee and the Holy Spirit, one God, for ever and ever.

or

O LORD our God, as we wait for the coming of thy Son our Lord, preserve us in watchfulness and faith: that when he shall appear he may not find us asleep in sin but active to serve him and joyful to praise him; through Jesus Christ thy Son our Lord, who liveth and reigneth with thee, in the unity of the Holy Spirit, one God, for ever and ever.

Second Sunday in Advent
BLESSED Lord, who hast caused all holy Scriptures to be written for our learning: grant that we may in such wise hear them, read, mark, learn, and inwardly digest them, that by patience and comfort of thy holy Word, we may embrace, and ever hold fast, the blessed hope of everlasting life, which thou hast given us in our Saviour Jesus Christ; who liveth and reigneth with thee, in the unity of the Holy Spirit, one God, for ever and ever.

Third Sunday in Advent
LORD, we beseech thee, give ear to our prayers: and by thy gracious visitation lighten the darkness of our heart; by our Lord Jesus Christ, who livest with the Father in the unity of the Holy Spirit, one God, for ever and ever.

or

O LORD Jesu Christ, who at thy first coming didst send thy messenger to prepare thy way before thee: grant that the ministers and stewards of thy mysteries may likewise so prepare and make ready thy way, by turning the hearts of the disobedient to the wisdom of the just, that at thy second coming to judge the world we may be found an acceptable people in thy sight; who livest and reignest with the Father in the unity of the Holy Spirit, one God, for ever and ever.

Fourth Sunday in Advent

O LORD, raise up (we pray thee) thy power, and come among us, and with great might succour us: that whereas, through our sins and wickedness, we are sore let and hindered in running the race that is set before us, thy bountiful grace and mercy may speedily help and deliver us; through the satisfaction of thy Son our Lord, to whom with thee and the Holy Spirit be honour and glory, for ever and ever.

Christmas Eve

O GOD, who makest us glad with the yearly remembrance of the birth of thy only Son Jesus Christ: grant that as we joyfully receive him for our redeemer, so we may with sure confidence behold him when he shall come to be our judge; who liveth and reigneth with thee and the Holy Spirit, one God, for ever and ever.

17 December – *O Sapientia*
O Wisdom, coming forth from the mouth of the Most High,
reaching from one end to the other mightily,
and sweetly ordering all things:
Come and teach us the way of prudence.

cf Sir 24:3; Wis 8:1

18 December – *O Adonai*
O Adonai, and leader of the House of Israel,
who appeared to Moses in the fire of the burning bush
and gave him the law on Sinai:
Come and redeem us with an outstretched arm.

cf Ex 3:2, 24:12

19 December – *O Radix Jesse*
O Root of Jesse, standing as a sign among the peoples;
before you kings will shut their mouths,
to you the nations will make their prayer:
Come and deliver us, and delay no longer.

cf Is 11:10, 45:14, 52:15; Rom 15:12

20 December – *O Clavis David*
O Key of David and sceptre of the House of Israel;
you open and no one can shut;
you shut and no one can open:
Come and lead the prisoners from the prison house,
those who dwell in darkness and the shadow of death.

cf Is 22:22, 42:7

21 December – *O Oriens*
O Morning Star,
splendour of light eternal and sun of righteousness:
Come and enlighten those who dwell in darkness
and the shadow of death.

cf Mal 4:2

22 December – *O Rex Gentium*
O King of the nations, and their desire,
the cornerstone making both one:
Come and save the human race,
which you fashioned from clay.

cf Is 28:16; Eph 2:14

23 December – *O Emmanuel*
O Emmanuel, our king and our lawgiver,
the hope of the nations and their Saviour:
Come and save us, O Lord our God.

cf Is 7:14

Advent Prose

Rorate cæli

Drop down ye heavens, from above,
and let the skies pour down righteousness:

1   Be not wroth very sore, O Lord,
neither remember iniquity for ever:
the holy cities are a wilderness,
Sion is a wilderness,
Jerusalem a desolation:
our holy and our beautiful house,
where our fathers praised thee.
Drop down &c.

2   We have sinned, and are as an unclean thing,
and we all do fade as a leaf:
and our iniquities, like the wind, have taken us away;
thou hast hid thy face from us:
and hast consumed us, because of our iniquities.
Drop down &c.

3   Ye are my witnesses, saith the Lord,
and my servant whom I have chosen;
that ye may know me and believe me:
I, even I, am the Lord, and beside me there is no Saviour
and there is none that can deliver out of my hand.
Drop down &c.

4   Comfort ye, comfort ye, my people,
my salvation shall not tarry:
I have blotted out as a thick cloud thy transgressions:
Fear not, for I will save thee:
for I am the Lord thy God,
the Holy One of Israel, thy Redeemer.
Drop down &c.

The service may proceed from West to East, from darkness to light, with various convenient stations for the readings. The psalmody throughout the service is used or omitted as expedient.

Processional Hymn

O come, O come Emmanuel!
  Redeem thy captive Israel,
That into exile drear is gone
  Far from the face of God's dear Son.
Rejoice! Rejoice! Emmanuel
Shall come to thee, O Israel.

O Sapientia

O come, thou Wisdom from on high!
  Who madest all in earth and sky,
Creating man from dust and clay:
  To us reveal salvation's way.

O Adonai

O come, O come, Adonaï,
  Who in thy glorious majesty
From Sinai's mountain, clothed with awe,
  Gavest thy folk the ancient law.

O Radix Jesse

O come, thou Root of Jesse! draw
  The quarry from the lion's claw;
From those dread caverns of the grave,
  From nether hell, thy people save.

O Clavis David

O come, thou Lord of David's Key!
 the royal door fling wide and free;
safeguard for us the heavenward road,
 and bar the way to death's abode.

O Oriens

O come, O come, thou Dayspring bright!
 pour on our souls thy healing light;
dispel the long night's lingering gloom,
 and pierce the shadows of the tomb.

O Rex Gentium

O come, Desire of nations! Show
 thy kingly reign on earth below;
thou Corner-stone, uniting all,
 restore the ruin of our fall.

O Emmanuel

O come, O come Emmanuel!
 redeem thy captive Israel,
that into exile drear is gone
 far from the face of God's dear Son.

Greeting

The night is far spent, and the day is at hand: let us therefore cast off the works of darkness, and let us put on the armour of light.

Rom 13:12

[The grace and peace of God our Father and the Lord Jesus
 Christ be with you.

People **And with thy spirit.**]

184

My brothers and sisters: how beautifully in this season the Church provides that we should recite the words and recall the longing of those who lived before our Lord's first coming. May we learn through their example to have a great longing for the day when he will come again. We do well to consider how much good our Lord did by his first coming, and how much more he will do for us by his second. This thought will help us to have a great love for that first coming of his and a great longing for his return. And if our conscience is not so perfect that we dare entertain such a desire, we ought at least to fear his second coming and, by means of that fear, to correct our faults, so that, if perhaps we cannot help being afraid here and now, we shall at least be secure and fearless when he comes again.

(Derived from a sermon by St Ælred of Rievaulx)

Let us pray.

ALMIGHTY God, give us grace that we may cast away the works of darkness, and put upon us the armour of light, now in the time of this mortal life in which thy Son Jesus Christ came to visit us in great humility: that in the last day, when he shall come again in his glorious majesty to judge both the quick and the dead, we may rise to the life immortal; through him who liveth and reigneth with thee and the Holy Spirit, one God, for ever and ever.

People   **Amen.**

Carol or Hymn

First Lesson

Bethlehem, from you shall come forth a ruler.

Mic 5:2-4

But you, O Bethlehem Ephrathah, who are little to be among the clans of Judah, from you shall come forth for me one who is to be ruler in Israel, whose origin is from of old, from ancient days. Therefore he shall give them up until the time when she who is in travail has brought forth; then the rest of his brethren shall return to the people of Israel. And he shall stand and feed his flock in the strength of the Lord, in the majesty of the name of the Lord his God. And they shall dwell secure, for now he shall be great to the ends of the earth.

At the end the following may be said

People   **Thanks be to God.**

Psalm

Ps 89:1-4

Misericordias Domini

1   My song shall be alway of the loving-kindness of the Lord :
     with my mouth will I ever be shewing thy truth from one
          generation to another.
2   For I have said, Mercy shall be set up for ever :
     thy truth shalt thou stablish in the heavens.
3   I have made a covenant with my chosen :
     I have sworn unto David my servant;
4   thy seed will I stablish for ever :
     and set up thy throne from one generation to another.

Carol or Hymn

Second Lesson

The wilderness and the dry land shall be glad.

Is 35

The wilderness and the dry land shall be glad, the desert shall rejoice and blossom; like the crocus shall blossom abundantly, and rejoice with joy and singing. The glory of Lebanon shall be given to it, the majesty of Carmel and Sharon. They shall see the glory of the Lord, the majesty of our God. Strengthen the weak hands, and make firm the feeble knees. Say to those who are of a fearful heart, 'Be strong, fear not! Behold, your God will come with vengeance, with the recompense of God. he will come and save you.' Then the eyes of the blind shall be opened, and the ears of the deaf unstopped; then shall the lame man leap like a hart, and the tongue of the dumb sing for joy. For waters shall break forth in the wilderness, and streams in the desert; the burning sand shall become a pool, and the thirsty ground springs of water; the haunt of jackals shall become a swamp, the grass shall become reeds and rushes. And a highway shall be there, and it shall be called the Holy Way; the unclean shall not pass over it, and fools shall not err therein. No lion shall be there, nor shall any ravenous beast come up on it; they shall not be found there, but the redeemed shall walk there. And the ransomed of the Lord shall return, and come to Zion with singing; everlasting joy shall be upon their heads; they shall obtain joy and gladness, and sorrow and sighing shall flee away.

At the end the following may be said

People   **Thanks be to God.**

187

Psalm

In convertendo

1   When the Lord turned again the captivity of Sion :
then were we like unto them that dream.

2   Then was our mouth filled with laughter :
and our tongue with joy.

3   Then said they among the heathen :
The Lord hath done great things for them.

4   Yea, the Lord hath done great things for us already :
whereof we rejoice.

5   Turn our captivity, O Lord :
as the rivers in the south.

6   They that sow in tears :
shall reap in joy.

7   He that now goeth on his way weeping,
and beareth forth good seed :
shall doubtless come again with joy,
and bring his sheaves with him.

Carol or Hymn

Third Lesson

I will fill this house with splendour.

Hag 2:5b-9

My Spirit abides among you; fear not. For thus says the Lord of hosts: Once again, in a little while, I will shake the heavens and the earth and the sea and the dry land; and I will shake all nations, so that the treasures of all nations shall come in, and I will fill this house with splendour, says the Lord of hosts. The silver is mine, and the gold is mine, says the Lord of hosts. The latter splendour of this house shall be greater than the former, says the Lord of hosts; and in this place I will give prosperity, says the Lord of hosts.

Alternative Third Lesson

Your Father judged the cause of the poor

Jer 22:13-16; 23:5-6

Woe to him who builds his house by unrighteousness, and his upper rooms by injustice; who makes his neighbour serve him for nothing, and does not give him his wages; who says, 'I will build myself a great house with spacious upper rooms,' and cuts out windows for it, paneling it with cedar, and painting it with vermilion. Do you think you are a king because you compete in cedar? Did not your father eat and drink and do justice and righteousness? Then it was well with him. he judged the cause of the poor and needy; then it was well. Is not this to know me? says the Lord. Behold, the days are coming, says the Lord, when I will raise up for David a righteous Branch, and he shall reign as king and deal wisely, and shall execute justice and righteousness in the land. In his days Judah will be saved, and Israel will dwell securely. And this is the name by which he will be called: 'The Lord is our righteousness.'

At the end the following may be said

People   **Thanks be to God.**

Psalm

Ps 96:7-12

7   Ascribe unto the Lord, O ye kindreds of the people :
       ascribe unto the Lord worship and power.

8   Ascribe unto the Lord the honour due unto his Name :
       bring presents, and come into his courts.

9   O worship the Lord in the beauty of holiness :
       let the whole earth stand in awe of him.

10   Tell it out among the heathen that the Lord is King :
       and that it is he who hath made the round world so fast that
          it cannot be moved;
       and how that he shall judge the people righteously.

11   Let the heavens rejoice, and let the earth be glad :
        let the sea make a noise, and all that therein is.
12   Let the field be joyful, and all that is in it :
        then shall all the trees of the wood rejoice before the Lord.

Carol or Hymn

Fourth Lesson

There shall come forth a shoot from the stump of Jesse.

Is 11:1-9

There shall come forth a shoot from the stump of Jesse, and a branch shall grow out of his roots. And the Spirit of the Lord shall rest upon him, the spirit of wisdom and understanding, the spirit of counsel and might, the spirit of knowledge and the fear of the Lord. And his delight shall be in the fear of the Lord. he shall not judge by what his eyes see, or decide by what his ears hear; but with righteousness he shall judge the poor, and decide with equity for the meek of the earth; and he shall smite the earth with the rod of his mouth, and with the breath of his lips he shall slay the wicked. Righteousness shall be the girdle of his waist, and faithfulness the girdle of his loins. The wolf shall dwell with the lamb, and the leopard shall lie down with the kid, and the calf and the lion and the fatling together, and a little child shall lead them. The cow and the bear shall feed; their young shall lie down together; and the lion shall eat straw like the ox. The sucking child shall play over the hole of the asp, and the weaned child shall put his hand on the adder's den. They shall not hurt or destroy in all my holy mountain; for the earth shall be full of the knowledge of the Lord as the waters cover the sea.

At the end the following may be said

People   **Thanks be to God.**

Psalm

10   For thy servant David's sake :
      turn not away the presence of thine Anointed.

11   The Lord hath made a faithful oath unto David :
      and he shall not shrink from it;

12   Of the fruit of thy body :
      shall I set upon thy seat.

13   If thy children will keep my covenant, and my testimonies
      that I shall learn them :
      their children also shall sit upon thy seat for evermore.

14   For the Lord hath chosen Sion to be an habitation for
      himself :
      he hath longed for her.

15   This shall be my rest for ever :
      here will I dwell, for I have a delight therein.

16   I will bless her victuals with increase :
      and will satisfy her poor with bread.

Carol or Hymn

Fifth Lesson

How beautiful upon the mountains!

How beautiful upon the mountains are the feet of him who brings
good tidings, who publishes peace, who brings good tidings of good,
who publishes salvation, who says to Zion, 'Your God reigns.' Hark,
your watchmen lift up their voice, together they sing for joy; for eye to
eye they see the return of the Lord to Zion. Break forth together into
singing, you waste places of Jerusalem; for the Lord has comforted his
people, he has redeemed Jerusalem. The Lord has bared his holy arm
before the eyes of all the nations; and all the ends of the earth shall see
the salvation of our God.

Alternative Fifth Lesson

A voice cries in the wilderness: Prepare the way of the Lord.

Is 40:1-11

Comfort, comfort my people, says your God. Speak tenderly to Jerusalem, and cry to her that her warfare is ended, that her iniquity is pardoned, that she has received from the Lord's hand double for all her sins. A voice cries: 'In the wilderness prepare the way of the Lord, make straight in the desert a highway for our God. Every valley shall be lifted up, and every mountain and hill be made low; the uneven ground shall become level, and the rough places a plain. And the glory of the Lord shall be revealed, and all flesh shall see it together, for the mouth of the Lord has spoken.' A voice says, 'Cry!' And I said, 'What shall I cry?' All flesh is grass, and all its beauty is like the flower of the field. The grass withers, the flower fades, when the breath of the Lord blows upon it; surely the people is grass. The grass withers, the flower fades; but the word of our God will stand for ever. Get you up to a high mountain, O Zion, herald of good tidings; lift up your voice with strength, O Jerusalem, herald of good tidings, lift it up, fear not; say to the cities of Judah, 'Behold your God!' Behold, the Lord God comes with might, and his arm rules for him; behold, his reward is with him, and his recompense before him. he will feed his flock like a shepherd, he will gather the lambs in his arms, he will carry them in his bosom, and gently lead those that are with young.

At the end the following may be said

People   **Thanks be to God.**

192

Psalm

Ps 85:8-13

8   I will hearken what the Lord God will say concerning me :
for he shall speak peace unto his people, and to his Saints,
  that they turn not again.

9   For his salvation is nigh them that fear him :
that glory may dwell in our land.

10   Mercy and truth are met together :
righteousness and peace have kissed each other.

11   Truth shall flourish out of the earth :
and righteousness hath looked down from heaven.

12   Yea, the Lord shall shew loving-kindness :
and our land shall give her increase.

13   Righteousness shall go before him :
and he shall direct his going in the way.

Carol or Hymn

Sixth Lesson

Christ took the form of a servant

Phil 2:5-11

Have this mind among yourselves, which is yours in Christ Jesus, who, though he was in the form of God, did not count equality with God a thing to be grasped, but emptied himself, taking the form of a servant, being born in the likeness of men. And being found in human form he humbled himself and became obedient unto death, even death on a cross. Therefore God has highly exalted him and bestowed on him the name which is above every, that at the name of Jesus every knee should bow, in heaven and on earth and under the earth, and every tongue confess that Jesus Christ is Lord, to the glory of God the Father.

At the end the following may be said

People   **Thanks be to God.**

Canticle

Magnificat

✠ MY soul doth magnify the Lord:
and my spirit hath rejoiced in God my Saviour.

2 For he hath regarded:
the lowliness of his hand-maiden.

3 For behold, from henceforth:
all generations shall call me blessed.

4 For he that is mighty hath magnified me:
and holy is his Name.

5 And his mercy is on them that fear him:
throughout all generations.

6 He hath shewed strength with his arm:
he hath scattered the proud
in the imagination of their hearts.

7 He hath put down the mighty from their seat:
and hath exalted the humble and meek.

8 He hath filled the hungry with good things:
and the rich he hath sent empty away.

9 He remembering his mercy hath holpen his servant Israel:
as he promised to our forefathers, Abraham and his seed for
ever.

Lk 1:46-55

Glory be to the Father, and to the Son :
and to the Holy Spirit;
As it was in the beginning, is now, and ever shall be :
world without end. Amen.

When the canticle **Magnificat** *is sung at this point, the altar may be censed in the usual fashion. If incense is used here it is used too at the Seventh Lesson.*

Carol or Hymn

Seventh Lesson

The Annunciation

Lk 1:26-38

In the sixth month the angel Gabriel was sent from God to a city of Galilee named Nazareth, to a virgin betrothed to a man whose name was Joseph, of the house of David; and the virgin's name was Mary. And he came to her and said, 'Hail, full of grace, the Lord is with you!' But she was greatly troubled at the saying, and considered in her mind what sort of greeting this might be. And the angel said to her, 'Do not be afraid, Mary, for you have found favour with God. And behold, you will conceive in your womb and bear a son, and you shall call his name Jesus. he will be great, and will be called the Son of the Most High; and the Lord God will give to him the throne of his father David, and he will reign over the house of Jacob for ever; and of his kingdom there will be no end.' And Mary said to the angel, 'How shall this be, since I have no husband?' And the angel said to her, 'The Holy Spirit will come upon you, and the power of the Most High will overshadow you; therefore the child to be born will be called holy, the Son of God. And behold, your kinswoman Elizabeth in her old age has also conceived a son; and this is the sixth month with her who was called barren. For with God nothing will be impossible.' And Mary said, 'Behold, I am the handmaid of the Lord; let it be to me according to your word.' And the angel departed from her.

At the end the following may be said

People **Thanks be to God.**

Carol or Hymn

Conclusion

	[The Lord be with you:
People	**and with thy spirit.**]

Let us pray.

	Lord, have mercy upon us.
People	**Christ, have mercy upon us.**
	Lord, have mercy upon us.

People   **OUR Father, who art in heaven, hallowed be thy name; thy kingdom come; thy will be done; on earth as it is in heaven. Give us this day our daily bread. And forgive us our trespasses, as we forgive those who trespass against us. And lead us not into temptation; but deliver us from evil. Amen.**

Collect of the Day

or

O LORD our God, as we wait for the coming of thy Son our Lord, preserve us in watchfulness and faith: that when he shall appear he may not find us asleep in sin but active to serve him and joyful to praise him; through Jesus Christ thy Son our Lord, who liveth and reigneth with thee, in the unity of the Holy Spirit, one God, for ever and ever. **Amen.**

Blessing

May God the Father, judge all-merciful,
make us worthy of a place in his kingdom.

People   **Amen.**

May God the Son, coming among us in power,
reveal in our midst the promise of his glory.

People   **Amen.**

May God the Holy Spirit make us steadfast in faith,
joyful in hope and constant in love.

People   **Amen.**

And the blessing of God almighty,
the Father, the Son and the Holy Spirit,
be upon you and remain with you always.

People   **Amen.**

Office

Opening Sentence

Behold, I bring you good tidings of great joy which shall be to all people: for unto you is born in the city of David, a Saviour, which is Christ the Lord. *Lk 2:10, 11*

CHRISTMAS DAY

Hymn

Morning & Evening Prayer   *Vespers*

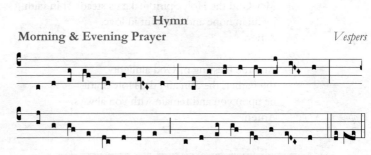

Christe Redemptor

1. Jesu, the Father's only Son,
   whose death for all redemption won;
   before the worlds of God most high
   begotten all ineffably.

2. The Father's light and splendour thou,
   their endless hope to thee that bow;
   accept the prayers and praise today
   that through the world thy servants pray.

3. Salvation's Author, call to mind
   how, taking form of humankind,
   born of a virgin undefiled,
   thou in man's flesh becam'st a child.

4. Thus testifies the present day,
   through every year in long array,
   that thou, salvation's source alone,
   proceedest from the Father's throne.

5. Whence sky, and stars, and sea's abyss,
   and earth, and all that therein is,
   shall still, with laud and carol meet,
   the Author of thine advent greet.

6. And we who, by thy precious blood
   from sin redeemed, are marked for God,
   on this the day that saw thy birth,
   sing the new song of ransomed earth.

7. For that thine advent glory be,
   O Jesu, virgin born, to thee;
   with Father, and with Holy Ghost,
   from men and from the heavenly host.Amen.

6th cent. Tr. J. M. Neale

198

A solis ortu cardine

1.From east to west, from shore to shore,
  let every heart awake and sing
the holy child whom Mary bore,
  the Christ, the everlasting King.

2.Behold, the world's Creator wears
  the form and fashion of a slave;
our very flesh our Maker shares,
  his fallen creature, man, to save.

3.For this how wondrously he wrought!
  A maiden, in her lowly place,
became, in ways beyond all thought,
  the chosen vessel of his grace.

4.She bowed her to the angel's word
  declaring what the Father willed,
and suddenly the promised Lord
  that pure and hallowed temple filled.

5. He shrank not from the oxen's stall,
  he lay within the manger-bed,
and he, whose bounty feedeth all,
  at Mary's breast himself was fed.

6. And while the angels in the sky
  sang praise above the silent field,
to shepherds poor the Lord Most High,
  the one great Shepherd, was revealed.

7. All glory for this blessed morn
  to God the Father ever be;
all praise to thee, O Virgin-born,
all praise, O Holy Ghost, to thee.

A- men.

Cœlius Sedulius, c. 450. Tr. *J. Ellerton*

See also EH 14 (modern tune), Puer nobis nascitur.

Post-Biblical Reading

A reading from the discourses of Blessed John Henry Newman

The Eternal Word, the Only-begotten Son of the Father, put off his glory, and came down upon earth, to raise us to heaven. Though he was God, he became man; though he was Lord of all, he became as a servant: 'though he was rich, yet for our sakes he became poor, that we, through his poverty, might be rich' (1 Cor 8:9). He came from heaven in so humble an exterior, that the self-satisfied Pharisees despised him, and treated him as a madman or an impostor. When he spoke of his father Abraham, and implied his knowledge of him, who was in truth but the creature of his hands, they said in derision, 'thou are not yet fifty years old, and hast thou seen Abraham?' (Jn 8:57). he made answer, 'Amen, amen, I say unto you, Before Abraham was made, I am' (Jn 8:58). He had seen Abraham, who lived two thousand years before; yet in truth he was not two thousand years old, more than he was fifty. He was not two thousand years old, because he had no years; he was the Ancient of days, who never had beginning, and who never will have an end; who is above and beyond time; who is ever young, and ever is beginning, yet never has not been, and is as old as he is young, and was as old and young when Abraham lived as when he came on earth in our flesh to atone for our sins. And hence he says, 'Before Abraham was, I *am*', and not 'I *was*'; because with him there is no past or future. It cannot be properly said of him, that he was, or that he will be, but that he is; he is always; always the same, no older because he has lived two thousand years in addition, not younger because he has not lived them.

My brethren, if we could get ourselves to enter into this high and sacred thought, if we really contemplated the Almighty in himself, then we should understand better what his incarnation is to us, and what it is in him. I do not mean, if we worthily contemplated him as he is; but, even if we contemplated him in such a way as is really possible to us, if we did but fix our thoughts on him, and make use of the reason which he has given us, we should understand enough of his greatness to feel the awfulness of his voluntary self-abasement. [...]

Bl. John Henry Newman, 'The Mystery of Divine Condescension' in John Henry Cardinal Newman, *Discourses addressed to Mixed Congregations* (London: Longmans, Green, 1902), pp. 284-285, 297, 298-299.

Such is the Creator in his Eternal Uncreated Beauty, that, were it given to us to behold it, we should die of very rapture at the sight. Moses, unable to forget the token of it he had once seen in the Bush, asked to see it fully, and on this very account was refused. 'he said, Show me thy glory; and he said, thou canst not see my Face; for man shall not see me and live' (Ex 33: 18, 20). When saints have been favoured with glimpses of it, it has thrown them into ecstasy, broken their poor frames of dust and ashes, and pierced them through which such keen distress, that they have cried out to God, in the very midst of their transports, that he would hold his hand, and, in tenderness to them, check the abundance of his consolations. What saints partake in fact, we enjoy in thought and imagination; and even that mere reflection of God's glory is sufficient to sweep away the gloomy, envious thoughts of him, which circle round us, and to lead us to forget ourselves in the contemplation of the All-beautiful. [...]

And if he has so constituted us, that, in spite of the abyss which lies between him and us, in spite of the mystery of his attributes and the feebleness of our reason, the very vision of him dispels all doubt, allures our shrinking souls, and is our everlasting joy, what shall we say, my brethren, when we are told that he has also condescended to take possession of us and to rule us by means of hope and gratitude, those 'cords of Adam', by which one man is bound to another? You say that God and man never can be one, that man cannot bear the sight and touch of his Creator, nor the Creator condescend to the feebleness of the creature; but blush and be confounded to hear, O peevish, restless hearts, that he has come down from his high throne and humbled himself to the creature, in order that the creature might be inspired and strengthened to rise to him. It was not enough to give man grace; it was little to impart to him a celestial light, and a sanctity such as Angels had received; little to create Adam in original justice, with a heavenly nature superadded to his own, with an intellect which could know God and a soul which could love him; he purposed even in man's first state of innocence a higher mercy, which in the fullness of time was to be accomplished in his behalf. It became the Wisdom of God, who is the eternally glorious and beautiful, to impress these attributes upon men by his very presence and personal dwelling in their flesh, that, as he was by nature the Only-begotten Image of the Father, so he might also become the 'First-born of every creature' (Col 1:15). It became him who is higher than the highest, to act as if even humility, if this dare be said, was in the number of his attributes, by taking Adam's nature upon himself, and manifesting himself to men and Angels in it.

Holy Family

A reading from Nicholas Love, *Mirror of the Blessed Life of Jesus Christ*

When our Lady with her Child and Joseph were on the way to Nazareth..., not knowing the privy counsel of God hereof, that Herod the king purposed to slay the Child Jesus, the angel of God appeared to Joseph in his sleep, bidding that he should flee to Egypt with the Child and his Mother for Herod would seek the Child to slay him. And anon Joseph, waking of his sleep, called our Lady and told her these hard tidings, and she in all haste took up her their Son and began to go, for she was full sore aghast at his word, and she wished not to be seen negligent in the keeping of him, wherefore anon in that night they took the way toward Egypt. And so fled that great lord the pursuit of his servant - more properly the devil's servant, there travelling with him his young and tender mother, and that old man Joseph by a troublesome way that was hard and diverse... And that way, as it is said, was by that desert in which the children of Israel led out of Egypt, dwelling there forty years.

Lord, how did they there of their livelihood, or where rested they or were harboured in the nights, for in that way found they full seldom any house. Here ought we to have inwardly compassion on them, and not be loath or think it troublesome to do penance for ourselves, because others took so great and so often travail for us, namely they that were so noble and so worthy.

[I]n this aforesaid narrative, if we take good heed we may see many good examples and notable doctrines for us. First, if we take good heed how our Lord Jesus took in his own person some times prosperity and wealth, and some times adversity and woe, we should not be stirred to impatience, what time that it befell us in the same manner, both in time of prosperity and comfort, so contrary-wise on the other side. If thou wouldst see an example hereof in Jesus: lo, first in his birth he was magnified to the herdsmen as God and honoured and worshipped by them as God, with joy, and soon after he was circumcised as would be a simple sinful man with sorrow. After, the kings, coming to him,

---

Nicholas Love, *Mirror of the Blessed Life of Jesus Christ*, X, in *Nicholas Love's 'Mirror of the Blessed Life of Jesus Christ'*. A Critical Edition based on Cambridge University Library Additional MSS 6578 and 6686, edited with introduction, notes and glossary by Michael G. Sargent (New York and London: Garland, 1992), pp. 51-52. Text slightly amended for modern readers.

worshipped him in sovereign manner both in their persons and in great gifts, and yet dwelt he still in that stable among beasts in poverty, weeping as any other child of a simple man. Afterwards, he was presented in the temple with joy, and great things were prophesied of him as of God almighty, and now he is bidden by the angel to flee from Herod into Egypt, as if he were a poor man without might.

And so, furthermore, we would find in all his life prosperity and adversity, mingled together for our example and teaching. For he sent us diverse comforts to lift up our hope that we fall not by despair, and therewith he sent us tribulation and discomforts to keep us in meekness that thereby knowing our own wretchedness we might stand always in his dread.

The second lesson that we may learn in this aforesaid narrative is touching the benefits and the special comforts of God, that he that feels them specially be not thereby elevated in his own sight, as holding himself more worthy than others that have them not, and also that he that feels not such special gifts and comforts be not therefore cast down by sorrow or envy of him that has them. For, as we see here, the angels, appearing and speaking of the Child, did so to Joseph and not to Our Lady, and nevertheless he was much more less in merit and unworthy than she. Also here we may learn that he that feels such special gifts of God though he have them not always as he would and after his desire, that therefore he complain not, nor be heavy with unkindness against God. For notwithstanding that Joseph was so near and acceptable to God, nevertheless the appearing of the angel and the revelations were not done to him openly and in waking but in the manner of dreams and in his sleeping.

SOLEMNITY OF MARY, MOTHER OF GOD

Corde natus ex Parentis

1.Of the Father's heart begotten
  ere the world from chaos rose,
he is Alpha: from that Fountain,
  all that is and hath been flows;
he is Omega, of all things
  yet to come the mystic Close,
  Evermore and evermore.

2.By his word was all created;
  he commanded and 'twas done;
earth and sky and boundless ocean,
  universe of three in one,
all that sees the moon's soft radiance,
  all that breathes beneath the sun,

3.* He assumed this mortal body,
  frail and feeble, doomed to die,
that the race from dust created
  might not perish utterly,
which the dreadful Law had sentenced
  in the depths of hell to lie,

4.O how blest that wondrous birthday,
  when the Maid the curse retrieved,
brought to birth mankind's salvation,
  by the Holy Ghost conceived,
and the Babe, the world's Redeemer,
  in her loving arms received,

5. This is he, whom seer and sybil
  sang in ages long gone by;
this is he of old revealed
  in the page of prophecy;
lo! he comes, the promised Saviour;
  let the world his praises cry

6.Sing, ye heights of heaven, his praises;
  angels and Archangels, sing!
Wheresoe'er ye be, ye faithful,
  let your joyous anthems ring,
every tongue his name confessing,
  countless voices answering,

7.*Hail! thou Judge of souls departed;
  hail! of all the living King!
on the Father's right hand throned,
  through his courts thy praises ring,
till at last for all offences
  righteous judgement thou shalt bring,

8.Now let old and young uniting
  chant to thee harmonious lays,
maid and matron hymn thy glory,
  infant lips their anthem raise,
boys and girls together singing
  with pure heart their song of praise,

204

9.Let the storm and summer sunshine,
gliding stream and sounding shore,
sea and forest, frost and zephyr,
day and night their Lord alone;
let creation join to laud thee
through the ages evermore,
Evermore and evermore

Latin, Prudentius, 348-413
Tr. R. F. Davis (1866-1937)
Tune: Divinum Mysterium,
Melody from Piæ Cantiones, *1582*

Post-Biblical Reading

A reading from the discourses of Blessed John Henry Newman

[I]f you would bring out distinctly and beyond mistake and evasion, the simple idea of the Catholic Church that God is man, could you do it better than by laying down in St John's words that 'God *became* man' (cf Jn 1:14), and again could you express this more emphatically and unequivocally than by declaring that he was *born* a man, or that he had a *Mother?* The world allows that God *is* man; the admission costs it little, for God is everywhere, and (as it may say) is everything; but it shrinks from confessing that God is the Son of Mary. It shrinks, for it is at once confronted with a severe fact, which violates and shatters its own unbelieving view of things; the revealed doctrine forthwith takes its true shape, and receives an historical reality; and the Almighty is introduced into his own world at a certain time and in a definite way. Dreams are broken and shadows depart; the Divine truth is no longer a poetical expression, or a devotional exaggeration, or a mystical economy, or a mythical representation.

'Sacrifice and offering', the shadows of the Law, 'thou wouldest not, but a body hast thou fitted to me' (Ps [39] 40:6). 'That which was from the beginning, which we have heard, which we have seen with our eyes, which we have diligently looked upon, and our hands have handled' (1 Jn 1:1). 'That which we have seen and have heard, declare we unto you' (1 Jn 1:3); - such is the record

Bl. John Henry Newman, 'The Glories of Mary for the sake of her Son', in *Discourses addressed to Mixed Congregations, by John Henry Cardinal Newman* (London: Longmans, Green, 1902), pp. 346-349.

of the Apostle, in opposition to those 'spirits' which denied that 'Jesus Christ had appeared in the flesh' (2 Jn 7), and which 'dissolved' him by denying either his human nature or his divine. And the confession that Mary is *Deipara*, or the Mother of God, is that safeguard wherewith we seal up and secure the doctrine of the Apostle from all evasion, and that test whereby we detect all the pretences of those bad spirits of 'Antichrist which have gone out into the world' (2 Jn 7). It declares that he is God; it implies that he is man; it suggests to us that he is God still, though he has become man, and that he is true man though he is God. By witnessing to the *process* of the union, it secures the reality of the two *subjects* of the union, of the divinity and of the manhood. If Mary is the Mother of God, Christ must be literally Emmanuel, God with us. [...]

You see, then, my brethren, in this particular, the harmonious consistency of the revealed system, and the bearing of one doctrine upon another; Mary is exalted for the sake of Jesus. It was fitting that she, as being a creature, though the first of creatures, should have an office of ministration. She, as others, came into the world to do a work, she had a mission to fulfil; her grace and her glory are not for her own sake, but for her Maker's; and to her is committed the custody of the Incarnation; this is her appointed office, - 'A Virgin shall conceive, and bear a Son, and they shall call his name Emmanuel' (Is 7: 14). As she was once on earth, and was personally the guardian of her Divine Child, as she carried him in her womb, folded him in her embrace, and suckled him at her breast, so now, and to the latest hour of the Church, do her glories and the devotion paid her proclaim and define the right faith concerning him as God and man. [...] Thus she is the *Turris Davidica*, as the Church calls her, 'the Tower of Davd'; the high and strong defence of the King of the true Israel; and hence the Church also addresses her in the Antiphon, as having 'alone destroyed all heresies in the whole world'.

A reading from Richard Rolle, *Of the Virtues of the Holy Name of Jesus*

'Oil outpoured is thy Name' (Song 1:3). As soon as the name of Jesus comes into the world it smells as oil outpoured. Oil, that is a token of everlasting salvation for which we hope. 'Jesus' indeed means Saviour or healthful. Therefore, what does 'Oil outpoured is thy Name' mean but 'Jesus is thy Name'? This name is oil outpoured because Jesus the Word of God has taken the nature of man.

O Jesus! Thou dost fulfil in work what thou are called in name. Verily, thou whom we call Saviour dost save man, and therefore Jesus is thy Name. Ah! that wonderful Name! Ah! that delectable Name! This is the Name that is above all names, the Name which is highest of all, without which no man hopes for salvation. This Name is sweet and joyful, giving veritable comfort to the heart of man. Verily, the Name of Jesus is in my mind a joyous song and heavenly music in mine ear, and in my mouth a honeyed sweetness. Wherefore no wonder I love that Name which gives comfort to me in all my anguish. [...]

This Name of Jesus, loyally kept in mind, draws up vices by the roots, implants virtues, sows charity, pours in the savour of heavenly things, destroys discord, re-establishes peace, gives everlasting rest, does away with the grievousness of fleshly desires, turns all earthly things to sorrow, and fills the lover with ghostly joy.

So it may well be said: 'All shall rejoice that love thy Name, for thou shalt bless the righteous' (Ps 5:11-12). Because the righteous have deserved to be blessed if they have truly loved the Name of Jesus. And therefore they are called righteous because they strove to love Jesus truly. Therefore, what can he lack who desires to love the Name of Jesus unceasingly? Indeed, he loves and yearns to love, for we know that the Love of God is of such a kind that the more we love the more we long to love.

Richard Rolle, *Of the Virtues of the Holy Name of Jesus*, in *Selected Works of Richard Rolle, Hermit*. Transcribed, with an introduction, by G. C. Heseltine (London: Longmans, Green 1930), pp. 81-83.

Second Sunday of Christmas

A reading from Roger of Byland, *The Milk of Babes*

For the empire of an earthly kind, believe me, all are so prompt and so trained in the livery of obedience, that they even long to hear his command. But God himself, the inexpressible, eternal Majesty and the incalculable Power summons us again and again. he even sends us sacred dispatches and the truly awesome letters of his commandments. Yet we do not immediately welcome them with joy and homage, nor do we consider as the highest blessing the rule of so great and glorious a Power, especially when not the advantage of the Commander but the good of his subject prompts the summons. Now what raises our minds more to higher thoughts, what frees us more from despair of immortality, than the fact that the eternal and immutable Word of God, should become flesh for us and dwell among us? What could arouse us to divine love more than the fact that the omnipotent and invariable Good, by whom all things were created from nothing and becomingly and beautifully arrayed, that the one and only supreme Good whose greatness is without end and whose wisdom is beyond counting, determined to become such a being as might experience the confinement of the womb, share the indignity of coming to birth, endure the bonds of swaddling clothes, suffer the weakness of the cradle and, though he was the Word, ask with tears for nourishment and, through he was the Author of all time and space, by subject to growing up through the ages of man.

By associating with us even in our flesh, he withdrew from us every alibi, he refuted all human sophistry. In fact, because devotees of pleasure perversely coveted the wealth of the people, he determined to be poor. They sighed for honours and power; he refused to be made a king. They thought children born of their flesh a great blessing; he scorned such marriage and progeny. They shrank from reproach; he endured reproaches of every kind. They thought insults insufferable, but what insult is greater than the condemnation of a just and innocent man? They abominated bodily pain; but he was scourged and mocked. They feared death; he was punished with death. They considered the cross the most ignominious form of death; he was crucified.

Roger of Byland, *The Milk of Babes*, 3-4, in *The Works of Gilbert of Hoyland IV. Treatises, Epistles, and Sermons, with a Letter of Roger of Byland,* The Milk of Babes, and an edition and translation of the works of Master Gilbert, Abbot, from MS Bodley 87, The Bodleian Library. Translated with an appendix by Lawrence C. Braceland, S. J. (Kalamazoo, MI: Cistercian Publications, 1981), pp. 110-111.

Hence his whole life on earth exemplified the right way for mankind, through the human form he so graciously assumed. Indeed no sin can be committed, except when man covets what he despised and shuns what he endured. When the rational soul, bound in the chains of death as a penalty for sin, was reduced to so weak a state that it depended upon suggestions from visible reality to reach invisible truth, then in fact the omnipotent, eternal, immense and invisible God, consented to become the visible food of a rational creature, not by the change of his own nature but by the assumption of ours, and he recalled souls from the quest for visible realities to the quest for his invisible Reality. Hence the soul found him in humility outside herself, whom in her pride she had abandoned within herself. By beginning to imitate his visible lowliness, the soul prepares to return to his invisible sublimity. Thus indeed man, though not yet equal to the angels, could eat the bread of angels, since the very Bread of angels consented to be made equal to man.

Short Readings for Prayer during the Day
in Christmastide

Sunday *1 Jn 4:9*
In this the love of God was made manifest among us, that God sent his only Son into the world, so that we might live through him.

Monday *Is 9:2, 6, 7*
The people who walked in darkness have seen a great light; those who dwelt in a land of deep darkness, on them has light shined. For to us a child is born, to us a son is given; and the government will be upon his shoulder, and his name will be called 'Wonderful Counsellor, Mighty God, Everlasting Father, Prince of Peace.' Of the increase of his government and of peace there will be no end, upon the throne of David, and over his kingdom, to establish it, and to uphold it with justice and with righteousness from this time forth and for evermore. The zeal of the Lord of hosts will do this.

Tuesday *Deut 4:7*
What great nation is there that has a god so near to it as the Lord our God is to us, whenever we call upon him?

Wednesday *Is 65:1*
I was ready to be sought by those who did not ask for me; I was ready to be found by those who did not seek me. I said, 'Here am I, here am I,' to a nation that did not call on my name.

Thursday *Gal 4:4-7*
When the time had fully come, God sent forth his Son, born of woman, born under the law, to redeem those who were under the law, so that we might receive adoption as sons. And because you are sons, God has sent the Spirit of his Son into our hearts, crying, 'Abba! Father!' So through God you are no longer a slave but a son, and if a son then an heir.

Friday _Tit 2:11-14_

The grace of God has appeared for the salvation of all men, training us to renounce irreligion and worldly passions, and to live sober, upright, and godly lives in this world, awaiting our blessed hope, the appearing of the glory of our great God and Saviour Jesus Christ, who gave himself for us to redeem us from all iniquity and to purify for himself a people of his own who are zealous for good deeds.

Saturday _Heb 1:1-3a_

In many and various ways God spoke of old to our fathers by the prophets; but in these last days he has spoken to us by a Son, whom he appointed the heir of all things, through whom also he created the ages. he reflects the glory of God and bears the very stamp of his nature, upholding the universe by his word of power.

Christmas Prayer during the Day

Almighty and everlasting God,
who stooped to raise fallen humanity
through the child-bearing of blessed Mary;
grant that we, who have seen thy glory
revealed in our human nature
and thy love made perfect in our weakness,
may daily be renewed in thine image
and conformed to the pattern of thy Son
Jesus Christ our Lord.

Collects

Christmas Day

ALMIGHTY God, who hast given us thy only-begotten Son to take our nature upon him, and as at this time to be born of a pure Virgin: grant that we, being regenerate and made thy children by adoption and grace, may daily be renewed by thy Holy Spirit; through Jesus Christ thy Son our Lord, who liveth and reigneth with thee and the same Spirit, for ever and ever.

Sunday after Christmas Day: Holy Family

HEAVENLY Father, whose blessed Son shared at Nazareth the life of an earthly home: grant to thy Church grace to live as one family, united in love and obedience, and at the last bring us all to our home in heaven; through Jesus Christ thy Son our Lord, who liveth and reigneth with thee in the unity of the Holy Spirit, one God, for ever and ever.

Second Sunday after Christmas

ALMIGHTY God, who hast poured upon us the new light of thine incarnate Word: grant that the same light enkindled in our hearts may shine forth in our lives; through Jesus Christ thy Son our Lord, who liveth and reigneth with thee in the unity of the Holy Spirit, one God, for ever and ever.

Solemnity of Mary, Mother of God (1 January)

O GOD, who didst vouchsafe that, as at this time, thy Word was made flesh in the womb of the Blessed Virgin Mary: grant to us thy humble servants that we, believing her to be indeed the Mother of God, may by her intercession find favour in thy sight; through the same Jesus Christ thy Son our Lord, who liveth and reigneth with thee and the same Spirit, for ever and ever.

2 January until the Epiphany

ALMIGHTY God, who didst wonderfully create man in thine own image, and didst yet more wonderfully restore him: grant, we beseech thee, that as thy Son our Lord Jesus Christ was made in the likeness of men, so we may be made partakers of the divine nature; through the same thy Son, who with thee and the Holy Spirit liveth and reigneth, one God, for ever and ever.

Most Holy Name of Jesus (3 January)

O GOD, who didst appoint thine only-begotten Son to be the Saviour of mankind, and didst command that he should be called Jesus: mercifully grant, that we, who venerate his holy name on earth, may also rejoice to behold him in heaven; we ask this through Jesus Christ thy Son our Lord, who liveth and reigneth with thee, in the unity of the Holy Spirit, one God, for ever and ever.

or

O GOD, who hast caused the most glorious Name of our Lord Jesus Christ, thine only-begotten Son, to be loved with the greatest affection by thy faithful, and to be terrible and fearful to evil spirits: mercifully grant that all they who devoutly venerate this Name of JESUS on earth may have part in the sweetness of holy consolations in this present life, and in the world to come may attain unto the fullness of joy and eternal praise; through the same Christ our Lord.

Processional Hymn

Bidding Prayer

Beloved in Christ, be it this Christmastide our care and delight to hear again the message of the angels, and in heart and mind to go even unto Bethlehem and see this thing which is come to pass, and the Babe lying in a manger.

Therefore let us read and mark in Holy Scripture the tale of the loving purposes of God from the first days of our disobedience unto the glorious redemption brought us by this Holy Child.†

But first let us pray for the needs of his whole world; for peace on earth and goodwill among all his people; for unity and brotherhood within the Church he came to build, and especially in this city [*town, village*] of.....

And because this of all things would rejoice his heart, let us remember in his name the poor and helpless, the cold, the hungry and the oppressed; the sick and them that mourn, the lonely and the unloved, the aged and the little children; all those who know not the Lord Jesus, or who love him not, or who by sin have grieved his heart of love.

Lastly let us remember before God all those who rejoice with us, but upon another shore, and in a greater light, that multitude which no man can number, whose hope was in the Word made flesh, and with whom in the Lord Jesus we are for ever one.

---

† *in churches dedicated to the Blessed Virgin Mary add:* and let us make this Church, dedicated to Mary, his most blessed Mother, glad with our carols of praise.

These prayers and praises let us humbly offer up to the throne of heaven, in the words which Christ himself has taught us:

People **Our Father, who art in heaven,**
hallowed be thy name;
thy kingdom come;
thy will be done,
on earth as it is in heaven.
Give us this day our daily bread.
And forgive us our trespasses,
as we forgive those who trespass against us.
And lead us not into temptation;
but deliver us from evil. Amen.

May the almighty God bless us with his grace; Christ give us the joys of everlasting life, and unto the fellowship of the citizens above may the King of angels bring us all.

People **Amen.**

Carol or Hymn

First Lesson

God tells sinful Adam that he has lost the life of Paradise and that his seed will bruise the serpent's head.

Gen 3:8-20

And they heard the sound of the Lord God walking in the garden in the cool of the day, and the man and his wife hid themselves from the presence of the Lord God among the trees of the garden. But the Lord God called to the man, and said to him, 'Where are you?' And he said, 'I heard the sound of you in the garden, and I was afraid, because I was naked; and I hid myself.' he said, 'Who told you that you were naked? Have you eaten of the tree of which I commanded you not to eat?' The man said, 'The woman whom you gave to be with me, she gave me fruit of the tree, and I ate.' Then the Lord God said to the woman, 'What is this that you have done?' The woman said, 'The serpent beguiled me, and I ate.' The Lord God said to the serpent, 'Because you have done this, cursed are you above all cattle,

215

and above all wild animals; upon your belly you shall go, and dust you shall eat all the days of your life. I will put enmity between you and the woman, and between your seed and her seed; he shall bruise your head, and you shall bruise his heel.' To the woman he said, 'I will greatly multiply your pain in childbearing; in pain you shall bring forth children, yet your desire shall be for your husband, and he shall rule over you.' And to Adam he said, 'Because you have listened to the voice of your wife, and have eaten of the tree of which I commanded you, 'You shall not eat of it,' cursed is the ground because of you; in toil you shall eat of it all the days of your life; thorns and thistles it shall bring forth to you; and you shall eat the plants of the field. In the sweat of your face you shall eat bread till you return to the ground, for out of it you were taken; you are dust, and to dust you shall return.' The man called his wife's name Eve, because she was the mother of all living.

At the end the following may be said

People **Thanks be to God.**

Carol or Hymn

Second Lesson

God promises to faithful Abraham that
in his seed shall all the nations of the earth be blessed.
Gen 22:15-18

And the angel of the Lord called to Abraham a second time from heaven, and said, 'By myself I have sworn, says the Lord, because you have done this, and have not withheld your son, your only-begotten son, I will indeed bless you, and I will multiply your descendants as the stars of heaven and as the sand which is on the seashore. And your descendants shall possess the gate of their enemies, and by your descendants shall all the nations of the earth bless themselves, because you have obeyed my voice.'

At the end the following may be said

People **Thanks be to God.**

216

Carol or Hymn

Third Lesson

The prophet foretells the coming of the Saviour.

Is 9:2, 6-7

The people who walked in darkness have seen a great light; those who dwelt in a land of deep darkness, on them has light shined. For to us a child is born, to us a son is given; and the government will be upon his shoulder, and his name will be called 'Wonderful Counsellor, Mighty God, Everlasting Father, Prince of Peace.' Of the increase of his government and of peace there will be no end, upon the throne of David, and over his kingdom, to establish it, and to uphold it with justice and with righteousness from this time forth and for evermore. The zeal of the Lord of hosts will do this.

At the end the following may be said

People   **Thanks be to God.**

Carol or Hymn

Fourth Lesson

The peace that Christ will bring is foreshown.

Is 11:1-9

There shall come forth a shoot from the stump of Jesse, and a branch shall grow out of his roots. And the Spirit of the Lord shall rest upon him, the spirit of wisdom and understanding, the spirit of counsel and might, the spirit of knowledge and the fear of the Lord. And his delight shall be in the fear of the Lord. he shall not judge by what his eyes see, or decide by what his ears hear; but with righteousness he shall judge the poor, and decide with equity for the meek of the earth; and he shall smite the earth with the rod of his mouth, and with the breath of his lips he shall slay the wicked. Righteousness shall be the belt of his waist, and faithfulness the belt of his loins. The wolf shall dwell with the lamb, and the leopard shall lie down with the kid, and

217

the calf and the lion and the fatling together, and a little child shall lead them. The cow and the bear shall feed; their young shall lie down together; and the lion shall eat straw like the ox. The sucking child shall play over the hole of the asp, and the weaned child shall put his hand on the adder's den. They shall not hurt or destroy in all my holy mountain; for the earth shall be full of the knowledge of the Lord as the waters cover the sea.

At the end the following may be said

People   **Thanks be to God.**

Alternative Fourth Lesson

The prophet Micah foretells the glory of little Bethlehem.

Mic 5:2-4

But you, O Bethlehem Eph'rathah, who are little to be among the clans of Judah, from you shall come forth for me one who is to be ruler in Israel, whose origin is from of old, from ancient days. Therefore he shall give them up until the time when she who is in travail has brought forth; then the rest of his brethren shall return to the people of Israel. And he shall stand and feed his flock in the strength of the Lord, in the majesty of the name of the Lord his God. And they shall dwell secure, for now he shall be great to the ends of the earth.

At the end the following may be said

People   **Thanks be to God.**

Carol or Hymn

Fifth Lesson

The angel Gabriel salutes the Blessed Virgin Mary.

Lk 1:26-38

In the sixth month the angel Gabriel was sent from God to a city of Galilee named Nazareth, to a virgin betrothed to a man whose name was Joseph, of the house of David; and the virgin's name was Mary. And he came to her and said, 'Hail, full of grace, the Lord is with you!' But she was greatly troubled at the saying, and considered in her mind what sort of greeting this might be. And the angel said to her, 'Do not be afraid, Mary, for you have found favour with God. And behold, you will conceive in your womb and bear a son, and you shall call his name Jesus. he will be great, and will be called the Son of the Most High; and the Lord God will give to him the throne of his father David, and he will reign over the house of Jacob for ever; and of his kingdom there will be no end.' And Mary said to the angel, 'How can this be, since I have no husband?' And the angel said to her, 'The Holy Spirit will come upon you, and the power of the Most High will overshadow you; therefore the child to be born will be called holy, the Son of God. And behold, your kinswoman Elizabeth in her old age has also conceived a son; and this is the sixth month with her who was called barren. For with God nothing will be impossible.' And Mary said, 'Behold, I am the handmaid of the Lord; let it be to me according to your word.' And the angel departed from her.

At the end the following may be said

People **Thanks be to God.**

Alternative Fifth Lesson

The prophet in exile foresees
the coming of the glory of the Lord.

Is 60:1-6, 19

Arise, shine; for your light has come, and the glory of the Lord has risen upon you. For behold, darkness shall cover the earth, and thick darkness the peoples; but the Lord will arise upon you, and his glory will be seen upon you. And nations shall come to your light, and kings to the brightness of your rising. Lift up your eyes round about, and see; they all gather together, they come to you; your sons shall come from far, and your daughters shall be carried in the arms. Then you shall see and be radiant, your heart shall thrill and rejoice; because the abundance of the sea shall be turned to you, the wealth of the nations shall come to you. A multitude of camels shall cover you, the young camels of Midian and Ephah; all those from Sheba shall come. They shall bring gold and frankincense, and shall proclaim the praise of the Lord. The sun shall be no more your light by day, nor for brightness shall the moon give light to you by night; but the Lord will be your everlasting light, and your God will be your glory.

Carol or Hymn

or

*When the Festival of Nine Lessons and Carols replaces the public celebration of Evening Prayer, the canticle **Magnificat** may be sung at this point, and the altar censed in the usual fashion. If incense is used here it is used too at the Ninth Lesson.*

Sixth Lesson

St Matthew tells of the birth of Jesus.

Mt 1:18-23

Now the birth of Jesus Christ took place in this way. When his mother Mary had been betrothed to Joseph, before they came together she was found to be with child of the Holy Spirit; and her husband Joseph, being a just man and unwilling to put her to shame, resolved to send her away quietly. But as he considered this, behold, an angel of the Lord appeared to him in a dream, saying, 'Joseph, son of David, do not fear to take Mary your wife, for that which is conceived in her is of the Holy Spirit; she will bear a son, and you shall call his name Jesus, for he will save his people from their sins.' All this took place to fulfil what the Lord had spoken by the prophet: 'Behold, a virgin shall conceive and bear a son, and his name shall be called Emmanuel' (which means, God with us).

At the end the following may be said

People   **Thanks be to God.**

Alternative Sixth Lesson

St Luke tells of the birth of Jesus.

Lk 2:1-7

In those days a decree went out from Cæsar Augustus that all the world should be enrolled. This was the first enrollment, when Quirin'i-us was governor of Syria. And all went to be enrolled, each to his own city. And Joseph also went up from Galilee, from the city of Nazareth, to Judea, to the city of David, which is called Bethlehem, because he was of the house and lineage of David, to be enrolled with Mary, his betrothed, who was with child. And while they were there, the time came for her to be delivered. And she gave birth to her first-born son and wrapped him in swaddling cloths, and laid him in a manger, because there was no place for them in the inn.

At the end the following may be said

People   **Thanks be to God.**

Carol or Hymn

Seventh Lesson

The shepherds go to the manger.

Lk 2:8-16

And in that region there were shepherds out in the field, keeping watch over their flock by night. And an angel of the Lord appeared to them, and the glory of the Lord shone around them, and they were filled with fear. And the angel said to them, 'Be not afraid; for behold, I bring you good news of a great joy which will come to all the people; for to you is born this day in the city of David a Saviour, who is Christ the Lord. And this will be a sign for you: you will find a babe wrapped in swaddling cloths and lying in a manger.' And suddenly there was with the angel a multitude of the heavenly host praising God and saying, 'Glory to God in the highest, and on earth peace among men with whom he is pleased!' When the angels went away from them into heaven, the shepherds said to one another, 'Let us go over to Bethlehem and see this thing that has happened, which the Lord has made known to us.' And they went with haste, and found Mary and Joseph, and the babe lying in a manger. And when they saw it they made known the saying which had been told them concerning this child; and all who heard it wondered at what the shepherds told them. But Mary kept all these things, pondering them in her heart. And the shepherds returned, glorifying and praising God for all they had heard and seen, as it had been told them.

At the end the following may be said

People   **Thanks be to God.**

222

Carol or Hymn

Eighth Lesson

The wise men are led by the star to Jesus.

Mt 2:1-12

Now when Jesus was born in Bethlehem of Judæa in the days of Herod the king, behold, Wise Men from the East came to Jerusalem, saying, 'Where is he who has been born king of the Jews? For we have seen his star in the East, and have come to worship him.' When Herod the king had heard these things, he was troubled, and all Jerusalem with him; and assembling all the chief priests and scribes of the people, he inquired of them where the Christ was to be born. They told him, 'In Bethlehem of Judæa; for so it is written by the prophet: "And you Bethlehem, in the land of Judah, are by no means least among the rulers of Judah; for out of you shall come a ruler, who will govern my people Israel." ' Then Herod summoned the Wise Men secretly and ascertained from them what time the star appeared; and he sent them to Bethlehem, saying, 'Go and search diligently for the child; and when you have found him, bring me word, that I too may come and worship him. When they had heard the king they went their way; and behold, the star, which they had seen in the East went before them, till it came to rest over the place where the child was. When they saw the star, they rejoiced exceedingly with great joy; and going into the house they saw the child with Mary his mother, and they fell down, and worshipped him. Then, opening their treasures, they offered him gifts, gold and frankincense and myrrh. And being warned in a dream not to return to Herod, they departed to their own country by another way.

At the end the following may be said

People   **Thanks be to God.**

Carol or Hymn

223

Ninth Lesson

St John unfolds the great mystery of the Incarnation.

Jn 1:1-14, 16-18

In the beginning was the Word, and the Word was with God, and the Word was God. He was in the beginning with God; all things were made through him, and without him was not any thing made that was made. In him was life, and the life was the light of men. The light shines in the darkness, and the darkness has not overcome it. There was a man sent from God, whose name was John. He came for testimony, to bear witness to the light, that all might believe through him. He was not the light, but came to bear witness of that light. The true light that enlightens every man was coming into the world. He was in the world, and the world was made through him, yet the world knew him not. He came to his own home, and his own people received him not. But to all who received him, who believed in his name, he gave power to become children of God; who were born, not of blood, nor of the will of the flesh, nor of the will of man, but of God. And the Word became flesh and dwelt among us, full of grace and truth; we have beheld his glory, glory as of the only-begotten Son from the Father. And from his fullness have we all received, grace upon grace. For the law was given through Moses; grace and truth came through Jesus Christ. No-one has ever seen God; the only-begotten Son, who is in the bosom of the Father, he has made him known.

At the end the following may be said

People **Thanks be to God.**

Carol or Hymn

Collect

People

[The Lord be with you:
and with thy spirit.]

Let us pray.

O GOD, who makest us glad with the yearly remembrance of the birth of thy only son, Jesus Christ: grant that as we joyfully receive him for our redeemer, so we may with sure confidence behold him, when he shall come to be our judge; who liveth and reigneth with thee and the Holy Spirit, one God, world without end. **Amen.**

Blessing

Christ, who by his incarnation gathered into one things earthly and heavenly, grant you the fullness of inward peace and goodwill, and make you partakers of the divine nature; and the blessing of God almighty, the Father, the Son and the Holy Spirit, be upon you and remain with you always. **Amen.**

Recessional Hymn

Epiphany of the Lord

Office

Opening Sentence

From the rising of the sun to its setting my name is great among the nations, and in every place incense is offered to my name, and a pure offering; for my name is great among the nations, says the Lord of hosts.

Mal 1:11

Hymn

Morning & Evening Prayer *Vespers*

(A simpler version of the melody is found on page 199)

Hostes Herodes impie

1.Why, impious Herod, shouldst thou fear
because the Christ is come so near?
He who doth heavenly kingdoms grant
thine earthly realm can never want.

2.Lo, sages from the East are gone
to where the star hath newly shone:
led on by light to Light they press,
and by their gifts their God confess.

3.The Lamb of God is manifest
again in Jordan's water blest,
and he who sin had never known
by washing hath our sins undone.

4.Yet het hat ruleth everything
can change the nature of the spring
and gives at Cana this for sign—
the water reddens into wine.

5.Then glory, Lord, to thee we pay
For thine Epiphany today;
all glory through eternity
to Father, Son, and Spirit be. Amen

C. Sedulius, *c.* 450. *Tr.* Percy Dearmer

Post-Biblical Reading

A reading from the sermons of Blessed John Henry Newman

Our Saviour said to the woman of Samaria, 'The hour cometh, when ye shall neither in this mountain, nor yet at Jerusalem, worship the Father' (Jn 4:21). And upon today's Festival I may say to you in his words on another occasion, 'This day is this scripture fulfilled in your ears' (Lk 4:21). This day we commemorate the opening of the door of faith to the Gentiles, the extension of the Church of God through all lands, whereas, before Christ's coming, it had been confined to one nation only. This dissemination of the Truth throughout the world had been the subject of prophecy. 'Enlarge the place of thy tent, and let them stretch forth the curtains of thine habitations: spare not, lengthen thy cords, and strengthen thy stakes; for thou shalt break forth in the right hand and on the left; and thy seed shall inherit the Gentiles, and make the desolate cities to be inhabited' (Is 54:2, 3). In these words the Church is addressed as Catholic, which is the distinguishing title of the Christian Church, as contrasted with the Jewish. [...]

This characteristic blessing of the Church of Christ, its Catholic nature, is a frequent subject of rejoicing with St Paul, who was the chief instrument of its propagation. In one Epistle he speaks of Gentiles being 'fellow heirs' with the Jews, 'and of the same body, and partakers of his promise in Christ by the Gospel' (Eph 3:6). In another he enlarges on 'the mystery now made manifest to the saints', viz. 'Christ among the Gentiles, the hope of glory' (Col 2:26-27).

The day on which we commemorate this gracious appointment of God's Providence, is called the Epiphany, or bright manifestation of Christ to the Gentiles; being the day on which the wise men came from the East under guidance of a star to worship him, and thus became the first-fruits of the heathen world. The name is explained by the words of the text, which occur in one of the lessons selected for today's service, and in which the Church is addressed. 'Arise, shine; for thy light is come, and the glory of the Lord is risen upon thee. For, behold, the darkness shall cover the earth, and gross darkness the people: but the Lord shall arise upon these, and his glory shall be seen upon thee. And the Gentiles shall come to thy light, and kings to the brightness of

---

Bl. John Henry Newman, 'The Glory of the Christian Church', in J. H. Newman, *Parochial and Plain Sermons* II (London: Rivingtons, 1880), pp. 79-81, 93-94.

thy rising…. thy people also shall be all righteous: they shall inherit the land for ever, the branch of my planting, the work of my hands that I may be glorified' (Is 60: 1-3, 21).

That this and other similar prophecies had their measure of fulfilment when Christ came, we all know; when his Church, built upon the Apostles and Prophets, wonderfully branched out from Jerusalem as a centre into the heathen world round about, and gathering into it men of all ranks, languages, and characters, moulded them upon one pattern, the pattern of their Saviour, in truth and righteousness. Thus the prophecies concerning the Church were fulfilled at that time in two respects, as regards its sanctity and its Catholicity.

It is often asked, have these prophecies had then and since their perfect accomplishment? Or are we to expect a more complete Christianizing of the world than has hitherto been vouchsafed it? And it is usual at the present day to acquiesce in the latter alternative, as if the inspired predictions certainly meant more than has yet been realized.

Now so much, I think, is plain on the face of them, that the Gospel is to be preached in all lands, before the end comes: 'This gospel of the kingdom shall be preached in all the world for a witness unto all nations; and then shall the end come' (Mt 24: 14). Whether it has been thus preached is a question of fact, which must be determined, not from the prophecy, but from history; and there we may leave it. But as to the other expectation, that a time of greater purity is in store for the Church, that is not easily to be granted. The very words of Christ just quoted, so far from speaking of the Gospel as tending to the conversion of the world at large, when preached in it, describe it only as a *witness* unto all the Gentiles, as if the many would not obey it. And this intimation runs parallel to St Paul's account of the Jewish Church, as realizing faith and obedience only in a residue out of the whole people; and is further illustrated by St John's language in the Apocalypse, who speaks of the 'redeemed from among men' being but a remnant, 'the first-fruits unto God and to the Lamb' (Apoc 14: 4). […]

While labouring to unite its fragments, which the malice of Satan has scattered to and fro, to recover what is cast away, to purify what is corrupted, to strengthen what is weak, to make it in all its parts what Christ would have it, a Church Militant, still (please God) we will not reckon on any visible fruit of our labour. We will be content to believe our cause triumphant, when we see it apparently defeated. We will silently bear the insults of the enemies of Christ,

228

and resign ourselves meekly to the shame and suffering which the errors of his followers bring upon us. We will endure offences which the early Saints would have marvelled at, and Martyrs would have died to redress. We will work with zeal, but as to the Lord and not to men; recollecting that even Apostles saw the sins of the Churches they planted; that St Paul predicted that 'evil men and seducers would wax worse and worse' (2 Tim 3:13); and that St John seems even to consider extraordinary unbelief as the very sign of the times of the Gospel, as if the light increased the darkness of those who hated it. 'Little children, it is the last time; and as ye have heard that Antichrist shall come, even now are there many Antichrists, whereby we know that it is the last time' (1 Jn 2:18).

Short Readings for Prayer during the Day
at Epiphany

Sunday *Mal 1:11*

From the rising of the sun to its setting my name is great among the nations, and in every place incense is offered to my name, and a pure offering; for my name is great among the nations, says the Lord of hosts.

Monday *Tob 14:7, 9*

All the Gentiles will praise the Lord, and his people will give thanks to God, and the Lord will exalt his people. And all who love the Lord God in truth and righteousness will rejoice, showing mercy to our brethren. But keep the law and the commandments, and be merciful and just, so that it may be well with you.

Tuesday *Is 60.1-3*

Arise, shine; for your light has come, and the glory of the Lord has risen upon you. For behold, darkness shall cover the earth, and thick darkness the peoples; but the Lord will arise upon you, and his glory will be seen upon you. And nations shall come to your light, and kings to the brightness of your rising.

Wednesday *2 Cor 4:5, 6*

What we preach is not ourselves, but Jesus Christ as Lord, with ourselves as your servants for Jesus' sake. For it is the God who said, 'Let light shine out of darkness,' who has shone in our hearts to give the light of the knowledge of the glory of God in the face of Christ.

Thursday

When we cry, 'Abba! Father!' it is the Spirit himself bearing witness with our spirit that we are children of God, and if children, then heirs, heirs of God and fellow heirs with Christ, provided we suffer with him in order that we may also be glorified with him.

Rom 8:15b-17

Friday *Eph 1:9-10*

The Father has made known to us in all wisdom and insight the mystery of his will, according to his purpose which he set forth in Christ as a plan for the fullness of time, to unite all things in him, things in heaven and things on earth.

Saturday *Rev 1:13-16*

In the midst of the lampstands one like a Son of man, clothed with a long robe and with a golden girdle round his breast; his head and his hair were white as white wool, white as snow; his eyes were like a flame of fire, his feet were like burnished bronze, refined as in a furnace, and his voice was like the sound of many waters; in his right hand he held seven stars, from his mouth issued a sharp two-edged sword, and his face was like the sun shining in full strength.

Epiphany Prayer during the Day

O good Jesu,
Word of the Father and
brightness of his glory,
whom angels desire to behold:
teach me to do thy will
that, guided by thy Spirit,
I may come to that blessed city of
 everlasting day,
where all are one in heart and mind,
where there is safety and eternal peace,
happiness and delight,
where thou livest with the Father and the Holy Spirit,
one God,
world without end.

after St Gregory the Great (604)

Collect

O GOD, who by the leading of a star didst manifest thy only-begotten Son to the Gentiles: mercifully grant, that we, which know thee now by faith, may after this life have the fruition of thy glorious Godhead; through Jesus Christ thy Son our Lord, who liveth and reigneth with thee in the unity of the Holy Spirit, one God, for ever and ever.

Office

Opening Sentence

From the rising of the sun to its setting my name is great among the nations, and in every place incense is offered to my name, and a pure offering; for my name is great among the nations, says the Lord of hosts.

Mal 1:11

Post-Biblical Reading

A reading from the sermons of Lancelot Andrewes

And so was he baptized. And he had a threefold immersion; one in Gethsemane, one in Gabbatha, and a third in Golgotha. In Gethsemane, in his sweat of blood. In Gabbatha, in the blood that came from the scourges and thorns; and in Golgotha, that which came from the nails and the spear. Specially, the spear. There, met the two streams of 'water and blood' (Jn 19:34), the true Jordan, the bath or laver, wherein we are purged 'from all our sins' (1 Jn 1:7). No sin of so deep a dye but this will command it, and fetch it out. This in Jordan, here now, was but an undertaking of that then; and in virtue of that, doth all our water-baptism work. And therefore are we baptized into it: not into his water-baptism, but into his cross-baptism; not into his baptism, but into his death. 'So many as are baptized, are baptized into his death' – it is the Apostle (Rom 6:3).

To take our leave of this point. This may be said: if it be 'justice' (Mt 3:15), that Christ comes to baptism, much more that the people. And how then comes it to pass that there is such sacrilegious pride in some of the people, that, as if no such thing were, set so light by it as they do? And that not John's, as this was, but Christ's own baptism? Be sure of this, if Christ thus did, to countenance

---

Lancelot Andrewes, 'A Sermon preached before the King's Majesty, at Greenwich, on the twenty-ninth of May, A. D. MDCXV, being Whit-Sunday, in *Ninety-Six Sermons by the right honourable and reverend father in God Lancelot Andrewes,* III (Oxford: Parker, 1850), pp. 247-249, 258.

and credit John's baptism because it was the ordinance of God, much more his mind is to give countenance, and to have countenance given, to his own, which is God's ordinance, of a far higher nature.

And if the Lord thought not much to come to the baptism of his servant, he will think much if the servant come not to the baptism of his Lord. This of his then is but a lesson to us, to invite us thereto; and we take it as the voice that spake to St Paul, 'And now why stay you?' (Acts 22:16). 'Up, wash away your sins', with all the speed you may. For if when the people was baptized, Christ was so, much more strongly it holds, when Christ himself is so, that then the people should and ought to be baptized. [...]

St Paul tells us, that besides the circumcision that was the manufacture, there was another 'made without hands' (Col 2:11). There is so, in baptism, besides the hand seen that casts on the water; the virtue of the Holy Ghost is there, working 'without hands' what here was wrought.

And for this Christ prays; that then it might, might then, and might ever, be joined to that of the water. Not in his baptism only, but in the people's; and as he afterwards enlarges his prayer, in all others' that 'should ever after believe in his name' (Jn 17:20). That what in his here was, in all theirs might be; what in this first, in all following; what in Christ's, in all Christians': Heaven might open, the Holy Ghost comes down, the Father be pleased to say over the same words, so oft as any Christian man's child is brought to his baptism.[...]

A great change; even from the state of servants, as by creation and generation we were, and so still under the law, into the state of 'sons;, as now we are, being ;new creatures' (2 Cor 5:17) in Christ, regenerate and translated into the state of 'grace wherein we stand' (Rom 5:2).

And not only a great change, but a great rise also. At the first, we were but washed from our sins, there was all; but here, from a baptized sinner to an adopted son is a great ascent. he came not down so low, but we go up as high for it. For 'if sons, then heirs', saith the Apostle (Rom 8:17) – so goes the tenor in Heaven; 'heirs' and 'joint heirs' of Heaven, 'with Christ', that is, for the possession and fruit of it, full every way as himself; and this he brings us to, before he leaves us.

Short Reading for Prayer during the Day   *Is 42:1*

Behold, my servant whom I uphold, my chosen in whom my soul delights; I have put my Spirit upon him, he will bring forth justice to the nations.

Collect

ETERNAL Father, who at the baptism of Jesus didst reveal him to be thy Son, anointing him with the Holy Spirit: grant that we, being born again by water and the Spirit, may be faithful to our calling as thine adopted children; through Jesus Christ thy Son our Lord, who liveth and reigneth with thee in the unity of the Holy Spirit, one God, for ever and ever.

Candlemas

Office

Opening Sentence

Behold, this child is set for the fall and rising of many in Israel, and for a sign that is spoken against.

Lk 2:34

Hymn

Evening Prayer   *Vespers*

Quod chorus vatum

1.All prophets hail thee,
   from of old announcing,
   by the inbreathèd
   Spirit of the Father,
God's Mother, bringing
   prophecies to fullness,
Mary the maiden.

3.In the high temple
   Simeon receives thee,
   takes to his bent arms
   with a holy rapture
that promised Saviour,
   vision of redemption,
Christ long awaited.

2.Thou the true Virgin
   Mother of the Highest,
bearing incarnate
   God in awed obedience,
meekly acceptest
   for a sinless offspring
purification.

4.Now the fair realm of
   Paradise attaining,
and to thy Son's throne,
   Mother of th' Eternal,
raisèd all glorious,
   yet in earth's devotion
join with us always.

5.Glory and worship
   to the Lord of all things
pay we unresting,
   who alone adored,
Father and Son and
   Spirit, in the highest
reigneth eternal. Amen.

9th Cent. Tr. T. A. Lacey

See also EH 209, Hail to the Lord who comes.

236

Post-Biblical Reading

A reading from the sermons of Blessed John Henry Newman

We commemorate on this day the Presentation of Christ in the Temple according to the injunction of the Mosaic Law, as laid down in the thirteenth chapter of the Book of Exodus and the twelfth of Leviticus. When the Israelites were brought out of Egypt, the first-born of the Egyptians (as we all know) were visited by death, 'from the first-born of Pharoah that sat on his throne, unto the first-born of the captive that was in the dungeon; and all the first-born of cattle' (Ex 12:29). Accordingly, in thankful remembrance of this destruction, and their own deliverance, every male among the Israelites who was the first-born of his mother, was dedicated to God; likewise, every first-born of cattle. Afterwards, the Levites were taken, as God's peculiar possession, instead of the first-born: but still the first-born were solemnly brought to the Temple at a certain time from their birth, presented to God and then redeemed or bought off at a certain price. At the same time certain sacrifices were offered for the mother, in order to her purification after child-birth; and therefore today's Feast, in memory of Christ's Presentation in the Temple, is commonly called the Purification of the Blessed Virgin Mary.

Our Saviour was born without sin. his Mother, the Blessed Virgin Mary, need have made no offering, as requiring no purification. On the contrary, it was that very birth of the Son of God which sanctified the whole race of woman, and turned her curse into a blessing. Nevertheless, as Christ himself was minded to 'fulfil all righteousness' (Mt 3:13), to obey all ordinances of the covenant under which he was born, so in like manner his Mother Mary submitted to the Law, in order to do it reverence.

This, then, is the event in our Saviour's infancy which we this day celebrate; his Presentation in the Temple when his Virgin Mother was ceremonially purified. It was made memorable at the time by the hymns and praises of Simeon and Anna, to whom he was then revealed. And there were others, besides these, who had been 'looking for redemption in Jerusalem' (Lk 2:38), who were also vouchsafed a sight of the Infant Saviour. But the chief importance of this event consists in its being a fulfilment of prophecy. Malachi had announced the

---

Bl. John Henry Newman, 'Secrecy and Suddenness of Divine Visitations', in J. H. Newman, *Parochial and Plain Sermons* II(London: Rivingtons, 1880), pp. 107-111.

Lord's visitation of his Temple in these words, 'The Lord whom ye seek shall suddenly come to his Temple' (Mal 3:1); words which, though variously fulfilled during his ministry, had their first accomplishment in the humble ceremony commemorated on this day. [...]

I say, we are to-day reminded of the noiseless course of God's providence, - his tranquil accomplishment, in the course of nature, of great events long designed; and again, of the suddenness and stillness of his visitations. Consider what the occurrence in question consists in. A little child is brought to the Temple, as all first-born children were brought. There is nothing here uncommon or striking so far. his parents are with him, poor people, bringing the offering of pigeons or doves, for the purification of the mother. They are met in the Temple by an old man, who takes the child in his arms, offers a thanksgiving to God, and blesses the parents; and next are joined by a woman of a great age, a widow of eighty-four years, who had exceeded the time of useful service, and seemed to be but a fit prey for death. She gives thanks also, and speaks concerning the child to other persons who are present. Then all retire.

Now, there is evidently nothing great or impressive in this; nothing to excite the feelings, or interest the imagination. We know what the world thinks of such a group as I have described. The weak and helpless, whether from age or infancy, it looks upon negligently and passes by. Yet all this that happened was really the solemn fulfilment of an ancient and emphatic prophecy. The infant in arms was the Saviour of the world, the rightful heir, come in disguise of a stranger to visit his own house. [...] Behold the glory; a little child and his parents, two aged persons, and a congregation without name or memorial. 'The kingdom of God cometh not with observation' (Lk 17:20).

Such has ever been the manner of his visitations, in the destruction of his enemies as well as in the deliverance of his own people; - silent, sudden, unforeseen, as regards the world, though predicted in the face of all men, and in their measure comprehended and waited for by his true Church.

Short Reading for Prayer during the Day *Is 42:13*

The Lord goes forth like a mighty man, like a man of war he stirs up his fury; he cries out, he shots aloud, he shows himself mighty against his foes.

Collect

ALMIGHTY and ever-living God, we humbly beseech thy majesty: that, as thy only-begotten Son was this day presented in the temple, in substance of our flesh, so we may be presented unto thee with pure and clean hearts; by thy Son Jesus Christ our Lord, who liveth and reigneth with thee in the unity of the Holy Spirit, one God, for ever and ever.

IV. Times and Seasons

Part II Temporale:

Time between
Epiphany and Lent

Time before Lent

Office Hymns for daily use are found on pages 388ff.

Office

Opening Sentence

O worship the Lord in the beauty of holiness:
let the whole earth stand in awe of him.

Psalm 96:9

Second Sunday after Epiphany

A reading from the sermons of Blessed Isaac of Stella

'There was a wedding-feast at Cana, in Galilee' (Jn 2:1). As I reflect on this wedding-feast, brothers, I am captivated not so much by the great and obvious miracle as by the hidden meaning of the miracle. The former goes to the building-up of one's faith, the latter does something even greater. While the first is a sign for unbelievers, the other has a mysterious message for believers. Both help our spiritual life and delight us; each is great, each is divine. [...]

It seems to me at the moment that there are three kinds of wedding feast – an outer, an inner and a higher. The first takes place externally, the second internally, and the third most intimately; the first between human beings, the second in human beings, and the third above human beings. The first kind of union is of the flesh; the second, of flesh and spirit; the third, of spirit and spirit. The first unites two distinct persons; 'they are no longer two, but one flesh' (Mt 19:60), Scripture tells us. The second achieves an even closer union between rational soul and flesh, two things so opposite in nature, and results in a single person. The third results in the highest possible union of incorporeal beings: 'The man who unites himself to God becomes one spirit with him' (1 Cor 6:17).

Isaac of Stella, *Sermons,* 9: 1, 8-10, 13-14, 18, 20, in Isaac of Stella, *Sermons on the Christian Year,* Volume 1. Translated by Hugh McCaffery, Monk of Mount Melleray (Kalamazoo, MI: Cistercian Publications, 1979), pp. 73, 75, 77-79.

In the first case, flesh joined to flesh becomes one flesh. In the second, call it flesh united to spirit or spirit united to flesh, the outcome is neither one flesh nor one spirit, but an individual human being. In the third case, spirit clinging to God becomes one with God, becomes what God is. This is precisely what the Son prays his Father to grant to his brothers: 'This, Father, is my desire, that they may be one with us as we are one' (Jn 17:21). This unity precedes, surpasses, and outlives every other; it is both source and purpose of all that is. Two in one flesh is union so close as to be no longer two but one flesh. Greater still is the unity that results in a single person from the two substances that go to make man. The greatest union of all, however, comes about when a person clings to God and two spirits are no longer two but become one.

The first kind of union begets existence; the second specifically determines a being's mode of existence; the third is the everlasting glory of existence itself. In the first man is begun, in the second he is formed, in the third, he is completed. First, he comes to be, then he subsists and naturally tends to union. To be one with God: that is the meaning of his coming to be, of his subsisting. Man comes from men that he may go to God

That this built-in bent towards God should in due time and through God's grace find fulfilment, there took place a mysterious marriage, intermediate between the second and third kinds and far distant from the first, a marriage whereby the Word and our nature, Christ and the Church were joined. [...] Jesus neither came from the first kind of wedding nor used it, for he was not born from it nor did he generate by means of it. Yet, when invited, he came to such a kind of wedding. He consecrated it by his presence and upheld it against its detractors by his miraculous power. His chief motive, however, was to stress its significance as a sign of the wedding that is his Incarnation and also the wedding that is the purpose of his Incarnation. For in the second and third kinds of marriage flesh and soul and the Word are all involved: three substances, two natures, God and man in one person. His coming was for the sake of the fourth sort of wedding, a wedding he had himself already achieved in a manner surpassing that of any other man. [...]

This should teach you to go step by step ever higher, from what is less to what is more, from flesh to spirit, from spirit to God; from the second kind of marriage (to which you came through the first kind of marriage) to the third kind, that of the Mediator, himself the ladder, to the fourth kind of marriage. [...]

And do not forget, dear friends, that the marriage to which you have been invited with Jesus (I take it you are his disciples and so apply to yourselves the words, 'Jesus himself, and his disciples, had been invited to the wedding', [Jn 2:2]), this marriage can take place only if you are zealous for conversion.

Third Sunday after Epiphany

A reading from John of Ford, *Sermons on the Final Verses of the Song of Songs*

The charity of God has more to it than sweet and loving premeditations. It is also powerful, and displays its strength in activity. It is well worthwhile to probe into its workings, to see its power, what value it has, what weight, what brightness, what solidity. Sometimes it is necessary for a reality of such deep deliberation and long-lasting silence to break into the open, and a mystery so purposely concealed will find it fitting to answer itself in a style in keeping with its magnificence. Following this principle, the Lord Jesus, when he lived among us, for a long time did not walk about in full view. For roughly thirty years he purposely kept to himself; his face was as it were hidden and despised, and in the meanwhile he made darkness his covering. But afterwards, in keeping with the words of Isaiah, he came 'like a rushing stream which the spirit of the Lord drives forward' (Is 59:19). He broke the long-standing silence by opening his mouth and distilling the honey of his lips, and he also broke for ever his peaceful retreat by opening his hands and displaying the power of his marvellous deeds. As the apostle says, at the time of his good pleasure, the charity of God came to reveal to his Church the mystery silent from immemorial ages and hidden in God alone. He came out of his marriage chamber to preach upon the housetops what had been whispered in the privacy of the inner room.

Those eternal ages were for our God like a time of contemplation and rest, indeed, like a Sabbath. Then the day came, in his own time, for him to come out into the open and for contemplation to display itself in action. What had

John of Ford, *Sermons on the Final Verses of the Song of Songs*, 13: 5-6, in John of Ford, *Sermons on the Song of Songs*, I. Translated by Wendy Mary Beckett (Kalamzoo, MI: Cistercian Publications, MI, 1977), pp. 240-241.

been for so long in labour at last came forth. Let the womb of that eternal love be opened, and let it bring forth for us a Saviour. Let it pour forth with him and after him the whole race of the chosen, conceived so long ago. This is in all reality exactly what happened. We have his own words, 'I have kept silence, I have restrained myself. I will cry out like a woman in child-birth (Is 42:14). And again: "'Shall I who bring others to birth, be sterile?", says the Lord God' (Is 66:9). 'As the earth brings forth its shoots, and as a garden causes what is sown in it to spring up, so the Lord God will cause righteousness and praise to spring up before all the nations'(Is 61:11). So the Wisdom of God as come, raising his voice in our streets, preaching to the world the charity of God. This is what he cries aloud: 'God so loved the world as to given his Only-begotten Son' (Jn 3:16).

Listen, O Church of God, listen and incline your ear! To you the words are spoken, and to you alone have been given ears that can hear.

Fourth Sunday after Epiphany

A reading from the sermons of John Keble

What was this possession with devils, of which we read so much in the New Testament? We cannot exactly say what it was, or is, but thus much is very plain concerning it, that, in many of the symptoms, it was very like the condition of those, who are unhappily out of their mind. All the mercy therefore, which our Lord shewed to any of the possessed, is a token and pledge of his great and never-failing care over those whose senses are disordered. In fevers for example, and in many other complaints, how distressing is it for the time to hear the sick persons wandering as they do! But depend upon it, they are not left to themselves: the Healer of sick souls, as well as of sick bodies, is with them. 'He tells', as the Psalmist says, 'all their flittings; he puts their tears into his bottle; these things are all noted in his Book' (Ps 56:8). He waits to be gracious and merciful to us, as soon as ever our own faith, or the faith of our friends, is such as he delights to answer. And never

---

John Keble, 'Sermon XLVII. Our Lord's Power over the Unseen World', in *Sermons for Christmas and Epiphany, by the late Rev. John Keble* (Oxford and London: Parker, 1875), pp. 477-479, 481-482.

need men despair of his mercy; not in the worst of cases, not in the worst of times; men, I mean, who try to be penitent. Could any case be worse than is described in the following sentences, 'There met him two possessed with devils, coming out of the tombs, exceeding fierce, so that no man might pass by that way', one of whom, for a long time, had had not one evil spirit but many, so that he said, his name was Legion, and this one wore no clothes, nor abode in any house, but in the tombs; no man could bind him, no not with chains, because that he had been often bound with fetters and chains, and the chains were torn in sunder of him, and the fetters broken in pieces, and no man could master him; and always, night and day, he was in the mountains and in the tombs, crying, and cutting himself with stones' (Mk 5:3-5).

See here, what the Evil one will do, if we once permit him to have dominion over us. He will strip us of our clothes, of that holy robe of Baptism, which is all in all to us, so long as we keep it pure. He will not let us abide in any house, no, not the Church of the Living God, the most sacred and comfortable abode of Christ and his Saints. He will not let men be good and happy at home, but encourages restless feelings of every kind. He drives them out among the tombs; teaches them to scorn the safe shelter, the happy home which God has provided, and to wander 'in desolate places like dead men' (Is 59:10): to feel their way about the miserable paths of this world, where all at best is dead and helpless, and can do them no real good. [...] So those who listen to Satan become proud, envious, anxious, and murmuring; neither God nor man can please them; they punish and torment themselves far more than any one else. [...]

And [Satan] is ever at hand, waiting to do us this mischief. He is like roaring lion that walketh about the fold to catch up and devour the stray sheep. Where we least think, there he lies in wait, 'like a lion greedy of its prey, or a lion's whelp lurking in secret places!' (Ps 17:12). So he is 'waiting in our way on every side, turning his eyes down to the ground' (Ps 17:11). The holy Psalms are full of such warnings concerning the Wicked one, and of prayers to God to deliver us from him: and one reason why the Church uses us to learn and say the Psalms so diligently is, because they greatly help us to watch and pray against him.

Let us then do so, my brethren. Night and day, let us keep our souls awake and our hearts lifted up to God. [...] If you strive in earnest to keep yourself inwardly and outwardly pure, you may say to him in the Name of Jesus, 'Get thee hence', and he shall depart, where he can have no more of his own way;

nor shall he ever be able to do you harm, so long as you continue with our Lord, clothed with his righteousness, and practicing his right and pure mind, either sitting at his Feet, or letting his light, by your good works, shine before men: as we read of the possessed person in this Gospel, that he was found with Jesus, 'sitting and clothed in his right mind', and that, when he did leave him, it was at his command, to tell his friends how great things Christ our God had done unto him.

Fifth Sunday after Epiphany

A reading from the sermons of Edward Bouverie Pusey

[A]ll prayer to God implies that we act as we pray. God wills to knit in one his own work and ours. He wills so to unite his creatures with himself, that he would bring about his own work through them. He could, if it seemed to him good, convert all to himself by his one word, as he converted Saul in his journey to Damascus. It might seem, that so would his glory be the more seen, if any one who notoriously hated and opposed the Gospel were, by his converting grace, suddenly and openly won to the faith, and 'preached the faith which they once destroyed' (Gal 1:23). It would avail as a display of his power; but it would not effect the purpose of his love. Every where, in our own souls, towards our neighbours, towards the Church or the whole race of his redeemed, he wills to blend in one our poor love with his boundless ocean of love; our weak efforts with his own Almightiness; our petty abilities with the depths of his Wisdom; our little mercifulness with his own Endless loving-kindness; our poor human words with the Fire of his Spirit, which he came on earth to kindle.

Nay more! God so willeth to admit us into a part of his own divine work, that *now* he scarce willeth to accomplish any thing, save through us. He willeth mostly so to hide his own glory, that he doth not accomplish himself one part, the great outstanding works of his grace and love, leaving to us, as it were, the gleanings of his Vintage; but he doth well-nigh everything *for* man *through* man.

E. B. Pusey, 'Sermon XXII. God advances his Kingdom through Man', in *Parochial and Cathedral Sermons, by the Rev. E. B. Pusey* (London: Walter Smith, 1883), pp. 321-324.

In the depths of his Wisdom and his Counsel, all things work his will. Even those who opposed his Will, accomplish, against their own will, his Will which they oppose. For in him we 'live and move and have our being' (Acts 17:28). *His* is the Only Power and Wisdom and Knowledge and Love; and only from his Wisdom and Power and Love can any created being have any love or power or wisdom lodged in them.[…]

Nay, what was the Incarnation of the Son of God himself, but his Will to accomplish our redemption itself 'through that Man whom he had ordained' (Acts 17:31), remedying man's disobedience through the obedience of man? Our dear Lord's sacred Manhood obeyed, suffered, bore for us the deserts of our sins, died: the Godhead, wherewith that manhood was united, gave to that Obedience, Suffering, Death for us, a value Infinite. After that pattern, he still worked invisibly, what visibly was wrought through man. Apostles spake; but the Spirit of their Father spake in them; they wrought miracles; but it was 'in the name if Jesus' (Acts 8:16); they taught in words given them by God; but God opened to receive their words the hearts which closed themselves not against them. God did every thing, and he willed that man should do every thing: but God did it, as he who alone hath in himself Power and Might and Wisdom and Goodness; men, as living instruments of his Will, willing freely, through the Grace of God, the Will of God.

Sixth Sunday after Epiphany

A reading from the sermons of Blessed John Henry Newman

The earth is full of the marvels of divine power' 'Day to day uttereth speech, and night to night showeth knowledge' (Ps 19 [18]: 2). The tokens of omnipotence are all around us, in the world of matter, and in the world of man: in the dispensation of nature, and in the dispensation of grace. To do impossibilities, I may say, is the prerogative of him, who made all things out of nothing, who foresees all events before they occur, and controls all wills without compelling them. In emblem of this his glorious attribute, he came to his disciples, …walking upon the sea (cf Mt 14:24-27), - the emblem or

---

Bl. John Henry Newman, 'Christ upon the Waters', in *Sermons preached on various Occasions, by John Henry Newman, D. D., of the Oratory* (London: Burns and Lambert, 1858, 2nd edition), pp. 62-165.

hieroglyphic among the ancients of the impossible; to show them that what is impossible with man, is possible with God. He who could walk the waters, could also ride triumphantly upon what is still more fickle, unstable, tumultuous, treacherous – the billows of human wills, human purposes, human hearts. The bark of Peter was struggling with the waves, and made no progress; Christ came to him walking upon them; he entered the boat, and by entering it he sustained it. He did not abandon himself to it, but he gathered it round himself; he did not merely take refuge in it, but he made himself the strength of it, and the pledge and cause of a successful passage. 'Presently', another gospel says, 'the ship was at the land, whither they were going' (Jn 6: 21).

Such was the power of the Son of God, the Saviour of man, manifested by visible tokens in the material world, when he came down upon earth; and such, too, it has ever since signally shown itself to be, in the history of that mystical ark which he then formed to float upon the ocean of human opinion. He told his chosen servants to form an ark for the salvation of souls: he gave them directions how to construct it, - the length, breadth, and height, its cabins and its windows; and the world, as it gazed upon it, forthwith began to criticise. It pronounced it framed quite contrary to the scientific rules of ship-building; it prophesied, as it still prophesies, that such a craft was not sea-worthy; that it was not water-tight; that it would not float; that it would go to pieces and founder. And why it does not, who can say, except that the Lord is in it? Who can say why so old a framework, put together eighteen hundred years ago, should have lasted, against all human calculation, even to this day; always going, and never gone; ever failing, yet ever managing to explore new seas and foreign coasts – except that he, who once said to the rowers, 'It is I, be not afraid' (Mk 6: 50), and to the waters, 'Peace' (Mk 4: 39), is still in his own ark, which he has made, to direct and to prosper her course?

Septuagesima

A reading from the sermons of John Keble

'Without faith it is impossible to please him: for he that cometh to God must believe that he is, and that he is a rewarder of them that diligently seek him.' (Heb 11:6). These two things, that God is, and that he is a rewarder, are the beginning of all religion: and therefore... they stand at the very threshold of the whole Bible: they are taught us in the very first chapter of God's Holy Book. 'In the beginning God created the heaven and the earth': that is, God *is*, one great Almighty Eternal being; before all things, and by whom all things consist. That is the first verse of this wonderful lesson, and the last is like unto it. 'God saw all that he had made, and behold it was very good.' On these two verses, as I said, hang all that we mean when we speak of religion, the whole of man's service done to God, both inward and outward. God is, else we could not serve him: God maketh and loveth what is good, he abhorreth and putteth down what is evil, else it were not worth while to serve him. Again, God is, and therefore the world was and is governed by him: God is good, and therefore the world is so governed as that it will surely be in the end well with the righteous and ill with the wicked.

These, as I said, are the foundation points, the very alphabet, of al, religion: and both of these, so St Paul tells us in the text, require our faith. 'He that cometh to God must believe that he is, and that he is a rewarder of them that diligently seek him'. He must *believe*; he cannot set it with his eyes, but with his mind's eye he must so look at, as if he could see it in very deed; he must not at all permit himself to doubt it. This is what Scripture means by faith: for as St Paul had said just before, 'faith is the substance', the realizing, as it is sometimes called, 'of things hoped for, the evidence of things not seen', i.e. venturing all upon them, as if you could see them. We do not use to say, we believe things which are in sight; no one in his senses would say, I believe it is now day and not night: we *see*, we *know*, we are *sure* of, such things as that, but 'what a man actually seeth, why doth he yet believe and hope for?' Now of course we cannot see God: no man may see his Face and live; no man hath seen him as he is at any time: there were indeed those who saw him in the form of the Man Christ Jesus, when he went in and out among us in the days of his flesh: but they did

---

John Keble, 'Sermon VIII. Faith the Foundation of all Religion', in *Sermons for Septuagesima to Ash Wednesday with Sermons for Confirmation and the Litany, by the Rev. John Keble* (Oxford and London: Parker, 1879), pp. 75-77.

not see him *as* God: and of them, as of all the rest, it might be said, God made himself known to them not by sight but by faith.

We must believe, then, for we cannot see, that God is: and we must also believe, for we cannot see, that he is always on the side of the good, the dutiful, the obedient, a rewarder of those that diligently seek him. Certainly it does not always appear so: certainly there are and always have been occasions wherein even the most contented and faithful spirits have been sorely tempted to cry out with the prophet Jeremiah, 'Wherefore doth the way of the wicked prosper? Wherefore are all they happy that deal very treacherously?', or with the Psalmist, 'I cleaned by heart in vain, and washed my hands in innocency'. But faith helps us to endure all this, as it has all along helped the holy martyrs and saints of God: teaching us to look not to the things which are seen, and which are merely for a time, but to the things unseen, which are for ever. Faith assures us of a day when he will come and judge the world in righteousness: he to whom the promise is made, 'I will put all things under his feet': then and not till then shall we see with our eyes that 'he is a rewarder of them that diligently seek him', but in the mean time 'we see not yet all things put under him'. God's perfect righteousness, as the just Governor of all - this, as well as his Being, is out of sight, and will be so as long as this imperfect world endures. He that cometh to God must *believe*, for he cannot *see*, that God is: he must *believe*, for he cannot see, that he is one who never fails to reward his dutiful servants.

Sexagesima

A reading from the sermons of Edward Bouverie Pusey

There are many ways to death; one only, a narrow way, to life. There are many false, deceiving, meteor hopes; one only, sure and steadfast; many, which end on this earth, one only 'which entereth into that within the veil', even the Heaven of heavens, binding the soul, amid all the tossings of this troublesome world, to the Throne of God. One only hope reaches already, yea and places us already there 'whither the Forerunner is' (not, as it were, for himself, so Scripture speaks, but) 'for us, entered'. That where he is gone, there we might

---

Edward Bouverie Pusey, 'Sermon II. Hope' in *Parochial Sermons by the Rev. E. B. Pusey* (Oxford and London: Parker, 1853), pp. 23-25, 26-27

enter in, might tread the way which he has trod before, follow after, where he is the Forerunner and holdeth wide open the Everlasting Doors, which lifted up their heads to receive him, a High Priest for ever after the order of Melchizedek, ever living to intercede for us.

This Hope is not a Gift only of God to cheer us on. It is also a virtue, one of the chief virtues, whose end is not man but God himself. If we be Christians indeed, we not only may, we *ought* to have this virtue of hope. Our Christian character is wanting without it. It does not merely make the difference of serving God with gladness of heart or with heaviness, as slaves or as sons; we do not merely with it part with a great stay in trouble, a great spur to noble devoted exertion; we lose a grace, and thereby our other graces and our whole tone of mind are impaired. [...]

Hope, as a Christian grace, it has been said, is 'a certain expectation of future blessedness, coming from the grace of God, amid well-doing', or 'a desire of heavenly good with a trustfulness of attaining it'. But then, as well as its sister graces, faith and charity, with which it is intwined by an indissoluble bond, it is capable of increase, degrees; so that the first trembling hope of the returning prodigal may be as different from the assured hope of Paul the aged, when he had 'fought the good fight', had 'finished his course', and 'the crown of Righteousness, laid up for' him, stood just before him, as may be their mansions in heaven, or the glory of one star above another. [...]

In a healthy state of the soul, then, faith, hope, and love will be born, live, thrive together. When the first good tidings of salvation come to one out of Christ, there must be hope for himself that he *may* so be saved, and love for him who died to save him, and faith in him, that he, as St Paul says, 'loved me and gave himself for me'. And so to one, again dead in trespasses and sins, the hope that, on repentance, he *can* be saved, shoots like an electric shock through the benumbed heart, and faith and love revive together, and the dried-up soul gushes forth anew in tears of penitential love, and cries to Jesus, '*my* Redeemer and *my* God'. [...]

And thus, in their continual flight by which they bear the soul heavenwards, these three divine Graces, are seen, as it were, at times this one, at times that, before the other; yet where one advances, the others follow; for, even if not seen, they hardly can but be together. All having their being from the same source, the love of God towards us; all are fixed on him; all return to him. They are a threefold way of grasping or 'apprehending' (as Scripture speaketh,) him by whom we have been apprehended; three modes of holding his who is Infinite, of containing him who containeth all things.

Quinquagesima

A reading from the sermons of John Keble

Lent is at hand, and the trumpet will soon sound again, the great and holy trumpet, of which it is written, 'Blow ye the trumpet in Zion, and sound an alarm in my holy mountain' (Joel 2:1). The sound of it will be heard next Wednesday, by all who have ears to hear. The true and dutiful children of the Church, the loyal soldiers of Christ Jesus will next Wednesday hear the call o their Leader's trumpet, rousing them up, as on all Ash-Wednesdays, to set about his work, to fight his battle, in earnest. It will be the old note, but you will not therefore scorn it, if you are true men and brave soldiers. You know it would never do for a soldier, when the trumpet or bugle sounds in the morning, to say, 'It is only the old call over again, what I have been used to so very often; I am not going to disturb myself for that', and so to stay quietly in his quarters. No more will it do for you, Christian warriors, to make light of your Lord's summons, now that he is calling upon you at the opening of another Lent; another holy season of penitent self-denial and prayers. He calls you morning by morning, and morning by morning, you must answer his call. And what is the note, the keen and ringing note, by which he would call you, and scatter your deadly sleep? The awakening note, the clear word of warning, is, as you know, 'Turn unto the Lord': that is, 'Prepare'. Prepare to meet thy God, O Israel'; so he cries aloud to the whole Church, and to every separate member of it: 'Prepare, get ready to meet him', as you soon must, face to face. Ready or not, you must and will meet him, he must and will come upon you. [...]

Christ our Lord asks a question of you, my brethren. He asks it of every one of you. Christ asks you a question: had you not better think how to answer it? He

---

John Keble, 'Sermon XXI. Preparation for Holy Communion, Preparation for Death and for Judgment', in *Sermons for Septuagesima to Ash-Wednesday, with Sermons for Confirmation and on the Litany, by the Rev. John Keble* (Oxford and London: Parker, 1879), pp. 209-210, 215-216.

says, 'I am coming, I am at hand, I shall presently be here: are you ready for me? How is he coming? And how are we to prepare to meet him? [...]

Yes, dear brethren, you know it in your hearts, however some of you may be accustomed to make light of the thought: nevertheless you know in your hearts, that you have indeed but one thing to do in the world, and that is, to prepare to meet your God first in death, and afterwards in judgment. If you ask, How am I to do this? Give me some short rule, which I may carry away with me, and remember and practice, for I am not learned, I must have something simple and plain. If you ask me this, I will give you such a rule as you ask: but, my brethren, will you practice it? You will, if you desire to deal honestly and justly and truly with your loving Saviour who bought you with his own Blood. But the rule is the same, whether you will mind it or not, for it is in God's own message, and when once it is delivered, upon you must be the burden of rejecting it, if you choose to do so. Well, the rule which will prepare you to meet your God in death and judgment is simply this: you must prepare to meet him, and really and regularly meet him, in his own great Sacrament; you must become a worthy communicant. If your own death is to find you ready for him, you must live in remembrance of his Death; and his Sacrament, you know, is his appointed Remembrance. And if judgment is to find you ready, you must judge yourself in time in self-examination before the Sacrament.

Consider a moment, and you will see that it stands to reason that the Holy Communion should be *the* true way of preparing to meet him. For it is in fact using yourself to meet him. He has promised to be there, as often as we 'do this in remembrance of' him. For he is 'that Bread of life' (Jn 6:48). He is there, that eating him, we may live by him. He is 'the true Vine' (Jn 15:1). He is there, that we may all of us drink of his Blood, his Blood of the New Testament, shed for us and for many for the remission of sins.

Short Reading for Prayer during the Day
between Epiphany and Lent

(see Prayer during the Day)

Collects

Week after Epiphany
Week 1 per annum

O LORD, we beseech thee mercifully to receive the prayers of thy people which call upon thee: and grant that they may both perceive and know what things they ought to do, and also may have grace and power faithfully to fulfil the same; through Jesus Christ thy Son our Lord, who liveth and reigneth with thee in the unity of the Holy Spirit, one God, for ever and ever.

Second Sunday after Epiphany
Sunday 2 per annum

ALMIGHTY and everlasting God, who dost govern all things in heaven and earth: mercifully hear the supplications of thy people, and grant us thy peace all the days of our life; through Jesus Christ thy Son our Lord, who liveth and reigneth with thee in the unity of the Holy Spirit, one God, for ever and ever.

• Third Sunday after Epiphany
Sunday 3 per annum

ALMIGHTY and everlasting God: mercifully look upon our infirmities, and in all our dangers and necessities stretch forth thy right hand to help and defend us; through Jesus Christ thy Son our Lord, who liveth and reigneth with thee in the unity of the Holy Spirit, one God, for ever and ever.

• From the third Sunday before Lent substitute *Septuagesima* (see below)

• Fourth Sunday after Epiphany

O GOD, who knowest us to be set in the midst of so many and great dangers, that by reason of the frailty of our nature we cannot always stand upright: grant to us such strength and protection as may support us in all dangers and carry us through all temptations; through Jesus Christ thy Son our Lord, who liveth and reigneth with thee in the unity of the Holy Spirit, one God, for ever and ever.

• Fifth Sunday after Epiphany

Sunday 5 per annum

O LORD, we beseech thee to keep thy Church and household continually in thy true religion: that they who do lean only upon the hope of thy heavenly grace may evermore be defended by thy mighty power; through Jesus Christ thy Son our Lord, who liveth and reigneth with thee in the unity of the Holy Spirit, one God, for ever and ever.

• Sixth Sunday after Epiphany

O GOD, whose blessed Son was manifested that he might destroy the works of the devil, and make us the sons of God, and heirs of eternal life: grant us, we beseech thee, that, having this hope, we may purify ourselves, even as he is pure; that, when he shall appear again with power and great glory, we may be made like unto him in is eternal and glorious kingdom; where with thee, O Father, and thee, O Holy Spirit, he liveth and reigneth, ever one God, world without end.

Septuagesima (Third Sunday before Lent)

O LORD, we beseech thee favourably to hear the prayers of thy people: that we, who are justly punished for our offences, may be mercifully delivered by thy goodness, for the glory of thy name; through Jesus Christ our Saviour who liveth and reigneth with thee, in the unity of the Holy Spirit, one God, for ever and ever.

Sexagesima (Second Sunday before Lent)

O LORD God, who seest that we put not our trust in any thing that we do: mercifully grant that by thy power we may be defended against all adversity; through Jesus Christ thy Son our Lord, who liveth and reigneth with thee in the unity of the Holy Spirit, one God, for ever and ever.

Quinquagesima (Sunday next before Lent)

O LORD, who hast taught us that all our doings without charity are nothing worth: send thy Holy Spirit and pour into our hearts that most excellent gift of charity, the very bond of peace and of all virtues without which whosoever liveth is counted dead before thee; grant this for thine only Son Jesus Christ's sake, who liveth and reigneth with thee, in the unity of the Holy Spirit, one God, for ever and ever.

IV. Times and Seasons

Part III Temporale:

Lent and Passiontide

Ash Wednesday

Office

Opening Sentences

To the Lord our God belong mercies and forgivenesses, though we have rebelled against him: neither have we obeyed the voice of the Lord our God, to walk in his laws which he set before us.

Dan 9:9, 10

Enter not into judgment with thy servant, O Lord; for in thy sight shall no man living be justified.

Ps 143:2

When the wicked man turneth away from his wickedness that he hath committed, and doeth that which is lawful and right, he shall save his soul alive.

Ezek 18:27

I acknowledge my transgressions, and my sin is ever before me.

Ps 51:3

Hide thy face from my sins, and blot out all mine iniquities.

Ps 51:9

O Lord, correct me, but with judgment; not in thine anger, lest thou bring me to nothing.

Jer 10:24; Ps 6:1

Rend your heart, and not your garments, and turn unto the Lord your God: for he is gracious and merciful, slow to anger, and of great kindness, and repenteth him of the evil.

Joel 2:13

Seven Penitential Psalms

The Seven Penitential Psalms may be used for the Divine Office on Ash Wednesday – Pss 6, 32, 38 and 51 at Morning Prayer and Pss 102, 130 and 143 at Evening Prayer. All seven may be used at the beginning of the Ash Wednesday ceremonies.

Antiphon
Remember not, Lord, our offences,
  nor the offences of our forefathers:
neither take thou vengeance of our sins.

[Morning Prayer]

Psalm 6

Domine, ne in furore

1   O LORD, rebuke me not in thine indignation :
    neither chasten me in thy displeasure.
2   Have mercy upon me, O Lord, for I am weak :
    O Lord, heal me, for my bones are vexed.
3   My soul also is sore troubled :
    but, Lord, how long wilt thou punish me?
4   Turn thee, O Lord, and deliver my soul :
    O save me for thy mercy's sake.
5   For in death no man remembereth thee :
    and who will give thee thanks in the pit?
6   I am weary of my groaning; every night wash I my bed :
    and water my couch with my tears.
7   My beauty is gone for very trouble :
    and worn away because of all mine enemies.
8   Away from me, all ye that work vanity :
    for the Lord hath heard the voice of my weeping.
9   The Lord hath heard my petition :
    the Lord will receive my prayer.
10 All mine enemies shall be confounded, and sore vexed :
    they shall be turned back, and put to shame suddenly.

Psalm 32

Beati, quorum

1 BLESSED is he whose unrighteousness is forgiven :
and whose sin is covered.

2 Blessed is the man unto whom the Lord imputeth no sin :
and in whose spirit there is no guile.

3 For while I held my tongue :
my bones consumed away through my daily complaining.

4 For thy hand is heavy upon me day and night :
and my moisture is like the drought in summer.

5 I will acknowledge my sin unto thee :
and mine unrighteousness have I not hid.

6 I said, I will confess my sins unto the Lord :
and so thou forgavest the wickedness of my sin.

7 For this shall every one that is godly make his prayer unto
thee,
in a time when thou mayest be found :
but in the great water-floods they shall not come nigh him.

8 Thou art a place to hide me in,
thou shalt preserve me from trouble :
thou shalt compass me about with songs of deliverance.

9 I will inform thee, and teach thee in the way wherein thou
shalt go :
and I will guide thee with mine eye.

10 Be ye not like to horse and mule, which have no
understanding :
whose mouths must be held with bit and bridle,
lest they fall upon thee.

11 Great plagues remain for the ungodly :
but whoso putteth his trust in the Lord,
mercy embraceth him on every side.

12 Be glad, O ye righteous, and rejoice in the Lord :
and be joyful, all ye that are true of heart.

Psalm 38

Domine, ne in furore

1 PUT me not to rebuke, O Lord, in thine anger :
  neither chasten me in thy heavy displeasure.

2 For thine arrows stick fast in me :
  and thy hand presseth me sore.

3 There is no health in my flesh, because of thy displeasure :
  neither is there any rest in my bones, by reason of my sin.

4 For my wickednesses are gone over my head :
  and are like a sore burden, too heavy for me to bear.

5 My wounds stink, and are corrupt :
  through my foolishness.

6 I am brought into so great trouble and misery :
  that I go mourning all the day long.

7 For my loins are filled with a sore disease :
  and there is no whole part in my body.

8 I am feeble, and sore smitten :
  I have roared for the very disquietness of my heart.

9 Lord, thou knowest all my desire :
  and my groaning is not hid from thee.

10 My heart panteth, my strength hath failed me :
   and the sight of mine eyes is gone from me.

11 My lovers and my neighbours did stand looking upon my
   trouble :
   and my kinsmen stood afar off.

12 They also that sought after my life laid snares for me :
   and they that went about to do me evil talked of wickedness,
   and imagined deceit all the day long.

13 As for me, I was like a deaf man, and heard not :
   and as one that is dumb, who doth not open his mouth.

14 I became even as a man that heareth not :
   and in whose mouth are no reproofs.

15 For in thee, O Lord, have I put my trust :
   thou shalt answer for me, O Lord my God.

16 I have required that they, even mine enemies, should not
   triumph over me :
   for when my foot slipped, they rejoiced greatly against me.

17	And I, truly, am set in the plague :
	and my heaviness is ever in my sight.
18	For I will confess my wickedness :
	and be sorry for my sin.
19	But mine enemies live, and are mighty :
	and they that hate me wrongfully are many in number.
20	They also that reward evil for good are against me :
	because I follow the thing that good is.
21	Forsake me not, O Lord my God :
	be not thou far from me.
22	Haste thee to help me :
	O Lord God of my salvation.

Psalm 51

Miserere mei, Deus

1 HAVE mercy upon me, O God, after thy great goodness :
according to the multitude of thy mercies do away mine
offences.

2 Wash me throughly from my wickedness :
and cleanse me from my sin.

3 For I acknowledge my faults :
and my sin is ever before me.

4 Against thee only have I sinned, and done this evil in thy
sight :
that thou mightest be justified in thy saying,
and clear when thou art judged.

5 Behold, I was shapen in wickedness :
and in sin hath my mother conceived me.

6 But lo, thou requirest truth in the inward parts :
and shalt make me to understand wisdom secretly.

7 Thou shalt purge me with hyssop, and I shall be clean :
thou shalt wash me, and I shall be whiter than snow.

8 Thou shalt make me hear of joy and gladness :
that the bones which thou hast broken may rejoice.

9 Turn thy face from my sins :
and put out all my misdeeds.

10 Make me a clean heart, O God :
and renew a right spirit within me.

11   Cast me not away from thy presence :
           and take not thy holy Spirit from me.

12   O give me the comfort of thy help again :
           and stablish me with thy free Spirit.

13   Then shall I teach thy ways unto the wicked :
           and sinners shall be converted unto thee.

14   Deliver me from blood-guiltiness, O God,
           thou that art the God of my health :
           and my tongue shall sing of thy righteousness.

15   Thou shalt open my lips, O Lord :
           and my mouth shall shew thy praise.

16   For thou desirest no sacrifice, else would I give it thee :
           but thou delightest not in burnt-offerings.

17   The sacrifice of God is a troubled spirit :
           a broken and contrite heart, O God, shalt thou not despise.

18   O be favourable and gracious unto Sion :
           build thou the walls of Jerusalem.

19   Then shalt thou be pleased with the sacrifice of
           righteousness,
           with the burnt-offerings and oblations :
           then shall they offer young bullocks upon thine altar.

---

*At the end of Morning Prayer psalmody on Ash Wednesday there
follows*

Glory be to the Father, and to the Son :
and to the Holy Spirit;
as it was in the beginning, is now, and ever shall be :
world without end. Amen.

**Remember not, Lord, our offences,
nor the offences of our forefathers:
neither take thou vengeance of our sins.**

[Evening Prayer]

If the psalmody begins here, this antiphon is used

Antiphon

Remember not, Lord, our offences, nor the offences of our
  forefathers:
neither take thou vengeance of our sins.

Psalm 102

Domine, exaudi

1   HEAR my prayer, O Lord :
     and let my crying come unto thee.

2   Hide not thy face from me in the time of my trouble :
     incline thine ear unto me when I call; O hear me,
     and that right soon.

3   For my days are consumed away like smoke :
     and my bones are burnt up as it were a firebrand.

4   My heart is smitten down, and withered liked grass :
     so that I forget to eat my bread.

5   For the voice of my groaning :
     my bones will scarce cleave to my flesh.

6   I am become like a pelican in the wilderness :
     and like an owl that is in the desert.

7   I have watched, and am even as it were a sparrow :
     that sitteth alone upon the house-top.

8   Mine enemies revile me all the day long :
     and they that are mad upon me
       are sworn together against me.

9   For I have eaten ashes as it were bread :
     and mingled my drink with weeping;

10   And that because of thine indignation and wrath :
     for thou hast taken me up, and cast me down.

11   My days are gone like a shadow :
     and I am withered like grass.

264

12	But thou, O Lord, shalt endure for ever : and thy remembrance throughout all generations.
13	Thou shalt arise, and have mercy upon Sion : for it is time that thou have mercy upon her, yea, the time is come.
14	And why? thy servants think upon her stones : and it pitieth them to see her in the dust.
15	The heathen shall fear thy name, O Lord : and all the kings of the earth thy majesty;
16	When the Lord shall build up Sion : and when his glory shall appear;
17	When he turneth him unto the prayer of the poor destitute : and despiseth not their desire.
18	This shall be written for those that come after : and the people which shall be born shall praise the Lord.
19	For he hath looked down from his sanctuary : out of the heaven did the Lord behold the earth;
20	That he might hear the mournings of such as are in captivity : and deliver the children appointed unto death;
21	That they may declare the name of the Lord in Sion : and his worship at Jerusalem;
22	When the people are gathered together : and the kingdoms also, to serve the Lord.
23	He brought down my strength in my journey : and shortened my days.
24	But I said, O my God, take me not away in the midst of mine age : as for thy years, they endure throughout all generations.
25	Thou, Lord, in the beginning hast laid the foundation of the earth : and the heavens are the work of thy hands.
26	They shall perish, but thou shalt endure : they all shall wax old as doth a garment;
27	And as a vesture shalt thou change them, and they shall be changed : but thou art the same, and thy years shall not fail.
28	The children of thy servants shall continue : and their seed shall stand fast in thy sight.

Psalm 130

De profundis

1   OUT OF the deep have I called unto thee, O Lord :
Lord, hear my voice.

2   O let thine ears consider well :
the voice of my complaint.

3   If thou, Lord, wilt be extreme to mark what is done amiss :
O Lord, who may abide it?

4   For there is mercy with thee :
therefore shalt thou be feared.

5   I look for the Lord; my soul doth wait for him :
in his word is my trust.

6   My soul fleeth unto the Lord :
before the morning watch, I say, before the morning watch.

7   O Israel, trust in the Lord, for with the Lord there is mercy :
and with him is plenteous redemption.

8   And he shall redeem Israel :
from all his sins.

Psalm 143

Domine, exaudi

1   HEAR my prayer, O Lord, and consider my desire :
hearken unto me for thy truth and righteousness' sake.

2   And enter not into judgment with thy servant :
for in thy sight shall no man living be justified.

3   For the enemy hath persecuted my soul;
  he hath smitten my life down to the ground :
he hath laid me in the darkness,
  as the men that have been long dead.

4   Therefore is my spirit vexed within me :
and my heart within me is desolate.

5   Yet do I remember the time past;
  I muse upon all thy works :
yea, I exercise myself in the works of thy hands.

6   I stretch forth my hands unto thee :
my soul gaspeth unto thee as a thirsty land.

7	Hear me, O Lord, and that soon, for my spirit waxeth faint : hide not thy face from me, lest I be like unto them that go down into the pit.
8	O let me hear thy loving-kindness betimes in the morning, for in thee is my trust : shew thou me the way that I should walk in, for I lift up my soul unto thee.
9	Deliver me, O Lord, from mine enemies : for I flee unto thee to hide me.
10	Teach me to do the thing that pleaseth thee, for thou art my God : let thy loving Spirit lead me forth into the land of righteousness.
11	Quicken me, O Lord, for thy name's sake : and for thy righteousness' sake bring my soul out of trouble.
12	And of thy goodness slay mine enemies : and destroy all them that vex my soul ; for I am thy servant.

Glory be to the Father, and to the Son :
and to the Holy Spirit;
as it was in the beginning, is now, and ever shall be :
world without end. Amen.

**Remember not, Lord, our offences, nor the offences of
our forefathers:
neither take thou vengeance of our sins.**

Deducant oculi mei lacrimam

1   LET my eyes run down with tears night and day :
    and let them not cease,

2   For the virgin daughter of my people is smitten with a great
        wound :
    with a very grievous blow.

3   If I go out into the field :
    behold, those slain by the sword!

4   And if I enter the city :
    behold, the diseases of famine!

5   For both prophet and priest ply their trade through the land :
    and have no knowledge.

6   Have you utterly rejected Judah? :
    Does your soul loathe Zion?

7   Why have you smitten us :
    so that there is no healing for us?

8   We looked for peace, but no good came :
    for a time of healing, but behold, terror.

9   We acknowledge our wickedness, O Lord,
        and the iniquity of our fathers :
    for we have sinned against you.

10 Do not spurn us, for your name's sake;
        do not dishonour your glorious throne :
    remember and do not break your covenant with us.

Jer 14:17-21

Post-Biblical Reading

A reading from the treatise of the Venerable Bede, *On the Temple*

The people liberated from Egypt as a figure of the present Church were subjected to many hardships for forty years in the desert, but at the same time were also regaled with heavenly bread, and in this way finally reached the land promised them of old. They were subjected to trials for forty years in order to draw attention to the hardships with which the Church contends throughout the whole world in observing the law of God; they were fed in manna from heaven for those forty years to demonstrate that the very sufferings which the Church endures in the hope of the heavenly denarius – that is, of eternal happiness – are to be alleviated when those who now 'hunger and thirst for righteousness will have their fill' (Mt 5:6) and as the same Church sings to its redeemer, 'But as for me, I will appear before your sight in righteousness; I shall be satisfied when your glory shall appear' (Ps 17 [16]:15). In the same way, then, the people of God is both subjected to adversities and regaled with manna to confirm the saying of the Apostle, 'Rejoicing in hope, patient in tribulation' (Rom 12:12).

In this figure too Our Lord fasted forty days before his bodily death and feasted forty more with his disciples after his bodily resurrection 'appearing to them by many proofs and speaking of the kingdom of God, and eating together with them' (Acts 1:3-4). For by fasting he showed in himself our toil, and by eating and drinking with his disciples he showed his consolation in our midst. While he was fasting he was crying out, as it were, 'Take heed lest perhaps your hearts be weighed down with dissipation and drunkenness and the cares of this life' (Lk 21:34), whereas while he was eating and drinking he was crying out, as it were, 'Behold I am with you all days even to the consummation of the world' (Mt 28:20); and: 'But I will see you again, and your heart shall rejoice, and your joy no one shall take from you' (Jn 16:22).

For as soon as we set our feet upon the way of the Lord we both fast from the vanity of the present world and are cheered with the promise of the world to

St Bede, *On the Temple* I. 10, in Bede, *On the Temple*. Translated with notes by Seán Connolly with an introduction by Jennifer O'Reilly (Liverpool: Liverpool University Press, 1995), pp. 39-40.

come, not setting our heart on the life here below but feeding our heart on the life up there.

Short Reading for Prayer during the Day   *Jer 3:12-14a*
Return, says the Lord. I will not look on you in anger, for I am merciful, says the Lord; I will not be angry for ever. Only acknowledge your guilt, that you rebelled against the Lord your God and that you have not obeyed my voice, says the Lord. Return, O faithless children, says the Lord; for I am your master.

Lent Prayer during the Day

Teach us, good Lord, to serve thee as thou deservest;
to give and not to count the cost;
to fight and not to heed the wounds;
to toil and not to seek for rest;
to labour and not to seek for any reward,
save that of knowing that we do thy will.

St Ignatius of Loyola (1556)

Collect

ALMIGHTY and everlasting God, who hatest nothing that thou hast made, and dost forgive the sins of all them that are penitent: create and make in us new and contrite hearts, that we worthily lamenting our sins, and acknowledging our wretchedness, may obtain of thee, the God of all mercy, perfect remission and forgiveness; through Jesus Christ thy Son our Lord, who liveth and reigneth with thee in the unity of the Holy Spirit, one God, for ever and ever.

Lent

From the day after Ash Wednesday until the Saturday after the Fourth Sunday in Lent

Office

Opening Sentences

I will arise and go to my father, and will say unto him, Father, I have sinned against heaven, and before thee, and am no more worthy to be called thy son.

Lk 15:18, 19

To the Lord our God belong mercies and forgivenesses, though we have rebelled against him: neither have we obeyed the voice of the Lord our God, to walk in his laws which he set before us.

Dan 9:9, 10

Enter not into judgment with thy servant, O Lord; for in thy sight shall no man living be justified.

Ps 143:2

When the wicked man turneth away from his wickedness that he hath committed, and doeth that which is lawful and right, he shall save his soul alive.

Ezek 18:27

O Lord, correct me, but with judgment; not in thine anger, lest thou bring me to nothing.

Jer 10:24; Ps 6:1

Repent ye; for the kingdom of heaven is at hand.

Mt 3:2

Rend your heart, and not your garments, and turn unto the Lord your God: for he is gracious and merciful, slow to anger, and of great kindness, and repenteth him of the evil.

Joel 2:13

Hymns

Sunday Evening Prayer *Vespers*

Audi benigne Conditor

1.O Kind Creator, bow thine ear
   to mark the cry, to know the tear
before thy throne of mercy spent
   in this thy holy fast of Lent.

2.Our hearts are open, Lord, to thee:
   thou knowest our infirmity;
pour out on all who seek thy face
   abundance of thy pardoning grace.

3.Our sins are many, this we know;
   spare us, good Lord, thy mercy show;
and for the honour of thy name
   our fainting souls to life reclaim.

4.Give us the self-control that springs
   from discipline of outward things,
that fasting inward secretly
   the soul may purely dwell with thee.

5.We pray thee, Holy Trinity,
   One God, unchanging Unity,
that we from this our abstinence
   may reap the fruits of penitence.

Asc. to St Gregory the Great, 6th cent. Tr. T. A. Lacey

272

Ex more docti mystico

1.The fast, as taught by holy lore,
  we keep in solemn course once more;
the fast to all men known, and bound
  in forty days of yearly round.

2.The law and seers that were of old
  in divers ways this Lent foretold
which Christ, all seasons' King and Guide,
  in after ages sanctified.

3.More sparing therefore let us make
  the words we speak, the food we take,
our sleep and mirth, and closer barred
  be every sense in holy guard.

4.In prayer together let us fall,
  and cry for mercy, one and all,
and weep before the Judge's feet,
  and his avenging wrath entreat.

5.Thy grace have we offended sore,
  by sins, O God, which we deplore;
but pour upon us from on high,
  O pardoning One, thy clemency.

6.Remember thou, though frail we be,
  that yet thine handiwork are we;
nor let the honour of thy Name
  be by another put to shame.

7.Forgive the sin that we have wrought;
  increase the good that we have sought;
that we at length, our wanderings o'er,
  may please thee here and evermore.

8.We pray thee, holy Trinity,
  One God, unchanging Unity,
that we from this our abstinence
  may reap the fruits of penitence. Amen.

c.6ᵗʰ cent. Tr. J. M. Neale

Iesu quadragenariæ

1.O Jesu Christ, from thee began
  this healing for the soul for man,
by fasting sought, by fasting found
  through forty days of yearly round;

2.That he who fell from high delight,
  borne down to sensual appetite,
by dint of stern control may rise
  to climb the hills of Paradise.

3.Therefore behold thy Church, O Lord,
  and grace of penitence accord
to all who seek with generous tears
  renewal of their wasted years.

4.Forgive the sin that we have done,
  forgive the course that we have run,
and show henceforth in evil day
  thyself our succour and our stay.

5.But now let every heart prepare,
  by sacrifice of fast and prayer,
to keep with joy magnifical
  the solemn Easter festival.

6.Father and Son and Spirit blest,
  to thee be every prayer addrest,
who art in threefold Name adored,
  from age to age, the only Lord. Amen.

c.9th cent. Tr. T. A. Lacey

A reading from the sermons of Blessed John Henry Newman

After this manner, then, must be understood his suffering, temptation, and obedience, not as if he ceased to be what he had ever been, but, having clothed himself with a created essence, he made it the instrument of his humiliation; he acted in it, he obeyed and suffered through it. Do we not see among men, circumstances of a peculiar kind throw one of our own race out of himself, so that he, the same man, acts as if his usual self were not in being, and he had fresh feelings and faculties, for the occasion, higher or lower than before? Far be it from our thoughts to parallel the incarnation of the Eternal Word with such an accidental chance! But I mention it, not to explain a Mystery…, but to facilitate your conception of him who is the subject of it, to help you towards contemplating him as God and man at once, as still the Son of God though he had assumed a nature short of his original perfection.

That Eternal Power, which, till then, had thought and acted as God, began to think and act as a man, with all man's faculties, affections, and imperfections, sin excepted. Before he came on earth he was infinitely above joy and grief, fear and anger, pain and heaviness; but afterwards all these properties and many more were his as fully as they are ours. Before he came on earth he was infinitely above joy and grief, fear and anger, pain and heaviness; but afterwards all these properties and many more were his as fully as they are ours. Before he came on earth, he had but the perfections of God, but afterwards he had also the virtues of a creature, such as faith, meekness, self-denial. Before he came on earth he could not be tempted of evil; but afterwards he had a man's heart, a man's tears, and a man's wants and infirmities. His Divine Nature indeed pervaded his manhood, so that every deed and word of his in the flesh savoured of eternity and infinity; but, on the other hand, from the time he was born of the Virgin Mary, he had a natural fear of danger, a natural shrinking from pain, though ever subject to the ruling influence of that Holy and Eternal essence which was in him. For instance, we read on one occasion of his praying that the cup might pass from him; and, at another, when Peter showed surprise at the prospect of his crucifixion, he rebuked him sharply, as if for tempting him to murmur and disobey.

Bl John Henry Newman, 'The Humiliation of the Eternal Son', in J. H. Newman, *Parochial and Plain Sermons* III (London: Rivingtons, 1881), pp. 165-167, 169-170.

Thus he possessed at once a double assemblage of attributes, divine and human. Still he was all-powerful, though in the form of a servant; still he was all-knowing, though seemingly ignorant; still incapable of temptation, though exposed to it; and if any one stumble at this, as not a mere mystery, but in the very form of language a contradiction of terms, I would have him reflect on those peculiarities of human nature itself, which I just now hinted at. Let him consider the condition of his own mind, and see how like a contradiction it is. Let him reflect upon the faculty of memory, and try to determine whether he docs or docs not know a thing which he cannot recollect, or rather, whether it may not be said of him, that one self-same person, that in one sense he knows it, in another he does not know it. This may serve to appease his imagination, if it startles at the mystery. […]

In truth, until we contemplate our Lord and Saviour, God and man, as a really existing being, external to our minds, as complete and entire in his personality as we allow ourselves to be to each other, as one and the same in all his various and contrary attributes, 'the same yesterday, to-day, and for ever', we are using words which profit not. Till then we do not realize that Object of faith, which is not a mere name on which titles and properties may be affixed without congruity and meaning, but has a personal existence and an identity distinct from everything else. In what true sense do we 'know' him, if our idea of him be not such as to take up and incorporate into itself the manifold attributes and offices which we ascribe to him? What do we gain from words, however correct and abundant, if they end with themselves, instead of lighting up the image of the Incarnate Son in our hearts?

Second Sunday in Lent

A reading from the sermons of Blessed John Henry Newman

I suppose it is scarcely necessary to prove to those who have allowed their minds to dwell on the Gospels, that the peculiar character of Our Lord's goodness, as displayed therein, is its tenderness and its considerateness. These

---

Source: Bl. John Henry Newman, 'A Particular Providence as revealed in the Gospel', in *Parochial and Plain Sermons, by J. H. Newman,* III (London: Rivingtons, 1881), pp. 119-120, 124-125.

qualities are the very perfection of kindness between man and man; but from the extent and complication of the world's system, and from its Maker's being invisible, our imagination scarcely succeeds in attributing them to him, even when our reason is convinced, and we wish to believe accordingly. His Providence manifests itself in general laws, it moves forward along the lines of truth and justice; it has no respect of persons, rewarding the good and punishing the bad, not as individuals but according to their character. How shall he who is Most Holy direct his love to this man or that for the sake of each, contemplating us one by one, without infringing on his own perfections? Or even were the Supreme Being a God of unmixed benevolence, how, even then, shall the thought of him come home to our minds with that constraining power which the kindness of a human friend exerts over us? [...]

Now at first sight, it is difficult to see how our idea of Almighty God can be divested of these earthly notions, either that his goodness is imperfect, or that it is fated and necessary; and wonderful indeed is the condescension by which he has met our infirmity. He has met and aided it in that same Dispensation by which he redeemed our souls. In order that we may understand that in spite of his mysterious perfections he has a separate knowledge and regard for individuals, he has taken upon him the thoughts and feelings of our own nature, which we all understand *is* capable of such personal attachments. By becoming man, he has cut short the perplexities and the discussions of our reason on the subject, as if he would grant our objections for argument's sake, and supersede them by taking our own ground.

The most winning property of our Saviour's mercy (if it is right so to speak of it), is its dependence on time and place, person and circumstance; in other words, its tender discrimination. It regards and consults for each individual as he comes before it. It is called forth by some as it is not by others, it cannot (if I may say so) manifest itself to every object alike; it has its peculiar shade and mode of feeling for each; and on some men it so bestows itself, as if he depended for his own happiness on their well-being. [...]

God beholds thee individually, whoever thou art. He 'calls thee by thy name' (Is 43:1). He sees thee, and understands thee, as he made thee. He knows what is in thee, all thy own peculiar feelings and thoughts, thy dispositions and likings, thy strength and thy weakness. He views thee in thy day of rejoicing, and thy day of sorrow. He sympathizes in thy hopes and thy temptations. He interests himself in all thy anxieties and remembrances, all the risings and fallings of thy spirit. He has numbered the very hairs of thy head and the cubits

277

of thy stature. He compasses thee round and bears thee in his arms; he takes thee up and sets thee down. [....]

Thou art not only his creature (though for the very sparrows he has a care, and pitied the 'much cattle' ([Jon 4:11] of Nineveh), thou art man redeemed and sanctified, his adopted son, favoured with a portion of that glory and blessedness which flows form him everlastingly unto the Only-begotten.

Third Sunday in Lent

A reading from Richard Rolle, *The Amending of Life*

That a man be rightly directed to the worship of God and to his own profit and that of his neighbour, four things are to be told:

Firstly, what it is that defiles a man. And that is three sins or kinds of sin – namely, of thought, of mouth, and of work. A man sins in thought when he thinks anything against God, if he occupy not his heart with the love and praise of God, but suffers it to be distracted with divers thoughts and allows it to wander about the world. He sins in mouth when he lies, when he forswears, when he curses, when he backbites, when he defends a wrong, when he brings forth fond, foul, vain or idle speech. He sins in deed in many ways: by lechery, sinfully touching or kissing, wilfully defiling himself, or procuring or sustaining without great cause occasions by which he knows he might be defiled; by robbing, stealing, beguiling, smiting, and so on.

Secondly, what is it that cleanses a man? And there are three things against the three aforesaid sins; that is to say: contrition of thought and the expulsion of desires that belong not to the praise or worship of God; confession of mouth, that ought to be timely, bare and whole; satisfaction of work, which has three parts – namely, fasting because he has sinned against himself, prayer because he has sinned against God, almsdeeds because he has sinned against his neighbour. Yet I say that he should not give alms of other men's goods, but he shall restore, for the sin is not forgiven unless that which is withdrawn is restored.

Richard Rolle, *The Amending of Life*, IV, in G. C. Heseltine, *Selected Works of Richard Rolle, Hermit*. Transcribed, with an introduction, by G. C. Heseltine (London: Longmans, Green, 1930), pp. 118-120.

Thirdly, what keeps cleanness of heart? And there are three things: first, a lively thought of God, that there be no time in which thou dost not think of God except in sleep, which is common to all; second, a careful keeping of thy outward wits, that tasting, smelling, hearing, and seeing be wisely restrained under the bridle of control; third, honest occupation, be it reading or talking of God, or writing, or other useful work. Similarly there are three things that keep cleanness of mouth: considered speech, to beware of much speech, and to hate lying. Also three things keep cleanness of working: moderation in food, avoiding evil company, and being often mindful of death.

Fourthly, what are the things that induce us to conform ourselves to God's will? And there are three: example of creatures, that we have by beholding them; familiarity with God, that is gained by meditation and prayer; and joy of the heavenly kingdom, that is felt in a manner by contemplation.

And so the man of God set to live in this wise shall be as a tree that is set by the running and flowing waters of grace, that shall always be green in virtue and never dry through sin, that shall give fruit in due time, that is good works for example, and good words to the worship of God, and this he shall not sell for vain-glory. He says 'in due time' against them that give example of fasting when it is time for eating, and the reverse way also; and against miserly men that give their fruit when it is rotten, or else do not give until they die.

Fourth Sunday in Lent

A reading from the sermons of Blessed John Henry Newman

St Paul speaks in plain terms of our one Mediator as 'the man Christ Jesus' (1 Tim 2:5), not to speak of our Lord's own words on the subject. Still, we must ever remember, that though he was in nature perfect man, he was not man in exactly the same sense in which any of us is a man. Though man, he was not, strictly speaking, in the English sense of the word, *a* man; he was not such as one of us, and one out of a number. He was man because he had our

---

Bl John Henry Newman, 'The Humiliation of the Eternal Son', in J. H. Newman, *Parochial and Plain Sermons* VI (London: Rivingtons, 1881), pp. 62-64.

human nature wholly and perfectly, but his Person is not human like ours, but divine. He who was from eternity, continued one and the same, but with an addition. His incarnation was a 'taking of the manhood into God'. As he had no earthly father, so has he no human personality. We may not speak of him as we speak of any individual man, acting from and governed by a human intelligence within him, but he was God, acting not only as God, but now through the flesh also, when he would. He was not a man made God, but God made man.

Thus, when he prayed to his Father, it was not the prayer of a man supplicating God, but of the Eternal Son of God who had ever shared the glory of the Father, addressing him, as before, but under far other circumstances, and in a new way, not according to those most intimate and ineffable relations which belonged to him who was in the bosom of the Father, but in the economy of redemption, and in a lower world, namely, through the feelings and thoughts of human nature, When he wept at the grave of Lazarus, or sighed at the Jews' hardness of heart, or looked round about in anger, or had compassion on the multitudes, he manifested the tender mercy, the compassion, the long-suffering, the fearful wrath of Almighty God, yet not in himself, as from eternity, but as if indirectly through the outlets of that manhood with which he had clothed himself.

When 'he spat on the ground, and made clay of the spittle, and he anointed the eyes of the blind man with the clay' (Jn 9:6), he exerted the virtue of his Divine essence through the properties and circumstances of the flesh. When he breathed on his disciples and said, 'Receive ye the Holy Ghost' (Jn 20:22), he vouchsafed to give his Holy Spirit through the breath of his human nature. When virtue went out of him, so that whoso touched him was made whole, here too, in like manner, he shows us that he was not an individual man, like any of us, but God acting through human nature as his assumed instrument.

When he poured out his precious blood upon the Cross, it was not a man's blood, though it belonged to his manhood, but blood full of power and virtue, instinct with life and grace, as issuing most mysteriously from him who was the Creator of the world. And the case is the same in every successive communication of himself to individual Christians. As he became the Atoning Sacrifice by means of his human nature, so is he our High Priest in heaven by means of the same. He is now in heaven, entered into the Holy place, interceding for us, and dispensing blessings to us. He gives us abundantly of his Spirit; but still he gives It not at once from his Divine nature, though from eternity the Holy Ghost proceeds from the Son as well as from the Father, but by means of that incorruptible flesh which he has taken on him.

Sunday   *Rom 6:3-5*

Do you not know that all of us who have been baptized into Christ Jesus were baptized into his death? We were buried therefore with him by baptism into death, so that as Christ was raised from the dead by the glory of the Father, we too might walk in newness of life. For if we have been united with him in a death like his, we shall certainly be united with him in a resurrection like his.

Monday   *Joel 2:12-14*

'Yet even now,' says the Lord, 'return to me with all your heart, with fasting, with weeping, and with mourning; and rend your hearts and not your garments.' Return to the Lord, your God, for he is gracious and merciful, slow to anger, and abounding in steadfast love, and repents of evil. Who knows whether he will not turn and repent, and leave a blessing behind him, a cereal offering and a drink offering for the Lord, your God?

Tuesday   *1 Cor 9:24-27*

Do you not know that in a race all the runners compete, but only one receives the prize? So run that you may obtain it. Every athlete exercises self-control in all things. They do it to receive a perishable wreath, but we an imperishable. Well, I do not run aimlessly, I do not box as one beating the air; but I pommel my body and subdue it, lest after preaching to others I myself should be disqualified.

Wednesday   *Rom 7:21-25a*

So I find it to be a law that when I want to do right, evil lies close at hand. For I delight in the law of God, in my inmost self, but I see in my members another law at war with the law of my mind and making me captive to the law of sin which dwells in my members. Wretched man that I am! Who will deliver me from this body of death? Thanks be to God through Jesus Christ our Lord!

Thursday   *Is 58:6-9a*

Is not this the fast that I choose: to loose the bonds of wickedness, to undo the thongs of the yoke, to let the oppressed go free, and to break every yoke? Is it not to share your bread with the hungry, and bring the homeless poor into your house; when you see the naked, to cover him, and not to hide yourself from your own flesh? Then shall your light break forth like the dawn, and your healing shall spring up speedily; your righteousness shall go before you, the glory of the Lord shall be your rear guard. Then you shall call, and the Lord will answer; you shall cry, and he will say, 'Here I am'. Is not this the fast that I choose: to loose the bonds of injustice, to undo the thongs of the yoke, to let the oppressed go free, and to break every yoke? Is it not to share your bread with the hungry, and bring the homeless poor into your house; when you see the naked, to cover them, and not to hide yourself from your own flesh? Then shall your light break forth like the dawn, and your healing shall spring up speedily; your righteousness shall go before you, the glory of the Lord shall be your rearguard. Then you shall call, and the Lord will answer; you shall cry for help, and he will say, 'Here I am'.

Friday   *Jer 3:12-14a*

Return, says the Lord. I will not look on you in anger, for I am merciful, says the Lord; I will not be angry for ever. Only acknowledge your guilt, that you rebelled against the Lord your God and that you have not obeyed my voice, says the Lord. Return, O faithless children, says the Lord; for I am your master.

Saturday   *Is 44:21-22*

Remember these things, O Jacob, and Israel, for you are my servant; I formed you, you are my servant; O Israel, you will not be forgotten by me. I have swept away your transgressions like a cloud, and your sins like mist; return to me, for I have redeemed you.

Lent Prayer during the Day

Teach us, good Lord, to serve thee as thou deservest;
to give and not to count the cost;
to fight and not to heed the wounds;
to toil and not to seek for rest;
to labour and not to seek for any reward,
save that of knowing that we do thy will.

St Ignatius of Loyola (1556)

Collects

First Sunday in Lent

O LORD, who for our sake didst fast forty days and forty nights: give us grace to use such abstinence, that, our flesh being subdued to the Spirit, we may ever obey thy godly motions in righteousness, and true holiness, to thy honour and glory; who livest and reignest with the Father and the Holy Spirit, one God, for ever and ever.

Second Sunday in Lent

ALMIGHTY God, who seest that we have no power of ourselves to help ourselves: Keep us both outwardly in our bodies and inwardly in our souls; that we may be defended from all adversities which may happen to the body and from all evil thoughts which may assault and hurt the soul; through Jesus Christ thy Son our Lord, who liveth and reigneth with thee in the unity of the Holy Spirit, one God, for ever and ever.

Third Sunday in Lent

WE BESEECH thee, almighty God: look upon the hearty desires of thy humble servants and stretch forth the right hand of thy Majesty, to be our defence against all our enemies; through Jesus Christ thy Son our Lord, who liveth and reigneth with thee in the unity of the Holy Spirit, one God, for ever and ever.

Fourth Sunday in Lent

GRANT, we beseech thee, almighty God: that we, who for our evil deeds do worthily deserve to be punished, by the comfort of thy grace may mercifully be relieved; through our Lord and Saviour Jesus Christ, who liveth and reigneth with thee and the Holy Spirit, one God, for ever and ever.

Lent Prose

Attende Domine
Hear us, O Lord, have mercy upon us:
for we have sinned against thee.

1   To thee, Redeemer, on thy throne of glory:
lift we our weeping eyes in holy pleadings:
listen, O Jesu, to our supplications.
Hear us &c.

2   O thou chief cornerstone, right hand of the Father:
way of salvation, gate of life celestial:
cleanse thou our sinful souls from all defilement.
Hear us &c.

3   God, we implore thee, in thy glory seated:
bow down and hearken to thy weeping children:
pity and pardon all our grievous trespasses.
Hear us &c.

4   Sins oft committed, now we lay before thee:
with true contrition, now no more we veil them:
grant us, Redeemer, loving absolution.
Hear us &c.

5   Innocent captive, taken unresisting:
falsely accused, and for us sinners sentenced,
save us, we pray thee, Jesu, our Redeemer.
Hear us &c.

Passion Sunday
and the first week of Passiontide

Office

Opening Sentence

Is it nothing to you, all ye that pass by? Behold, and see if there be any sorrow like unto my sorrow.

Lam 1:12

Hymns

Evening Prayer

Vespers

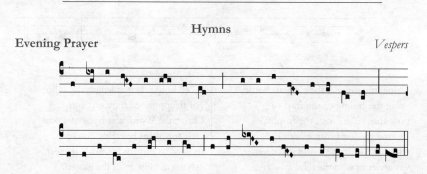

Vexilla regis prodeunt

1.The royal banners forward go,
  the cross shines forth in mystic glow;
where he in flesh, our flesh who made,
  our sentence bore, our ransom paid.

2.Where deep for us the spear was dyed,
  life's torrent rushing from his side,
to wash us in that precious flood,
  where mingled water flowed, and blood.

3.Fulfilled is all that David told
  in true prophetic song of old,
amidst the nations, God, saith he,
  hath reigned and triumphed
    from the tree.

4.O tree of beauty, tree of light!
  O tree with royal purple dight!
elect on whose triumphal breast
  those holy limbs should find their rest.

5.On whose dear arms, so widely flung,
  the weight of this world's ransom hung:
the price of humankind to pay,
  and spoil the spoiler of his prey.

6.O cross, our one reliance, hail!
  Still may thy power with us avail
to give new virtue to the saint,
  and pardon to the penitent.

7.To thee, eternal Three in One,
  let homage meet by all be done:
whom by the cross thou dost restore,
  preserve and govern evermore.

1-5 Venantius Fortunatus, *Tr.* J. M. Neale

Pange, lingua, gloriosi prœlium

1.Sing, my tongue, the glorious battle,
  sing the ending of the fray;
now above the cross, the trophy,
  sound the loud triumphant lay:
tell how Christ the world's Redeemer,
  as a victim won the day.

2.He, our Maker, deeply grieving
  that the first made Adam fell,
when he ate the fruit forbidden
  whose reward was death and hell,
marked e'en then this Tree the ruin
  of the first tree to dispel.

3.Tell how, when at length the fullness,
  of th'appointed time was come,
Christ, the Word, was born of woman,
  left for us his heavenly home;
showed us human life made perfect,
  shone as light amid the gloom.

4.Lo! He lies an Infant weeping,
  where the narrow manger stands,
while the Mother-Maid his members
  wraps in mean and lowly bands,
and the swaddling-cloth is winding
  round his helpless feet and hands.

5.To the Trinity be glory
  everlasting, as is meet:
equal to the Father, equal
  to the Son and Paraclete:
Trinal Unity, whose praises
  all created things repeat. Amen.

Venantius Fortunatus, *Tr.* Percy Dearmer and J. M. Neale

or

En acetum fel arundo

1.Lo, with gall his thirst he quenches!
  see the thorns upon his brow!
Nails his tender flesh are rending!
  see his side is opened now!
Whence, to cleanse the whole creation,
  Streams of blood and water flow.

2.Faithful Cross! above all other,
  one and only noble Tree!
None in foliage, none in blossom,
  None in fruit thy peers may be;
Sweetest wood and sweetest iron!
  Sweetest Weight is hung on thee!

3.Lofty tree, bend down thy branches,
  to embrace thy sacred load;
Oh, relax the native tension
  of that all too rigid wood;
gently, gently bear the members
  of thy dying King and God.

4.Tree, which solely wast found worthy
  the world's Victim to sustain.
Harbour from the raging tempest!
  Ark, that saved the world again!
Tree, with sacred blood anointed
  of the Lamb for sinners slain.

5.Blessing, honour, everlasting,
  to the immortal Deity;
to the Father, Son, and Spirit,
  equal praises ever be;
glory through the earth and heaven
  to Trinity in Unity. Amen.

Venantius Fortunatus, *Tr.* E Caswall

Passion Sunday

A reading from the sermons of Lancelot Andrewes

To consider his sufferings, and to begin with the first: the pains of his body, his wounds and his stripes.

Our very eye will soon tell us that no place was left in his body, where he might be smitten and was not. His skin and flesh rent with the whips and scourges, his hands and feet wounded with the nails, his head with the thorns, his very heart with the spear-point; all his senses, all his parts laden with whatsoever wit or malice could invent. His blessed body given as an anvil to be beaten upon with the violent hands of those barbarous miscreants, till they brought his into this case of 'if ever there were sorrow like my sorrow' (Lam 1:12). For Pilate's *Ecce Homo!*' (Jn 19:5), his shewing him with an *Ecce*, as if he should say, Behold, look if ever you saw the like rueful spectacle; this very shewing of his sheweth plainly, he was then come into woeful plight – so woeful as Pilate verily believed his very sight so pitiful, as it would have moved the hardest heart of them all to have relented and said, This is enough, we desire no more. And this for the wounds of his body, for on this we stand not.

In this peradventure some 'like' may be found, in the pains of the body; but in the second, the sorrow of the soul, I am sure, none. And indeed, the pain of the body is but the body of pain; the very soul of sorrow and pain is the soul's sorrow and pain. Give me any grief, save the grief of the mind, saith the Wise Man; for, saith Solomon, 'The spirit of a man will sustain all his other infirmities, but a wounded spirit, who can bear? (Prov 18:14). And of this, this of his soul, I dare make a case, 'If there be any sorrow…'.

'He began to be troubled in soul' saith St John (Jn 12:27); 'to be in an agony', saith St Luke (Lk 22:44); 'to be in anguish of mind and deep distress', saith St Mark (Mk 14:33). To have his soul round about on every side environed with sorrow, and that sorrow to the death. Here is trouble, anguish, agony, sorrow, and deadly sorrow; but it must be such, as never the like: so it was too.

Lancelot Andrewes, 'A Sermon preached before the King's Majesty, at Whitehall, on the sixth of April, A. D. MDCIV, being Good-Friday', in *Ninety-Six Sermons by the Right Honourable and Reverend Father in God Lancelot Andrewes,* II (Oxford: Parker, 1849), pp. 143-145.

The estimate whereof we may take from the second word of melting, that is, from his sweat in the garden; strange, and the like whereof was never heard or seen.

No manner violence offered him in body, no man touching him or being near him; in a cold night, for they were fain to have a fire within doors, lying abroad in the air and upon the cold earth, to be all of a sweat, and that sweat to be blood; and not as they call it 'a thin faint sweat', but 'of great drops'; and these so many, so plenteous, as they went through his apparel and all; and through all streamed to the ground, and that in great abundance; - read, enquire, and consider, 'if ever there were sweat like this sweat of his'. Never the like sweat certainly, and therefore never the like sorrow. Our translation is: 'done unto me'; but we said the word properly signifieth, and so St Jerome and the Chaldean paraphrase read it, 'melted me'. And truly it should seem by this fearful sweat of his he was near some furnace, the feeling whereof was able to cast him into that sweat, and to turn his sweat into drops of blood. And sure it was so; for see, even in the very next words of all to this verse, he complaineth of it: 'that a fire was sent into his bones' (Lam 1:13) which melted him, and made that bloody sweat to distil from him. That hour, what his feelings were, it is dangerous to define; we know them not, we may be too bold to determine of them. To very good purpose it was, that the ancient Fathers of the Greek Church in their Liturgy, after they have recounted all the particular pains, as they are set down in his Passion, and by all, and by every one of them called for mercy, do after all shut up all with this, 'By thine unknown sorrows and sufferings, felt by thee, but not distinctly known by us, Have mercy upon us, and save us!'

Short Readings for Prayer during the Day
in Passiontide

Sunday *Heb 2:10-12*

It was fitting that he, for whom and by whom all things exist, in bringing many sons to glory, should make the pioneer of their salvation perfect through suffering. For he who sanctifies and those who are sanctified have all one origin. That is why he is not ashamed to call them brethren, saying, 'I will proclaim your name to my brethren, in the midst of the congregation I will praise you.'

Monday *Jer 11:19-20*

I was like a gentle lamb led to the slaughter. I did not know it was against me they devised schemes, saying, 'Let us destroy the tree with its fruit, let us cut him off from the land of the living, that his name be remembered no more.' But, O Lord of hosts, who judge righteously, who test the heart and the mind, let me see your vengeance upon them, for to you have I committed my cause.

Tuesday *Is 53:4-6*

Surely he has borne our griefs and carried our sorrows; yet we esteemed him stricken, smitten by God, and afflicted. But he was wounded for our transgressions, he was bruised for our iniquities; upon him was the chastisement that made us whole, and with his stripes we are healed. All we like sheep have gone astray; we have turned every one to his own way; and the Lord has laid on him the iniquity of us all.

Wednesday *1 Cor 1:18, 22-25*

The word of the cross is folly to those who are perishing, but to us who are being saved it is the power of God. For Jews demand signs and Greeks seek wisdom, but we preach Christ crucified, a stumbling block to Jews and folly to Gentiles, but to those who are called, both Jews and Greeks, Christ the power of God and the wisdom of God. For the foolishness of God is wiser than men, and the weakness of God is stronger than men.

Thursday   *1 Pet 2:24, 25*

Christ himself bore our sins in his body on the tree, that we might die to sin and live to righteousness. By his wounds you have been healed. For you were straying like sheep, but have now returned to the Shepherd and Guardian of your souls.

Friday   *Rom 5:6-8*

While we were yet helpless, at the right time Christ died for the ungodly. Why, one will hardly die for a righteous man - though perhaps for a good man one will dare even to die. But God shows his love for us in that while we were yet sinners Christ died for us.

Saturday   *1 Jn 2:1b-2*

If any one does sin, we have an advocate with the Father, Jesus Christ the righteous; and he is the expiation for our sins, and not for ours only but also for the sins of the whole world.

Passiontide Prayer during the Day

Soul of Christ, sanctify me,
Body of Christ, save me,
Blood of Christ, inebriate me,
Water from the side of Christ, wash me.
Passion of Christ, strengthen me.
O good Jesus, hear me:
within thy wounds, hide me;
let me never be separated from thee;
from the wicked enemy, defend me.
in the hour of my death, call me
and bid me come to thee;
that with thy Saints I may praise thee
for ever and ever.

Anima Christi (14th cent.)

Collects

Fifth Sunday in Lent
WE BESEECH thee, almighty God, mercifully to look upon thy people: that by thy great goodness they may be governed and preserved evermore, both in body and soul; through Jesus Christ thy Son our Lord, who liveth and reigneth with thee in the unity of the Holy Spirit, one God, for ever and ever.

or

MOST merciful God, who by the death and resurrection of thy Son Jesus Christ hast delivered and saved the world: grant that by faith in him who suffered on the cross we may triumph in the power of his victory; through Jesus Christ thy Son our Lord, who liveth and reigneth with thee, in the unity of the Holy Spirit, one God, for ever and ever.

Palm Sunday

Office

Opening Sentence

Is it nothing to you, all ye that pass by? Behold, and see if there be any sorrow like unto my sorrow.

Lam 1:12

Post-Biblical Reading

A reading from John of Ford, *Sermons on the Last Verses of the Song of Songs*

Whatever the Lord Jesus endured or still endures or will one day endure, either in himself or in his body, it is the eve of the great Sabbath, a preparation for eternal peace and freedom and a lesson in how to attain that paschal joy. So the Lord's blessed bride, who has already greeted from far off the peaceful freedom of this great Sabbath, now prepares for herself whatever is needed for that solemn day, coming in advance to anoint the body of Jesus, which she is herself, for burial. And since she is well aware that she cannot rise with Christ unless she has first been buried with him, and that she cannot be buried with him unless she has been crucified with him, unless she has died with him, she chooses 'crucifixion' for her soul and death for her bones.

But now, when she voluntarily takes up the cross and her hands and feet are nailed to it with his, now the cross indeed triumphs in his members, at least for the most part. Now, though sin may tempt her, she consents in neither mind nor act, for she has something in which she greatly glories, and that is the cross of her Lord, Jesus Christ. Of course, while her soul is still within her, she cannot yet glory in it wholly. But when the Spirit of God divides soul from body with his sword, then all that is animal in her through concupiscence will be swallowed up by the spiritual. Only then will she be able to consider herself dead with Christ, only then will she venture to triumph over death and cry with Christ: 'It is consummated' (Jn 19:30).

John of Ford, *Sermons on the Last Verses of the Song of Songs*, 99: 3-4, in John of Ford, *Sermons on the Song of Songs*, VI. Translated by Wendy Mary Beckett (Kalamazoo, MI: Cistercian Publications, 1984), pp. 204-206.

But what is the soul to do who certainly has the wish to lay down her life, but is absolutely without the power to do so? It seems to me that there is only one thing that helps, while we are still on earth, to prepare the soul for the death and burial which she longs for, and that is never to come down from the cross. Whatever the persuasion of evil spirits, whatever the flattery of friends, (and however many of them are) whatever the incitements of the enemy, the soul must not come down from the cross, but must stretch out her arms all day long and say with Paul, 'With Christ I am nailed to the cross' (Gal 2:19). She must say with Andrew: 'Never permit me, Lord, to be taken down from this cross'. She must say with David: 'Pierce my flesh with your fear' (Ps 119:20). Then she must make confession with the crucified thief, a twofold confession; she must frequently confess to the High Priest who hangs with her on the cross both her own sinfulness and the immaculate innocence which is his alone. And if she persists in these two confessions, she will win from the cross of Jesus to her own cross, yes, she will truly win not only forgiveness for her guilt but even the promise of life. Further, Jesus does not put off his promises; not in the distant future, but here and now he gives forgiveness and, after a little while, that is, on the very same day, he gives life.

Short Reading for Prayer during the Day   *Heb 2:10-12*

It was fitting that he, for whom and by whom all things exist, in bringing many sons to glory, should make the pioneer of their salvation perfect through suffering. For he who sanctifies and those who are sanctified have all one origin. That is why he is not ashamed to call them brethren, saying, 'I will proclaim your name to my brethren, in the midst of the congregation I will praise you.'

Collect

ALMIGHTY and everlasting God, who, of thy tender love towards mankind, hast sent thy Son, our Saviour Jesus Christ, to take upon him our flesh, and to suffer death upon the cross, that all mankind should follow the example of his great humility: mercifully grant, that we may both follow the example of his patience, and also be made partakers of his resurrection; through Jesus Christ thy Son our Lord, who liveth and reigneth with thee in the unity of the Holy Spirit, one God, for ever and ever.

Monday to Wednesday
in Holy Week

Office

Opening Sentence
Is it nothing to you, all ye that pass by? Behold, and see if there be any sorrow like unto my sorrow.

Lam 1:12

Short Readings for Prayer during the Day
in Passiontide

Monday in Holy Week   *Jer 11:19-20*
I was like a gentle lamb led to the slaughter. I did not know it was against me they devised schemes, saying, 'Let us destroy the tree with its fruit, let us cut him off from the land of the living, that his name be remembered no more.' But, O Lord of hosts, who judge righteously, who test the heart and the mind, let me see your vengeance upon them, for to you have I committed my cause.

Tuesday in Holy Week   *Is 53:4-6*
Surely he has borne our griefs and carried our sorrows; yet we esteemed him stricken, smitten by God, and afflicted. But he was wounded for our transgressions, he was bruised for our iniquities; upon him was the chastisement that made us whole, and with his stripes we are healed. All we like sheep have gone astray; we have turned every one to his own way; and the Lord has laid on him the iniquity of us all.

Wednesday in Holy Week   *1 Cor 1:18, 22-25*

The word of the cross is folly to those who are perishing, but to us who are being saved it is the power of God. For Jews demand signs and Greeks seek wisdom, but we preach Christ crucified, a stumbling block to Jews and folly to Gentiles, but to those who are called, both Jews and Greeks, Christ the power of God and the wisdom of God. For the foolishness of God is wiser than men, and the weakness of God is stronger than men.

Passiontide Prayer during the Day

Soul of Christ, sanctify me,
Body of Christ, save me,
Blood of Christ, inebriate me,
Water from the side of Christ, wash me.
Passion of Christ, strengthen me.
O good Jesus, hear me:
within thy wounds, hide me;
let me never be separated from thee;
from the wicked enemy, defend me.
in the hour of my death, call me
and bid me come to thee;
that with thy Saints I may praise thee
for ever and ever.

Anima Christi (14th cent.)

Collects

Monday in Holy Week
ALMIGHTY God, whose most dear Son went not up to joy but first he suffered pain, and entered not into glory before he was crucified: mercifully grant that we, walking in the way of the cross, may find it none other than the way of life and peace; through Jesus Christ thy Son our Lord, who liveth and reigneth with thee in the unity of the Holy Spirit, one God, for ever and ever.

Tuesday in Holy Week
O LORD God, whose blessed Son, our Saviour, gave his back to the smiters and hid not his face from shame: grant us grace to take joyfully the suffering of the present time, in full assurance of the glory that shall be revealed; through Jesus Christ thy Son our Lord, who liveth and reigneth with thee in the unity of the Holy Spirit, one God, for ever and ever.

Wednesday in Holy Week
ASSIST us mercifully with thy help, O Lord God of our salvation: that we may enter with joy upon the meditation of those mighty acts, whereby thou hast given us life and immortality; through Jesus Christ thy Son our Lord, who liveth and reigneth with thee in the unity of the Holy Spirit, one God, for ever and ever.

Maundy Thursday

Morning Prayer

Opening Sentence

A new commandment I give to you, that you love one another, as I have loved you.

Jn 13:34

Vigils Pss 69 (*or* 69, 70, 71)
Lauds Pss 80, 81

First Lesson†

Lam 1:1-4

Here begins the Lamentation over Jerusalem by the Prophet Jeremiah

Part I

ALEPH How lonely sits the city that was full of people! How like a widow has she become, she that was great among the nations! She that was a princess among the cities has become a vassal.

BETH She weeps bitterly in the night, tears on her cheeks; among all her lovers she has none to comfort her; all her friends have dealt treacherously with her, they have become her enemies.

GHIMEL Judah has gone into exile because of affliction and hard servitude; she dwells now among the nations, but finds no resting place; her pursuers have all overtaken her in the midst of her distress.

---

† The readings set out in this section for Morning Prayer in the Easter Triduum come from the *Tenebræ* series. The readings otherwise are as found in the Office Lectionary.

DALETH The roads to Zion mourn, for none come to the appointed feasts; all her gates are desolate, her priests groan; her maidens have been dragged away, and she herself suffers bitterly.

HE Her foes have become the head, her enemies prosper, because the Lord has made her suffer for the multitude of her transgressions; her children have gone away, captives before the foe.

Jerusalem, Jerusalem, return to the Lord your God.

Part II

Lam 1:5-9

VAU From the daughter of Zion has departed all her majesty. Her princes have become like deer that find no pasture; they fled without strength before the pursuer.

ZAYIN Jerusalem remembers in the days of her affliction and bitterness all the precious things that were hers from days of old. When her people fell into the hand of the foe, and there was none to help her, the foe gloated over her, mocking at her downfall.

HETH Jerusalem sinned grievously, therefore she became filthy; all who honoured her despise her, for they have seen her nakedness; yes, she herself groans, and turns her face away.

TETH Her uncleanness was in her skirts; she took no thought of her doom; therefore her fall is terrible, she has no comforter. 'O Lord, behold my affliction, for the enemy has triumphed!'

Jerusalem, Jerusalem, return to the Lord your God.

Canticle

Quis est iste qui venit de Edom

1 WHO IS this that comes from Edom :
   from Bozrah in garments stained crimson?
2 Who is this glorious in his apparel :
   marching in the greatness of his strength?
3 It is I, announcing vindication :
   It is I, says the Lord, mighty to save.
4 Why are your robes red :
   and your garments like those who tread the wine press?
5 I have trodden the wine press alone :
   and from the peoples no one was with me.
6 I looked, but there was no one to help :
   I stared, but there was no one to sustain me,
      so my own arm brought me victory.
7 I will recount the merciful love of the Lord,
   the praises of the Most High.
8 According to all that the Lord has granted us :
   and the great favour to the house of Israel;
9 That he has shewn them according to his mercy :
   according to the abundance of his steadfast love.
10 For he said, Surely they are my people,
   sons who will not deal falsely :
   and he became their Saviour in all their distress.
11 It was no messenger or angel :
   but his presence that saved them.
12 In his love and in his pity he redeemed them :
   he lifted them up and carried them all the days of old.

Is 63:1-3a, 5, 7-9

Second Lesson

1 Cor 11:17-34

A reading from the First Letter of Saint Paul to the Corinthians.

In the following instructions I do not commend you, because when you come together it is not for the better but for the worse. For, in the first place, when you assemble as a church, I hear that there are

303

divisions among you; and I partly believe it, for there must be factions among you in order that those who are genuine among you may be recognized. When you meet together, it is not the Lord's supper that you eat. For in eating, each one goes ahead with his own meal, and one is hungry and another is drunk. What! Do you not have houses to eat and drink in? Or do you despise the church of God and humiliate those who have nothing? What shall I say to you? Shall I commend you in this? No, I will not.

For I received from the Lord what I also delivered to you, that the Lord Jesus on the night when he was betrayed took bread, and when he had given thanks, he broke it, and said, 'This is my body which is for you. Do this in remembrance of me.' In the same way also the chalice, after supper, saying, 'This chalice is the new covenant in my blood. Do this, as often as you drink it, in remembrance of me.' For as often as you eat this bread and drink the chalice, you proclaim the Lord's death until he comes.

Whoever, therefore, eats the bread or drinks the cup of the Lord in an unworthy manner will be guilty of profaning the body and blood of the Lord. Let a man examine himself, and so eat of the bread and drink of the cup. For any one who eats and drinks without discerning the body eats and drinks judgment upon himself. That is why many of you are weak and ill, and some have died. But if we judged ourselves truly, we should not be judged. But when we are judged by the Lord, we are chastened so that we may not be condemned along with the world.

So then, my brethren, when you come together to eat, wait for one another -- if any one is hungry, let him eat at home -- lest you come together to be condemned. About the other things I will give directions when I come

Prayer during the Day

Short Reading *Heb 7:26-27*
It was fitting that we should have such a high priest, holy, blameless, unstained, separated from sinners, exalted above the heavens. Jesus has no need, like those high priests, to offer sacrifices daily, first for his own sins and then for those of the people; he did this once for all when he offered up himself.

Collect

ALMIGHTY and everlasting God, who, of thy tender love towards mankind, hast sent thy Son, our Saviour Jesus Christ, to take upon him our flesh, and to suffer death upon the cross, that all mankind should follow the example of his great humility: mercifully grant, that we may both follow the example of his patience, and also be made partakers of his resurrection; through Jesus Christ thy Son our Lord, who liveth and reigneth with thee in the unity of the Holy Spirit, one God, for ever and ever.

Evening Prayer is not said by those who participate in the evening Mass.

Morning Prayer

Opening Sentence

God showed his love for us, in that, while we were still sinners Christ
died for us.

Rom 5:8

Vigils Pss 2, 22, 38 (*or* 2, 22, 27)
Lauds Pss 51, 147:12-20

First Lesson

A reading from the Lamentation over Jerusalem by the Prophet
Jeremiah

Part I

Lam 2:8-11

HETH The Lord determined to lay in ruins the wall of the daughter
of Zion; he marked it off by the line; he restrained not his hand from
destroying; he caused rampart and wall to lament, they languish
together.

TETH Her gates have sunk into the ground; he has ruined and
broken her bars; her king and princes are among the nations; the law
is no more, and her prophets obtain no vision from the Lord.

YODH The elders of the daughter of Zion sit on the ground in
silence; they have cast dust on their heads and put on sackcloth; the
maidens of Jerusalem have bowed their heads to the ground.

CAPH My eyes are spent with weeping; my soul is in tumult; my heart
is poured out in grief because of the destruction of the daughter of my
people, because infants and babes faint in the streets of the city.

Jerusalem, Jerusalem, return to the Lord your God.

LAMEDH They cry to their mothers, 'Where is bread and wine?' as they faint like wounded men in the streets of the city, as their life is poured out on their mothers' bosom.

MEM What can I say for you, to what compare you, O daughter of Jerusalem? What can I liken to you, that I may comfort you, O virgin daughter of Zion? For vast as the sea is your ruin; who can restore you?

NUN Your prophets have seen for you false and deceptive visions; they have not exposed your iniquity to restore your fortunes, but have seen for you oracles false and misleading.

SAMECH All who pass along the way clap their hands at you; they hiss and wag their heads at the daughter of Jerusalem; 'Is this the city which was called the perfection of beauty, the joy of all the earth?'

Jerusalem, Jerusalem, return to the Lord your God.

Part III

ALEPH I am the man who has seen affliction under the rod of his wrath; he has driven and brought me into darkness without any light; surely against me he turns his hand again and again the whole day long.

BETH He has made my flesh and my skin waste away, and broken my bones; he has besieged and enveloped me with bitterness and tribulation; he has made me dwell in darkness like the dead of long ago.

GHIMEL He has walled me about so that I cannot escape; he has put heavy chains on me; though I call and cry for help, he shuts out my prayer; he has blocked my ways with hewn stones, he has made my paths crooked.

Jerusalem, Jerusalem, return to the Lord your God.

Canticle

Domine, audivi auditionem tuam

1   LORD, I have heard of your renown :
and I stand in awe, O Lord, of your work.

2   In the midst of the years renew it;
    in the midst of the years make it known :
in wrath remember mercy.

3   God came from Teman,
    and the Holy One from Mount Paran :
his glory covered the heavens,
    and the earth was full of his praise.

4   His brightness was like the sun :
rays flashed from his hand; there he veiled his power.

5   You came forth to save your people :
to save your anointed.

6   You trampled the sea with your horses :
churning the mighty waters.

7   I hear, and my belly trembles :
my lips quiver at the sound;

8   Rottenness enters into my bones :
and my steps totter beneath me.

9   I will quietly wait for the day of trouble :
to come upon the people that invade us.

10   Though the fig tree does not blossom,
    nor fruit appear on the vines :
the produce of the olive fail, and the fields yield no food,

11   Though the flock be cut off from the fold :
and there be no herd in the stalls,

12   Yet will I rejoice in the Lord :
I will exult in the God of my salvation.

13   God, the Lord, is my strength :
he makes my feet like hinds' feet,
    and makes me tread upon the high places.

Hab 3:2-4, 13a, 15-19

Second Lesson

Heb 4:9 – 5:10

A reading from the Letter to the Hebrews.

So then, there remains a sabbath rest for the people of God; for whoever enters God's rest also ceases from his labours as God did from his.

Let us therefore strive to enter that rest, that no one fall by the same sort of disobedience. For the word of God is living and active, sharper than any two-edged sword, piercing to the division of soul and spirit, of joints and marrow, and discerning the thoughts and intentions of the heart. And before him no creature is hidden, but all are open and laid bare to the eyes of him with whom we have to do.

Since then we have a great high priest who has passed through the heavens, Jesus, the Son of God, let us hold fast our confession. For we have not a high priest who is unable to sympathize with our weaknesses, but one who in every respect has been tempted as we are, yet without sin.

Let us then with confidence draw near to the throne of grace, that we may receive mercy and find grace to help in time of need.

For every high priest chosen from among men is appointed to act on behalf of men in relation to God, to offer gifts and sacrifices for sins. He can deal gently with the ignorant and wayward, since he himself is beset with weakness. Because of this he is bound to offer sacrifice for his own sins as well as for those of the people. And one does not take the honour upon himself, but he is called by God, just as Aaron was.

So also Christ did not exalt himself to be made a high priest, but was appointed by him who said to him, 'You are my Son, today I have begotten you'; as he says also in another place, 'You are a priest for ever, after the order of Melchiz'edek.'

In the days of his flesh, Jesus offered up prayers and supplications, with loud cries and tears, to him who was able to save him from death, and he was heard for his godly fear. Although he was a Son, he learned obedience through what he suffered; and being made perfect he became the source of eternal salvation to all who obey him, being designated by God a high priest after the order of Melchiz'edek.

Prayer during the Day

Short Reading

Is 53:2-7

For he grew up before him like a young plant, and like a root out of dry ground; he had no form or comeliness that we should look at him, and no beauty that we should desire him. He was despised and rejected by men; a man of sorrows, and acquainted with grief; and as one from whom men hide their faces he was despised, and we esteemed him not. Surely he has borne our griefs and carried our sorrows; yet we esteemed him stricken, smitten by God, and afflicted. But he was wounded for our transgressions, he was bruised for our iniquities; upon him was the chastisement that made us whole, and with his stripes we are healed. All we like sheep have gone astray; we have turned every one to his own way; and the Lord has laid on him the iniquity of us all. He was oppressed, and he was afflicted, yet he opened not his mouth; like a lamb that is led to the slaughter, and like a sheep that before its shearers is dumb, so he opened not his mouth.

Collect

ALMIGHTY God, we beseech thee graciously to behold this thy family: for whom our Lord Jesus Christ was contented to be betrayed, and given up into the hands of wicked men, and to suffer death upon the cross; who now liveth and reigneth with thee and the Holy Spirit, ever one God, world without end.

The Solemn Liturgy of the Passion is celebrated according to the Roman Rite.

Evening Prayer is not said by those who participate in the afternoon Liturgy.

Morning Prayer

Opening Sentence

Rest in the Lord and wait patiently for him; and he will give you your heart's desire.

Ps 37:7, 4

Vigils Pss 4, 16, 24, 95 (*or* 4, 15, 16)
Lauds Pss 64, 150

First Lesson

A reading from the Lamentation over Jerusalem by the Prophet Jeremiah

Part I

Lam 3:22-31

HETH The steadfast love of the Lord never ceases, his mercies never come to an end; they are new every morning; great is your faithfulness. 'The Lord is my portion,' says my soul, 'therefore I will hope in him.'

TETH The Lord is good to those who wait for him, to the soul that seeks him. It is good that one should wait quietly for the salvation of the Lord. It is good for a man that he bear the yoke in his youth.

YODH Let him sit alone in silence when he has laid it on him; let him put his mouth in the dust -- there may yet be hope; let him give his cheek to the smiter, and be filled with insults. For the Lord will not cast off for ever.

Jerusalem, Jerusalem, return to the Lord your God.

Lam 4:1-6

ALEPH How the gold has grown dim, how the pure gold is changed! The holy stones lie scattered at the head of every street.

BETH The precious sons of Zion, worth their weight in fine gold, how they are reckoned as earthen pots, the work of a potter's hands!

GHIMEL Even the jackals give the breast and suckle their young, but the daughter of my people has become cruel, like the ostriches in the wilderness.
DALETH The tongue of the nursling cleaves to the roof of its mouth for thirst; the children beg for food, but no one gives to them.

HE Those who feasted on dainties perish in the streets; those who were brought up in purple lie on ash heaps.

VAU For the chastisement of the daughter of my people has been greater than the punishment of Sodom, which was overthrown in a moment, no hand being laid on it.

Jerusalem, Jerusalem, return to the Lord your God.

Lam 5:1-11

Remember, O Lord, what has befallen us; behold, and see our disgrace!

Our inheritance has been turned over to strangers, our homes to aliens.

We have become orphans, fatherless; our mothers are like widows.
We must pay for the water we drink, the wood we get must be bought.

With a yoke on our necks we are hard driven; we are weary, we are given no rest.

We have given the hand to Egypt, and to Assyria, to get bread enough.

Our fathers sinned, and are no more; and we bear their iniquities.

Slaves rule over us; there is none to deliver us from their hand.

We get our bread at the peril of our lives, because of the sword in the wilderness.

Our skin is hot as an oven with the burning heat of famine.

Women are ravished in Zion, virgins in the towns of Judah.

Jerusalem, Jerusalem, return to the Lord your God.

Canticle

Ego dixi: in dimidio dierum meorum

1   I SAID, In the noontide of my days I must depart;
     I am consigned to the gates of Sheol :
      for the rest of my years.

2   I said, I shall not see the Lord :
     in the land of the living;

3   I shall look upon man no more :
     among the inhabitants of the world.

4   My dwelling is plucked up and removed from me :
     like a shepherd's tent;

5   Like a weaver I have rolled up my life :
     he cuts me off from the loom;

6   From day to night you bring me to an end :
     I cry for help until morning;

7   Like a lion he breaks all my bones :
     from day to night you bring me to an end.

8   Like a swallow or a crane I clamour :
     I moan like a dove.

9   My eyes are weary with looking upward :
     O Lord, I am oppressed; be my security!

10   Behold, it was for my welfare :
     that I had great bitterness;

11	But you have held back my life :
	from the pit of destruction,
12	For you have cast all my sins :
	behind your back.
13	For Sheol cannot thank you :
	death cannot praise you;
14	Those who go down to the pit :
	cannot hope for your faithfulness.
15	The living, the living, he thanks you, as I do this day :
	the father makes known to the children your faithfulness.
16	The Lord will save me, and we will sing to stringed
	instruments :
	all the days of our life, at the house of the Lord.

Is 38:10-1, 17-20

Second Lesson

Heb 9:11-22

A reading from the Letter to the Hebrews.

When Christ appeared as a high priest of the good things that have come, then through the greater and more perfect tent (not made with hands, that is, not of this creation) he entered once for all into the Holy Place, taking not the blood of goats and calves but his own blood, thus securing an eternal redemption. For if the sprinkling of defiled persons with the blood of goats and bulls and with the ashes of a heifer sanctifies for the purification of the flesh, how much more shall the blood of Christ, who through the eternal Spirit offered himself without blemish to God, purify your conscience from dead works to serve the living God.

Therefore he is the mediator of a new covenant, so that those who are called may receive the promised eternal inheritance, since a death has occurred which redeems them from the transgressions under the first covenant. For where a will is involved, the death of the one who made it must be established. For a will takes effect only at death, since it is not in force as long as the one who made it is alive. Hence even the first covenant was not ratified without blood. For when every commandment of the law had been declared by Moses to all the people, he took the blood of calves and goats, with water and scarlet wool and hyssop, and sprinkled both the book itself and all the people, saying, 'This is the blood of the covenant which God commanded you.' And in the same way he sprinkled with the blood both the tent and all the vessels used in worship. Indeed, under the law almost everything is purified with blood, and without the shedding of blood there is no forgiveness of sins

---

Prayer during the Day

Short Reading   *1 Jn 1:8-9; 2:1b-2; 8b-10*

If we say we have no sin, we deceive ourselves, and the truth is not in us. If we confess our sins, he is faithful and just, and will forgive our sins and cleanse us from all unrighteousness.

If any one does sin, we have an advocate with the Father, Jesus Christ the righteous; and he is the expiation for our sins, and not for ours only but also for the sins of the whole world.

The darkness is passing away and the true light is already shining. He who says he is in the light and hates his brother is in the darkness still. He who loves his brother abides in the light, and in it there is no cause for stumbling.

Collect

GRANT, O Lord, that as we are baptized into the death of thy blessed Son our Saviour Jesus Christ, so by continual mortifying our corrupt affections we may be buried with him: and that through the grave and gate of death, we may pass to our joyful resurrection; for his merits, who died, and was buried, and rose again for us, thy Son Jesus Christ our Lord, who now liveth and reigneth with thee and the Holy Spirit, ever one God, world without end.

IV. Times and Seasons

Part IV Temporale:

Easter until Trinity,
Solemnities after Easter

Office

Opening Sentence

Blessed be the God and Father of our Lord Jesus Christ, who according to his great mercy hath begotten us again unto a living hope by the resurrection of Jesus Christ from the dead.

1 Pet 1:3

Hymns

Evening Prayer   *Vespers*

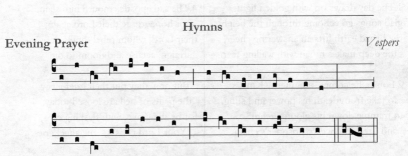

Ad cenam Agni providi

1. The Lamb's high banquet we await
   in snow-white robes of royal state;
   and now, the Red Sea's channel passed,
   to Christ, our Prince, we sing at last.

2. Upon the altar of the Cross
   his Body hath redeemed our loss;
   and tasting of his roseate Blood,
   our life is hid with him in God.

3. That paschal eve God's arm was bared;
   the devastating angel spared:
   by strength of hand our hosts went free
   from Pharoah's ruthless tyranny.

4. Now Christ our Passover is slain,
   the Lamb of God that knows no stain;
   the true oblation offered here,
   our own unleavened Bread sincere.

5. O thou from whom hell's monarch flies,
   O great, O very Sacrifice,
   thy captive people are set free,
   and endless life restored in thee.

6. For Christ, arising from the dead,
   from conquered hell victorious sped;
   he thrusts the tyrant down to chains,
   and paradise for man regains.

7. Maker of all, to thee we pray,
   fulfill in us thy joy today;
   when death assails, grant, Lord, that we
   may share thy paschal victory.

8. To thee who, dead, again dost live,
   all glory, Lord, thy people give;
   all glory, as is every meet,
   to Father and to Paraclete. Amen.

7th cent. Tr. J. M. Neale

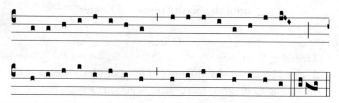

Aurora lucis rutilat

1.The day draws on with golden light,
  glad songs go echoing through the height,
the broad earth lifts an answering cheer,
  the deep makes moan with wailing fear.

2.For lo, he comes, the mighty King,
  to take from death his power and sting,
to trample down his gloomy reign
  and break the weary prisoner's chain.

3.Enclosed he lay in rocky cell,
  with guard of armèd sentinel;
but thence returning, strong and free,
  he comes with pomp of jubilee.

4.The sad apostles mourn him slain,
  nor hope to see their Lord again;
their Lord, whom rebel thralls defy,
  arraign, accuse and doom to die.

5.But now they put their grief away,
  the pains of hell are loosed today;
for by the grave, with flashing eyes,
  "Your Lord is ris'n," the angel cries.

6.Maker of all, to thee we pray,
  fulfill in us thy joy today;
when death assaults, grant, Lord, that we
  may share thy paschal mystery.

7.To thee, who, dead, again dost live,
  all glory, Lord, thy people give;
  all glory, as is ever meet,
  to Father and to Paraclete. Amen.

4th or 5th cent. Tr. T. A. Lacey

A reading from the sermons of Blessed John Henry Newman

Such then is our risen Saviour in himself and towards us: - conceived by the Holy Ghost; holy from the womb; dying, but abhorring corruption; rising again the third day by his own inherent life; exalted as the Son of God and Son of man, to raise us after him; and filling us incomprehensibly with his immortal nature, till we become like him; filling us with a spiritual life which may expel the poison of the tree of knowledge, and restore us to God. How wonderful a work of grace! Strange it was that Adam should be our death, but stranger still and very gracious, that God himself should be our life, by means of that human tabernacle which he has taken on himself.

O blessed day of the Resurrection, which of old time was called the Queen of Festivals, and raised among Christians an anxious, nay contentious diligence duly to honour it! Blessed day, once only passed in sorrow, when the Lord actually rose, and the disciples believed not; but ever since a day of joy to the faith and love of the Church! In ancient times, Christians all over the world began it with a morning salutation. Each man said to his neighbour, 'Christ is risen'; and his neighbour answered him, 'Christ is risen indeed, and hath appeared unto Simon'. Even to Simon, the coward disciple who denied him thrice, Christ is risen; even to us who long ago vowed to obey him, and yet so often denied him before men, so often taken part with sin, and followed the world, when Christ called us another way.

'Christ is risen indeed, and hath appeared to Simon!': to Simon Peter the favoured Apostle, on whom the Church is built, Christ appeared. He has appeared to his Holy Church first of all, and in the Church he dispenses blessings, such as the world knows not of. Blessed are they if they knew their blessedness, who are allowed, as we are, week after week, and Festival after Festival, to seek and find in that Holy Church the Saviour of their souls! Blessed are they beyond language or thought, to whom it is vouchsafed to receive those tokens of his love, which cannot otherwise be gained by man, the pledges and means of his special presence, in the Sacrament of his Supper; who are allowed to eat and drink the food of immortality, and receive life from the bleeding side of the Son of God!

Bl. John Henry Newman, 'Christ, a Quickening Spirit', in J. H. Newman, *Parochial and Plain Sermons* II (London: Rivingtons, 1880), pp. 147-149.

Alas! By what strange coldness of heat, or perverse superstition is it, that any one called Christian keeps away from that heavenly ordinance? Is it not very grievous that there should be any one who fears to share in the greatest conceivable blessing which could come upon sinful men? What in truth is that fear, but unbelief, a slavish sin-loving obstinacy, if it leads a man to go year after year without the spiritual sustenance which God has provided for him? Is it wonderful that, as time goes on, he should learn deliberately to doubt of the grace therein given? That he should no longer look upon the Lord's Supper as a heavenly feast, or the Lord's Minister who consecrates it as a chosen vessel, or that Holy Church in which he ministers as a Divine Ordinance, to be cherished as the parting legacy of Christ to a sinful world? Is it wonderful that seeing he sees not, and hearing he hears not; and that, lightly regarding all the gifts of Christ, he feels no reverence for the treasure-house wherein they are stored?

But we, who trust that so far we are doing God's will, inasmuch as we are keeping to those ordinances and rules which his Son has left us, we may humbly rejoice in this day, with a joy the world cannot take away, any more than it can understand.

Monday in Easter Week

A reading from John Pearson, *Exposition of the Creed*

That Christ did thus rise from the dead, is a most necessary article of Christian faith, which all are obliged to believe and profess: to the meditation whereof the apostle hath given us a particular injunction: 'Remember that Jesus of the seed of David was raised from the dead' (2 Tim 2:8). First, because without it our faith is vain, and by virtue of it strong. By this we are assured that he which died was the Lord of life; and though he were 'crucified through weakness, yet he liveth by the power of God' (2 Cor 13:4). By this resurrection from the dead, he 'was declared to be the Son of God' (Rom 1:4); and upon the morning of

---

John Pearson, *Exposition of the Creed*, V, 267-268, in *An Exposition of the Creed, by John Pearson*. Revised and corrected by the Rev. Temple Chevallier (Cambridge, Cambridge University Press, 1859, 2nd edition), pp. 500-502.

the third day did those words of the Father manifest a most important truth, 'Thou art my Son, this day have I begotten thee; (Acts 13:33). In his death he assured us of his humanity, by his resurrection he demonstrated his Divinity.

Secondly, by his resurrection we are assured of the justification of our persons; and 'if we believe in him that raised up Jesus our Lord from the dead', it will be 'imputed to us for righteousness', for he 'was delivered for our offences, and was raised again for our justification' (Rom 4:24-26). By his death we know that he suffered for sin, by his resurrection we are assured, that the sins for which he suffered were not his own. Had no man been a sinner he had not died; had he been a sinner, he had not risen again; but dying for those sins which we committed, he rose from the dead to shew that he had made full satisfaction for them, that we believing in him might obtain remission of our sins, and justification of our persons.[...]

Thirdly, it was necessary to pronounce the resurrection of Christ, as an article of our faith, that thereby we might ground, confirm, strengthen, and declare our hope. [...] He laid down his life, but it was for us; and being to take up his own, he took up ours. We are the members of that body, of which Christ is the Head; if the Head be risen, the members cannot be far behind. He is the 'first-born from the dead' (Col 1:18), and we 'the sons of the resurrection' (Lk 20:36). The Spirit of Christ abiding in us maketh us the members of Christ, and by the same Spirit we have a full right and title to rise with our Head. [...] Thus the resurrection of Christ is the cause of our resurrection by a double causality, as an efficient, and as an exemplary cause. As an efficient cause, in regard our Saviour by and upon his resurrection hath obtained power and right to raise all the dead: 'For as in Adam all die, so in Christ shall all be made alive' (1 Cor 15:22). As an exemplary cause, in regard that all the saints of God shall rise after the similitude and in conformity to the resurrection of Christ: 'For I we have been planted together in the likeness of his death, we shall be also in the likeness of his resurrection' (Rom 6:5).

Fourthly, it is necessary to profess our faith in Christ risen from the dead, that his resurrection may effectually work its proper operation in our lives. For as it is efficient and exemplary to our bodies, so is it also to our souls.

A reading from the sermons of Blessed John Henry Newman

Now observe what was the nature of his presence in the Church after his Resurrection. It was this, that he came and went as he pleased; that material substances, such as fastened doors, were no impediments to his coming; and that when he was present his disciples did not, as a matter of course, know him. St Mark says he appeared to the two disciples who were going into the country, to Emmaus, 'in another form' (Mk 16:12). St. Luke, who gives the account more at length, says, that while he talked with them the heart burned within them. And it is worth remarking, that the two disciples do not seem to have been conscious of this at the time, but on looking back, they recollected that as having been, which did not strike them while it was. 'Did not', they say, 'did not our heart burn within us, while he talked with us by the way, and while he opened to us the Scriptures?' (Lk 24:32). But at the time, their hearts seem to have been holden (if we may use the expression) as well as their eyes. They were receiving impressions, but could not realize to themselves that they were receiving them; afterwards, however, they became aware of what had been.

Let us observe, too, when it was that their eyes were opened; here are we suddenly introduced to the highest and most solemn Ordinance of the Gospel, for it was when he consecrated and brake the Bread that their eyes were opened. There is evidently a stress on this, for presently St. Luke sums up his account of the gracious occurrence with an allusion to it in particular, 'They told what things were done in the way, and how he was known of them in breaking of bread' (Lk 24: 35). For so it was ordained, that Christ should not be both seen and known at once; first he was seen, then he was known. Only by faith is he known to be present; he is not recognized by sight. When he opened his disciples' eyes, he at once vanished. He removed his visible presence, and left but a memorial of himself. He vanished from sight that he might be present in a sacrament; and in order to connect his visible presence with his presence invisible, he for one instant manifested himself to their open eyes; manifested himself, if I may so speak, while he passed from his hiding-place of sight without knowledge, to that of knowledge without sight.

Bl. John Henry Newman, 'The Spiritual Presence of Christ in the Church', in *Parochial and Plain Sermons, by J. H. Newman* VI (London: Rivingtons, 1881), pp. 131-133.

A reading from Arthur Michael Ramsey, *The Resurrection of Christ*

The Christian Gospel was not first addressed to people who had no belief in the future state. [...] But nowhere, either for Greek or for Jew, was belief in the future life vivid, immediate, central and triumphant. Nowhere did the belief combine a conscious nearness of the world to come with a moral exalting of life in this present world. This was what Christianity brought. Its doctrine was not a flight to another world that left this world behind, nor was it a longing for another world that would come when this world was ended. It was the very near certainty of another world, with which the Christians were already linked and into which the life of the world would be raised up.

For the Christian belief about the future state centred in Jesus Christ. He had been seen and loved in this life; and he had been seen and loved also as one who had conquered death. He had become vividly known as the Lord both of the living and the dead; and the conviction of his people concerning the future life rested upon their conviction about him in whose life they shared. It was an intense and triumphant conviction that where he was there also would his people be. [...]

While there was the glorifying of his body to which the narratives testify, there was also the continuity of the whole manhood, body and spirit, raised from death. The Son of God took upon him the whole of human nature (often in the New Testament the word 'flesh' is so used) in order that the whole might be raised in glory. [...]

It is insufficient and misleading to present the Old Testament as the story of the growth of man's ideas about God, without the primacy of the greater theme of God's own acts and God's own utterances in the events of Israel's history that makes the Old Testament what it is. It is equally misleading to present the Gospel as the conception of God taught by Jesus, without due reference to the mighty act of God himself in the Passion and Resurrection. Read in its own light, the Bible has the Resurrection as its key. Its God is the God who raised up Jesus Christ from the dead, and in so doing vindicated his word in the Old

---

Arthur Michael Ramsey, *The Resurrection of Christ. A Study of the Event and its meaning for the Christian Faith* (London: Collins, 1965 [1961], 2nd edition).

Testament and in the Cross of Christ. It is only in virtue of the Resurrection that the Bible is one, and that the message of the Bible is coherent and true.

But though the revelation in the Bible is unique and breaks into the world from above, it is not 'wholly other'. For the God who there reveals himself is also the God who created the world. Therefore the theme of the Gospel, Life-through-Death, does not come as wholly strange to the world. Rather is it like a pattern already woven into nature and into the life of man. Though it is blurred by human sinfulness the pattern is not obliterated; and throughout all life there runs, however faintly perceived, a law of living through dying, a law whose presence testifies that man is made in the image of God. The Gospel of the glory of God in the face of Jesus Christ is both strange to mankind and yet nearer to mankind than the breath which they breathe. For the truth in him is also the truth in them.

Thursday in Easter Week

A reading from the sermons of Blessed John Henry Newman

St Paul says that whereas Christ is risen, he 'hath raised us up together, and made us sit together in heavenly places in Christ Jesus' (Eph 2:6). This is what we have still to learn; to know our place, position, situation as 'children of God, members of Christ, and inheritors of the kingdom of heaven'. We are risen again, and we know it not. We begin our catechism by confessing that we are risen, but it takes a long life to apprehend what we confess. We are like people waking from sleep, who cannot collect their thoughts at once, or understand where they are. By little and little the truth breaks upon us. Such are we in the present world; sons of light, gradually waking to a knowledge of themselves. For this let us meditate, let us pray, let us work, - gradually to attain to a real apprehension of what we are.

Thus, as time goes on, we shall gain first one thing, then another. By little and little we shall give up shadows and find the substance. Waiting on God day by day, we shall make progress day by day, and approach to the true and clear view of what he has made us to be in Christ. Year by year we shall gain something,

---

Bl. John Henry Newman, 'Difficulty of Realizing Sacred Privileges', in *Parochial and Plain Sermons, by J. H. Newman* VI (London: Rivingtons, 1881), pp. 99-100.

and each Easter, as it comes, will enable us more to rejoice with heart and understanding in that great salvation which Christ then accomplished.

This we shall find to be one great providential benefit arising from those duties which he exacts of us. Our duties to God and man are not only duties done to him, but they are means of enlightening our eyes and making our faith apprehensive. Every act of obedience has a tendency to strengthen our convictions about heaven. Every sacrifice makes us more zealous; every self-denial makes us more devoted. This is a use, too, of the observance of sacred seasons; they wean us from this world, they impress upon us he reality of the world which we see not. We trust, if we thus proceed, we shall understand more and more where we are. We humbly trust that, as we cleanse ourselves from this world, our eyes will be enlightened to see the things which are only spiritually discerned. We hope that to us will be fulfilled in due measure the words of the beatitude, 'Blessed are the pure in heart, for they shall see God' (Mt 5:8).

Friday in Easter Week

A reading from Thomas Traherne, *Centuries of Meditations*

No man loves, but he love another more than himself. In mean instances this is apparent. If you come into an orchard with a person you love, and there be but one ripe cherry you prefer it to the other. If two lovers delight in the same piece of meat, either takes pleasure in the other, and the more esteems the beloved's satisfaction. What ails men that they do not see it? In greater cases this is evident. A mother runs upon a sword to save her beloved. A father leaps into the fire to fetch out his beloved. Love brought Christ from heaven to die for his beloved. It is in the nature of love to despise itself, and to think only of its beloved's welfare. Look to it, it is not right love that is otherwise. Moses and St. Paul were no fools. God made me one of their number. I am sure nothing is more acceptable to him, than to love others so as to be willing to imperil even one's own soul for their benefit and welfare.

Thomas Traherne, *Centuries of Meditations*, IV. 56-59, in Thomas Traherne, *Centuries* (London and Oxford: Mowbrays, 1975 [1960]), pp. 193-195.

Nevertheless it is infinitely rewarded, though it seemeth difficult. For by this love do we become heirs of all men's joys, and co-heirs with Christ. For, what is the reason of your own joys, when you are blessed with benefits? Is it not self-love? Did you love others as you love yourself, you would be as much affected with their joys. Did you love them more, more. For according to the measure of your love to others will you be happy in them. For according thereto you will be delightful to them, and delighted in your felicity. The more you love men, the more delightful you will be to God, and the more delight you will take in God, and the more you will enjoy him. So that the more like you are to him in goodness, the more abundantly you will enjoy his goodness. By loving others you live in others to receive it.

Shall I not love him infinitely for whom God made the world and gave his Son? Shall I not love him infinitely who loveth me infinitely? Examine yourself well, and you will find it a difficult matter to love God so as to die for him, and not to love your brother so as to die for him in the same manner. Shall I not love him infinitely whom God loveth infinitely, and commendeth to my love, as the representative of himself, with such a saying, 'What ye do to him is done unto Me'? (cf Mt 25: 40). And if I love him so, can I forbear to help him? Verily, had I but one crown in the world, being in an open field, where both he and I were ready to perish, and 'twere necessary that one of us must have it all or be destroyed, though I know not where to have relief, he should have it, and I would die with comfort. I will not say, How small a comfort so small a succour is did I keep it: but how great a joy, to be the occasion of another's life! Love knows not how to be timorous, because it receives what it gives away, and is unavoidably the end of its own afflictions and another's happiness. Let him that pleases keep his money, I am rich in this noble charity to all the world, and more enjoy myself in it than he can be in both the Indies.

Is it unnatural to do what Jesus Christ hath done?

Saturday in Easter Week

A reading from the sermons of Austin Farrer

'I believe in the forgiveness of sins', says the Apostles' Creed, making the article hang upon belief in Holy Church Universal and Communion of Saints. One of our oldest authorities for the origins of the Apostles' Creed speaks of 'remission of sins through Holy Church' as that which the candidate for baptism was asked to believe. The creed, after all, is a baptismal creed, and baptism is a washing for the remission of sins, administered by Holy Church. It was reasonable enough that the candidate should be required to profess belief in the very rite he came there to undergo. And so we have it without ambiguity in the parallel form of the Church's ancient creed called Nicene; 'I believe in one baptism for the remission of sins', we recite every Sunday in the Holy Eucharist.

When the Holy Ghost moved the Church to put these articles into her professions of faith, it was never supposed that the intention was anything so vague or platitudinous as to declare that God bears no grudges, or that he would much rather see men repent than see them go to the devil. No, the intention was to proclaim that God had taken certain measures to make his forgiveness effective. He had taken a pair of human hands with which to turn our stiff-necked heads, and bring our eyebeams into the line of his own. And in accomplishing this – so gentle he was, yet so strong – he died and he conquered; that was the price of it, for that was the means to it; that indeed was the act of it. The death of Jesus is the forgiveness of God taking effect, the very act of our remission. The judge on the bench speaks acquittal, the Saviour bleeds forgiveness on the cross.

But, says the theology of the creeds, don't imagine that you can creep into quiet corner, and make your peace with God. You may indeed begin that way, you can't end that way. You must come out into the open, you must give yourself up, must surrender to visible justice; for the Christ who turns your face to his own is still in the world, and you must meet him there. He has a mystical body, a Catholic Church, a Communion of Saints. And if you will not surrender to his

Austin Farrer, 'All Souls' Examination', in *Austin Farrer. The Essential Sermons.* Selected and edited by Leslie Houlden (London: Society for the Promotion of Christian Knowledge, 1991), pp. 29-30.

327

human body, you are not reconciled to his divine person. In the Catholic Church you meet the very symbols, the very stuff of his saving passion: bathe in the waters of the font as in the stream that flowed from Christ's side, take the bread as his body, hear the absolution as from his lips; above all, love the Christians as Christ; for what you are to love in them is Christ – Christ fashioned and growing in them, as he begins also to grow in you.

Morning Prayer *Lauds*

Chorus novæ Ierusalem

1.Ye choirs of new Jerusalem,
   your sweetest notes employ,
 the Paschal victory to hymn
   in strains of holy joy.

2.For Judah's Lion bursts his chains,
   crushing the serpent's head;
 and cries aloud through death's domains
   to wake the imprisoned dead.

3.From hell's devouring jaws the prey
   alone our Leader bore;
 his ransomed hosts pursue their way
   where Jesus goes before.

4.Triumphant in his glory now
   to him all power is given;
 to him in one communion bow
   all saints in earth and heaven.

5.While we, his soldiers, praise our King,
   his mercy we implore,
 within his palace bright to bring
   and keep us evermore.

6.All glory to the Father be,
   all glory to the Son,
 all glory, Holy Ghost, to thee,
   while endless ages run. Alleluia! Amen.

St Fulbert of Chartres, *c. 1000 Tr.* R. Campbell.
Tune: St Fulbert, H. J. Gauntlett

1.Christ the Lord is risen again!
   Christ hath broken every chain!
hark, the angels shout for joy,
   singing evermore on high,
                    Alleluia!

2.He who gave for us his life,
   who for us endured the strife,
is our Paschal Lamb to-day!
   we too sing for joy, and say
                    Alleluia!

3.He who bore all pain and loss
   comfortless upon the Cross,
lives in glory now on high,
   pleads for us, and hears our cry.
                    Alleluia!

4.He whose paths no records tell,
   who descended into hell;
Who the strong man armed hath bound,
   now in highest heaven is crowned.
                    Alleluia!

5.Now he bids us tell abroad
   how the lost may be restored,
how the penitent forgiven,
   how we too may enter heaven.
                    Alleluia!

6.Thou, our Paschal Lamb indeed,
   Christ, to-day thy people feed;
take our sins and guilt away,
   that we all may sing for ay,
                    Alleluia!

Words: Michael Weisse, *c. 1480-1534. Tr.* C. Winkworth
Tune: Orientis Partibus, Mediæval French Melody

Second Sunday of Easter (Low Sunday)

A reading from the sermons of Lancelot Andrewes

A brotherhood, we grant, was begun then at Christmas by his birth, as upon that day, for 'lo then was he born'. But so was he now also at Easter; born then too, and after a better manner born. His resurrection was a second birth, Easter a second Christmas. 'Today I have begotten thee' (Ps 2:7), as true of this day as of that. The Church appointeth for the first Psalm this day the second Psalm, the Psalm of 'Today I have begotten thee'. The Apostle saith expressly, when he rose from the dead, then was 'Today I have begotten thee' fulfilled in him, verified of him. Then he was 'God's first-begotten from the dead' (Col 1:18). And upon this latter birth doth the brotherhood of this day depend.

There was then a new begetting this day. And if a new begetting, a new paternity, and fraternity both. But the 'Today I have begotten thee' of Christmas, how soon was he born of the Virgin's womb he became our brother, sin except, subject to all our infirmities; so to mortality, and even to death itself. And by death that brotherhood had been dissolved, but for this day's rising. By the 'Today I have begotten thee' of Easter, as soon as he was born again of the womb of the grave, he begins a new brotherhood, founds a new fraternity straight; adopts us, we see, anew again by his 'my brethren' (Jn 20:17), and thereby he that was 'first-begotten from the dead' becomes 'the first-begotten' in this respect 'among many brethren' (Rom 8:20). Before he was ours, now we are his. That was by the mother's side; – so, he ours. This is by 'your Father', the Father's side; - so, we his. But half-brothers before, never of whole blood till now. Now by father and mother both, twin brothers, most fraternal brothers, we cannot be more.

To shut up all in a word, that of Christmas was the fraternity rising out of 'my God and your God'; so then brethren. This of Easter, adopting us to his Father, was the fraternity of 'my Father and your Father'; so brethren now. This day's is the better birth, the better brotherhood by far; the fore-wheels are the less, the hinder the larger ever. For first, that of ours was when he was mortal; but his adoption he deferred, he would not make it while he was

---

Lancelot Andrewes, 'A Sermon preached before the King's Majesty, at Whitehall, on the twenty-first of April, A. D. MDCXXII, being Easter-Day', in *Ninety-Six Sermons by the Right Honourable and Reverend Father in God Lancelot Andrewes*, III (Oxford: Parker, 1850), pp. 56-58.

mortal; reserved it till he was risen again, and was even upon his ascending, and then he made it. So mortal he was, when he ours; but now when we his, he is immortal, and we brethren to him in that state, the state of immortality. Brethren before, but not to 'I am ascending'; now to 'I am ascending' and all. Death was in danger to have dissolved that, but death hath now no power on him, or on this; this shall never be in danger of being dissolved any more. That without this is nothing.

But we shall not need to stand in terms of comparison, since then it was but one of these; now it is both. His Father is now become our Father, to make us joint-heirs with him of his heavenly Kingdom; his God likewise become our God, to make us 'partakers' with them both 'of the divine nature' (2 Pet 1:4). 'My Father' and 'your Father', 'my God' and 'your God', run both merrily together, and 'I am ascending' upon them both.

Whereof, I mean of the partaking of his divine nature, to give us full and perfect assurance, as he took our flesh and became our Brother, flesh of our flesh then, so he gives us his flesh, that we may become his brethren, flesh of his flesh now; and it gives us now upon this day, the very day of our adoption into this fraternity. By taking our flesh – so begun his; by giving his flesh; - so begins ours. For requisite it was, that since we drew our death from the first Adam by partaking his substance, similarly and in like sort we should partake the substance of the second Adam; that so we might draw our life from him; should be engrafted into him, as the branches into the vine, that we might receive his sap – which is his similitude; should be flesh of his flesh, not he of ours as before, but we of his now; that we might be vegetate with his Spirit, even with his Divine Spirit. For now in him the Spirits are so united, as partake one and partake the other withal.

Third Sunday of Easter

A reading from the sermons of John Keble

'The Lamb which is in the midst of the throne shall feed them, and shall lead them unto living fountains of waters: and God shall wipe away all tears from their eyes' (Rev 7:17). What is the throne, but the throne of God, the place where he reigns in the light which no man can approach unto? And who is the Lamb in the midst of it, but our Lord Jesus Christ, God made Man, first redeeming us on the Cross, then returning with his human nature to his Father's right hand, and sitting down with him on the throne of his glory? The Lamb of God, who taketh away the sins of the world, is here shewn to us as our Shepherd, sparing and dealing gently with his people, whom he hath redeemed with his precious blood. He is our Shepherd, to feed and to lead us.

We know that it is one great part of a shepherd's business to give his flock fodder from time to time, and to shew them and conduct them on the way to clear and wholesome waters. So our Lord Jesus Christ, as it is in the Psalm, 'feeds us in a green pasture, and leads us forth beside the waters of comfort' (Ps 23:2). He feeds us with his own Body and Blood, he causes us to drink of his Spirit. As the shepherd searches out for his sheep the best and freshest pasture, as he attends particularly to the diseased and feeble, as he goes before them shewing them where they should be, and preparing and fencing in the most healthful and convenient places, as he finds out wholesome waters for their drink, and takes care that all may come to them; so does our Lord Jesus Christ, in his Church, for the sheep of his pasture, which are men, baptized, Christian men. He cares for all their needs; the heavenly food which he provides seems to us one and the same to all, but it is marvellously tempered and ordered as is said of the manna of old, to suit each person's own particular wants. The waters of his Spirit are divided to every man severally as he wills, and he wills what he knows will profit.

Now as his tender care is exercised particularly over those who are in trouble and destitution, in seeking the lost, bringing back the misguided, binding up the broken, strengthening the sick, carrying the lambs that are in his arms, and gently leading those that are with young, so the Holy Scripture seems especially

---

John Keble, 'God's Returns of Comfort', in *Sermons for the Sundays after Trinity. Part II. Sundays XIII-End, by the late Rev. John Keble* (Oxford and London: Parker, 1878), pp. 229-231, 233.

to point out the constancy and regular returns of his mercy, as being that circumstance which above all others makes it the proper comfort and relief of the afflicted. Why may the sheep so entirely depend upon the shepherd? Because his care of them is so unfailing, so regular, so constant. He does not neglect them one day, and remember them another; he does not provide them now and then with a full meal, and then leave them for a long time to take care of themselves; but as regularly as the day comes, he feeds them in green pastures, and leads them beside the still waters; they look for him at the appointed hour, and know that they may depend upon him; we see them gathering by the gate where he comes, their faces turned all the same way; they follow where he leads, and make no doubt of finding the wholesome herbage and fresh and living waters, which they long for.

Now what is it which answers to this in the Church and kingdom of heaven. Surely nothing so much as the regular returns of Church services and holy Sacraments. [...]

You are hungry and thirsty, you want refreshment and good, cool waters and tender grass; what so plain and natural, what so sure to obtain a blessing, as to come early and late where the Good Shepherd has promised to be, if not in body, yet in heart and mind? Kneel down before him, say those prayers to him which he has himself taught you by his Church, praise and adore him in the words of his divine psalms – the prayer-book, as it has been well called, which he and all his used have used, from the day when he taught us to pray; listen reverently to his holy lessons, observe the times, weeks, hours, and days which he hallowed by his death and resurrection, and by the gifts of his Holy Spirit; do this diligently, not once or twice, but as the rule of your life, with a reverent and obedient heart; try to do it always as in his presence, and see if the comfort and refreshment which you long for will not come.

Fourth Sunday of Easter

A reading from Gilbert of Hoyland, *Sermons on the Song of Songs*

Why does Jesus need a door? He says in the Gospel, 'I am the door'! (Jn 10:7). Here is a surprising paradox. He is the door and he knocks at the door. He wishes to enter, but through him 'whoever enters will be saved and find pasture' (Jn 10:9). There is a great difference between one door and another. For there is a door of one kind in the evidence of nature; there is another door in the sacraments of the Church; there is a third door in the experiences of grace.

At the first door, by the guidance of natural reason, wisdom acting through its works makes itself known to us; we gain access to some share of truth; we gather some knowledge of the Godhead, not however of the distinction of Persons in the Godhead. At this door the distinction of Persons is not made nor is grace conferred. Therefore at this door one should not delay forever or knock too long.

Through the second door, by our initiation into the saving sacraments, we enter the unity of the Church and the Communion of Saints. At this door some so stand inside as to be half outside, until they approach the third door, which we interpret as a familiar access through the affection of charity to some enjoyment and contemplation of the Beloved. This door, so secret, so intimate, does not lie open to all but is reserved for the bride alone...

However, it makes little difference, I suppose, whether you visit him or her visits you, except that you then seem to visit him, when you take the first step and are the first to call upon him. But he visits you, when he takes the lead, knocks at your affections, slips in unexpected, and, when you have no such visit in mind, moves you with a touch of delicacy beyond your hopes.

When he knocks in this way at your door, do not delay. Arise, hasten, lest perhaps he turn away. For this happens even in our verse; 'I opened the bolt of my door to my beloved, but he had turned away and gone' (Song 5:6). Why go off, good Jesus? Why turn away? Why cheat the beloved of her desire? Do you

---

Gilbert of Hoyland, *Sermons on the Song of Songs,* 44: 2-3, in Gilbert of Hoyland, *Sermons on the Song of Songs, III.* Translated and introduced by Lawrence C. Braceland, S. J., (Kalamazoo, MI: Cistercian Publications, 1979), pp. 529-530.

prompt her desire and withdraw her delight? Or perhaps, in this way, do you draw out her yearnings to greater keenness and warmer desire by withdrawing your presence? It is so. It is obviously so. All the disappointments of love add more fuel to love itself, and all the deceptive wiles raise love to its peak.

Fifth Sunday of Easter

A reading from the sermons of Blessed John Henry Newman

The heavenly gift of the Spirit fixes the eyes of our mind upon the Divine Author of our salvation. By nature we are blind and carnal; but the Holy Ghost by whom we are new-born, reveals to us the God of mercies, and bids us recognize and adore him as our Father with a true heart. He impresses on us our Heavenly Father's image, which we lost when Adam fell, and disposes us to seek his presence by the very instinct of our new nature. He gives us back a portion of that freedom in willing and doing, of that uprightness and innocence, in which Adam was created. He unites us to all holy beings, as before we had relationship with evil. He restores for us that broken bond, which, proceeding from above, connects together into one blessed family all that is anywhere holy and eternal, and separates it off from the rebel world which comes to nought. Being then the sons of God, and one with him, our souls mount up and cry to him continually. This special characteristic of the regenerate soul is spoken of by St Paul soon after the text, 'Ye have received the Spirit of adoption, whereby we cry, Abba, Father' (Rom 8:15). [...]

The indwelling of the Holy Ghost raises the soul, not only to the thought of God, but of Christ also. St John says, 'Truly our fellowship is with the Father, and with his Son Jesus Christ' (1 Jn 1:3). And our Lord himself, 'If a man love me, he will keep my words; and my Father will love him, and We will come unto him, and make our abode with him' (Jn 14:23). Now, not to speak of other and higher ways in which these texts are fulfilled, one surely consists in that exercise of faith and love in the thought of the Father and Son, which the Gospel, and the Spirit revealing it, furnish to the Christian. The Spirit came specially to 'glorify' Christ; and vouchsafes to be a shining light within the Church and the individual Christian, reflecting the Saviour of the world in all

---

Bl. John Henry Newman, 'The Indwelling Spirit', in J. H. Newman, *Parochial and Plain Sermons* II (London: Rivingtons, 1880), pp. 224-225, 226-228.

his perfections, all his offices, all his works. He came for the purpose of unfolding what was yet hidden, whilst Christ was on earth; and speaks on the house-tops what was delivered in closets, disclosing him in the glories of his transfiguration, who once had no comeliness in his outward form, and was but a man of sorrows and acquainted with grief.

First, he inspired the Holy Evangelists to record the life of Christ, and directed them which of his words and works to select, which to omit; next, he commented (as it were) upon these, and unfolded their meaning in the Apostolic Epistles. The birth, the life, the death and resurrection of Christ, has been the text which he has illuminated. He has made history to be doctrine; telling us plainly, whether by St John or St Paul, that Christ's conception and birth was the real Incarnation of the Eternal Word, – his life, 'God manifest in the flesh,' – his death and resurrection, the Atonement for sin, and the Justification of all believers.

Nor was this all: he continued his sacred comment in the formation of the Church, superintending and overruling its human instruments, and bringing out our Saviour's words and works, and the Apostles' illustrations of them, into acts of obedience and permanent Ordinances, by the ministry of Saints and Martyrs. Lastly, he completes his gracious work by conveying this system of Truth, thus varied and expanded, to the heart of each individual Christian in which he dwells. Thus he vouchsafes to edify the whole man in faith and holiness: 'casting down imaginations and every high thing that exalteth itself against the knowledge of God, and bringing into captivity every thought to the obedience of Christ' (2 Cor 10:5). By his wonder working grace all things tend to perfection. Every faculty of the mind, every design, pursuit, subject of thought, is hallowed in its degree by the abiding vision of Christ, as Lord, Saviour, and Judge. All solemn, reverent, thankful and devoted feelings, all that is noble, all that is choice in the regenerate soul, all that is self-denying in conduct, and zealous in action, is drawn forth and offered up by the Spirit as a living sacrifice to the Son of God.

A reading from the sermons of Edward Bouverie Pusey

All which our Lord has is ours, if we are indeed his. As Man, he received Gifts, that he might give them to men. To him, as Man, though God, 'was given all Power in Heaven and on earth' (Mt 28:18), that he might bestow on his all things in Heaven and earth; that all things, in both, might work and serve together to the good of his Elect. As Man, he received the Holy Spirit, that he might again dwell in man, clothe us with the Robe of supernatural Grace and Holiness, which we lost in Adam, and were found naked. For our sakes he sanctified himself, that we also might be sanctified by the Truth. He sanctified his Human Nature by his Indwelling Godhead, that so he might sanctify our nature by himself, who is the Word of Truth. For us the Spirit of God rested upon him with his Sevenfold Gifts, 'the Spirit of Wisdom and Understanding, the Spirit of Counsel and Might, the Spirit of Knowledge and True Godliness, the Spirit of Holy Fear' (Is 11:2), that through him It might stream down through all his members, as the holy oil which was poured upon Aaron's head 'went down to the skirts of his clothing' (Ps 133:2), hallowing, and giving a sweet savour to all his body. For us, the Spirit was 'given without measure to him' (Jn 3:34), that from him It might be parted to us his members, as we severally need, or are found worthy. [...] For us, 'though he were a Son, yet learned he obedience by the things which he suffered', that, being made perfect, he might become 'the Author of Eternal Salvation to all them that obey him' (Heb 5:8, 9). His shame is our glory; his Blood is our ransom; his Sweat our refreshment; the Streams from his Side our Sacraments; his Wounded Side our hiding-place from our own sins, and Satan's wrath; his Death our life.

And what, then, on this 'our triumphant Holy Day' should his Life be? What but the sealing to us of all which he had wrought for us? What but the bursting of the bars of our prison-house, the restoration of our lost Paradise, the opening of the Kingdom of Heaven, the earnest of our Endless Life, the binding of the strong man, and letting us, his lawful prisoners, free, the bringing in of Incorruption, the Conquest, in the Head, of the last enemy, that he may, one by one, be conquered in us too, and the death of our bodies may be the deliverance from 'this body of death', our souls' perfected life?

E. B. Pusey, 'Sermon XVI. The Christian's Life in Christ', in *Sermons during the Season from Advent to Whitsuntide, by the Rev. E. B. Pusey* (Oxford and London: Parker, 1848), pp. 230-233.

Can there be more than this? There can. The text unfolds to us a yet deeper Mystery, that all this is to us 'in Christ', 'in Christ shall all be made alive' (1 Cor 15:22). The Endless Life, which they shall live who are counted worthy of it, shall then not be a life such as men seem to live here where our true life is unseen, as if we were so many creatures of God's Hand, each having his own existence wholly separate from his fellows, upheld in being by God, yet, as it seems, apart from God, having his own wills, affections, tastes, pursuits, passions, love, hatred, interests, joys, sufferings. Our life then shall not be, as it seems here, and as it truly is in the ungodly, separate from God, and in the good indistinctly and imperfectly united with him. It shall be a life 'in God'. '*In* Christ shall all be made alive'. We shall live then, not only as having our souls restored to our bodies, and souls and bodies living on in the Presence of Almighty God. Great and unutterable as were this Blessedness, there is a higher yet in store, - to live on 'in Christ'. For this implies Christ's living on in us. [...] To dwell *in* God is not to dwell *on* God only. It is no mere lifting up of our affections to him, no being enwrapt in the contemplation of him, no going forth of ourselves to cleave to him. All this is our seeking him, not his taking us up; our stretching after him, not our attaining him; our knocking, not his Opening. To dwell in God must be by his Dwelling in us. He takes us out of our state of nature, in which we were, fallen, estranged, in a far country, out of and away from him, and takes us up into himself. He cometh to us, and if we will receive him, he dwelleth in us, and maketh his Abode in us. He enlargeth our hearts by his Sanctifying Spirit which he giveth us, by the obedience which he enables us to yield, by the acts of Faith and love which he strengthens us to do, and then dwelleth in those who are his more largely. By dwelling in us, he makes us parts of himself, so that in the Ancient Church they could boldly say, 'he deifieth me'; that is, he makes me part of him, of his Body, who is God.

Short Readings for Prayer during the Day
in Eastertide

Sunday *1 Pet 1:3-5*

Blessed be the God and Father of our Lord Jesus Christ! By his great mercy we have been born anew to a living hope through the resurrection of Jesus Christ from the dead, and to an inheritance which is imperishable, undefiled, and unfading, kept in heaven for you, who by God's power are guarded through faith for a salvation ready to be revealed in the last time.

Monday *Zeph 3:14-18*

Sing aloud, O daughter of Zion; shout, O Israel! Rejoice and exult with all your heart, O daughter of Jerusalem! The Lord has taken away the judgments against you, he has cast out your enemies. The King of Israel, the Lord, is in your midst; you shall fear evil no more. On that day it shall be said to Jerusalem: 'Do not fear, O Zion; let not your hands grow weak. The Lord, your God, is in your midst, a warrior who gives victory; he will rejoice over you with gladness, he will renew you in his love; he will exult over you with loud singing as on a day of festival. 'I will remove disaster from you, so that you will not bear reproach for it.'

Tuesday *1 Cor 15:42-44a, 47-49*

So is it with the resurrection of the dead. What is sown is perishable, what is raised is imperishable. It is sown in dishonour, it is raised in glory. It is sown in weakness, it is raised in power. It is sown a physical body, it is raised a spiritual body. The first man was from the earth, a man of dust; the second man is from heaven. As was the man of dust, so are those who are of the dust; and as is the man of heaven, so are those who are of heaven. Just as we have borne the image of the man of dust, we shall also bear the image of the man of heaven.

Wednesday *Col 3:1-4*

If then you have been raised with Christ, seek the things that are above, where Christ is, seated at the right hand of God. Set your minds on things that are above, not on things that are on earth. For you have died, and your life is hid with Christ in God. When Christ who is our life appears, then you also will appear with him in glory.

Thursday   *Tit 3:5-7*

God saved us, not because of deeds done by us in righteousness, but in virtue of his own mercy, by the washing of regeneration and renewal in the Holy Spirit, which he poured out upon us richly through Jesus Christ our Saviour, so that we might be justified by his grace and become heirs in hope of eternal life.

Friday   *Job 19:23-27a*

Job said, 'Oh that my words were written! Oh that they were inscribed in a book! Oh that with an iron pen and lead they were graven in the rock for ever! For I know that my Redeemer lives, and at last he will stand upon the earth; and after my skin has been thus destroyed, then from my flesh I shall see God, whom I shall see on my side, and my eyes shall behold, and not another'.

Saturday   *Rev 1:12, 13, 17, 18*

I turned to see the voice that was speaking to me, and on turning I saw seven golden lampstands, and in the midst of the lampstands one like a son of man, clothed with a long robe and with a golden girdle round his breast. When I saw him, I fell at his feet as though dead. But he laid his right hand upon me, saying, 'Fear not, I am the first and the last, and the living one; I died, and behold I am alive for evermore, and I have the keys of Death and Hades.

Easter Prayer during the Day

Christ yesterday and today,
the beginning and the end,
Alpha and Omega,
all time belongs to you,
and all ages;
to you be glory and power
through every age and for ever.

from the Easter Vigil

Easter Sunday

ALMIGHTY God, who through thine only-begotten Son Jesus Christ hast overcome death and opened unto us the gate of everlasting life: we humbly beseech thee, that as by thy special grace preventing us thou dost put into our minds good desires, so by thy continual help we may bring the same to good effect; through Jesus Christ thy Son our Lord, who liveth and reigneth with thee in the unity of the Holy Spirit, one God, for ever and ever.

or

GOD, who for our redemption didst give thine only-begotten Son to the death of the cross, and by his glorious resurrection hast delivered us from the power of our enemy: grant us so to die daily unto sin that we may evermore live with him in the joy of his risen life; through the same thy Son Christ our Lord who liveth and reigneth with thee and the Holy Spirit, one God, for ever and ever.

Easter Week

GRANT, we beseech thee, almighty God: that we who celebrate with reverence the paschal feast, may be found worthy to attain to everlasting joys; through Jesus Christ thy Son our Lord, who liveth and reigneth with thee, in the unity of the Holy Spirit, one God, for ever and ever.

Second Sunday of Easter

ALMIGHTY Father, who has given thine only Son to die for our sins, and to rise again for our justification: grant us so to put away the leaven of malice and wickedness, that we may alway serve thee in pureness of living and truth; through the merits of the same thy Son Jesus Christ our Lord, who liveth and reigneth with thee, in the unity of the Holy Spirit, one God, for ever and ever.

Third Sunday of Easter

ALMIGHTY God, who has given thine only Son to be unto us both a sacrifice for sin, and also an ensample of godly life: give us grace that we may always most thankfully receive that his inestimable benefit, and also daily endeavour ourselves to follow the blessed steps of his most holy life; through Jesus Christ thy Son our Lord, who liveth and reigneth with thee, in the unity of the Holy Spirit, one God, for ever and ever.

Fourth Sunday of Easter

ALMIGHTY God, who shewest to them that be in error the light of thy truth, to the intent that they may return into the way of righteousness: grant unto all them that are admitted into the fellowship of Christ's religion, that they may eschew those things that are contrary to their profession, and follow all such things as are agreeable to the same; through Jesus Christ thy Son our Lord, who liveth and reigneth with thee, in the unity of the Holy Spirit, one God, for ever and ever.

Fifth Sunday of Easter

O ALMIGHTY God, who alone canst order the unruly wills and affections of the sinful: grant unto thy people that they may love the thing which thou commandest and desire that which thou dost promise, that so, among the sundry and manifold changes of the world, our hearts may surely there be fixed where true joys are to be found; through Jesus Christ thy Son our Lord, who liveth and reigneth with thee, in the unity of the Holy Spirit, one God, for ever and ever.

Sixth Sunday of Easter (Rogation Sunday)

O LORD, from whom all good things do come: grant to us thy humble servants, that by thy holy inspiration we may think those things that be good and, by thy merciful guiding may perform the same; through Jesus Christ thy Son our Lord, who liveth and reigneth with thee, in the unity of the Holy Spirit, one God, for ever and ever.

Rogation Days

Office

Opening Sentence
The earth is the Lord's, and the fullness thereof.

Ps 24:1

Short Readings for Prayer during the Day

Monday   *Zeph 3:14-18*

Sing aloud, O daughter of Zion; shout, O Israel! Rejoice and exult
with all your heart, O daughter of Jerusalem! The Lord has taken away
the judgments against you, he has cast out your enemies. The King of
Israel, the Lord, is in your midst; you shall fear evil no more. On that
day it shall be said to Jerusalem: 'Do not fear, O Zion; let not your
hands grow weak. The Lord, your God, is in your midst, a warrior
who gives victory; he will rejoice over you with gladness, he will renew
you in his love; he will exult over you with loud singing as on a day of
festival. 'I will remove disaster from you, so that you will not bear
reproach for it.'

Tuesday   *1 Cor 15:42-44a, 47-49*

So is it with the resurrection of the dead. What is sown is perishable,
what is raised is imperishable. It is sown in dishonour, it is raised in
glory. It is sown in weakness, it is raised in power. It is sown a
physical body, it is raised a spiritual body. The first man was from the
earth, a man of dust; the second man is from heaven. As was the man
of dust, so are those who are of the dust; and as is the man of heaven,
so are those who are of heaven. Just as we have borne the image of
the man of dust, we shall also bear the image of the man of heaven.

If then you have been raised with Christ, seek the things that are above, where Christ is, seated at the right hand of God. Set your minds on things that are above, not on things that are on earth. For you have died, and your life is hid with Christ in God. When Christ who is our life appears, then you also will appear with him in glory.

Collects

ALMIGHTY God, Lord of heaven and earth: we humbly pray that thy gracious providence may give and preserve to our use the harvests of the land and of the seas, and may prosper all who labour to gather them, that we, who constantly receive good things from thy hand, may always give thee thanks; through Jesus Christ thy Son our Lord, who liveth and reigneth with thee, in the unity of the Holy Spirit, one God, for ever and ever.

or

ALMIGHTY God and Father, who hast ordered our life in common dependence one on another: prosper those who work in commerce and industry and direct their minds and their hands that they may rightly use thy gifts in the service of others; through Jesus Christ thy Son our Lord, who liveth and reigneth with thee, in the unity of the Holy Spirit, one God, for ever and ever.

or

O GOD our Father, who dost never cease from the work that thou hast begun, and dost prosper with thy blessing all human labour: make us wise and faithful stewards of thy gifts, that we may serve the common good, maintain the fabric of the world, and seek that justice where all may share the good things thou dost pour upon us; through Jesus Christ thy Son our Lord, who liveth and reigneth with thee, in the unity of the Holy Spirit, one God, for ever and ever.

Ascension Day

Office

Opening Sentence

Seeing that we have a great high priest that is passed into the heavens,
Jesus the Son of God, let us come boldly unto the throne of grace,
that we may obtain mercy and find grace to help in time of need.

Heb 4:14, 16

Post-Biblical Reading

A reading from the sermons of Blessed John Henry Newman

'It is Christ that died, yea rather, that is risen again, who is even at the right
hand of God, who also maketh intercession for us' (Rom 8:34). The Ascension
of our Lord and Saviour is an event ever to be commemorated with joy and
thanksgiving, for St Paul tells us in the text that he ascended to the right hand
of God, and there makes intercession for us. Hence it is our comfort to know,
that 'if any man sin, we have an Advocate with the Father, Jesus Christ the
righteous, and he is the propitiation for our sins' (1 Jn 2:1, 2). As the Jewish
High Priest, after the solemn sacrifice for the people on the great day of
Atonement, went into the Holy of Holies with the blood of the victim, and
sprinkled it upon the Mercy-Seat, so Christ has entered into heaven itself, to
present (as it were) before the Throne that sacred Tabernacle which was the
instrument of his passion, - his pierced hands and wounded side, - in token to
the atonement which he has effected for the sins of the world.

Wonder and awe must always mingle with the thankfulness which the revealed
dispensation of mercy raises in our minds. And this, indeed, is an additional
cause of thankfulness, that Almighty God has disclosed to us enough of his
high Providence to raise such sacred and reverent feelings. Had he merely told
us that he had pardoned us, we should have had overabundant cause for
blessing and praising him; but in showing us something of the means, in
vouchsafing to tell us what cannot wholly be told, in condescending to abase

---

Bl. John Henry Newman, 'Mysteries in Religion', in J. H. Newman, *Parochial and Plain Sermons* II (London: Rivingtons, 1880), pp. 206-207, 211-212.

heavenly things to the weak and stammering tongues of earth, he had enlarged our gratitude, yet sobered it with fear. We are allowed with Angels to obtain a glimpse of the mysteries of Heaven, 'to rejoice with trembling'. Therefore, so far from considering the Truths of the Gospel as a burden, because they are beyond our understanding, we shall rather welcome them and exult in them, nay, and feel an antecedent stirring of heart towards them, for the very reason that they are above us.[…]

We are not given to see the secret shrine in which God dwells. Before him stand the Seraphim, veiling their faces. Christ is within the veil. We must not search curiously what is his present office, what is meant by his pleading his sacrifice, and by his perpetual intercession for us. And since we do not know, we will studiously keep to the figure given us in Scripture; we will not attempt to interpret it, or change the wording of it, being wise above what is written. We will not neglect it, because we do not understand it. We will hold it as a Mystery, or (what was anciently called) a Truth Sacramental; that is, a high invisible grace lodged in an outward form, a precious possession to be piously and thankfully guarded for the sake of the heavenly reality contained in it. Thus much we see in it, the pledge of a doctrine which reason cannot understand, viz. of the influence of the prayer of faith upon the Divine counsels. The Intercessor directs or stays the hand of the Unchangeable and Sovereign Governor of the World; being at once the meritorious cause and the earnest of the intercessory power of his brethren. 'Christ rose again for our justification', 'The effectual fervent prayer of a righteous man availeth much', are both infinite mercies, and deep mysteries.

Short Reading for Prayer during the Day
Christ has entered, not into a sanctuary made with hands, a copy of the true one, but into heaven itself, now to appear in the presence of God on our behalf.

Heb 9:24

Iesu nostra redemptio

1. O Christ, our hope, our hearts' desire,
   redemption's only spring;
   Creator of the world art thou,
   its Saviour and its King.

2. How vast the mercy and the love
   which laid our sins on thee,
   and led thee to a cruel death
   to set thy people free.

3. But now the bonds of death are burst,
   the ransom has been paid;
   and thou art on thy Father's throne
   in glorious robes arrayed.

4. O may thy mighty love prevail
   our sinful souls to spare;
   O may we come before thy throne,
   and find acceptance there!

5. O Christ, be thou our present joy,
   our future great reward;
   our only glory may it be
   to glory in the Lord.

6. All praise to thee, ascended Lord;
   all glory every be
   to Father, Son and Holy Ghost,
   through all eternity. Amen.

c.8th cent. Tr. J Chandler
Tune: Metzler's Redhead, R. Redhead

Collect

GRANT, we beseech thee, almighty God: that like as we do believe thy only-begotten Son our Lord Jesus Christ to have ascended into the heavens so we may also in heart and mind thither ascend, and with him continually dwell; who liveth and reigneth with thee and the Holy Spirit, one God, for ever and ever.

From the Day after Ascension Day
until the Day of Pentecost

Office

Opening Sentence

The love of God has been shed abroad in our hearts through the Holy
Spirit which was given unto us.

Rom 5:5

Hymns

Evening Prayer   *Vespers*

Veni Creator Spiritus

1. Come, Holy Ghost, our souls inspire,
   and lighten with celestial fire.
   Thou the anointing Spirit art,
   who dost thy sevenfold gifts impart.

2. Thy blessed unction from above
   is comfort, life, and fire of love.
   Enable with perpetual light
   the dullness of our blinded sight.

3. Anoint and cheer our soilèd face
   with the abundance of thy grace.
   Keep far our foes, give peace at home:
   where thou art guide, no ill can come.

4. Teach us to know the Father, Son,
   and thee, of both, to be but One,
   that through the ages all along,
   this may be our endless song:

Praise to thy eternal merit,
Father, Son, and Holy Spirit.

Before 10ᵗʰ cent. Tr. John Cosin (1594-1672)
Tune: Veni Creator ('Mechlin Version')

The last two lines begin thus:

Praise   to thy   e-ter-nal mer-it,   Fa-ther,&c.

Another version of this hymn is found on page 357.

349

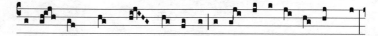

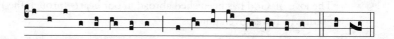

Æterne Rex altissime

1.Eternal Monarch, King most high,
  whose blood hath brought redemption nigh,
by whom the death of Death was wrought,
  and conquering Grace's battle fought.

2.Ascending to the throne of might,
  and seated at the Father's right,
all power in heaven is Jesu's own,
  that here his manhood had not known.

3.That so, in nature's triple frame,
  each heavenly and each earthly name,
and things in hell's abyss abhorred,
  may bend the knee and own him Lord.

4.Yea, angels tremble when they see
  how changed is our humanity;
that flesh hath purged what flesh had stained,
  and God, the flesh of God, hath reigned.

5.Be thou our joy and strong defence,
  who art our future recompense:
so shall the light that springs from thee
  be ours through all eternity.

6.O risen Christ, ascended Lord,
  all praise to thee let earth accord,
who art, while endless ages run,
  with Father and with Spirit One. Amen.

c.5th cent. Tr. J.M. Neale

A reading from Walter Hilton, *The Scale of Perfection*

The saints say, and rightly, that there are two sorts of spiritual love. One is called uncreated and the other created. Uncreated Love is God himself, the Third Person of the Trinity, that is the Holy Ghost. He is uncreated Love: as St John says, 'God is love' (1 Jn 4:8) that is the Holy Ghost. Created love is the love that the Holy Ghost arouses in a soul at the sight of truth - that is, of God. This love is called created because it is brought about by the Holy Ghost. Being created it is not God himself, but it is the love which the soul feels at the contemplation of God, when it is drawn to him alone.

Now you can see how created love is not the cause of a soul coming to the contemplation of God. For there are some who think that they can love God so ardently, as it were by their own powers, that they can merit the contemplation of him, but it is not so. It is uncreated Love, that is God himself, who is the cause of all this knowledge. For owing to sin and the weakness of its human nature the poor, blind soul is so far from the clear knowledge of God and the enjoyment of his love that it would never be able to attain them, if it were not for the infinite greatness of God's love. But because he loves us so much, he gives us his love that is the Holy Ghost. He is both the giver and the gift, and by that gift makes us know and love him. This is the love that I said you should desire, this uncreated Love that is the Holy Ghost. And indeed a lesser gift than he will not avail to bring us to the blessed knowledge of God. Therefore we should desire and ask of God only this gift of Love; that in the greatness of his blessed love he would illumine our hearts with his incomprehensible light that we may know him, and that he may impart his blessed love to us, that as he loves us, so we may love him in return. St John says, 'Let us love God now, for he has first loved us' (1 Jn 4:19). He loved us much when he made us in his likeness, but he loved us more when he redeemed us from the power of the devil and from the pains of hell through his precious blood by voluntarily undergoing death in his human nature. But he loves us most when he gives us the gift of the Holy Ghost, that is Love. By which we know him and love him and are assured that we are his sons chosen for salvation.

Walter Hilton, *The Scale of Perfection* II. 34, in Walter Hilton, *The Scale of Perfection*. Translated into Modern English, with an Introduction and Notes, by Dom Gerard Sitwell, O. S. B. (London: Burns Oates, 1953), pp. 248-250.

We are more bound to him for this love than for any other that he has shown is, either in creating or redeeming us. For though he had created us and redeemed us, if he had not saved us as well, what profit would it have been for us? None indeed.

Pentecost (Whitsunday)

A reading from the sermons of Lancelot Andrewes

We are this day, beside our weekly due of the Sabbath, to renew and to celebrate the yearly memory of the sending down the Holy Ghost. One of 'the great and wonderful benefits of God' (Acts 2:11); indeed, a benefit so great and so wonderful as there were not tongues enough upon earth to celebrate it withal, but there were fain to be more sent from Heaven to help to sound it out thoroughly, even a new supply of tongues from Heaven. For all the tongues in earth were not sufficient to magnify God for his goodness, in sending down to men the gift of the Holy Ghost.

This we may make a several benefit by itself, from those of Christ's. And so the Apostle seemeth to do. First, 'God sent his Son' in one verse (Gal 4:4); and then after 'God sent the Spirit of his Son' in another (Gal 4:6).

Or we may hold our continuation still, and make this the last of Christ's benefits; for 'he went up on high' is not the last, there is still one remaining, which is, 'he gave gifts to me' (Ps 68:18). And that is this day's peculiar; wherein were given to men many and manifold both graces and gifts, and all in one gift, the gift of the Holy Ghost.

Howsoever we make it, sure it is that all the rest, all the feasts hitherto in the return of the year from his incarnation to the very last of his ascension, though all o them be great and worthy of all honour in themselves, yet to us they are as

---

Lancelot Andrewes, 'A Sermon preached before the King's Majesty at Greenwich, on the eighth day of June, A. D. MDCVI, being Whit-Sunday', in *Ninety-Six Sermons by the Right Honourable and Reverend Father in God Lancelot Andrewes,* III (Oxford: Parker, 1850), pp. 107-109.

nothing, any of them or all of them, even all the feasts in the Calendar, without this day, the feast which now we hold holy to the sending of the Holy Ghost.

Christ is the Word, and all of him but words spoken or words written, there is no seal put to till this day; the Holy Ghost is the seal or signature, 'in whom you were sealed' (Eph 4:30). A testament we have and therein many fair legacies, but till this day nothing administered – 'The administrations are the Spirit's' (1 Cor 12:5). In all these of Christ's there is but the purchase made and paid for, and as they say, 'the right to the thing' acquired; but 'the right in the thing', 'a sending into possession', livery and seizing, that is reserved till this day; for the Spirit is the 'earnest' (2 Cor 5:5) or the investiture of all that Christ hath done for us.

These, if we should compare them, it would not be easy to determine, whether the greater of these two: 1. that of the Prophet, 'to us a son is given' (Is 9:6); 2. or that of the Apostle, 'The Spirit has been given to us' (Rom 5:5); the ascending of our flesh, or the descending of his Spirit; the mystery of his incarnation, or the mystery of our inspiration. For mysteries they are both and 'great mysteries of godliness' both; and in both of them 'God manifested in the flesh' (1 Tim 3:16). 1. In the former, by the union of his Son; 2. In the latter, by the communion of his Blessed Spirit.

But we will not compare them, they are both above all comparison. Yet this we may safely say of them: without either of them we are not complete, we have not our accomplishment; but by both we have, and that fully, even by this day's royal exchange. Whereby, as before he of ours, so now we of his are made partakers. He clothed with our flesh, and we invested with his Spirit. The great promise of the Old Testament accomplished, that he should partake our human nature; and the great and precious promise of the New, that we should 'partake his divine nature' (2 Pet 1:4), both are this day accomplished. That the text well beginneth 'when the days were fulfilled' (Acts 2:1), for it is our complement indeed; and not only ours but the very Gospel's too. It is Tertullian: 'the coming of Christ was the fulfilling of the Law, the coming of the Holy Ghost is the fulfilling of the Gospel'.

Friday after Ascension
Heb 2:8b-10

As it is, we do not yet see everything in subjection to him. But we see Jesus, who for a little while was made lower than the angels, crowned with glory and honour because of the suffering of death, so that by the grace of God he might taste death for every one. For it was fitting that he, for whom and by whom all things exist, in bringing many sons to glory, should make the pioneer of their salvation perfect through suffering.

Saturday after Ascension
Rom 8:38, 39

I am sure that neither death, nor life, nor angels, nor principalities, nor things present, nor things to come, nor powers, nor height, nor depth, nor anything else in all creation, will be able to separate us from the love of God in Christ Jesus our Lord.

Sunday after Ascension
Eph 2:4-6

God, who is rich in mercy, out of the great love with which he loved us, even when we were dead through our trespasses, made us alive together with Christ (by grace you have been saved), and raised us up with him, and made us sit with him in the heavenly places in Christ Jesus.

Monday before Pentecost
Is 40:28-31

Have you not known? Have you not heard? The Lord is the everlasting God, the Creator of the ends of the earth. He does not faint or grow weary, his understanding is unsearchable. He gives power to the faint, and to him who has no might he increases strength. Even youths shall faint and be weary, and young men shall fall exhausted; but they who wait for the Lord shall renew their strength, they shall mount up with wings like eagles, they shall run and not be weary, they shall walk and not faint.

Tuesday before Pentecost
1 Cor 12:4-7

Now there are varieties of gifts, but the same Spirit; and there are varieties of service, but the same Lord; and there are varieties of working, but it is the same God who inspires them all in every one. To each is given the manifestation of the Spirit for the common good.

Wednesday before Pentecost

Joel 2:28, 29

And it shall come to pass afterward, that I will pour out my spirit on all flesh; your sons and your daughters shall prophesy, your old men shall dream dreams, and your young men shall see visions. Even upon the menservants and maidservants in those days, I will pour out my spirit.

Thursday before Pentecost

Col 1:11-14

May you be strengthened with all power, according to his glorious might, for all endurance and patience with joy, giving thanks to the Father, who has qualified us to share in the inheritance of the saints in light. He has delivered us from the dominion of darkness and transferred us to the kingdom of his beloved Son, in whom we have redemption, the forgiveness of sins.

Friday before Pentecost

2 Cor 1:20-22

All the promises of God find their Yes in him. That is why we utter the men through him, to the glory of God. But it is God who establishes us with you in Christ, and has commissioned us; he has put his seal upon us and given us his Spirit in our hearts as a guarantee.

Saturday before Pentecost

2 Cor 3:17, 18

Now the Lord is the Spirit, and where the Spirit of the Lord is, there is freedom. And we all, with unveiled face, beholding the glory of the Lord, are being changed into his likeness from one degree of glory to another; for this comes from the Lord who is the Spirit.

Pentecost (Whitsunday)

2 Cor 1:21-22

It is God who establishes us with you in Christ, and has commissioned us; he has put his seal upon us and given us his Spirit in our hearts as a guarantee.

355

Ascension to Pentecost Prayer during the Day

O King enthroned on high,
Comforter and Spirit of truth,
you that are in all places and fill all things,
the treasury of blessings and the giver of life,
come and dwell with us,
cleanse us from every stain
and save our souls, O gracious One.

Byzantine Rite

Veni creator Spiritus

1.Come, O Creator Spirit, come,
  and make within out heart thy home;
to us thy grace celestial give,
  who of thy breathing move and live.

2.O Comforter, that name is thine,
  of God most high the gift divine;
the well of life, the fire of love,
  our souls' anointing from above.

3.Thou dost appear in sevenfold dower
  the sign of God's almighty power;
the Father's promise, making rich
  with saving truth our earthly speech.

4.Our senses with thy light inflame,
  our hearts to heavenly love reclaim;
our bodies' poor infirmity
  with strength perpetual fortify.

5.Our mortal foes afar repel,
  grant us henceforth in peace to dwell;
and so to us, with thee for guide,
  no ill shall come, no harm betide.

6.May we by thee the Father learn,
  and know the Son, and thee discern,
who art of both; and thus adore
  in perfect faith for evermore. Amen.

Before 10th *cent. Tr. and rev. Yattendon Hymnal*

Beata nobis gaudia

1.Rejoice! the year upon its way
  has brought again that blessèd day,
when on the chosen of the Lord
  the Holy Spirit was outpoured.

2.On each the fire, descending, stood
  in quivering tongues' similitude—
tongues, that their words might ready prove,
  and fire, to make them flame with love.

3.To all in every tongue they spoke;
  amazement in the crowd awoke,
who mocked, as overcome with wine,
  those who were filled with power divine.

4.These things were done in type that day,
  when Eastertide had passed away,
the number told which once set free
  the captive at the jubilee.

5.And now, O holy God, this day
  regard us as we humbly pray,
and send us, from thy heavenly seat,
  the blessings of the Paraclete.

6.To God the Father, God, the Son,
  and God the Spirit, praise be done;
may Christ the Lord upon us pour
  the Spirit's gift forevermore. Amen.

c 4th cent. Tr. R.E. Roberts

Collects

Seventh Sunday of Easter

O GOD the King of glory, who hast exalted thine only Son Jesus Christ with great triumph unto thy kingdom in heaven: we beseech thee, leave us not comfortless; but send to us thine Holy Spirit to comfort us, and exalt us unto the same place whither our Saviour Christ is gone before; who liveth and reigneth with thee and the Holy Spirit, one God, for ever and ever.

Pentecost

GOD, who as at this time didst teach the hearts of thy faithful people, by the sending to them the light of thy Holy Spirit: grant us by the same Spirit to have a right judgment in all things, and evermore to rejoice in his holy comfort; through the merits of Christ Jesus our Saviour, who liveth and reigneth with thee, in the unity of the same Spirit, one God, for ever and ever.

Office

Opening Sentence

God is love; and he that abides in love abides in God and God in him.

1 Jn 4:16

Post-Biblical Reading

Monday after Whitsunday

A reading from the sermons of Blessed John Henry Newman

Christ has promised he will be with us to the end, - be with us, not only as he is in the unity of the Father and the Son, not in the Omnipresence of the Divine Nature, but personally, as the Christ, as God and man; not present with us locally and sensibly, but still really, in our hearts and to our faith. And it is by the Holy Ghost that this gracious communion is effected. How he effects it we know not; in what precisely it consists, we know not. We see him not; but we are to believe that we possess him, - that we have been brought under the virtue of his healing hand, of his life-giving breath, of the manna flowing from his lips, and of the blood issuing from his side. And hereafter, on looking back, we shall be conscious that we have been thus favoured.

Such is the Day of the Lord in which we find ourselves, as if in fulfilment of the words of the prophet, 'The Lord my God shall come, and all the saints with thee. And it shall come to pass in that Day, that the light shall not be clear, nor dark: but it shall be one day which shall be known to the Lord, not day, nor

---

Bl.. John Henry Newman, 'The Spiritual Presence of Christ in the Church', in *Parochial and Plain Sermons, by J. H. Newman* VI (London: Rivingtons, 1881), pp. 133-135.

night: but it shall come to pass, that at evening time it shall be light' (Zech 14: 5-7). Nay, even before the end comes, Christians, on looking back on years past, will feel, at least in a degree, that Christ has been with them, though they knew it not, only believed it, at the time. They will even recollect then the burning of their hearts. Nay, though they seemed not even to believe any thing at the time, yet afterwards, if they have come to him in sincerity, they will experience a sort of heavenly fragrance and savour of immortality, when they least expect it, rising upon their minds, as if in token that God had been with them, and investing all that has taken place, which before seemed to them but earthly, with beams of glory.

And this is true, in one sense, of all the rites and ordinances of the Church, of all providences that happen to us; that, on looking back on them, though they seemed without meaning at the time, elicited no strong feeling, or were even painful and distasteful, yet if we come to them and submit to them in faith, they are afterwards transfigured, and we feel that it has been good for us to be there; and we have a testimony, as a reward of our obedience, that Christ has fulfilled his promise, and, as he said, is here through the Spirit, though he be with the Father.

Tuesday after Whitsunday

A reading from the sermons of Lancelot Andrewes

The Holy Ghost is the Alpha and Omega of all our solemnities. In his coming down all the feasts began; at his annunciation, when he descended on the Blessed Virgin, whereby the Son of God did take our nature, the nature of man. And in the Holy Ghost's coming they end, even in his descending this day upon the sons of men, whereby they actually become 'partakers of his nature, the nature of God' (2 Pet 1:4). Of which his last and great coming, in this text is the promise, and at this time the performance; that as promise and performance, so the text and time agree.

Lancelot Andrewes, 'A Sermon preached before the King's Majesty, at Whitehall, on the twenty-seventh of May, A. D. MDCX, being Whit-Sunday', in *Ninety-Six Sermons by the Right Honourable and Reverend Father in God Lancelot Andrewes,* III (Oxford: Parker, 1850), pp. 145-147.

Every promise is glad tidings, but every promise is not gospel; nor is it good to make a text of it while it is in suspense. But when it is 'so said and so done' (Ps 33:9), then it is a gospel, and may be preached on. Being then made good this day, the Church hath made it the Gospel of this day, it being the feast whereon it was to be and whereon it was paid.

This promise grew thus. They were to be deprived of Christ's presence: he to be gone. They were troubled with it, troubled at the very heart. In that state they needed comfort. A 'Comforter' he promiseth them. His promise is in manner of a deed; not absolute, but as it were with articles on both parts. A covenant on his part, a condition on theirs. He covenants two things; the one supposed, love, - 'If ye love me'. The other imposed – then 'keep my commandments' (Jn 14:15). These two on their part well and truly performed and kept, he stands bound to pray, and praying to procure them a 'Comforter', another in his stead. And that they might not be every other while to seek for a new one, that should not leave them as he did, but 'abide with them for ever' (Jn 14:16).

Many are the benefits that come to us by the Holy Ghost, and so his titles many. He is here expressed in the title of a 'Comforter'. Comfort never comes amiss, but it is most welcome to men in their estate here, troubled in mind. It may be, our estate is not as theirs was, and we have our little earthly consolations, which yet serve our turn well enough. But there is none of us but the day will come, when we shall need him and his comfort. It will be good to look after him; and the sooner the better. He came here, we see, before 'the third hour of the day' (Acts 2:15), that is, nine in the morning: let us not put him off till nine at night. It will be too late to seek for our oil when the bridegroom is coming.

These same articles were here drawn for them; but he that liketh the same conditions, may have title to the same covenant to the world's end. For to the world's end this covenant here holdeth; and the Holy Ghost offered to be sent – though not in visible manner as this day; it was meet it should be with some solemnity at his first coming, for the more credit, yet – sensibly to them that receive him.

Wednesday after Whitsunday

A reading from the writings of Dom Gregory Dix

In the primitive conception there is but one *eschaton*, one 'coming', the 'coming to the Father' of redeemed mankind, which is the realization of the Kingdom of God. That Kingdom is realized in its fullness in the sacrifice of Christ and its acceptance – his death and resurrection – of which the Eucharist is the *anamnesis* [the re-calling]. 'In him' all the redeemed enter into that Kingdom. That is the purpose and meaning of all history, however long it may continue. The Eucharist is the contact of time with the eternal fact of the Kingdom of God through Jesus. In it the Church within time continually, as it were, enters into its own eternal being in that Kingdom, 'in him', as Body of Christ, through his act. [...] If this interpretation of the original meaning of the Eucharist be correct, viz. that it is the contact of the Church within time with the single *eschaton*, the coming of the Kingdom of God beyond time, it should follow that one consequence within time should be the gift to the Church of that 'Spirit' by which, so to speak, the Church maintains itself in time as the Body of Christ. [...] As St Paul said, 'We have all been made to drink of one Spirit' (1 Cor 12:13), as Israel long before in the desert 'did all eat the same spiritual meat and did all drink the same spiritual drink' (1 Cor 10:4). [...]

At the root of all primitive eschatology lies the paradox that by the Christian life in this world you must strive 'to become what you are'. It is by the sacraments that you receive 'what you are', your true Christian being; it is by your life that you must 'become' what they convey. By baptism a Christian even in this world truly is 'a member of Christ, a child of God and an inheritor (not "heir") of the Kingdom of heaven'. But because he is in the Body of Christ within time, the gift of the Spirit is given to him in confirmation that by his life in time he may become these things in eternal fact. The Church is in the sight of God the Body of Christ; at the Eucharist and by the Eucharist for a moment it truly fulfils this, its eternal being; it becomes what it is. And the Church goes out from the Eucharist back to daily life in this world having 'received the Spirit of adoption, whereby we cry "Abba, Father"' (Rom 8:15), - the syllables always upon the lips of the Son when he dwelt in time. As St Thomas said, the 'spiritual benefit' received in this sacrament 'is the unity of the mystical body', -

Gregory Dix, *The Shape of the Liturgy* (London: Adam and Charles Black, 1982 [1945], 2nd edition), pp. 265-267.

and in the New Testament this unity is above all 'the unity of the Spirit' (Eph 4:3).

Thursday after Whitsunday

A reading from the sermons of Blessed John Henry Newman

If we consider the variety and dignity of the gifts ministered by the Spirit, we shall, perhaps, discern in a measure, why our state under the Gospel is called a state of glory. It is not uncommon, in the present day, to divide the works of the Holy Ghost in the Church into two kinds, miraculous and moral. By 'miraculous' are meant such as he manifested in the first ages of the Gospel, marvels out of the course of nature, addressed to our senses; such as the power of healing, of raising the dead, and the like; or again, such as speaking with tongues and prophecy. On the other hand, by 'moral' operations or influences are meant such as act upon our minds, and enable us to be what we otherwise could not be holy and accepted in all branches of the Christian character; in a word, all such as issue in sanctification, as it is called. [....] Granting then that the gift of the Spirit mentioned in Scripture includes in it both the miracles of the first ages and the influences of grace; granting also that the sanctifying grace bestowed in each Christian is given with far greater fullness, variety, and power, than it was vouchsafed to the Jews (whether it be eventually quenched or not); granting, too, that holiness is really the characteristic of that gift which the Holy Spirit ministers now, as miracles were its outward manifestation in the first ages; still all this is not a sufficient account of it; it is not equivalent to our great Gospel privilege, which is something deeper, wider, and more mysterious, though including both miracles and graces.

In truth, the Holy Ghost has taken up his abode in the Church in a variety of gifts, as a sevenfold Spirit. For instance, is the gift of the body's immortality miraculous or moral? Neither, in the common sense of the words; yet it is a gift bestowed on us in this life, and by the power of the Holy Ghost, according to the texts, 'Your body is the temple of the Holy Ghost (1 Cor 6:19), and 'He that raised up Christ from the dead shall also quicken your mortal bodies

---

Bl. John Henry Newman, 'The Gift of the Spirit', in *Parochial and Plain Sermons, by J. H. Newman* III (London: Rivingtons, 1881), pp. 258-260.

by his indwelling Spirit' (Rom 8:11). Again, is justification, or the application of Christ's merits to the soul, moral or miraculous? Neither; yet we are told that we are 'washed, hallowed, justified in the name of the Lord Jesus, and by the Spirit of our God' (1 Cor 6:11). Or is the gift of the Holy Ghost in Ordination miraculous or moral? It is neither the one nor the other, but a supernatural power of ministering effectually in holy things. Once more, is communion with Christ miraculous or moral? On the contrary, it is a real but mysterious union of nature with him, according to the text, 'We are members of his body' (Eph 5:30), from his flesh, and from his bones.

Such reflections as these are calculated, perhaps, to give us somewhat of a deeper view than is ordinarily admitted, of the character of that Gift which attends on the presence of the Holy Ghost in the Church, and which is called the gift of glory. I do not say that anything that has been just said has been sufficient to define it; rather I would maintain, that it cannot be defined. It cannot be limited; it cannot be divided, and exhausted by a division. This is the very faultiness of the division into miraculous and moral, useful as this may be for particular purposes, that it professes to embrace what is in fact incomprehensible and unfathomable. I would fain keep from the same mistake; and the instances already given may serve this purpose, enlarging our view without bounding it. The gift is denoted in Scripture by the vague and mysterious term 'glory'; and all the descriptions we can give of it can only, and should only, run out into a mystery.

Friday after Whitsunday

A reading from the sermons of Lancelot Andrewes

Among divided men or minds he will not dwell. Not but where unity and love is. In vain we talk of the Spirit without these. Aaron's ointment and the dew of Hermon – both types of him – ye know what psalm they belong to; it begins with 'brethren dwelling in unity' (Ps 133:1). It is in this psalm before, 'where men are of one mind in a house' (Ps 68:6) – there he delights to be. This very

---

Lancelot Andrewes, 'A Sermon preached before the King's Majesty, at Greenwich, on the twelfth of June, A. D. MDCXIV, being Whit-Sunday', in *Ninety-Six Sermons by the Right Honourable and Reverend Father in God Lancelot Andrewes,* III (Oxford: Parker, 1850), pp. 238-239.

day, they that received him were 'with one accord in one place' (Acts 1:14). That 'with one accord' is the adverb of the feast. And the Apostle in his comment on this verse – no better way, saith he, to preserve the 'unity of the Spirit', or the Spirit of unity, choose you whether, than in the 'bond of peace' (Eph 4:3). To say truth, who would be hired 'to dwell in Mesech' (Ps 120:5) where nothing is but continual jars and quarrels? Such places, such men, are even as torrid zones, not habitable by the Spirit, by this Spirit. But for the other spirit, the spirit of division, they are; a fit place for the devil, to dwell among such. Think of this seriously, and set it down, that 'at Salem is his Tabernacle' (Ps 76:2), and Salem is 'peace', and so the Fathers read it, in peace has been made his place. Make him that place and he will say, Here is my rest, 'here will I dwell, for I have delight therein'.

We said even now: to 'dwell among us', he must dwell *in* us; and in us he will 'dwell', if the fruits of his Spirit be found in us. And of his fruits the very first is love. And the fruit is as the tree is. For he himself is love, the essential love, and love-knot of the undivided Trinity.

Now to work love, the undoubted both sign and means of his dwelling, what better way, or how sooner wrought, than by the sacrament of love, at the feast of love, upon the feast-day of love; when Love descended with both his hands full of gifts for very love, to take up his dwelling with us?

You shall observe: there ever was and will be a near alliance between 'the gifts he sent' and 'the gifts he left us'. He left us the gifts of his body and blood. His body broken, and full of the characters of love all over. His blood shed, every drop whereof is a great drop of love. To those which were sent, these which were left, love, joy, peace, have a special connatural reference, to breed and to maintain each other. His body the Spirit of strength, his blood the Spirit of comfort; both, the Spirit of love.

A reading from Thomas Traherne, *Centuries of Meditations*

O thou who ascendest up on high, and ledst captivity captive, and gavest gifts unto men, as after thy ascension into heaven thou didst send thy Holy Spirit down upon thine Apostles in the form of a rushing mighty wind, and in the shape of cloven fiery tongues; send down the Holy Ghost upon me: breathe upon me, inspire me, quicken me, illuminate me, enflame me, fill me with the Spirit of God; that I may overflow with praises and thanksgivings as they did. Fill me with the riches of thy glory that Christ may dwell in my heart by faith, that I being rooted and grounded in Love may speak the wonderful Works of God. Let me be alive unto them: let me see them all, let me feel them all, let me enjoy them all: that I may admire the greatness of thy love unto my soul, and rejoice in communion with thee for evermore.

How happy, O Lord, am I, who am called to a communion with God the Father, Son, and Holy Ghost, in all their works and ways, in all their joys, in all their treasures, in all their glory! Who have such a Father, having in him the Fountain of Immortality, Rest, and Glory, and the joy of seeing him creating all things for my sake! Such a Son, having in him the means of peace and felicity, and the joy of seeing him redeeming my soul, by his sufferings on the cross, and doing all things that pertain to my salvation between the Father and me. Such a Spirit and such a Comforter dwelling in me to quicken, enlighten, and enable me, and to awaken all the powers of my soul that night and day the same mind may be in me that was in Christ Jesus! [...]

O let me know thee, thou Spirit of Truth, be thou always with me, and dwell within me. How is it possible, but thou shouldst be an infinite Comforter; who givest me a being as wide as eternity; a well-being as blessed as the Deity; a temple of glory in the omnipresence of God, and a light wherein to enjoy the New Jerusalem! An immoveable inheritance, and an everlasting Kingdom that cannot be shaken! Thou art he who shewest me all the treasures in heaven and earth, who enablest me to turn afflictions into pleasures, and to enjoy mine enemies! Thou enablest me to love as I am beloved, and to be blessed in God: thou sealest me up unto the Day of Redemption, and givest me a foretaste of heaven upon earth. Thou art my God and my exceeding joy, my Comforter and

Thomas Traherne, *Centuries of Meditations*, I. 95, 98, in Thomas Traherne, *Centuries* (London and Oxford: Mowbrays, 1975 [1960]), pp. 49-50, 51-52.

my strength for evermore. Thou representest all things unto me, which the Father and the Son hath done for me. Thou fillest me with courage against all assaults, and enablest me to overcome in all temptations; thou makest me immoveable by the very treasures and the joys which thou shewest in me. Oh never leave me nor forsake me, but remain with me, and be my comfort forever!

Short Readings for Prayer during the Day

Monday after Whitsunday   *Is 40:28-31*
Have you not known? Have you not heard? The Lord is the everlasting God, the Creator of the ends of the earth. He does not faint or grow weary, his understanding is unsearchable. He gives power to the faint, and to him who has no might he increases strength. Even youths shall faint and be weary, and young men shall fall exhausted; but they who wait for the Lord shall renew their strength, they shall mount up with wings like eagles, they shall run and not be weary, they shall walk and not faint.

Tuesday after Whitsunday   *1 Cor 12:4-7*
Now there are varieties of gifts, but the same Spirit; and there are varieties of service, but the same Lord; and there are varieties of working, but it is the same God who inspires them all in every one. To each is given the manifestation of the Spirit for the common good.

Wednesday after Whitsunday   *Joel 2:28, 29*
And it shall come to pass afterward, that I will pour out my spirit on all flesh; your sons and your daughters shall prophesy, your old men shall dream dreams, and your young men shall see visions. Even upon the menservants and maidservants in those days, I will pour out my spirit.

Thursday after Whitsunday   *Col 1:11-14*

May you be strengthened with all power, according to his glorious might, for all endurance and patience with joy, giving thanks to the Father, who has qualified us to share in the inheritance of the saints in light. He has delivered us from the dominion of darkness and transferred us to the kingdom of his beloved Son, in whom we have redemption, the forgiveness of sins.

Friday after Whitsunday   *2 Cor 1:20-22*

All the promises of God find their Yes in him. That is why we utter the men through him, to the glory of God. But it is God who establishes us with you in Christ, and has commissioned us; he has put his seal upon us and given us his Spirit in our hearts as a guarantee.

Saturday after Whitsunday   *2 Cor 3:17, 18*

Now the Lord is the Spirit, and where the Spirit of the Lord is, there is freedom. And we all, with unveiled face, beholding the glory of the Lord, are being changed into his likeness from one degree of glory to another; for this comes from the Lord who is the Spirit.

Pentecost Prayer during the Day

O King enthroned on high,
Comforter and Spirit of truth,
you that are in all places and fill all things,
the treasury of blessings and the giver of life,
come and dwell with us,
cleanse us from every stain
and save our souls, O gracious One.

Byzantine Rite

369

Collect

O LORD, from whom all good things do come: grant to us thy humble servants, that by thy holy inspiration we may think those things that be good and, by thy merciful guiding may perform the same; through Jesus Christ thy Son, our Lord, who liveth and reigneth with thee, in the unity of the Holy Spirit, one God, for ever and ever.

Trinity Sunday

Office

Opening Sentence

God is love; and he that abides in love abides in God and God in him.

1 Jn 4:16

Post-Biblical Reading

A reading from St Anselm, *The Proslogion*

You alone then, Lord are what you are and you are who you are. For what is one thing as a whole and another as to its parts, and has in it something mutable, is not altogether what it is. And what began to exist from non-existence, and can be thought not to exist, and returns to non-existence unless it subsists through some other, and what has had a past existence but does not now exist, and a future existence but does not yet exist – such a thing does not exist in a strict and absolute sense. But you are what you are, for whatever you are at any time and in any way this you are wholly and forever.

And you are the being who exists in a strict and absolute sense because you have neither past nor future existence but only present existence; nor can you be thought not to exist at any time. And you are life and light and wisdom and blessedness and eternity and many suchlike good things; and yet you are nothing save the one and supreme good, you who are completely sufficient unto yourself, needing nothing, but rather he whom all things need in order that they may have being and well-being.

You are this good, O God the Father; this is your Word, that is to say, your Son. For there cannot be any other than what you are, or any thing greater or lesser than you, in the Word by which you utter yourself. For your Word is true as you are truthful and is therefore the very truth that you are and that is not other than you. And you are so simple that there cannot be born of you any other than what you are. This itself is the Love, one and common to you and to

---

St Anselm, *Proslogion* 22-24, in *Anselm of Canterbury. The Major Works.* Edited with an Introduction by Brian Davies and G. R. Evans (Oxford: Oxford University Press, 1998), pp. 99-101.

your Son, that is the Holy Spirit proceeding from both. For this same Love is not unequal to you or to your Son since your love for yourself and him, and his Love for you and himself, are as great as you and he are. Nor is that other than you and than him which is not different from you and him; nor can there proceed from your supreme simplicity what is other than that from which it proceeds. Thus, whatever each is singly, that the whole Trinity is altogether, Father, Son, and Holy Spirit; since each singly is not other than the supremely simple unity and the supremely unified simplicity which can be neither multiplied nor differentiated.

'Moreover, one thing is necessary' (Lk 10:42). This is, moreover, that one thing necessary in which is every good, or rather, which is wholly and uniquely and completely and solely good.

Now, my soul, rouse and lift up your whole understanding and think as much as you can on what kind and how great this good is. For if particular goods are enjoyable, consider carefully how enjoyable is that good which contains the joyfulness of all goods; not a joy such as have experienced in created things, but as different from this as the Creator differs from the creature. For if life that is created is good, how good is the Life that creates? If the salvation that has been brought about is joyful, how joyful is the Salvation that brings about all salvation? If wisdom in the knowledge of things that have been brought into being is lovable, how lovable is the Wisdom that has brought all things into being out of nothing? Finally, if there are many great delights in delightful things, of what kind and how great is the delight in him who made these same delightful things?

Short Reading for Prayer during the Day *Gal 4:4-7*
When the time had fully come, God sent forth his Son, born of woman, born under the law, to redeem those who were under the law, so that we might receive adoption as sons. And because you are sons, God has sent the Spirit of his Son into our hearts, crying, 'Abba! Father!' So through God you are no longer a slave but a son, and if a son then an heir.

Collect

ALMIGHTY and everlasting God, who hast given unto us thy servants grace, by the confession of a true faith to acknowledge the glory of the eternal Trinity, and in the power of thy Divine Majesty to worship the Unity: we beseech thee, that thou wouldst keep us steadfast in this faith, and evermore defend us from all adversities; who livest and reignest, one God, for ever and ever.

Corpus Christi

Office

Opening Sentence

Every time we eat this bread and drink this cup, we proclaim the Lord's death until he comes.

cf 1 Cor 11:26

Hymns

Pange lingua gloriosi corporis

1.Of the glorious Body telling,
  O my tongue, its mysteries sing,
and the Blood, all price excelling,
  which the world's eternal King,
in a noble womb once dwelling
  shed for the world's ransoming.

2.Given for us, descending,
  of a Virgin to proceed,
Man with man in converse blending,
  scattered he the Gospel seed,
till his sojourn drew to ending,
  which he closed in wondrous deed.

3.At the last great Supper lying
  circled by his brethren's band,
meekly with the law complying,
  first he finished its command;
then, immortal Food supplying,
  gave himself with his own hand.

4.Word made Flesh, by word he maketh
  very bread his Flesh to be;
man in wine Christ's Blood partaketh:
  and if senses fail to see,
faith alone the true heart waketh
  to behold the mystery.

5.Therefore we, before him bending,
  this great Sacrament revere;
types and shadows have their ending,
  for the newer rite is here;
faith, our outward sense befriending,
  makes the inward vision clear.

6.Glory let us give, and blessing
  to the Father and the Son;
honour, might and praise addressing,
  while eternal ages run;
ever too his love confessing,
  who, from both, with both is one.

Amen.

St Thomas Aquinas,
Tr. J.M. Neale, E. Caswall, *and others*

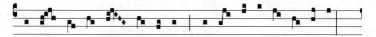

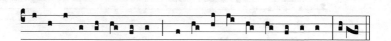

Verbum supernum prodiens

1. The Word of God, proceeding forth
   yet leaving not his Father's side,
and going to his work on earth,
   had reached at length life's eventide;

2. By false disciple to be given
   to foemen for his blood athirst.
himself, the living Bread from heaven,
   he gave to his disciples first.

3. In twofold form of sacrament
   he gave his Flesh, he gave his Blood,
yhat man, of twofold substance blent,
   might wholly feed on mystic food.

4. In birth man's fellow-man was he,
   his meat while sitting at the board;
he died, his ransomer to be,
   he reigns to be his great reward.

5. O saving Victim! opening wide
   the gate of heaven to man below,
our foes press hard on every side,
   thine aid supply, thy strength bestow.

6. All praise and thanks to thee ascend
   for evermore, blest One in Three;
O grant us life that shall not end
   in our true native land with thee. Amen.

St Thomas Aquinas.
Tr. J. M. Neale, E. Caswall, *and others.*

Post-Biblical Reading

A reading from Nicholas Love, *Mirror of the Blessed Life of Jesus Christ*

When he had washed his disciples' feet, and was again up with them where he before sat at the Supper, as it is said, as for an end of the sacrifices of the Old Law and beginning of the New Testament, making himself our Sacrifice, he took bread in his holy hands and lifted up his eyes to his Father, God almighty, and blessed the bread and said the words of consecration there over, by virtue of the which words, bread was turned into his Body, and then he gave it to his disciples and said, 'Take and eat for truly this is my Body that shall be taken and given for you'. And after in the same manner, taking the chalice with wine said, 'Take and drink all hereof, for this is my Blood that shall be outpoured for you and for many in remission of sins'. And afterwards he gave them power of that consecration and made priests of them all and said, 'This do ye as often as ye take it in commemoration and mind of me'.

Take now good heed here, thou Christian man, but specially thou priest, how devoutly, how diligently and truly, the Lord Jesus Christ first made this precious Sacrament and after with his blessed hands ministered it, and communicated that blessed - and his beloved - company. And on the other side, take heed with what devout wonder they first saw him make that wonderful and excellent Sacrament, and after with what dread and reverence they took it and received it of him. Truly at this time they left all their natural human reason, and only rested in true belief to all that he said and did, believing without any doubt that he was God and could not err. And so must thou do that would feel and have the virtue and the spiritual sweetness of this blessed Sacrament.

This is that sweet and precious Memorial that in sovereign manner makes man's soul worthy and pleasing to God, as often as it is duly received, either by true and devout meditation of his Passion or else, and that more especially, in sacramental eating thereof. Wherefore with reason this excellent gift of love should kindle man's soul and inflame it all wholly into the Giver thereof, our

Nicholas Love, *Mirror of the Blessed Life of Jesus Christ*, XXXIX, in *Nicholas Love's Mirror of the Blessed Life of Jesus Christ*. A Critical Edition based on Cambridge University Library Additional MSS 6578 and 6686, edited with introduction, notes and glossary by Michael G. Sargent (New York and London: Garland, 1992), pp. 151-152. Text slightly amended for modern readers.

Lord Jesus Christ. For there is nothing that he might give or leave to us that is more dear, more sweet, more profitable, than himself. For without any doubt he that we receive in the Sacrament of the altar is himself God's Son, Jesus, that took flesh and blood and was born of the Virgin Mary and that suffered death on the Cross for us, and rose the third day from death to life and after went up into heaven and sits on the Father's right side, and that shall come in the day of doom and judge all mankind. In whose power is both life and death, that made both heaven and hell and that only may save us or damn us forever without end.

And so he that is himself God and man is contained in that little Host that thou seest in form of bread, and every day is offered up to the Father of heaven for our spiritual health, and everlasting salvation.

Short Reading for Prayer during the Day *Wis 16:20*
You gave your people the food of angels, and without their toil you supplied them from heaven with bread ready to eat, providing every pleasure and suited to every taste.

Collect
O GOD, who under a wonderful sacrament hast left unto us a memorial of thy passion: grant us, we beseech thee, so to venerate the sacred mysteries of thy Body and Blood, that we may ever perceive within ourselves the fruit of thy redemption; who livest and reignest for ever and ever.

or

GRANT, O Lord, we pray: that we may delight for all eternity in that share in thy divine life, which is foreshadowed in the present age by our reception of thy precious Body and Blood; who livest and reignest for ever and ever.

Roman Missal (adapted)

As the Blessed Sacrament is exposed for veneration, the following or some other suitable hymn may be sung.

O salutaris hostia

O SAVING VICTIM, opening wide
   the gate of heaven to man below:
our foes press hard on every side;
   thine aid supply, thy strength bestow.

All praise, O Lord, to thee ascend
   for evermore blest One in Three:
O grant us life that shall not end,
   in our true native land with thee.

Tr. J.M.Neale, E.Caswall, and others

There may follow a litany, prayers or a period of silent prayer

The following or some other suitable hymn may be sung.

Tantum ergo

THEREFORE WE, before him, bending,
   this great Sacrament revere;
types and shadows have their ending,
   for the newer rite is here;
faith, our outward sense befriending,
   makes the inward vision clear.

Glory let us give, and blessing
   to the Father and the Son;
honour, might and praise addressing,
   while eternal ages run;
ever too his love confessing,
   who from both, with both, is one.

Tr. J.M.Neale, E.Caswall, and others

379

	Thou gavest them bread from heaven: (Alleluia.)
People	**containing in itself all sweetness. (Alleluia.)**

Alleluia is added in Eastertide and at Corpus Christi.

The collect follows.

Let us pray.

O GOD, who under a wonderful Sacrament hast left unto us a memorial of thy passion: grant us, we beseech thee, so to venerate the sacred mysteries of thy Body and Blood, that we may ever perceive within ourselves the fruit of thy redemption; who livest and reignest for ever and ever.

The Priest makes the sign of the cross over the people with the monstrance.

Other devotions may follow.

The Divine Praises

Blessed be God.
Blessed be his holy name.
Blessed be Jesus Christ, true God and true man.
Blessed be the name of Jesus.
Blessed be his most sacred heart.
Blessed be his most precious blood.
Blessed be Jesus in the most holy sacrament of the altar.
Blessed be the Holy Spirit the Paraclete.
Blessed be the great Mother of God, Mary most holy.
Blessed be her holy and immaculate conception.
Blessed be her glorious assumption.
Blessed be the name of Mary, Virgin and mother.
Blessed be Saint Joseph, her spouse most chaste.
Blessed be God in his angels and in his saints.

Louis Felici SJ

Psalm 117

Antiphon
Let us adore for ever
the most holy Sacrament.

1   O praise the Lord, all ye heathen :
     praise him, all ye nations.
2   For his merciful kindness is ever more and more towards us :
     and the truth of the Lord endureth for ever. Praise the Lord.

     Glory be to the Father, and to the Son :
     and to the Holy Spirit;
     as it was in the beginning, is now, and ever shall be :
     world without end. Amen.

Let us adore for ever
the most holy Sacrament.

*During the reposition of the Blessed Sacrament the following, or some
other suitable texts, are used.*

Adoration of Christ in the Blessed Sacrament

Blessed and praised be Jesus Christ in the most holy
  sacrament.
Hosanna, hosanna, hosanna in excelsis.

or

Blessed, hallowed and adored
be Jesus Christ on his throne of glory
and in the most holy sacrament of the altar.
(Alleluia. Alleluia.) Amen.

Office

Opening Sentence

God, who is rich in mercy, out of the great love with which he loved us, made us alive together with Christ, that he might show the immeasurable riches of his grace in kindness toward us in Christ Jesus.

Ephesians 2:4, 5, 7

Post-Biblical Reading

A reading from the *Meditation of the Five Wounds of Jesu Christ*

Behold especially the five most notable wounds, two in his blessed hands, and two in his blessed feet, and the most open wound in his right side.

Into these wounds of Christ's blessed hands and feet (with Thomas of India) put in thy fingers, - that is to say, thy most subtle thoughts and desires.

And in the wounds of Christ's blessed side, since it is the largest and deepest, put in all thine hand, - that is to say, all thy love and all thy works; and there feel Christ's blessed heart so hot, loving thee; and there feel Christ's blessed heart-blood shed for thee and to ransom thy soul; also there feel the water of Christ's side streaming out, as of a well of life, for to wash thee and all mankind of sin.

And then seize up water of everlasting life without end out of these five most open wounds of Christ, as out of five well-springs.

And understand, see and behold and learn, that the wound in Christ's right hand is the well of wisdom: the wound in Christ's left hand is the well of mercy: the wound in Christ's right foot is the well of grace: the wound in

---

Anonymous, *A Meditation of the Five Wounds of Jesu Christ* (MS University College, 87, f. 262), in *A Book of the Love of Jesus. A Collection of Ancient English Devotions in Prose and Verse*, compiled and edited by Robert Hugh Benson (London: Pitman, 1906), pp. 82-83; 85-86.

Christ's left foot is the well of ghostly comfort: the largest and deepest wound, that which is in Christ's right side, is the well of everlasting life. […]

Out of the largest and deepest well of everlasting life in the most open wound in Christ's blessed side seize up deepest and heartliest water of joy and bliss without end, beholding there inwardly how Christ Jesu, God and man, to bring thee to everlasting life, suffered that hard and hideous death on the cross, and suffered his side to be opened and himself to be pierced to the heart with that dreadful spear; - and so with that dole-full stroke of the spear there gushed out of Christ's side that blissful flood of water and blood to ransom us, water of his side to wash us, and blood of his heart to buy us.

For love of these blessed wounds creep into this hot bath of Christ's heart-blood, and there bathe thee: for there was never sin of man nor of woman, thought nor wrought, that was laved with lovely sorrow and hearty repentance, that there is not in this well full remission to buy it, and water of life fully to cleanse and wash it.

Therefore rest thee here, comfort thee here, live in Christ's heart without end.

Short Reading for Prayer during the Day   *Rom 5:8-9*
God shows his love for us in that while we were yet sinners Christ died for us. Since, therefore, we are now justified by his blood, much more shall we be saved by him from the wrath of God.

Collect
O LORD Jesu Christ, Son of the living God, who didst come down from heaven to earth from the bosom of the Father, and didst bear five wounds on the cross, and didst pour forth thy precious blood for the remission of our sins: we humbly beseech thee that at the day of judgment we may be set at thy right hand, and hear from thee that most comfortable word, Come, ye blessed into my Father's kingdom; who livest and reignest with the Father in the unity of the Holy Spirit, one God, for ever and ever.

Dedication Festival

and the Feast of the Dedication of the Basilica
of Saint John Lateran (9th November)

Office

Opening Sentence

How awesome is this place! This is none other than the house of
God, and this is the gate of heaven.

Gen 28:17

Post-Biblical Reading

A reading from the sermons of John Mason Neale

'And Peter answered him and said, Lord, if it be thou, bid me come unto thee
on the water. And he said, Come. And when Peter was come down out of the
ship he walked on the water to go to Jesus' (Mt 14:28-29). Can heart of man
conceive anything more beautiful than that midnight walk of our Lord over the
stormy waves? than the solitude, and wildness and desolation of the scene. On
the one hand, deep calling to deep because of the voice of the waterpipes, the
rushing and raging of the billows, the howling of the wind the drifting of the
dark, angry clouds over the moon: on the other – the holiness and majesty of
that presence, the resting of those feet on the surge, those blessed feet
afterwards to be anointed and kissed by that happy penitent, afterwards to be
fastened with cruel nails to the bitter Cross; shedding peace, as it were, around
them; turning, for the time being, the angry swell into a very haven of peace.
'Thy way is in the sea, and thy paths in the great waters, and thy footsteps are
not known' (Ps 77:19).

And see how, in its mystical sense, this journey of our Lord's corresponds with
that other time when his disciples were still toiling on the sea; but he had done

---

John Mason Neale, 'Sermon XIII. He said, Come', in *Occasional Sermons, Preached
in Various Churches,* by the Rev. J. M. Neale, (London: Hayes, 1873), pp. 143-
147.

with it for ever. 'When the morning was now come, Jesus stood on the shore' (Jn 21:4). Now it was night, deep dark night, and he was surrounded by the raging waves. Oh how well then, in the night of this world, he knows how to sympathise with his tempest-tossed followers! Oh how well he understands their cry: 'Let not the water-flood drown me, neither let the deep swallow me up!' (Ps 69:15) And oh, how well also he knows what is that glory, what is that peace, what is that Beatific Vision when the storms of this world shall be passed, and the morning of the resurrection shall have some, and we also shall stand with him on the shore of our true and everlasting Country!

And why did he thus enter on that wonderful path, treading down the waters beneath him – he, the true light in that darkness: he, the true peace in that turmoil: he, the rest and repose of every faithful heart on that tossing and heaving deep? Why? He had a little band that loved him toiling on those same waters: in hard labour, in much peril, constrained by him to enter into them and then, - so it seemed to flesh and blood, deserted by him on them. It is them that he seeks; for them he labours: in all their afflictions he is afflicted; and he goes, not by an angel now, but in his own dear presence, to save them.

My brethren, the likeness is not far to seek; and the day reminds me of it. This day we commemorate the dedication of a Church, not only endeared to you by many and many a tie of hallowed recollections, of seasons in which you have been very near to God: of times when the Immaculate Lamb was sacrificed on your Altar, when you yourselves felt that you were indeed incorporate with him – a Church dear to you, I say, for man and many such a season, - but dear to us all, a comfort to us all, yes, and an example and a pattern. It is hard for you to imagine, you who have the great privilege of joining in God's service here, of enduring in common the reproach of Christ, of fighting in common that battle which all true Catholics are now more especially called to fight; you cannot imagine, when one is in the habit of bearing the burden and heat of the day alone, with strong enemies and weak friends, isolated from human help and sympathy, isolated, yes, and, but for the God of all consolation, desolate, - what is the joy, and gladness, and encouragement of looking as such a congregation as this now before me, and to feel that the seven thousand in Israel still remain, Yes, you may be, like the Apostles, in the storm, in the night, in peril, in fear; but the ear of faith can already hear the footfall of the Lord Jesus on the billows, as he comes to your assistance. 'O, thou afflicted, tossed with tempest, and not comforted; behold, I will lay thy stones with fair colours, and will lay thy foundations with sapphires' (Is 54:11). God grant it! God grant that your beloved priest may year by year see the living temple of elect souls grow higher and higher about him, display lovelier and lovelier hues, still it become a part of the house not made with hands, eternal in the heavens!

Short Reading for Prayer during the Day   *1 Cor 3:16-17*

Do you not know that you are God's temple and that God's Spirit dwells in you? If any one destroys God's temple, God will destroy him. For God's temple is holy, and that temple you are.

Collect

ALMIGHTY God, to whose glory we celebrate the dedication of this house of prayer: we praise thee for the many blessings thou hast given to those who worship thee here: and we pray that all who seek thee in this place may find thee, and, being filled with the Holy Spirit, may become a living temple acceptable to thee; who liveth and reigneth with thee, in the unity of the Holy Spirit, one God, for ever and ever.

IV. Times and Seasons

Part V Temporale:

Time after Trinity

Time after Trinity

During Time after Trinity, *the Roman Lectionary and Propers, Sundays and* weeks per annum, *are the norm. Where the series of Sundays after Trinity is followed, the non-scriptural readings in this section will be pertinent and useful.*

Office

Opening Sentence *(General)*
God is Spirit: and they that worship him must worship him in spirit and in truth.

Jn 4:24

Hymns

Morning Prayer (General)   *Prime*

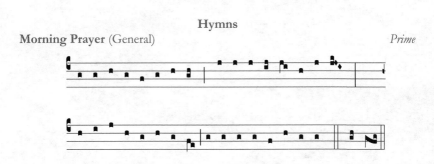

Iam lucis orto sidere

1.Now that the daylight fills the sky,
  we lift our hearts to God on high,
that he, in all we do or say,
  would keep us free from harm today.

2.Would guard our hearts and tongues from strife,
  from anger's din would hide our life,
from all ill sights would turn our eyes;
  would close our ears from vanities.

3.Would keep our inmost conscience pure
  our souls from folly would secure,
would bid us check the pride of sense
  with due and holy abstinence.

4.So we, when this new day is gone,
  and night in turn is drawing on,
with conscience by the world unstained
  shall praise his name for victory gained

5.All laud to God the Father be;
  all praise, eternal Son, to thee;
all glory, as is ever meet,
  to God the holy Paraclete. Amen.

5th cent. Tr. J.M. Neale

388

Rerum Deus tenax vigor

1.O Strength and Stay upholding all creation,
  who ever dost thyself unmoved abide;
 yet day by day the light in due gradation
  from hour to hour through all its changes guide.

2.Grant to life's day a calm unclouded ending,
  an eve untouched by shadows of decay,
 the brightness of a holy deathbed blending
  with dawning glories of the eternal day.

3.Hear us, O Father, gracious and forgiving,
  through Jesus Christ thy co-eternal Word,
 who, with the Holy Ghost, by all things living
  now and to endless ages art adored. Amen.

Ascribed to St Ambrose, Tr. J. Ellerton, F. J. A. Hart
Tune: Strength and Stay, J. B. Dykes

Evening Prayer I   *Vespers I*

Deus creator omnium

1. Creator of the earth and sky,
    ruling the firmament on high,
   clothing the day with robes of light,
    blessing with gracious sleep the night,

2. That rest may comfort weary men,
    and brace to useful toil again,
   and soothe awhile the harassed mind,
    and sorrow's heavy load unbind:

3. Day sinks; we thank thee for thy gift;
    night comes; and once again we lift
   our prayers and vows and hymns, that we
    against all ills may shielded be.

4. Thee let the secret heart acclaim,
    thee let our tuneful voices name,
   round thee our chaste afflictions cling,
    thee sober reason own as King.

5. That when black darkness closes day,
    and shadows thicken round our way,
   faith may no darkness know, and night
    from faith's clear beam may borrow light.

6. Rest not, my heaven-born mind and will;
    rest, all ye thoughts and deeds of ill;
   may faith its watch unwearied keep,
    and cool the dreaming warmth of sleep.

7. From cheats of sense, Lord, keep me free,
    and let my heart's depth dream of thee;
   let not my envious foe draw near,
    to break my rest with any fear.

8. Pray we the Father and the Son,
    and Holy Ghost: O Three in One,
   blest Trinity, whom all obey,
    guard thou thy sheep by night and day. Amen.

St Ambrose, *Tr.* Charles Bigg

390

Æterne rerum conditor

1. Transcendent God in whom we live,
   the Resurrection and the Light,
   we sing for you a morning hymn
   to end the silence of the night.

2. When early cock begins to crow
   and everything from sleep awakes,
   new life and hope spring up again
   while our of darkness colour breaks.

3. Creator of all things that are,
   the measure and the end of all,
   forgiving God, forget our sins,
   and hear our prayers before we call.

4. Praise Father, Son and Holy Ghost,
   blest Trinity and source of grace,
   who call us out of nothingness
   to find in you our resting-place. Amen.

St Ambrose, *Tr. Stanbrook Abbey Hymnal*

Lucis creator optime

1.O blest Creator of the light,
 who mak'st the day with radiance bright,
and o'er the forming world didst call
 the light from chaos first of all.

2.Whose wisdom joined in meet array
 the morn and eve, and named them day:
night comes with all its darkling fears;
 regard thy people's prayers and tears.

3.Lest, sunk in sin, and whelmed with strife,
 they lose the gift of endless life;
while thinking but the thoughts of time,
 they weave new chains of woe and crime.

4.But grant them grace that they may strain
 the heavenly gate and prize to gain:
each harmful lure aside to cast,
 and purge away each error past.

5.O Father, that we ask be done,
 through Jesus Christ, thine only Son;
who, with the Holy Ghost and thee,
 doth live and reign eternally. Amen.

6th cent. Tr. J. M. Neale

Monday

Morning Prayer *Lauds*

Splendor paternæ Gloria

1.O splendour of God's glory bright,
  O thou that bringest light from light;
O Light of light, light's living spring,
  O day, all days illumining.

2.O thou true Sun, on us thy glance
  let fall in royal radiance;
the Spirit's sanctifying beam
  upon our earthly senses stream.

3.The Father, too, our prayers implore,
  Father of glory evermore;
the Father of all grace and might,
  to banish sin from our delight.

4.To guide whate'er we nobly do,
  with love all envy to subdue;
to make ill fortune turn to fair,
  and give us grace our wrongs to bear.

5.Our mind be in his keeping placed
  our body true to him and chaste,
where only faith her fire shall feed,
  to burn the tares of Satan's seed.

6.And Christ to us for food shall be,
  from him our drink that welleth free,
the Spirit's wine, that maketh whole,
  and, mocking not, exalts the soul.

7.Rejoicing may this day go hence;
  like virgin dawn our innocence,
like fiery noon our faith appear,
  nor known the gloom of twilight drear.

8.Morn is in rosy chariot borne;
  let him come forth our perfect morn,
the Word in God the Father one,
  the Father perfect in the Son.

9.All laud to God the Father be;
  all praise, eternal Son, to thee;
all glory, as is ever meet,
  to God the holy Paraclete.

St Ambrose, *Tr. Yattendon Hymnal*

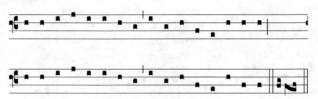

Immense cæli conditor

1.O boundless Wisdom, God most high,
  O Maker of the earth and sky,
who bid'st the parted waters flow
  in heaven above, on earth below.

2.The streams on earth, the clouds in heaven,
  by thee their ordered bounds were given,
lest 'neath the untempered fires of day
  the parched soil should waste away.

3.E'en so on us who seek thy face
  pour forth the waters of thy grace;
renew the fount of life within,
  and quench the wasting fires of sin.

4.Let faith discern the eternal Light
  beyond the darkness of the night,
and through the mists of falsehood see
  the path of truth revealed by thee.

5.O Father, that we ask be done,
  through Jesus Christ, thine only Son;
who, with the Holy Ghost and thee,
  doth live and reign eternally. Amen.

c.6th cent. Tr. Gabriel Gillett (1873-1948)

Ales diei nuntius

1.The wingèd herald of the day
   proclaims the morn's approaching ray:
and Christ the Lord our souls excites,
   and so to endless life invites.

2.Take up thy bed, to each he cries,
   who sick or wrapped in slumber lies;
and chaste and just and sober stand
   and watch: my coming is at hand.

3.With earnest cry, with tearful care,
   call we the Lord to hear our prayer;
while supplication, pure and deep,
   forbids each chastened heart to sleep.

4.Do thou, O Christ, our slumbers wake;
   do thou the chains of darkness break:
purge thou our former sins away,
   and in our souls new light display.

5.All laud to God the Father be,
   all praise, eternal Son, to thee;
all glory, as is ever meet,
   to God the holy Paraclete

Prudentius, *Tr.* J. M. Neale

395

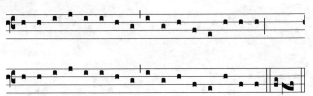

Telluris ingens conditor

1.Earth's mighty Maker, whose command
  raised from the sea the solid land,
and drove each billowy heap away,
  and bade the earth stand firm for ay.

2.That so, with flowers of golden hue,
  the seeds of each it might renew;
and fruit trees bearing fruit might yield--
  and pleasant pasture of the field;

3.Our spirit's rankling wounds efface
  with dewy freshness of thy grace:
that grief may cleanse each deed of ill,
  and o'er each lust may triumph still.

4.Let every soul thy law obey,
  and keep from every evil way;
rejoice each promised good to win
  and flee from every mortal sin.

5.O Father, that we ask be done,
  through Jesus Christ, thine only Son;
who, with the Holy Ghost and thee,
  doth live and reign eternally. Amen.

c.7th cent. Tr Anon (1854)

Nox et tenebræ et nubile

1. Ye clouds and darkness, hosts of night,
   that breed confusion and affright,
begone! o'erhead the dawn shines clear,
   the light breaks in, and Christ is here.

2. Earth's gloom flees broken and dispersed,
   by the sun's piercing shafts coerced:
the day-star's eyes rain influence bright,
   and colours glimmer back to sight.

3. Thee, Christ, alone we know; to thee
   we bend in pure simplicity;
our songs with tears to thee arise;
   prove thou our hearts with thy clear eyes.

4. Though we be stained with blots within,
   thy quickening rays shall purge our sin;
light of the Morning Star, thy grace
   shed on us from thy cloudless face.

5. All laud to God the Father be,
   all praise, eternal Son, to thee;
all glory, as is ever meet,
   to God the holy Paraclete. Amen.

Prudentius, *Tr.* Robert Martin Pope (1865-1944)

Cæli Deus sanctissime

1.Most holy Lord and God of Heaven,
   who to the glowing sky hast given
the fires that in the east are born
   with gradual splendours of the morn;

2.Who, on the fourth day, didst reveal
   the sun's enkindled flaming wheel,
didst set the moon her ordered ways,
   and stars their ever-winding maze;

3.That each in its appointed way
   might separate the night from day,
and of the seasons through the year
   the well-remembered signs declare;

4.Illuminate our hearts within,
   and cleanse our minds from stain of sin;
unburdened of our guilty load
   may we, unfettered, serve our God.

5.O Father, that we ask be done,
   through Jesus Christ, thine only Son;
who, with the Holy Ghost and thee,
   doth live and reign eternally. Amen.

4th or 5th cent. Tr. Maurice Frederick Bell (1862-1931)

Magnæ Deus potentiæ

1. Almighty God, who from the flood
   didst bring to light a twofold brood;
   part in the firmament to fly,
   and part in ocean's depths to lie;

2. Appointing fishes in the sea,
   and fowls in open air to be,
   that each, by origin the same,
   its separate dwelling place might claim:

3. Grant that thy servants, by the tide
   of blood and water purified,
   no guilty fall from thee may know,
   nor death eternal undergo.

4. Be none submerged in sin's distress,
   none lifted up in boastfulness;
   that contrite hearts be not dismayed,
   nor haughty souls in ruin laid.

5. O Father, that we ask be done,
   through Jesus Christ thine only Son;
   who, with the Holy Ghost and thee,
   doth live and reign eternally. Amen.

6th or 7th cent. Tr. J. M. Neale

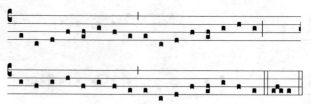

Æterna cæli gloria

1. Eternal Glory of the sky,
   blest Hope of frail humanity,
the Father's sole begotten One,
   yet born a spotless Virgin's Son!

2. Uplift us with thine arm of might,
   and let our hearts rise pure and bright,
and, ardent in God's praises, pay
   the thanks we owe him every day.

3. The day-star's rays are glittering clear,
   and tell that day itself is near:
the shadows of the night depart;
   thou, holy Light, illume the heart!

4. Within our senses ever dwell,
   and worldly darkness thence expel;
long as the days of life endure,
   preserve our souls devout and pure.

5. The faith that first must be possessed,
   root deep within our inmost breast;
and joyous hope in second place,
   then charity, thy greatest grace.

6. All laud to God the Father be,
   all praise, eternal Son, to thee;
all glory, as is ever meet,
   to God the holy Paraclete. Amen.

St Ambrose, *Tr.* J. M. Neale

Friday

Vespers

Plasmator hominis Deus

1.Maker of man, who from thy throne
  dost order all things, God alone;
By whose decree the teeming earth
  To reptile and to beast gave birth:

2.The mighty forms that fill the land,
  instinct with life at thy command,
sre giv'n subdued to humankind
  for service in their rank assigned.

3.From all thy servants drive away
  whate'er of thought impure today
hath been with open action blent,
  or mingled with the heart's intent.

4.In heaven thine endless joys bestow,
  and grant thy gifts of grace below;
from chains of strife our souls release,
  bind fast the gentle bands of peace.

5.O Father, that we ask be done,
  through Jesus Christ, thine only Son;
who, with they Holy Ghost and thee,
  doth live and reign eternally. Amen.

c.7th cent. Tr. J. D. Chamber (1805-93)

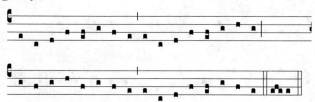

Aurora iam spargit polum

1. Dawn purples all the east with light;
   day o'er the earth is gliding bright;
   morn's sparkling rays their course begin;
   farewell to darkness and to sin!

2. Each evil dream of night, depart,
   each thought of guilt, forsake the heart!
   let every ill that darkness brought
   beneath its shade, now come to naught!

3. So that last morning, dread and great,
   which we with trembling hope await,
   with blessèd light for us shall glow,
   who chant the song we learnt below.

4. To God the Father glory be,
    and to his sole-begotten Son;
   glory, O Holy Ghost, to thee,
    while everlasting ages run. Amen.

PECUSA Hymnal 1871 (Tr. Anon.)
Doxology: E. Caswall (*English Hymnal*)

First Sunday after Trinity

A reading from the sermons of John Keble

We have lately finished the solemn course of the Church's great days, beginning with Advent and ending on Trinity Sunday. Those days have brought before us, one after another, the great truths of the Creed, the several parts of that 'Catholic Faith, which except a man keep whole and undefiled, without doubt he shall perish everlastingly'.

If we have seriously turned our hearts to them as they came before us one by one; if we have earnestly tried to believe and love Christ, conceived by the Holy Ghost, and born of the Virgin Mary, Christ suffering, crucified, dead and buried, Christ descending into hell, rising again the third day, ascending into heaven, sitting at the Right Hand of the Father; Christ sending his holy Spirit to set up his Holy Catholic Church, and call us to partake therein of the Communion of saints and the Forgiveness of sins; finally, Christ coming at the end of the world to judge the quick and the dead; raising our bodies, and endowing saints with life everlasting: if we have gone on believing and loving our Lord and Saviour in all these manifestations of himself; so far it is well: we may hope we have the right Faith; we have made a good beginning in the way of holiness.

We cannot be too thankful to him, who, without any works or deserving of ours, hath bestowed on us so great a gift; and the best way of shewing our thankfulness will of course be this; not to stand waiting, but at once to set about doing whatever God would have us to do next.

'My heart hath talked of thee' (Ps 27:8), says the Psalmist; and surely many a heart here must have talked deeply within itself, of the astonishing mercies which God made Man has wrought for us: 'my heart hath talked of thee: seek ye my Face'. We have felt his secret silent voice within us, entreating, urging, pressing us, by all his goodness, and by all our hopes, to look away from the world and to look after him; to turn away from the false, miserable delights which the flesh and the devil pretend to offer us, and to seek what he offers to

John Keble, 'Sermon I. Steps towards Heaven', in *Sermons for the Sundays after Trinity. Part I. Sundays I-XII, by the late Rev. John Keble* (Oxford and London: Parker, 1878), pp. 1-3.

his saints, - the light of his countenance, the ineffable joy of beholding him, face to face.

Our heart hath talked of God: 'Seek ye my face'; let us not be slow to answer, 'thy face, Lord, will I seek'. Thou hast drawn us, and we will 'run after thee'; thou hast called to us, as to Saul, from heaven; we see the light which is 'above the brightness of the sun' (Acts 26:13). What other answer can be make than St Paul's own? 'Lord, what wilt thou have me to do?' (Acts 9:6).

Surely, if we have a spark of true love, we shall not be content merely to receive so great blessings, and admire God's mercy in giving them to us so unworthy persons, and not try to do some little for his sake. We shall not surely rest, until we have done some little, towards the further coming of that glorious and blessed kingdom, which we feel to be all the world to ourselves. There must be something added to our faith, else we shall be neither safe nor perfect.

Second Sunday after Trinity

A reading from the sermons of Mark Frank

Worldly honour may consist with Christ's; our greatest estate with the true riches; our lawful busiest vocations with his service; our secular learning with heavenly knowledge; the care of our bodies with the salvation of our souls; our lives with his death: only they must not stand in competition for time and place, but be all left to his disposing; and when at any time they cannot either stand with his service or hinder it, then leave them all we must to follow him, as occasions and opportunities shall require the forsaking of any of them, be it life itself. Alas! he loves not Christ at all that loves anything above him, anything equal with him that prefers anything to him, or will not readily leave it for him.

We have read of many who have left their thrones and cast away their sceptres; many who have thrown away their riches, and deserted their estates; many who have given over all their thriving ways; many who have bid adieu to all secular studies; many who have in strange austerities and mortifications neglected, nay,

---

Mark Frank, 'A Sermon on St Andrew's Day', in *Sermons by Mark Frank,* II (Oxford: John Henry Parker, 1849), pp. 384-385.

crucified their bodies, and others that have run to death as to a wedding, that so they might the easier follow, or the more happily attain to their Master's steps: but these are singular and particular heights; the ordinary course of Christianity is by a lower way. Yet is the way good too. Says St Jerome: 'he also verily forsakes all that desires none', nothing but Jesus Christ; who 'has crucified the flesh with all the affections and lusts' as the Apostle speaks (Gal 5:24), the world with all the desires thereof; who though he has all he can desire, yet desires nothing but what God will have him attain.

Sometimes it may fall out that we must leave our callings to go after him, when they be either truly sinful or evidently dangerous; and our wealth, when it is unjustly gotten or unrighteously held, we must restore and leave to the right owners of it. Sometimes again it may be lawful for us to have both estates and callings, though we be not bound to it; as when we plainly see we can thereby serve our Master better, and he seems to point us to it; when we perceive we cannot else perform the task or calling he has designed us to, or the business he has already set us upon.

Third Sunday after Trinity

A reading from Thomas Ken, *Practice of Divine Love*

For whom, O Unutterable Goodness, didst thou suffer the extreme bitterness of sorrow, but for the vilest of all thy creatures, sinful man, and for me one of the worst of sinners? and therefore I praise and love thee.

For what end didst thou suffer, O Most Ardent Charity, but to save sinners from all things that were destructive, the curse of the law, the terrors of death, the tyranny of sin, the power of darkness, and torments eternal, to purchase for us all things conducible to our happiness, pardon and grace, consolation and acceptance, and the everlasting joys and glories of the Kingdom of Heaven? and therefore I praise and love thee.

Thomas Ken, *The Practice of Divine Love being an Exposition of the Church Catechism*, in *The Prose Works of the Right Reverend Thomas Ken*. Now first collected and edited with a biographical notice by the Rev. W. Benham (London: Griffith, Farran, 1889), pp. 135-136.9

Out of what motive didst thou suffer, O Boundless Benignity, but out of thy own preventing Love, free Mercy, and pure Compassion? and therefore I praise and love thee.

When no other sacrifice could atone thy Father's anger, O thou the Beloved Son of God, and reconcile divine justice and mercy together, but the Sacrifice of God Incarnate, who as Man was to die, and to suffer in our stead, as God was to merit and make satisfaction for our sins; 'twas then that thou, O Son of God, didst become Man, the very meanest of men, didst 'take upon thee the form of a servant' (Phil 2: 7), and didst on the Cross show us the mystery and the miracle of love, God crucified for sinners, and sinners redeemed by the Blood of God.

O thou propitious Wonder, God Incarnate on the Cross, by what names shall I adore thee? All are too short, too scanty to express thee; Love only, nothing but Love will reach thee, thou art Love, O Jesus, thou art all Love, O Tenderest, O Sweetest, O Purest, O Dearest Love, soften, sweeten, refine, love me into all Love like thee!

By the love of thy Cross, O Jesu, I live, and that I will only glory, that above all things will I study, that before all things will I value; by the love of thy Cross I will take up my cross, daily and follow thee, I will persecute and torment and crucify my sinful affections and lusts, which persecuted, tormented and crucified thee; and if thy Love calls me to it, I will suffer on the Cross for thee, as thou hast done for me.

How illustrious and amiable were thy Graces amidst all thy sufferings O thou afflicted Jesu; I admire, and I love thy profound Humility, unwearied Patience, Lamb-like Meekness, immaculate Innocence, invincible Courage, absolute Resignation, compassionate Love of souls, and perfect Charity to thy enemies. O my Love, I cannot Love thee but I must desire above all things to be like my Beloved; O give me grace to tread in thy steps, and conform me to thy Divine Image, that the more I grow like thee, the more I may love thee, and the more I may be loved by thee.

Fourth Sunday after Trinity

A reading from the sermons of Henry Edward Manning

The great law of mutual forgiveness is founded both on the law of nature, and on the fact of the still greater forgiveness which we have received at God's hand. If he have forgiven us so much, what is there that we shall not forgive our brother? If he have forgiven us so often, how can we ever refuse forgiveness? 'Seventy times seven' (Mt 18:22), seven times in a day, what is this to those who have the forgiveness of God through the blood of Jesus Christ.

But the point I wish to draw attention to is, not the duty of forgiveness as it is here enjoined, but the character of Christ which is revealed in these words. It is plain that he does not lay on us a rule of mercy by which he does not proceed himself. He has not two measures, or an unequal balance. As he would have us measure to others, so he will mete to us. The law he here lays down is a transcript of himself: this seventy times sevenfold remission, what is it but his unwearied mercy? And what is this 'seven times in a day' but his all-enduring patience?

Now it is this particular truth which distinguishes the Gospel from all religions of nature, and even from all other measures of the earlier revelations of God. The great truth here revealed to us is, the love, clemency, forgiveness of God to sinners. All this was, indeed, exhibited before in promises and prophecies, and in God's manifest dealings with his chosen people of old; but it was never so fully revealed as by the Incarnation and atonement of Christ. It may be said with truth, that a full perception of this great mystery of mercy is the very life of faith; and that there is nothing we are slower and more willing to believe than in its truth and fullness. The greatness of it is too large for our narrow hearts.

It is very easy to say, God is merciful, Christ is full of compassion; but these general truths, as we utter them, are limited and overcast by others not less certain. For if the Gospel has revealed God's mercy, it has also revealed God's holiness; if it has taught us that God is Love, it has also taught us that he is 'a consuming fire'. With the atonement, we have learned the judgment to come; with the sacrifice of Christ, we have learned the guilt of sin; with the gift of regeneration, the defilement of the inmost soul; if baptism has brought us

---

Henry Edward Manning, 'Sermon XIX. The Long-suffering of Christ', in *Sermons, by Henry Edward Manning. II* (London: James Burns, 1846), pp. 361-365.

remission, it has made sins after baptism more fearful. The Gospel is an aweful twofold light, before which even faithful Christians tremble, and often see but in part, and, through weakness and fear, and the earthliness of their hearts, often believe and speak amiss. It seems inconceivable that God should pardon so great sins as ours; or if he pardon us one, that he should pardon us when we fall again. […]

Now I am not going to argue against this feeling, so far as it promotes in us bitterness of repentance, fear, humiliation, and prayer for pardon. It is to be corrected only when it clashes with the perfect revelation of our Lord's character, and of his dealings with us. Too much humbled we cannot be, too tender of conscience, too fearful to offend; but we may dishonour him by unworthy and faithless mistrust, by thinking that he is verily such an one as ourselves, and that his forgiveness is no readier and broader than the perception we form if it in our hearts, f there be any one thing of vital force in a life of Christian obedience, it is a true and full knowledge of him whom we obey. His character is our very law; it imposes on us the conditions of our whole life, in thought, word and deed, and defines the whole of our relations to him. Now these words of his… reveal to us that to those who repent, howsoever often they have sinned, there is perpetual forgiveness; that as often as we turn to him, saying in truth, 'I repent' he will take us back again, And this is, indeed, the very grace and mystery of the Gospel.

Fifth Sunday after Trinity

A reading from the sermons of Mark Frank

Though we omit no pains, but even toil and labour what we can, nor slip no time, but even break our sleep, and take in the nights; nor fail of any opportunity, but take every hour of the night, ready all the night long, upon the least occasion; nor neglect any policy or art to help us, but make it our whole labour and business every way to gain our intentions, though we be never so great or good, so wise or subtle, so many or so powerful, we shall gain nothing but labour and sorrow by the hand, unless God be with us.

Mark Frank, 'The Second Sermon on the Calling of St Peter', in *Sermons by Mark Frank*, II (Oxford: John Henry Parker, 1849), pp. 308-309.

Toil itself, and labour, catches nothing; 'We have toiled all night and caught nothing' (Lk 5:5); all our labour is but as the running round of a mill, or the turning of a door on the hinges, never the further for all its motion. 'Consider your ways', says the prophet, 'you have sown much and bring in little'; 'he that earneth wages earns it to put it into a bag with holes' (Hab 1:6). He gains somewhat, as he thinks, and lays it up; but when he looks again for it, it is come to nothing. He that gave his mind to seek out the nature and profit of every labour under the sun, returns home empty, only with this experimental saying in his mouth: 'What has a man of all his labour, and of the vexation of his heart, wherein he hath laboured under the sun? for all his days are sorrows, and his travail grief'. A goodly catch for all his pains.

All the attendances upon times and seasons will effect no more, if you separate from God's special benediction; 'We have toiled all night and yet caught nothing'. Let a man serve seven years for a fortune or preferment, as Jacob did for Rachel, and in the morning his fair and longed for Rachel will prove but blear-eyed Leah at the best. Whatever it is he gets, it will be but misery to him, or a false happiness. Or let him lie waiting with the bed-rid man at the pool of Bethesda eight and thirty years for the moving of the waters, he will always be prevented – be never able to get in – till Christ come to him; yea, let him wait out all his years, and draw out his days in perpetual expectations and attendances for some happy planet, some propitious hour; he will never see it, unless God speak the word and command it to him. These fishers, in the text had even chose their time and spent it out to the last minute – the best time to fish; when the eye of the sporting fish could not see the net that was spread to entangle them, nor perceive the hand or shadow of him who subtly laid wait to take them – the time of night; and they pursued their labour till the day came on, 'all the night', says the text, yet nothing they could catch; they lost their labour and their hope. Just thus it is, when men having, as they think, diligently made use of the opportunity, and expected it out, having never thought of God all the while, find themselves at last no nearer the end of their desires than they were at the beginning. Your own eyes see it by many daily experiences that it thus oft falls out.

Policy comes ever and anon as short of its aim where God is set aside. Though men be oft so cunning in all the artist of thriving, that nothing seems to escape their reach; though the net seem full with fish, their fields stand thick with corn, and their garners full and plenteous with all manner of store; yet draw up the net when the night is gone, when the clear day appears to show all things as they are, and, behold, in all these they have taken nothing: their souls, the best fish, are lost and gone by their unjust and wicked gains; the true fish is slipt away, and there is nothing but the scales and slime, a little glittering earth, or slimy pleasure left behind,. Thus mere policy, I mean such as God is not remembered in, proves ever at the last.

Sixth Sunday after Trinity

A reading from Thomas Ken, *A Manual of Prayers for Winchester Scholars*

O Blessed Saviour! what more powerful Motives can I have to persuade me to Communicate, than thy Command, and the admirable effects of the Holy Sacrament?

But alas! my corrupt Nature is apt to suggest to me low and base inducements to this Duty, such as are, fear of my Superior's displeasure, if I abstain, or shame of not appearing as devout as my equals, or the mere custom of the Place, or of the Season! But, Lord, I do from my Heart renounce all these and the like carnal considerations, and I come to thy Altar to renew my Baptismal Covenant with thee, of which thy Sacrament is the Seal.

I come to testify my sense of thy Love, O Heavenly Father, in so loving the World, as to give up thy only Son to die for me. I come to testify my Faith in thee, and my Love towards thee, O Blessed Saviour, and thankfully to commemorate thy wonderful Love in dying for me. I come, Lord, to testify my steadfastness in the Communion of thy Church, and my Charity to all the World. I come to thy Table, O Lord, out of the sense I have of the want of that spiritual Food, to which thou there invitest me.

Alas, alas! I am soon apt to grow weary of well-doing: a few Prayers, every little Duty is apt to tire me, every slight Temptation is apt to overcome me, and I know there is no food can strengthen my Soul but thy Body, no cordial can revive my drooping Obedience, but thy Blood; - and it is thy most Blessed

---

Thomas Ken, *A Manual of Prayers for Winchester Scholars* in *The Prose Works of the Right Reverend Thomas Ken*. Now first collected and edited with a biographical notice by the Rev. W. Benham (London: Griffith, Farran, 1889), pp. 240-242.

Body and Blood I hunger and thirst after: - O gracious Lord, grant that I and all that communicate with me, may feel its saving efficacy. O Feed, O refresh, O Nourish our Souls with it to Life Everlasting, and that for thy Own infinite Mercy's sake, which moved thee to offer up thy Body and Blood for us. […]

O Heavenly Father, clothe me with the wedding-garment, even the Graces of my Blessed Saviour, for then am I sure to be welcome guest to thy Table, when I shall come thither in the Likeness of thy only well-beloved Son, in whom thou art always well pleased.

O Heavenly Father, fill me with a lively Faith, profound Humility, filial Obedience, inflamed Affections, and universal Charity; O raise in my Soul all those heavenly Transports of Zeal and devotion, of Love and Desire, of Joy and Delight, of Praise and thanksgiving, which become the remembrance of a Crucified Saviour, - which become one redeemed by the Blood of God, and that for his sake only who redeemed me.

Seventh Sunday after Trinity

A reading from the sermons of John Keble

The doings of Jesus Christ are the doings of God: of the Almighty God, Son of the Father, made Man for our sake. Therefore you may be sure there is much more in them that we can understand at once; yea more a great deal than we could understand, if we spent ever so much time in thinking of them. So in this miraculous feast there is a great deal more meaning, you may be sure, than the mere act of bounty and power, such as a great king or rich nobleman on earth might practice, by way of doing a very kind and good-natured action, making people happy for the moment, and so an end. Depend upon it, the Saviour of our souls, the great King of heaven and earth, had a deeper meaning than that, in performing this mighty work. […]

John Keble, 'Sermon XXIV. The Feeding of the Four Thousand', in *Sermons for the Sundays after Trinity. Part I, Sundays I-XII, by the late Rev. John Keble* (Oxford and London: Parker, 1878), pp. 255, 259-261, 263.

411

Now I want you to observe, how in all these proceedings, wonderful and divine as they were, our Lord did everything in order: in the same order whereby he provides for us in what is called the common course of nature. It is all done… through men like ourselves. Our Lord received the loaves of the disciples, and employed the hands of the disciples to distribute them; he did not give them to the multitude with his own hands, telling them to approach him one by one, but he formed the multitudes into companies, and sent the disciples, one to each company; much as he does in his Church, in respect of spiritual blessings. He might have given us his Word and Sacraments directly from himself, without any clergy to convey them; but it hath pleased him to do otherwise. And it is not the less his gift, because it comes through his ministers, neither will it do our souls the less good: even as that bread and fish was quite as effectual to nourish the persons who partook of it, given them, as it was, by some one of the Apostles, as it would have been, had our blessed Lord in each case given it with his own hand. There is the same condescension in his thus employing ministers, as in his not creating all the bread which he gave them, but making a beginning, small though it were, yet a real beginning, from those seven loaves, which he caused to go as far as they could.

Then observe that he does it all by benediction. He took the seven loaves, and blessed, and brake, and distributed. Afterwards when the few small fishes were brought forward, he blessed, and commanded to set them also before them. Nothing would he give them without his blessing. Surely we must be very dull, if we do not learn hereby to ask God's blessing on all our meals, all our pursuits, all our undertakings, whether for the good of others or for our own. If his blessing be not upon it, how can it do us good? And if even the great Lord and Creator did not account what he gave his people sufficiently sanctified by his touch, but used also word and prayer, why should we think much to say grace devoutly before and after all our principal meals?

And he teaches us in the same way not to be wasteful. 'Gather up the fragments that remain that nothing be lost'. What was it to him, the Maker and Owner of all, him who 'openeth his hand and filleth all things living with plenteousness' (Ps 104:28), whether those few crumbs, which remained over and unto them that had eaten, were carefully preserved or no? To him it could make no difference: the difference is to us his reasonable creatures, whether we will deal reverently and gratefully, with the provision which his love makes for us, or whether we will waste it, as no object to us. […]

Now that which is true concerning earthly relief and nourishment, is even much more true, as concerning spiritual relief and nourishment. If it needed humble trust, and patient waiting for the men, women and children of that company to partake of Christ's outward and visible feasts, surely he will expect us to be trustful and patient, in respect of the Bread which cometh down from heaven. What that Bread is, we know: it is 'the Body and Blood of our Saviour Christ, verily and indeed taken and received by the faithful in the Lord's Supper'. That is the seven loaves, the sevenfold or perfect feast, the feast full of all the rich gifts of the Holy Ghost, which he has miraculously provided to sustain us here in the wilderness of this present world.

Eighth Sunday after Trinity

A reading from the sermons of Henry Edward Manning

Our lives are chiefly determined for good or ill by the first choice we make upon the very threshold: and our choice will be wise, and safe, just in the measure in which we repress the importunate solicitations of our own minds, and follow in faith what seems to us to be the leading of God's providential hand.

With many of us this act of choice is past. For good or ill it is over: to some of us it is irrevocable – I mean, to us who have received Holy Orders. We cannot choose again; but we may learn much from what I have endeavoured to express. We may learn to look more fixedly, year by year, on the one aim of our life; to cast off unnecessary burdens; to draw ourselves within straiter lines, and to live more singly, and with fuller dedication of all we have and all we are, to the service of the Church.

But I had rather speak to those who have this one great choice still to make.

Brethren, you are come to the point where your life must soon take its determination for ever. Hitherto you have been walking in a vain show; a little

---

Henry Edward Manning, 'Sermon III. The work appointed us', in *Sermons preached before the University of Oxford, by Henry Edward Manning* (Oxford: Parker, and London: Rivngton, 1844), pp. 57-60.c

while, and your life will be turned to a reality. A change will soon have passed on you, which you have not imagination now to conceive. Your present life will seem to you to be a very dream, a playing at life rather than living. For some of you the choice of your future path (though not actually made) is already predisposed. [...] Be that position, be that career what it may be, there is one governing law, which must alike control you and the most consecrated servant of God, No rank, or wealth, or secular dignities; no high office, or great employments of state; no successful administration of civil functions; will set you free from the law which binds you to live absolutely and supremely for the glory of God. The civil state (though not the highest in God's kingdom) may nevertheless be so related to the mystical body of Christ, as they that ministered to him on earth were related to his Divine person. Personal holiness, therefore, and the devotion of our best and chiefest powers to the service of God, is not the duty of the Priesthood only, but of the whole Church. In this the layman is bound no less than we... 'Ye are bought with a price, therefore glorify God in your bodies, and in your spirits, which are God's' (1 Cor 6:2)). In this there is but one law for all members of his kingdom. The example and the blood-shedding of Christ bind all alike.

Of those among you that are still free to decide, I would fain ask, On what principle, on what view of life have you been preparing to choose your future profession?

The example of our Lord Jesus Christ not only lays down for us a rule of self-devotion; it reveals to us, further, what is the highest work to which the powers and life of man can be devoted. The most perfect office in this world of sin, is that to which he was consecrated – the Priesthood of the atonement, the ministry of reconciliation, which he has entrusted to his Church. So far as the redeemed could partake in the work of their redeemer, he associated his Apostles with himself. They partook of the Divine commission which he had received of the Father: and in them he associated with himself all who should succeed him to the end of the world. There is no other office so nearly related to his Cross, his Sacrifice, and his Throne; none which so takes up into itself the whole being of him that bears it; none so near to the work of ministering angels; none so real, changeless, or blissful, nor in so full a harmony with the will of God in Christ Jesus.

Ninth Sunday after Trinity

A reading from the sermons of Henry Parry Liddon

The Everlasting Spirit fills the world, not merely to stablish, strengthen, and settle the faithful, not merely to build up and sanctify Christ's own through the sacraments, or ministry, or Scriptures of the Church, but to hover with quickening power and love, with gentle breathing and strong agonizing solicitations, around souls which, like the prodigal, have wasted their substance, their natural advantages and their spiritual endowments, in riotous living, and have 'begun to be in want'.[...]

That memory of the happy past, of the spiritual plenty of his deserted home, of the fresh joyousness of the days which he spent beneath his father's roof; that keen, strong perception of the nothingness of what the world can offer him, which sets on one side its education and its good taste, and its refinement, and its wealth, and its activity, and its grace of manner, and its affectation of principle, and its hold upon the multitude, and the homage it receives from the press, and the votaries it numbers among the great and the powerful, and penetrates straight down to the void which opens like a chasm beneath, to that loss of all real peace, real faith, real hope, real love, - to that inner existence, which is only superficially so active because it is at bottom so aimless, to that felt, that miserable, that present banishment from the Face of God, coupled with the torturing memory of his gracious smile in bygone says, and with the knowledge that thousands are at this moment basking beneath its warmth and brightness, - all this has not been given him for nothing. Though he be wandering in the streets of Jerusalem with Peter, or mixing with the world's gaiety like the Magdalen, or in the last agony with the thief on the cross, he will arise and go to his Father. He will make an effort, and at the moment; he will seek the home of his early affections; rebel that he is, he will throw himself upon One whose nature and property it is to have mercy and to forgive; he will turn a deaf ear to the scorn of his companions, to the polished ridicule of the world, to the false prudence of the half-hearted, to the faithless murmurings of his own aching heart; he will not tamper with light which has been vouchsafed that he may obey it, and which may be dimmed or withdrawn if obedience is

---

Henry Parry Liddon, 'Christ's Welcome to the Penitent', in *Sermons preached on Special Occasions, 1860-1889, by H. P. Liddon* (London: Longmans, Green, 1897), pp. 4, 6-8.

delayed; he will go to a Father who is a Father still, even to him, and ease his heart, even if he may not do more, by a full outpouring of its wounds and miseries, by an unreserved and broken-hearted confession: 'While I held my tongue, my bones consumed away through my daily complaining. I will acknowledge my sins unto thee, and mine unrighteousness have I not hid' (Ps 22:3, 5). [...]

It has been remarked that there is no trace in this parable of a Mediator who is sought, and who leads the sinner to the Father's presence-chamber. It has been urged in reply that the agency of a Mediator, if not expressed, is implied and understood, both from the evangelic tenderness of the reception, and from the explicit assertion of Scripture elsewhere. And certainly, as when the Apostle speaks of our being justified freely through the Father's grace, we might have supposed that the Father pardoned without sacrifice or atonement, if it were not added 'through the redemption that is in Christ Jesus, whom God hath set forth to be a propitiation through faith in his Blood' (Rom 8:24-25); so here the prodigal is received only in virtue of infinite merits and sacred sorrows, to describe which does not fall within the scope of the parable, though such description is given elsewhere. It is God the Holy Trinity, the Father, the Son, and the Holy Ghost, who receives the penitent; it is 'the death and passion of our Saviour Christ, both God and Man', which secures the reception. Nay, more, it is our Saviour, who, besides announcing to our race the welcome which awaits sinners at the hands of God, administers that welcome in his own human nature, since 'God was in Christ reconciling' (2 Cor 5: 19); administers it whether in the days of his flesh, or through the ordinances and ministers of his Church; administers it with a love which is as divine as it is human and as human as it is divine.

Tenth Sunday after Trinity

A reading from the sermons of Thomas Wilson

And God knows, we have great reason ... to mourn, whether we consider the general state of Christianity, or the wicked lives of particular Christians. [...] To see people, for instance, who profess to have here no abiding-place, yet setting

---

Thomas Wilson, 'Sermon XLIII', in *The Works of the Right Reverend Father in God Thomas Wilson,* II (Oxford: John Henry Parker, 1847), pp. 486-487.

up their rest upon earth, as if they were sure, as if they desired, never to leave it; to see Christians, who are bound by their profession to love one another, rejoicing and taking pleasure in the misery and ruin of each other; to hear people beg of God to forgive them their trespasses, as they are ready to forgive others, and at the same time resolving not to forgive the least offence against themselves without full satisfaction; to see the rich oppressing the poor, and the poor envying the rich, as if the rich were not accountable to God, nor the poor expected any amends in the next world for what they want in this; to see parents educating their children after such a manner as if they intended their eternal ruin; teaching them to love the world, instead of renouncing it; gratifying them in every thing that is vain and sinful, and suffering them to content themselves with a bare outward form of religion, without knowing any thing of its power, or of that 'holiness without which no man may see the Lord' (Heb 12:14); to see pastors as little concerned for the flocks committed to their charge, as if, in truth, they were so many beasts whose souls would die with their bodies, and for which they were never to give an account; in one word, to see the greatest part of Christians live without faith, without hope, without charity, without fear; that is, without any true religion; to see them living at this rate, without apprehending any manner of danger, neglecting the day of grace which God has afforded them for their salvation, and never considering 'that the night cometh when no man can work; (Jn 9:4): can any Christian see and consider all this, and where it must end, and not be moved with sorrow and compassion, as our Lord was, for the eternal miseries which unthoughtful Christians are bringing upon themselves? Can they forebear to mourn in secret and beg of God to pity and cure these disorders, and the blindness of sinners, who do not see the danger of neglecting the time of visitation, and the day of grace?

It was this that moved our Lord's compassion for Jerusalem, because she 'knew not the time of her visitation' (Lk 19:44), and because that was the occasion of her ruin. She knew not; that is, she would not know it. She would not see the sin that occasioned it; she would not believe the Prophets that foretold it; she would not receive the Son of God, who came to warn her of her approaching ruin, and who would, no doubt of it, have delivered her from it, would she have improved the means of salvation so mercifully afforded her; for it was as easy for God to have saved that whole nation from destruction, as he did those few that believed, whom he delivered as by a miracle from that desolation which soon after followed.

Now, these things, good Christians, were written for our example that we may see the danger of not knowing the day of visitation. For that is an appointed time in which God offers grace to sinners, and an opportunity of working out their salvation; and that when this is neglected and past, sinners have nothing to expect but judgment without mercy; that this is so, is plain from this, and from many other instances and parts of holy Scripture.

Eleventh Sunday after Trinity

A reading from the sermons of Mark Frank

If we peruse the speeches of humble souls in Scripture, by which they accosted their God or their superiors, we shall see variety of expression indeed, but little difference in the upshot of the words. 'I am but dust and ashes' (Gen 18:27), says Father Abraham. Now, how can dust and ashes, with their light scattering atoms, endure the last breath of the Almighty? The Prophet Isaiah 'saw the Lord' in a vision, 'sitting upon a throne', and presently he cries out, 'Woe is me! for I am undone, because I am a man of unclean lips: for mine eyes have seen the King, the Lord of hosts' (Is 6:5). What! undone, Isaiah? Yes, 'Woe is me, I am undone, for mine eyes have seen the Lord of hosts'. Who certainly cannot but consume me, for so boldly beholding him. 'I m not worthy', says the centurion to Christ, 'that thou shouldest come under the roof of my house: speak the word only'; as if his presence were so great he might not bear it. And St Paul, as soon as he had told us that he had seen Christ, tells us he was 'one born out of due time;, was ;'the least of the Apostles', and 'not meet to be called an Apostle' (1 Cor 15:8), as if the very seeing of Christ had made him worth nothing. Indeed, it makes us think ourselves so, of whom we ever think too much, till we look up to God. Then it befalls us, as it fell out to Job, 'I have heard thee by the hearing of the ear', but that was nothing, 'now mine eye seeth thee: wherefore I abhor myself, and repent in dust and ashes' (Job 42:5, 6). Hither it is always that the sight of God depresses us, to think humbly of ourselves, that we profess our just deserts to be no other than to be deprived of his presence.

Mark Frank, 'A Sermon on the Calling of St Peter', in *Sermons by Mark Frank*, II (Oxford: John Henry Parker, 1849), pp. 291-292, 298.

There are like expressions of humble minds towards our superiors too in Holy Writ. 'When Rebekah saw Isaac coming towards her, she lighted down from her camel, and covered herself with her veil; (Gen 24:65), as if either her humility or her modesty would not suffer her suddenly to look upon his face who was presently to be her lord. But Abigail's complimental humility surpasses. When David sent to take her to him to wife, 'she arose and bowed herself to the earth, and said, Behold, let thine handmaid be a servant to wash the feet of the servants of my lord' (1 Sam 25:41). And Mephibosheth, though not so courtly, yet as deeply undervalues himself in the sight of his lord and king, when he thus answers David's proferred kindness, 'What is thy servant that thou shouldest look upon such a dead dog as I am?' (2 Sam 9:8).

Now if Rebekah descend from her camel, and veil her face at the sight of her designed husband; if Abigail term herself the servant of the servants of David, even to the meanest office, to wash their feet; if Mephibosheth count himself a dog in the presence of King David, each of these thus expressing their humility, it is no wonder if St Peter, at the presence of his Saviour, it is but just that we, in the presence of our God and Saviour, descend from our camels, from our chairs of state, from our seats of ease, from the stools whereon we sit, and bow down our eyes, our hearts and bodies in all humility, as unworthy to look up to heaven, to look him in the face whom we have so offended, willing to wash the feet of his poorest servants, to serve him in anything, in the poorest, meanest way or office, ready to profess ourselves among the vilest of his creatures, who cannot so much as expect a good look from him. [...]

Yet we are men, thy creatures, the work of thine own hands, the price of thine own blood. Spare us, therefore, good Lord, and though thou hast departed from us, for a long, too long a season, return again and save us, for we are sinful men, people that have need of thy presence, never so much as now, who cannot be without it, who though we are not worthy to be with thee, yet we cannot but desire to be with thee for ever and ever. Turn thee then, O Lord, and be gracious unto thy servants, cleanse us from our sins, free us from our iniquities, fit us for thy presence, compass us with thy mercy, and visit us with thy salvation: salvation here and salvation hereafter, where we may enjoy they blessed and glorious presence for evermore.

<hr>

Twelfth Sunday after Trinity

A reading from the sermons of Robert Isaac Wilberforce

Now in what manner can the limited be brought into relation with the unlimited? How can the finite become one with the Infinite? Is this a process which is confined to man's intellect alone? Is it a privilege allowed to the superior part of his being, which his inferior nature does not share? What were this but the error of the Gnostics; and how singular to recognize the ancient delusion among those who smile at the fanciful shape in which their own opinions were formerly dressed? For what was the alleged opposition between matter and God, but the idea that in the limitations of our finite being lay the origin of evil, and that to escape from them was to enter at once upon a higher mode of existence. And this is identical with the thought, that though our complex nature is bound down to earth by the law of its material being, yet in the mind we have an open door, which enables us at once to enter into communion with God. If this were so, then would the alienation, which has separated man from God, be attributable, not to the perverseness of his will, but to the conditions of his nature. It would seem as though the pure spirit, which could range unchecked through the regions of the infinite, were contaminated by its imprisonment in those material frames, which gave to its several portions an individual life, and separate consciousness. So that the material structure would be the true cause of debasement, and man would be separated from his Maker by the accident of isolation, and not by the malignity of sin. [...] Such is the necessary result of denying that sacramental system which is built upon the notion of our Lord's humanity. [...]

Is it asked how can things, which are wholly diverse, be brought into relation with one another, how can the finite become one with the Infinite? The answer is given in one word, through the Incarnation of Christ. Let us confess only that 'Jesus Christ is come in the flesh', and however far we may be from comprehending this mystery, we cannot choose but believe it. For was not this the very work which was effected by 'the taking of the manhood into God?' Were not the finite and the infinite bound together by that personal existence, whereby man and God were united in the instant of his taking flesh? Thus did Deity become capable, in the human nature of the Word, of sympathizing with

---

Robert Isaac Wilberforce, 'Sermon XIX. The Sacramental System', in *Sermons on the New Birth of Man's Nature, by Robert Isaac Wilberforce* (London: John Murray, 1850), pp. 230-233.

human sorrows; and manhood became capable of being the seed of grace, through its being taken into God. The one was able to participate through its inferior nature in the weakness of limited humanity; the other through its alliance with a superior nature was endured with heavenly efficacy. Thus did our Lord's humanity become that very source of life, which is distributed through Sacraments as the life of his brethren: the Infinite Head communicates himself through these channels to his finite brethren: God is in Christ reconciling to himself the world: so that the efficacy of these ordinances depends wholly upon our estimate of him, with whom they ally us: and to accept his mediation as a truth is to receive that sacramental system, where by he is come in the flesh as the re-creator of mankind.

Thirteenth Sunday after Trinity

A reading from the sermons of John Keble

'Take care of him: and whatsoever thou spendest more, when I come again, I will repay thee' (Lk 10:35). Our Lord in the Gospel this day tells a history in which five different persons are concerned. First there is a poor man in distress; secondly, one who passes by and pays no regard at all to him; thirdly, another who passes by, and thinks of him a little, but does him no good at all; fourthly, the good Samaritan who not only notices him but does for him all that he can, all that the poor man needs; and fifthly, there is the Host or keeper of the Inn, to whose care the charitable Samaritan commits the poor traveller; as we read in the text, 'On the morrow when he departed, he took out two-pence and gave them to the host, and said, Take care of him: and whatsoever thou spendest more, when I come again, I will repay thee'. It is of this last, the host or landlord, entrusted by the good Samaritan with the care of the traveller, it is of *him* especially that I now wish to speak, and of the words which were spoken to him, for indeed we are all of us greatly concerned in those words.

For who is this good Samaritan but he who came down from heaven to be our Saviour? That was his journey which he took, and he made himself a Samaritan,

John Keble, 'All Christians concerned in the Good Samaritan's Charge to his Host', in *Sermons for the Sundays after Trinity. Part II. Sundays XIII-End, by the Rev. John Keble* (Oxford and London: James Parker, 1878), pp. 21-23.

that is, poor and despised, a scorn of men and an outcast of the people. And who is the poor man by the road side, but each of us miserable sinners? Who the robbers, but those evil spirits who stripped our first father of his robe of righteousness, the Image of God in which he was created, and gave him the deadly wound of wilful sin? Who the priest and Levite, but the imperfect helps which God ordained for his people for a time in the Old Testament, which could only look at them and pass by, not having power really to deliver them? And thus the way was prepared for him who not only saw but had compassion: and not only had compassion but came unto us, became Emmanuel, and not only came unto us but bound up our wounds, pouring in oil and wine, healing our past sins and giving us grace, and not only tended us where we lay, but put us on his own beast, and took us like lost sheep on his shoulders, and brought us to an inn, his Church, his House of refuge, and is even now taking care of us.

The Samaritan in the parable came as it were by chance where the wounded traveller lay: but our Good Samaritan took the journey on purpose, he came along that road, the road of earthly trouble, the Highway of the Cross, because he knew that on either side of it the children of Adam were lying in their misery. And the Samaritan in the parable made us of the inn which others had made ready for him on the road, but the true Samaritan himself prepared the Inn to which he takes us for refuge, his holy Church, the house of sinners on their trial, till he come again and take them with him to his own home, where he hath prepared a place for each one of them.

Who then is the master of the inn? Those to whom he hath given the care of his Church: all Christians in their measure and place, but most especially Christian ministers. We who in one respect are as the poor traveller in the parable, in another respect are as the master of the inn. Sinners ourselves, redeemed, and brought into God's house, we are commanded to be continually shewing mercy on other sinners. Every brother whom God's Providence puts in our way comes to us with our Lord's word, 'Take care of him', 'I give thee something, fear not to spend it on him or even more if need be': and does not our brother come to us with our Lord's promise too, 'Whatsoever thou spendest more, when I come again, I will repay thee?' Yes, surely he does: and this is the point which I desire especially now to consider. I wish that you and I and all Christians should regard each one himself as the host, to whom the good Samaritan brought the poor man, and should order his ways to his poor brethren accordingly.

Fourteenth Sunday after Trinity

A reading from the writings of Thomas Traherne

Lord Jesus, what love shall I render unto thee, for thy love unto me! Thy eternal love! Oh what fervour, what ardour, what humiliation, what reverence, what joy, what adoration, what zeal, what thanksgiving! Thou that art perfect in Beauty, thou that art the King of Eternal Glory, thou that reignest in the Highest heavens came down from Heaven to die for me! And shall I not live unto thee? O my joy! O my Sovereign Friend! O my life and my all! I beseech thee let those trickling drops of blood that ran down thy flesh drop upon me. O let thy love enflame me. Which is so deep and infinite, that thou didst suffer the wrath of God for me: And purchase all nations and Kingdoms to be my treasures. O thou that redeemed me from Hell, and when thou hadst opened the Kingdom of Heaven to all believers; what shall I do unto thee: what shall I do for thee, O thou preserver of Men? Live, Love, and Admire; and learn to become such unto thee as thou unto me, O Glorious Soul; whose comprehensive understanding at once contains all Kingdoms and Ages! O Glorious Mind! Whose love extendeth to all creatures! O miraculous and eternal Godhead, now suffering on the cross for me: as Abraham saw thy Day and was glad, so didst thou see me and this Day from all Eternity, and seeing me wast Gracious and Compassionate towards me. (All transient things are permanent in God.) 'Thou settest me before thy face forever' (Ps 41:12). O let me this day see thee, and be united to thee in thy Holy Sufferings. Let me learn, O God, such lessons from thee, as may make me wise, and blessed as an Angel of God!

Why, Lord Jesus, dost thou love men; why are they all thy treasures? What wonder is this, that thou shouldest so esteem them as to die for them? Shew me the reasons of thy love, that I may love them too. O Goodness ineffable! They are the treasures of thy goodness. Who so infinitely lovest them that thou gavest thyself for them. Thy Goodness delighted to be communicated to them whom thou hast saved. O thou who art most glorious in Goodness, make me abundant n this Goodness like unto thee. That I may as deeply pity others' misery, and as ardently share thirst for their happiness as thou dost. Let the same mind be in me as is in Christ Jesus. For he that is not led by the spirit of Christ is none of his. Holy Jesus I admire thy love unto me also. O that I could

Thomas Traherne, *Centuries of Meditations*, I. 62-63, in Thomas Traherne, *Centuries* (London and Oxford: Mowbrays, 1975 [1960]), pp. 30-31.

see it through all those wounds! O that I could feel it in those stripes! O that I could hear it in all those groans! O that I could taste it beneath the gall and vinegar! O that I could smell the savour of thy sweet ointments, even in this Golgotha, or place of a skull. I pray thee teach me first thy love unto me, and then unto mankind! But in thy love unto mankind I am beloved.

Fifteenth Sunday after Trinity

A reading from *The Cloud of Unknowing*

St Luke tells us that when our Lord was in the house of Martha her sister, all the time that Martha was busying herself preparing his meal, Mary sat at his feet. And as she listened to him she regarded neither her sister's busy-ness (and it was a good and holy business; is it not the first part of the active life?) nor his priceless and blessed physical perfection, nor the beauty of his human voice and words (and this is an advance, for this is the second part of the active life, as well as the first part of the contemplative). But what she was looking at was the supreme wisdom of his Godhead shrouded by the words of his humanity.

And on this she gazed with all the love of her heart. Nothing she saw or heard could budge her, but there she sat, completely still, with deep delight, and an urgent love eagerly reaching out in that high cloud of unknowing that was between her and God.

I want to say this: no one in this life, however pure, and however enraptured with contemplating and loving God, is ever without this intervening, high, and wonderful cloud. It was in this same cloud that Mary experienced the many secret movements of her love. Why? Because this is the highest and holiest state of contemplation we can know on earth.

From 'this part' (Lk 10:42) nothing on earth could move her. So much so, that when her sister Martha complained to our Lord, and told him to tell her to get up and help her, and not leave her to do all the work by herself, Mary sat

---

The Cloud of Unknowing, 17 and 20, in *The Cloud of Unknowing*. Translated into modern English with an introduction by Clifton Wolters (Harmondsworth: Penguin, 1961), pp. 75-76, 78-79.

completely still and silent, showing not the least indication of any grumble or complaint she might have against her sister. It is not surprising: she had other work to do that Martha did not understand, and she had no time to spare for her, or for answering her complaint. […]

I think, therefore, that they who set out to be contemplatives should not only excuse actives when they complain but themselves be so spiritually occupied that they pay little or no attention to what men say or do to them. Mary, who is our example in al this, did this when her sister Martha complained to our Lord, and if we will do the same, our Lord will do for us today what he then did for Mary.

And what was that? Surely this: our loving Lord Jesus Christ, from whom no secrets are hidden, when Martha demanded that he should act as judge and tell Mary to get up and help her serve him, because he saw that Mary's spirit was ardently loving his Godhead, with great courtesy and propriety himself answered for her. She would not leave her love for him in order to answer for herself. How did he answer? Certainly not as the judge to whom Martha appealed, but as an advocate he lawfully defended her who loved him, and said 'Martha, Martha!' (Lk 10:41). He named her name twice for her good, for he wanted her to listen and attend to his words. 'Thou art very busy', he said, 'and concerned about many things'. (Actives have to be busy and concerned about a whole variety of matters to provide for their own needs, and for their deeds of mercy to fellow Christians, as Christian charity requires). He said this to Martha because he wanted her to know that what she was doing was good and useful to her spiritual health. But in order that she might not think that what she was doing was the highest and best that man could so, he added, 'But one thing is necessary'.

What is that one thing? Surely that God is loved and praised for himself alone, above all else that a man can do, physically or spiritually. And to stop Martha thinking that she could love and praise God above all else whatsoever, and still be busied in the affairs of this life, and to settle her question whether or not she could serve God in a physical way and a spiritual at the same time – she could do it imperfectly, but not perfectly – he added that Mary had 'chosen the best part, which should never be taken from her'. For that perfect outreaching of love which begins here on earth is the same as that which shall last eternally in the blessedness of heaven; it is all one.

425

Sixteenth Sunday after Trinity

A reading from the sermons of Robert Isaac Wilberforce

In the fullness of time, the Second Person in the Ever-Blessed Trinity took man's nature in the womb of the Blessed Virgin, of her substance, that as he had at first made man out of the dust of the earth, so he might re-make him out of the fallen elements of his frail humanity. Thus did he himself become the new Adam, the second man, the pattern and type of mortality, the first-begotten from the dead, the first-born of every creature, that in bringing many sons to glory, the Captain of their salvation might be made perfect through sufferings.

Thus was the Eternal Son exhibited in the flesh as the model and centre of man's nature, even as prophecy had declared in ancient days that when he stooped to mingle with creation, he should be the beginning of God's works. For we must not fancy of him as a mere common man, as a single grain out of the garner of mortality, seeing that in him not this individual or that but manhood itself was taken into God. Thus as he was by right the representative of Godhead, and shared in its whole glorious nature, as he was the brightness of his Father's glory and the express image of his person, so did he by choice become the representative of mankind, 'for the first man is of the earth, earthy, the second man is the Lord from heaven' (1 Cor 15:47).

Now from this brief statement it follows at once why Our Lord's miracles, when in the flesh, were a real fulfilment of that which had been spoken in ancient days concerning his nature. For their characteristic is, that in them human sympathy was perfectly divested of human weakness. They show such absolute lordship over the powers of nature, as might have sufficed to empty the whole ocean of material suffering. He who fed thousands, why could he not banish all want? He who healed men by his thought, why could not he avert every sickness? Doubtless he would have done so, but that the stopping these outlets of natural calamity would only have increased the more intense malignity of moral woe. There will be no more pain where is no more sin. To natural sympathy, then, Our Lord gave its proper weight: he could shed a tear near the grave of Bethany, and show pity at the gates of Nain; - these

---

Robert Isaac Wilberforce, 'Sermon VIII. Christmas', in *Sermons on the New Birth of Man's Nature, by Robert Isaac Wilberforce* (London: John Murray, 1850), pp. 94-96.

concessions he made to the sinless affections of our common nature; but they interfered not with those other qualities, which personal union with Deity communicated to his man's soul. For justice also and holiness are attributes of God, to them we may adapt the words of our greatest English writer, and say that their 'seat is the bosom of God, their voice the harmony of the world, that all things in heaven and earth do them homage'. These, then, must find their expressions in the acts of him, who knew what was in man; and what so wonderful as that their entire possession should have interfered not one whit with the perfection of sympathy for human sorrows? [...]

Are men in pain or grief, in fear or loneliness; does the thought of sin overpower, or he dread of death confound them – here then is one, who to all the attributes of a God, unites all the compassion of a brother.

Seventeenth Sunday after Trinity

A reading from the sermons of John Keble

However great and wise we may think ourselves, and be in the eye of the world, and however mean and worthless and low our neighbours may be, yet there is certain to be some one point or more in which we should be glad to change places with him, in which he is really superior to us: and searching out these matters, and dwelling upon them, is in fact taking the lowest room; it is giving up freely any advantage you seem to have'; it is owning yourselves, as the patriarch Jacob did, 'less than the least of Gods' mercies' (Gen 32:10), or as the Apostle St Paul did, 'less than the least of all saints' (Eph 3:8). To have this feeling constantly settled in one's heart is indeed a great and rare virtue. To speak well of it, and to profess it, is very easy: very easy in words to call one's self the chief of sinners, but really and constantly to mean it, is perhaps one of the hardest exercises of virtue: and it has a great blessing accordingly. He who makes himself really lowest, and not only pretends to do so, has first of all the express promise of Almighty God to be made highest of all. 'Whosoever shall

John Keble, 'Sermon XV. The lowest place our proper place', in *Sermons for the Sundays after Trinity. Part II. Sundays XIII-End, by the late Rev. John Keble* (Oxford and London: James Parker, 1978), pp. 158-161.

humble himself as this little child, the same is greatest in the kingdom of heaven' (Mt 18:4). [...]

Lowliness is that special grace which recommends us most, especially to the regard and favour of our God. It recommends us also, most especially, to the favour and respect of all the good and glorious spirits, our fellow creatures, Angels and Saints, who are in God's household and about his royal throne: just as the contrary, pride and conceit, and taking all the best to one's self, causes them all to dislike such persons and draw back from their society. [...]

The holy Angels and Saints will one day or other come to know the full amount of that humility which is practised daily by Christ's faithful servants in earth: they will enter into the mind of Christ: whom he honours, they will delight to honour: they will give that man *worship*, I mean respect and praise, as they sit together at Christ's Table. As Job's friends did when they were reconciled to hum, when were sure by God's own gracious interference, of Job's innocency and of his lowliness; when they heard how he professed himself vile and said he would lay his hand upon his mouth, they 'gave him a piece of money, and every one an earring of gold' (Job 42:11): so the good spirits of every kind, are preparing crowns and palms for such as are truly endeavouring to take the lowest rooms.

Eighteenth Sunday after Trinity

A reading from Richard Rolle, *The Fire of Love*

Since the human soul is capable of receiving God alone, nothing less than God can fill it; which explains why lovers of earthly things are never satisfied. The peace known by lovers of Christ comes from their heart being fixed, in longing and in thought, in the love of God; it is a peace that sings and loves and burns and contemplates. Very sweet indeed is the quiet which the spirit experiences. Music, divine and delectable, comes to rejoice it; the mind is rapt in sublime and gay melody and sings the delights of everlasting love. Now from human lips sounds forth again the praise of God – the praise, too, of the Blessed

---

Richard of Rolle, *The Fire of Love*, 11, in Richard Rolle, *The Fire of Love*. Translated into modern English with an introduction by Clifton Wolters (London: Penguin, 1988 [1972]), pp. 76-78.

Virgin in whom he glories beyond measure. This need occasion no surprise, for the heart of the singer is altogether ablaze with heavenly fire. And he is transformed into the likeness of him in whom is all melody and song, and is transported by loving desire for the taste of heaven. A man overflows with inner joy, and his very thought sings as he rejoices in the warmth of his love.

All this, to be sure, is meaningless to those who are 'dead', and an outsider cannot understand how anything so sweet and lovely is experienced by a man in a decaying body, limited by its very mortality. But even the one who has all this himself wonders at it, and rejoices at the unspeakable goodness of God who 'gives liberally and does not upbraid' (Jas 1:5), for it is from him the experience comes. Moreover, when he has once had experience of that great thing (and it is a great thing, completely unknown by dying men) he knows that when it is missing he is never at ease, but is always pining for love. So he remains vigilant, and sings and thinks of his love and his Beloved – and if he is on his own sings all the more blithely!

Once a man has known some such experience, he is never thereafter wholly without it, for there always remains a sort of glow, some song or sweetness, even if these are not all present together in equal strength. Yet all are present, unless illness catches him, or he is gripped by intolerable hunger or thirst, or is held up by cold, or heat, or travel. It behoves him then who would sing his love for God and rejoice fervently in such singing, to pass his days in solitude. Yet the abstinence in which he lives should not be excessive, nor on the other hand should he display too much extravagance. Better for him slightly to exceed the limit if it is done in ignorance and with the sound intention of sustaining the body, then that he should falter by over strict fasting, and through physical weakness be unable to sing. But, to be sure, he who is chosen for his life is not overcome by the devil's deceits whether he eats or abstains. The true lover of Christ, one who is taught by him, does not worry overmuch whether there is too much or too little. He will deserve infinitely more by his joyous song, by his prayer and contemplation, by his reading and meditations, yes, and by his discretion in eating, than if, without it, he were ever fasting, or only eating bread and vegetables while he prayed and read. I myself have eaten and drunk things that are considered delicacies – not because I love such dainties, but in order to sustain my being in the service of God, and in the joy of Christ. For his sake I conformed quite properly to those with whom I was living lest I should invent a sanctity where none existed, lest men should over-praise me where I was less worthy of praise.

A reading from St Thomas More's *Dialogue of Comfort*

Since all our principal comfort must come from God, we must first presuppose, in him to whom we shall give any effectual comfort with any ghostly counsel, one ground to begin with, on which all that we shall build may be supported and stated; that is, the ground and foundation of faith. Without this, had ready before, all the spiritual comfort that anyone may speak of can never avail a fly.

For just as it would be utterly vain to lay natural reasons of comfort to him who hath no wit, so would it undoubtedly be frustrate to lay spiritual causes of comfort to him who hath no faith. For unless a man first believe that holy scripture is the word of God, and that the word of God is true, how can he take any comfort in that which the scripture telleth him? A man must needs take little fruit of scripture, if he either believe not that it be the word of God, or else think that, though it were, it might yet for all that be untrue! As this faith is more strong or more faint, so shall the comforting words of holy scripture stand the man in more stead or less.

This virtue of faith can no man give himself, nor yet any man to another. But though men may with preaching be ministers unto God therein; and though a man can, with his own free will, obeying freely the inward inspiration of God, be a weak worker with almighty God therein; yet is the faith indeed the gracious gift of God himself. For, as St James saith, 'Every good gift and every perfect gift is given from above, descending from the Father of lights' (Jas 1:17). Therefore, feeling our faith by many tokens very faint, let us pray to him who giveth it to us, that it may please him to help and increase it. And let us first say with him in the gospel, 'I believe, good Lord, but help thou the lack of my belief' (Mk 9:24). And afterwards, let us pray with the apostles, 'Lord, increase our faith' (Lk 17:5). And finally, let us consider, by Christ's saying unto them, that, if we would not suffer the strength and fervour of our faith to wax lukewarm – or rather key-cold – and lost its vigour by scattering our minds abroad about so many trifling things that we very seldom think of the matters of our faith, we should withdraw our thought from the respect and regard of all

St Thomas More, *Dialogue of Comfort against Tribulation*, I. ii, in St Thomas More, *Dialogue of Comfort against Tribulation*, edited by Monica Stevens (London: Sheed and Ward, 1986 [1951]), pp. 8-10.

worldly fantasies, and so gather our faith together into a little narrow room. And like the little grain of mustard seed, which is by nature hot, we should set it in the garden of our soul, all weeds being pulled out for the better feeding of our faith. Then shall it grow, and so spread up in height that the birds – that is, the holy angels of heaven – shall breed in our soul, and bring forth virtues in the branches of our faith. And then, with the faithful trust that through the true belief of God's word we shall put in his promise, we shall be well able to command a great mountain of tribulation to void from the place where it stood in our heart, whereas with a very feeble faith and faint, we shall be scantly able to remove a little hillock.

And therefore, as for the first conclusion, since we must of necessity before any spiritual comfort presuppose the foundation of faith, and since no man can give us faith but only God, let us never cease to call upon God for it.

Twentieth Sunday after Trinity

A reading from the sermons of Blessed John Henry Newman

Nothing is more clearly brought out in Scripture, or more remarkable in itself than this, that in every age, out of the whole number of persons blessed with the means of grace, few only have duly availed them of this great benefit. So certain, so uniform is the fact that it is almost stated as a doctrine. 'Many are called, few are chosen' (Mt 20:16). Again, 'Strive to enter in at the strait gate; for many, I say unto you, shall seek to enter in, and shall not be able' (Lk 13:24). And again, 'Wide is the gate, and broad is the way, that leadeth to destruction, and many there be which go in thereat... Strait is the gate, and narrow is the way that leadeth unto life, and few there be that find it' (Mt 7:13,14). And St Paul seems expressly to turn the historical fact into a doctrine, when he says, by way of remark upon his own day as compared with former ages of the Church, 'Even so then, at this present time also', that is, as formerly, 'there is a *remnant*, according to the election of grace' (Rom 11:5). [...]

Bl. John Henry Newman, 'Many called, few chosen', in *Parochial and Plain Sermons, by John Henry Newman*, V (London: Rivingtons, 1820, pp. 254-256, 264, 268-269.

This rule in God's dispensations is most abundantly and awfully illustrated in their history. At the time of the Flood, out of a whole world, in spite of Adam's punishment, in spite of Enoch's preaching, in spite of Noah's setting about the ark, eight only found acceptance with God, and even one of these afterwards incurred a curse. When the Israelites were brought out of Egypt by miracle, two only of the whole generation entered the land of promise. Two tribes alone out of twelve remained faithful at the time of the great schism and continued in possession of God's covenanted mercies. And when Christ came, the bulk of his own people rejected him, and his Church came but of the scanty remnant, 'as a root out of a dry ground' (Is 53:2). [...]

And it need scarcely be added, that the same bountifulness on God's part, the same ingratitude on the part of man, the same scarcity of faith, sanctity, truth, and conscientiousness, have marked the course of the Christian Dispensation, as well as of those former ones of which the inspired volume is the record. [...]

The doctrine... that few are chosen though many be called, properly understood, has no tendency whatever to make us fancy ourselves secure and others reprobate. We cannot see the heart, we can but judge from externals, from words and deeds, professions and habits. But these will not save us, unless we persevere in them to the end; and they are no evidence that we shall be saved, except so far as they suggest hope that we shall persevere. They are but a beginning; they tell for nothing till they are completed. Till we have done all, we have done nothing; we have but a prospect, not possession. If we ultimately do attain, every good things we shall have done will have tended to that attainment, as a race tends to a goal; but, unless we attain, it will not have so tended; and, therefore, from no good thing which we do can we argue that we are sure to attain. [...]

Of course we must not press the words of Scripture: we do not know the exact meaning of the word 'chosen'; we do not know what is meant by being saved 'so as by fire' (1 Cor 3:15); we do not know what is meant by 'few'. But still the few can never mean the many; and to be called without being chosen cannot but be a misery. We know that the man, in the parable, who came to the feats without a wedding garment, was 'cast into outer darkness' (Mt 22:13). Let us then set at nought the judgment of the many, whether about truth and falsehood, or about ourselves, and let us go by the judgment of that line of Saints, from the Apostles; times downwards, who were ever spoken against in their generation, ever honoured afterwards, - singular in each point of time as it came, but continuous and the same in the line of their history, - ever protesting against the many, ever agreeing with each other. And, in proportion as we attain to their judgment of things, let us pray God to make it live in us; so that at the Last Day, when all veils are removed, we may be found among those who are inwardly what they seem outwardly, - who... have 'borne and had patience, and for his Name-sake laboured and not fainted' (Apoc 2:3), watched in all things, done the work of an Evangelist, fought a good fight, finished their course, kept the faith.

Twenty-First Sunday after Trinity

A reading from the sermons of Henry Parry Liddon

Although our Lord was born into a province of the Roman empire, marked by the very strongest peculiarity of race and thought, he does not exclusively belong to it. His character is just as intelligible to the Greeks or the Romans or the Germans, as to the Syrians or the Arabs. No Jewish sect could claim him as an adherent; no Jewish teacher has left on him a narrowing impress; no popular errors, among the people of whom he was, received any sanction at his hands. [...] Still less has any Roman or Greek or Indian thinker shaped him into an intellectual mould. He rises above all the dividing lines of that or any previous or subsequent age. He speaks to the human soul in all countries and ages with the authority of one in whom every soul finds, at last its ideal representative. Although he wore the dress of a Jewish rabbi, and accommodated himself to the usages of Jewish life, all his ordinary words and actions, although altogether suitable to his age and country, are yet also equally adapted to all people and all climes; and thus his character – let me repeat it – his character is correspondent to his world-wide claim, and in all quarters of the world men have recognized in him an absolutely universal type of human goodness. And if any have dared, of his grace, to say with his apostle, 'Be ye followers of me', they have quickly added, 'even as I also am of Christ'.

There is, indeed, one side of our Lord's bearing towards men – I mean his literally boundless claims upon their faith and their obedience – which would be fatal to the ideal which is presented to us if it did not depend upon a fact,

---

Henry Parry Liddon, 'Christ the Pattern Man', in *Sermons, by the Rev. H. P. Liddon* (London: Swan Sonnenschein, 1892), pp. 46-47.

upon a necessity, of his being as one higher than any of the sons of men. As it is, his self-assertion is only a part of his perfect veracity. He would not have been true to himself – he would not have been true to us, if he could have shrunk from claiming to be the judge of the world, and already one with the everlasting Father in those distant times when, as yet, Abraham, the patriarch of Israel, had not been born. [...]

If our Lord is thus the pattern Man, the four holy Gospels are, on this account, the most precious of all books in existence; they are the inner sanctuary of Scripture; they are its holy of holies. Certainly the Eternal Spirit moves and breathes everywhere in the sacred volume, but his organs are very various. Elsewhere we are in presence of legislators, of historians, of prophets, of apostles; here we meet – we listen to – the Master himself, as one and the same figure, so gracious and so awful, as reflected in four distinct yet ultimately harmonious types of teaching, Like those four mysterious beings whom Ezekiel and the beloved disciple successively beheld in vision, highest and nearest to the throne of the Uncreated, as representing the loftiest forms of created life, so the four evangelists stand alone in the book of God, because they narrate the life of the perfect moral being – the life of Jesus.

Twenty-Second Sunday after Trinity

A reading from the sermons of William Beveridge

Now, according to this the true notion of faith, described by the Holy Ghost himself, as we hope for pardon and justification from Christ, according to the promises which God hath made us in him, upon our believing in him for it, we are accordingly pardoned and justified by him, because we are thereby actually stated in him, and made partakers of him, and of all that he hath merited for that purpose; as the apostle saith, 'We are partakers of Christ, if we hold the beginning of our confidence steadfast unto the end' (Heb 3: 14). So that if we

---

William Beveridge, 'Sermon XVIII: 'Christ's resurrection the cause of our justification', in *Twenty-six Sermons on Various Subjects, selected from the works of William Beveridge* (London: Society for the Promotion of Christian Knowledge, 1850), pp. 384-387.

continue steadfastly to believe in Christ, we are thereby partakers of him; and if of him, then, be sure, of all that is in him, as is our Mediator and Redeemer.

Hence they who truly believe in him are said to be 'one with him' (Jn 17:21), to be 'joined to him' (1 Cor 6:17); to be 'in him' (2 Cor 5:17, Rom 16:7, Phil 1:1); 'to dwell in him' (1 Jn 4:13); to abide in him' (1 Jn 3:6); 'as a branch abideth in the vine' (Jn 15:4-6); and a member in the body, for 'he is the head of the body, the church' (Col 1:18), and believers are all members, 'every one in particular' (1 Cor 12:27), yea, they are 'members of his body, of his flesh, and of his bones' (Eph 5:30), and so are united and joined to him, as a wife is to her husband.

This is that mystical union that is betwixt Christ and his Church, betwixt Christ and all that truly believe in him. By their believing in him they are thus united to him; and by virtue of this their union to him they partake of all his merits: as a branch partakes of the sap and juice that is in the stock; as a member partakes of the spirit that is in the head; as a wife partakes of all the honours, estate, and privileges of her husband; so doth a believer partake of all the merits of Christ, by reason of his being joined to him, and abiding always in him. He was crucified with him, and he rose again with him. He was in him, and with him, in all he did or suffered; and so he in him satisfied God's justice for his sins, he in him fulfilled all righteousness and therefore he in him may justly be accounted righteous before God himself. He cannot but be so, upon that very account – because he is in Christ, 'for there is no condemnation to them which are in Christ Jesus' (Rom 8: 1). And if they be not condemned, they must needs be justified; and if they be justified, or accounted righteous, before God, it must be by that righteousness they have in him in whom they are so, for they have no other which can be truly so accounted; but in him they have most absolute and perfect righteousness, because his was so. And being his in whom they are by their believing in him, it is reckoned theirs, too, as effectually, to all intents and purposes, as if it had been performed in their own persons. [...]

But here we must observe, that all who are being thus in Christ are justified by his merit, they are also sanctified by the Spirit that is in him. As there is 'no condemnation to them which are in Christ Jesus', so they 'walk not after the flesh, but after the Spirit' (Rom 8: 1): and 'if any man be in Christ, he is a new creature' (2 Cor 5: 17); therefore 'a new creature' because in him, who is 'made to us wisdom and sanctification', as well as 'righteousness and redemption'; and all that are of him partake of all that is in him; of his wisdom to make them wise, and his grace to make them holy in themselves, as well as of his righteouness and merit to justify them before God. [...]

435

And this is that which St James means, where he treats upon this subject, wherein some have thought he contradicts St Paul; but that is a great mistake: for St Paul saith, that 'we are justified by faith without the deeds of the law' (Rom 3: 28). St James doth not say, that we are justified by the works of the law without faith, he only saith, that 'a man is justified by works, and not by faith only' (Jas 2: 24); where he plainly asserts our justification by faith, and only denied that we are justified by faith *only*, or by such a faith as is *alone,* without good works.

---

*For the Twenty-Third and Twenty-Fourth Sundays after Trinity,
see page 442 onwards.*

Short Reading for Prayer during the Day

(see Prayer during the Day)

Collects

First Sunday after Trinity
Sunday 11 per annum

O GOD, the strength of all them that put their trust in thee: mercifully accept our prayers and, because through the weakness of our mortal nature we can do no good thing without thee, grant us the help of thy grace that, in keeping of thy commandments, we may please thee, both in will and deed; through Jesus Christ thy Son our Lord, who liveth and reigneth with thee, in the unity of the Holy Spirit, one God, for ever and ever.

Second Sunday after Trinity
Sunday 12 per annum

O LORD, who never failest to help and govern them who thou dost bring up in thy steadfast fear and love: keep us, we beseech thee, under the protection of thy good providence, and make us to have a perpetual fear and love of thy holy Name; through Jesus Christ thy Son our Lord, who liveth and reigneth with thee, in the unity of the Holy Spirit, one God, for ever and ever.

Third Sunday after Trinity

O LORD, we beseech thee mercifully to hear us: and grant that we, to whom though hast given an hearty desire to pray, may be comforted in all dangers and adversities; through Jesus Christ thy Son our Lord, who liveth and reigneth with thee, in the unity of the Holy Spirit, one God, for ever and ever.

Fourth Sunday after Trinity
Sunday 17 per annum

O GOD, the protector of all that trust in thee, without whom nothing is strong, nothing is holy: increase and multiply upon us thy mercy that, thou being our ruler and guide, we may so pass through things temporal that we lose not our hold on things eternal; grant this, O heavenly Father, for Jesus Christ's sake our Lord, who liveth and reigneth with thee, in the unity of the Holy Spirit, one God, for ever and ever.

Fifth Sunday after Trinity

Sunday 8 per annum

GRANT, O Lord, we beseech thee: that the course of this world may be so peaceably ordered by thy governance that thy Church may joyfully serve thee in all godly quietness; through Jesus Christ thy Son our Lord, who liveth and reigneth with thee, in the unity of the Holy Spirit, one God, for ever and ever.

Sixth Sunday after Trinity

Sunday 20 per annum

O GOD, who hast prepared for them that love thee such good things as pass our understanding: pour into our hearts such love toward thee that we, loving thee in all things and above all things, may obtain thy promises which exceed all that we can desire; through Jesus Christ thy Son our Lord, who liveth and reigneth with thee, in the unity of the Holy Spirit, one God, for ever and ever.

Seventh Sunday after Trinity

Sunday 22 per annum

LORD of all power and might, who art the author and giver of all good things: graft in our hearts the love of thy name, increase in us true religion, nourish us with all goodness, and of thy great mercy keep us in the same; through Jesus Christ thy Son our Lord, who liveth and reigneth with thee, in the unity of the Holy Spirit, one God, for ever and ever.

Eighth Sunday after Trinity

O GOD, whose never-failing providence ordereth all things both in heaven and earth: we humbly beseech thee to put away from us all hurtful things, and to give us those things which be profitable for us; through Jesus Christ thy Son our Lord, who liveth and reigneth with thee, in the unity of the Holy Spirit, one God, for ever and ever.

Ninth Sunday after Trinity

Sunday 7 per annum

GRANT to us, Lord, we beseech thee the spirit to think and do always such things as be rightful: that we, who cannot do any thing that is good without thee, may by thee be enabled to live according to thy will; through Jesus Christ thy Son our Lord, who liveth and reigneth with thee, in the unity of the Holy Spirit, one God, for ever and ever.

Tenth Sunday after Trinity

LET thy merciful ears, O Lord, be open to the prayers of thy humble servants: and that they may obtain their petitions make them to ask such things as shall please thee; through Jesus Christ thy Son our Lord, who liveth and reigneth with thee, in the unity of the Holy Spirit, one God, for ever and ever.

Eleventh Sunday after Trinity

Sunday 26 per annum

O GOD, who declarest thy almighty power most chiefly in shewing mercy and pity: mercifully grant unto us such a measure of thy grace that we, running the way of thy commandments, may obtain thy gracious promises and be made partakers of thy heavenly treasure; through Jesus Christ thy Son our Lord, who liveth and reigneth with thee, in the unity of the Holy Spirit, one God, for ever and ever.

Twelfth Sunday after Trinity

Sunday 27 per annum

ALMIGHTY and everlasting God, who art always more ready to hear than we to pray, and art wont to give more than either we desire or deserve: pour down upon us the abundance of thy mercy, forgiving us those things whereof our conscience is afraid and giving us those good things which we are not worthy to ask; but through the merits and mediation of Jesus Christ thy Son our Lord, who liveth and reigneth with thee, in the unity of the Holy Spirit, one God, for ever and ever.

Thirteenth Sunday after Trinity

ALMIGHTY and merciful God, of whose only gift it cometh that thy faithful people do unto thee true and laudable service: grant, we beseech thee, that we may so faithfully serve thee in this life, that we fail not finally to attain thy heavenly promises; through the merits of Jesus Christ our Lord, who liveth and reigneth with thee, in the unity of the Holy Spirit, one God, for ever and ever.

Fourteenth Sunday after Trinity

Sunday 30 per annum

ALMIGHTY and everlasting God, give unto us the increase of faith, hope, and charity: and, that we may obtain that which thou dost promise, make us to love that which thou dost command; through Jesus Christ thy Son our Lord, who liveth and reigneth with thee, in the unity of the Holy Spirit, one God, for ever and ever.

Fifteenth Sunday after Trinity

KEEP, we beseech thee, O Lord, thy Church with thy perpetual mercy: and, because our human frailty without thee cannot but fall, keep us ever by thy help from all things hurtful and lead us to all things profitable to our salvation; through Jesus Christ thy Son our Lord, who liveth and reigneth with thee, in the unity of the Holy Spirit, one God, for ever and ever.

Sixteenth Sunday after Trinity

O LORD, we beseech thee, let thy continual pity cleanse and defend thy Church: and, because it cannot continue in safety without thy succour, preserve it evermore by thy help and goodness; through Jesus Christ thy Son our Lord, who liveth and reigneth with thee, in the unity of the Holy Spirit, one God, for ever and ever.

Seventeenth Sunday after Trinity

Sunday 28 per annum

LORD, we pray thee that thy grace may always precede and follow us: and make us continually to be given to all good works; through Jesus Christ thy Son our Lord, who liveth and reigneth with thee, in the unity of the Holy Spirit, one God, for ever and ever.

Eighteenth Sunday after Trinity

LORD, we beseech thee, grant thy people grace to withstand the temptations of the world, the flesh, and the devil: and with pure hearts and minds to follow thee the only God; through Jesus Christ thy Son our Lord, who liveth and reigneth with thee, in the unity of the Holy Spirit, one God, for ever and ever.

Nineteenth Sunday after Trinity

O GOD, forasmuch as without thee we are not able to please thee: mercifully grant, that thy Holy Spirit may in all things direct and rule our hearts; through Jesus Christ thy Son our Lord, who liveth and reigneth with thee, in the unity of the Holy Spirit, one God, for ever and ever.

Twentieth Sunday after Trinity

Sunday 32 per annum

O ALMIGHTY and most merciful God, of thy bountiful goodness keep us, we beseech thee, from all things that may hurt us: that we, being ready both in body and soul, may cheerfully accomplish those things that though wouldest have done; through Jesus Christ thy Son our Lord, who liveth and reigneth with thee, in the unity of the Holy Spirit, one God, for ever and ever.

Twenty-First Sunday after Trinity

GRANT, we beseech thee, merciful Lord, to thy faithful people pardon and peace: that they may be cleansed from all their sins and serve thee with a quiet mind; through Jesus Christ thy Son our Lord, who liveth and reigneth with thee, in the unity of the Holy Spirit, one God, for ever and ever.

Twenty-Second Sunday after Trinity

LORD, we beseech thee to keep thy household the Church in continual godliness: that through thy protection it may be free from all adversities, and devoutly given to serve thee in good works, to the glory of thy Name; through Jesus Christ thy Son our Lord, who liveth and reigneth with thee, in the unity of the Holy Spirit, one God, for ever and ever.

For the Twenty-Third and Twenty-Fourth Sundays after Trinity, see page 443 onwards.

From the day after All Souls' Day
until the day before Christ the King

Office

Opening Sentence

Blessed are the poor in spirit,
for theirs is the kingdom of heaven.

Mt 5:3

For the readings for the Twenty-First and Twenty-Second Sundays after Trinity, see pages 433 and 434.

Twenty-Third Sunday after Trinity

When this Sunday falls on the solemnity of Christ the King, the Sunday next before Advent, it (and any remaining Sundays after Trinity) is superseded.

A reading from the sermons of William Laud

'Arise, O God, (plead or) maintain thine own cause: remember how the foolish man (reproacheth or) blasphemeth thee daily' (Ps 74:22). [...] Now 'the cause of God' meant here, though it be proposed as one cause, yet it is very large, and comprehends many particulars under it. Some directly concern God, and some only by reflex. But God is so tender of his justice and his honour, that nothing can so much as touch upon him, but it is God's cause presently: 'Inasmuch as ye have done it, or not done it, to one of these little ones, ye have done it, or not done it, to me' (Mt 25:45). And so goes the text, 'God's cause', all, and but one, whether it be directed against him, or reflected upon him; whether it be the reproach which the Son of God suffered for us, or the troubles and afflictions which we suffer for him, it is God's cause still, and accounted as one.

As one: and yet I find three things agreed upon, to be principally contained in this cause of God. First, the magistrate, and his power and justice. And resist either of these, and you resist 'the power, and the ordinance of God' (Rom 13:2). There is God's cause plain. And the eye of nature could see somewhat that was divine in the governors and orderers of commonwealths. In their very office; inasmuch as they are singled out to be the ministers of divine Providence upon earth; and are expressly called the officers of God's kingdom...And here Kings may learn, if they will, I am sure it is fit they should, that those men which are sacrilegious against God and his Church are, for the very neighbourhood of sin, the likeliest men to offer violence to the honour of princes first, and their persons after.

Secondly: the cause of the Church, in what kind soever it be, be it in the cause of truth, or in the cause of unity, or in the cause of right and means, it is God's cause too; and it must needs be so; for Christ and his Church are 'head and body' (Eph 1:22, 23), and therefore, they must needs have one common cause.

William Laud, 'Sermon V. Preached before his Majesty, at Whitehall, on Wednesday, the 5th of July, 1626, at the solemn fast then held', in *The Works of the most reverend father in God, William Laud, I. Sermons* (Oxford: John Henry Parker, 1857), pp. 121, 131-134.

One cause; and you cannot corrupt the Church in her truth, or persecute her for it, nor distract her from her unity, nor impoverish and abuse her in her means, but God suffers in the oppression. Nay more, no man can wilfully corrupt the Church in her doctrine, but he would have a false God; nor persecute the profession of the Church, but he would have no God; nor rend the Church into sects, but he would have many gods, nor make the Church base, but he would pluck God as low, were God as much in his power as the Church is; and therefore, the Church's cause is God's cause. [...]

Now this ever holds true, in whatsoever the Church suffers for the name of God and Christ, And therefore if either State or Church will have their 'cause' God's, the State must look their proceedings be just, and the Church must look their devotions and actions be pious. Else, if the State be all in wormwood and injustice; if the Church savour of impurity and irreligion, if either of these threaten either body, neither can call God upon them. For sin is their own and the devil's 'cause', no 'cause' of God's, who punishes sin ever, but never 'causes' it.

Thirdly: it is 'God's cause', which is directly against himself, when injustice that he will not, or weakness that he cannot, 'arise' and 'help', are most unworthily, nay, blasphemously, cast upon him. The very text you see, calls it no less than 'blasphemy'. And as Saint Basil tells us, it was most audaciously cast into the face of God. But how, I pray? How? why, they persecuted the Church of Christ with great extremities, and then because God did not always and in all particulars, deliver it, they accused God of impotency. Rabshakeh's case, before Christ in the flesh: 'Which of the gods have delivered the nations that serve then, that the Lord should deliver Jerusalem?' (2 Kings*18:35). Pilate's case to Christ: 'Have I not power to crucify thee, and power to loose thee?' (Jn 19:10). Julian's case, after Christ: for while he raged against the Christians, he turned the contumely upon God; and charged Omnipotence with weakness. So you see the 'cause of God' what it ism and withal that it is many, and but one. Many in the circumference of his creatures, which fill up the State and the Church; and yet but one in the point of that indivisible centre, which is himself.

---

*Sometimes known as 4 Kings

Twenty-Fourth Sunday after Trinity

When this Sunday falls on the solemnity of Christ the King, the Sunday next before Advent, it is superseded. If there are more than twenty-four Sundays after Trinity, use is made of the Sundays omitted after the Epiphany.

A reading from the sermons of William Beveridge

That which I look upon as most observable of all is, that [Christ] did not only speak, but act, in his own name, and by his own power. He saith, I confess, in one place, 'I am come in my Father's name' (Jn 5:43). And in another, 'The works that I do in my Father's name, they bear witness of me' (Jn 10:25). But we must observe, that he doth not say, 'In the name of God', but 'of his Father'. If he had said, 'In the name of God', some might have been apt to think, though without ground, that he himself was not God; for, if he was, it would have been more proper to have said, he came or acted in his own name. But, to prevent that mistake, he saith only 'in the name of the Father', and so he acted even as God in the name of the Father, because he received his divine essence, and so the power by which he acted, from the Father. In which sense he saith, 'I can of myself do nothing' (Jn 5:30). And 'I do nothing of myself, but as my Father hath taught me, I speak these things' (Jn 5:30). And, 'If I do not the works of my Father, believe me not' (Jn 10:37). And so all along he speaks of the Father, as the person from whom he received his power, as being his Son; but still he acted by that power immediately from himself, as being God.

To prove this, we need go no farther than the works of creation, wherein God did most clearly exert and shew forth his power and Godhead, in producing all things out of nothing by a word of his mouth: he only said, 'Let there be light: and there was light' (Gen 1:3). 'Let the waters under the heavens be gathered together in one place; and it was so' (Gen 1:9). 'Let the earth bring forth grass: and it was so' (Gen 1:11). Thus the whole creation was finished, only by God;' expressing and signifying his will, that everything should be as he pleased, and so it was; which was such an act of divine power, that no creature could ever pretend to it, nor, indeed, can be capable of it, it being an incommunicable

William Beveridge, 'Sermon XX; Faith in Christ, the only means of overcoming the world', in *Twenty-six Sermons on Various Subjects, selected from the works of William Beveridge* (London: Society for the Promotion of Christian Knowledge, 1850), pp. 427-430.

perfection of the Divine nature to act so immediately in, and of itself, and perfectly to its own will.

And yet this was the way Christ acted when he was upon earth, and so demonstrated his divine power and glory the same way as God had done it in making of the world. For when there came a leper to him, saying, 'If thou wilt, thou canst me clean', Jesus only said, 'I will; be thou clean', and it was so; 'immediately his leprosy was cleansed' (Mt 8:2-3) [...] When he came to Jairus' house, and found his daughter lying dead, he only said, 'Talitha cumi', ('Damsel, arise') and it was so; 'straightway the damsel arose, and walked (Mk 5:41). When they brought to him one that was deaf, and had an impediment in his speech, he only said, 'Ephphatha, be opened; and it was so; for 'straightway his ears were opened, and the string of his tongue was loosed, and he spake plain' ((Mk 7:34,35). [...] When he came near the city of Nain, and saw a dead man carried out to be buried, he only said, 'Young man, I say unto thee, Arise' and it was so; for, 'he that was dead sat up and began to speak' (Lk 7:14). When Lazarus had been dead four days, and was laid in his grave, he only said, 'Lazarus, Come forth', and it was so; 'he that was dead came forth' (Jn 11:43). There are many instances to be found in the Gospel, of Christ's acting merely by his word. And which, if it be possible, is more remarkable, he did the same by his apostles, who wrought miracles only in his name.[...]

In all which it is to be observed, that Christ had no sooner spoke the word with his own mouth, or by his apostles, but the thing was done; which plainly shews, that he could so what he would, only by willing it should be done. Which, as it is the proper notion of Omnipotence, so it is an indeniable argument and demonstration of his Godhead. From all which it appears, that God himself in the Holy Scriptures, hath declared both by his word and works, that Jesus Christ is his own natural or essential Son, of the same nature and substance with himself; and therefore, whosoever would believe aright, according to his own word, must thus believe, that 'Jesus is the Son of God'.

Short Readings for Prayer during the Day

Sunday *Rev 4:9-11*

Whenever the living creatures give glory and honour and thanks to him who is seated on the throne, who lives for ever and ever, the twenty-four elders fall down before him who is seated on the throne and worship him who lives for ever and ever; they cast their crowns before the throne, singing, 'Worthy art thou, our Lord and God, to receive glory and honour and power, for thou didst create all things, and by thy will they existed and were created.'

Monday *Phil 4:4-7*

Rejoice in the Lord always; again I will say, Rejoice. Let all men know your forbearance. The Lord is at hand. Have no anxiety about anything, but in everything by prayer and supplication with thanksgiving let your requests be made known to God. And the peace of God, which passes all understanding, will keep your hearts and your minds in Christ Jesus.

Tuesday *Heb 12:22-24*

You have come to Mount Zion and to the city of the living God, the heavenly Jerusalem, and to innumerable angels in festal gathering, and to the assembly of the first-born who are enrolled in heaven, and to a judge who is God of all, and to the spirits of just men made perfect, and to Jesus, the mediator of a new covenant, and to the sprinkled blood that speaks more graciously than the blood of Abel.

Wednesday *Is 65:18-19*

Be glad and rejoice for ever in that which I create; for behold, I create Jerusalem a rejoicing, and her people a joy. I will rejoice in Jerusalem, and be glad in my people; no more shall be heard in it the sound of weeping and the cry of distress.

Thursday *Eph 4:11-13*

His gifts were that some should be apostles, some prophets, some evangelists, some pastors and teachers, to equip the saints for the work of ministry, for building up the body of Christ, until we all attain to the unity of the faith and of the knowledge of the Son of God, to mature manhood, to the measure of the stature of the fullness of Christ.

Friday *Heb 12:1, 2*

Since we are surrounded by so great a cloud of witnesses, let us also lay aside every weight, and sin which clings so closely, and let us run with perseverance the race that is set before us, looking to Jesus the pioneer and perfecter of our faith, who for the joy that was set before him endured the cross, despising the shame, and is seated at the right hand of the throne of God.

Saturday *Dan 12:2, 3*

Many of those who sleep in the dust of the earth shall awake, some to everlasting life, and some to shame and everlasting contempt. And those who are wise shall shine like the brightness of the firmament; and those who turn many to righteousness, like the stars for ever and ever.

All Saints until Advent Prayer during the Day

Bring us, O Lord God, at our last awakening
into the house and gate of heaven,
to enter that gate and dwell in that house,
where there shall be no darkness nor dazzling,
  but one equal light;
no noise nor silence, but one equal music;
no fears nor hopes, but one equal possession;
no ends nor beginnings, but one equal eternity;
in the habitations of thy glory and dominion,
world without end.

Eric Milner White (1963)
after John Donne (1631)

Twenty-First Sunday after Trinity

GRANT, we beseech thee, merciful Lord, to thy faithful people pardon and peace: that they may be cleansed from all their sins and serve thee with a quiet mind; through Jesus Christ thy Son our Lord, who liveth and reigneth with thee, in the unity of the Holy Spirit, one God, for ever and ever.

Twenty-Second Sunday after Trinity

LORD, we beseech thee to keep thy household the Church in continual godliness: that through thy protection it may be free from all adversities, and devoutly given to serve thee in good works, to the glory of thy Name; through Jesus Christ thy Son our Lord, who liveth and reigneth with thee, in the unity of the Holy Spirit, one God, for ever and ever.

Twenty-Third Sunday after Trinity

O GOD, our refuge and strength, who art the author of all godliness: be ready, we beseech thee, to hear the devout prayers of thy Church, and grant that those things which we ask faithfully we may obtain effectually; through Jesus Christ thy Son our Lord, who liveth and reigneth with thee, in the unity of the Holy Spirit, one God, for ever and ever.

Twenty-Fourth Sunday after Trinity

O LORD, we beseech thee, absolve thy people from their offences: that through thy bountiful goodness we may all be delivered from the bands of those sins, which by our frailty we have committed; grant this, O heavenly Father, for Jesus Christ's sake, our blessed Lord and Saviour.

Twenty-Fifth Sunday after Trinity *(as needed)*

(Fifth Sunday after Epiphany)

O LORD, we beseech thee to keep thy Church and household continually in thy true religion: that they who do lean only upon the hope of thy heavenly grace may evermore be defended by thy mighty power; through Jesus Christ thy Son our Lord, who liveth and reigneth with thee in the unity of the Holy Spirit, one God, for ever and ever.

Twenty-Sixth Sunday after Trinity *(as needed)*

(Sixth Sunday after Epiphany)

O GOD, whose blessed Son was manifested that he might destroy the works of the devil, and make us the sons of God, and heirs of eternal life: grant us, we beseech thee, that, having this hope, we may purify ourselves, even as he is pure, that, when he shall appear again with power and great glory, we may be made like unto him in his eternal and glorious kingdom; where with thee, O Father, and thee, O Holy Spirit, he liveth and reigneth, ever one God, world without end.

Office

Opening Sentence

The Lord is King, and has put on glorious apparel:
the Lord has put on his glory and girded himself with strength.

Ps 93:1

Post-Biblical Reading

A reading from the sermons of Blessed John Henry Newman

There are three favoured servants of God in particular, special types of the Saviour to come, men raised from low estate to great honour, in whom it was his will that his pastoral office should be thus literally fulfilled. And the first is Jacob, the father of the patriarchs, who appeared before Pharoah... But at the first he was, as his descendants solemnly confessed, year by year, 'a Syrian ready to perish' (Deut 26:5); and what was his employment? the care of sheep; and with what toil and suffering, and for how many years, we learn from his expostulation with his hard master and relative, Laban – 'This twenty years have I been with thee', he says, 'thy ewes and thy she-goats have not cast their young, and the rams of thy flock have I not eaten. That which was torn of beasts I brought not unto thee; I bare the loss of it; of my hand didst thou require it, whether stolen by day, or stolen by night, Thus I was; in the day the drought consumed me, and the frost by night; and my sleep departed from mine eyes. Thus have I been twenty years in thy house; ... and thou hast changed my wages ten times' (Gen 31:38-41).

Who is more favoured than Jacob, who was exalted to be a Prince with God, and to prevail by intercession? Yet, you see, he is a shepherd, to image to us the mystical and true Shepherd and Bishop of souls who was to come. Yet there is a second and a third as highly favoured in various ways. The second is Moses, who drove away the rival shepherds and helped the daughters of the Priest of

Bl. John Henry Newman, 'The Shepherd of our Souls', in *Parochial and Plain Sermons, by John Henry Newman*, VIII (London: Rivingtons, 1882), pp. 236-238, 240-241, 243.

Midian to water their flock; and who, while he was keeping the flock of Jethro, his father-in-law, saw the Angel of the Lord in a flame of fire in the bush. And the third is David, the man after God's own heart. He was 'the man who was raised up on high, the anointed of the God of Jacob, and the sweet Psalmist of Israel (2 Sam 23:1), but he was found among the sheep. [...]

Jacob endured, Moses meditated – and David wrought. Jacob endured the frost, and heat, and sleepless night, and paid the price of the lost sheep; Moses was taken up into the mount for forty days; David fought with the foe, and recovered the prey – he rescued it from the mouth of the lion, and the paw of the bear, and killed the ravenous beasts. Christ, too, not only suffered with Jacob, and was in contemplation with Moses, but fought and conquered with David. David defended his father's sheep at Bethlehem; Christ, born and heralded to the shepherds at Bethlehem, suffered on the Cross in order to conquer. He came 'from Edom, with dyed garments from Bozrah', but he was 'glorious in his apparel', for he trod the people 'in his anger, and trampled them in his fury, and their blood was sprinkled upon his garments, and he stained all his raiment' (Is 63:1-3). Jacob was not as David, nor David as Jacob, nor either of them as Moses; but Christ was all three, as fulfilling all types, the lowly Jacob, the wise Moses, the heroic David, all in one – Priest, Prophet, and King. [...]

Blessed are they who give the flower of their days, and their strength of soul and body to him; blessed are they who in their youth turn to him who gave his life for them, and would fain give it to them and implant it in them, that they may live for ever. Blessed are they who resolve – come good, come evil, come sunshine, come tempest, come honour, come dishonour – that he shall be their Lord and Master, their King and God!

Short Reading for Prayer during the Day *Col 1:12-20*

Give thanks to the Father, who has qualified us to share in the inheritance of the saints in light. He has delivered us from the dominion of darkness and transferred us to the kingdom of his beloved Son, in whom we have redemption, the forgiveness of sins. He is the image of the invisible God, the first-born of all creation; for in him all things were created, in heaven and on earth, visible and invisible, whether thrones or dominions or principalities or authorities - all things were created through him and for him. He is before all things, and in him all things hold together. He is the head of the body, the church; he is the beginning, the first-born from the dead, that in everything he might be pre-eminent. For in him all the fullness of God was pleased to dwell, and through him to reconcile to himself all things, whether on earth or in heaven, making peace by the blood of his cross.

Collect

ALMIGHTY Father, whose will is to restore all things in thy beloved Son, the king of all: govern the hearts and minds of those in authority and bring the families of the nations, divided and torn apart by the ravages of sin, to be subject to his just and gentle rule; who liveth and reigneth with thee, in the unity of the Holy Spirit, one God, for ever and ever.

Office

Opening Sentence
Thou shalt shew me the path of life;
in thy presence is the fullness of joy:
and at thy right hand there is pleasure for evermore.

Ps 16:12

Short Reading for Prayer during the Day

(see Prayer during the Day)

All Saints until Advent Prayer during the Day

Bring us, O Lord God, at our last awakening
into the house and gate of heaven,
to enter that gate and dwell in that house,
where there shall be no darkness nor dazzling,
  but one equal light;
no noise nor silence, but one equal music;
no fears nor hopes, but one equal possession;
no ends nor beginnings, but one equal eternity;
in the habitations of thy glory and dominion,
world without end.

Eric Milner White (1963)
after John Donne (1631)

Collect
STIR up, we beseech thee, O Lord, the wills of thy faithful people:
that they, plenteously bringing forth the fruit of good works, may of
thee be plenteously rewarded; through Jesus Christ thy Son our Lord,
who liveth and reigneth with thee, in the unity of the Holy Spirit, one
God, for ever and ever.

IV. Times and Seasons

Part VI Sanctorale:

Propers of the
General Calendar

(1) Propers of the General Calendar

For the National Calendar and the Calendar set out for this Customary, see page 550. For the Proper of Saints from the General Calendar, who are celebrated also in the National and Local Calendar, see the Calendar of the Customary of Our Lady of Walsingham.†

These Propers are for the Use of this Customary, and not for use with the Roman Missal or the Liturgy of the Hours. Some celebrations in the General Calendar are not represented here: memorias of saints of other countries and cultures are usually omitted and where the memorias are of obligation resort should be made to the Liturgy of the Hours and the Roman Missal.

Complementary material also should be drawn from the Common of Saints below (see page 658) and from the Roman Missal or the Liturgy of the Hours.

---

† The exceptions are the Propers of St Andrew, of the Patrons of Europe (SS Cyril and Methodius, St Catherine of Siena, St Benedict, St Bridget, St Teresa Benedicta of the Cross), and of St Elizabeth of Hungary, which, though in the National Calendar, remain in the General Calendar section. St Gregory the Great, a national feast in England, is in the Calendar of this Customary.

Saint Andrew, Apostle, Patron of Scotland
(30 November)

Proper of the Day and Common of Apostles

A reading from the sermons of Blessed John Henry Newman

These are the facts before us. St Andrew was the first convert among the apostles; he was especially in our Lord's confidence; thrice is he described as introducing others to him; lastly, he is little known in history, while the place of dignity and the name of highest renown have been allotted to his brother Simon, whom he was the means of bringing to the knowledge of his Saviour.

Our less, then, is this: that those men are not necessarily the most useful men in their generation, nor the most favoured by God, who make the most noise in the world, and who seem to be principals in the great changes and events recorded in history; on the contrary, that even when we are able to point to a certain number of men as the real instruments of any great blessings vouchsafed to mankind, our relative estimate of them, one with another, is often very erroneous: so that, on the whole, if we would trace truly the hand of God in human affairs, and pursue his bounty as displayed in the world to its original sources, we must unlearn our admiration of the powerful and distinguished, our reliance on the opinion of society, our respect for the decisions of the learned or the multitude, and turn our eyes to private life, watching in all we read or witness for the true signs of God's presence, the graces of personal holiness manifested in his elect; which, weak as they may seem to mankind, are mighty through God, and have an influence upon the course of his Providence, and bring about great events in the world at large, when the wisdom and strength of the natural man are of no avail. [...]

Who taught the doctors and saints of the Church, who, in their day, or in after times, have been the most illustrious expounders of the precepts of right and wrong, and, by word and deed, are the guides of our conduct? Did Almighty Wisdom speak to them through the operation of their own minds, or rather,

---

Bl. John Henry Newman, 'The World's Benefactors', in *Parochial and Plain Sermons, by John Henry Newman* II (London: Rivingtons, 1880), pp. 4-6, 9-20.

did it not subject them to instructors unknown to fame, wiser perhaps even than themselves? Andrew followed John the Baptist, while Simon remained at his nets. Andrew first recognized the Messiah among the inhabitants of despised Nazareth; and be brought his brother to him. Yet to Andrew Christ spake no word of commendation which has been allowed to continue on record; whereas to Simon, even on his first coming, he gave the honourable name by which he is now designated, and afterwards put him forward as the typical foundation of his Church. Nothing indeed can hence be inferred, one way or the other, concerning the relative excellence of the two brothers; so far only appears, that, in the providential course of events, the one was the secret beginner, and the other the public instrument, of a great divine work. [...]

[A]re not the blessed angels unknown to the world: and is not God himself, the Author of all good, hid from mankind at large, partially manifested and poorly glorified, in a few scattered servants here and there? And his Spirit, do we know whence it cometh, and whither it goeth? And though he has taught men whatever these has been of wisdom among them from the beginning, yet when he came on earth in visible form, even then it was said of him, 'The world knew him not'. His marvellous providence works beneath a veil, which speaks but an untrue language; and to see him who is the Truth and the Life, we must stoop underneath it, and so in our turn hide ourselves from the world. [...] Hid are the saints of God; if they are known to men, it is accidentally, in their temporal offices, as holding some high earthly station, or effecting some mere civil work, not as saints, St Peter has a place in history, far more as a chief instrument of a strange revolution in human affairs, than in his true character, as a self-denying follower of his Lord, to whom truths were revealed which flesh and blood could not discern.

Collect

ALMIGHTY God, who didst give such grace unto thy apostle Saint Andrew that he readily obeyed the calling of thy Son Jesus Christ and followed him without delay: grant unto us all that we, being called by thy holy word, may forthwith give up ourselves obediently to fulfil thy holy commandments; through Jesus Christ thy Son our Lord, who liveth and reigneth with thee, in the unity of the Holy Spirit, one God, for ever and ever.

Saint Nicholas, Bishop
(6 December)

Proper of the Day and Common of Pastors

ALMIGHTY Father, lover of souls, who didst choose thy servant Nicholas to be a bishop in the Church, that he might give freely out of the treasures of thy grace: through his intercession, make us mindful of the needs of others and, as we have received, so teach us also to give; through Jesus Christ thy Son our Lord, who liveth and reigneth with thee, in the unity of the Holy Spirit, one God, for ever and ever.

Saint Ambrose, Bishop, Doctor of the Church
(7 December)

Proper of the Day and Common of Pastors
or of Doctors of the Church

LORD God of hosts, who didst call Ambrose from the governor's throne to be a bishop in thy Church and a courageous champion of thy faithful people: mercifully grant that, through his prayers, as he fearlessly rebuked rulers, so we may with like courage contend for the faith which we have received; through Jesus Christ thy Son our Lord, who liveth and reigneth with thee, in the unity of the Holy Spirit, one God, for ever and ever.

Immaculate Conception of the Blessed Virgin Mary
(8 December)

Proper of the Day and Common of the Blessed Virgin Mary

A reading from the writings of Blessed John Henry Newman

What is the great rudimental teaching of Antiquity from its earliest date concerning her [the Blessed Virgin]. By 'rudimental teaching' I mean the *prima facie* view of her person and office, the broad outline laid down of her, the aspect under which she comes to us, in the writings of the fathers. She is the Second Eve. [...] She holds, as the Fathers teach us, that office in our restoration which Eve held in our fall: - now, in the first place, what were Eve's endowments to enable her to enter upon her trial? She could not have stood against the wiles of the devil, though she was innocent and sinless, without the grant of a large grace. And this she had; - a heavenly gift, which was over and above and additional to that nature of hers, which she had received from Adam, a gift which had been given to Adam also before her, at the very time (as it is commonly held) of his original formation. [...] Now, taking this for granted, because I know that you and those who agree with you maintain it as well as we do, I ask you, have you any intention to deny that Mary was as fully endowed as Eve? Is it any violent inference, that she, who was to co-operate in the redemption of the world, at least was not less endowed with power from on high, than she who, given as a helpmate to her husband, did in the event but co-operate with him for its ruin? If Eve was raised above human nature by that indwelling moral gift which we call grace, is it rash to say that Mary had even a greater grace? And this consideration gives significance to the Angel's salutation of her as 'full of grace', - and interpretation of the original word which is undoubtedly the right one, as soon as we resist the common Protestant assumption that grace is a mere external approbation or acceptance, answering to the word 'favour', whereas it is, as the Fathers teach, a real inward condition or superadded quality of soul. And if Eve had this supernatural inward gift given her from the first moment of her personal existence, is it possible to deny that Mary too had this gift from the very first moment of her personal existence? I do not know how to resist this inference: - well, this is simply and

Bl. John Henry Newman, *A Letter addressed to the Rev. E. B. Pusey, D. D., on the Occasion of his Eirenicon*, in John Henry Cardinal Newman, *Certain Difficulties felt by Anglicans in Catholic Teaching* (London: Longmans, Green and Co, 1907), II., pp. 31, 44-45, 48-49.

literally the doctrine of the Immaculate Conception. I say the doctrine of the Immaculate is in its substance this, and nothing more or less than this (putting aside the question of degrees of grace); and it really does seem to me bound up in the doctrine of the Fathers, that Mary is the second Eve. [...]

Mary could not merit... the restoration of that grace; but it was restored to her by God's free bounty, from the very first moment of her existence, and thereby, in fact, she never came under the original curse, which consisted in the loss of it. And she had this special privilege, in order to fit her to become the Mother of her and our Redeemer, to fit her mentally, spiritually for it; so that, by the aid of the first grace, she might so grow in grace, that, when the Angel came and her Lord was at hand, she might be 'full of grace', prepared as far as a creature could be prepared, to receive him into her bosom.

Collect

O GOD, who through the immaculate Conception of the Virgin didst prepare a habitation meet for thy Son: we beseech thee that, as thou, foreseeing the death of thy Son, didst preserve her from all stain, so by her intercession thou wouldest suffer us also to attain in purity to thee; through the same Jesus Christ thy Son our Lord, who liveth and reigneth with thee, in the unity of the Holy Spirit, one God, for ever and ever.

Saint Lucy, Virgin, Martyr
(13 December)

Proper of the Day and Common of Martyrs

O GOD our redeemer, who gavest light to the world that was in darkness by the healing power of the Saviour's cross: we beseech thee to shed that light on us that with thy martyr Lucy we may, by the purity of our lives, reflect the light of Christ and, by the merits of his passion, attain to the light of everlasting life; through Jesus Christ thy Son our Lord, who liveth and reigneth with thee, in the unity of the Holy Spirit, one God, for ever and ever.

**Saint John of the Cross, Priest,
Doctor of the Church
(14 December)**

*Proper of the Day and Common of Pastors
or of Doctors of the Church*

O GOD, the judge of all, who gavest to thy servant John of the Cross
a warmth of nature, a strength of purpose and a mystical faith that
sustained him even in the darkness: through his prayers shed thy light
on all who love thee, granting them union of body and soul in thy Son
Jesus Christ our Lord; who liveth and reigneth with thee, in the unity
of the Holy Spirit, one God, for ever and ever.

**Saint Stephen, First Martyr
(26 December)**

Proper of the Day and Common of Martyrs

A reading from the sermons of Blessed John Henry Newman

St Stephen, who was one of the seven Deacons, is called the Protomartyr, as
having first suffered death in the cause of the Gospel. Let me take the
opportunity of his festival to make some remarks upon martyrdom generally.

The word 'martyr' properly means 'a witness', but is used to denote exclusively
one who has suffered death for the Christian faith. Those who have witnessed
for Christ without suffering death are called confessors: a title which the early
martyrs often made their own, before their last solemn confession unto death,
or martyrdom. Our Lord Jesus Christ is the chief and most glorious of martyrs,
as having 'before Pontius Pilate witnessed a good confession' (1 Tim 6:13), but
we do not call him a martyr as being much more than a martyr. True it is, he
died for the truth; but that was not the chief purpose of his death. He died to
save us sinners from the wrath of God. He was not only a martyr; he was an
atoning Sacrifice.

Bl. John Henry Newman, 'Martyrdom', in *Parochial and Plain Sermons, by John
Henry Newman* II (London: Rivingtons, 1880), pp. 41-43; 48-49.

He is the supreme object of our love, gratitude, and reverence. Next to him we honour the noble army of martyrs; not indeed comparing them with him, 'who is above all, God blessed for ever' (Rom 9:5), or as if they in suffering had any part in the work of reconciliation, but because they have approached most closely to the pattern of all his servants. They have shed their blood for the Church, fulfilling the text, 'He laid down his life for us, and we ought to lay down our lives for the brethren' (1 Jn 3:16). They have followed his steps, and claim our grateful remembrance. [...]

Now it may be said, that many men suffer pain, as great as martyrdom, from disease, and in other ways: again, that it does not follow that those who happened to be martyred were always the most useful and active defenders of the faith; and therefore, that in honouring the martyrs, we are honouring with especial honour those to whom indeed we may be peculiarly indebted (as in the case of apostles), but nevertheless who may have been but ordinary men, who happened to stand in the most exposed place, in the way of persecution, and were slain as if by chance, because the sword met them first. But this, it is plain, would be a strange way of reasoning in a parallel case. We are grateful to those who have done us favours, rather than to those who might or would, if it had so happened. We have no concern with the question, were the martyrs the best of men or not, or whether others would have been martyrs too, had it been allowed them. We are grateful to those who were such, from the plain matter of fact that they were such, that they did go through much suffering, in order that the world might gain an inestimable benefit, the light of the Gospel. [...]

It is useful to reflect on subjects such as that I have now laid before you, in order to humble ourselves. 'We have not resisted unto blood, striving against sin' (Heb 12:4). What are our petty suffering, which we make so much of, to their pains and sorrows, who lost their friends, and then their own lives for Christ's sake; who were assaulted by all kinds of temptations, the sophistry of Antichrist the blandishments of the world, the terrors of the sword, the weariness of suspense, and yet fainted not. How far about ours are both their afflictions, and their consolations under them! Now I know that such reflections are at once, and with far deeper reason, raised by the thought of the sufferings of Christ himself; but commonly, his transcendent holiness and his depth of woe do not immediately affect us, from their very greatness. We sum them up in a few words, and we speak without understanding. On the other hand, we rise somewhat towards the comprehension of them, when we make use of that heavenly ladder by which his saints have made their way towards him. By contemplating the lowest of his true servants, and seeing how far any of them surpasses ourselves, we learn to shrink before his ineffable purity, who is infinitely holier than the holiest of his creatures; and to confess ourselves wit a sincere mind to be unworthy of the least of all his mercies. Thus his martyrs lead us to himself, the chief of martyrs and the King of saints.

Collect

GRANT us, O Lord, to learn to love our enemies: by the example of thy martyr Saint Stephen, who prayed to thee for his persecutors; who livest and reignest with the Father and the Holy Spirit, ever one God, world without end.

or

GRANT, O Lord, that in all our sufferings here upon earth for the testimony of thy truth, we may steadfastly look up to heaven, and by faith behold the glory that shall be revealed: and, being filled with the Holy Spirit, may learn to love and bless our persecutors by the example of thy first martyr Saint Stephen, who prayed for his murderers to thee, O blessed Jesus; who standest at the right hand of God to succour all those that suffer for thee, our only mediator and advocate.

Evening Prayer is of the Octave Day of Christmas unless the feast of Saint Stephen is celebrated as a solemnity.

Saint John, Apostle, Evangelist
(27 December)

Proper of the Day and Common of Apostles and of Evangelists

A reading from the sermons of John Keble

'Therefore that disciple whom Jesus loved saith unto Peter, It is the Lord' (Jn 21:7). […] This is the point, to which I would draw your attention: that St John knew Jesus before the rest; knew him to be the Lord by signs and tokens, which had somehow not been understood by the rest. The rest all saw the miraculous draught of fishes, all saw the Lord standing on the shore, all heard his grave and kind voice, giving them directions. But they knew him not: it came not as yet into their minds that this was another visit of their Master to them, now that he was risen from the dead. They knew him not. Only St John knew him. What was the reason of this? It was not that St John had been longer acquainted with our Lord. There was as it seems but one's day difference in St John's and St Peter's introduction to him, and St Andrew and St John followed him, by the Baptist's direction, both on the same day. And all three, with St James, were called at the same moment to forsake all and follow him.

The reason, therefore, of St John's knowing our Saviour, when the rest knew him not, was not his having a longer and more perfect acquaintance with him. But it is contained, I suppose, in the words, 'The disciple, whom Jesus loved'. Because Jesus loved St John especially, therefore St John was in a manner always on the look out for him, ever watching for his signs and tokens, ever expecting and longing for his presence, and could not well miss him when he came. Why will a child know its mother at a distance sooner than another personal would? Of course, because she loves it so dearly, and it is used to depend so entirely on her. Wherever it goes, it thinks of her; sees her in dreams, imagines her at hand very often, when she is away, discovers in every thing somewhat to remind it of her. This, and no other, was the reason by St John perceived Christ sooner than the rest could. There was in him, we may well believe, more of that tender yearning affection, which a young child feels towards its mother and its nurse. He felt that he could not do without our Saviour: therefore his eyes sought him eagerly, wherever he was; and in the most unlikely places, he would still be fancying, 'What if this should be my

John Keble, 'The Intuition of Love', in *Sermons for the Saints' Days and other Festivals, by the late Rev. John Keble* (Oxford and London: Parker, 1877), pp. 68-71.

Master's token? What if he should even now shew himself?' The constant employment of his heart was such as is described in that beautiful verse of the psalmist, 'My soul waiteth for the Lord, more than they that watch for the morning'. When we are expecting any dear friend, how anxiously do we look out long before, how often imagine that we see him before he arrives! And why? Because we love him so much, and long so earnestly to set eyes upon him.

Collect

MERCIFUL Lord, we beseech thee to cast thy bright beams of light upon thy Church: that it being enlightened by the doctrine of thy blessed apostle and evangelist Saint John may so walk in the light of thy truth, that it may at length attain to the light of everlasting life; through Jesus Christ thy Son our Lord, who liveth and reigneth with thee in the unity of the Holy Spirit, one God, for ever and ever.

Evening Prayer is of the Octave Day of Christmas unless the feast of Saint John is celebrated as a solemnity.

Holy Innocents
(28 December)

Hymn

Morning Prayer

OR

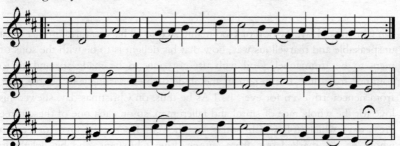

Hymnum canentes

1. The hymn for conquering martyrs raise,
   the victor Innocents we praise,
   whom in their woe earth cast away,
   but Heav'n with joy received today;
   whose angels see the Father's face
   world without end, and hymn his grace;
   and while they chant unceasing lays,
   the hymn for conquering martyrs raise.

2. A voice from Ramah was there sent,
   a voice of weeping and lament,
   when Rachel mourned the children's care
   whom for the tyrant's sword she bare.
   triumphal is their glory now,
   whom earthly torments could not bow,
   what time, both far and near that went,
   a voice from Ramah there was sent.

3. Fear not, O little flock and blest,
   the lion that your life opprest!
   To heavenly pastures ever new
   the heavenly Shepherd leadeth you;

who, dwelling now on Zion's hill,
   the Lamb's dear footsteps follow still;
   by tyrant there no more distrest,
   fear not, O little flock and blest.

4. And every tear is wiped away
   by your dear Father's hands for ay;
   death hath no power to hurt you more,
   whose own is life's eternal store.
   who sow their seed, and sowing weep,
   in everlasting joy shall reap,
   what time they shine in heavenly day,
   and every tear is wiped away.

5. O city blest o'er all the earth,
   who gloriest in the Saviour's birth,
   who are his earliest martyrs dear,
   by kindred and by triumph here;
   none from henceforth may call thee small,
   of rival towns thou passest all:
   in whom our Monarch had his birth,
   O city blest o'er all the earth!

The Venerable Bede, *Tr.* J. M. Neale
*Tune: Wer da wonet, Melody in St Gall Gesangbuch',
from* Vehe's *Gesangbüchlein*

Post-Biblical Reading

A reading from the sermons of John Keble

On Christmas-Day, the Son of God manifested to all his creatures, in that most unspeakable and marvellous way, how that his delight is to be with the sons of men, to be Emmanuel, God with us: not only to be made so, and so to continue for a time, but to remain and abide such everlastingly: to be true man, from henceforth even for ever. [...] As he thus, on Christmas-day, shewed his love for the whole race of sinful and fallen man, so on each one of these three great days which follow Christmas, he sheweth his special love for certain whom he has marked out, from among other Christians, and his delight in being with them. For it is the nature and the proof of love, as you know, to delight in being with the beloved person.

Which then are the three sorts of Christians, whom our Lord thus specially favours? First, his martyrs and those who give up all for his sake: of whom St Stephen is the type and pattern. Next, his virgin-disciples: those who for his sake, being able to stand steadfast in their heart, have kept themselves single and chaste: the leader of whom, among Christian men, has always been considered in the Church to be St John, his own beloved disciple. Thirdly, the babes, and little children, of whom the first fruits were those Innocents, whose remembrance we keep to-day.[...]

And he makes haste, as we acknowledge to-day, which is only the fourth day from his Birth, to shew to men and angels this his great love for young children by allowing those babes at Bethlehem to be in some sense his first martyrs, the first who shed their blood for him. For the cause of their death, as you know, was no other than their belonging to Christ, as being born near the same time, and in the same place. Therefore, as a great king would feel himself bound to provide not only or the soldiers or sailors or other persons who devoted their lives and endured wounds or hardships in his service, but also for their children, who could as yet do nothing at all for him: so our Lord, and the Captain of our salvation, hath of his royal bounty, glorified these Innocents, and made them saints in heaven, as truly as he glorified St Stephen and St John,

John Keble, 'Christ's Love for Little Children and our Duty toward Them', in *Sermons for the Saints' Days and other Festivals, by the late Rev. John Keble* (Oxford and London: Parker, 1877), pp. 77-80.

and the rest of his holy martyr, and virgins, who went after him, knowing better whither they went.

Collect

ALMIGHTY God, whose praise this day the young innocents thy witnesses hath confessed and shewed forth, not in speaking but in dying: mortify and kill all vices in us, that in our conversation our life may express thy faith, which with our tongues we do confess; through Jesus Christ thy Son our Lord, who liveth and reigneth with thee and the same Spirit, for ever and ever.

or

O ALMIGHTY God, who out of the mouths of babes and sucklings hast ordained strength, and madest infants to glorify thee by their deaths: mortify and kill all vices in us, and so strengthen us by thy grace, that by the innocency of our lives, and constancy of our faith even unto death, we may glorify thy holy Name; through Jesus Christ thy Son our Lord, who liveth and reigneth with thee and the Holy Spirit, for ever and ever.

Evening Prayer is of the Octave Day of Christmas unless the feast of Holy Innocents is celebrated as a solemnity.

Saints Basil the Great and Gregory Nazianzen, Bishops, Doctors of the Church
(2 January)

Proper of the Day and Common of Pastors
or of Doctors of the Church

ALMIGHTY God, whose servants Basil and Gregory proclaimed the mystery of thy Word made flesh, that thy Church might be built up in wisdom and strength: grant that we, through their prayers and rejoicing in his presence among us, may with them be brought to know the power of thine unending love; through Jesus Christ thy Son our Lord, who liveth and reigneth with thee, in the unity of the Holy Spirit, one God, for ever and ever.

Saint Hilary, Bishop, Doctor of the Church
(13 January)

Proper of the Day and Common of Pastors
or of Doctors of the Church

EVERLASTING God, whose servant Hilary steadfastly confessed thy Son Jesus Christ to be both human and divine: grant us his gentle courtesy to bring to all the message of redemption in the incarnate Christ; who liveth and reigneth with thee, in the unity of the Holy Spirit, one God, for ever and ever.

Saint Antony of Egypt, Abbot
(17 January)

Proper of the Day and Common of Saints: for an Abbot

MOST gracious God, who didst call thy servant Antony to sell all that he had and to serve thee in the solitude of the desert: grant that we, through his intercession and following his example, may learn to deny ourselves and to love thee before all things; through Jesus Christ thy Son our Lord, who liveth and reigneth with thee, in the unity of the Holy Spirit, one God, for ever and ever.

Saint Agnes, Virgin, Martyr
(21 January)

Proper of the Day and Common of Martyrs

ETERNAL God, Shepherd of thy sheep, by whose grace thy child Agnes was strengthened to bear witness, in her life and in her death, to the true love of her redeemer: grant us, by her prayers, the power to understand, with all thy saints, what is the breadth and length and height and depth and to know the love that passeth all knowledge; even Jesus Christ thy Son our Lord who liveth and reigneth with thee, in the unity of the Holy Spirit, one God, for ever and ever.

471

Saint Francis de Sales, Bishop,
Doctor of the Church
(24 January)

Proper of the Day and Common of Pastors
or of Doctors of the Church

GOD of all holiness, who didst call thy bishop Francis de Sales to bring many to Christ through his devout life, and to renew thy Church with patience and understanding: grant that through his intercession, we may, by word and example, reflect thy gentleness and love to all those whom we meet; through Jesus Christ our Saviour, who liveth and reigneth with thee, in the unity of the Holy Spirit, one God, for ever and ever.

Conversion of Saint Paul
(25 January)

Proper of the Day and Common of Apostles

A reading from the sermons of John Keble

St Paul's day is, in one respect, different from most of the saints' days of the holy Church universal. We keep, not only the anniversary of his martyrdom, which took place the same day with that of St Peter, but also that of his Conversion to the faith of Christ.

One reason for this, no doubt, is the special appearance of our Lord Jesus Christ at his conversion; and, for a like reason, we observe the day of St John the Baptist's Nativity, not the day of his martyrdom: taking that point in the history of both saints, which marks them our most, as especial instruments for the glory of our divine Saviour, and brings him, as it were, nearest to them.

John Keble, 'Apostolical Sympathy', in *Sermons for the Saints' Days and other Festivals, by the late Rev. John Keble* (Oxford and London: Parker, 1877), pp. 100-102, 104-105.

Another and a very manifest reason for this distinction in the case of St Paul, is the knowledge we have of the particular purpose, for which God raised him up; namely, to be the apostle of the Gentiles, and to bestow by him on the Church very great and remarkable blessings. It has pleased Providence that his example and character should be much more fully set before us, than that of any other saint of the New Testament. In him, more than in any other, we are given to see the Church of God, such as she was intended to be in her conflict with the wicked world. I mean the Church of God in action: enduring toils; overcoming difficulties; silencing blasphemies; directing consciences; winning her way against opposers; casting down unholy or proud imaginations; bringing into captivity every thought to the obedience of Jesus Christ. […]

Among other things which particularly fitted him to govern and guide the flock of God, is that which is mentioned in the text; that he was 'made all things to all men' (1 Cor 9:22). This is an expression which might easily be mistaken, and has been so before now: as though St Paul recommended, by his advice and example, a sort of craft in religious matters, pretending to agree with men when you really do not, humouring them in bad ways, concurring with them to a certain length in what you know or fear to be wrong; but all the whole for their benefit, and with a view of doing, on the whole, more good in the end. […]

[T]he difference may be put in a word: it is not accommodation which St Paul encourages, but sympathy. He does not say that he practised what would please others, to win them, but he says that he always had an eye to them; he put himself in their place. He thought with himself, 'Were I a heathen, or a Jew, a young man or an old, an advanced or an imperfect Christian, a rich man or a poor, a master or a servant; what would my thoughts, and feelings, and fancies be, when such and such holy truths, or divine commandments, were made known to me?' And according to what his wise and charitable heart, guided by the Holy Spirit, told him of the needs and feelings of other persons, so he ordered his ways towards them, and his manner of speaking to them, and dealing with them.

As he says to the Galatians, he was accustomed to 'change his voice' (Gal 4:20); not always to please and soothe them. Sometimes it was quite the other way: as when he smote Elymas with blindness, calling him 'the child of the devil, the enemy of righteousness' (Acts 13:10). He knew that such fearful words, and the judgment which accompanied them, 'not seeing the sun for a season', was just what the case of that unhappy person required. And we may remember, St Paul himself knew well, what were the feelings of a person struck blind, and how such a stroke of God's anger might lead to repentance. For he himself was blind for three days after his conversion, 'and did neither eat nor drink' (Acts 9:9); and what he went through in that time, no man knows; but we know how he served God afterwards.

Collect

O GOD, who, through the preaching of the blessed apostle Saint Paul, hast caused the light of the gospel to shine throughout the world: grant, we beseech thee, that we, having his wonderful conversion in remembrance, may shew forth our thankfulness unto thee for the same, by following the holy doctrine which he taught; through Jesus Christ thy Son our Lord, who liveth and reigneth with thee, in the unity of the Holy Spirit, one God, for ever and ever.

Saints Timothy and Titus, Bishops
(26 January)

Proper of the Day and Common of Pastors

HEAVENLY Father, who didst send thine apostle Paul to preach the gospel, and gavest him Timothy and Titus to be his companions in the faith: grant that, through their prayers, our fellowship in the Holy Spirit may bear witness to the name of Jesus; who liveth and reigneth with thee, in the unity of the Holy Spirit, one God, for ever and ever.

Saint Thomas Aquinas, Priest,
Doctor of the Church
(28 January)

Proper of the Day and Common of Doctors of the Church

EVERLASTING God, who didst enrich thy Church with the learning and holiness of thy servant Thomas Aquinas: grant to all who seek thee a humble mind and a pure heart that they may know thy Son Jesus Christ to be the way, the truth and the life; who liveth and reigneth with thee, in the unity of the Holy Spirit, one God, for ever and ever.

Saint Anskar, Bishop
(3 February)

Proper of the Day and Common of Pastors: for Missionaries

ALMIGHTY and gracious God, who didst send thy servant Anskar to spread the gospel among the Nordic people: through his intercession raise up, in this our generation, messengers of thy good tidings and heralds of thy kingdom, that the world may come to know the immeasurable riches of our Saviour Jesus Christ; who liveth and reigneth with thee, in the unity of the Holy Spirit, one God, for ever and ever.

Saints Cyril, Monk, and Methodius, Bishop,
Patrons of Europe
(14 February)

Proper of the Day and Common of Pastors: for Missionaries

O LORD of all, who gavest to thy servants Cyril and Methodius the gift of tongues to proclaim the gospel to the Slavic people: we pray that thy whole Church may be one as thou art one, that all who confess thy name may honour one another, and that from east and west all may acknowledge one Lord, one faith, one baptism, and thee, the God and Father of all; through Jesus Christ thy Son our Lord, who liveth and reigneth with thee, in the unity of the Holy Spirit, one God, for ever and ever.

Chair of Saint Peter the Apostle (22 February)

Proper of the Day and Common of Apostles

A reading from the writings of Henry Edward Manning

Our Divine Lord restored man and society in his person when he deified our manhood, our intelligence, heart, will, our whole nature, soul and body. When he gathered his disciples about him, he elevated them also… Their heart, mind, and will were gradually transfigured into his own likeness; and as he changed them into his own likeness, so he united them together. They became of one mind, one heart, one will; they had one faith, one vision of God, one Guide, one Teacher, one law. There was wrought in them an internal change, which perfectly united them one with another; so that their thoughts, affections, volitions, being subject by faith to the sovereignty of their Divine Master, were assimilated to each other. There grew up an internal unity in the hearts of the disciples; and therefore the external unity with which they adhered to him and to one another, was the result and consequence of this intrinsic unity of mind and will.

He thus organized them together. He made one of them to be the first, and all the rest to be equal. He gave to that one a chief authority, and he gave to them all a participation, not of that sole primacy, but of all other powers which he gave to Peter, and so knit them into one perfect society, of which he himself was the visible Head whilst on earth, and his Vicar when he ascended into heaven. This is what we call his Church, or Mystical Body.

… When he ascended into heaven and sent the Holy Ghost, his disciples and all who believed in him were united to him by the indwelling of the Spirit of God. He thereby became their Head. They became his members, and were members one with another in one organized body, so compacted and fitted together, that as the body of a man, quickened and animated by one life, grows to its perfection, so with the Mystical Body of Christ. He bestowed on it a participation of his own prerogatives: it became imperishable, because he has immortal life; it became indissolubly one, because he is the only Son of God; it became infallible, because he is the Divine Truth, and cannot err; it became

---

Henry Edward Manning, *The Fourfold Sovereignty of God* (London: Burns and Oates, 1871), pp. 64-71.

sovereign in the world, because it is the representative of himself, and, in his Name, exercises his sovereignty among the nations of the earth.

… As they were united, so they were organized together; and there grew up in the world the one Vine and the branches, – the one world-wide organisation, the one life-giving society of men – united by baptism, faith, and worship; by submission to one authority; by the recognition of one visible Head – the sole fountain of supernatural knowledge and supernatural power. There was one hand which held the two keys of jurisdiction and of science – that is, of supreme power and of the perfect knowledge of faith: and that one hand was the hand of him who bears the representative character of the Vicar of his Divine Master.

Collect

O ALMIGHTY God, who by thy Son Jesus Christ didst give to thy apostle Saint Peter many excellent gifts and commandest him earnestly to feed thy flock: make we beseech thee, all bishops and pastors diligently to preach thy holy Word, and the people obediently to follow the same, that they may receive the crown of everlasting glory; through Jesus Christ thy Son our Lord, who liveth and reigneth with thee, in the unity of the Holy Spirit, one God, for ever and ever.

Saint Polycarp, Bishop, Martyr
(23 February)

Proper of the Day and Common of Martyrs

ALMIGHTY God, who gavest to thy servant Polycarp boldness to confess the name of our Saviour Jesus Christ before the rulers of this world and courage to suffer death for his faith: grant that, through his prayers, we too may be ready to give an answer for the faith that is in us and to suffer gladly for the sake of our Lord Jesus Christ; who liveth and reigneth with thee, in the unity of the Holy Spirit, one God, for ever and ever.

Saints Perpetua and Felicity and their Companions
Martyrs
(7 March)

Proper of the Day and Common of Martyrs

O HOLY God, who gavest great courage to Perpetua, Felicity and
their companions: grant that, through their prayers, we may be worthy
to climb the ladder of sacrifice and be received into the garden of
peace; through Jesus Christ thy Son our Lord, who liveth and reigneth
with thee, in the unity of the Holy Spirit, one God, for ever and ever.

Saint Joseph, Spouse of the Blessed Virgin Mary
(19 March)

Proper of the Day and Common of Saints

A reading from the sermons of John Keble

No man that we read of in Scripture was so highly favoured as Saint Joseph, in
respect of being constantly near the Person of our Saviour. From Christ's birth
to his own death, which was at least more than twelve years, and very likely a
good deal longer, Joseph was the entrusted guardian of our Lord; the minister
of God, especially called and raised up to watch over that holiest Childhood
and Youth, and to protect his blessed Mother. Judging from God's ordinary
dealings in Scripture, we cannot but suppose that he must have been more than
almost any one prepared and made meet for God's Kingdom, who was
permitted for so long a time to exercise a ministry so near to God himself.

Again, we cannot but delight in imagining to ourselves the part which Joseph
bore in that holy Family: how tenderly, how reverently he watched over the

---

John Keble, 'Sermon XV: Our Lord's Nursing Father', in *Sermons for Christmas
and Epiphany, by the late Rev. John Keble* (Oxford and London: Parker, 1975), pp.
150-152.

blessed Mother, and the Most Blessed and Divine Child: and we naturally look out for all that Holy Scripture tells us, that may help us to draw in our hearts that sacred picture.

The first thing we read in the Gospel concerning Saint Joseph is, that the Virgin Mother of our Lord was espoused to him. For it pleased him, when he would redeem our poor fallen manhood by taking it into his own nature, to be born of a betrothed Virgin, not of one altogether free. And of this the holy writers of old give several reasons. It protected the Blessed Mary from the evil report which she would otherwise have had to endure. It provided her with a friend, comforter, and helper in her poor and lowly life, and anxious care of the Holy Child. It veiled from the eyes of men, as yet unfit to bear it, the aweful mystery of the Incarnation of God the Son: and accordingly we find that our Lord was all along spoken of by ordinary acquaintance as 'the son of Joseph', 'the carpenter's son'.

Again, some have thought it might be in God's purpose to hide from the evil spirits the glory of the Divine Child, and that this was done by ordering things so, that Satan might imagine him to be the Son of Joseph and Mary; upon which he dared to tempt him, and so, being defeated and baffled, was, against his will, the cause of a great blessing to mankind.

And lastly, it may have been one point more in our Lord's exceeding humiliation, that he would be subject, in his childhood and youth, not to his Mother only, but to her husband also: whereas we proud sinners think it a great and happy thing to free ourselves, as much as possible, from submission and obedience; to be, as far as possible, our own masters.

It being then the will of our Lord that his Mother should be a betrothed, not a disengaged person, consider what manner of man he was whom he so chose to be his guardian. He was a poor hard-working man, a carpenter: so poor, that, as it may seem, he had not wherewithal to pay for a lodging at Bethlehem. Yet he was a person of high family, the very highest among the Jews. Both he and his espoused wide were of the house and lineage of David. These are circumstances very trying to the pride of man. Many feel to themselves as if they could bear poverty, but cannot bear decay and degradation; cannot bear to be in a lower place than they or their fathers have been used to. Not such, we may be sure, was the holy Joseph: and for his humble contentment, see how he was rewarded: he became the foster-father of the King of kings: the Almighty Lord of heaven and earth lodged in his house for many years.

Collect

O GOD our Father, who from the house of thy servant David didst raise up Joseph the carpenter to be the guardian of thine incarnate Son and husband of the Blessed Virgin Mary: give us grace to follow him in faithful obedience to thy commands; through Jesus Christ thy Son our Lord, who liveth and reigneth with thee, in the unity of the Holy Spirit, one God, for ever and ever.

Annunciation of the Lord *(Lady Day)*
(25 March)

Proper of the Day

Office

Opening Sentence

A virgin shall conceive and bear a Son: and his name shall be called Emmanuel, God-is-with-us.

Is 7:14; Mt 1:23

Post-Biblical Reading

A reading from the meditations of Blessed John Henry Newman

Mary is called the *Gate* of Heaven, because it was through her that our Lord passed from heaven to earth. The Prophet Ezekiel, prophesying of Mary, says, 'The gate shall be closed, it shall not be opened, and no man shall pass through it, since the Lord God of Israel has entered through it – and it shall be closed for the Prince, the Prince himself shall sit in it' (Ezek 44:2-3).

Now this is fulfilled, not only in our Lord having taken flesh from her, and being her Son, but moreover, in that she had a place in the economy of

---

Bl. John Henry Newman, 'On the Annunciation. Mary is the *Janua Coeli*, the Gate of Heaven', in *Meditations and Devotions of the Late Cardinal Newman* (London: Longmans, Green and Co, 1907), pp. 51-54.

Redemption; it is fulfilled in her spirit and will, as well as in her body. Eve had a part in the fall of man, though it was Adam who was our representative, and whose sin made us sinners. It was Eve who began, and who tempted Adam. Scripture says, 'The woman saw that the tree was good to eat, and fair to the eyes, and delightful to behold; and she took of the fruit thereof, and did eat, and gave to her husband, and he did eat' (Gen 3:6). It was fitting then in God's mercy that, as the woman began the *destruction* of the world, so woman should also begin its *recovery*, and that, as Eve opened the way for the fatal deed of the first Adam, so Mary should open the way for the great achievement of the second Adam, even our Lord Jesus Christ, who came to save the world by dying on the cross for it. Hence Mary is called by the holy Fathers a second and a better Eve, as having taken that first step in the salvation of mankind which Eve took in its ruin.

How, and when, did Mary take part, and the initial part, in the world's restoration? It was when the Angel Gabriel came to her to announce to her the great dignity which was to be her portion. Saint Paul bids us 'present our bodies to God as a reasonable service' (Rom 12:1). We must not only pray with our lips, and fast, and do outward penance, and be chaste in our bodies; but we must be obedient, and pure in our minds. And so, as regards the Blessed Virgin, it was God's will that she should undertake *willingly* and with *full understanding* to be the Mother of our Lord, and not to be a mere passive instrument whose maternity would have no merit and no reward. The higher our gifts, the heavier our duties. It was no light lot to be so intimately near to the Redeemer of men, as she experienced afterwards when she suffered with him. Therefore, weighing well the Angel's words before giving her answer to them – first she asked whether so great an office would be a forfeiture of that Virginity which she had vowed. When the Angel told her no, then, with the full consent of a full heart, full of God's love to her and her own lowliness, she said, 'Behold the handmaid of the Lord, be it done unto me according to thy word' (Lk 1:38). It was by this consent she became the *Gate of Heaven*.

Short Reading for Prayer during the Day   *1 Jn 4:10*
In this is love, not that we loved God but that he loved us and sent his Son to be the expiation of our sins.

Collect

WE BESEECH thee, O Lord, pour thy grace into our hearts: that, as we have known the incarnation of thy Son Jesus Christ by the message of an angel, so by his cross and passion we may be brought unto the glory of his resurrection; through Jesus Christ thy Son our Lord, who liveth and reigneth with thee, in the unity of the Holy Spirit, one God, for ever and ever.

Saint Mark, Evangelist
(25 April)

Proper of the Day and Common of Apostles and of Evangelists

A reading from the sermons of Blessed John Henry Newman

The chief points of St Mark's history are these: first, that he was sister's son to Barnabas, and taken with him and St Paul on their first apostolical journey; next, that after a short time he deserted them and returned to Jerusalem; then, that after an interval, he was St Peter's assistant at Rome, and composed his Gospel there principally from the accounts which he received from that apostle; lastly, that he was sent by him to Alexandria, in Egypt, where founded one of the strictest and most powerful churches of the primitive times.

The points of contrast in his history are as follows: that first he abandoned the cause of the Gospel as soon as danger appeared; afterwards, he proved himself, not merely as an ordinary Christian, but a most resolute and exact servant of God, founding and ruling that strictest Church of Alexandria. And the instrument of this change was, as it appears, the influence of St Peter, a fit restorer of a timid and backsliding disciple.

The encouragement which we derive from these circumstances in St Mark's history is, that the feeblest among us may through God's grace become strong. And the warning to be drawn from it is, to distrust ourselves; and again, not to despise weak brethren, or to despair of them, but to bear their burdens and help them forward, if so be we may restore them. Now let us attentively consider the subject thus brought before us.

Some men are naturally impetuous and active; others love quiet and readily yield. The ever-earnest must be sobered, and the indolent must be roused. The history of Moses supplies s with an instance of a proud and rash spirit, tamed down to an extreme gentleness of deportment. In the greatness of the change wrought in him, when from a fierce, though honest, avenger of his brethren, he

---

Bl. John Henry Newman, 'Religious Cowardice', in *Parochial and Plain Sermons, by John Henry Newman*, II (London: Rivingtons, 1880), pp. 174-177.

became the meekest of men on earth, he evidences the power of faith, the influence of the Spirit on the heart. St Mark's history affords a specimen of the other, and still rare change, from timidity to boldness.

Difficult as it is to subdue the more violent passions, yet I believe it to be still more difficult to overcome a tendency to sloth, cowardice, and despondency. These evil dispositions cling about a man, and weigh him down. They are minute chains, binding him on every side to the earth, so that he cannot even turn himself or make an effort to rise. It would seem as if right principles had yet to be planted in the indolent mind; whereas violent and obstinate tempers had already something of the nature of firmness and zeal in them, or rather what will become so with care, exercise, and God's blessing. Besides, the events of life have a powerful influence in sobering the ardent or self-confident temper. Disappointments, pain, anxiety, advancing years, bring with them some natural wisdom as a matter of course, and, though such tardy improvement bespeaks but a weak faith, yet we may believe that the Holy Ghost often blesses these means, however slowly and imperceptibly. On the other hand, these same circumstances do but increase the defects of the timid and irresolute, who are made more indolent, selfish, and faint-hearted by advancing years and find a sort of sanction of their unworthy caution in their experience of the vicissitudes of life.

St Mark's change, therefore, may be considered even more astonishing in its nature than that of the Jewish Lawgiver. 'By faith', he was 'out of weakness made strong', and becomes a memorial of the more glorious and marvellous gifts of the last and spiritual Dispensation.

Collect
ALMIGHTY God, who hast instructed thy holy Church with the heavenly doctrine of thy evangelist Saint Mark: give us grace, that, being not like children carried away with every blast of vain doctrine, we may be established in the truth of thy holy gospel; through Jesus Christ thy Son our Lord, who liveth and reigneth with thee, in the unity of the Holy Spirit, one God, for ever and ever.

Saint Catherine of Siena, Virgin, Doctor of the Church, Patron of Europe
(29 April)

*Proper of the Day and Common of Virgins
or of Doctors of the Church*

O MERCIFUL God, who gavest to thy servant Catherine of Siena a wondrous love of the passion of Christ: grant that, through her prayers, we thy people may be united to him in his majesty and rejoice for ever in the revelation of his glory; who liveth and reigneth with thee, in the unity of the Holy Spirit, one God, for ever and ever.

Saint Athanasius, Bishop, Doctor of the Church
(2 May)

Proper of the Day and Common of Pastors
or of Doctors of the Church

EVER-LIVING God, whose servant Athanasius bore witness to the mystery of the Word made flesh for our salvation: give us grace, with all thy saints, to contend for the truth and to grow into the likeness of thy Son, Jesus Christ our Lord; who liveth and reigneth with thee, in the unity of the Holy Spirit, one God, for ever and ever.

Saints Philip and James, Apostles (3 May)

Proper of the Day and Common of Apostles and of Evangelists

A reading from the sermons of John Keble

Over and above all the other glorious privileges and tokens, by which our Lord has from the beginning blessed and glorified his Spouse and Body, the Church; that it is One, as being the mystical Body of the One Lord Jesus Christ; Catholic, as belonging alike to all nations; Apostolic, as built upon the foundation of the Apostles and prophets; Holy, as made up of persons entirely dedicated to him, and meant to be altogether like him: I say, over and above all these, the Apostles' Creed sets before us two especial privileges and gifts to be found in the Church and nowhere else: the one the Communion of saints, the other the Forgiveness of sins.

On the one hand we are brought into nearest communion and intercourse with those who have pleased God from the beginning of the world; the salt of the

---

John Keble, 'The Communion of Saints', in *Sermons for the Saints' Days and other Festivals, by the late Rev. John Keble* (Oxford and London: Parker, 1877), pp. 224-226.

earth, the best and holiest of mankind, whether living or in paradise. On the other hand, there is in the Church, by his exceeding unspeakable mercy, forgiveness and remission of all sins, even the worst; not only forgiveness in Baptism, for whatever has gone before, for all offences committed in men's heathen and unregenerate state: but forgiveness also, entire absolution, for all sins committed after Baptism, but truly and entirely repented of.

The holy Church is the mother of us all, but her motherly love is especially shewn towards two classes of her children, saints and penitents: the perfect, to help them on toward higher perfection: and the backsliders, to recover them and to welcome them when recovered. Our privilege, my brethren, is exceeding great, whether, having by God's mercy an earnest desire to be perfect, we are encouraged by the assurance that we are in communion with the holy souls of all ages and nations; or whether (as is, alas!, far more likely) we have grievously sinned since our Baptism, and can but hope to save our souls as by fire.

The full type and pattern of this our highly favoured calling may be seen in those places, where the holy Gospel sets before us our Lord making himself a companion of publicans and sinners. 'Many publicans and sinners, drew near, and sat down with Jesus and his disciples' (Mt 9:10). Then might be seen in one room, at one table, the Holy Saviour of the world, and his saints with him, and also many who had been living the worst and most discreditable lives: even as in the holy Church and kingdom of the same Saviour, ever since, there has been both the Communion of saints and the Forgiveness of sins: no perfection too high to be hoped for, no sin too bad to be forgiven, if only men would turn to Christ, and dutifully abide with him.

At present, the plan by which our catechisings have been ordered, would lead us to speak only of the first of these two privileges, the Communion of saints: and this, you will perceive, suits well with the day; for it is a day consecrated to two of the chief of Christ's saints, and the lessons appointed for it, tell us not a little of our Lord's dealings with his saints; what sort of persons they are, whom he commonly chooses out to bring near unto himself; and in what sort of ways he trains them. He chooses out the simple, teachable, and guileless, and he trains them in temptations bids them trust him, and teaches them how to pray. And into communion with such as these he invites us all, even the mere beginners and children, promising continually, You 'shall see great things than these' (Jn 1:50).

Collect

O ALMIGHTY God, whom truly to know is everlasting life: grant us perfectly to know thy Son Jesus Christ to be the way, the truth and the life: that, following the steps of thy holy apostles, Saint Philip and Saint James, and assisted by their prayers, we may steadfastly walk in the way that leadeth to eternal life; through Jesus Christ thy Son our Lord, who liveth and reigneth with thee, in the unity of the Holy Spirit, one God, for ever and ever.

Saint Matthias, Apostle (14 May)

Proper of the Day and Common of Apostles

A reading from the sermons of Blessed John Henry Newman

This is the only saint's day which is to be celebrated with mingled feelings of joy and pain. It records the fall as well as the election of an apostle. St Matthias was chosen in place of the traitor Judas. In the history of the latter we have the warning recorded in very deed, which our Lord in the text gives us in word, 'Hold that fast which thou hast, that no man take thy crown' (Rev 3:11). And doubtless many were the warnings such as this, addressed by our Lord to the wretched man who in the end betrayed him. Not only did he call him to reflection and repentance by the hints which he let drop concerning him during the Last Supper, but in the discourses previous to it he may be supposed to have intended a reference to the circumstances of his apostate disciple. 'Watch ye, therefore', he said, 'lest suddenly coming, he find you sleeping' (Mt 24:42). I called Judas just now 'wretched'; for we must not speak of sinners, according to the falsely charitable way of some, styling them 'unfortunate' instead of wicked, lest we thus learn to excuse sin in ourselves. He was doubtless inexcusable, as we shall be, if we follow his pattern; and he must be viewed, not with pity, but with fear and awe.

The reflection which rises in the mind on a consideration of the election of St Matthias is this: how easily God may effect his purposes without us, and put others in our place, if we are disobedient to him. It often happens that those

---

Bl. John Henry Newman, 'Divine Decrees', in *Parochial and Plain Sermons, by John Henry Newman*, II (London: Rivingtons, 1880), pp.117-118, 119-120.

who have long been in his favour grow secure and presuming. They think their salvation certain, and their service necessary to him who has graciously accepted it. They consider themselves as personally bound up with his purposes of mercy manifested in the Church; and so marked out that, if they could fall, his word would fail. They come to think they have some peculiar title or interest in his promises, over and above other men (however derived, it matters not, whether from his eternal decree, or, on the other hand, from their own especial holiness and obedience), but practically such an interest that the very supposition that they can possibly fall offends them. Now, this feeling of self-importance is repressed all through the Scriptures, and especially by the events we commemorate today. [...]

All his twelve apostles seemed, from the letter of his words, to be predestined to life; nevertheless in a few months, Matthias held the throne and crown of one of them. And there is something remarkable in the circumstance itself, that our Lord should have made up their number to a full twelve, after one had fallen; and, perhaps, there may be contained in it some symbolical allusion to the scope of his decrees, which we cannot altogether enter into. Surely, had he willed it, eleven would have accomplished his purposes as well as twelve. Why, when one had fallen, should he accurately fill up the perfect number? Yet not only in the case of the apostles, but in that of the tribes of Israel also, if he rejects one, he divides another into two. Why is this, but to show us, as it would appear, that in this election of us, he does not look at us as mere individuals, but as a body, as a certain definite whole, of which the parts may alter in the process of disengaging them from this sinful world - with reference to some glorious and harmonious design upon us, who are the immediate objects of his bounty, and shall be the fruit of his love, if we are faithful? Why, but to show us that he could even find other apostles to suffer for him – and, much more, servants to fill his lower thrones, should we be wanting and transgress his strict and holy law.

Collect

O ALMIGHTY God, who into the place of the traitor Judas didst choose thy faithful servant Matthias to be of the number of the twelve apostles: grant that thy Church, being alway preserved from false apostles, may be ordered and guided by faithful and true pastors; through Jesus Christ thy Son our Lord, who liveth and reigneth with thee, in the unity of the Holy Spirit, one God, for ever and ever.

Visitation of the Blessed Virgin Mary
to Elizabeth
(31 May)

Proper of the Day and Common of the Blessed Virgin Mary

A reading from the writings of Eric Lionel Mascall

Mary's relation to us who are Christ's members is compounded out of her relation to Christ and his relation to us; it is, to use a term of modern logic, the logical product of those two relations. Mary is our mother, because we are members of her Son, because we have, not just metaphorically but really, been adopted into him. By our baptism we have been incorporated into the human nature which he took from her and which still continues to exist in its ascended glory. If Christ had ceased to be man at his ascension – and it is to be feared that only too many Christians unreflectively assume that he did – then Mary would have ceased to be his mother, our incorporation into him would be a mere fiction, and so would our relation to him. But the Catholic doctrine of the Incarnation declares that the eternal Son of God, who at one moment in the world's history took human nature in the womb of Blessed Mary, is, in that human nature, man for evermore. [...] Mary is the mother of Jesus and of those who are incorporated into him, the mother of the Church which is his Mystical Body and which, because a man and his bride are one flesh, is also Christ's bride.

The Incarnation took place at the Annunciation, when in response to Mary's *Fiat*, the Word was made very man in her womb. But the further fact of her relation to the Church and its members had to wait for the Ascension and for the descent of the Spirit at Pentecost, when the Church, whose archetypal substance already existed in the manhood of Jesus, was fully and visibly constituted in power. In the Ascension the Lord's human nature was withdrawn from human sight and touch. From then until Pentecost the apostolic group was the Church in expectancy and potentiality, awaiting its activation by the Spirit and the communication to it of the full reality of Christ's manhood. When the Spirit descended in tongues of fire, it was to make the waiting group into the mystical Body of Christ in a way analogous to that in

---

E. L. Mascall, '*Theotokos*: The Place of Mary in the Work of Salvation', in E. L. Mascall and H. St Box (ed.), *The Blessed Virgin Mary. Essays by Anglican Writers* (London: Darton, Longman, and Todd, 1963), pp. 23-25.

which the descent of the Spirit upon Mary at her Annunciation had formed the natural body of Christ in her womb. Nevertheless, although the Mystical Body came into being by this new descent of the Spirit, there was not a new incarnation, Christ was not becoming man a second time, he was not assuming a new human nature; the human nature which he had taken from his mother, in which he had died for our sins and risen again for our justification, was being made present under a new mode. There are not, strictly speaking, two bodies of Christ, a natural and a mystical, but one body of Christ which is manifested in two forms.

Nor does the story end here, for that part of the Mystical Body which is on earth needs to be continually nourished and sustained, as Christ's natural body did before its glorification. It is through the Eucharistic Body of the Blessed Sacrament that this takes place. Here again, there is not a new incarnation, but in the Eucharist the human nature which Christ took from his mother is made present in yet another form, a form through which that part of the Mystical Body which is still *in via* on earth is repeatedly sustained and renewed.

In all these modes of manifestation, the human nature of Christ is the human nature which he took from Mary. The descent of the Holy Spirit on Mary at the Annunciation first formed it, the descent of the Holy Spirit upon the Apostles at Pentecost released it, so to speak, in the world as the Mystical Body of the Church, and the descent of the Holy Spirit upon the Eucharistic elements brings it to us as the Sacramental Body. But in all these manifestations and expressions it is one and the same Body, the Body which was formed in Mary's womb, and so when we return from the Altar, having received the sacramental Body of Christ and having thereby been received more firmly into his Mystical Body, we can say with a new emphasis the words that, in the Genesis story, Adam said after he had tasted the food given him by the first Eve: 'The woman gave me, and I did eat' (Gen 3:12). For it is the very body, the human nature, which Christ took from his mother, on which we are fed in the Holy Eucharist. And Jesus and his members are one Body, the Whole Christ, and Mary is his mother and theirs.

Collect

O GOD, who didst lead the Blessed Virgin Mary to visit Elizabeth, to their exceeding joy and comfort: grant unto thy people, that as Mary did rejoice to be called the Mother of the Lord, so, by her intercession, they may ever rejoice to believe the incarnation of thine only-begotten Son; to whom with thee and the Holy Spirit be all honour and glory, world without end.

Saint Justin, Martyr
(1 June)

Proper of the Day and Common of Martyrs

O GOD our redeemer, who through the folly of the cross didst teach thy martyr Justin the surpassing knowledge of Jesus Christ: free us, we beseech thee, from every kind of error, that we, like him, may be firmly grounded in the faith, and make thy name known to all peoples; through Jesus Christ thy Son our Lord, who liveth and reigneth with thee, in the unity of the Holy Spirit, one God, for ever and ever.

Saint Barnabas, Apostle
(11 June)

Proper of the Day and Common of Apostles

A reading from the sermons of John Keble

'They sent forth Barnabas, that he should go as far as Antioch: who, when he came, and had seen the grace of God, was glad, and exhorted them all, that with purpose of heart they would cleave unto the Lord' (Acts 11:22-23). The character, in which St Barnabas is here presented to us, is that of a person greatly rejoicing in other men's goodness. He was glad, when he saw the grace of God in his brethren. Of his doing so, there are several other instances; indeed, almost the whole of his conduct towards St Paul is full, from the beginning, of such generous and affectionate joy.

He, you may observe, was the first person at Jerusalem, who was able to convince himself of St Paul's truly being converted. When that great Apostle came to Jerusalem, where he was known before only as a persecutor of the

---

John Keble, 'Apostolic Generosity in Encouraging Others', in *Sermons for the Saints' Days and other Festivals, by the late Rev. John Keble* (Oxford and London: Parker, 1877), pp. 234-235, 236, 238-239.

Name of Christ, 'he assayed to join himself to the disciples; but they were all afraid of him, and believed not that he was a disciple. But Barnabas took him, and brought him to the Apostles, and declared unto them how he had seen the Lord in the way'.

Almost ever afterwards, he continued the affectionate companion and friend of St Paul. Presently after the visit to Antioch, in the text, we find him departing to Tarsus to seek Saul, and when he had found him, bringing him to Antioch. No doubt he was well aware that St Paul was, humanly speaking, a much greater and more noticeable person than himself; that by seeking him, and bringing him forward, he was as it were throwing himself into the background: according to what is said afterwards, that wherever they went, Paul was 'the chief speaker'. But this made no difference to his affection for St Paul, or his wish to have him with him. He rejoiced to see the grace of God, even when its light shone so brightly in others, as quite to eclipse and drown his own light.

All this is the more to be observed, because this feeling, in the Apostle of Consolation is especially attributed by the Holy Scripture to the sanctifying Spirit of God. 'He was glad when he saw the grace of God, and exhorted them all, that with purpose of heart they would cleave unto the Lord: for he was a good man, and full of the Holy Ghost and of faith'. So that the 'charity;' which 'envieth not' the spiritual attainments of others, is an especial token 'of the Holy Ghost and of faith'. [...]

But concerning this disposition to rejoice in other men's goodness, it is much easier to see how amiable it looks in others, than to practice it one's self in good earnest. Do not men envy others, not merely for their outward advantages, but for their goodness itself: especially for those parts of goodness, which they themselves have not the heart to imitate? [...]

The Christian, Catholic, renewed heart is altogether different from this; it is not at all satisfied, as men of the world are, with persons going on decently and quietly; it wants them to be inwardly sound and pure; first of all, to have a good 'purpose of heart', and then to persevere in that purpose, 'cleaving' to our Lord and Saviour continually. [...]

And it will ever keep in view the growth of the Church and kingdom of Jesus Christ, as being the one thing for which it works; and our Lord and Saviour himself, as being the one Master whom it serves. It works not for a sect or party, but for the holy apostolical Church herself: as St Barnabas, not regarding his own or another Apostle's name, laboured only to have 'much people added unto the Lord'.

Collect

O LORD God almighty, who didst endue thy holy apostle Barnabas with singular gifts of the Holy Spirit: leave us not, we beseech thee, destitute of thy manifold gifts, nor yet of grace to use them always to thy honour and glory; through Jesus Christ thy Son our Lord, who liveth and reigneth with thee, in the unity of the Holy Spirit, one God, for ever and ever.

Nativity of Saint John the Baptist
(24 June)
Proper of the Day and Common of Pastors
Hymn
Morning & Evening Prayer   *Vespers*

Ut queant laxis

1.Let thine example, holy John, remind us,
   ere we can meetly sing thy deeds of wonder,
hearts must be chastened, and the bonds that bind us
            broken asunder!

2.Lo! a swift angel, from the skies descending,
   tells to thy father what shall be thy naming;
all thy life's greatness to its bitter ending
            duly proclaiming.

3.But when he doubted what the angel told him,
   came to him dumbness to confirm the story;
at thine appearing, healed again behold him,
            chanting thy glory!

4.Oh! what a splendour and a revelation
   came to each mother, at they joyful leaping,
greeting thy Monarch, King of every nation,
            in the womb sleeping.

5.Angels in orders everlasting praise thee,
   God, in thy triune Majesty tremendous;
hark to the prayers we, penitents, upraise thee:
            save and defend us. Amen.

Paul the Deacon, 730-99, *Tr* Richard Ellis Roberts (1879-1953)

Post-Biblical Reading

A reading from the sermons of Blessed Isaac of Stella

This Birthday is more of a celebration than the feasts of other saints precisely because it is so clearly symbolic and prophetic. Since by his preaching and baptizing, yes, and by his way of living, and by the manner of his death and the miracle of his birth the Voice foretold the Word, the Forerunner ran before the Lord, the Prophet prefigured the Coming One, the More-than-a-Prophet actually pointed out the actual Lord, the Messenger was able to pick out the very One he heralded, and not just for the benefit of those in this world but for those in the other one.

So it was that one born contrary to the laws of nature prefigured to some extent the One who would be born beyond such laws; the former against the normal, the latter beyond the natural; the unusual in the first case, the unique in the other. While there had never been an instance of the latter, there had been a few of the former. Elizabeth's sterility partly prefigured Mary's virginity. There is pregnant sterility on the one hand, fruitful virginity on the other. The old wife brought forth an only son for the sake of the one and only Son the young virgin gave birth to.

John's father was decrepit with age. Christ's Father knows nothing of age. For just as the lack of any Scripture genealogy for Melchizedek typifies the indescribable birth of Christ, Zachary's old age suggests Christ's not having a human father. An old man begets in the former, no man begets in the latter instance. The one unable to beget by nature did so by grace; neither nature nor grace did any begetting when the Giver of grace and nature's Maker alone effected everything.

Thus it was only right that the foreshadowing should ever decrease and the actual fact should ever increase. Shadows, as you now, are longer at morning and evening, and shorter at midday than the bodies that cast them. This holds when morning stands for prophecy, evening for memory and midday or the actuality of Christ. Consequently it was for John to grow less while Christ grew

---

Isaac of Stella, *Sermons*, 46: 5-8, in *The Selected Works of Isaac of Stella. A Cistercian Voice from the Twelfth Century.* Edited by Daniel Deme (Aldershot: Ashgate, 2007), pp. 126-127.

greater, for Christ to be lifted up in death while John became less by decapitation, for Christ to be born as day increased, and John as day decreased.

Collect

ALMIGHTY God, by whose providence thy servant John Baptist was wonderfully born, and sent to prepare the way of thy Son our Saviour, by preaching of repentance: make us so to follow his doctrine and holy life, that we may truly repent according to his preaching and, after his example, constantly speak the truth, boldly rebuke vice and patiently suffer for the truth's sake; through Jesus Christ thy Son our Lord, who liveth and reigneth with thee, in the unity of the Holy Spirit, one God, for ever and ever.

Saint Irenæus, Bishop, Martyr
(28 June)

Proper of the Day and Common of Martyrs

O GOD of peace, who through the ministry of thy servant Irenæus didst strengthen the true faith and bring harmony to thy Church: keep us steadfast in thy true religion and renew us in faith and love, that, by his prayers, we may ever walk in the way that leadeth to everlasting life; through Jesus Christ thy Son our Lord, who liveth and reigneth with thee, in the unity of the Holy Spirit, one God, for ever and ever.

Saints Peter and Paul, Apostles (29 June)

Proper of the Day and Common of Apostles

Hymn

Morning and Evening Prayer

Aurea luce

1.With golden splendour and with roseate hues of morn,
   O gracious Saviour, Light of light, this day adorn,
which brings to ransomed sinners hopes of that far home
   where saints and angels sing the praise of martyrdom.

2.Lo, the Keybearer, lo the Teacher of mankind,
   lights of the world and judges sent to loose and bing,
alike triumphant or by cross or sword-stroke found,
   in life's high Senate stand with victor's laurel crowned.

3.Good Shepherd, Peter, unto whom the charge was given
   to close or open ways of pilgrimage to heaven,
in sin's hard bondage held may we have grace to know
   the full remission thou wast granted to bestow.

4.O noble Teacher, Paul, we trust to learn of thee
   both earthly converse and the flight of ecstasy;
till from the fading truths that now we know in part
   we pass to fullness of delight for mind and heart.

5.Twin olive branches, pouring oil of gladness forth,
   your prayers shall aid us, that for all our little worth,
believeing, hoping, loving, we for whom ye plead,
   thus body dying, may attain to life indeed.

6.Now to the glorious Trinity be duly paid
   worship and honour, praise and service unafraid,
  who in unchanging Unity, one Lord sublime,
   hath ever lived as now and to unending time. Amen.

Ascribed to Elpis, 5th cent., Tr T. A. Lacey (1853-1931)

A reading from the sermons of Saint John Fisher

When you see a tree stand upright upon the ground and its branches spread abroad, full of leaves and fruit, if the sun shine clear this tree maketh a shadow in the which shadow you may perceive a figure of the branches of the leaves and of the fruit. Everything that is in the tree hath somewhat answering unto it in the shadow. And contrary-wise, every part of the shadow hath something answering unto it in the tree. A man's eye may lead him from every part of the tree to every part of the shadow, and again from every part of the shadow to every part of the tree answering thereto. Every man may point to any certain part of the shadow and say, this is the shadow of such a branch, and this is the shadow of such a leaf, and this is the shadow of the bole of the tree and this is the shadow of the top of the tree. But so it that the law of Moses and the governance of the synagogue of the Jews was but a shadow of the governance of the universal Church of Christ. So saith Saint Paul: 'The law had but a shadow of the things for to come' (Heb 10:1). All their governance was but a figure and shadow of the Church. Now then to my purpose. In the governance were twain heads appointed, one under another, Moses and Aaron, to conduct that people through the desert unto the country that was promised them. We know that that people of the Jews was a shadow of the Christian people, and that their journey by the desert toward the country promised them was a shadow of our journey through this wretched world unto the country of heaven. But Moses and Aaron, which were the heads of that people whereof be they shadow? Without doubt they must be the shadow of Christ and of his vicar Saint Peter which under Christ was also the head of Christian people.

And you will see this more manifestly by three likenesses. First, Moses and Aaron both of them were priests. Moses was made by God, and Aaron made

---

Saint John Fisher, 'The Sermon *Cum venerit Paraclitus*', in *English Works of John Fisher, Bishop of Rochester (1469-1535). Sermons and Other Writings, 1520-1535*. Edited by Cecilia A. Hart (Oxford: Oxford University Press, 2002), pp. 78-80.

by Moses at the commandment of God, to whom was committed the cure of the Jews in the absence of Moses. So Christ and Saint Peter both were priests of the New Law, Christ made by his Father, almighty God, as it is written of him, 'Thou art a priest for ever according to the order of Melchizedek' (Heb 5:6). And Peter was made by Christ, to whom he committed in his absence the cure of the Christian people saying, 'Feed my sheep… Feed… feed' (Jn 21:15, 16, 17).

The second likeness is this: Moses was the mean between Almighty God and Aaron for the causes of the people, and Aaron was the mean between Moses and the people touching the causes of God. So Scripture teacheth: Almighty God said unto Moses speaking of Aaron, 'He shall speak in thy stead unto the people and thou shalt be for him again in those causes that pertain to God' (Ex 4:15-16). You will see how Christ was the mouth of Peter towards Almighty God. He said to Saint Peter, 'Simon, Simon, Satan hath coveted greatly to sift thee as a man sifteth his wheat. But I have prayed for thee to the intent that thy faith do not fail. And thou, once turned to the stable way, confirm thy brethren (Lk 22:32). See now here whether Christ was not the mouth of Peter when he promoted his cause before Almighty God the Father and prayed for him that his faith should not finally perish. And contrary-wise was not Peter the mouth of Christ when he to the true way did confirm his brethren? Here note well what authority was given to Peter upon them to confirm all the other of his brethren in the stable way.

The third likeness is this: Moses ascended unto the mountain to speak with Almighty God and Aaron remained behind to instruct the people. Did not Christ likewise ascend unto his Father unto the great mount of heaven: and to what intent I pray you? Saint Paul telleth: 'to appear before the face of [Almighty] God for us' (Heb 9:24), and there to be our advocate as Saint John saith (1 Jn 2:1). And did not Peter remain behind to teach the people the which our Saviour committed unto his charge, like as Aaron was left for to do the people of the Jews when Moses was above in the mount with God?

Thus every man may see how that shadow and this thing agreeth one to another fully and clearly.

Collect

ALMIGHTY God, whose blessed apostles Peter and Paul glorified thee in their death as in their life: grant that thy Church, inspired by their teaching and example, aided by their prayers, and made one by thy Spirit, may ever stand firm on the one foundation which is thy Son, Jesus Christ our Lord; who liveth and reigneth with thee, in the unity of the Holy Spirit, one God, for ever and ever.

Saint Thomas, Apostle
(3 July)

Proper of the Day and Common of Apostles

A reading from the sermons of John Keble

'For the more confirmation of our faith' [St Thomas] was suffered to be without full faith for a time. Our Lord, in his mercy, permitted him both to see and touch his glorious and saving Wounds, and so all doubt was taken away, which might have lingered in any person's mind from the manner of his appearing to the other disciples before. Coming and going, as he did, in a shadowy manner, the doors being shut, some might think they had only see a spirit. But now there could be no doubt that it was his very Body: no doubt, that we too shall see that same Body with the same marks of his Wounds in it. We shall see them in the Last Day, to our condemnation if we have crucified him anew, and opened those Wounds, so to speak, afresh by our sins: we shall see him and them to our everlasting bliss and joy, if, through his mercy, we have remembered them in time, denied ourselves, and overcome the flesh. This we are quite sure of; the more sure and certain, for that unbelief of St Thomas: and so far, it was ordered providentially for our good.

Yet, in itself, there can be no doubt that his unbelief was, at least, an error; and a great loss to him for the time. It was an error, not to have noted more exactly the many sayings of our Lord, by which, from time to time, he had been preparing his disciples to expect his real Resurrection: - not to trust their report, so many and so good as they were, who declared that they had seen him, after he was risen. And it was a great loss, surely, to abide for a whole week in doubt and fear, while the rest were thankfully enjoying the unspeakable work of mercy which God had wrought for them. It was a great loss, to be separated, even for those few days, from the favoured company of Christ's believing people; from his Mother and the rest of the holy women, and from the Apostles whom he had breathed on, and sent, as his Father had sent him. And we may well imagine how St Peter and St John, and the rest of that faithful and affectionate

---

John Keble, 'The Unbelief of Christians in their Supernatural Condition', in *Sermons for the Saints' Days and other Festivals, by the late Rev. John Keble* (Oxford and London: Parker, 1877), pp. 20-22, 23-24.

company, must have grieved and prayed for him during that week; how they must have rejoiced, when, on the second Lord's Day, our Saviour made his appearance again, and graciously quieted St Thomas' doubting mind, making the whole eleven again to be one happy and believing company. [...]

Why did St Thomas not believe? And why are so many of us Christians unable to realize their true condition and privileges? It is much the same reason in both cases. Our own senses, our own experiences, do not confirm what we are called on to believe. St Thomas was told by his fellow-disciples that they had seen the Lord, but his timid spirit was not content with their report: he wanted to see him his own self, to see his Wounds, and not only to see, but to feel them: then, he said, he could believe, but not otherwise. So we Christians are taught in the Catechism that we are 'members of Christ, children of God, and inheritors of the kingdom of heaven', but we do not see it, nor feel it: we see and feel the same as unbaptized people do. The world is about us, as it is about them, with its wants and pains and cares and pleasures; and there is in too many of us an evil heart of unbelief, a sullen obstinate spirit, to whisper, 'Seeing is believing', and you do not see the things which Clergymen and good books so positively tell you of; why then need you trouble yourself much about them? They say you are in the kingdom of heaven, but you do not find or feel the difference: why then need you attend to them? Then the Evil One helps our corrupt hearts to reason with us: and so it comes to pass that Christians go on for ten, twenty, forty, sixty years, living like heathens and yet take it as a matter of course: they are not ashamed, they scarce care to deny or excuse themselves; they think they are no saints, and what better could be expected of them? If they could see with their eyes such things as the Apostles saw, heaven opened, the dead raised, all sorts of miracles wrought, then perhaps, they think they should believe: but as it is, they do not, and cannot, They walk by sight, not by faith: and see, what they lose by it.

Collect
ALMIGHTY and eternal God, who, for the more confirmation of the faith, didst suffer thy holy apostle Thomas to be doubtful in thy Son's resurrection: grant us so perfectly, and without all doubt, to believe in thy Son Jesus Christ, that our faith in thy sight may never be reproved. Hear us, O Lord, through the same Jesus Christ, to whom, with thee and the Holy Spirit, be all honour and glory, for ever and evermore.

Saint Benedict, Abbot, Patron of Europe (11 July)

Proper of the Day and Common of Saints: for an Abbot

O ETERNAL God, who made Benedict a wise master in the school of thy service, and a guide to many called into the common life to follow the rule of Christ: grant that we may put thy love above all things, and seek with joy the way of thy commandments; through Jesus Christ thy Son our Lord, who liveth and reigneth with thee, in the unity of the Holy Spirit, one God, for ever and ever.

Saint Mary Magdalen (22 July)

Proper of the Day and Common of Saints

Collect

O ALMIGHTY God, whose blessed Son did call and sanctify Mary Magdalen to be a witness to his resurrection: mercifully grant that by thy grace, and assisted by her prayers, we may be healed of all our infirmities, and always serve thee in the power of his endless life; who with thee and the Holy Spirit liveth and reigneth, one God, world without end.

Saint Bridget of Sweden, Religious,
Patron of Europe
(23 July)

Proper of the Day and Common of Saints: for an Abbess

ALMIGHTY God, by whose grace Bridget, enkindled with the fire of thy love, became a burning and a shining light in the Church: inflame us with the same spirit of discipline and love, that, rejoicing in her prayers, we may ever walk before thee as children of light; through Jesus Christ thy Son our Lord, who liveth and reigneth with thee, in the unity of the Holy Spirit, one God, for ever and ever.

Saint James, Apostle (25 July)

Proper of the Day and Common of Apostles

A reading from the sermons of John Keble

The collect for the day points out to us, as usual with our Church on saints' days, a part of St James's example for our particular imitation. We pray that, as 'he, leaving his father and all that he had, without delay was obedient unto the calling of Christ, and followed him, so we, forsaking all worldly and carnal affections, may be evermore ready to follow his holy commandments'. Thus our thoughts are carried back to the time, when it seemed good to the Son of God, in his divine foresight, to call four fishermen from their work on the shore of the sea of Galilee to be his apostles, and chief foundations of his Church. 'Follow me', he said, first to St Peter and St Andrew, 'and I will make you fishers of men' (Mt 4:19). 'They drew their nets to land, forsook all, and followed him'. Presently after, going a little further, he saw their partners also, 'James, the son of Zebedee, and John his brother, in a ship with Zebedee their father, mending their nets: and he called them: and they immediately left the ship and their father, and followed him' (Mt 4:21-22). [...]

John Keble, 'Profit and Home Forsaken for Christ', in *Sermons for the Saints' Days and other Festivals, by the late Rev. John Keble* (Oxford and London: Parker, 1877), pp. 305-306, 308-309.

It would appear as if Zebedee and his sons were what the world calls 'better off' than Simon and Andrew, the sons of Jonah. For of these latter, when our Lord finally summoned them, it is only said, that 'when they had brought their ships to land, they forsook all and followed him': but of James and John that 'they left their father Zebedee in the ship with the hired servants, and followed after Jesus'. [...]

St James, then, may be regarded as affording an example and encouragement to those who follow Christ, in two sorts of trials more particularly: those which arise from a thriving condition in the world, and those which attend, sometimes, on a quiet and comfortable home. To obey our Lord's call, he left 'both the ship and his father': both the business to which he had been brought up, and on which he might depend, if not for wealth, at least for a comfortable maintenance; and the consolation of being with his parents, and living peaceably at home with them.

And for this, his double self-denial, how greatly was he rewarded! Our Lord received him to be not only a disciple, but an apostle; and not only an apostle, but one of three whom he particularly favoured above the other apostles, keeping them near him on the highest and holiest occasions, when the rest were bade remain at the threshold, so to speak, of his glories. St Peter, St James, and St John were alone with him, when he raised Jairus's daughter, and restored her to her afflicted parents; alone with him in the holy Mount, when he was transfigured, and had Moses and Elias talking with him: alone (except St Andrew) with him, when he uttered those aweful prophecies concerning the end of the world; alone with him, finally, when he submitted himself to his agony in the garden, and 'his sweat was, as it were great drops of blood falling down to the ground, and there appeared unto him an Angel from heaven strengthening him' (Lk 22:44). St James, in each case, is the second namely of the highly-favoured ones, whom he chose among living men, to be his witnesses on these solemn occasions. [...]

It might seem almost sinful presumption, for such as we are, to take to ourselves, as if intended for our pattern, the example of so great and holy a saint, one brought so very near the person of our divine Saviour himself. But we know it is not presumption, since even Christ's own example, and that of the Eternal Father, are set before us for our study and imitation. We are bid to do to one another as Christ did to his disciples; and to 'be perfect, as our Father which is in heaven is perfect' (Mt 5:48). Much less then must we shrink from contemplating the pattern of any saint or apostle, how holy and glorious so ever, as one which we ought to copy; since we shall surely be judged by all such patterns, once made known to us by God's Providence, in his holy Scriptures or his Church. They will be reckoned among the talents, which will burthen and sink us into earth at the last day, if we be found to have neglected the due improvement of them now.

Collect

GRANT, O merciful God, that as thine holy apostle Saint James, leaving his father and all that he had, without delay was obedient unto the calling of thy Son Jesus Christ, and followed him: so we, forsaking all worldly and carnal affections, may be evermore ready to follow thy holy commandments; through Jesus Christ thy Son our Lord, who liveth and reigneth with thee, in the unity of the Holy Spirit, one God, for ever and ever.

Saints Joachim and Anne,
Parents of the Blessed Virgin Mary
(26 July)

Proper of the Day and Common of Saints

O LORD, God of our Fathers, who bestowed on Saints Joachim and Anne this grace, that of them should be born the Mother of thine incarnate Son: grant that, through their prayers, we may attain the salvation which thou hast promised to thy people; through Jesus Christ thy Son our Lord, who liveth and reigneth with thee, in the unity of the Holy Spirit, one God, for ever and ever.

Saint Martha
(29 July)

Proper of the Day and Common of Saints

ALMIGHTY and ever-living God, whose Son was pleased to be welcomed as a guest in the house of thy servant Saint Martha: grant, we pray, that, through her intercession, serving Christ faithfully in our brethren we may merit to be received by thee in the halls of heaven; through Jesus Christ thy Son our Lord, who liveth and reigneth with thee, in the unity of the Holy Spirit, one God, for ever and ever.

**Transfiguration of the Lord
(6 August)**

Proper of the Day

Hymns

Evening Prayer *Vespers*

O nata lux de lumine

1.O light of light, by love inclined,
  Jesu, Redeemer of mankind,
with loving-kindness deign to hear
  from suppliant voices praise and prayer.

2.Thou who to raise our souls from hell
  didst deign in fleshly form to dwell,
vouchsafe us, when our race is run,
  in thy fair Body to be one.

3.More bright than day thy face did show,
  thy raiment whiter than the snow,
when on the mount to mortals blest
  man's Maker thou wast manifest.

4.Two prophets, that had faith to see,
  with thine elect found company,
where unto each, divinely shown
  the Godhead veiled in form was known.

5.The heavens above his glory named,
  the Father's voice the Son proclaimed;
to whom, the King of glory now,
  all faithful hearts adoring bow.

6.May all who seek thy praise aright
  through purer lives show forth thy light;
so to the brightness of the skies
  by holy deeds our hearts shall rise.

7.Eternal God, to thee we raise,
  the King of kings, our hymn of praise,
who Three in One and One in Three
  doth live and reign eternally. Amen.

10ᵗʰ cent. Tr. Laurence Housman (1865-1959)

511

Dulcis Iesu memoria

1.Jesu! – The very thought is sweet!
  in that dear name all heart-joys meet;
but sweeter than the honey far
  the glimpses of his presence are.

2.No word is sung more sweet than this:
  no name is heard more full of bliss:
no thought brings sweeter comfort nigh
  than Jesus, Son of God most hight.

3.Jesu! the hope of souls forlorn!
  how good to them for sin that mourn.
to them that seek thee, O how kind!
  But what art thou to them that find?

4.Jesu, thou sweetness, pure and blest,
  Truth's Fountain, Light of souls distrest,
Surpassing all that heart requires,
  Exceeding all that soul desires!

5.No tongue of mortal can express,
  no letters write its blessedness:
alone who hath thee in his hearth
  knows, love of Jesus! what thou art.

6.O Jesu! King of wondrous might!
  O Victor, glorious from the fight!
sweetness that may not be exprest,
  and altogether loveliest!

7.Remain with us, O Lord, to-day!
  in every heart thy grace display:
that now the shades of night are fled,
  on thee our spirits may be fed.

8.All honour, laud and glory be,
  O Jesu, Virgin-born, to thee!
all glory, as is ever meet,
  to Father and to Paraclete. Amen.

11th cent. Tr. J. M. Neale

A reading from the sermons of Blessed John Henry Newman

Our Lord often passed the night in prayer, and as afterwards in that sad night before his Passion he took with him three Apostles to witness his prayer in

Bl. John Henry Newman, 'The World and Sin', in *Catholic Sermons of Cardinal Newman*. Published, for the first time, from the Cardinal's autograph manuscripts. Edited at the Birmingham Oratory (London: Burns and Oates, 1957), pp. 80-83, 88-90.

agony, so at an earlier time he took the same favoured three with him to witness his prayer in ecstasy and glory. On the one occasion he fell on his face and prayed more earnestly till he was covered with a sweat of blood which rolled down upon the cold earth. In the other, as he prayed his countenance became bright and glorious, and he was lifted off the earth. So he remained communing with his Father, ministered to by Moses and Elias, till a voice came from the cloud, which said: 'This is my beloved Son, hear ye him' (Lk 9:35). The sight had been so wonderful, so transporting, that St Peter could not help crying out. He knew not what he said. He did not know how to express his inward feelings, nor did he understand in a moment all the wonders about him. He could but say, 'Lord, it is good for us to be here' (Lk 9:33a). Simple words, but how much they contain in them. It was good, it was the good of man, it was the great good, it was our good. He did not say that the sight was sublime and marvellous. He was not able to reflect upon it and describe it. his reason did not speak, but his affections. He did but say that it was good to be there. And he wished that great good to continue to him ever. He said, 'Let us build three tabernacles, one for thee, one for Moses, and one for Elias' (Lk 9:33b). He wished to remain there for ever, it was so good. He was loath the vision should come to an end. He did not like to descend from the mount and return to those whom he had left behind.

Now let us see what was taking place below while they were above. When they reached the crowd, they found a dispute going on between the rest of the Apostles and the Scribes. The subject of it seems to have been the poor demoniac, who is next spoken of. A father had brought his son to be cured by the Apostles. He was a frightful maniac, possessed by the devil. None could hold him. The spirit took away his voice and hearing. He was ordinarily deaf and dumb, but sometimes he dashed himself to the ground, threw himself into the fire or into the water. The devil was too much for the Apostles. They could not master him, they could not cast him out. They were reduced to a sort of despair, and this was the occasion, as it appears, of their dispute with the Scribes, who might be taunting them with their failure. Oh the contrast between what St Peter had come from and what he had now come to! he had left peace, stillness, contemplation, the vision of heavens, and he had come into pain, grief, confusion, perplexity, disappointment, and debate.

Now this contrast… between the Mount of Transfiguration and the scene at its foot fitly represents to us the contrast between the world and the Church, between the things seen and the things unseen.

I will not dwell on the mere physical evils of this life, though they are enough to appal us, the miseries of sickness, pain, want, cold, hunger; but let us dwell upon the moral evils which it contains. The poor youth who was brought to Christ to be cured was possessed by the devil, and alas! is not a great portion, is not the greatest portion of mankind at this day possessed by the devil too?[...] [A]s the poor epileptic in the Gospel was under the mastery of the evil spirit, so that his eyes, his ears, his tongue, his limbs were not his own, so does that same miserable spirit possess the souls of sinners, ruling them impelling them here and there, doing what he will with them, but indeed doing the same with everyone, some he moves one way, some in another, but all in some pitiable, horrible, and ungodly way. [...] When, then, St Peter, St James, and St John came down from the Mount and saw the miserable youth tormented by an evil spirit, they saw in that youth a figure and emblem of that world of sinners to whom in due time they were to be sent to preach. [...]

There is an immense weight of evil in the world. We Catholics, and especially we Catholic priests, have it in charge to resist, to overcome the evil; but we cannot do what we would, we cannot overcome the giant, we cannot bind the strong man. We do a part of the work, not all. It is a battle which goes on between good and evil, and though by God's grace we do something, we cannot do more. There is confusion of nations and perplexity. It is God's will that it should be so, to show his power. He alone can heal the soul. He alone can expel the devil. And therefore we must wait for a good deal, till he comes down from his seat on high, his seat in glory, to aid us and deliver us.

Collect
O GOD, who before the passion of thine only-begotten Son didst reveal his glory upon the holy mount: grant unto us thy servants, that in faith beholding the light of his countenance, we may be strengthened to bear the cross, and be changed into his likeness from glory to glory; through the same Jesus Christ our Lord, who liveth and reigneth with thee, in the unity of the Holy Spirit, one God, for ever and ever.

Saint Dominic, Priest
(8 August)

Proper of the Day and Common of Saints

ALMIGHTY God, whose servant Dominic grew in the knowledge of thy truth, and formed an order of preachers to proclaim the faith of Christ: by thy grace grant to all thy people a love for thy word and a longing to share the gospel, that the whole world may be filled with the knowledge of thee and of thy Son Jesus Christ our Lord; who liveth and reigneth with thee, in the unity of the Holy Spirit, one God, for ever and ever.

Saint Teresa Benedicta of the Cross (Edith Stein), Virgin, Martyr, Patron of Europe
(9 August)

Proper of the Day and Common of Martyrs

ALMIGHTY God, by whose grace and power thy holy martyr Teresa Benedicta of the Cross triumphed over suffering and was faithful unto death: strengthen us with thy grace, that, assisted by her prayers, we may endure reproach and persecution and faithfully bear witness to the name of Jesus Christ thy Son our Lord; who liveth and reigneth with thee, in the unity of the Holy Spirit, one God, for ever and ever.

Saint Laurence, Deacon, Martyr
(10 August)

Proper of the Day and Common of Martyrs

ALMIGHTY God, who didst make Laurence a loving servant of thy people and a wise steward of the treasures of thy Church: inflame us, by his example, to love as he loved and, aided by his prayers, to walk in the way that leads to everlasting life; through Jesus Christ thy Son our Lord, who liveth and reigneth with thee, in the unity of the Holy Spirit, one God, for ever and ever.

Saint Clare, Virgin,
(11 August)

Proper of the Day and Common of Virgins

O GOD of peace, who in the poverty of the blessed Clare gavest us a clear light to shine in the darkness of this world: give us grace so to follow in her footsteps that, by her intercession, we may, at the last, rejoice with her in thine eternal glory; through Jesus Christ thy Son our Lord, who liveth and reigneth with thee, in the unity of the Holy Spirit, one God, for ever and ever.

Assumption of the Blessed Virgin Mary
(15 August)

Proper of the Day and Common of the Blessed Virgin Mary

A reading from Mother Julian, *Revelations of Divine Love*

And with this same appearance of mirth and joy our good Lord looked down on his right, and brought to my mind where our Lady stood at the time of his Passion, and he said: Do you wish to see her? And these sweet words were as if he had said, I know well that you wish to see my blessed mother, for after myself she is the greatest joy that I could show you, and the greatest delight and honour to me, and she is what all my blessed creatures most desire to see. And because of the wonderful, exalted and singular love that he has for this sweet maiden, his blessed mother, our Lady Saint Mary, he reveals her bliss and joy through the sense of these sweet words, as if he had said, do you wish to see how I love her, so that you could rejoice with me in the love which I have in her and she has in me?

And for greater understanding of these sweet words our good Lord speaks in love to all mankind who will be saved, addressing them all as one person, as if he said, do you wish to see in her how you are loved? It is for love of you that I have made her so exalted, so noble, so honourable; and this delights me. And I wish it to delight you. For next to him, she is the most blissful to be seen. But in this matter I was not taught to long to see her bodily presence while I am here, but the virtues of her blessed soul, her truth, her wisdom, her love, through which I am taught to know myself and reverently to fear my God.

And when our good Lord had revealed this, and said these words: Do you wish to see her? I answered and said: Yes, good Lord, great thanks, yes, good Lord, if it be your will. Often times I had prayed for this, and I had expected to see her in a bodily likeness; but I did not see her so. And Jesus, saying this, showed me a spiritual vision of her. Just as before I had seen her small and simple, now he showed her high and noble and glorious and more pleasing to him than all

Mother Julian, *Revelations of Divine Love*, 25 (Long Text), in Julian of Norwich, *Showings*. Translated from the critical text with an introduction by Edmund Colledge, O. S. A. and James Walsh, S. J. (New York: Paulist, 1978), pp. 221-223.

creatures. And so he wishes it to be known that all who take delight in him should take delight in her, and in the delight that he has in her and she in him.

And for greater understanding he showed this example, as if, when a man loves some creature particularly, more than all other creatures, he will make all other creatures to love and delight in that creature whom he loves so much. And in these words which Jesus said: Do you wish to see her? it seemed to me that these were the most delectable words which he could give me in this spiritual vision of her which he gave me. For our Lord showed me no particular person except our Lady Saint Mary, and he showed her on three occasions. The first was as she conceived, the second was as she had been under the Cross, and the third was as she is now, in delight, honour and joy.

Collect

O GOD, who hast taken to thyself the blessed Virgin Mary, mother of thy incarnate Son: grant that we, who have been redeemed by his blood, may, through her intercession, share with her the glory of thine eternal kingdom; through the same thy Son, Jesus Christ our Lord, who liveth and reigneth with thee, in the unity of the Holy Spirit, one God, for ever and ever.

Saint Bernard, Abbot, Doctor of the Church (20 August)

Proper of the Day and Common of Doctors of the Church

O MERCIFUL redeemer, who, by the life and preaching of thy servant Bernard, didst rekindle the radiant light of thy Church: grant that, through his prayers, we in our generation may be inflamed with the same spirit of discipline and love and ever walk before thee as children of light; through Jesus Christ thy Son our Lord, who liveth and reigneth with thee, in the unity of the Holy Spirit, one God, for ever and ever.

Saint Bartholomew, Apostle (24 August)

Proper of the Day and Common of Apostles

A reading from the sermons of Blessed John Henry Newman

When Philip told him that he had found the long-expected Messiah of whom Moses wrote, Nathanael (that is, Bartholomew) at first doubted. He was well read in the Scriptures, and knew that Christ was to be born in Bethlehem; whereas Jesus dwelt at Nazareth, which Nathanael supposed in consequence to be the place of his birth, - and he knew of no particular promises attached to that city, which was a place of evil report, and he thought no good could come out of it. Philip told him to come and see; and he went to see, as a humble single-minded man, sincerely desirous to get at the truth. In consequence, he was vouchsafed an interview with our Saviour, and was converted.

Now, from what occurred in this interview, we gain some insight into St Bartholomew's character. Our Lord said of him, 'Behold an Israelite indeed, in whom is no guile!' (Jn 1:47) and it appears, moreover, as if, before Philip called him to come to Christ, he was engaged in meditation or prayer, in the privacy which a fig-tree's shade afforded him. [...]

'Behold an Israelite indeed, in whom is no guile!' This is just the character which (through God's grace) they may attain most fully who live out of the world in the private way I have been describing - which is made last account of by man, and thought to be in the way of success in life, though our Saviour chose it to make head against all the power and wisdom of the world. Men of the world think an ignorance of its ways is a disadvantage or disgrace; as if it were somehow unmanly and weak to have abstained from all acquaintance with its impieties and lax practices. How often do we hear them say that a man must do so and so, unless he would be singular and absurd; that he must not be too strict, or indulge high-flown notions of virtue, which may be good to talk about, but are not fit for this world!

But the guileless man has a simple boldness and a princely heart; he overcomes dangers which others shrink from, merely because they are no dangers to him, and thus he often gains even worldly advantages, by his straightforwardness,

---

Bl. John Henry Newman, 'Guilelessness', in *Parochial and Plain Sermons, by John Henry Newman*, II (London: Rivingtons, 1880), pp. 335, 337, 339-40, 341-342.

which the most crafty persons cannot gain, though they risk their souls for them. It is true such single-hearted men often get into difficulties, but them usually get out of them as easily; and are almost unconscious both of their danger and their escape.[...]

Innocence must be joined to prudence, discretion, self-command, gravity, patience, perseverance in well-doing, as Bartholomew doubtless learned in due season under his Lord's teaching; but innocence is the beginning. Let us then pray God to fulfil in us 'all the good pleasure of his goodness, and the work of faith with power' (2 Thess 1:11), that if it should please him suddenly to bring us forward to great trials, as he did his apostles, we may not be taken by surprise, but be found to have made a private or domestic life a preparation for the achievements of Confessors and Martyrs.

Collect

O ALMIGHTY and everlasting God, who didst give to thine apostle Bartholomew grace truly to believe and to preach thy word: grant, we beseech thee, unto thy Church, to love that Word which he believed, and both to preach and receive the same; through Jesus Christ thy Son our Lord, who liveth and reigneth with thee, in the unity of the Holy Spirit, one God, for ever and ever.

Saint Monica
(27 August)

Proper of the Day and Common of Saints

O FAITHFUL God, who didst strengthen Monica, the mother of Augustine, with wisdom, and by her steadfast endurance didst draw him to seek after thee: grant us to be constant in prayer that, through her prayers, those who stray from thee may be brought to faith in thy Son Jesus Christ our Lord; who liveth and reigneth with thee, in the unity of the Holy Spirit, one God, for ever and ever.

Saint Augustine of Hippo, Bishop, Doctor of the Church
(28 August)

Proper of the Day and Common of Pastors
or of Doctors of the Church

O MERCIFUL Lord, who didst turn Augustine from his sins to be a faithful bishop and teacher: grant that we may follow him in penitence and godly discipline, till our restless hearts find their rest in thee; through Jesus Christ thy Son our Lord, who liveth and reigneth with thee, in the unity of the Holy Spirit, one God, for ever and ever.

Beheading of Saint John the Baptist
(29 August)
Proper of the Day and Common of Martyrs

Hymn

Morning and Evening Prayer   *Vespers*

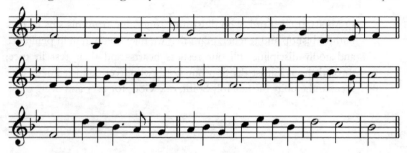

Præcessor almus gratiæ

1. Hail, harbinger of morn: thou that art this day born,
   and heraldest the Word with clarion voice!
   Ye faithful ones, in him behold the dawning dim
   of the bright day, and let your hearts rejoice.

2. John; - by that chosen name to call him, Gabriel came
   by God's appointment from his home on high:
   what deeds that babe should do to manhood when he grew,
   God sent his angel forth to testify.

3. There is none greater, none, than Zechariah's son;
   than this no mightier prophet hath been born:
   of prophets he may claim more than a prophet's fame;
   sublimer deeds than theirs his brow adorn.

4. 'Lo, to prepare thy way,' did God the Father say,
   'before thy face my messenger I send,
   thy coming to forerun; as on the orient sun
   doth the bright daystar morn by morn attend.'

5. Praise therefore God most high; praise him who came to die
   for us, his Son that liveth evermore;
   and to the Spirit raise, the Comforter, life praise,
   while time endureth, and when time is o'er.

Tune: Hail, Harbinger of Morn, W. H. Bell (1873-1946)
Words: St Bede, *Tr.* Charles Calverley (1831-84)

522

Collect

ALMIGHTY God, who didst call thy servant John the Baptist to be in birth and death the forerunner of thy blessed Son: strengthen us by thy grace that, as he suffered for the truth, so may we boldly withstand corruption and vice and receive with him the unfading crown of glory; through Jesus Christ thy Son our Lord, who liveth and reigneth with thee, in the unity of the Holy Spirit, one God, for ever and ever.

Nativity of the Blessed Virgin Mary
(8 September)

Proper of the Day and Common of the Blessed Virgin Mary

A reading from John of Ford, *Sermons on the Final Verses of the Song of Songs*

When Jesus was speaking to the crowds, it was not one of the band of the apostles, not one of the council of elders, but simply one of the women there in the crowd who 'lifted up her voice' (Lk 11:27), and proclaimed that the womb that bore him was blessed. The example of this woman has given me the courage to dare, in my turn, to say something about the blessedness of this womb. And in sober truth, above all that can be said or thought, that womb is blessed indeed, pregnant with so sacred an offspring, heavy with so light a burden, guardian of a trust so precious. That womb is a marriage chamber of very great tenderness, rich in the most noble seed, and it contains a great and holy secret. It has knowledge of great mystery and it bears very great dignity.

But clearly, that womb was blessed even before it carried the Lord. Day and night, with a most pure desire and the longing of a holy and consecrated love, it prepared itself to bear its holy burden. In the silence of her heart, Mary said to herself: 'Let him kiss me with the kiss of his mouth' (Song 1:1). There has never been another soul, or rather, there has never been one of the blessed spirits, not even from that most blissful of the nine choirs that takes its name from the fire of charity and refreshes the heat of its immense love by the continual contemplation of eternity and the ceaseless praise of the holy Trinity: no, not even among the cherubim has any one made progress like hers in desiring and receiving this kiss.

So then, to make her ready for such grace, from her mother's womb she was fashioned by him who establishes the heavens, and every single moment, during the successive stages by which God established her, the fullness of grace was built up. One day she would become God's mother, and then an angel would call her 'full of grace' (Lk 1: 28). So her womb is blessed in the very

John of Ford, *Sermons on the Final Verses of the Song of Songs*, 70: 3-5, in John of Ford, *Sermons on the Song of Songs*, V. Translated by Wendy Mary Beckett (Kalamazoo, MI: Cistercian Publications, 1983), pp. 98-101.

manner of its establishment in blessedness, yet it is far more blessed when it finally, in a divine and indescribable way, receives its most blessed burden. Blessed indeed, though, most blessed, is that womb when it bore him, when it formed him, when it was in labour with him, when it brought him to birth.

[…] So, 'all the glory of the king's daughter is from within' (Ps 45:13). It came from within, but no part of that glory went to waste within or retreated from within. Every single one of the gifts of God's mother, whether interior or exterior, all are signs of salvation. Grace was added to grace, glory was heaped on glory, and as her crowning virtue grew, nothing went to waste, not even the least touch of her humility. Although 'full of grace', she could always be enriched by a new increase of fullness, but however this increase overflowed, no suggestion of vanity had power to spoil its bloom, not for an instant. God 'looked on' the purity of his mother, just as he had 'looked on the humility of his handmaid' (Lk 1:48).

Yes, God 'looked on' her, and while he looked, he enriched her and strengthened her and rewarded her. He looked indeed, and saw that, just as this most blessed of mothers kept her virginity intact despite the glory of her fruitfulness, so did her humility remain intact and untouchable, through she has reached the heights of perfection. And it was in this way that most blessed womb poured out its blessedness far and wide. […]

In short, just as all grace and glory flowed from this woman's body, so it can be said that every generation of saints truly arose from her by what we can only call the wonderful mystery of divine fruitfulness. Let me repeat it: the mother of Jesus is not only the mother of our glorious head, Jesus Christ, mediator between God and man, but she is also the mother of all who love Jesus, of the whole of Jesus' sacred body.

Collect

ALMIGHTY and everlasting God, who stooped to raise fallen humanity through the child-bearing of blessed Mary: grant that we, who have seen thy glory revealed in our human nature and thy love made perfect in our weakness, may daily be renewed in thine image and conformed to the pattern of thy Son Jesus Christ our Lord; who liveth and reigneth with thee, in the unity of the Holy Spirit, one God, for ever and ever.

Most Holy Name of Mary
(12 September)

Proper of the Day and Common of the Blessed Virgin Mary

GRANT, we beseech thee, almighty God: that thy faithful people who rejoice in the name and protection of the most holy Virgin Mary, may by her loving intercession be delivered from all evils on earth and be found worthy to come to everlasting joys in heaven; we ask this through Jesus Christ thy Son our Lord, who liveth and reigneth with thee, in the unity of the Holy Spirit, one God, for ever and ever.

Saint John Chrysostom, Bishop,
Doctor of the Church
(13 September)

Proper of the Day and Common of Pastors
or of Doctors of the Church

O GOD of truth and love, who gavest to thy servant John Chrysostom eloquence to declare thy righteousness in the great congregation and courage to bear reproach for the honour of thy name: mercifully grant to the ministers of thy word such excellence in preaching that all people may share with them in the glory that shall be revealed; through Jesus Christ thy Son our Lord, who liveth and reigneth with thee, in the unity of the Holy Spirit, one God, for ever and ever.

Exaltation of the Holy Cross (Holy Cross Day)
(14 September)

Proper of the Day

For the Hymn, Vexilla Regis, *see page 287.*

A reading from the sermons of Saint John Fisher

The prophet Ezekiel tells that he saw a book spread before him which was written both within and without, and there was written also in it 'lamentations, song, and woe'. This was a wonderful book, and much to be marvelled upon. Much comfortable knowledge and sweetness this prophet got by this book (as he says in the chapter next ensuing, 'this book was in my mouth as sweet as honey'). This book to our purpose may be taken to be unto us the Crucifix, the which doubtless is a marvellous book, as we shall shew hereafter.

In the which if we do exercise our admiration, we shall come to wonderful knowledge. Marvelling was the cause why that the philosophers came to so great knowledge as they had. They beheld and saw many wonderful things and effects in this world, as the marvellous earthquakes, thunders, lightnings, snow, rain, and frosts, blazing stars, the eclipse of the sun and of the moon, and such other effects. And those marvellous wonders moved them to search for the causes of the same. And so by diligent search and inquisition, they came to great knowledge and cunning, which cunning men call 'philosophy natural'. But there is another higher philosophy which is above nature, which is also got with marvelling. And this is the very philosophy of Christian people.

And doubtless amongst all other things concerning a Christian man, it is a thing much marvellous, and most wonderful, that the Son of God, for the love that he had unto the soul of man, would suffer himself to be crucified, and so to take upon him that most villainous death upon the Cross. Of this the prophet Habakkuk says, 'Marvel, and wonder you, for a work is done in your days, which when it shall be shown, no man will believe'.

Saint John Fisher, *A Sermon preached on a Good Friday*, in *English Works of John Fisher, Bishop of Rochester (1469-1535). Sermons and Other Writings, 1520-1535.* Edited by Cecilia A. Hart (Oxford: Oxford University Press, 2002), pp. 300-301.

Is it not a wonderful thing, that he which is most to be dreaded and feared, would be in so much fear, that, for very fear and dread of pain he had to suffer, he sweated water and blood? Is it not a wonderful thing, that he that was most inestimable in price, and most precious, would suffer his body to be sold for so little a price, as for the value of thirty pence? Is it not a wonderful thing, that he that is the Lord of heaven and earth and all other creatures, would suffer himself to be bound of those villains with ropes like a thief? Is it not a wonderful thing that he that has so great might and power, would suffer himself to be taken of his cruel and mortal enemies, and so led into all these pains? Is it not a wonderful thing, that he that is the Judge of all the world, should thus wrongfully be judged? Is it not a wonderful thing, that he that had in him all wisdom, would thus be mocked and reputed a fool? Is it not a wonderful thing, that he that is so strong and mighty, would be made so weak, and feeble, that he fell under the weight and burden of the Cross? Is it not a wonderful thing, that he that is the Lord of angels, would be spat at and bobbed of a sort of laurels in that most despiteful manner? Is it not a wonderful thing, that he that is the King of everlasting glory would suffer his head in mockery to be crowned with thorns? Is it not a wonderful thing, that he that gives life to every creature, would suffer this most shameful, sorrowful and so painful death? Is it not a wonderful thing, that he that is the Lord, and Author of all liberty, would thus be bound with ropes, and nailed hand and foot unto the Cross?

Thus who that lists with a meek heart, and a true faith, to muse and to marvel at this wonderful book (I say of the Crucifix) he shall come to more fruitful knowledge, than many other which daily study upon their common books. Thus book may suffice for the study of a true Christian man, all the days of his life.

Collect

ALMIGHTY God, who in the passion of thy blessed Son hast made an instrument of painful death to be for us the means of life and peace: grant us so to glory in the cross of Christ that we may gladly suffer for his sake; who liveth and reigneth with thee, in the unity of the Holy Spirit, one God, for ever and ever.

Saint Matthew, Apostle, Evangelist
(21 September)

Proper of the Day and Common of Apostles and of Evangelists

A reading from the sermons of John Keble

'It came to pass, as Jesus sat at eat in the house, behold, many publicans and sinners came and sat down with him and his disciples' (Mt 9:10). See here the extreme condescension and tender love of Jesus Christ, for the worst and most miserable sinners. The holy evangelist St Matthew seems himself astonished at the remembrance of it. *Behold*, says he; as if it were something wonderful, something more than could be looked for, even from Christ's unspeakable mercy: that he should sit at meat in a publican's and sinner's house, and that many of the like sort should be permitted to come and sit down with him. Such, no doubt, had been St Matthew's feeling at the time: and such it continued, so long afterwards, twenty or thirty years perhaps, when he came to write it down in his Gospel. For he, St Matthew's own self, was the person to whom this great thing happened.

He had been, a little before, called suddenly by Jesus Christ, when sitting at his ordinary work. Like a rich merchant, a lawyer, or a shop-keeper, who has many various accounts to settle; whose time is taken up, from morning till night, with calls of business which he is forced to attend to: all of them, more or less, turning his thoughts towards money, as if the gain, or the loss of it were the great business of life: such was Matthew, as he sat at the receipt of custom: and if you would wonder to see such a one rise up suddenly at the call of some holy man, leave his accounts, his treasures, and his gainful employments, and devote himself entirely to the more immediate service of God, you may in some measure judge, with what adoring love and thankfulness the great Apostle, Evangelist would remember the moment of his call: all the loving looks, gracious words, and merciful condescension of his God and Saviour towards him.

We know how Abraham rejoiced, when he had entertained angels unawares: but here is the God and Creator of the angels coming to sit down to meat in

---

John Keble, 'Our Lord's Condescending Kindness to Penitents', in *Sermons for the Saints' Days and other Festivals, by the late Rev. John Keble* (Oxford and London: Parker, 1877), pp. 352-354.

the house of one, whom he had no long before called out of the dangerous ways of the wicked heathen world. For the publicans, or Roman tax-gatherers, were not only wicked persons, generally speaking, but even positive heathens; and St Matthew, though a Jew, must have been, by his calling, brought into frequent companionship with such. How then must he have been transported and overpowered, what a bowing down of heaven to earth must it have appeared to him, when the holy Jesus vouchsafed to enter under his roof: to sit at meat there, where so often profane and wicked persons had been, indulging in profane and wicked discourse: and not only so, but as the publicans and sinners, one by one, entered in, and took their places at the same board with the holy and divine Visitor: how must the saint's heart have been filled with the thought of the same mercy offered to each of them, whereof he had himself so happily partaken! What joy to him to hope, that by inviting them to meet our Lord, he might do something, under God, unworthy as he was, towards changing their hearts, and saving their souls! And then what an enduring inexhaustible comfort, to perceive that his Redeemer's purpose was, not only to call sinners once for all, but to abide with them, after he had called them: to be their helper as well as their converter: to abide with them not only in church-services, and where they appear before him solemnly as penitents, but also in all the ordinary concerns of life, in their business and refreshment, their meals and conversations.

Collect

O ALMIGHTY God, who by thy blessed Son didst call Matthew from the receipt of custom to be an apostle and evangelist: grant us grace to forsake all covetous desires and inordinate love of riches, and to follow the same thy Son Jesus Christ, who liveth and reigneth with thee and the Holy Spirit, one God, for ever and ever.

Saint Vincent de Paul, Founder of the Lazarists
(27 September)

Proper of the Day and Common of Pastors or of Saints: for a Saint Noted for Works of Mercy

O MERCIFUL God, whose servant Vincent de Paul, by his ministry of preaching and pastoral care, brought thy love to the sick and the poor: by his prayers, grant to all thy people a heart of compassion, that by serving the needs of others they may serve thee in word and deed; through Jesus Christ thy Son our Lord, who liveth and reigneth with thee, in the unity of the Holy Spirit, one God, for ever and ever.

SS Michael, Gabriel, and Raphael, Archangels (29 September)

Proper of the Day

Hymn

Morning and Evening Prayer   *Lauds*

Tibi Christe splendor Patris

1.Thee, O Christ, the Father's splendour,
  life and virtue of the heart,
in the presence of the angels
  sing we now with tuneful art,
meetly in alternate chorus
  bearing our responsive part.

2.Thus we praise with veneration
  all the armies of the sky;
chiefly him, the warrior Primate,
  of celestial chivalry,
Michael, who in princely virtue,
  cast Abaddon from on high.

3.By whose watchful care repelling –
  King of everlasting grace –
every ghostly adversary,
  all things evil, all things base,
grant us of thine only goodness
  in thy paradise a place.

4.Laud and honour to the Father,
  laud and honour to the Son,
laud and honour to the Spirit,
  ever Three and ever One,
consubstantial, co-eternal,
  while undending ages run. Amen.

Ascr. to Rabanus Maurus, 9ᵗʰ cent., Tr J. M. Neale

Post-Biblical Reading

A reading from John Pearson, *An Exposition of the Creed*

Whatsoever hath any being is either made or not made: whatsoever is not made is God; whatsoever is not God is made. One uncreated and independent essence; all other depending on it, and created by it. One of eternal and necessary existence; all other indifferent, in respect of actual existing, either to be or not to be, and that indifferency determined only by the free and voluntary act of the first Cause.

Now because to be thus made includes some imperfection, and among the parts of the world, some are more glorious than others; if those which are most perfect presuppose a Maker, then can we not doubt of a creation where we find far less perfection. This house of God, though uniform, yet is not all of the same materials, the footstool and the throne are not of the same mould; there is a vast difference between the heavenly expansions. This first aerial heaven, where God setteth up his pavilion, where 'he maketh the clouds his chariot, and walketh upon the wings of the wind' (Ps 104:3), is not so far inferior in place as it is in glory to the next, the seat of the sun and moon, the two great lights, and stars innumerable, far greater than the one of them. And yet that second heaven is not so far above the first as beneath the third, into which St Paul was caught. The brightness of the sun doth not so far surpass the blackness of a wandering cloud, as the glory of that heaven of presence surmounts the fading beauty of the starry firmament. For in this great temple of the World, in which the Son of God is the high-priest, the heaven which we see is but the veil, and that which is above, the Holy of Holies. This veil indeed is rich and glorious, but one day to be rent, and then to admit us into a far greater glory, even to the Mercy-seat and Cherubim. For this third heaven in the 'proper habitation' (Jude 6) of the blessed angels, which constantly attend upon the throne. And if those most glorious and happy spirits, those 'morning-stars which sang together, those sons of God which shouted for joy when the foundations of the earth were laid' (Job 38:7, 4), if they and their habitation were made; then can we no ways doubt of the production of all other creatures so much inferior to them.

John Pearson, *Exposition of the Creed*, I. 49-50, in *An Exposition of the Creed, by John Pearson. Revised and corrected by the Rev. Temple Chevallier* (Cambridge, Cambridge University Press, 1859, 2nd edition), pp. 93-94.

Forasmuch then as the angels are termed 'the sons of God', it sufficiently denoteth that they are from him, not of themselves; all filiation inferring some kind of production: and being God hath but one proper and only-begotten Son, whose propriety and singularity consisteth in this, that he is of the same increated essence with the Father, all other offspring must be made, and consequently even the angels created sons; of whom the Scripture speaking saith, 'Who maketh his angels spirits, and his ministers a flame of fire' (Ps 104: 4). For although those words, as first spoken by the Psalmist, do rather express the nature of the wind and the lightning,: yet being the author of the Epistle to the Hebrews hath applied the same to the angels properly so called, we cannot but conclude upon his authority, that the same God who 'created the wind' (Amos 4: 13), and 'made a way for the lightning of the thunder' (Job 28: 26), hath also produced those glorious spirits; and as he furnished them with that activity there expressed, so did he frame the subject of it, their immaterial and immortal essence.

Collect
O EVERLASTING God, who hast ordained and constituted the services of angels and mortals in a wonderful order: mercifully grant that, as thy holy angels alway do thee service in heaven, so by thy appointment they may succour and defend us on earth; through Jesus Christ thy Son our Lord, who liveth and reigneth with thee, in the unity of the Holy Spirit, one God, for ever and ever.

Saint Francis of Assisi
(4 October)

Proper of the Day and Common of Saints: for Religious

O GOD, who ever delightest to reveal thyself to the childlike and lowly of heart: grant that, following the example of the blessed Francis, and aided by his prayers, we may count the wisdom of this world as foolishness and know only Jesus Christ and him crucified; who liveth and reigneth with thee, in the unity of the Holy Spirit, one God, for ever and ever.

Saint Teresa of Jesus, Virgin, Doctor of the Church (15 October)

*Proper of the Day and Common of Virgins
or of Doctors of the Church*

MERCIFUL God, who by thy Spirit didst raise up thy servant Teresa of Avila to reveal to thy Church the way of perfection: grant that her teaching may awaken in us a longing for holiness until, assisted by her intercession, we attain to the perfect union of love in Jesus Christ thy Son our Lord, who liveth and reigneth with thee, in the unity of the Holy Spirit, one God, for ever and ever.

Saint Ignatius, Bishop, Martyr
(17 October)

Proper of the Day and Common of Martyrs

FEED us, O Lord, with the living bread and make us drink deep of the cup of salvation: that, following the teaching of thy bishop Ignatius, and rejoicing in the faith with which he embraced the death of a martyr, we may be nourished for that eternal life which he ever desired; through Jesus Christ thy Son our Lord, who liveth and reigneth with thee, in the unity of the Holy Spirit, one God, for ever and ever.

Saint Luke, Evangelist (18 October)

Proper of the Day and Common of Apostles and of Evangelists

A reading from the sermons of John Keble

Our Church, in the collect to-day, reminds us that St Luke was a physician as well as an evangelist, and the yearly return of his martyrdom may well be taken by all good and dutiful hearts, as a call from Almighty God to thank him very earnestly and sincerely for his tender care of our poor frail bodies, in providing us with medicines and persons to apply them. [...] Sickness, as well as death, is part of the punishment denounced in the beginning against sin: but our gracious Maker, by the ways of his good providence, so loving and gentle, has turned the punishment to a blessing; providing physicians, and giving them skill to wait on us: he wounds that he may heal in the end. [...] You may judge of your Maker's goodness in so relieving you, by just considering for a moment what is the first thought, when you find yourself or anyone belonging to you seriously ill. What a difference does it then make, whether or no you know of any physician, in whom you have confidence! Whether or no he is within reach, and when he has been sent for, how earnestly is his presence longed for, and

---

John Keble, 'The Touch of Christ an Infallible Cure', in *Sermons for the Saints' Days and other Festivals, by the late Rev. John Keble* (Oxford and London: Parker, 1877), pp. 362-384; 389-390.

how eagerly do people welcome his footsteps, when they perceive him to be at the door! Their longing after him is such as St Paul expresses when he calls Luke the 'beloved' physician, signifying how long the time seems, till he makes his appearance, and how the sufferer feels as if he could not do without him. [...] All surely, who have felt this for themselves are bound to make it an occasion of special thanksgiving to God: and what more natural than they should remember to do so, on the memorial day of that saint, whom Holy Scripture recommends to us as the pattern of a Christian physician?

But St Luke was not only the beloved physician: he was also an evangelist and physician of the soul. When he came into the room to visit a sick person, he was (if one may so speak) the clergyman and physician in one, bringing peace and health to body and soul alike: and by how much the soul is more precious than the body, and eternity worth more than time, by so much ought our praise and thanksgiving, this day, to go up more earnestly to Almighty God for his healing mercies in the Gospel, than even for all that he has done and is doing for our poor frail distempered bodies. [...]

[Christ] was manifested to take away our sins, to take our infirmities and bear our sicknesses, first by making himself one of us, then by suffering on the Cross the penalty due to our transgressions, and lastly by applying himself to us, one by one, to be the life and light, the righteousness, sanctification, and redemption, of each several Christian, man, woman and child: Christ dwelling in us and we in him. These are the wholesome medicines of the doctrine delivered by all evangelists and physicians of the soul, whereby, if it be not our fault, all the diseases of our souls may and will be healed: and in particular these are the medicines prescribed to us by Luke the beloved physician, seeing that in his Gospel the Incarnation of our Lord, the history of his Conception and Birth, is set forth more at large than in either of the other three. St Luke's is also in a special sense the Gospel of Sacrifice and pardon, the Gospel for penitent sinners: being the only one of the four which has in it the history of the penitent thief, of Zacchaeus, and of the woman which was a sinner, and the comfortable parable of the prodigal son: places, most healing surely, and full of all consolation to souls deeply wounded and smarting, grieved and wearied with the burden of their sins.

Collect

ALMIGHTY God, who calledst Luke the physician, whose praise is in the gospel, to be an evangelist and physician of the soul: may it please thee that, by the wholesome medicines of the doctrine delivered by him, all the diseases of our souls may be healed; through the merits of thy Son Jesus Christ our Lord, who liveth and reigneth with thee and the Holy Spirit, one God, for ever and ever.

Saints Simon and Jude, Apostles
(28 October)

Proper of the Day and Common of Apostles

A reading from the sermons of Blessed John Henry Newman

St Simon is called Zelotes, which means the Zealot; a title given him (as is supposed) from his belonging before his conversion to the Jewish sect of Zealots, which professed extraordinary zeal for the law. Anyhow, the appellation marks him as distinguished for this particular Christian grace. St Jude's Epistle, which forms part of the service of the day, is almost wholly upon the duty of manifesting zeal for Gospel truth, and opens with a direct exhortation to 'contend earnestly for the faith once delivered to the saints' (Jude 3). The collect also indirectly reminds us of the same duty, for it prays that all the members of the Church may be united in spirit by the Apostles' doctrine; and what are these but the words of zeal, viz. of a love for the truth and the Church so strong as not allow that man should divide what God hath joined together?

However, it will be a more simple account of zeal, to call it the earnest desire for God's honour, leading to strenuous and bold deeds in his behalf; and that in spite of all obstacles. [...] [Z]eal is one of the elementary religious qualifications; that is, one of those which are essential in the very notion of a religious man. A man cannot be said to be in earnest in religion, till he magnifies his God and Saviour; till he so far consecrates and exalts the thought of him in his heart, as an object of praise, and adoration, and rejoicing, as to be pained and grieved at dishonour shown to him, and eager to avenge him. In a

---

Bl. John Henry Newman, 'Christian Zeal', in *Parochial and Plain Sermons, by John Henry Newman* II (London: Rivingtons, 1880), pp. 379-382; 384-387.

word, a religious temper is one of loyalty towards God; and we all know what is meant by being loyal from the experience of civil matters. To be loyal is not merely to obey; but to obey with promptitude, energy, dutifulness, disinterested devotion, disregard of consequences. And such is zeal, except that it is ever attended with that reverential feeling which is due from a creature and a sinner towards his Maker, and towards him alone. It is the main principle in all religious service to love God above all things; now, zeal is to love him above all men, above our dearest and most intimate friends. [...]

Zeal is the very consecration of God's ministers to their office. Accordingly, our blessed Saviour, the one great High Priest, the antitype of all priests who went before him and the Lord and strength of all who come after, began his manifestation of himself by two acts of zeal. When twelve years old he deigned to put before us in representation the sacredness of this duty, when he remained in the Temple 'while his father and mother sought him sorrowing', and on their finding him, returned answer, 'Wist ye not that I must be about my Father's business?' (Lk 2:48-49). And again, at the opening of his public ministry, he went into the Temple, and 'made a scourge of small cords, and drove out the sheep and oxen, and overthrew the changers' tables' that profaned it (Jn 2:15): thus fulfilling the prophecy contained in the text, 'The zeal of thine house hath eaten Me up' (Jn 2:17). [...] Being thus consumed by zeal himself, no wonder he should choose his followers from among the zealous.

It is the present fashion to call zeal by the name of intolerance, and to account intolerance the chief of sins; that is, any earnestness for one opinion above another concerning God's nature, will, and dealings with man – or, in other words, any earnestness of the faith once delivered to the saints, any earnestness for revelation as such. Surely, in this sense, the Apostles were the most intolerant of men; what is it but intolerance in this sense of the word to declare, that 'he who hath the Son hath life, and he that hath not the Son of God hath not life' (1 Jn 5:12); that 'they that obey not the Gospel of our Lord Jesus Christ... shall be punished with everlasting destruction from the presence of the Lord' (2 Thess 1:8, 9); that 'neither fornicators, nor idolaters, nor adulterers, nor covetous, nor revilers, nor extortioners, shall inherit the kingdom of God' (1 Cor 6:9, 10); that we must not even 'eat with a brother who is one of such; that we may not 'receive into our houses', or 'bid God speed; to any one who comes to us without the 'doctrine of Christ' (2 Jn 10, 11)? [...] Such is zeal, a Christian grace to the last, while it is also an elementary virtue; equally belonging to the young convert and the matured believer; displayed by Moses at the first, when he slew the Egyptian, and by St Paul in his last hours, while he was reaching forth his hand for his heavenly crown.

On the other hand, zeal is an imperfect virtue; that is, in our fallen state, it will ever be attended by unchristian feelings, if it is cherished by itself. [...] Hence it appropriately fills so prominent a place in the Jewish dispensation, which was intended to lay the foundations, as of Christian faith so of the Christian character. Whether we read the injunctions delivered by Moses against idolatry and idolaters, or trace the actual history of God's chosen servants, such as Phinehas, Samuel, Elijah, and especially David, we find that the Law was peculiarly a covenant of zeal. [...] [T]he Gospel brings out into its full proportions, that perfect temper of mind, which the law enjoined indeed, but was deficient both in enforcing and creating – love; that is, love or charity, as described by St Paul in his first Epistle to the Corinthians, which is not merely brotherly-love (a virtue ever included in the notion of zeal itself), but a general temper of gentleness, meekness, sympathy, tender consideration, openheartedness towards all men, brother or stranger, who come in our way. In this sense, zeal is of the Law and love of the Gospel: and love perfects zeal, purifying and regulating it. Thus the saints of God go on unto perfection. Moses ended his life as 'the meekest of men' (Num 12:3), though he began it with undisciplined zeal, which led him to a deed of violence. St John, who would call down fire from heaven, became the Apostle of love; St Paul, who persecuted Christ's servants, 'was made all things to all men' (1 Cor 9:22); yet neither of them lost their zeal, though they trained it to be spiritual.

Collect

O ALMIGHTY God, who hast built thy Church upon the foundation of the apostles and prophets, Jesus Christ himself being the head cornerstone: grant us so to be joined together in unity of spirit by their doctrine, that we may be made an holy temple acceptable unto thee; through Jesus Christ thy Son our Lord, who liveth and reigneth with thee, in the unity of the Holy Spirit, one God, for ever and ever.

All Saints' Day
(1 November)

Proper of the Day

Office

Opening Sentence

You have come to Mount Zion and to the city of the living God, the heavenly Jerusalem, to the spirits of the righteous made perfect, and to Jesus, the mediator of a new covenant.

Heb 12:22a, 23b, 24a

Hymn

Morning and Evening Prayer   *Lauds*

Iesu salvator sæculi

1.O Saviour Jesu, not alone
  we plead for help before thy throne;
thy Mother's love shall aid our prayer
  to win for us that healing care.

2.For souls defaulting supplicate
  all orders of the Angel state,
the Patriarchs in line to thee,
  the Prophets' goodly company.

3.For souls in guilt ensnared pray
  the Baptist, herald of thy way,
the wielder of the heavenly keys,
  the apostolic witnesses.

4.For souls polluted intercede
  thy Martyrs, hallowed in their deed,
Confessors high in priestly power,
  and they who have the virgin dower.

5.Let all who served thy Church below,
  and now thy heavenly freedom know,
give heed to help our lingering strife
  and claim for us the crown of life.

6.To God the Father, God the Son,
  and God the Spirit, Three in One,
all honour, praise, and glory be
  from age to age eternally. Amen.

9th cent., Tr. T. A. Lacey

Post-Biblical Reading

A reading from the Commentary of the Venerable Bede
on the First Letter of Saint Peter

'And you yourselves like living stones are to be built into the edifice, spiritual houses' (1 Pet 2:5). [The apostle] says that they are being added to the building, because without the Lord Jesus Christ, namely the Living Stone, no spiritual building is able to stand. 'For no one can lay another foundation except' him (1 Cor 3:11). By being joined with him, the faithful are made into living stones, who because of their unfaithfulness had been dead stones, namely, hard and unfeeling. To them it was rightly said, 'I shall take away from you your heart of stone and give you a heart of flesh' (Ezek 36:26). But they are fitted like living stones into the spiritual building when at the discrimination of a learned teacher they have their undesirable actions and thoughts cut off and are squared off by the blow of a hammer, as it were. And just as some rows of stones in a wall are held up by others, so all the faithful in the Church are held up by the righteous who preceded them, while they themselves by their teaching and support hold up those who come after even to the last righteous person. He, though he is held up by those who went before, will have no one coming after him whom he ought to hold up; but he who holds up the entire building and is himself held up by no one is the Lord Christ – hence he is also called by the prophet a precious stone laid in the foundation.

[The apostle] likewise calls the elect living stones that he may indicate the struggle of good intent or action in which they ought always to be engaged with the grace of God preceding and accompanying them. For when dead, that is, material, stones are being prepared or laid up on a building, they cannot help the builder's work in any way and can do nothing but fall; but however and wherever they are laid by the builder, they stay there in the same place without any feeling or they even slip down and fall. But blessed Peter does not wish us to imitate the hardness and lack of feeling of such stones but to be built into a building as living stones on the foundation of Christ that, with the help of his grace, namely, by living soberly and righteously and godly, we may work together with him after the example of him who said, 'And his grace was not without effect in me, but I laboured more than all those' (1 Cor 15:10). For a

Saint Bede, Commentary on I Peter 2: 5, in *The Commentary on the Seven Catholic Epistles of Bede the Venerable*. Translated by David Hurst, Monk of Portsmouth Abbey (Kalamazoo, MI: Cistercian Publications, 1985), pp. 82-84.

living stone in the building of holy Church was he who strove to labour diligently lest he have received the grace of God in vain; and lest he appear to have attributed anything of the same devoted labour to himself, he added carefully, 'It was not I, however, but the grace of God with me'. Therefore, anyone who with his gift and help takes care to press on untiringly in his good works is being built by Christ as a living stone into his house. But anyone who, after being incorporated into holy Church through the grace of rebirth, has striven to do no further work towards his salvation is, like a dead stone, unworthy of the heavenly building, in a word, and therefore to be rejected by the divine judgment; and another who is worthy is to be substituted in his place – according to the command of Leviticus by which the leprous stones of houses are commanded to be inspected by a priest, and if they cannot be made clean, to be then counted as unclean and removed from the course of clean stones.

Short Reading for Prayer during the Day   *Rev 21:10-12; 22:3b-4*
In the Spirit the angel carried me away to a great, high mountain, and showed me the holy city Jerusalem coming down out of heaven from God, having the glory of God, its radiance like a most rare jewel, like a jasper, clear as crystal. The throne of God and of the Lamb shall be in the city, and his servants shall worship him; they shall see his face, and his name shall be on their foreheads.

Collect
O ALMIGHTY God, who hast knit together thine elect in one communion and fellowship, in the mystical body of thy Son Christ our Lord: grant us grace so to follow thy blessed saints in all virtuous and godly living, that we may come to those unspeakable joys, which thou hast prepared for them that unfeignedly love thee; through Jesus Christ thy Son our Lord, who liveth and reigneth with thee, in the unity of the Holy Spirit, one God, for ever and ever.

Commemoration of the Faithful
Departed (All Souls' Day)
(2 November)

Proper of the Day

Office

Opening Sentence

All that the Father gives to me will come to me;
and the one who comes to me, I will not cast out.

Jn 6:37

Post-Biblical Reading

A reading from Saint Thomas More, *The Supplication of Souls*

Consider you our pains, and pity them in your hearts, and help us with
pilgrimages, and other almsdeeds: and of all things in special procure us the
suffrages and blessed oblation of the Holy Mass, whereof no man living so well
can tell the fruit, as we that here feel it. The comfort that we have here, except
our continual hope in Our Lord God, comes at season from Our Lady, with
such glorious saints, as either ourselves with our own devotion while we lived
or ye with yours for us since our decease and departing have made intercessors
for us.

And among other right especially be we beholden to the blessed spirits our own
proper good angels, whom, when we behold coming with comfort to us, albeit
that we take great pleasure and greatly rejoice therein, yet is it not without much
confusion and shamefastness, to consider how little we regarded our good
angels, and how seldom we thought upon them while we lived. They carry up
our prayers to God and good saints for us, and they bring down from them the
comfort and consolation to us with which, when they come and comfort us,

---

Saint Thomas More, *The Supplication of Souls* 70-71, in *The Supplication of Souls.
Thomas More. His reply to* The Supplication of Beggards *by Simon Fish.* A
transcription from black letter by Eileen Morris (London: Primary Publications,
1970), pp. 154-155.

only we and God know the joy it is to our hearts and how heartily we pray for you.

And therefore, if God accept the prayer after his own favour borne towards him that prays, and the affection that he prays with, our prayer must needs be profitable, for we stand sure of his grace. And our prayer for you is so fervent, that ye can nowhere find any such affection on earth.

And therefore since we lie sore in pains and have in our great necessity so great need of your help, and that ye may so well do it whereby shall also rebound upon yourself an inestimable profit: let never any slothful oblivion raze us out of your remembrance, or malicious enemy of ours cause you to be careless of us, or any greedy mind upon your good withdraw your gracious alms from us. Think how soon ye shall come hither to us; think what great grief and rebuke would then your unkindness be to you, what comfort on the contrary part when all we shall thank you, what help ye shall have here of your good sent hither.

Remember what kin ye and we be together, what familiar friendship has ere this been between us, what sweet words ye have spoken and what promise ye have made us. Let now your words appear and your fair promise be kept. Now, dear friends, remember how nature and Christendom binds you to remember us. If any point of your old favour, any piece of your old love, any kindness of kindred, any care of acquaintance, any favour of old friendship, any spark of charity, any tender point of pity, any regard of charity, any respect of Christendom, be left in your breasts: let never the malice of a few fond fellows, a few pestilent persons borne towards priesthood, religion, and your Christian Faith raze out of your heart the care of all your kindred, all force of your old friends, and all remembrance of all Christian souls.

Remember our thirst while ye sit and drink, our hunger while ye be feasting, our restless watch while ye be sleeping, our sore and grievous pain while ye be playing, our hot burning fire while ye be in pleasure and sporting. So must God make your offspring after remember you: so God keep you hence, or not long here, but bring you shortly to that bliss, to which for Our Lord's love help you to bring us, and we shall set hand to help you thither to us.

Short Reading for Prayer during the Day
(All Souls) *Job 19:25-27*
I know that my redeemer lives, and at last he will stand upon the earth; and after my skin has been thus destroyed, then from my flesh I shall see God, whom I shall see on my side, and my eyes shall behold, and not another.

Short Reading for Prayer during the Day
(Office for the Dead) *Wis 1:13b-15*
God did not make death, and he does not delight in the death of the living. For he created all things that they might exist, and the creatures of the world are wholesome, and there is no destructive poison in them; and the dominion of Hades is not on earth. For righteousness is immortal.

Collect
EVERLASTING God, our maker and redeemer, grant us, with all the faithful departed, the sure benefits of thy Son's saving passion and glorious resurrection: that, in the last day, when thou dost gather up all things in Christ, we may with them enjoy the fullness of thy promises; through Jesus Christ thy Son our Lord, who liveth and reigneth with thee, in the unity of the Holy Spirit, one God, for ever and ever.

Saint Leo the Great, Pope, Doctor of the Church
(10 November)

Proper of the Day and Common of Pastors
or of Doctors of the Church

O GOD our Father, who madest thy servant Leo strong in the defence of the faith: we humbly beseech thee so to fill thy Church with the spirit of truth that, being guided by humility and governed by love, she may prevail against the powers of evil; through Jesus Christ thy Son our Lord, who liveth and reigneth with thee, in the unity of the Holy Spirit, one God, for ever and ever.

Saint Martin of Tours, Bishop
(11 November)

Proper of the Day and Common of Pastors

ALMIGHTY God, who didst call Martin from the armies of this world to be a faithful soldier of Christ: give us grace to follow him in his love and compassion for those in need, and empower thy Church to claim for all people their inheritance as the children of God; through Jesus Christ thy Son our Lord, who liveth and reigneth with thee, in the unity of the Holy Spirit, one God, for ever and ever.

Saint Elizabeth of Hungary, Religious
(18 November)

Proper of the Day and Common of Saints: for Religious

O LORD God, who didst teach Elizabeth of Hungary to recognize and to reverence Christ in the poor of this world: grant that we, being strengthened by her example and assisted by her prayers, may so love and serve the afflicted and those in need that we may honour thy Son, the servant king; who liveth and reigneth with thee, in the unity of the Holy Spirit, one God, for ever and ever.

Presentation of the Blessed Virgin Mary
(21 November)

Proper of the Day and Common of the Blessed Virgin Mary

O GOD, who didst will that blessed Mary ever-Virgin, the dwelling-place of the Holy Spirit, should this day be presented in the temple: grant, we beseech thee, that by her intercession we may be worthy to be presented in the temple of thy glory; through Jesus Christ thy Son our Lord, who liveth and reigneth with thee, in the unity of the same Holy Spirit, one God, for ever and ever.

St Cecilia, Virgin, Martyr
(22 November)

Proper of the Day and Common of Martyrs

O GOD, who makest us glad with the yearly solemnity of blessed Cecilia thy Virgin and Martyr: grant that we who venerate her in our service, may also follow the example, of her godly conversation; through Jesus Christ thy Son our Lord, who liveth and reigneth with thee, in the unity of the Holy Spirit, one God, for ever and ever.

Saint Clement, Pope, Martyr
(23 November)

Proper of the Day and Common of Martyrs

ETERNAL Father, creator of all, whose martyr Clement bore witness with his blood to the love that he proclaimed and the gospel that he preached: give us thankful hearts as we celebrate thy faithfulness, revealed to us in the lives of thy saints, and strengthen us in our pilgrimage as we follow thy Son, Jesus Christ our Lord; who liveth and reigneth with thee, in the unity of the Holy Spirit, one God, for ever and ever.

IV. Times and Seasons

Part VII Sanctorale:

Propers for the
Customary of
Our Lady of Walsingham

PROPERS FOR THE CALENDAR OF
OUR LADY WALSINGHAM

Including Second Readings and Responsories for Saints for whom no Proper
Readings and Responsories are found in the Roman Liturgy of the Hours

The reference to the Proper of the Day and Commons, here and hereafter, is
both to the Proper of the Day and Commons in the Roman Rite and, as
appropriate, the Proper of the Day and Commons in this Customary.

Saint Ælred of Rievaulx, Abbot
(12 January)

Proper of the Day and Common of Saints: for Religious

A reading from Saint Ælred, *The Mirror of Charity*

God has spread out his heaven over us like a curtain, and there his stars shine, to give us light in our dark world, where forest beasts roam about, seeking to devour us. Above the heavens are the great waters, from whence the rains come to soften the parched earth, which is the soul of man, and to bring forth fruits of oil and wheat and wine. We would labour in vain without the help of God who gives us our daily bread, but we have only to seek in order to find, and when we have found we have only to taste and see how sweet thou art, O Lord. My soul, unproductive through its dryness, thirsts for thy gentle rain, so that there may spring up in it that heavenly bread that feeds the angels. Then it will taste a true delight, and cast aside its yearning for the fleshpots of Egypt, the land where Pharoah demanded a daily toll of bricks, though he gave no straw for their making. O Good Jesus, let thy voice sound in my ears so that my heart and mind and my inmost soul may learn to love thee, and the very depths of my heart cleave to thee, who art my one delight and joy.

But what is this love which I desire, O my God? Unless I am much misled, it is a wonderful delight in the soul, which is the more sweet for being unsullied by passion, more sincere if it is tender, and a source of joy when it embraces all our fellow men. Love may truly be called the heart's own sense of taste, since it enables us to feel thy sweetness. Love is the eye by means of which we can see that thou art good. Love is a capacity for God who transcends all things, and whoever loves God gathers God to himself. The more we love God, the more we possess him, simply because God *is* love: he is charity. Love is God's rich banquet, that so gratifies those who eat at his table and drink deep, that they forget and lose themselves, only to find themselves in him. And how shall this be done, unless they love him?

Geoffrey Webb and Adrian Walker (translated and arranged), *The Mirror of Charity. The* Speculum Caritatis *of Saint Ælred of Rievaulx* (London: Mowbray, 1962), pp. 1-2.

I beg thee, Lord, to let but a touch of this delight penetrate my soul, and turn the bread of bitterness to sweetness. Give me the smallest morsel of it as a foretaste of what I yearn for in this mortal life, or rather let my hunger and thirst be that foretaste, for to eat is to hunger still more, and to drink is to thirst still more. Let me eat and drink my fill when all may see the glory and delight that are hidden at the present time, and revealed only to those who love thee. Meanwhile I shall seek thee by loving thee, since to advance in thy love is certainly to seek thee, and to love thee perfectly is to have found thee. Indeed, justice demands that thy creatures love thee, for their capacity to love is a gift that thou hast given them. The irrational and insensible creation cannot love thee, for that is beyond its nature. It is not called upon to share man's purpose, which is to be happy, and to love thee. Instead, the beauty and goodness of creatures, with all their different functions, serve rather to help man to find happiness and love.

Pss [30:20] 31:19; [35:9] 36:8

℞. How abundant are your treasures of loving-kindness, O Lord, *
    which you give to those who fear you.
℣. They delight in the abundance of your house, they drink the waters
    of contentment* which you give to those who fear you.

Collect
ALMIGHTY God, who didst endow the blessed abbot Ælred with the gift of Christian friendship and the wisdom to lead others into the way of holiness: grant to thy people that same spirit of mutual affection, that in loving one another we may know the love of Christ and rejoice in the eternal possession of thine unsurpassable goodness; through Jesus Christ thy Son our Lord, who liveth and reigneth with thee, in the unity of the Holy Spirit, one God, for ever and ever.

Saint Benedict Biscop, Abbot
(12 January)

Proper of the Day and Common of Saints: for Religious

A reading from the Venerable Bede,
Lives of the Abbots of Wearmouth and Jarrow

Benedict Biscop, a devout follower of Christ, inspired by grace from on high, founded a monastery in honour of the most blessed Peter, Prince of the Apostles, on the north bank of the Wear, towards the mouth of the river, with the help of the venerable and holy King Egfrid who donated the land for it. For sixteen years, despite the heavy toll exacted by his many illnesses and the burden of all his travels, Benedict ruled over it with the same care and conscientiousness he had given to its construction. To quote the words of the blessed Pope Gregory when he says, in praise of an abbot of the same name, 'He was a man of venerable life, rightly called Benedict since so much blessed by God. Even as a boy he had the outlook of an old man, his behaviour belying his age, and never gave himself to sensual pleasure.' He came of noble Angle lineage and his mind – no less noble than his birth – was constantly fixed on the life of Heaven. He was about twenty-five and one of King Oswiu's thegns when the king gave him possession of the amount of land due to his rank; but he put behind him the things that perish so that he might gain those that last forever, despising earthly warfare with its corruptible rewards so that he might fight for the true king and win his crown in the heavenly city. He left country, home, and family for the sake of Christ and the gospel so that he might receive a hundredfold in return and gain eternal life. He rejected the bond of earthly marriage so that in the kingdom of Heaven he might follow the Lamb of spotless virginity. He refused to bring forth children in the flesh, being predestined by Christ to raise up for him sons nurtured in spiritual doctrine who would life forever in the world to come. [...]

He was untiring in his efforts to see his monastery well provided for: the ornaments and images he could not find in France he sought out in Rome. Once his foundation had settled down to the ordered life of the Rule, he went off on a fourth visit to Rome, returning with a greater variety of spiritual

---

Bede, *Lives of the Abbots of Wearmouth and Jarrow* 1 and 6, in *The Age of Bede*, edited with an introduction by D. H. Farmer (London: Penguin, 2004 [1988]), pp. 187-188; 192-193.

treasures than ever before. In the first place he returned with a great mass of books of every sort. Secondly, he brought back an abundant supply of relics of the blessed apostles and Christian martyrs which were to prove such a boon for many churches in the land. Thirdly, he introduced in his monastery the order of chanting and singing the psalms and conducting the liturgy according to the practice in force at Rome. To this end Pope Agatho, at Benedict's request, offered him the services of the chief cantor of Saint Peter's and abbot of the monastery of Saint Martin, a man called John. Benedict brought him back to Britain to be choirmaster in the monastery. John taught the monks at first hand how things were done in the churches in Rome and also committed a good part of his instruction to writing. This is still preserved in memory of him in the monastery library. The fourth benefit Benedict brought back, and not one to be despised, was a letter of privilege from the venerable Pope Agatho, sought with Egfrid's permission and indeed at his wish and exhortation, guaranteeing the monastery's complete safety and independence by a grant of perpetual exemption from external interference. Fifthly, he brought back many pictures of the saints to adorn the church of Saint Peter he had built: a painting of the Mother of God, the Blessed Mary ever-Virgin, and one of each of the twelve apostles which he fixed round the central arch on a wooden entablature reaching from wall to wall: pictures of incidents in the gospels with which he decorated the south wall, and scenes from Saint John's vision of the apocalypse for the north wall. Thus all who entered the church, even those who could not read, were able, whichever way they looked, to contemplate the dear face of Christ and his saints, even if only in a picture, to put themselves more firmly in mind of the Lord's Incarnation and, as they saw the decisive moment of the Last Judgment before their very eyes be brought to examine their conscience with all due severity.

Sir 31:8,11,10

℟.Blessed is the man who is found blameless, and who does not go
    after gold nor place his trust in hoards of money. * his fortune will
be firmly based on the Lord.
  ℣. He had the power to sin and has not sinned, to wrong another and
  has not done it, * his fortune will be firmly based on the Lord.

Saint Kentigern (Mungo), Bishop
(13 January)

Proper of the Day and Common of Pastors: for a Bishop

From the *Life of Saint Kentigern* by Jocelyn of Furness

Emulating the fervour of certain of the holy fathers, nay, rather following the footsteps of Elias and John the Baptist, and of the Saviour himself, he retired to desert places every Lent, and so by withdrawing himself from the sight of the sons of men, and remaining in a solitude of body and soul, he dwelt with himself. There, more freely giving himself up to the contemplation of God, he rested under the shadow of the Face of the Almighty, safe from the disturbance of man, from the strife of tongues and worldly converse. Therefore sitting solitary, he lifted himself above himself, and often abiding in the caverns of the earth, and standing in the entering in of his save, and praying, after the great and strong wind and the earthquake, he heard the still small whisper of thin air breathing upon him, and bathing him in and filling him with unspeakable sweetness. Wherefore he went about the streets of the heavenly Jerusalem seeking for himself him whom his soul loved, and offering for himself, in his heart, a sacrifice of jubilation, he mortified his most holy members which were upon the earth. Offering himself a living victim, holy, well-pleasing unto the Lord, he afflicted his most innocent body by a continual martyrdom as a sweet savour. With what and what sort of food he sustained his life on those days he revealed to none, or at least to few, and to these by his episcopal authority he forbade that they should ever reveal the mystery to mortal man.

Yet once he spoke, and two of his disciples heard a word not to be recalled, once only, and simply uttered from his lips. 'I knew', said he, 'a certain man, who during Lent sustained life on the roots of herbs only, and sometimes, the Lord giving him strength, he passed the whole of that time without the support of earthly food'. Neither of them doubted that he spoke this of himself; but the man of God suppressed his name, to avoid vainglory, which he everywhere sought to shun. At length, for a long time before Maundy Thursday, and after

---

Jocelyn of Furness, *Life of Saint Kentigern*, XVII, in *Lives of Saint Ninian and Saint Kentigern*, compiled in the twelfth century, edited from the best mss. by Alexander Penrose Forbes, D. C. L., Bishop of Brechin (Edinburgh: Edminston and Douglas, 1874), pp. 61-62.

that, on the Saturday before Palm Sunday, he returned to his home and to his people to fulfil his episcopal office, and he was received by them all as an angel of peace and light.

Wherefore he was used to pass that week with his disciples, and on Maundy Thursday, after the composition of the holy chrism and oil, he washed with his own hands the feet of a multitude of poor men first, and then of lepers, bathing them with his tears, wiping them with his hair, comforting them with many kisses, and afterwards he waited upon the people diligently at table. Then sitting for their consolation with the reconciled penitents at a banquet, he consoled himself and them with spiritual and bodily refreshment. Thereafter from that hour till after the celebration of Mass on Easter Day he always remained fasting. Verily, on Good Friday he crucified himself with the Crucified One with incredible torture, and with scourging, nakedness, and frequent genuflection, scarcely ever sitting down, he passed the day and the night, bearing about in his body the marks of the Lord Jesus, with great affliction of body and soul.

But on the Holy Saturday, as if dead to the world, burying in a double tomb, the true Abraham, the Ancient of Days along with himself, and entering the sepulchre in the abundance of inward contemplation, he rested from all the tumult of this stormy world, except that he appeared to celebrate the Office of the day. Them, renewed in the spirit of his mind, he awaited with the sweet spices of holy virtues so diligently prepared, the most sacred day of the Lord's resurrection, In a way rising again with Christ, he feasted on the Flesh of the Immaculate Lamb, in the unleavened bread of sincerity and truth. And in the day which the Lord had made a day of joy in earth and heaven, he rejoiced with all spiritual joy, and feasted with the brethren and a great multitude of poor.

1 Cor 9:16-22

℞. If I preach the gospel, I can claim no credit for it; I cannot help myself;* it would be a misery to me not to preach.

℣. I have become everything in turn to men of every sort, so that in some way or another I may save some;* it would be a misery to me not to preach.

Saint Wulstan, Bishop
(19 January)

Proper of the Day and Common of Pastors: for a Bishop

A reading from the *Life of Saint Wulfstan* by William of Malmesbury

Wulfstan immediately on his elevation as bishop put his mind to works of piety. There was no delay: the day after his ordination he dedicated a church to the blessed Bede, an excellent choice for his first dedication, for Bede had been the prince of English letters. That day Wulfstan's flow of preaching so watered the people that it was not in doubt that he owed to the Holy Spirit his command of an eloquence that had once moved the tongue of Bede. And indeed all his life long, not just on this occasion, the people were so seduced by the report of his preaching that you might have seen them flocking in droves whenever it was reported that he was to dedicate a church.

For his part, he went out of his way to collect material that would enable him always to speak of Christ, always to put Christ before his hearers, and finally to bring Christ over to his side even (if I may put it so) when Christ was reluctant. For he persevered with such determination in fasts and vigils, and flung such violent prayers at Heaven, that it was not without reason that the Lord said of him and his followers, 'The kingdom of heaven suffereth violence, and the violent take it' (Mt 11:12).

His life held to so fine a balance that he held to both professions without losing either: he was the bishop without abjuring the monk in his religious practice, and the monk while preserving a bishop's authority. He was far removed indeed from the ways of the men produced in our century. If he was asked for his advice, he was excellent at giving it; if he was begged for something, he was ready to listen.

When a request had to be considered, he was thorough in his deliberation but swift to come to a view. When judgment had to be given, he leaned towards

---

[St Wulstan is also known in some sources and translations as Wulfstan. In the National Calendar of England, he is called Wulstan.] William of Malmesbury, *Life of Saint Wulfstan*, 14, in William of Malmesbury, *Saints' Lives. Lives of Saints Wulfstan, Dunstan, Patrick, Benignus and Indract*, by M. Winterbottom and R. M. Thomson (Oxford: Clarendon Press, 2002), pp. 51-53

justice, neither flattering the rich for the sake of money, nor oppressing the poor because of their poverty. He was not given to flattering, and showed no favour to those who flattered him. He never turned aside from what was just for fear of princes, and never responded to their love for him by giving them more honour than was due to them. If he was praised for the good he did, he rejoiced in receiving the grace of God, with no thought for his own pride. If he criticized, he forgave his critics' error and rejoiced in the knowledge of his own rectitude. But that happened but rarely, for, just as he cherished every man as his own child out of love of charity, so they all in return loved him as a parent.

In his lightness of heart and cheerfulness of countenance he had a foretaste of the joys above, and his hope allowed him to draw in advance on the fountain of heavenly pleasure which he now in very fact drains without stint. Though he was constantly concerned with inner things, men did not find him dilatory or sluggish when it came to outer things. Many were the churches throughout the diocese that he began with vigour and completed to an excellent standard, not least his own cathedral, which he started from the foundations and put the finishing touches to, increasing the number of the monks and making them behave in accordance with the Rule.

1 Pet 5:2,3,4; Acts 20:28

℟. Tend the flock of God that is your charge; be examples to them,*
   and when the chief shepherd appears, you will receive the unfading crown of glory.
℣. Keep watch over all the flock of which the Holy Spirit has given
   you charge, as shepherds of the Church of God,* and when the chief shepherd appears, you will receive the unfading crown of glory.

Collect

O LORD God, who didst raise up Wulfstan to be a bishop among thy people and a leader in thy Church: give us grace, after his example and assisted by his prayers, to live simply, to work diligently, and to make thy kingdom known; through Jesus Christ thy Son our Lord, who liveth and reigneth with thee, in the unity of the Holy Spirit, one God, for ever and ever.

Saint Brigid of Kildare, Abbess
(1 February)

Proper of the Day and Common of Virgins or Saints:
for Religious

A reading from the *Life of Saint Brigid* by Cogitosus

Holy Brigid, whom God had chosen beforehand to be conformed and predestined to his image, was born of noble Christian parents. As the chosen of God, she was indeed a girl of great modesty, who as she grew in years grew also in serenity. [...]

Once a wild boar which was being hunted charged out of the forest, and in the course of its panicked flight careered into a herd of pigs that belonged to the most blessed Brigid. She noticed its presence and she blessed it. Immediately the creature lost its sense of fear and settled down quietly among the herd of pigs. See, my friends, how even the wild beasts and animals could not resist either her bidding or her will, but served her docilely and humbly. [...]

On another occasion the blessed Brigid felt a tenderness for some ducks that she saw swimming on the water and occasionally taking wing. She bid them fly to her, and a great flock of them flew towards her, without any fear, as if they were humans under obedience to her. She touched them with her hand and embraced them tenderly. She then released them and they flew into the sky. And as they did so she praised God the Creator of all living things, to whom all life is subject, and for the service of whom all life is a gift. [...]

From these and many other episodes which demonstrated her power, it is certain that blessed Brigid could command the affections of wild animals, cattle and the birds of the air.

Cogitosus, *Life of Brigid, Patrologia Latina* 72, cols. 775, 782-783, in *Celebrating the Saints. Daily spiritual readings to accompany the Calendars of The Church of England, The Church of Ireland, The Scottish Episcopal Church and The Church in Wales*, compiled and introduced by Robert Atwell (Norwich: Canterbury Press, 2004, enlarged edition), pp. 75-76.

℟. All those who abandon the Lord shall perish. * To be near God is my happiness; I have made him my refuge.

℣. He who is united to the Lord becomes one spirit with him. * To be near God is my happiness; I have made him my refuge.

Saint Gilbert of Sempringham, Religious (4 February)

Proper of the Day and Common of Saints: for Religious

A reading from the Book of Saint Gilbert

After lauds, when he had recited the martyrdoms of the saints and the collect for the dead, he made a humble and lengthy confession, both on his own behalf and that of the whole flock entrusted to his charge; from the brothers he asked for absolution of all offences and himself absolved those who were absent as well as those who were present; afterwards he bestowed his blessing in the manner of Job, offering a daily sacrifice on behalf of each one of his sons. He permitted no part of the day to drift idly by, but divided the passing hours evenly, alternately engaged in prayer, spiritual reading, contemplation, and good deeds. He gave his whole attention to every single thing that happened, viewing it in context rather than in isolation, and he shunned no part of his proper responsibility for what followed. In looking after others he did not forget his own salvation, nor neglect the divine for the human; and his concern over things within did not lessen through preoccupation with those outside. He was very close to all men in sympathy but far above them all in contemplative prayer. He would weep during hymns and spiritual songs; he was beguiled by the voices which rang so sweetly through the church, but he took greater pleasure in the sense of the words. To ensure that no external happening or inner train of thought distracted his attention from the savour and meaning of the divine word, as he expounded it or listened to it, he invented for himself signs upon his fingers, and, attributing to each joint

---

The Book of Saint Gilbert, 23, in R. Foreville and G. Keir, *The Book of Saint Gilbert* (Oxford: Clarendon Press, 1987), pp. 65-67.

individual words or prayers, by this device he impressed the memory of what was recited more firmly upon his mind.

His piety taught him this, the piety of a mind discharged of every taint, which persuaded him to concentrate on looking at the Bridegroom alone, and embracing him in all his limbs, poured out all the bowels of charity. Just as he wept out of devotion, rejoicing in God's love, so he grieved with the unfortunate, weeping out of compassion for his neighbour. We observed that when someone offended so gravely that he set himself apart and then returned to seek pardon, Gilbert at first opposed him, appearing almost relentlessly severe in his determination to test the penitent's contrition, to purge his fault completely, and to inspire fear in everyone else; but when he understood that the penitent's change of heart was total and sincere, he wept before them all and, summoning his brethren and friends on behalf of the sheep or the coin which had been lost but was found, he would rejoice deeply and cause them all to rejoice with him. Thus by abasing himself and sharing in the sufferings of the afflicted, he followed after Jesus with his cross.

1 Pet 3:8, 9; Rom 12:10-11

℟. Be one in thought and feeling; love the brothers, be compassionate and self-effacing: * this is what you have been called to do, so that you may inherit a blessing.

℣. Love each other as much as brothers should, and have a profound respect for each other. Work for the Lord with untiring effort and with great earnestness of spirit: * this is what you have been called to do, so that you may inherit a blessing.

Saint David, Bishop, Patron of Wales
(1 March)

Proper of the Day and Common of Pastors: for a Bishop

A reading from Rhigyfarch's *Life of Saint David*

Waking up at cock-crow [David's monastic community] apply themselves to prayer on bended knees, and spend the remainder of the night till morning without sleep… From Saturday evening till daybreak at the first hour of Sunday, they give themselves to watchings, prayers and genuflexions, except for one hour after matins on Saturday. They reveal their thoughts to the father, and obtain his permission even for the requirements of nature. All things are in common; there is no 'mine' or 'thine' for whosoever should say 'my book; or 'my anything else' would be straightaway subjected to a severe penance. They wore clothes of mean quality, mainly skins. There was unfailing obedience to the father's command: great was their perseverance in the performance of duties, great was their uprightness in all things.

[…] There was no superfluity: voluntary poverty was loved: for whosoever desired their manner of life, nothing of his property, which he had forsaken in the world when he renounced it, would the holy father accept for the use of the monastery, not even one penny, so to speak; but naked, as though escaping from a shipwreck, was he received, so that he should not by any means extol himself, or esteem himself above the brethren or, on grounds of his wealth, refuse his equal share of toil with the brethren; nor, if he should throw off his monk's robes, might be by force extort what he had left to the monastery, and drive the patience of the brethren into anger.

But the father himself, overflowing with daily fountains of tears, and fragrant with sweet-smelling offerings of prayers, and radiant with a twofold flame of charity, consecrated with pure hands the due oblation of the Lord's Body. After matins, he proceeded alone to hold converse with the angels. Immediately

---

Rhigyfarch, *Life of Saint David* 27-28, 3031, in J. W. James, *Rhigyfarch's 'Life of Saint David'. The Basic Mid Twelfth-Century Latin Text with Introduction, Critical Apparatus and Translation* (Cardiff: University of Wales Press, 1967), pp. 37-38.

afterwards, he sought cold water, remaining in it sufficiently long to subdue all the ardours of the flesh. The whole of the day he spent, inflexibly and unweariedly, in teaching, praying, genuflecting, and in care for the brethren; also in feeding a multitude of orphans, wards, widows, needy, sick, feeble, and pilgrims: so he began; so he continued; so he ended. As for the other aspects of the severity of the discipline, although a necessary ideal for imitation, this brief abbreviation forbids us to enlarge upon it. But he imitated the monks of Egypt, and lived a life like theirs.

Mt 19:21; Lk 14:33

℞ If you wish to be perfect, go and sell what you own and give the money to the poor, and you will have treasure in heaven; * then come, follow me.

℣ None of you can be my disciple unless he give up all his possessions; * then come, follow me.

Collect

ALMIGHTY God, who didst call thy servant David to be a faithful and wise steward of thy mysteries for the people of Wales: in thy mercy, grant that, following his purity of life and zeal for the gospel of Christ, and assisted by his prayers, we may with him receive the crown of everlasting life; through Jesus Christ our Lord, to whom with thee and the Holy Spirit be all honour and glory, world without end.

Saint Piran, Abbot
(5 March)

Proper of the Day and Common of Saints: for Religious

A reading from Saint Aldhelm, *On Virginity*

If the glory of holy virginity is believed to be next kin to angelic beatitude, and the beauteous company of the heavenly citizens wins praise for the merit of chastity, it ought to be extolled with the acclaim which is its due, since among the other ranks of the virtues it is singled out to wield the sceptre of the highest sovereignty and the sway of government; since, indeed, just as the taste of honeyed sweetness quite incomparably excels everything that is experienced as pleasing and delectable when brought to human mouths and the palate of mortals, so the divine majesty – though I speak, however, with the peace and indulgence of those saints once bound by the ties of matrimony – set the special attribute of virginity before all the ranks of virtues in general which are enumerated in the list of the gifts of the Holy Spirit. A clear enough proof of this exists, since, when from the highest summit of the heavens the venerable Offspring of God descended to rescue the straying sheep and to recover the lost farthing, he entered the womb of an uncontaminated mother, made capable of virginal birth without danger to her perpetual purity or loss of her chastity.

For this reason I think also that the holy recliner on the Lord's breast and the 'fourth river of Paradise' [that is, John, author of the fourth gospel], who above all others irrigated the seven churches of Asia with the inexhaustible waters of divine doctrine, deserved the special prerogative of divine love and the intimate lavishing of affection before all the renown of the other apostles, since he offered up to Christ – who is a passionate lover of chastity and a jealous teacher of holiness – the welcome sacrifice of virginity made with spontaneous devotion.

For this reason the true Physician, when, considering the wounds of evil and the scars of sin by which the souls of the sick were prostrated by a cruel overthrow, he mixed a health-giving potion and vitally administered an antidote

---

Saint Aldhelm of Malmesbury, *On Virginity* VII, in Aldhelm, *The Prose Works*. Translated by Michael Lapidge and Michael Herren (Ipswich: Brewer, 1979), pp. 63-64.

of celestial medicine to the fibres mortally affected with a virulent dose of spiritual wickedness, and when, ascending the summit of the gallows on the sixth day after the Sabbath – that is, the 'day of preparation' – he was suffering, mindful of reverence towards his mother, he dutifully enjoined the disciple who was awaiting the outcome of things among the dangers presented by the perfidious soldiers to look after his mother – as can not inappropriately be expressed in a rhythmical poem,

> Christ, having suffered on the cross
> and the hiding places of death,
> himself a virgin commended a virgin [Mary]
> to a virgin [John] for safe-keeping.

Afterwards, when decades had elapsed, John, having been banished as an exile to Patmos by Diocletian – who at that time, reliant on his imperial power, was inflicting the cruel pains of torture upon the worshippers of the true faith – and having been transported in a vision of ecstasy, was found worthy to hear the 144, 000 virgins singing a new song with sweet-sounding harmonies of melody and to behold them with his pure eyes. Of them it is said, 'For they are virgins; these follow the Lamb whithersoever he goeth' (Apoc 14:4). The rest of the faithful are to hear, but these are to sing the holy songs, and to walk with the Lamb through the august glory of the heavenly kingdom.

R̰. This holy man did all that God asked of him, * and God said to him: 'Out of all the nations, it is you alone whom I have found just in my sight. Come in and rest with me'.
V̰. This saint spurned a life of worldliness, and attained the kingdom of heaven, * and God said to him: 'Out of all the nations, it is you alone whom I have found just in my sight. Come in and rest with me'.

Saint Patrick, Bishop, Patron of Ireland
(17 March)

Proper of the Day and Common of Pastors: for a Bishop

ALMIGHTY God, who in thy providence chose thy servant Patrick to be the apostle of the people of Ireland: keep alive in us the fire of faith which he kindled, and in this our earthly pilgrimage strengthen us to gain the light of everlasting life; through Jesus Christ thy Son our Lord, who liveth and reigneth with thee, in the unity of the Holy Spirit, one God, for ever and ever.

Saint Magnus of Orkney, Martyr (16 April)

Proper of the Day and Common of Martyrs

A reading from the *Life of Saint Magnus* by an anonymous Icelandic author

When the holy Earl Magnus saw that the treachery of Haakon was about to show itself, he went with his men up into the island to a church to pray, and was there through the night, not because of fear or dread, but rather to commit all his care to God. his men offered to defend him, and fight against Haakon. But he answered, 'I will not place your lives in danger for me. And if peace cannot be made between us two kinsmen, then let it be as God wills; for rather will I suffer evil and treachery than do it to others'. For this noble martyr, when saying this, knew that all guile and deceit is returned to him who does it. Now thought his men most true that which he had before said to them about the treachery of Haakon. But as Earl Magnus knew before of his death, whether it were of his foresight or of divine revelation, he wished neither to fly nor to go far from the meeting of his enemies, and he went for no other reason to the holy church than for religion. Earl Magnus watched long in prayer during the night and meditated on his salvation, and prayed earnestly; he committed all his cause and himself into the hands of God. In the morning he let Mass be sung, and received in that Mass the *Corpus Domini*. And this his deed was necessary for the highest reason, that in that place he should become an offering to God, as was offered the redeeming sacrifice of Body and blood of our Lord Jesus Christ for the salvation of the whole world. [...]

The same morning that Earl Haakon had come up on to the island with his evil-doers, he sent four of his men, the worst of his servants, who were the fiercest and most eager to work ill, to seize earl Magnus wherever he was. These four, who, from their ferocity, may rather be called the wildest wolves than rational men, always thirsting for bloodshed, leapt into the church just as Mass was ending. Snatched they at once the holy Earl Magnus with great violence, uproar, and clamour, out of the peace and bosom of Holy Church, as

The Life of Saint Magnus, 25 & 27, in *Ancient Lives of Scottish Saints*, translated by W. M. Metcalfe (Fellinfach: Llanerch, 1998 [1895]), Part Two, pp. 348-349, 350-351.

the gentlest sheep of the fold. The saint was holden of the thralls of sin, the righteous was bound, dragged unjustly by the unjust, and then led away before the greedy judge, Earl Haakon. But this strong champion had such great steadfastness in all these wrestlings, that neither his body shook from fear, nor his mind with dread or grief, for he forsook this thorny world with all its fruitless flowers. He hoped that God would recompense his patience with an ineffable crown; but their cruelty and fury with everlasting torture in the hot fire of hell, because of their inhuman wickedness and monstrous greed. He was as glad and cheerful when they took him, as if he had been bidden to a banquet, and had so settled a heart and mind that he spoke to his enemies with no bitterness, anger, or tremor in his voice. [...]

Then begged the blessed Earl Magnus leave to pray first, and it was granted him. He fell then to the ground and gave himself into the power of God, offering himself to him in sacrifice. Not alone for himself prayed he, but rather for his enemies and murderers as well; and forgave them he all with his whole heart that which they were misdoing against him; and confessed he all his sins to God, and prayed that they might all be washed away by the shedding of his blood; and he commended his spirit into the hands of God, praying God's angels to come to meet it, and bear it to the rest of Paradise. Then when this noble martyr of God had ended his prayer, he said to Lifolf: 'Stand before me and hew me on the head a great wound; for it beseems not to behead chiefs like thieves. Be strong, man, and weep not, for I have prayed God to pardon thee'. Lifolf struck him on the head a great blow with an axe. Then said Earl Magnus, 'Saintrike again'. Then struck Lifolof into the same wound. Then fell the holy Earl Magnus on his knees, and fared with this martyrdom from the miseries of this world to the everlasting joys of the kingdom of heaven. And him whom the murderer took out of the earth, Almighty God led reign with him in heaven. his body fell to the earth, but his spirit was gloriously taken up into the heavenly glory of the angels.

The spot where the holy Earl Magnus was slain was stony and mossy. But a little after his merits before God were made manifest, so that since then there is a green field, fair and smooth, and God showed by this token, that Earl Magnus was slain for righteousness' sake, and gained the fairness and greenness of Paradise in the land of the living.

℞. Fearless in the sight of wicked men, this saint died in defence of the law of God, * for he was built on rock.

℣. This is he who rejected the life of this world and gained the kingdom of heaven,* for he was built on rock.

Saint Alphege, Bishop, Martyr
(19 April)

*Proper of the Day and Common of Martyrs or
Common of Pastors: for a Bishop*

A reading from Eadmer's *Life of Saint Anselm*

The things which were said and done... between the revered prelate Lanfranc and Abbot Anselm will require no explanation to those who knew the lives and habits of both; but those who did not know them may form some idea from the fact that – in my opinion and that of many others – there was nobody at that time who excelled Lanfranc in authority and breadth of learning, or Anselm in holiness and the knowledge of God. Moreover, Lanfranc, as an Englishman, was still somewhat green, and some of the customs which he found in England had not yet found acceptance with him. So he changed many of them, often with good reason, but sometimes simply by the imposition of his own authority. While, therefore, he was giving his attention to these changes, he had Anselm with him, a friend and brother with whom he was of one mind; and talking with him informally one say, he said, 'These Englishmen among whom we are living have set up for themselves certain saints whom they revere. But sometimes when I turn over in my mind their own accounts of who they were, I cannot help having doubts about the quality of their sanctity. Now one of them lies here in the holy church over which by God's will I now preside. He was called Alphege, a good man certainly, and in his day archbishop of this place. This man they not only number among the saints, but even among the martyrs, although they do not deny that he was killed, not for professing the name of Christ, but because he refused to buy himself off with money. For – to use the words of the English themselves – when his foes, the

---

Eadmer, *The Life of Anselm*, xxx, in *The Life of Saint Anselm, Archbishop of Canterbury, by Eadmer,* edited with introduction, notes and translation by R. W. Southern (Oxford: Clarendon Press, 1962), pp. 50-53.

pagan enemies of God, had captured him, out of respect for his dignity they gave him the possibility of buying himself off, and demanded in return an immense sum of money from him. But since he could only have obtained this by despoiling his own men and possibly reducing some of them to a wretched state of beggary, he preferred to lose his life rather than to keep it on such conditions. Now, my brother, I should like to hear what you think about this.' Thus, talking as a recent citizen of England, he briefly outlined the case and submitted it to Anselm.

If, however, we look on the matter historically, we see that this was not the only cause of Saint Alphege's death, but that there was another and more fundamental one. It was not only because he refused to buy himself off with money, but also because like a Christian freeman he stood out against his pagan persecutors, and tried to convert them from their infidelity, when they were burning the city of Canterbury and the church of Christ which stands there, and when they were putting the innocent citizens to a horrible death, - it was for this that they seized him and put him to death with cruel torture. But Anselm, replying simply to the question put to him, as one prudent man to another, spoke as follows: 'It is clear that a man, who has no hesitation in dying rather than sin against God even in a small matter, would very much rather die than anger God by committing some grave sin. And certainly it appears to be a graver sin to deny Christ than for any lord of earth to injure his men by taking away their money. But it was the lesser of these evils which Alphege refused to commit. Much less therefore would he have denied Christ, if furious men had laid hands on him, threatening him with death unless he did so. From this we can understand the wonderful hold which justice had in his breast, since he preferred to give his life rather than to throw aside charity and become a cause of scandal to his neighbours. How far from him then is that "woe" which the Lord threatened 'to him by whom scandal comes' (Mt 18:7). And, in my view, it is not unfitting that one who is truthfully pronounced to have suffered death voluntarily for so great a love of justice should be numbered among the martyrs. For John the Baptist also, whom the whole church of God believes to be the chief of martyrs and venerates as such, was killed, not because he refused to deny Christ, but because he refused to dissemble the truth. Indeed, what difference is there between dying for justice and dying for truth? Moreover, there is the witness of Holy Scripture as you, Father, very well know, that Christ is both truth and justice; so he who dies for truth and justice dies for Christ But he who dies for Christ is, as the Church holds, a martyr. Now Saint Alphege as truly suffered for justice as Saint John did for truth. So why should anyone have more doubt about the true and holy martyrdom of the one than of the other, since a similar cause led both of them to suffer death? These arguments, revered father, so far as I can see, are what reason itself teaches me to be sound. But it is for your judgment to correct and restrain me if you feel differently, and to teach and declare to the church of God a better way of looking on this important matter.' To this Lanfranc replied, 'I acknowledge – I approve and deeply respect the subtlety and insight of your mind and now that have been instructed by your solid argument, I trust that I shall, by God's grace, henceforth worship and venerate Saint Alphege with all my heart, as a truly great and glorious martyr of Christ'.

1 Thess 2:8; Gal 4:19

℟. In our great longing for you, we desired nothing better than to
     offer you our own lives, as well as God's gospel,* so greatly had we
     learned to love you.
℣. My little children, I am in travail over you afresh, until I can see
     Christ's image formed in you,* so greatly had we learned to love you.

Collect

O MERCIFUL God, who didst raise up thy servant Alphege to be a pastor of thy people and gavest him grace to suffer for justice and true religion: grant that we who celebrate his martyrdom may know the power of the risen Christ in our hearts and share his peace in lives offered to thy service; through Jesus Christ thy Son our Lord, who liveth and reigneth with thee, in the unity of the Holy Spirit, one God, for ever and ever.

Saint Anselm, Bishop, Doctor of the Church
(21 April)

Proper of the Day and Common of Pastors: for a Bishop

Reading and Responsory as in the Liturgy of Hours

O EVERLASTING God, who gavest to thy servant Anselm singular gifts as a pastor and teacher: grant that we, like him, may desire thee with our whole heart and, so desiring, may seek thee and, seeking, may find thee; through Jesus Christ thy Son our Lord, who liveth and reigneth with thee, in the unity of the Holy Spirit, one God, for ever and ever.

Saint George, Martyr, Patron of England
(23 April)

Proper of the Day and Common of Martyrs (Eastertide)

The following passage may be read in the Divine Office according to the Use of this Customary but not at the Office of Readings in the Liturgy of Hours of the Roman Rite.

A reading from the writings of Blessed John Henry Newman

A country which is given up whether to heresy or schism… is far from being in the miserable state of a heathen population; it has portions of the truth remaining in it; it has some supernatural channels of grace; and the results are such as can never be known till we have all passed out of this visible scene of things, and the accounts of the world are finally made up for the last tremendous day. While, then, I think it plain that the existence of large Anti-

---

Bl. John Henry Newman, *Lectures on the Difficulties of Anglicans* XI, in *Certain Difficulties felt by Anglicans in Catholic Teaching Considered, by John Henry Cardinal Newman*, I. (London: Longmans, Green, 1908), pp. 352-353, 354-355, 356-357.

Catholic bodies professing Christianity are as inevitable, from the nature of the case, as infidel races or states, except under some extraordinary dispensations of divine grace, while there must ever be in the world false prophets and Antichrists, standing over against the Catholic Church, yet it is consolatory to reflect how the schism or heresy, which the self-will of a monarch or of a generation has caused, does not suffice altogether to destroy the work for which in some distant age Evangelists have left their homes, and Martyrs have shed their blood. Thus, the blessing is inestimable to England, so far as among us the Sacrament of Baptism is validly administered to any portion of the population. [...]

Among the most bitter railers against the Church in this country, may be found those who are influenced by divine grace, and are at present travelling towards heaven, whatever be their ultimate destiny. Among the most irritable disputants against the Sacrifice of the Mass or Transubstantiation, or the most impatient listeners to the glories of Mary, there may be those for whom she is saying to her Son, what he said on the cross to his Father, 'Forgive them, for they know not what they do' (Lk 23:34). [...]

As to the prospect of those countless multitudes of a country like this, who apparently have no supernatural vision of the next world at all, and die without fear because they die without thought, with these, alas! I am not here concerned. But the remarks I have been making suggest much of comfort, when we look out into what is called the religious world in all its varieties, whether it be the High Church section, or the Evangelical, whether it be in the Establishment, or in Methodism, or in Dissent, so far as there seems to be real earnestness and invincible prejudice. One cannot but hope that that written Word of God, for which they desire to be jealous, though exhibited to them in a mutilated form and in a translation unsanctioned by Holy Church, is of incalculable blessing to their souls, and may be, through God's grace, the divine instrument of bringing many to contrition and to a happy death who have received no sacrament since they were baptized in their infancy. One cannot hope but that the Anglican Prayer Book with its Psalter and Catholic prayers, even though these, in the translation, have passed through heretical intellects, may retain so much of its old virtue as to co-operate with divine grace in the instruction and salvation of a large remnant.

In these and many other ways, even in England, ... the difficulty is softened which is presented to the imagination by the view of such large populations, who, though called Christian, are not Catholic or orthodox in creed.

Collect

O GOD of hosts, who didst so kindle the flame of love in the heart of thy servant George that he bore witness to the risen Lord by his life and by his death: grant us the same faith and power of love that we, who rejoice in his triumphs, may come to share with him the fullness of the resurrection; through Jesus Christ thy Son our Lord, who liveth and reigneth with thee, in the unity of the Holy Spirit, one God, for ever and ever.

Saint Mellitus, Bishop
(24 April)

Proper of the Day and Common of Pastors: for a Bishop

A reading from the letters of Pope Saint Gregory the Great

Gregory, servant of the servants of God, greets his most beloved son and abbot, Mellitus.

Since the departure of our monks, who accompany you, we have been made extremely anxious, because it has happened that we have heard nothing about the success of your journey. But when almighty God has led you to that most reverend man, our brother Bishop Augustine, tell him what I have long pondered over, while thinking about the case of the English. That is, that the temples of the idols among that people ought not to be destroyed at all, but the idols themselves, which are in them, should be destroyed. Let water be blessed and sprinkled in the same temples, and let altars be constructed and relics placed there. For if those temples have been well constructed, it is necessary that they should be changed from the cult of demons to the worship of the true God, so that, while that race sees itself that its temples are not being destroyed, it may remove errors from its people's hearts, and by knowing and adoring the

---

Saint Gregory the Great, *Letters* XI. 56, in *The Letters of Gregory the Great*, translated with Introduction and Notes, by John R. C. Martyn, Volume 3. Books 10-14 (Toronto: Pontifical Institute of Mediæval Studies, 2004), pp.802-803.

true God, they may come together in their customary places in a more friendly manner.

And because they are accustomed to killing many oxen while sacrificing to their demons, some solemn rites should be changed for them over this matter. On the day of a dedication, or on the birthdays of holy martyrs, whose relics are placed there, they should make huts for themselves around those churches that have been converted from shrines, with branches of trees, and they should celebrate the festival with religious feasting. And they should not sacrifice animals to the devil any more, but kill animals for eating in praise of God, and offer thanks to the Giver of all things for their sufficiency. Thus, while some joys are reserved for them externally, they might more readily consent to internal joys. For there is no doubt that it is impossible to cut away everything at the same time from hardened minds, because anyone who strives to ascend to the highest place, relies on ladders or steps. He is not lifted up in one leap.

Even so, the Lord certainly made himself known to the people of Israel in Egypt, and yet he kept their use of sacrifices, which they used to offer to the devil in worshipping him, so as to order them to slaughter animals for their own sacrifice. He thereby changed their hearts, and they left aside one aspect of the sacrifice and retained another, so that, although they were the same animals that they used to sacrifice, yet by killing them for the true God, and not for the idols, they would no longer be the same sacrifices.

It is necessary, therefore, for your Beloved to say all of this to our aforesaid brother, so that as he is present there, he may consider how he ought to arrange everything. May God preserve you in safety, most beloved son.

Rom 15:15-16; 1:9

℟. God has given me this special grace: he has appointed me as a
   priest of Jesus Christ, and I am to carry out my priestly duty by
bringing the Good News from God to the pagans, * and so make
   them acceptable as an offering, sanctified by the Holy Spirit.
℣. I offer God the humble service of my spirit by preaching the Good
   News of his Son to the pagans, * and so make them acceptable as an
offering, sanctified by the Holy Spirit.

The English Martyrs
(4 May)

Proper of the Day and Common of Martyrs

A reading from the homily of Pope Paul VI
at the canonization of the Forty Martyrs of England and Wales

To all those who are filled with admiration in reading the records of these Forty Holy Martyrs, it is perfectly clear that they are worthy to stand alongside the greatest martyrs of the past; and this is not merely because of their fearless faith and marvellous constant, but by reason of their humility, simplicity and serenity, and above all the spiritual joy and that wondrously radiant love with which they accepted their condemnation and death.

The unity existing between these men and women depends from the deeply spiritual cast of mind which they had in common. In so many other respects they were completely different – as different as any large group usually is: in age and sex, in culture and education, in social status and occupation, in character and temperament, in their qualities, natural and supernatural, in the external circumstances of their lives. So we find among these Forty Holy Martyrs priests, secular and regular, religious of different orders and grades; and we have, amongst the laity, men of the highest nobility and those who rank as ordinary, married women and mothers of families. What unites them all is that interior quality of unshakeable loyalty to the vocation given them by God – the sacrifice of their lives as a loving response to that call.

The high tragedy in the lives of these martyrs was that their honest and genuine loyalty came into conflict with their fidelity to God and with the dictates of their conscience illumined by the Catholic faith. Two truths especially were involved: the Holy Eucharist and the inalienable prerogatives of the successor of Peter who, by God's will, is the universal shepherd of Christ's Church. Faced with the choice of remaining steadfast in their faith and of dying for it, or of saving their lives by denying that faith, without a moment's hesitation and with a truly supernatural strength they stood for God and joyfully confronted

---

The Office of Readings, 25 October (England and Wales), in *The Divine Office, Volume III* (London: Collins, 2006), pp. 440*-41*

martyrdom. At the same time such was the greatness of their spirit that many of them died with prayers on their lips for the country they loved so much, for the King or Queen, and not least for those directly responsible for their capture, their sufferings, and the degradation and ignominy of their cruel deaths.

May our thanksgiving go up to God who, in his providential goodness, saw fit to raise up these martyrs.

Collect
O MERCIFUL God, who, when thy Church on earth was torn apart by the ravages of sin, didst raise up men and women in this land who witnessed to their faith with courage and constancy: give unto thy Church that peace which is thy will, and grant that those who have been divided on earth may be reconciled in heaven and be partakers together in the vision of thy glory; through Jesus Christ thy Son our Lord, who liveth and reigneth with thee, in the unity of the Holy Spirit, one God, for ever and ever.

St John the Apostle in Eastertide
(formerly St John *ante portam Latinam*)
(6 May)

Proper of St John, 27 December, and Common of Apostles in Eastertide

A reading from the sermons of John Keble

'Therefore that disciple whom Jesus loved saith unto Peter, It is the Lord' (Jn 21:7). […] This is the point, to which I would draw your attention: that St John knew Jesus before the rest; knew him to be the Lord by signs and tokens, which had somehow not been understood by the rest. The rest all saw the miraculous draught of fishes, all saw the Lord standing on the shore, all heard his grave and kind voice, giving them directions. But they knew him not: it came not as yet into their minds that this was another visit of their Master to them, now that he was risen from the dead. They knew him not. Only St John

---

John Keble, 'The Intuition of Love', in Sermons for the Saints' Days and other Festivals, by the late Rev. John Keble (Oxford and London: Parker, 1877), pp. 68-71.

knew him. What was the reason of this? It was not that St John had been longer acquainted with our Lord. There was as it seems but one's day difference in St John's and St Peter's introduction to him, and St Andrew and St John followed him, by the Baptist's direction, both on the same day. And all three, with St James, were called at the same moment to forsake all and follow him.

The reason, therefore, of St John's knowing our Saviour, when the rest knew him not, was not his having a longer and more perfect acquaintance with him. But it is contained, I suppose, in the words, 'The disciple, whom Jesus loved'. Because Jesus loved St John especially, therefore St John was in a manner always on the look out for him, ever watching for his signs and tokens, ever expecting and longing for his presence, and could not well miss him when he came. Why will a child know its mother at a distance sooner than another personal would? Of course, because she loves it so dearly, and it is used to depend so entirely on her. Wherever it goes, it thinks of her; sees her in dreams, imagines her at hand very often, when she is away, discovers in every thing somewhat to remind it of her. This, and no other, was the reason by St John perceived Christ sooner than the rest could. There was in him, we may well believe, more of that tender yearning affection, which a young child feels towards its mother and its nurse. He felt that he could not do without our Saviour: therefore his eyes sought him eagerly, wherever he was; and in the most unlikely places, he would still be fancying, 'What if this should be my Master's token? What if he should even now shew himself?' The constant employment of his heart was such as is described in that beautiful verse of the psalmist, 'My soul waiteth for the Lord, more than they that watch for the morning'. When we are expecting any dear friend, how anxiously do we look out long before, how often imagine that we see him before he arrives! And why? Because we love him so much, and long so earnestly to set eyes upon him.

Collect

MERCIFUL Lord, we beseech thee to cast thy bright beams of light upon thy Church: that it being enlightened by the doctrine of thy blessed apostle and evangelist Saint John may so walk in the light of thy truth, that it may at length attain to the light of everlasting life; through Jesus Christ thy Son our Lord, who liveth and reigneth with thee in the unity of the Holy Spirit, one God, for ever and ever.

**Saint Dunstan, Bishop
(19 May)**

Proper of the Day and Common of Pastors: for a Bishop

A reading from the Life of Saint Dunstan by Eadmer

Secure in the joy of his Lord and eternal felicity that was imminent for him, Dunstan rejoiced with thanks in the Lord and was filled with spiritual happiness towards everyone. Now the time for the daily office was upon him and the bishop advanced towards the altar in festive manner intending to celebrate it. As if inspired by God to come together in a larger number than usual in order to hear something special, a crowd of people filled the church so that its walls were scarcely able to contain the multitude on every side. And when the gospel for the Mass had been read the bishop came forward to preach to the people and with the Holy Spirit controlling his heart and tongue he spoke as he had never spoken before. Then, returning to the altar, by the immaculate blessing he changed the bread and wine into the body and blood of Jesus Christ But when the time came for the blessing of the people he departed from the altar to preach again to the people, and inebriated with the Spirit of God he expounded concerning the real existence of the body of Christ and about the future resurrection and eternal life, so that you might have thought that it was a citizen of that same perpetual life speaking, had you not known the speaker earlier.

He made no mention of his own death, however, among the things he was saying, because he was infused with holy tenderness of spirit and gentle holiness and did not wish to heap a double blow of sadness upon them, for whom he deemed the day of his death would be a sufficiently sad blow on its own. When the sermon was finished he returned to the altar and bestowed his pontifical blessing upon the people. At the same time he was acutely wounded in his mind because he feared that his dearest friends, whom he was leaving behind, would suffer more grievously if pierced by the unforeseen lance of his death than if they had been aware of it before the blow befell them. Then when he had given the blessing, to everyone's amazement, he advanced towards the people a third time. As soon as he opened his mouth to speak to them,

Eadmer, *Life of Saint Dunstan*, 65, in Eadmer of Canterbury, *Lives and Miracles of Saints Oda, Dunstan, and Oswald* , edited and translated by Andrew J. Turner and Bernard J. Muir (Oxford: Clarendon Press, 2006), pp. 153-155.

however, his face was resplendent with such great radiance that there was no one in that whole congregation who was able to look directly at him without having to turn their eyes aside.

I know that it is impossible for anyone to describe either with voice or in writing what sweetness, what delight, what happiness filled the hearts and mouths of everyone present there who merited to understand what was being said. But when the servant of God began to reveal that the day of his death was upon him, all the exultation was shattered by grief, and with such great grief that the father, who was now being admitted to the eternal joys, was moved with admirable compassion – for which he was renowned – and himself seemed to be one of the mourners. Yet with strength filling his spirit, though weeping he consoled those weeping, and said to them among other things that they ought not to mourn over the death of one who would be received by neither pain or punishment, but rather by rest and eternal glory. He said, moreover, that there was no one firmly grounded in true love who cherished his own temporal comfort more than the eternal profit of one close to him. And in order to console them more, in the hope of God's grace and mercy he promised them that though he might be absent from them in body, his spiritual presence would never be absent from among them. And when he had finished speaking in this manner he commended them all to Christ, and finally with them still longing for his glorious countenance he ascended to the table of the Lord where he would feast upon his life.

Lk 12:35-36; Mt 24:42

℟. Be ready for action, with belts fastened, lamps alight.* Be like men waiting for their master to return from the wedding feast

℣. Stay awake, because you do not know the day when your master is coming.* Be like men waiting for their master to return from the wedding feast

Collect
ALMIGHTY God, who didst raise up Dunstan to be a true shepherd of the flock, a restorer of monastic life and a faithful counsellor to kings: grant, we beseech thee, to all pastors the like gifts of thy Holy Spirit that they may be true servants of Christ and of all his people; through Jesus Christ thy Son our Lord, who liveth and reigneth with thee, in the unity of the Holy Spirit, one God, for ever and ever.

Saint Helena
(21 May)

Proper of the Day and Common of Saints

A reading from the 'Shorter Socrates'

Helen, the emperor's mother, is even more worthy of record for good deeds. There is a History concerning her which those who wish may study, but I shall relate briefly her actions. Constantine adorned the town of his mother, Drepanum, as a famous city with buildings and splendour, and called the town 'city of Helen' after his mother's name. She, blessedly firm in all respects, was God-loving, pious, and wise; totally firm in the faith and in her conduct she was even more worthy of praise. This blessed Helen received a command from God in a night vision to go to Jerusalem and seek the wood of Christ's Cross and build the churches of God: the Tomb, Sion, Ascension, Golgotha, Resurrection, the Nativity of Christ at Bethlehem, the church of the holy Mother of God where she died, Lazarus and Saint Stephen. She related to Constantine this vision and God's command. He readily and with faith accepted the words of his mother, gave her much gold and silver, and sent her to Jerusalem with a large escort to seek the Cross and to build the churches of the vision as had been shown her.

She came and found Jerusalem, according to the prophecy (Is 1:8), like a tent for fruits and like a shade among melon-gardens, and like a city made desolate by foreign peoples. Gathering the Jews, she requested the word of the Cross of Christ, as the History indicates. The finding of the Cross and nails I reckon superfluous to write down. The emperor's mother Helen restored the New Jerusalem with churches according to the indication of the vision from God. She adorned it with wonderful constructions and much splendour in accordance with the liturgical function of each one, to the glory of Christ's name.

In fear and awe of God she was perpetually fasting and praying together with many women and numerous holy virgins, with whom she properly carried out

---

'Shorter Socrates', 19, in *The Armenian Adaptation of the Ecclesiastical History of Socrates Scholasticus [Proper of the Day and Commonly known as 'The Shorter Socrates']*. Translation of the Armenian Text and Commentary by Robert W. Thomson (Leuven: Peeters, 2001), pp. 49-51.

her continuous prayers. She used to fill the poor and needy, and adorned the churches with notable vessels. She used to celebrate the joyful feasts according to each one's liturgy for each of the churches. She also arranged ministers so that the worship of God would be performed without interruption. Then she took leave of the ministers and the holy churches. A part of the holy Cross she left at Jerusalem; taking the rest with her, she brought it to Constantinople with the nails. They celebrated the encænia on the 13 September; and on the following day, 14 September, the feast of the holy Cross. Then the holy Cross was shown to the people, and the emperor kissed it. He enclosed it, and this was like a covering for the Cross; and he rejoiced and blessed God. With such spiritual celebration and joy they praised God. When these things had thus taken place to the glory of God, the blessed Helen went to her own city. With consecrated virgins she lived in undisturbed fasting and prayer. Aged eighty, she died. The emperor took her body and laid it to rest in Rome, in the tombs of the kings, with great honour to the glory and praise of our God.

cf Ruth 3:10,11; Jud 13:25

℟. The Lord has blessed you, * for the people all know your worth.
℣. The Lord has made your name so famous that you shall never pass from the memories of men, * for the people all know your worth.

Saint Godric of Finchale, Religious
(21 May)

Proper of the Day and Common of Saints: for Religious

A reading from Reginald of Durham,
The Little Book of the Life and Miracles of Saint Godric, Hermit of Finchale

It happened on one occasion that a hunting party of Ralph, the Bishop of Durham, had viewed a stag of unusual form, a very monarch of the forest; and once sighted the hunt turned completely from every other animal in the field,

---

Reginald of Durham, *The Little Book of the Life and Miracles of Saint Godric, Hermit of Finchale,* in Francis Rice, *The Hermit of Finchale. The Life of Saint Godric* (Durham, Pentland Press, 1994), pp. 233-234.

and gave chase to this one stag alone. The creature swerved and turned this way and that, terrified by the clamour of the horns, and the baying of the hounds, and in despair it ran hard for the hermit, 'whom it knew'. Wondering at once at the unusual uproar he opened his door, and heard at once the hounds, and the horns of the hunters; but he saw also the distress of the magnificent stag with its tongue hanging out, heavily panting and gasping. Godric went down on his knees and begged the Lord to save the animal he had instructed to come to his abode; and then he arose and indicating by the appropriate sounds and gestures, he bade the animal to spare its tears, and come right in. It clearly saw the welcome, and spread itself at Godric's feet.

Meanwhile the pack of hounds was coming closer, and seemed no more than a stone's thrown away. At this, the man of God came out of his house, closing the door carefully behind him, and sat under his tree. When the hounds reached him they turned in the direction of the sound of their masters, and barked for them to come. These had been delayed, for they would not venture into the inaccessible forest full of undesirable wild life. Instead they dismounted and circled the wood on foot to reach the hermit's hut, and came upon the man of God, wrapped in vile rags.

After they had politely exchanged greetings they asked him if he had seen a stag coming his way, and were given this reply: 'God knows where it is; for all animals on earth whether wild or tamed are under his dominion.' They recognized the spirit of God in this man, and all were both surprised and embarrassed. So apologizing for their rash intrusion they asked his pardon and went their way.

When it was growing dusk the man of God once again opened wide his door and let the stag go free, ducking its antlers to roam the woods at will. For some years the stag would return to the servant of God and lie in comfort beside him, like any well-trained domestic animal. It may be this was the stag's way of showing its respect and thanking the one who saved its life.

Deut 2:7; 8:5

℟. The Lord your God has blessed you in everything you have undertaken; he has watched your journey through the vast wilderness; * the Lord your God has been with you.
℣. As a man disciplines his son, he has disciplined you; * the Lord your God has been with you.

Proper of the Day and Common of Saints: for Religious

A reading from Saint Aldhelm, *On Virginity*

In the conflict of the eight principal vices, although Pride is placed last, yet like a fierce queen she is known to usurp for herself the authority of tyrannical power and the sway of government more so than the others, since without any wavering uneasiness of ambiguity it is to be truly believed that Lucifer – surrounded by parasitic accomplices and hemmed in by apostate followers – fell reeling into the profound abyss of pride and the foul pit of swollen arrogance, before the first-created man, the inhabitant of the newly made Paradise and the inexperienced owner of all the earthly creation which the smooth circling of the heavens encircles like a whirling sling, tasting the forbidden nourishment with stuffed cheeks and smacking lips, fell cruelly into the chasm of gluttony. Now if the angelic loftiness of heavenly citizens, swelling so greatly with the arrogance of pride, was deprived of the blessed companionship of the other angels and its share in contemplating the Godhead, how much more will the frail weakness of mortals be unhappily defrauded of the wedding-feast of the celestial Bride-groom, if it has swelled up like an inflated bladder with the merit of its own attainments, and has taken on the notoriety of vainglory because of its virginal chastity – as if it were some special sanctity?

Virgins of Christ and raw recruits of the Church must therefore fight with muscular energy against the horrendous monster of Pride and the same time against those seven wild beasts of the virulent vices, who with teeth rabid and venomous strive to mangle violently whoever is unarmed and despoiled of the breastplate of virginity and stripped of the shield of modesty; and they must struggle zealously with the arrows of spiritual armament and the iron-tipped spears of the virtues as if against the most ferocious armies of barbarians, who do not desist from battering repeatedly the shield-wall of the young soldiers of Christ with the catapult of perverse deceit.

Saint Aldhelm of Malmesbury, *On Virginity* XI, in Aldhelm, *The Prose Works*. Translated by Michael Lapidge and Michael Herren (Ipswich: Brewer, 1979), pp. 67-68.

In no way let us sloppily offer to these savage enemies the backs of our shoulder-blades in place of shield-bosses, after the fashion of timid soldiers effeminately fearing the horror of war and the battle-calls of the trumpeter! Rather, as combatants in the monastic army, boldly offering our foreheads armed with the banner of the Cross among the ranks of our competitors, and carrying tightly the warlike instruments of armament – which the distinguished warrior Saint Paul enumerates, that is to say, the sword of the Holy Word and the impenetrable breast-plate of faith – and protected by the secure shield against the thousand harmful tricks of spiritual wickedness, we shall then blessedly rejoice in the heavenly kingdom, revelling in celestial glory and ready to receive the due triumph of victory from Christ our paymaster – if we now fight strenuously in the forefront of the battle as rulers of the world or as warriors of the Lord, steadfastly struggling with steadfast foes, against the dominion of Leviathan and the powers of darkness.

Phil 3:17; 4:9; 1 Cor 1:10

℞. My friends, join in imitating me. You have us for a model; watch
   those whose way of life conforms to it. * The lessons I taught you,
   the tradition I have passed on, all that you heard me say or saw me do,
   put into practice, and the God of peace will be with you.
℣. I appeal to you, my brothers, in the name of our Lord Jesus Christ,
   agree among yourselves. * The lesson I taught you, the tradition I
have passed on, all that you heard me say or saw me do, put into
   practice, and the God of peace will be with you.

Saint Aldhelm, Bishop
(24 May)

Proper of the Day and Common of Pastors: for a Bishop

A reading from the letters of Saint Aldhelm

To the most glorious king Geraint, the lord who guides the sceptre of the western kingdom, whom I embrace with fraternal charity – as he who

---

Letter IV, to Geraint, in Aldhelm, *The Prose Works,* translated by Michael Lapidge and Michael Herren (Ipswich: Brewer, 1979), pp. 155-156.

scrutinizes my heart and inwards is witness – and likewise to all the bishops of God abiding throughout Devon, Aldhelm, performing the office of abbot without distinction of merits, sends his wishes for the salvation that we hope for in the Lord.

Recently, when I was present at an episcopal council, where, out of almost the entirety of Britain, an innumerable company of the bishops of God came together, having assembled for this purpose expressly, that out of concern for the churches and the salvation of souls, the decrees of the canons and the statutes of the Fathers might be discussed by all and be maintained in common, with Christ offering his protection – when these matters were duly accomplished, the entire episcopal council compelled my insignificant self with like precept and similar sentiment to direct epistolatory letters to the presence of your Loyalty, and, through the style of writing, to intimate their fatherly request and wholesome suggestion, that is, respecting the unity of the Catholic Church and the harmony of the Christian religion, without which an indifferent faith grows sluggish and future gain is exhausted. For what profit the emoluments of good works, if they are performed outside the Catholic Church, even if someone should meticulously carry out the rules of practice of a rigid life according to monastic discipline, or with fixed purpose decline the companionship of mortals and pass a life of contemplative retirement away in some squalid wilderness? Therefore that your Wisdom may be able to grasp more surely to what purposes my Mediocrity has directed these writings to you, I shall explain them briefly and succinctly.

For indeed we have heard and received report from the relation of diverse rumours that your bishops are not at all in harmony with the rule of the Catholic Faith according to the precepts of Scripture, and, on account of their animosities and verbal assaults, a grave schism and cruel scandal may arise in the Church of Christ, which the maxim of the Psalmist detests that says, 'Much peace have they that love thy law and to them there is no stumbling block' (Ps [118] 119:165). For truly, obedient harmony in religious matters unites with charity, just as harsh strife contaminates it. For the Psalmist enjoins the unity of brotherhood upon the followers of truth, saying, 'God who maketh men of one manner to dwell in a house' (Ps [67:7] 68:6). This house, according to allegory, is understood to be the Church, spread throughout all points of the world. For indeed, heretics and schismatics, foreign to the society of the Church, sprouting up in the world and like, so to speak, the dreadful seed of darnels sown in the midst of a fertile crop, defile the harvest of the Lord by their contentious arguments. But the Apostolic Trumpet [Saint Paul] curbs the disgrace of altercation of this sort: 'But if any man seems to be contentious', he says, 'we have no such custom nor does the Church of God' (1 Cor 11:16), 'which does not have spot or wrinkle' (Eph 5:27). Indeed, the evangelical oracles proclaim that peace is the mother of Catholics and the authoress of the children of God: 'Blessed are the peace-makers, for they shall be called the children of God' (Mt 5:9). Hence, when our Lord and Saviour came down from the highest summit of heaven in order to erase 'the handwriting of the decree that was against us' (Col 2:14), and to reconcile the world through mediating peace, the angelic melody sang out: 'Glory to God in the highest and on earth peace to men of good will' (Lk 2: 14); and the Psalmist: 'Let peace be thy strength and abundance in thy towers' (Ps [121] 122:7).

Jn 17:11, 23, 22

℟.Jesus prayed: Holy Father, keep them safe by the power of your name, the name you gave me, * so that they may be completely one, in order that the world may know that you sent me.
℣.I gave them the same glory you gave me, * so that they may be completely one, in order that the world may know that you sent me.

Saint Bede the Venerable, Priest and Doctor of the Church (25 May)

Proper of the Day and Common of Doctors of the Church

Reading and Responsory as in the Liturgy of Hours

ALMIGHTY God, maker of all things, whose Son Jesus Christ gave to thy servant Bede grace to drink in with joy the word which leadeth us to know thee and to love thee: in thy goodness grant that, through his prayers, we also may come at length to thee, the source of all wisdom, and stand before thy face; through Jesus Christ thy Son our Lord, who liveth and reigneth with thee, in the unity of the Holy Spirit, one God, for ever and ever.

Saint Augustine, first Bishop of Canterbury
(27 May)

The following passage may be read in the Divine Office according to the Use of this Customary but not at the Office of Readings in the Liturgy of Hours of the Roman Rite.

A reading from the Venerable Bede,
The Ecclesiastical History of the English People

So Augustine, strengthened by the encouragement of St Gregory, in company with the servants of Christ, returned to the work of preaching the word, and came to Britain. At that time, Æthelberht, king of Kent, was a very powerful monarch. The lands over which he exercised his suzerainty stretched as far as the great river Humber, which divides the northern from the southern Angles. Over against the eastern districts of Kent there is a large island called Thanet which, in English reckoning, is six hundred hides in extent. It is divided from the mainland by the river Wantsum, which is about three furlongs wide, can be crossed in two places only, and joins the sea at either end. Here Augustine, the servant of the Lord, landed with his companions, who are said to have been nearly forty in number. They had acquired interpreters from the Frankish race according to the command of Pope St Gregory. Augustine sent to Æthelberht to say that he had come from Rome bearing the best of news, namely the sure and certain promise of eternal joys in heaven and an endless kingdom with the living and true God to those who received it. On hearing this, the king ordered them to remain on the island where they had landed and be provided with all things necessary until he had decided what to do about them. [...]

Some days afterwards the king came to the island and, sitting in the open air, commanded Augustine and his companions to come thither to talk with him. He took care that they should not meet in any building for he held the traditional superstition that, if they practised any magic art, they might deceive him and get the better of him as soon as he entered. But they came endowed with divine not devilish power and bearing as their standard a silver cross and

St Bede, *Ecclesiastical History of the English People*, I. 25, in Bede, *The Ecclesiastical History of the English People, The Greater Chronicle, Bede's Letter to Egbert*, edited with an introduction and notes by Judith McClure and Roger Collins (Oxford: Oxford University Press, 2008 [1994]), pp. 39-40.

the image of our Lord and Saviour painted on a panel. They chanted litanies and uttered prayers to the Lord for their own eternal salvation and the salvation of those for whom and to whom they had come.

At the king's command, they sat down and preached the word of life to himself and all his counts there present. Then he said to them, 'The words and the promises you bring are fair enough, but because they are new to us and doubtful, I cannot consent to accept them and forsake those beliefs which I and the whole English race have held so long. But as you have come on a long pilgrimage and are anxious, I perceive, to share with us things which you believe to be true and good, we do not wish to do you harm; on the contrary, we will receive you hospitably and provide what is necessary for your support; nor do we forbid you to win all you can to your faith and religion by your preaching.' So he gave them a dwelling in the city of Canterbury, which was the chief city of all his dominions; and, in accordance with his promise, he granted them provisions and did not refuse them permission to preach.

Saint Boniface (Wynfrith) of Crediton, Bishop and Martyr (5 June)

Proper of the Day and Common of Martyrs

Reading and Responsory as in the Liturgy of Hours

O GOD our redeemer, who didst call thy servant Boniface to preach the gospel among the German people and to build up thy Church in holiness: grant that we may hold fast in our hearts that faith which he taught with his words and sealed with his blood, and profess it in lives dedicated to thy Son, Jesus Christ our Lord, who liveth and reigneth with thee, in the unity of the Holy Spirit, one God, for ever and ever.

Saint Columba, Abbot of Iona, Missionary (9 June)

Proper of the Day and Common of Saints: for Religious

A reading from Adomnan's *Life of Columba*

Going from there, he climbed a small hill overlooking the monastery, and stood on its summit for a little while. And as he stood he raised both hands, and blessed his monastery, saying: 'On this place, small and mean though it be, not only the kings of the Irish with their peoples, but also the rulers of barbarous and foreign nations, with their subjects, will bestow great and especial honour; also especial reverence will be bestowed by saints even of other churches.'

Adomnan, *Life of Columba* III. 23, in *Adomnan's Life of Columba*, edited with translation and notes by the late Alan Orr Anderson and by Marjorie Ogilvie Anderson, revised by Marjorie Ogilvie Anderson (Oxford: Clarendon Press, 1991), pp. 223-227.

After these words, he descended from that little hill, returned to the monastery, and sat in the hut, writing a psalter. And when he came to that verse of the thirty-third Psalm where it is written, 'But they that seek the Lord shall not want for anything that is good',* he said, 'Here, at the end of the page, I must stop. Let Baithene write what follows'.

[...] After he had written the former verse, at the end of the page, the saint entered the church for the vesper office of the Lord's-night. As soon as that was finished, he returned to his lodging, and reclined on his sleeping-place, where all the night he used to have for bed, the bare rock; and for pillow, a stone, which even today stands beside his burial-place as a kind of grave-pillar. So while reclining there, he gave his last commands to the brothers, in the hearing of his attendant alone, and said: 'I commend to you, my children, these latest words, that you shall have among yourselves mutual and unfeigned charity, with peace. If you follow this course after the example of the holy fathers, God, who gives strength to the good, will help you; and I, abiding with him, shall intercede for you. And not only will the necessaries of this life be sufficiently provided by him, but also the rewards of eternal good things will be bestowed, that are prepared for those who follow the divine commandments.'

We have carried down to this point, briefly told, the last words of the venerable patron, when he was, as it were, crossing over to the heavenly country from this weary pilgrimage.

After them the saint was silent for a little, as the happy latest hour drew near. Then, when the beaten bell resounded at midnight, he rose in haste and went to the church and, running, entered in advance of the others, alone; and bowing his knees in prayer he sank down beside the altar. In that moment Diormit, the attendant, following later, saw from a distance the whole church filled inside with angelic light about the saint. As Diormit approached the doorway, the light that he had seen quickly faded. A few more of the brothers also had seen it, when they too were a little way off.

So Diormit entering the church cried in a tearful voice, 'Where are you, where are you, father?' And groping in the darkness, since the lamps of the brothers had not yet been brought, he found the saint lying before the altar. Raising him a little, and sitting down beside him, he placed the holy head upon his lap. Meanwhile the company of monks ran up with lights; and when they saw that

---

*In the Hebrew numbering, Ps 34:10

their father was dying they began to lament. And as we have learned from some men who were present there, the saint, whose soul had not yet departed, opened his eyes, and looked around on either side, with wonderful joy and gladness of countenance; for he was gazing upon the holy angels that had come to meet him. Then Diormit raised the holy right hand, to bless the saints' company of monks. And the venerable father himself at the same time moved his hand, as much as he was able, in order that he might be seen to bless the brothers even by the movement of his hand, a thing that in the departure of his soul be could not do by voice. And after the holy benediction thus expressed he presently breathed out his spirit.

When that had left the tabernacle of the body, his face continued to be ruddy, and in a wonderful degree gladdened by the vision of angels, so much that it seemed like the face not of a dead man, but of a living sleeper.

Lk 6:47,48; Sir 25:15

℟. If anyone comes to me and listens to my commandments and
　carries them out, I will tell you what he is like; * he is like a man who,
when building a house, digs deep and lays the foundation upon rock.
℣. Blessed is he who fears the Lord; he has no equal; * he is like a man
　who, when building a house, digs deep and lays the foundation upon
　rock.

Collect
ALMIGHTY God, who didst fill the heart of Columba with the joy of the Holy Spirit, and with deep love for those in his care: grant to thy pilgrim people grace to follow him, strong in faith, sustained by hope, and made one in the love that binds us to thee; through Jesus Christ thy Son our Lord, who liveth and reigneth with thee, in the unity of the Holy Spirit, one God, for ever and ever.

Saint Richard, Bishop of Chichester, 1253
(16 June)

Proper of the Day and Common of Pastors: for a Bishop

A reading from the *Life of Saint Richard* by Ralph Bocking

God had so completely filled [blessed Richard's] heart with the virtue of hospitality that he would open the lap of his mercy to all who approached him and as far as possible receive them under the roof of his worldly house and give instructions that they should be afforded the necessities of this life appropriate to persons of their station, for he was always careful o remember the saying of Our Lord which, as he himself bears witness, will be recalled at the Last Judgment: 'I was a stranger and you took me in' (Mt 25:35). Indeed, he well understood what the commentator Haymo says about the verse which describes the bishop as 'given to hospitality' (1 Tim 3:2): 'A layman or any other churchman fulfils the duty of hospitality if he receives two or three poor persons. But a bishop is regarded as lacking hospitality if he does not receive all men.' Accordingly, his generosity and charity were not limited to the great palaces in which he dwelt and, not content with the crowds who came to him, he regarded himself as in debt to all poor men and, wherever of his journeys he might find the poor, he strove to provide them with all their needs. Whenever he entered the boroughs or townships of his diocese, he would make careful enquiry after any poor persons who were sick or infirm and it was his habit to afford them not only the gifts of his charity but also the comfort of his own presence and feed them upon the spiritual nourishment of the word of God, teaching them patience and counselling them that the hard road of poverty removes all taint of sin and showing them what great joys in the next life follow upon true and voluntary poverty. He regarded this duty of spiritual refreshment as a task especially his own and sought to add the savour of God's word to the nourishment with which he fed Christ's poor. Moreover, he often strove to fulfil this duty in person, but he sometimes did so through the Friars Preachers or Friars Minors.

In truth the Father of Mercies had so amplified and enlarged the bowels of his mercy that, although restrained by the bounds of a three-fold poverty – that is

---

Ralph Bocking, *The Life of Saint Richard Bishop of Chichester* I. 21, in D. Jones (ed.), *Saint Richard of Chichester. The Sources for his Life* (Lewes: Sussex Record Society, 1995), pp. 180-181.

to say the pressing obligations of his debts, the confiscation of the property of his diocese, and above all the pressures of dearth and famine – he could never restrain the natural kindness of his heart which was filled with the generosity of true charity. For instance, Sir Richard de Bagendon, a prudent man who belonged to a military order and who was the saint's brother according to the flesh, was entrusted with the care of the bishop's estates. On one occasion he remarked that the bishop had scarcely enough to provide for his own and therefore should not give so lavishly to such great numbers of the poor; the bishop, however, overflowed in the bowels of his goodness and replied, 'My dear brother Richard is it just or right in the sight of God that we should eat and drink from vessels of gold and silver while Christ in his poor is crucified with hunger and the poor are faint and dying from lack of nourishment?' And he added, 'I know very well how to eat and drink from a wooden bowl or platter, just as my father did. Therefore, let these gold and silver vessels be taken and sold and with the money feed the limbs of Christ who redeemed us and ours not with corruptible gold and silver but with his own precious blood. My horse, too, is a fine and valuable animal. Let him be sold as well and let the money he fetches be used to feed Christ's poor.'

Ps [88:20, 21-23] 89:19, 20-21; Jer 3:15

℟.To your friends the prophets you said, I have exalted one chosen
   from the people. I have found David, my servant; * with my holy oil
I have anointed him, and my hand shall always be with him.
℣. I will give you shepherds after my own heart, and these shall feed
   you on knowledge and discretion; * with my holy oil I have anointed
him, and my hand shall always be with him.

Collect
MOST merciful redeemer, who gavest to thy bishop Richard a love of learning, a zeal for souls and a devotion to the poor: grant that, encouraged by his example, and aided by his prayers, we may know thee more clearly, love thee more dearly, and follow thee more nearly, day by day; who livest and reignest with the Father, in the unity of the Holy Spirit, ever one God, world without end.

Saint Alban, first Martyr of Britain
(20 June)

Proper of the Day and Common of Martyrs

Reading and Responsory as in the Liturgy of Hours

O ETERNAL Father, who, when the gospel of Christ first came to our land, didst gloriously confirm the faith of Alban by making him the first to win the martyr's crown: grant that, assisted by his prayers and following his example in the fellowship of the Saints, we may worship thee, the living God, and faithfully witness to Jesus Christ thy Son our Lord, who liveth and reigneth with thee, in the unity of the Holy Spirit, one God, for ever and ever.

Saint John Fisher, Bishop, and
Saint Thomas More, Martyrs
(22 June)

The following passage may be read in the Divine Office according to the Use of this Customary but not at the Office of Readings in the Liturgy of Hours of the Roman Rite.

A reading from St John Fisher, *Exposition of the Seven Penitential Psalms*

To take the office of a doctor or teacher of God's laws is no small charge. It is a great jeopardy, and when I myself remember it, I am often afraid. For many times I think on Saint Paul's saying, if I do not teach the people God's laws, I shall be damned (cf 1 Cor 9:16). I fear that if we hide that gift of God, if we do not give a good account of the talent he left us, it shall be said to us at the dreadful Day of Judgment, as it is written in the Gospel, 'Why did you not give

---

St John Fisher, *Exposition of the Seven Penitential Psalms*, 'Psalm Fifty', in *Saint John Fisher, Exposition of the Seven Penitential Psalms.* In modern English and with an introduction by Anne Barbeau Gardiner (San Francisco: Ignatius, 1998), pp. 126-128.

me a true and just account of my money?' (Lk 19:23), that is to say, of the learning I gave you, with which you should have taught the people my laws. Also, even if we teach and help the hearers by it, yet a great peril remains, when any praise is given us for our learning, that we not be stricken with pride or vainglory by knowing ourselves praised. The miserable corruption of our nature makes us so liable to fall that when we do anything, no matter how little praiseworthy, it is a marvel if we do not offend with vainglory.

But in truth, if a due order is kept in our teaching of others, as we said before, every man according to his learning and ability, that is to say, if first we endeavour to amend our own lives, purge our own souls, try as much as we can to learn the wisdom of our Lord, and by our earnest prayer ask God for clean hearts and the grace of the Holy Ghost by which to order our own steps in the way of God, not for the vain praise of the world, but only to bring those who err into the right way, that they by our living and doctrine may be turned to that blessed Lord, then what we do shall be to the honour of God and the profit to our neighbour. And so, it follows, 'I will teach the unjust thy ways, and the wicked shall be converted to thee' (Ps 50: 15), as he might say: blessed Lord, if you look not upon my sins but remove my wickedness, create a new heart in me and endow me with the gift of the Holy Ghost, then I shall teach those who err, bring them into your ways, and they will be turned to worship you.

Truly, the prophet, after his great offence, kept this same order. Saint Paul also, having been made clean and inspired with the Holy Ghost after his great persecution of Christ's Church, taught all people openly the right way to come to heaven and made plain to all wicked creatures the ways of almighty God. Christ our Saviour gives us all warning to do so, saying, if your neighbour or brother offend you, correct him charitably (cf Mt 18:15). Therefore, let each of us ask Almighty God for a clean heart and the Holy Ghost, so that we may teach wicked people the ways of salvation and they may the sooner by our doctrine turn to him.

Saint Etheldreda (Audrey), Abbess
(23 June)

Proper of the Day and Common of Saints: for Religious

A reading from the Venerable Bede,
The Ecclesiastical History of the English People

King Ecgfrith married a wife named Etheldreda, the daughter of Anna, king of the East Angles, who has often been referred to, a very religious man and noble both in mind and deed. She had previously been married to an ealdorman of the South Gyrwe, named Tondberht. But he died shortly after the marriage and on his death she was given to King Ecgfrith. Though she lived with him for twelve years she still preserved the glory of perfect virginity. When I asked Bishop Wilfrid of blessed memory whether this was true, because certain people doubted it, he told me that he had the most perfect proof of her virginity; in fact Ecgfrith had promised to give him estates and money if he could persuade the queen to consummate their marriage, because he knew that there was none whom she loved more than Wilfrid himself. [...]

For a long time she had been asking the king to allow her to relinquish the affairs of this world and to serve Christ, the only true King, in a monastery; when at length and with difficulty she gained his permission, she entered the monastery of the Abbess Æbbe, Ecgfrith's aunt, which is situated in a place called Coldingham, receiving the veil and habit of a nun from Bishop Wilfrid. A year afterwards she was herself appointed abbess in the district called Ely, where she built a monastery and became, by the example of her heavenly life and teaching, the virgin mother of many virgins dedicated to God. It is related of her that, from the time she entered the monastery, she would never wear linen but only woollen garments and would seldom take a hot bath except just before the greater feasts, such as Easter, Pentecost, and Epiphany, and then last of all, after the other handmaidens of Christ who were present had washed themselves, assisted by herself and her attendants. She rarely ate more than once a day except at the greater festivals or because of urgent necessity; she

---

Bede, *The Ecclesiastical History of the English People* IV/ 19 (17), in Bede, *The Ecclesiastical History of the English People, The Greater Chronicle, Bede's Letter to Egbert*, edited with an introduction and notes by Judith McClure and Roger Collins (Oxford: Oxford University Press, 2008 [1994]), pp. 202-203.

always remained in the church at prayer from the office of matins until dawn, unless prevented by serious illness.

There are indeed some who say that, by the spirit of prophecy, she not only foretold the plague that was to be the cause of her death but also openly declared, in the presence of all, the number of those of the monastery who were to be taken from the world by the same pestilence. She was taken to the Lord in the midst of her people, after holding the rank of abbess for seven years. When she died she was buried by her own command in a wooden coffin, in the ranks of the other nuns, as her turn came.

cf Phil 4:8-9

℟. Do all that is true, all that is noble, all that is just and pure, all that
is lovable and gracious,* and the God of peace will be with you.
℣. If there is any excellence, if there is anything worthy of praise,
think about these things,* and the God of peace will be with you.

Collect
O ETERNAL God, who didst bestow such grace on thy servant Etheldreda that she gave herself wholly to the life of prayer and to the service of thy true religion: grant that, through her intercession, we may in like manner seek thy kingdom in our earthly lives, that by thy guidance we may be united in the glorious fellowship of thy Saints; through Jesus Christ thy Son our Lord, who liveth and reigneth with thee, in the unity of the Holy Spirit, one God, for ever and ever.

Saint Oliver Plunket, Bishop, Martyr
(1 July)

Proper of the Day and Common of Martyrs

Reading and Responsory as in the Liturgy of Hours

O GOD our Father, who didst fill Saint Oliver with thy Spirit of fortitude, enabling him to feed thy flock with his word, and to lay down his life for the faith. Keep us strong in the same true faith and help us to proclaim it everywhere. We ask this through Jesus Christ thy Son our Lord, who liveth and reigneth with thee, in the unity of the Holy Spirit, one God, for ever and ever.

Saint Swithun, Bishop
(15 July)

Proper of the Day and Common of Pastors: for a Bishop

From the anonymous *Life of Saint Swithun, Bishop and Confessor*

Saint Swithun, the patron and supporter of the Holy Catholic Church, was possessed of the burning desire to construct churches by the generous provision of funding in those places where they previously did not exist; and where churches lay in ruins, their walls collapsed and dilapidated, he very eagerly restored them to the service of the Lord. When the opportunity fell to him of consecrating some such church, on that occasion just as always he provided an attractive example for everyone of his humility and devoutness. For he did not employ any mule- or horse-drawn vehicle, nor did he make any display of worldly ceremony, but accompanied only by his own clergy and household he humbly – as was his custom – walked barefoot to the church he was to consecrate. But he did this not by day but by night, wisely avoiding the

---

Vita sancti Swithuni episcopi et confessoris, 7-8, in M. Lapidge, *The Cult of Saint Swithun*, with contributions by John Crook, Robert Deshman, and Susan Rankin (Oxford: Clarendon Press, 2003), pp. 637-638.

acclamation and praise of human adulation, not wishing to be considered with or among those of whom it is said that, since they loved men's praise, they 'received their reward'. He took his meals not with the rich but with the poor and needy. He always kept his mouth open in readiness to invite sinners to penitence, and urged, through the varied store of his discourse, those standing in a secure situation to avoid a fall, and the fallen moreover that they make an effort to get up. He took food sparingly and moderately, not to stuff but to sustain himself; he allowed himself only a little sleep, so that he could rise refreshed for God's service, and so that he would not expire after so many vigils and other exertions; he was always intent on psalmody and plain-chant, and never relinquished his fervour for ceaseless prayer; he always spoke to his neighbour as if to himself, in humble and modest speech, about what useful, virtuous, devout or holy course is to be followed in matters of ecclesiastical law.

Saint Swithun, God's holy servant, lived therefore for the true fulfilment of God's commandments from the beginnings of his youth up to his departure from this life, preserving his heart with every vigilance in spiritual cleanness and purity, remaining an irreproachable guardian of catholic and apostolic doctrine, and a watchful instructor and teacher of all his sons who were spiritually reborn in the pursuit of the religious vocation. And although there was virtually no moral excellence whose summit he had not himself attained, he nevertheless remained especially zealous in his attachment to humility and gentleness; pursuing peace and holiness he thirsted for the fountain of life and eternal beatitude; aspiring to the prize of his heavenly calling, he sought to end his life in peace. When, therefore, he had disposed properly arranged – according to ecclesiastical ceremony – the house and church of God, over which he had presided as holy patron and pastor, this victor of the flesh and fugitive of the world, secure in his crown, departed blessedly from his habitation in this world, in the third year of the reign of Æthelberht, king of the English and the son of glorious King Æthelwulf; he departed exulting and rejoicing, because it was said to him by the Lord God, 'Well done, good and faithful servant, because thou hast been faithful over a few things, enter thou into the joy of thy Lord' (Mt 25: 21).

Ps [88:20, 21-23] 89:19, 20-21; Jer 3:15

℟ To your friends the prophets you said, I have exalted one chosen
   from the people, I have found David, my servant; * with my holy oil
I have anointed him, and my hand shall always be with him.
℣ I will give you shepherds after my own heart, and these shall feed
   you on knowledge and discretion; * with my holy oil I have anointed
him, and my hand shall always be with him.

Collect

ALMIGHTY God, by whose grace we celebrate again the feast of thy
servant Swithun: grant that, as he governed with gentleness the people
committed to his care, so we, assisted by his prayers and rejoicing in
our inheritance in Christ, may ever seek to build up thy Church in
unity and love; through Jesus Christ thy Son our Lord, who liveth and
reigneth with thee, in the unity of the Holy Spirit, one God, for ever
and ever.

Saint Osmund, Bishop
(16 July)

Proper of the Day and Common of Pastors: for a Bishop

From the Anonymous *Life of Saint Osmund*

The holy Osmund… on his return to his parental home, used to have no
thought for anything of the world, anything of earth, but found leisure only for
continual prayer and meditation. And knowing, as he did, what risks are
commonly incurred by piety in the midst of wealth, by chastity amid luxury, by
humility among honours, he, therefore, gave his mind to soberness, humility,
and mercy, jealously guarding himself from the snares the world, the flesh, and
the devil; and, after the example of the apostle, keeping under his body and
bringing it into subjection, he compelled it, by a manifold discipline, to be in
obedience to his spirit. For during a long time he used to wear a hair shirt next
his skin, and when, on account of the excessive debility of his body, he left it

Anon, *Vita Beati Osmundi*, translated in H. T. Armfield, *The Legend of Christian
Art, illustrated in the Statutes of Salisbury Cathedral* (Salisbury: Brown; London:
Simpkin, Marshall; 1869), pp. 141-143.

off, he exchanged the practice for other works of piety, expending upon the poor, for instance, a certain sum of money which no one could definitely ascertain. He used to fast always on Wednesdays and Fridays, but especially in Advent and Lent, on which days he used to abstain from fish and fruit, and used to take only bread soaked in water, subduing himself continually with very many secret abstinences.

In short, the radiancy of every virtue was so brilliant in him that, in proportion to the nobility of his parentage, like a second David, he bore himself with the greater humility, and in the presence of God seemed the more vile in his own eyes. For every Saturday he was accustomed in secret to wash, wipe, and humbly kiss the feet and likewise the hands of certain poor people, giving to every one of them at the same time a certain sum of money. Oftentimes, also, on solemn vigils and certain other days before that he took a meal himself he used to furnish ample dishes for twenty poor people.

Once as he was going alone to church the Devil appeared to him, and tried to prevent his going any further. Then said Osmund to him, 'Who art thou?' And to him the Devil replied, 'I am the Devil, who at thy hands suffer much harm; and therefore I was just now wishing to turn thee from thy holy purpose'. Osmund said, 'What harm dost thou suffer at my hands?' The Devil replied, 'In one trifle thou hast the better of me. For though thou fastest, neither do I eat; thou watchest, and I without exception do not sleep; thou toilest, and I never rest; but there is one thing in which thou hast the better of me'. 'What is that?', said Osmund. 'thy humility', replied the Devil, 'on account of which I cannot get thee in my power'. And with these words the Devil vanished. Osmund, however, took no vain-glory from this incident, but, having before given his mind to humility, he was afterwards most humble, and gave God thanks.

Mal 2:7; Tit 1:7, 9

℟ Men listen eagerly to the words of the priest, seeking knowledge
    and instruction from him,* because he is the messenger of the Lord
    of hosts.
℣ A bishop should be God's steward, capable of giving instruction in
    sound doctrine,* because he is the messenger of the Lord of hosts.

Collect

O GOD, whose miracles of old we perceive to shine forth even in our days to the magnifying of thy name, and the praise and honour of Saint Osmund, Confessor and Bishop: mercifully grant us, at the intercession of him whose feast we keep, both to glorify thee in this present world, and to enjoy thy presence in that which is to come; through Jesus Christ thy Son our Lord, who liveth and reigneth with thee, in the unity of the Holy Spirit, one God, for ever and ever.

Saint Oswald, Martyr
(5 August)

Proper of the Day and Common of Martyrs

A reading from the Venerable Bede,
The Ecclesiastical History of the English People

Oswald, as soon as he had come to the throne, was anxious that the whole race under his rule should be filled with the grace of the Christian faith of which he had so wonderful an experience in overcoming the barbarians. So he sent to the Irish elders among whom he and his thegns had received the sacrament of baptism when he was an exile. He requested them to send a bishop by whose teaching and ministry the race over whom he ruled might learn the privileges of faith in our Lord and receive the sacraments. his request was granted without delay. They sent him Bishop Aidan, a man of outstanding gentleness, devotion, and moderation, who had a zeal for God though not entirely according to knowledge. For after the manner of his race, as we have often mentioned, he was accustomed to celebrate Easter Sunday between the fourteenth and the twentieth day of the moon. The northern province of the Irish and the whole nation of the Picts were still celebrating Easter Sunday according to this rule right up to that time, thinking that in this observance they were following the writings of the esteemed and holy father, Anatolius. Every instructed person can very easily judge whether this is true or not. But the Irish peoples who lived in the southern part of Ireland had long before learned to observe Easter according to canonical custom, through the teaching of the pope.

On the bishop's arrival, the king gave him a place for his Episcopal see on the island of Lindisfarne, in accordance with his wishes. As the tide ebbs and flows, this place is surrounded twice daily by the waves of the sea like an island and twice, when the shore is left dry, it becomes again attached to the mainland. The king humbly and gladly listened to the bishop's admonitions in all matters,

---

Bede, *The Ecclesiastical History of the English People* III. 3 and 6 in Bede, *The Ecclesiastical History of the English People, The Greater Chronicle, Bede's Letter to Egbert,* edited with an introduction and notes by Judith McClure and Roger Collins (Oxford: Oxford University Press, 2008 [1994]), pp. 113-114, 118-119.

diligently seeking to build up and extend the Church of Christ in his kingdom. It was indeed a beautiful sight when the bishop was preaching the gospel, to see the king acting as interpreter of the heavenly word for his ealdormen and thegns, for the bishop was not completely at home in the English tongue, while the king had gained a perfect knowledge of Irish during the long period of his exile.

From that time, as the days went by, many came from the country of the Irish into Britain and to those English kingdoms over which Oswald reigned, preaching the word of faith with great devotion. [...]

With such a man as bishop to instruct them, King Oswald, together with the people over which he ruled, learned to hope for those heavenly realms which were unknown to their forefathers; and also Oswald gained from the one God who made heaven and earth greater earthly realms than any of his predecessors had possessed. In fact, he held under his swat all the peoples and kingdoms of Britain, divided among the speakers of four different languages, British, Pictish, Irish, and English.

Though he wielded supreme power over the whole land, he was always wonderfully humble, kind, and generous to the poor and to strangers. For example, the story is told that on a certain occasion, one Easter Day, when he had sat down to dinner with Bishop Aidan, a silver dish was placed on the table before him full of rich foods. They had just raised their hands to ask a blessing on the bread when there came in an officer of the king, whose duty it was to relieve the needy, telling him that a very great multitude of poor people from every district were sitting in the precincts and asking alms of the king. He at once ordered the dainties which had been set in front of him to be carried to the poor, the dish to be broken up, and the pieces divided amongst them. The bishop, who was sitting by, was delighted with this pious act, grasped him by the right hand, and said, 'May this hand never decay'. his blessing and his prayer were fulfilled in this way: when Oswald was killed in battle, his hand and arm were cut off from the rest of his body, and they have remained uncorrupt until this present time; they are in fact preserved in a silver shrine in Saint Peter's church, in the royal city which is called after Queen Bebba (Bamburgh) and are venerated with fitting respect by all.

℟. The saint will blossom like the lily; * he will flourish for ever in the presence of our God.

℣. Planted in the house of the Lord, established in the courts of our God, * he will flourish for ever in the presence of our God.

Collect

O LORD God almighty, who didst so kindle the faith of thy servant King Oswald with thy Spirit that he set up the sign of the cross in his kingdom and turned his people to the light of Christ: grant that we, being fired by the same Spirit, may ever bear our cross before the world and be found faithful servants of the gospel; through Jesus Christ thy Son our Lord, who liveth and reigneth with thee, in the unity of the Holy Spirit, one God, for ever and ever.

Blessed Dominic of the Mother of God (Dominic Barberi), Priest (26 August)

Proper of the Day and Common of Pastors

Reading and Responsory as in the Liturgy of Hours

O GOD of salvation, thou chosest the blessed Dominic Barberi to be a minister of thy love, so that his teaching and example might help many to find peace and reconciliation in thy Church; guide our steps along the same way of love until we come to its eternal reward. We ask this through Jesus Christ thy Son our Lord, who liveth and reigneth with thee, in the unity of the Holy Spirit, one God, for ever and ever.

**Saints Margaret Clitherow, Anne Line,
and Margaret Ward, Virgin, Martyrs
(30 August)**

Proper of the Day and Common of Martyrs

A reading from the *Life of Margaret Clitherow* by John Mush

About eight of the clock the sheriffs came to her, and she being ready expecting them, having trimmed up her head with new inkle, and carrying on her arm the new habit of linen with inkle strings, which she had prepared to bind her hands, went cheerfully to her marriage, as she called it; dealing her alms in the street, which was so full of people that she could scarce pass by them. She went barefoot and barelegged, her gown loose about her. Fawcet, the sheriff, made haste and said, 'Come away, Mrs. Clitherow'. The martyr answered merrily, 'Good Master Sheriff, let me deal my poor alms before I go now, for my time is but short'. They marvelled all to see her joyful countenance.

The place of execution was the tollbooth, six or seven yards distant from the prison. There were present at her martyrdom the two sheriffs of York, Fawcet and Gibson, Frost, a minister, Fox, Mr Cheeke's kinsman, with another of his men, the four sergeants, which had hired certain beggars to do the murder, three or four men, and four women.

The martyr coming to the place, kneeled her down, and prayed to herself. The tormentors bade her pray with them, and they would pray with her. The martyr denied, and said, 'I will not pray with you, and you shall not pray with me; neither will I say Amen to your prayers, nor shall you to mine'. Then they willed her to pray for the Queen's majesty. The martyr began in this order. First, in the hearing of them all, she prayed for the Catholic Church, then for the Pope's Holiness, Cardinals and other Fathers which have charge of souls, and then for all Christian princes. At which words the tormentors interrupted her, and willed her not to put her majesty among that company; yet the martyr proceeded in this order, 'and especially for Elizabeth, Queen of England, that God turn her to the Catholic faith, and that after this mortal life she may

John Mush, *Life of Margaret Clitherow*, XX, in J. Morris, SJ, *The Troubles of our Catholic Forefathers related by Themselves* , 3rd series (Westmead: Gregg, 1970 [1877], pp. 430-432.

receive the blessed joys of heaven. For I wish as much good', quoth she, 'to her majesty's soul as to my own'. Sheriff Gibson, abhorring the cruel fate, stood weeping at the door. Then said Fawcet, 'Mrs Clitherow, you must remember that you die for treason'. The martyr answered, 'No, no, Mr. Sheriff, I die for the love of my Lord Jesu;' which last words she spoke with a loud voice.

Then Fawcet commanded her to put off her apparel; 'For you must die', said he, 'naked, as judgment was given and pronounced against you'. The martyr with the other women requested him on their knees that she might die in her smock, and that for the honour of womanhood they would not see her naked; but that would not be granted. Then she requested that women might unapparel her, and that they would turn their faces from her for that time.

The women took off her clothes, and put upon her the long habit of linen. Then very quietly she laid her down upon the ground, her face covered with a handkerchief, the linen habit being placed over her as far as it would reach, all the rest of her body being naked. The door was laid upon her, her hands she joined towards her face. Then the sheriff said, 'Nay, you must have your hands bound'. The martyr put forth her hands over the door still joined. Then two sergeants parted them, and with the inkle strings, which she had prepared for that purpose, bound them to two posts, so that her body and her arms made a perfect cross. They willed her again to ask the Queen's majesty's forgiveness, and to pray for her. The martyr said she prayed for her. They also willed her to ask her husband's forgiveness. The martyr said, 'If ever I have offended him, but for my conscience, I ask him forgiveness'.

After this they laid weight upon her, which when she first felt, she said, 'Jesu! Jesu! Jesu! have mercy upon me!,' which were the last words she was heard to speak. She was in dying one quarter of an hour. A sharp stone, as much as a man's fist, put under her back; upon her was laid to the quantity of seven or eight hundred-weight at the least which, breaking her ribs, caused them to burst forth of the skin. Thus most victoriously this gracious martyr overcame all her enemies, passing [from] this mortal life with marvellous triumph into the peaceable city of God, there to receive a worthy crown of endless immortality and joy.

Rom 8:34-35, 37

℟. Christ Jesus is at God's right hand and pleads our cause. * Then what can separate us from the love of Christ? Can affliction or hardship? Can persecution, hunger, nakedness, peril or the sword?
℣. These are the trials through which we triumph, by the power of him who loved us. * Then what can separate us from the love of Christ? Can affliction or hardship? Can persecution, hunger, nakedness, peril or the sword?

Collect

STEADFAST God, as we honour the fidelity in life and constancy in death of thy holy martyrs Margaret Clitherow, Anne Line and Margaret Ward: we pray thee to raise up in our day women of courage and resource to care for thy household; Jesus Christ thy Son our Lord, who liveth and reigneth with thee, in the unity of the Holy Spirit, one God, for ever and ever.

Saint Aidan, Bishop, and Saints of Lindisfarne (31 August)

Proper of the Day and Common of Pastors: for a Bishop or Common of Saints: for Missionaries or for Religious

A reading from the Venerable Bede,
The Ecclesiastical History of the English People

Aidan taught the clergy many lessons about the conduct of their lives but above all he left them a most salutary example of abstinence and self-control; and the best recommendation of his teaching to all was that he himself practised among his fellows. For he neither sought after nor cared for worldly possessions but he rejoiced to hand over at once, to any poor man he met, the gifts which he had received from kings or rich men of the world. He used to travel everywhere, in town and country, not on horseback but on foot, unless

---

Bede, *The Ecclesiastical History of the English People* III. 5 in Bede, *The Ecclesiastical History of the English People, The Greater Chronicle, Bede's Letter to Egbert*, edited with an introduction and notes by Judith McClure and Roger Collins (Oxford: Oxford University Press, 2008 [1994]), pp. 116-117.

compelled by urgent necessity to do otherwise, in order that, as he walked along, whenever he saw people whether rich or poor, he might at once approach them and, if they were unbelievers, invite them to accept the mystery of the faith; or, if they were believers, that he might strengthen them in the faith, urging them by word and deed to practise almsgiving and good works.

Aidan's life was in great contrast to our modern slothfulness; all who accompanied him, whether tonsured or laymen, had to engage in some form of study, that is to say, to occupy themselves with either reading the scriptures or learning the psalms. This was the daily task of Aidan himself and of all who were with him, wherever they went. And if it happened, as it rarely did, that he was summoned to feast with the king, he went with one or two of his clergy, and, after taking a little food, he hurried away either to read with his people or to pray. At that time a number of men and women, instructed by his example, formed the habit of prolonging their fast on Wednesdays and Fridays throughout the year, until the ninth hour, with the exception of the period between Easter and Pentecost. Neither respect nor fear made him keep silence about the sins of the rich, but he would correct them with a stern rebuke. He would never give money to powerful men of the world, but only food on such occasions as he entertained them; on the contrary he distributed gifts of money which he received from the rich either, as we have said, for the use of the poor or for the redemption of those who had been unjustly sold into slavery. In fact, many of those whom he redeemed for a sum of money he afterwards made his disciples and, when he had trained and instructed them, he ordained them priests.

Sir 45:3; Ps [77] 78:70, 71

℣ The Lord enhanced his reputation with kings. He gave him
  commandments for his people, * and showed him a vision of his
  own glory.
℟ The Lord chose him to be his servant, to be the shepherd of Israel
  his possession, * and showed him a vision of his own glory.

Collect
O EVERLASTING God, who didst send thy gentle bishop Aidan to proclaim the gospel in this land: grant that, aided by his prayers, we may live after his teaching in simplicity, humility and love for the poor; through Jesus Christ thy Son our Lord, who liveth and reigneth with thee, in the unity of the Holy Spirit, one God, for ever and ever.

Saint Gregory the Great, Pope, Doctor of the Church
(3 September)

Proper of the Day and Common of Pastors
or of Doctors of the Church

The following passage may be read in the Divine Office according to the Use of this
Customary but not at the Office of Readings in the Liturgy of Hours of the
Roman Rite.

A reading from the Venerable Bede,
The Ecclesiastical History of the English People

We must not fail to relate the story about St Gregory which has come down to us as a tradition of our forefathers. It explains the reason why he showed such earnest solicitude for the salvation of our race. It is said that one day, soon after some merchants had arrived in Rome, a quantity of merchandise was exposed for sale in the market-place. Crowds came to buy and Gregory too was amongst them. As well as other merchandise he saw some boys put up for sale, with fair complexions, handsome faces, and lovely hair. On seeing them he asked, so it is said, from what region or land they had been bought. He was told that they came from the island of Britain, whose inhabitants were like that in appearance. He asked again whether those islanders were Christians or still entangled in the errors of heathenism. He was told that they were heathen. Then with a deep-drawn sigh he said, 'Alas that the author of darkness should have men so bright of face in his grip, and that minds devoid of inward grace should bear so graceful an outward form'. Again he asked for the name of the race. He was told that they were called *Angli*. 'Good', he said, 'they have the faces of angels, and such men should be fellow-heirs of the angels in heaven'. 'What is the name', he asked, 'of the kingdom from which they have been

---

St Bede, *Ecclesiastical History of the English People* II. 1, in Bede, *The Ecclesiastical History of the English People, The Greater Chronicle, Bede's Letter to Egbert*, edited with an introduction and notes by Judith McClure and Roger Collins (Oxford: Oxford University Press, 2008 [1994]), pp. 70-71.

brought?' He was told that the men of the kingdom were called *Deiri*. '*Deiri*', he replied, '*De ira!* Good! Snatched from the wrath of Christ and called to his mercy. And what is the name of the king of the land?' He was told that it was Ælle; and playing on the name he said, 'Alleluia! The praise of God the Creator must be sung in those parts'.

So he went to the bishop of Rome and of the apostolic see, for he himself had not yet been made pope, and asked him to send some ministers if the word to the race of the Angles in Britain to convert them to Christ. He added that he himself was prepared to carry out the task with the help of the Lord provided that the pope was willing. But he was unable to perform this mission, because although the pope was willing to grant his request, the citizens of Rome could not permit him to go so far away from the city. Soon after he had become pope, he fulfilled the task which he had long desired. It is true that he sent other preachers, but he himself helped their preaching to bear fruit by his encouragement and prayers. I have thought it proper to insert this story into this Church History, based as it is on the tradition which we have received from our ancestors.

Collect

O MERCIFUL Father, who didst choose thy bishop Gregory to be a servant of the servants of God: grant that, like him, we may ever desire to serve thee by proclaiming thy gospel to the nations, and may ever rejoice to sing thy praises; through Jesus Christ thy Son our Lord, who liveth and reigneth with thee, in the unity of the Holy Spirit, one God, for ever and ever.

Saint Cuthbert, Bishop
(4 September)

Proper of the Day and Common of Pastors: for a Bishop

A reading from the *Life of Cuthbert* by the Venerable Bede

As soon as Christmas was over Cuthbert sought out his island home once more. A crowd of the brethren gathered to see him off, one of whom, an old monk, strong in the faith though wasted away through dysentery, said to him, 'Tell us, my lord, when we may expect to see you again'. The answer came back as plain as the question (for Cuthbert knew it was true): 'When you bring back my corpse'. He was given almost two months to rediscover the delights of the quiet life and to fit mind and body into the strict discipline of his old routine; then he was suddenly felled by disease, to be prepared by the fires of internal pain for the joys of everlasting bliss. Let me tell you of his death verbatim, just as I had it from Herefrith, a sincerely devout priest and present abbot of Lindisfarne.

'After being wracked by three weeks of continual illness, he met his end in the following way. He took ill, you know, on a Wednesday, and it was on a Wednesday too that the disease conquered and he went to his Lord. [...] I went in to him', Herefrith continued, 'about the ninth hour and found him lying in a corner of the oratory opposite the altar. I sat down beside him. He said very little, for the weight of affliction made it hard for him to speak. But when I asked him rather urgently what counsel he was going to leave us as his testament or last farewell, he launched into a brief but significant discourse on peace and humility, and exhorted us to be on our guard against those who, far from delighting in these virtues, actively foster pride and discord.'

'"Preserve among yourselves unfailing divine charity, and when you have to hold council about your common affairs let your principal aim be to reach a unanimous decision. Live in mutual concord with all other servants of Christ; do not despise those of the household of faith who come to you seeking hospitality. Receive them, put them up, and set them on their way with kindness, treating them as one of yourselves. Do not think yourselves better than the rest of your companions who share the same faith and follow the

---

Saint Bede, *Life of Cuthbert* 37, 39, in J. F. Webb, *Lives of the Saints,* translated with an introduction (Harmondsworth: Penguin, 1965), pp. 116, 120-121.

monastic life. With those who have wandered from the unity of the Catholic faith, either through not celebrating Easter at the proper time or through evil living, you are to have no dealings. Never forget that if you should ever be forced to make the choice between two evils I would much rather you left the island, taking my bones with you, than that you should be a party to wickedness on any pretext whatsoever, bending your necks to the yoke of schism. Strive most diligently to learn the Catholic statutes of the fathers and put them into practice. Make it your special care to carry out those rules of the monastic life which God in his divine mercy has seen fit to give you through my ministry. I know that, though some might think my life despicable, none the less after my death you will see that my teachings are not to be easily dismissed."'

'These and like sayings he uttered at intervals, because the gravity of the disease, as I said before, had weakened his speech. He passed the day quietly till evening, awaiting the joys of the world to come, and went on peacefully with his prayers throughout the night. At the usual time for night prayer I gave him the sacraments that lead to eternal life. Thus fortified with the Lord's Body and Blood in preparation for the death he knew was now at hand, he raised his eyes heavenwards, stretched out his arms aloft, and with his mind rapt in the praise of the Lord sent forth his spirit to the bliss of Paradise'.

1 Tim 4:2,5; Acts 20:28

℟.Proclaim the message and, welcome or unwelcome, insist upon it;
refute falsehood, correct error, summon to obedience, but do all
with the patience that the work of teaching requires; * face suffering,
work to spread the gospel.

℣. Keep watch over the flock of which the Holy Spirit has given you
charge, as shepherds of the Church of God; * face suffering, work to
spread the gospel.

Collect

ALMIGHTY God, who didst call thy servant Cuthbert from following the flock to follow thy Son and to be a shepherd of thy people: in thy mercy, grant that we may so follow his example that we may bring those who are lost home to thy fold; through Jesus Christ thy Son our Lord, who liveth and reigneth with thee, in the unity of the Holy Spirit, one God, for ever and ever.

Saint Ninian, Bishop
(16 September)

Proper of the Day and Common of Pastors: for a Bishop

A reading from the Preface to the *Life of Saint Ninian*, by Saint Ælred

Divine authority, which from the beginning is acknowledged to have constituted the holy patriarch Abraham a father of many nations, and a prince of the faith predestined from ancient times by such an oracle as this – 'Get thee out of thy country, and from thy kindred, and from thy father's house, unto a land that I shall show thee, and I will make of thee a great nation' (Gen 12:1), recommends to us the glorious life of the most holy Ninian, on this wise, that this most blessed one leaving his country, and his father's house, learnt in a foreign land that which afterwards he taught unto his own, 'being placed by God over the nations and kingdoms, to root out, and to pull down, and to destroy, and to throw down, to build, and to plant (Jer 1:10). Of this most holy man, the Venerable Bede, calling attention in a very few words to the sacred beginnings of his life, the tokens of his sanctity, the dignity of his office, the fruit of his ministry, his most excellent end, and the reward of his toil, thus writes concerning him:-

'In the year after the incarnation of the Lord 565, at the time when Justin the Less, after Justinian, had received the government of the Roman Empire, there came to Britain out of Ireland a presbyter and abbot, remarkable for his monastic habit and rule, by name Columba, with the intention of preaching the word of God in the provinces of the Northern Picts; that is, to whose who were separated from the southern regions by lofty and rugged ranges of mountains. For the Southern Picts themselves, who dwell on this side of the same mountains, had long before abandoned idolatry, and embraced the faith in the truth, by the preaching of the word by bishop Ninian, a most reverend and holy man, of the nation of the Britons, who had at Rome been regularly instructed in the faith and mysteries of the truth; the seat of whose episcopate, dedicated to Saint Martin, and a remarkable church, where he rests in the body along with many saints, the nation of the Angles now possesses. That province,

---

Saint Ælred, 'Preface', *Life of Saint Ninian*, in *Lives of Saint Ninian and Saint Kentigern*, compiled in the twelfth century, edited from the best mss. by Alexander Penrose Forbes, D. C. L., Bishop of Brechin (Edinburgh: Edminston and Douglas, 1874), pp. 6-7.

appertaining to the province of the Bernicii, is vulgarly called "At the White House", for that there he built a church of stone in a way unusual among the Britons.'

On the trustworthy testimony of this great author, we have been made acquainted with the origin of Saint Ninian, in that he states that he was of the race of the Britons, trained in the rules of the faith in the Holy Roman Church; with his office, in that he declares him to have been a bishop and a preacher of the word of God; with the fruit of his labours, in that he proves that the Southern Picts were converted from idolatry to the true religion by his toil; and, with his end, in that he witnesses that he rests along with many saints in the church of Saint Martin.

1 Tim 6:11-12; Tit 2:1

℟. As a man dedicated to God, you must aim to be saintly and
    religious, filled with faith and love, patient and gentle. * Fight the good fight of the faith and win for yourself eternal life.
℣. What you preach must be in keeping with wholesome doctrine. *
    Fight the good fight of the faith and win for yourself eternal life.

Collect
ALMIGHTY and everlasting God, who didst call thy servant Ninian to preach the gospel to the people of northern Britain: raise up, we beseech thee, in this and every land, heralds and evangelists of thy kingdom, that thy Church may make known the immeasurable richesof thy Son our Saviour Jesus Christ, who liveth and reigneth with thee, in the unity of the Holy Spirit, one God, for ever and ever.

Saint Edith of Wilton, Religious
(16 September)

Proper of the Day and Common of Virgins

A reading from Goscelin, *The Life of the Holy Virgin Edith*

Edith made donations to everybody with the greatest charity, from her mother's hand and her own, as if she would have been willing to give away all the chattels of the monastery, if it could be granted to her that by using rough haircloth and abstinence she could give to the poor soft clothing and alms.

She was wounded by the pains of all; if anyone was scandalized, she was on fire. She put on the bowels of mercy, in him who bore our griefs in his conscious suffering. The condemned knew her as their refuge, captives knew her as one who would redeem them. She suffered on behalf of thieves as much as if they were her brothers Edward or Æthelred. She interposed herself between the sword and the neck so that the executioner would have to strike an innocent woman, or spare the guilty. She broke through the adamantine decrees of the laws and judgments; she overcame ferocious throngs with prayers, tears, kindness, gifts; and the prey was snatched from the very jaws of death. Whatever she demanded from her pious father by delegates or by her own speaking, this was in her heart – that he should increase the number of churches, support them with riches, extend the embrace of his mercy to all needs, and set free by his clemency those who were to be punished or sold into slavery. Her pity and concern did not seek any gifts for herself, but the well being of others. Nor was it difficult to obtain her requests from the indulgence of that father, whose throne has been prepared in mercy, whose judgment preferred to pardon rather than to punish (provided only the people's peace was preserved), so that the grace of his daughter would put aside his sword, even when it had been drawn. He, indeed, was dominated by justice and mercy; she was driven forward by mercy alone, by which the whole law is fulfilled.

She also gathered together an innumerable household of wild animals, loving with compassion all those works of the Creator in the spirit of his love, who is kind to all things, and whose mercies are over all his works, who hates none of

---

Goscelin, *The Life of the Holy Virgin Edith, 64,* in S. Hollis (ed.), *Writing the Wilton Women. Goscelin's* Legend of Edith *and* Liber confortatorius (Turnhout: Brepols, 2004), pp. 40-41.

the things which he has made, and preserves both men and beasts, and fills with blessing every living creature; who is not only wonderful on high, in holy places and in the stars of heaven, but also in the very worms of the earth. Their courtyard was attached to the wall of the monastery on the southern side, and here in its wide embrace they had their territories and their district outside the walls. The virgin of the Lord, as untouched by the evils of the world as she was innocent of them, had here enclosed her exotics and natives, the gifts of the mighty, and she, the pet lamb of Christ, looked after that wild sheepfold and untamed herd with daily provisioning; to prevent the jealousy of Judas from snarling at these little enclosures, she was generous to the animals after attending to the Lord's poor.

cf Rev 1:5, 6; Eph 5:2

℟. Christ loved us and washed away our sins with his blood; * he made of us a royal house, priests to serve his God and Father.

℣. Follow Christ by loving as he loved us, when he gave up his life for us; * he made of us a royal house, priests to serve his God and Father.

Saint Theodore of Canterbury
(19 September)

Proper of the Day and Common of Pastors: for a Bishop

A reading from the Venerable Bede,
The Ecclesiastical History of the English People

Theodore came to his church [at Canterbury] on Sunday 27 May [668], in the second year after his consecration, and there he spent twenty-one years, three months, and twenty-six days. Soon after he arrived, he visited every part of the island where the English peoples lived and was gladly welcomed and listened to by all. He was accompanied everywhere and assisted by Hadrian, as he gave

---

Bede, *The Ecclesiastical History of the English People* IV/ 2, in Bede, *The Ecclesiastical History of the English People, The Greater Chronicle, Bede's Letter to Egbert,* edited with an introduction and notes by Judith McClure and Roger Collins (Oxford: Oxford University Press, 2008 [1994]), pp. 172-173.

instruction on the ordering of a holy life and the canonical custom of celebrating Easter. He was the first of the archbishops whom the whole English Church consented to obey. And because both of them were extremely learned in sacred and secular literature, they attracted a crowd of students into whose minds they daily poured the streams of wholesome learning. They gave their hearers instruction not only in the books of holy Scripture but also in the art of metre, astronomy, and ecclesiastical computation. As evidence of this, some of their students still survive who know Latin and Greek just as well as their native tongue. Never had there been such happy times since the English first came to Britain; for having such brave Christian kings, they were a terror to all the barbarian nations, and the desires of all men were set on the joys of the heavenly kingdom of which they had only lately heard; while all who wished for instruction in sacred studies had teachers ready to hand.

[…] So Theodore journeyed to every district, consecrating bishops in suitable places and, with their help, correcting whatever he found imperfect. Among these he made it clear to Bishop Chad that his consecration had not been regular, whereupon the latter humbly replied, 'If you believe that my consecration was irregular, I gladly resign from the office; indeed I never believed myself to be worthy of it. But I consented to receive it, however unworthy, in obedience to the commands I received.' When Theodore heard his humble reply, he said that he ought not to give up his office; but he completed his consecration a second time after the catholic manner. At the same time, when Deusdedit was dead and while a bishop for the church at Canterbury was being sought for, consecrated, and sent, Wilfrid was also sent to Gaul from Britain to be consecrated and, since he returned before Theodore's arrival, he ordained priests and deacons even in Kent until such time as the archbishop arrived at his own see. When Theodore came soon afterwards to the city of Rochester, where the bishopric had long been vacant after the death of Damian, he consecrated a man whose name was Putta. The latter was very learned in ecclesiastical matters but showed little interest in secular affairs and was content with a simple life. He was especially skilled in liturgical chanting after the Roman manner, which he had learned from the disciples of the blessed Pope Gregory.

2 Tim 4:2,5; Acts 20:28

℟.Proclaim the message and, welcome or unwelcome, insist upon it; refute falsehood, correct error, summon to obedience, but do all with the patience that the work of teaching requires; * face suffering, work to spread the gospel.

℣. Keep watch over the flock of which the Holy Spirit has given you charge, as shepherds of the Church of God; * face suffering, work to spread the gospel.

Collect

O GOD, whose servant Theodore was called to this land, to set the Church on a firm foundation: by his prayer, build us always anew on the rock that is Christ, and keep thy household faithful to the call we have received; we ask this through Jesus Christ thy Son our Lord, who liveth and reigneth with thee, in the unity of the Holy Spirit, one God, for ever and ever.

Our Lady of Walsingham
(24 September)

Proper of the Day and Common of the Blessed Virgin Mary

A reading from the prayers and meditations of Saint Anselm

Mary, great Mary, most blessed of all Marys, greatest among women, great Lady, great beyond all measure, I long to love you with all my heart, I want to praise you with my lips, I desire to venerate you in my understanding, I love to pray you from my deepest being, I commit myself wholly to your protection.

Heart of my soul, stir yourself up as much as ever you can (if you can do anything at all), and let all that is within me praise the good Mary has done, love the blessing she has received, wonder at her loftiness, and beseech her kindness; for I need her defence daily, and in my need I desire, implore, and

---

Saint Anselm, 'Prayer to Saint Mary (3), to ask for her and Christ's love', in *The Prayers and Meditations of Saint Anselm with the Proslogion*. Translated and with an introduction by Sister Benedicta Ward, S. L. G. (London: Penguin, 1988 [1973]), pp. 115-117.

beseech it, and if it is not according to my desire, at least let it be above, or rather contrary to, what I deserve.

Queen of angels, Lady of the world, Mother of him who cleanses the world, I confess that my heart is unclean, and I am rightly ashamed to turn towards such cleanness, but I turn towards it to be made clean, in order to come to it. Mother of him who is the light of my heart, nurse of him who is the strength of my soul, I pray to you with my whole heart to the extent of my powers. Hear me, Lady, answer me, most mighty helper; let this filth be washed from my mind, let my darkness be illuminated, my lukewarmness blaze up, my listlessness be stirred. For in your blessed holiness you are exalted above all, after the highest of all, your Son, through you omnipotent Son, with your glorious Don, by your blessed Son. So as being above all after the Lord, who is my God and my all, your Son, in my heart I know and worship you, love you and ask for your affection, not because of my imperfect desires, but because it belongs to your Son to make and to save, to redeem and bring back to life.

Mother of the life of my soul, nurse of the redeemer of my flesh, who gave suck to the saviour of my whole being – but what am I saying? My tongue fails me, for my love is not sufficient. Lady, Lady, I am very anxious to thank you for so much, but I cannot think of anything worthy to say to you, and I am ashamed to offer you anything unworthy. How can I speak worthily of the mother of the Creator and Saviour, by whose sanctity my sins are purged, by whose integrity incorruptibility is given me, by whose virginity my soul falls in love with its Lord and is married to its God. What can I worthily tell of the mother of my Lord and God by whose fruitfulness I am redeemed from captivity, by whose child-bearing I am brought forth from eternal death, by whose offspring I who was lost am restored, and led back from my unhappy exile to my blessed homeland.

℟. Blessed is the holy Virgin Mary, and most worthy of all praise; *
through her has risen the Sun of Justice, Christ our God, by whom we are saved and redeemed.
℣. Let us joyfully celebrate this feast of the Blessed Virgin Mary, *
Through her has risen the Sun of Justice, Christ our God, by whom we are saved and redeemed.

Collect

O LORD God, in the mystery of the incarnation Mary conceived thy Son in her heart before she conceived him in her womb: grant that, as we, thy pilgrim people, rejoice in her patronage, we also may welcome him into our hearts, and so, like her, be made a holy house fit for his eternal dwelling; we ask this through Jesus Christ thy Son our Lord, who liveth and reigneth with thee, in the unity of the Holy Spirit, one God, for ever and ever.

Saint Thomas of Hereford, Bishop
(3 October)

Proper of the Day and Common of Pastors: for a Bishop

A reading from the evidence of Hugh le Barber
at the canonization proceedings of Saint Thomas Cantilupe

As to discretion and prudence, Hugh could speak only in general terms. He knew of his humility from personal experience. The lord Thomas spoke humbly to the poor and called them his brothers. He frequently chided Hugh and others of his household when they did not call them brothers. One day, when the lord Thomas was at a meal and had before him half-a-dozen poor people, he sent Robert le Whytacre of his household to the gate, to see if there were any brothers there and to bring two of their number up. Robert went to the gate and found no men in Religious Orders there, which was what he thought was meant by 'brothers', so returned and told the lord Thomas there were none. To this the lord Thomas replied by saying, 'What, none like these?', pointing out the poor men eating before him. Robert answered that there were twenty such, and was then asked to bring up five of them. This happened at Hampton in the diocese of Worcester, in the presence of Hugh and many others, about sixteen years before the lord Thomas became bishop.

He was humble in dress and bearing, but nevertheless made use of good clothing for himself and his household, and had beautiful palfreys. He was not ashamed to conform to what was suitable.

He was meek and gentle as a lamb, debonair, patient and kind. Hugh knew this from his manner of living and because he never knew him angered. When he reproved Hugh or any of his household and any made a rough reply, he taught them charitably so that they should mend their ways. Asked if he showed patience with the earl of Gloucester, Hugh replied that the strongest words he

Meryl Jancey, 'A Servant speaks of his Master. Hugh le Barber's Evidence in 1307', in idem (ed.), *Saint Thomas Cantilupe, Bishop of Hereford. Essays in his Honour* (Hereford: Friends of Hereford Cathedral, Publications Committeee for the Dean and Chapter, 1982), pp. 196-197, 199.

spoke were, 'Lord earl, lord earl, say what you please about me, I will not let the rights of my church go by on account of your menaces'.[…]

The lord Thomas was very sedulous in contemplation, studied much and pored over his books. It displeased him to be much interrupted at his studies. Hugh often saw him in chapel kneeling and prostrate and believes that at those times he was pleading with God. Asked if this was by day or by night, he replied that it was by day, before Mass, and afterwards, while he was at the universities.

When asked if Cantilupe was just and God-fearing, Hugh said that he knew that he was from talking with him. He never entered upon litigation unless his case was good. When he was sure of this, he pursued the cause vigorously to the end. He was greatly displeased to hear of any injustice. his fear of God was noticeable in his hatred of liars, luxury lovers, and unjust and evil men.

Mt 11:52; Prov 14:33

℟. When a teacher of the law has become a learner in the kingdom of heaven, he is like a householder, * who can produce from his store both the new and the old.
℣. Wisdom instructs even fools, but she makes her home in the heart of a discerning man, * who can produce from his store both the new and the old.

Blessed John Henry Newman, Priest
(9 October)

Proper of the Day and Common of Pastors

A reading from the writings of Blessed John Henry Newman, Priest

From the time that I became a Catholic, of course I have no further history of my religious opinions to narrate. In saying this, I do not mean to say that my mind has been idle, or that I have given up thinking on theological subjects; but

---

Bl. John Henry Newman, *Apologia pro Vita Sua* (London: Longmans, Green, 1864), pp. 238-239, 250-251.

that I have had no variations to record, and have had no anxiety of heart whatever. I have been in perfect peace and contentment; I never have had one doubt. I was not conscious to myself, on my conversion, of any change, intellectual or moral, wrought in my mind. I was not conscious of firmer faith in the fundamental truths of Revelation, or of more self-command; I had not more fervour; but it was like coming into port after a rough sea; and my happiness on that score remains to this day without interruption.

Nor had I any trouble about receiving those additional articles, which are not found in the Anglican Creed. Some of them I believed already, but not any one of them was a trial to me. I made a profession of them upon my reception with the greatest ease, and I have the same ease in believing them now. I am far of course from denying that every article of the Christian Creed, whether as held by Catholics or by Protestants, is beset with intellectual difficulties; and it is simple fact, that, for myself, I cannot answer those difficulties. Many persons are very sensitive of the difficulties of Religion; I am as sensitive of them as any one; but I have never been able to see a connexion between apprehending those difficulties, however keenly, and multiplying them to any extent, and on the other hand doubting the doctrines to which they are attached. Ten thousand difficulties do not make one doubt, as I understand the subject; difficulty and doubt are incommensurate. There of course may be difficulties in the evidence; but I am speaking of difficulties intrinsic to the doctrines themselves, or to their relations with each other. A man may be annoyed that he cannot work out a mathematical problem, of which the answer is or is not given to him, without doubting that it admits of an answer, or that a certain particular answer is the true one. Of all points of faith, the being of a God is, to my own apprehension, encompassed with most difficulty, and yet borne in upon our minds with most power.

People say that the doctrine of Transubstantiation is difficult to believe; I did not believe the doctrine till I was a Catholic. I had no difficulty in believing it, as soon as I believed that the Catholic Roman Church was the oracle of God, and that she had declared this doctrine to be part of the original revelation. It is difficult, impossible, to imagine, I grant; - but how is it difficult to believe? [...]

I believe the whole revealed dogma as taught by the Apostles, as committed by the Apostles to the Church, and as declared by the Church to me. I receive it, as it is infallibly interpreted by the authority to whom it is thus committed, and (implicitly) as it shall be, in like manner, further interpreted by that same authority to the end of time. I submit, moreover, to the universally received traditions of the Church, in which lies the matter of those new dogmatic definitions which are from time to time made, and which in all times are the clothing and the illustration of the Catholic dogma as already defined. And I submit myself to those other decisions of the Holy See, theological or not, through the organs which it has itself appointed, which, waiving the question of their infallibility, on the lowest ground come to me with a claim to be accepted and obeyed. Also, I consider that, gradually and in the course of ages, Catholic inquiry has taken certain definite shapes, and has through itself into the form of a science, with a method and a phraseology of its own, under the intellectual handling of great minds, such as Saint Athanasius, Saint Augustine, and Saint Thomas; and I feel no temptation at all to break in pieces the great legacy of thought thus committed to us for these latter days.

Eph 3:7, 10; Jn 16:13

℟. Of this gospel I was made a minister according to the gift of God's grace which was given me by the working of his power, * that through the Church the manifold wisdom of God might be made known.

℣. When the Spirit of Truth comes, he will guide you into all the truth, * that through the Church the manifold wisdom of God might be made known.

Collect

O GOD, who didst bestow upon thy priest, Blessed John Henry Newman, the grace to follow thy kindly light and find peace in thy Church: graciously grant that, through his intercession and example, we may be led out of shadows and images into the fullness of thy truth; through Jesus Christ thy Son our Lord, who liveth and reigneth with thee, in the unity of the Holy Spirit, one God, for ever and ever.

Saint Paulinus of York, Bishop
(10 October)

Proper of the Day and Common of Pastors: for a Bishop

A reading from the Venerable Bede,
The Ecclesiastical History of the English People

Since Bishop Augustine had advised him that the harvest was great and the workers were few, Pope Gregory sent more colleagues and ministers of the word together with his messengers. First and foremost among these were Mellitus, Justus, Paulinus, and Rufinianus; and he sent with them all such things as were generally necessary for the worship and ministry of the Church, such as sacred vessels, altar cloths and church ornaments, vestments for priests and clerks, relics of the holy apostles and martyrs, and very many manuscripts.

[...] At this time the Northumbrian race, that is the English race which dwelt north of the river Humber, together with their king Edwin, also accepted the word of faith through the preaching of Paulinus already mentioned. [...] The occasion of the conversion of this race was that Edwin became related to the kings of Kent, having married King Æthelbehrt's daughter Æthelburh, who was also called Tate. When he first sent ambassadors to ask her in marriage from her brother Eadbald, who was then king of Kent, the answer was that it was not lawful for a Christian maiden to be given in marriage to a heathen for fear that the faith and mysteries of the heavenly King might be profaned by a union with a king who was an utter stranger to the worship of the true God. When Edwin heard the messengers' reply he promised that he would put no obstacles of any kind in the way of the Christian worship which the maiden practised; on the other hand, he would allow her and all who came with her, men and women, priests or retainers, to follow the faith and worship of their religion after the Christian manner; nor did he deny the possibility that he might accept the same religion himself if, on examination, it was judged by his wise men to be a holier worship and more worthy of God.

Bede, *The Ecclesiastical History of the English People* II. 9, in Bede, *The Ecclesiastical History of the English People, The Greater Chronicle, Bede's Letter to Egbert*, edited with an introduction and notes by Judith McClure and Roger Collins (Oxford: Oxford University Press, 2008 [1994]), pp. 84-85.

Thereupon the maiden was betrothed to Edwin and, in accordance with the agreement, Paulinus, a man beloved of God, was consecrated bishop to accompany her and to make sure by daily instruction and the celebration of the heavenly sacraments that she and her companions were not polluted by contact with the heathen.

Paulinus was consecrated bishop by Archbishop Justus, on 21 July in the year of our Lord 625, was so in the princess's train he came to Edwin's court, outwardly bringing her to her marriage according to the flesh. But more truly his whole heart was set on calling the people to whom he was coming to the knowledge of the truth; his desire was to present it, in the words of the apostle, as a pure virgin to be espoused to one husband, even Christ

cf 1 Pet 2:4, 5; Ps [117] 118:22

℟. Come to the Lord, our living corner-stone. * Come, and let
yourselves be built up on him, as stones that live and breathe.
℣. He is the stone which has become the apex of the building. *
Come, and let yourselves be built up on him, as stones that live and
breathe.

Collect
O GOD our Saviour, who didst send thy servant Paulinus to preach and to baptize, and so to build up thy Church in this land: grant that, being inspired by his example, we may proclaim to the whole world thy truth, that with him we may receive the reward thou hast prepared for all thy faithful servants; through Jesus Christ thy Son our Lord, who liveth and reigneth with thee, in the unity of the Holy Spirit, one God, for ever and ever.

Saint Ethelburga, Abbess
(11 October)

Proper of the Day and Common of Saints: for Religious

A reading from the Venerable Bede,
The Ecclesiastical History of the English People

Before Erconwald was made bishop, he founded two famous monasteries, one for himself and the other for his sister Ethelburga, and established an excellent form of monastic Rule and discipline in both. his own was in the kingdom of Surrey near the river Thames at a place called Chertsey, that is, the island of *Ceorot*. his sister's monastery he established at a place called Barking in the kingdom of the East Saxons where she was to love as mother and nurse of a company of women devoted to God. When she had undertaken the rule of this monastery, she proved herself worthy in all things of her brother the bishop, both by her own holy life and by her sound and devoted care for those who were under her rule, and of this heavenly miracles were the witness. [...]

When Ethelburga, the devout mother of that devoted congregation, was herself about to be taken from the world, a marvellous vision appeared to one of the sisters whose name was Torhtgyth. She had lived for many years in the monastery, always seeking to serve God herself in all humility and sincerity and endeavouring to help the mother to keep the discipline of the Rule by teaching or reproving the younger ones. Now in order that her strength, like the apostle's, might be made perfect in weakness, she was suddenly afflicted with a most serious bodily disease and for nine years was sorely tried, under the good providence of our Redeemer, so that any traces of sin remaining among her virtues through ignorance or carelessness might be burnt away by the fires of prolonged suffering. One evening at dusk, as she left the little cell in which she lived, she saw distinctly what seemed to be a human body, wrapped in a shroud and brighter than the sun, being apparently raised up from within the house in which the sisters used to sleep. She looked closely to see how this glorious visionary body was raised up and saw that it was lifted as it were by cords, brighter than gold, until it was drawn up into the open heavens and she could

---

Bede, *The Ecclesiastical History of the English People* IV/ 6; 9 in Bede, *The Ecclesiastical History of the English People, The Greater Chronicle, Bede's Letter to Egbert*, edited with an introduction and notes by Judith McClure and Roger Collins (Oxford: Oxford University Press, 2008 [1994]), pp. 183-184, 186-187.

see it no longer. As she thought over the vision there remained no doubt in her mind that some member of the community was about to die whose soul would be drawn up to the skies by the good deeds she had done, as though be golden cords. And so it came to pass. Not many days afterwards the mother of the congregation, Ethelburga, beloved of God, was taken from the prison-house of the flesh; and such was her record that none who knew her can doubt that, as she departed this life, the gates of her heavenly country were opened for her.

1 Cor 2:9-10

℟. What no eye has seen, nor ear heard, tings beyond our imagining –
   all that God has prepared for those who love him: * these are the very things that God has revealed to us through the Spirit.
℣. The Spirit reaches the depths of everything, even the depths of
   God: * these are the very things that God has revealed to us through the Spirit.

Saint Wilfrid, Bishop
(12 October)

Proper of the Day and Common of Pastors: for a Bishop

From the *Life of Wilfrid* by Eddius Stephanus

We looked on our holy bishop as a great man and a faithful servant of Christ, but our Lord, by the miracles worked on his behalf, made it known that he was no less than a saint living with him in glory. It happened one day that all the abbots came to Oundle to carry away the body in a carriage. Some of them wanted to wash the corpse and have it decently vested (as indeed was only right and proper) and obtained permission to do so. Abbot Bacula spread out his robe on the ground and the brethren laid the body on it. After the washing and vesting, which the abbots themselves performed, it was taken with great reverence to the place appointed. And lo, once again from over the monastery came the sound of birds alighting and taking off with a gentle, almost musical

---

Eddius Stephanus, *Life of Wilfrid* 66, in J. F. Webb, *Lives of the Saints, translated with an introduction* (Harmondsworth: Penguin, 1965), pp. 203-204.

flapping of wings, The wiser members of the community were convinced that Michael had come with his choirs of angels to lead our bishop's soul to Paradise. The washing had been done outside the monastery buildings in a tent put up for the purpose and the water had been emptied out in the same place. The monks erected a cross to mark the spot and many miracles were later performed there. Our monks wrapped up the holy remains in linen, placed them in the carriage, and brought it to Ripon, chanting as they came. The community came out with the holy relics to honour the cortège and hardly any of them managed to fight back his tears. They found voice, nevertheless, to sing the hymns and canticles for the reception of the corpse and led it into the basilica he himself had built and dedicated to Saint Peter. There he was buried with all honour in the seventy-sixth year of his age and the fortieth of his episcopate. Who can tell how many bishops, priests, and deacons he had consecrated and ordained or count the churches he has dedicated during all those years? his glory shall endure for ever. After the funeral his worthy successor Tatberht was led in surrounded by all the other bishops.

The abbot who had given his cloak for Wilfrid to be laid on told his servant lad to take it to Wilfrid's abbess, Cynithrith. It was rather dirty from being trodden on during the washing. Cynithrith's orders were to keep it just as it was, folded up, till the abbot should visit her. At first she did as she was bidden but after a while decided to have it washed. There was a poor nun in the convent who, like the mason in the gospel, had gone about for years with a withered hand. Hearing what the abbess was doing she came and knelt before her with tears in her eyes.

'In the name of the Lord Jesus Christ', she begged, 'and by the soul of your dear bishop, let me bathe my shrivelled limb in the washing water. I have unshakeable faith in the power of this water, mixed as it is with the saint's sweat, to cure my crooked hand and withered arm.'

The abbess, being a pious woman, dared hardly refuse the sister. To show her faith she at once picked up the lifeless hand with her good one and plunged it into the warm soapy water and rubbed it with the cloak. And, lo and behold, the fingers straightened out, the hand regained its vitality, and she got back the use of her whole arm. Like Moerisa, the woman in the gospel who was cured of an issue of blood by touching the hem of Christ's garment, her faith had made her whole, and like her prototype she gave thanks to God, praising him for his wonderful works.

Ps [88:20, 21-23] 89:19, 20-21; Jer 3:15

℟. To your friends the prophets you said, I have exalted one chosen
from the people. I have found David, my servant; * with my holy oil
I have anointed him, and my hand shall always be with him.
℣. I will give you shepherds after my own heart, and these shall feed
you on knowledge and discretion; * with my holy oil I have anointed
him, and my hand shall always be with him.

Collect

ALMIGHTY God, who didst call our forebears to the light of the
gospel by the preaching of thy servant Wilfrid: grant us, who keep his
life and labour in remembrance, to glorify thy name by following the
example of his zeal and perseverance; through Jesus Christ thy Son
our Lord, who liveth and reigneth with thee, in the unity of the Holy
Spirit, one God, for ever and ever.

Saint Edward the Confessor
(13 October)

Proper of the Day and Common of Saints: for Christian Rulers

Reading and Responsory as in the Liturgy of Hours

O SOVEREIGN God, who didst set thy servant Edward upon the
throne of an earthly kingdom and didst inspire him with zeal for the
kingdom of heaven: grant that we may so confess the faith of Christ
by word and deed, that we may, with all thy Saints, inherit thine
eternal glory; through Jesus Christ thy Son our Lord, who liveth and
reigneth with thee, in the unity of the Holy Spirit, one God, for ever
and ever.

Saint Frideswide, Abbess
(19 October)

Proper of the Day and Common of Saints: for Religious

A reading from the early twelfth century life of Saint Frideswide

When the English people had been taught and baptized through blessed Augustine's preaching, priests and deacons were appointed, and churches were built and dedicated throughout the nation. So 'the multitude of believers grew', and through the whole land of the English the church abounded with new offspring.

Long afterwards there was a king of Oxford named Didan. He took a wife named Sefrida, a godly woman diligent in all good works. They rejoiced together in the flower of their youth, and the Lord made them fruitful. So revered Sefrida conceived, and in due time produced a daughter. When the king heard this he rejoiced greatly and ordered that she should be re-born with water and the Holy Spirit.

So she was baptized and they called her Frideswide. This king's daughter was carefully brought up, and after five years they entrusted her to a woman called Aelgifu to learn her letters. The maiden, whom God was already preparing to be a vessel of the Holy Spirit, so applied herself to her studies that within six months she knew the whole Psalter. So the blessed virgin Frideswide grew from strength to strength, striving wholeheartedly to make herself amiable to all, and always clung as well as she could to the thresholds of Holy Church. She stored up the precepts of Holy Scripture in the depths of her heart, often repeating this prayer, that she might dwell in the house of the Lord all the days of her life, and might see and work his will.

Her mother died, gripped by bodily sickness and seized by a heavy fever. Then King Didan built a church in the town of Oxford, and had it dedicated in honour of the Holy Trinity, the spotless Virgin Mary and All Saints. Revered Frideswide asked her father, the same King Didan, to give her the church, and he gave her the church. After her mother's death the religious virgin studied to

---

The Early Twelfth Century Life of Saint Frideswide, in *Saint Frideswide, Patroness of Oxford*. The earliest texts edited and introduced by John Blair (Oxford: Perpetua Press, 2004, 2nd edition), pp. 31-33.

serve God day and night in vigils and prayers, always striving to forget bodily food, and to absorb spiritual food with all her might. Viewing the passing pomp and glory of this world, and valuing it all as dung, the virgin Frideswide gave everything that she had to the poor. She always wore a hair-shirt, and her food was a little barley-bread with a few vegetables and water. Meanwhile, all the English people marvelled at such virtue in one so young, and the king rejoiced, seeing and understanding that his only daughter was a vessel of the Holy Spirit.

The blessed virgin besought her father, saying, 'Sweetest father, help me to become worthy of the nun's habit, to praise and bless God's name forever in his temple'. King Didan rejoiced greatly when he heard his daughter and summoning a certain religious man named Orgar, bishop of Lincoln, he caused him to consecrate his daughter Frideswide to God. With her were also hallowed twelve virgins, all of noble family. Then the same king caused houses suitable for nuns to be built, namely a refectory, a dormitory and a cloister, and assigned religious men to serve them.

1 Cor 7:34; Ps [72] 73:26

℟.An unmarried woman, like a young girl, can devote herself to the Lord's affairs; * her aim is to be dedicated to him in body as in spirit.
℣.God is the strength of her heart; he is hers for ever. * Her aim is to be dedicated to him in body as in spirit.

Collect
ALMIGHTY and eternal God, source of truth and lover of virginity: grant us, we beseech thee, that the merits of Saint Frideswide, thy virgin so pleasing to thee, may be as a commendation of us to thee whose life by its chastity gave to thee such satisfaction; through Jesus Christ thy Son our Lord, who liveth and reigneth with thee in the unity of the Holy Spirit, one God, for ever and ever.

Saint Chad, Bishop
and Saint Cedd, Bishop
(26 October)

Proper of the Day and Common of Pastors: for Bishops

A reading from the Venerable Bede,
The Ecclesiastical History of the English People

While Cedd was acting as bishop of the East Saxons, he used very often to revisit his own land, the kingdom of Northumbria, to preach. Œthelwald, son of King Oswald who reigned over Deira, seeing that Cedd was a wise, holy, and upright man, asked him where he himself might frequently come to pray and hear the Word and where he might be buried; for he firmly believed that the daily prayers of those who served God there would greatly help him. This king had previously had with him, Cælin, Cedd's brother, a man equally devoted to God, who had been accustomed to minister the word and the sacraments of the faith to himself and his family; for he was a priest It was through him chiefly that the king had got to know and had learned to love the bishop. So, in accordance with the king's desire, Cedd chose himself a site for the monastery amid some steep and remote hills which seemed better fitted for the haunts of robbers and the dens of wild beasts than for human habitation; so that, as Isaiah says, 'In the habitations where once dragons lay, shall be grass with reeds and rushes' (Is 35:7), that is, the fruit of good works shall spring up where once beasts dwelt or where men lived after the manner of beasts.

The man of God was anxious first of all to cleanse the site which he had received for the monastery from the stain of former crimes by prayer and fasting, before laying the foundations. So he asked the king to grant him permission and opportunity to spend the whole of the approaching season of Lent there in prayer. Every day except Sunday he prolonged his fast until evening as his custom was and then he took nothing but a small quantity of bread, one hen's egg, and a little milk mixed with water. He explained that this was a custom of those from whom he had learned the discipline of a Rule that, when they had received a site for building a monastery or a church, they should

---

Bede, *The Ecclesiastical History of the English People* III. 23 in Bede, *The Ecclesiastical History of the English People, The Greater Chronicle, Bede's Letter to Egbert,* edited with an introduction and notes by Judith McClure and Roger Collins (Oxford: Oxford University Press, 2008 [1994]), pp. 148-149.

first consecrate it to the Lord with prayer and fasting. But ten days before the end of Lent, a messenger came to summon him to the king. Thereupon in order that this holy labour might not be interrupted because of the king's affairs, he asked his own brother Cynebill, who was a priest, to complete the sacred task. The latter gladly agreed and, when the work of fasting and prayer was ended, he built a monastery now called Lastingham and established in it the religious observances according to the usage of Lindisfarne where he had been brought up.

When Cedd had been bishop in the kingdom for many years and had borne the responsibility of this monastery, having appointed priors, he happened to come to it while the plague was raging there, fell sick and died. He was first of all buried outside the walls, but in course of time a stone church was built in the monastery in honour of the blessed Mother of God, and his body was buried in it on the right side of the altar.

The bishop left the monastery to be governed after him by his brother Chad who was afterwards consecrated bishop as we shall hear later. There were then four brothers whom we have mentioned, Cedd, Cynebill, Cælin and Chad, who were all famous priests of the Lord, a very rare thing to happen, and two of them reached the rank of bishop.

1 Thess 2:8; Gal 4:19

℟. With all our hearts we desired nothing better than to offer you our
    own lives, as well as God's gospel, * so greatly had we learned to
    love you.
℣. My little children, I am in travail over you afresh, until I can see
    God's image formed in you, * so greatly had we learned to love you.

Collect
ALMIGHTY God, from the first fruits of the English nation who turned to Christ thou didst call thy servants Chad and Cedd to minister as bishops to their people: give us grace to follow their peaceable nature, humble spirit and prayerful life, that, aided by their prayers, we may truly commend to others the faith which we ourselves profess; through Jesus Christ thy Son our Lord, who liveth and reigneth with thee, in the unity of the Holy Spirit, one God, for ever and ever.

Saint Winefride, Virgin
(3 November)

Proper of the Day and Common of Saints: for Religious

A reading from the *Life and Translation of Saint Winefride*
by Robert Pennant, Prior of Shrewsbury

[W]hen the brothers mentioned before were led to this place, as they were about to have that for which they had come and to obtain their wish, the aforementioned prior went ahead of his companions by the inspiration of the Holy Spirit, I believe, with no one leading him or showing the way beforehand, and he came by a straight way to Saint Winefride's tomb. And he who had never before been there nor known before the place of the tomb by anyone describing it, entered that churchyard first, with God guiding him, and came straight to the sepulchre of the holy maiden. [...] When this was found, with devout souls they gave thanks to God, and after the bones had been extracted from the dust, as then it was a convenient time for them, they placed them properly bound, in mantles. And so, saying farewell to those remaining in that district they began to return home with immense joy. [...]

[C]oming on the seventh day to the city of Shrewsbury, from which they had been sent, they dispatched messengers to the monastery to announce that they had what they had gone for. Indeed, when this was heard, the whole community rejoiced much, and declaring that it would be unsuitable for so great a treasure to be received in the monastery without the authority and blessing of the bishop and a great gathering of people from the entire province, the community determined that the most holy relics should be placed in Saint Giles' church, which is situated at the city gate. This speech pleased all, and they again dispatched the prior to the bishop to confirm by his authority what they were going to do concerning the sacred relic consigned to them by Heaven. Meanwhile, brothers from the convent were assigned to celebrate with

---

Robert Pennant, *Life and Translation of Saint Winefride,* 9, 11-12, in *Two Mediæval Lives of Saint Winefride.* Translated by Robert Pepin and Hugh Feiss, OSB (Eugene, OR: Wipf and Stock, 2004 [2000],) pp. 88-89, 90-93.

devout souls the offis of night and day in the presence of the blessed maiden's body. [...]

Then a day was designated and announced throughout the assemblies of the neighbouring parishes; all were urged to come on this day who wished to be present at the translation of the venerable saint. Thus, on the appointed day, while the brothers were processing along the way with crosses and candles and a numerous throng of people, the most holy body of the blessed maiden, Winefride, was brought, with all the people genuflecting, and many were unable to refrain from weeping for great joy. [...]

Then, after the reception of the holy relics, when the brothers had begun to go back to the monastery, it pleased all that the aforementioned prior who had brought them should address the crowd and instruct everyone about how great were the virtues or what were the merits of the maiden whose translation had taken place there. And when he had done this at length, while the clouds were hovering in the air nearby and threatening their downpour and wetting the surrounding country with rain, the body of the most holy maiden was received by the brothers withProper reverence while the praises of God were resounding on high. It was brought to the monastery and reverently placed upon the altar which had been built in honour of the holy apostles, Peter and Paul, where, to show the special privilege of the blessed maiden, cures are granted to the sick, and countless miracles happen for the glory and praise of God, to whom be honour, glory and dominion for ever and ever. Amen.

℟. The Lord has saved me and strengthened me; * with his help I will profess my loyalty to him to the end.
℣. In his loving-kindness the sinless Lord has consecrated to himself a spotless handmaid; * with his help I will profess my loyalty to him to the end.

Collect
O GOD of steadfast love, when thou didst will that thy Son be born of Mary thou revealedst to us the beauty of virginity: as we honour the memory of the virgin Winefride, may we enjoy, through her prayers, thy gifts of healing; through Jesus Christ thy Son our Lord, who liveth and reigneth with thee, in the unity of the Holy Spirit, one God, for ever and ever.

Saint Willibrord, Bishop
(7 November)

Proper of the Day and Common of Pastors: for a Bishop

A reading from the *Life of Saint Willibrord* by Alcuin

In the thirty-third year of his age the fervour of his faith had reached such an intensity that [Willibrord] considered it of little value to labour at his own sanctification unless he could preach the gospel to others and bring some benefit to them. He had heard that in the northern regions of the world the harvest was great but the labourers few. Thus it was that, in fulfillment of the dream which his mother stated she had seen, Willibrord, fully aware of hi own purpose but ignorant as yet of divine preordination, decided to sail for those parts and, if God so willed, to bring the gospel message to those people who through unbelief had not been stirred by its warmth. Some of these afterwards gained the martyr's crown through their constancy in preaching the gospel, others were later to become bishops and, after their labours in the holy work of preaching, have since gone to their rest in peace.

So the man of God, accompanied by his brethren, as we have already said, set sail, and after a successful crossing they moored their ships at the mouth of the Rhine. Them, after they had taken some refreshment, they set out of the Castle of Utrecht, which lies on the bank of the river, where some years afterwards, when by divine favour the faith had increased, Willibrord placed the seat of his bishopric. But as the Frisian people, among whom the fort was situated, and Radbod, their king, still defiled themselves by pagan practices, the man of God thought it wiser to set out for Francia and visit Pippin, the king of that country, a man of immense energy, successful in war and of high moral character. The duke received him with every mark of respect; and as he was unwilling that he and his people should lose the services of so eminent a scholar, he made over to him certain localities within the boundaries of his own realm, where he could uproot idolatrous practices, teach the newly converted people and so fulfil the command of the prophet, 'Drive a new furrow and sown no longer among the briars'.

The Anglo-Saxon Missionaries in Germany. Being the Lives of Saints Willibrord, Boniface, Sturm, Leoba and Lebuin, together with the Hodoeporicon *of Saint Willibald and a selection from the correspondence of Saint Boniface*, translated and edited by C. H. Talbot (London and New York: Sheed and Ward, 1954), pp. 6-8.

After the man of God had systematically visited certain localities and carried out the task of evangelization, and when he seed of life watered by the dews of heavenly grace had, though his preaching, borne abundant fruit in many hearts, the aforesaid King of the Franks, highly pleased at Willibrord's burning zeal and the extraordinary growth of the Christian faith, and having in view the still greater propagation of religion, thought it wise to send him to Rome in order that he might be consecrated bishop by Pope Sergius, one of the holiest men of that time. Thus, after receiving the apostolic blessing and mandate and being filled with greater confidence as the Pope's emissary, he would return to preach the gospel with even greater vigour, according to the words of the Apostle, 'How shall they preach unless they be sent?'

But when the king tried to persuade the man of God to do this he was met by a refusal. Willibrord said that he was not worthy to wield such great authority, and, after enumerating the qualities which Saint Paul mentioned to Timothy, his spiritual son, as being essential for a bishop, asserted that he fell far short of such virtues. On his side, the king solemnly urged what the man of God had already humbly declined. At length, moved by the unanimous agreement of his companions, and, what is of more importance, constrained by the divine will, Willibrord acquiesced, anxious to submit to the counsel of many rather than obstinately to follow his own will.

Mk 16:15, 16; Jn 3:5

℟. Go out to the whole world; proclaim the Good News to all
    creation: * he who believes and is baptized will be saved.
℣. No one can enter the kingdom of God without being born from
    water and Spirit, * he who believes and is baptized will be saved.

Collect

O GOD the Saviour of all, who didst send thy bishop Willibrord from this land to proclaim the gospel to many peoples and confirm them in their faith: strengthen us, we beseech thee, to witness to thy steadfast love by word and deed so that thy Church may increase and grow strong in holiness; through Jesus Christ thy Son our Lord, who liveth and reigneth with thee, in the unity of the Holy Spirit, one God, for ever and ever.

All Saints *of England*
(8 November)

Proper of the Day and Common of Martyrs
Other countries and particular Religious Communities would substitute a reading
appropriate to the nation or community.

A reading from *The Life and Martyrdom of Father Edmund Campion,*
by Robert Persons

He said that his commission was to preach the gospel of Christ Jesus freely and without all earthly interest, to administer the sacraments of the Catholic Church, to instruct the unlearned in the true ancient religion, to exhort the wicked from their sinful ways, to convince errors and heresies, to strengthen and confirm the good, and in one word to sound the sacred trumpet of spiritual and ghostly war against the tyranny of foul vice and proud ignorance wherewith a number of his dear countrymen were oppressed. [...]

Considering that this only was his end and cause of his coming, he desireth most humbly of their honours that they would vouchsafe for better informing themselves to hear him treat and dispute with all modesty of these important points in their presence as also in the presence of the learned Divines and lawyers of the land for that he did not doubt by the help and assistance of Almighty God that he should be able to show by all authority both of holy Scriptures, General Councils, holy Fathers, Ecclesiastical Histories and ancient laws which unto this day were in force within the land that the old Catholic faith of our forefathers was the only true faith and religion and all novelties raised up since was nothing else but falsehood and vanity.

He desired their honours most humbly to pardon this earnest offer of trial and disputation for that it proceeded not of any confidence of his own ability which was the least of thousands of his brethren in the Catholic Church, and much less of arrogancy or of vain worldly glory which he so much contemned as he had utterly renounced the world and was ready to cast himself at the feet of any for the service of his Master Jesus, whose only glory was that which had moved him to this enterprise, and the hope of his assistance gave him courage and confidence in the same, together with the known weakness and ignorance of

---

'Of the Life and Martyrdom of Father Edmund Campion', I. 24, in *Letters and Notices* XII (Roehampton: Manresa Press, 1879), pp. 48-50.

the teachers of heresies, who the better they should come prepared to this trial the more glad he would be, for that so the truth should better appear. [...]

Turning his speech to the Councillors themselves, he besought them as men of great wisdom and experience in worldly affairs to consider deeply this matter that so much concerned their souls and the salvation of infinite others that depended of them, that they should ponder the weak foundations which their new religion was grounded on, and why they had left the holy and honourable course of all their ancestors, kings, princes, and councillors of this realm since it was first converted to the Christian faith; that they should weigh with what love, zeal, and piety men of their own nation came hence from beyond the seas to teach and maintain this faith not respecting the danger of persecution and death but holding up their hands daily to God for their good and salvation and that it is impossible by temporal torments to extinguish this zealous offspring which every day increased and would by God's help continue to the end and that his Order of religious had fully purposed by the help of Jesus Christ to prosecute this most heavenly enterprise of doing good to England so long as they should have subjects to employ in the same which no doubt would never cease, and that the account of this was already made seeing the fine thereof was but paying of blood which would always be ready if the Queen and Council continued their persecution,

Lastly, he concluded, touching his own person, that if all these protestations, offers, and reasons would not serve to procure him grace nor grateful audience with them, then would he turn himself only to Almighty God that knew his thoughts and desires and would beseech him to take his cause and labours in protection and would extend his mercy to their honours until the last universal and great accounting day at what time they should well perceive with what integrity of mind and perfect love towards them, his prince, and country he had spoken then, and then there should be no memory of hatred nor suspicion of enmity between them.

Rev 19:5, 6; Ps [32] 33:1

℟. Praise our God, all you his servants, you who fear him, small and great, * for the reign of our Lord God, the Almighty, has begun.

℣. Rejoice in the Lord, O you just ones! Praise is fitting for loyal hearts, * for the reign of our Lord God, the Almighty, has begun.

Collect

WE BESEECH thee, O Lord, to multiply thy grace upon us who commemorate the Saints of our nation: that, as we rejoice to be their fellow-citizens on earth, so we may have fellowship also with them in heaven; through Jesus Christ thy Son our Lord, who liveth and reigneth with thee, in the unity of the Holy Spirit, one God, for ever and ever.

or

O GOD, whom the glorious company of the redeemed adore, gathered from all times and places of thy dominion: we praise thee for the Saints of our own land, and for the lamps that were lit by their holiness; and we beseech thee that, at the last, we too may be numbered among those who have done thy will and declared thy righteousness; through Jesus Christ thy Son our Lord, who liveth and reigneth with thee, in the unity of the Holy Spirit, one God, for ever and ever.

Saint Edmund of Abingdon, Bishop
(16 November)

Proper of the Day and Common of Pastors: for a Bishop

From the *Life of Saint Edmund* by Matthew Paris

It was with Blessed Edmund as we read of Saint Martin: he was poor and modest in his demeanour, but magnificently rich in heavenly grace; a prelate, yet a servant to others; great in the sight of God, but of small account in his own eyes; conscious of the gravity of his office, but jovial in his looks, affable, and charming in his speech. He always rejected any gifts proffered by those seeking advantage; he knew how to be thankful and content with his own means. He was tireless in works of mercy. On becoming a bishop he never faltered in the abounding goodness he always displayed towards the poor and

---

C. H. Lawrence, *The Life of Saint Edmund by Matthew Paris. Translated, edited, and with a biography* (London: Sandpiper, 1999), pp. 135-137.

afflicted. The abundant means and income he acquired with his office were barely enough to support the poor of Christ, to whom his helping hand was ever extended. For he would not suffer any beggar to leave his gates at any time empty-handed or forsaken. Lest anyone should be disturbed by my comparison of Blessed Edmund to Saint Martin, out of reverence for so great a saint, I shall examine in each of them their remarkably similar virtues.

For Martin, while he was still a catechumen, divided his cloak and clothed a shivering pauper, and in doing so, clothed Christ Edmund, to the best of his ability, clothed a numerous crowd of poor people every year, even before he had obtained a benefice. Many more he adorned with the garment of faith and doctrine. Martin revealed the glory of the Trinity to the heathen in the lands of the west Edmund, as a renowned doctor of theology, gave the light of doctrine to the land of England, and by his preaching sowed far and wide a seed that bore fruit, leaving his writing or the profit of posterity. A holy contention arose over the desire to possess the body of Saint Martin. A holy contention arose over possession of Saint Edmund's body, as will later be told. Martin was the shining flower of the Franks; Edmund the jewel of the English. Martin was distinguished as the archbishop of Tours, Edmund as archbishop of Canterbury. Martin, while yet living, by the power of the Trinity gloriously raised three people to life from death. Edmund, while still living, recalled three people to life from death, commanding no one to mention it during his lifetime. What else should I mention? Both fought their fight for one and the same King, and were sanctified by the one Spirit. Faithfully serving the one Lord, they merited to be 'made rulers over many things' [cf Mt 25:23].

Let us therefore praise God who has thus glorified his saint. England is to be congratulated on having borne so great a denizen of heaven and on having fostered such a happy child in her bosom. Let France rejoice that she has merited to keep the tomb that holds the body of so great a patron. Let the angels and all the knights of the court of heaven exult in the company of so great a fellow warrior. For by his teaching he shone upon the earth like the sun, and the news of his deeds was like the perfume of incense, so that he fulfilled the saying of the Apostle, 'As you speak, so do' (Jas 2:2). And like another John the Baptist in the desert of England, having been made a preacher general, he preached unceasingly, devoutly and effectively exhorting crowds of people – knights and townsmen, religious and clergy, and the faithful of either sex. Indeed he was for all a shining pattern of good living, an excellent mirror of sanctity, a zealous teacher of justice, a master of piety, the true form of doctrine, the consecration of learning, an example of religion. In him there is an ideal for every sex, age, condition or rank to choose; and from his holiness all receive a fullness of light. In him boyhood finds something to imitate, men see what to strive for and admire, the clergy are taught the ideal for which they should strive.

℟. The instruction he gave was true, and no harmful words ever fell
  from his lips; * he walked in harmony with me and in purity of life.
℣. My hand shall be ready to help him and my arm to give him
  strength; * he walked in harmony with me and in purity of life.

Collect

O GOD of justice, by whose inspiration Saint Edmund was vigilant for the cause of integrity in public office and discipline in religious life: grant, we pray thee, through his intercession, that same spirit of constancy to thy Church and make it fearless to proclaim the righteousness that thou demandest of all; through Jesus Christ thy Son our Lord, who liveth and reigneth with thee, in the unity of the Holy Spirit, one God, for ever and ever.

Saint Margaret of Scotland
(16 November)

Proper of the Day and Common of Saints: for Christian Rulers

Reading and Responsory as in the Liturgy of Hours

O GOD, the ruler of all, who didst call thy servant Margaret to an earthly throne and gavest to her both zeal for thy Church and love for thy people, that she might advance thy heavenly kingdom: mercifully grant that we who commemorate her example may be fruitful in good works and, with her prayers, attain to the glorious crown of thy Saints; through Jesus Christ thy Son our Lord, who liveth and reigneth with thee, in the unity of the Holy Spirit, one God, for ever and ever.

Saint Hugh of Lincoln, Bishop
(17 November)

Proper of the Day and Common of Pastors: for a Bishop

A reading from the *Life of Saint Hugh of Lincoln* by Adam of Evesham

When three full months had passed since his election and the envoys so often mentioned before had returned from Chartreuse, he, who had long ago left his country and kindred was forced by this third summons to depart from his home. He set out to be consecrated as a bishop, after which he would come to the mountain the Lord would show him, a lofty mountain indeed, not Lebanon but Lincoln, nay rather both Lebanon and Lincoln, not the Lebanon in the land of the Phoenicians, but the Lebanon of mystical whiteness, which the man clad in white raiment had come to cleanse whiter than snow. Outwardly, he was white in habit, appearance and countenance, inwardly he was much more so by his virtue, and he cleansed Lincoln by his teaching, example and holiness, by the fame of a group of illustrious men. On this mount like the magnificent and peace-loving Solomon he was to build a splendid temple, where like the faithful and obedient Abraham he would often offer sacrifice most acceptable to almighty God. There too like the valiant and comely David, he was to find a tomb which would finally be renowned and bring benefits to all the faithful who visited it.

Although he was on his way to receive the highest of the ecclesiastical orders, his utter humility remained unchanged. He acted on the advice of the sage [Sirach], which was always in his thoughts, that the greater a man was and the higher he rose, the greater should be his humility. Maintaining his usual seriousness and the external signs of the poverty of his order, his horse had no ornamental bridle or breastplate and had on its back behind the saddle, the roll of skins and rough blankets which he used during the day and night. Thus, the elect of God rode accompanied by his clerks whose horses had gold-embroidered saddle bags, and who tried to invent pretexts to transfer his bundle to one of their sumpter horses. Permission could not be extorted from him, either by serious requests or jests, for he had scruples about neglecting or

Adam of Evesham, *The Life of Saint Hugh of Lincoln* III. 5, in *Magna Vita Sancti Hugonis. The Life of Saint Hugh of Lincoln.* Volume One, edited by the late Decima L. Douie and David Hugh Farmer (Oxford: Clarendon Press, 1985), pp. 101-103.

making the least change in his former way of life before his elevation to a higher order. The humility of this spiritual man put their worldliness to the blush.

When they were approaching the city of Winchester, where they would be met by the king's household and a great throng of citizen, one of the clerks, whose vanity made him bold, secretly cut the strap by which the bundle I have already mentioned was fastened to the saddle, and thus robbed him without his knowledge of the burden which he had been carrying. At length they reached London, and there on Saint Matthew's day, he was consecrated bishop, and most fittingly raised to the apostolic order to preach the gospel to the poor.

1 Pet 5:2,3,4; Acts 20:28

℟. Tend the flock of God that is your charge; be examples to them, *
  and when the Chief Shepherd appears, you will receive the unfading
  crown of glory.
℣. Keep watch over all the flock of which the Holy Spirit has given
  you charge, as shepherds of the Church of God, * and when the
  Chief Shepherd appears, you will receive the unfading crown of glory.

Collect
O GOD, who didst endow thy servant Hugh with a wise and cheerful boldness and didst teach him to commend to earthly rulers the discipline of a holy life: by his intercession, give us grace like him to be bold in the service of the gospel, putting our confidence in Christ alone: who liveth and reigneth with thee, in the unity of the Holy Spirit, one God, for ever and ever.

Saint Hilda, Abbess
(17 November)

Proper of the Day and Common of Saints: for Religious

A reading from the Venerable Bede,
The Ecclesiastical History of the English People

In the year of our Lord 680, Hilda who, as previously stated, was abbess at the monastery called Whitby and a most devoted servant of Christ, departed on 17 November, after having done many heavenly deeds on earth, to receive the rewards of the heavenly life, at the age of sixty-six. Her career falls into two equal parts, for she spent her first thirty-three very nobly in the secular habit, while she dedicated an equal number of years still more notably to the Lord in the monastic life. She was of noble birth, being the daughter of Hereric, King Edwin's nephew. It was in company with Edwin that she received the faith and the mysteries of Christ through the teaching of Paulinus of blessed memory, the first bishop of the Northumbrians, and she preserved that faith inviolate until she was counted worthy to behold him.

When she had decided to give up the secular habit and serve the Lord alone, she withdrew to the kingdom of the East Angles, for she was a relation of a king of that land. It was her wish, if possible, to live as a stranger for the Lord's sake in the monastery of Chelles, so that she might the more easily attain to her eternal home in heaven. Her sister Hereswith, mother of Ealdwulf, king of the East Angles, was at that time living in the monastery under the discipline of the Rule and awaiting her heavenly crown. Inspired by her sister's example, Hilda continued a whole year in the kingdom of the East Angles with the intention of going abroad; but then Bishop Aidan called her home and she received a hide of land on the north side of the river Wear, where, for another year, she lived the monastic life with a small band of companions.

After this she was made abbess in the monastery called Hartlepool which had been founded not long before by Heiu, a devoted handmaid of Christ, who is said to have been the first woman in the Northumbrian kingdom to take the

Bede, *The Ecclesiastical History of the English People* IV/ 23 (21), in Bede, *The Ecclesiastical History of the English People, The Greater Chronicle, Bede's Letter to Egbert*, edited with an introduction and notes by Judith McClure and Roger Collins (Oxford: Oxford University Press, 2008 [1994]), pp. 210-211.

vows and habit of a nun, having been ordained [that is, blessed] by Bishop Aidan… Hilda, the handmaiden of Christ, was appointed to rule the monastery and at once set about establishing there a Rule of life in all respects like that which she had been taught by many learned men; for Bishop Aidan and other devout men who knew her visited her frequently, instructed her assiduously, and loved her heartily for her innate wisdom and her devotion to the service of God.

When she had ruled over the monastery for some years, wholly occupied in establishing a Rule of life there, it happened that she undertook either to found or to set in order a monastery at a place called Whitby, a task imposed upon her which she carried out with great industry. She established the same Rule of life as in the other monastery, teaching them to observe strictly the virtues of justice, devotion, and chastity and other virtues too, but above all things to continue in peace and charity. After the example of the primitive church, no one was rich, no one was in need, for they had all things in common and none had any private property. So great was her prudence that not only ordinary people but kings and princes sometimes sought and received her counsel when in difficulties. She compelled those under her direction to devote so much time to the study of the holy Scriptures and so much time to the performance of good works, that there might be no difficulty in finding many there who were fitted for holy orders, that is, for the service of the altar.

cf Ruth 3:10,11; Jud 13:25

℟. The Lord has blessed you, * for the people all know your worth.
℣. The Lord has made your name so famous that you shall never pass from the memories of men, * for the people all know your worth.

Collect

O ETERNAL God, who madest the abbess Hilda to shine as a jewel in our land and through her holiness and leadership didst bless thy Church with newness of life and unity: so assist us by thy grace that we, like her, may yearn for the gospel of Christ and bring reconciliation to those who are divided; through Jesus Christ thy Son our Lord, who liveth and reigneth with thee, in the unity of the Holy Spirit, one God, for ever and ever.

Saint Edmund, Martyr
(20 November)

Proper of the Day and Common of Martyrs

A reading from the *Life of Saint Edmund* by Abbo of Fleury

In King Æthelred's day a certain very learned monk named Abbo came over the sea from the south, from Saint Benedict's resting-place to Archbishop Dunstan, three years before Dunstan died. During their conversation Dunstan related the story of Saint Edmund just as Edmund's sword-bearer related it to King Æthelstan when Dunstan was a young man and the sword-bearer was an aged man. Abbo recorded the entire story in a single book, and when the book came to us, we translated it into English, just as it stands now. [...]

Edmund the Blessed, King of East Anglia, was wise and worthy, and exalted among the noble servants of the almighty God. He was humble and virtuous and remained so resolute that he would not turn to shameful vices, nor would be bend his morality in any way, but was ever-mindful of the true teaching: 'If you are installed as a ruler, do not puff yourself up, but be among them just like one of them'. He was charitable to poor folk and widows, just like a father, and with benevolence he guided his people always towards righteousness, and restrained the cruel, and lived happily in the faith.

Eventually it happened that the Danes came with a ship-army, harrying and slaying widely through the land, as is their custom. In the fleet were the foremost chieftains Ivar and Ubbi, united through the devil. They landed warships in Northumbria, and wasted that country and slew the people. Then Ivar went [south-]east with his ships and Halfdan remained in Northumbria gaining victory with slaughter. Ivar came rowing to East Anglia in the year in which prince Alfred – he who afterwards became the famous West Saxon king – was twenty-one. The aforementioned Ivar suddenly invaded the country, just like a wolf, and slew the people, men and women and innocent children, and ignominiously harassed innocent Christians. Soon afterward he sent to king Edmund a threatening message, that Edmund should submit to his allegiance, if he cared for his life. The messenger came to king Edmund and boldly

---

Abbo of Fleury, *Life of Saint Edmund*, in the version of Ælfric of Eynsham, Sweet, *Anglo-Saxon Primer* (Oxford: Oxford University Press, 1961, 9th edition), translated by Kenneth Cutler, *Internet Medieval Source Book*, 1998.

announced Ivar's message: 'Ivar, our king, bold and victorious on sea and on land, has dominion over many peoples, and has now come to this country with his army to take up winter-quarters with his men. He commands that you share your hidden gold-hoards and your ancestral possessions with him straightaway, and that you become his vassal-king, if you want to stay alive, since you now do not have the forces that you can resist him.'

Then king Edmund summoned a certain bishop with whom he was most intimate, and deliberated with him how he should answer the fierce Ivar. The bishop was afraid because of this emergency, and he feared for the king's life, and counselled him that he thought that Edmund should submit to what Ivar asked of him. [...] Then said king Edmund, since he was completely brave: 'This I heartily wish and desire, that I not be the only survivor after my beloved thegns are slain in their beds with their children and wives by these pirates. It was never my way to flee. I would rather die for my country if I need to. Almighty God knows that I will not ever turn from worship of him, nor from love of his truth. If I die, I live.'

After these words he turned to the messenger whom Ivar had sent him, and, undaunted, said to him, 'In truth, you deserve to be slain now, but I will not defile my clean hands with your vile blood, because I follow Christ who so instructed us by his example; and I happily will be slain by you if God so ordain it. Go now quickly and tell your fierce lord: 'Never in this life will Edmund submit to Ivar the heathen war-leader, unless he submit first to the belief in the Saviour Christ which exists in this country'. Then the messenger went quickly on his way, and met along the road the cruel Ivar with all his army hastening towards Edmund, and told the impious one how he had been answered. Ivar then arrogantly ordered that the pirates should all look at once for the king who scorned his command, and seize him immediately.

King Edmund, against whom Ivar advanced, stood inside his hall, and mindful of the Saviour, threw out his weapons. He wanted to match the example of Christ, who forbade to win the cruel Jews with weapons. Lo! The impious one then bound Edmund and insulted him ignominiously, and beat him with roads, and afterwards led the devout king to a firm living tree, and tied him there with strong bonds, and beat him with whips. In between the whip lashes, Edmund called out with true belief in the Saviour Christ Because of his belief, because he called to Christ to aid him, the heathens became furiously angry. They then shot spears at him. As if it were a game, until he was entirely covered with their missiles, like the bristles of a hedgehog (just like Saint Sebastian was).

When Ivar the impious pirate saw that the noble king would not forsake Christ, but with resolute faith called after him, he ordered Edmund beheaded, and the heathens did so. While Edmund still called out to Christ, the heathen dragged the holy man to his death, and with one stroke struck of his head, and his soul journeyed happily to Christ There was a man near at hand, kept hidden by God, who heard all this, and told of it afterward, just as we have told it here.

℟. Fearless in the sight of wicked men, this saint died in defence of the law of God, * for he was built on rock.
℣. This is he who rejected the life of this world and gained the kingdom of heaven,* for he was built on rock.

Collect
O ETERNAL God, whose servant Edmund kept faith to the end, both with thee and with his people, and glorified thee by his death: grant us the same steadfast faith, that, together with the noble army of martyrs, we may come to the perfect joy of the resurrection life; through Jesus Christ thy Son our Lord, who liveth and reigneth with thee, in the unity of the Holy Spirit, one God, for ever and ever.

Saint Edmund Campion, Priest and Martyr
(1 December)

Proper of the Day and Common of Martyrs

The following passage may be read in the Divine Office according to the Use of this Customary but not at the Office of Readings in the Liturgy of Hours of the Roman Rite.

A reading from the Acts of Martyrdom of St Edmund Campion

He said that his commission was to preach the gospel of Christ Jesus freely and without all earthly interest, to administer the sacraments of the Catholic Church, to instruct the unlearned in the true ancient religion, to exhort the wicked from their sinful ways, to convince errors and heresies, to strengthen and confirm the good, and in one word to sound the sacred trumpet of spiritual and ghostly war against the tyranny of foul vice and proud ignorance wherewith a number of his dear countrymen were oppressed. […]

Considering that this only was his end and cause of his coming, he desireth most humbly of their honours that they would vouchsafe for better informing themselves to hear him treat and dispute with all modesty of these important points in their presence as also in the presence of the learned Divines and lawyers of the land for that he did not doubt by the help and assistance of Almighty God that he should be able to show by all authority both of holy Scriptures, General Councils, holy Fathers, Ecclesiastical Histories and ancient laws which unto this day were in force within the land that the old Catholic faith of our forefathers was the only true faith and religion and all novelties raised up since was nothing else but falsehood and vanity.

He desired their honours most humbly to pardon this earnest offer of trial and disputation for that it proceeded not of any confidence of his own ability which was the least of thousands of his brethren in the Catholic Church, and much less of arrogancy or of vain worldly glory which he so much contemned as he had utterly renounced the world and was ready to cast himself at the feet of any

'Of the Life and Martyrdom of Father Edmund Campion', I. 24, in *Letters and Notices* XII (Roehampton: Manresa Press, 1879), pp. 48-50.

for the service of his Master Jesus, whose only glory was that which had moved him to this enterprise, and the hope of his assistance gave him courage and confidence in the same, together with the known weakness and ignorance of the teachers of heresies, who the better they should come prepared to this trial the more glad he would be, for that so the truth should better appear. [...]

Turning his speech to the Councillors themselves, he besought them as men of great wisdom and experience in worldly affairs to consider deeply this matter that so much concerned their souls and the salvation of infinite others that depended of them, that they should ponder the weak foundations which their new religion was grounded on, and why they had left the holy and honourable course of all their ancestors, kings, princes, and councillors of this realm since it was first converted to the Christian faith; that they should weigh with what love, zeal, and piety men of their own nation came hence from beyond the seas to teach and maintain this faith not respecting the danger of persecution and death but holding up their hands daily to God for their good and salvation and that it is impossible by temporal torments to extinguish this zealous offspring which every day increased and would by God's help continue to the end and that his Order of religious had fully purposed by the help of Jesus Christ to prosecute this most heavenly enterprise of doing good to England so long as they should have subjects to employ in the same which no doubt would never cease, and that the account of this was already made seeing the fine thereof was but paying of blood which would always be ready if the Queen and Council continued their persecution,

Lastly, he concluded, touching his own person, that if all these protestations, offers, and reasons would not serve to procure him grace nor grateful audience with them, then would he turn himself only to Almighty God that knew his thoughts and desires and would beseech him to take his cause and labours in protection and would extend his mercy to their honours until the last universal and great accounting day at what time they should well perceive with what integrity of mind and perfect love towards them, his prince, and country he had spoken then, and then there should be no memory of hatred nor suspicion of enmity between them.

Collect

ALMIGHTY and ever-living God, who gavest thy servant Edmund Campion courage to witness to the Gospel of Christ even to the point of giving his life for it: grant that, by his prayers, we may endure all suffering for love of thee, and may seek thee with all our hearts, for thou alone art the source of life; through Jesus Christ thy Son our Lord, who liveth and reigneth with thee, in the unity of the Holy Spirit, one God, for ever and ever.

Saint Thomas of Canterbury, Martyr
(29 December)

Proper of the Day and Common of Pastors: for a Bishop

The following passage may be read in the Divine Office according to the Use of tis Customary but not at the Office of Readings in the Liturgy of Hours of the Roman Rite.

A reading from the writings of Thomas Stearns Eliot

Dear children of God, my sermon this morning will be a very short one. I wish only that you should ponder and meditate the deep meaning and mystery of our masses of Christmas Day. For whenever Mass is said, we re-enact the Passion and Death of Our Lord; and on this Christmas Day we do this in celebration of his Birth. So that at the same moment we rejoice in his coming for the salvation of men, and offer again to God his Body and Blood in sacrifice, oblation and satisfaction for the sins of the whole world. It was in this same night that has just passed, that a multitude of the heavenly host appeared before the shepherds at Bethlehem, saying, 'Glory to God in the highest and on earth peace, good will toward men'; at this same time of all the year that we celebrate at once the Birth of Our Lord and his Passion and Death upon the Cross. Beloved, as the World sees, this is to behave in a strange fashion: For who in the World will both mourn and rejoice at once and for the same reason? For either joy will be overborne by mourning, or mourning will be cast out by joy; so it is only in these our Christian mysteries that we can rejoice and mourn at once for the same reason. [...]

Thomas Stearns Eliot, 'Interlude', in *Murder in the Cathedral, by T. St Eliot* (London: Faber and Faber, 1935), pp. 47-50.

Consider also one thing of which you have probably never thought. Not only do we at the feast of Christmas celebrate at once Our Lord's Birth and his Death: but on the next day we celebrate the martyrdom of his first martyr, the blessed Stephen. Is it an accident, do you think, that the day of the first martyr follows immediately the day of the Birth of Christ? By no means. Just as we rejoice and mourn at once, in the Birth and in the Passion of Our Lord; so also, in a smaller figure, we both rejoice and mourn in the death of martyrs. We mourn, for the sins of the world that has martyred them; we rejoice, that another soul is numbered among the Saints in Heaven, for the glory of God and for the salvation of men. [...]

Beloved, we do not think of a martyr simply as a good Christian who has been killed because he is a Christian: for that would be solely to mourn. We do not think of him simply as a good Christian who has been elevated to the company of the Saints: for that would be simply to rejoice: and neither our mourning nor our rejoicing is as the world's is. [...]

A martyr, a saint, is always made by the design of God, for his love of men, to warn them and to lead them, to bring them back to his ways. A martyrdom is never the design of man; for the true martyr is he who has become the instrument of God, who has lost his will in the will of God, not lost but found it, for he has found freedom in submission to God. The martyr no longer desires anything for himself, not even the glory of martyrdom. So thus as on earth the Church mourns and rejoices at once, in a fashion that the world cannot understand; so in Heaven the Saints are most high, having made themselves most low, seeing themselves not as we see them, but in the light of the Godhead from which they draw their being.

Collect
O LORD God, who gavest to thy servant Thomas Becket grace to put aside all earthly fear and be faithful even unto death: grant that we, caring not for worldly esteem, may fight against evil, uphold thy rule, and serve thee to our life's end; through Jesus Christ thy Son our Lord, who liveth and reigneth with thee, in the unity of the Holy Spirit, one God, for ever and ever.

Evening Prayer is of the Octave Day of Christmas unless the feast of Saint Thomas is celebrated as a solemnity.

IV. Times and Seasons

Part VIII Sanctorale:

Common of Saints

Various Needs
and Occasions

Common of the Blessed Virgin Mary

Office

Opening Sentence

Blessed are you Mary, for you believed that there would be a fulfillment of what was spoken to you from the Lord.

cf Lk 1:45

Short Reading for Prayer during the Day   *Zech 9:9*

Rejoice greatly, O daughter of Zion! Shout aloud, O daughter of Jerusalem! Behold, your king comes to you; triumphant and victorious is he.

Collect

ALMIGHTY and everlasting God, who stooped to raise fallen humanity through the child-bearing of blessed Mary: grant that we, who have seen thy glory revealed in our human nature and thy love made perfect in our weakness, may daily be renewed in thine image and, through her constant intercession, conformed to the pattern of thy Son Jesus Christ our Lord; who liveth and reigneth with thee, in the unity of the Holy Spirit, one God, for ever and ever.

Office

Opening Sentence

The righteous shall be had in everlasting remembrance; the memory of the just is blessed.

Ps 112:6; Prov 10:7

Short Readings for Prayer during the Day

Common of Apostles
Acts 5:12-14

Many signs and wonders were done among the people by the hands of the apostles. And they were all together in Solomon's Portico. None of the rest dared join them, but the people held them in high honour. And more than ever believers were added to the Lord, multitudes both of men and women.

Common of Evangelists
Acts 1:1b, 2

I have dealt with all that Jesus began to do and teach, until the day when he was taken up, after he had given commandment through the Holy Spirit to the apostles who he had chosen.

Common of Martyrs
Wis 3:1-3

The souls of the righteous are in the hand of God, and no torment will ever touch them. In the eyes of the foolish they seemed to have died, and their departure was thought to be an affliction, and their going from us to be their destruction; but they are at peace.

Common of Pastors
1 Tim 1:12

I thank him who has given me strength for this, Christ Jesus our Lord, because he judged me faithful by appointing me to his service.

Common of Doctors of the Church
1 Tim 4:13, 14

Attend to the public reading of Scripture, to preaching, to teaching. Do not neglect the gift you have, which was given you by prophetic utterance when the elders laid their hands upon you.

Common of Virgins
Rev 19:6b-8

The Lord our God the Almighty reigns. Let us rejoice and exult and give him the glory, for the marriage of the Lamb has come, and his Bride has made herself ready; it was granted her to be clothed with fine linen, bright and pure for the fine linen is the righteous deeds of the saints.

Common of Saints: for Religious
Phil 4:8, 9

Finally, brethren, whatever is true, whatever is honourable, whatever is just, whatever is pure, whatever is lovely, whatever is gracious, if there is any excellence, if there is anything worthy of praise, think about these things. What you have learned and received and heard and seen in me, do; and the God of peace will be with you.

Common of Saints:
for a Saint Noted for Works of Mercy
Gal 6:7b-10

Whatever a man sows, that he will also reap. For he who sows to his own flesh will from the flesh reap corruption; but he who sows to the Spirit will from the Spirit reap eternal life. And let us not grow weary in well-doing, for in due season we shall reap, if we do not lose heart. So then, as we have opportunity, let us do good to all men and especially to those who are of the household of faith.

Common of Saints: for an Educator
1 Tim 4:15, 16

Practise these duties, devote yourself to them, so that all may see your progress. Take heed to yourself and to your teaching; hold to that, for by so doing you will save both yourself and your hearers.

Common of Saints
1 Cor 9:24, 25

Do you not know that in a race all the runners compete, but only one receives a prize? So run that you may obtain it. Every athlete exercises self-control in all things. They do it to receive a perishable wreath, but we an imperishable.

Collects

Common of Apostles and Evangelists

O ALMIGHTY God, who hast built thy Church upon the foundation of the apostles and prophets, Jesus Christ himself being the head cornerstone: grant us so to be joined together in unity of spirit by their doctrine, that, by their intercession, we may be made an holy temple acceptable unto thee; through Jesus Christ thy Son our Lord, who liveth and reigneth with thee, in the unity of the Holy Spirit, one God, for ever and ever.

Common of Martyrs

ALMIGHTY God, by whose grace and power thy holy martyr *N.* triumphed over suffering and was faithful unto death: strengthen us with thy grace, that, assisted by *his/her* prayers we may endure reproach and persecution and faithfully bear witness to the name of Jesus Christ thy Son our Lord; who liveth and reigneth with thee, in the unity of the Holy Spirit, one God, for ever and ever.

Common of Pastors: for a Pope

O EVERLASTING Shepherd, look down in mercy on thy flock: and as thou didst choose blessed *N.* to be supreme pastor and ruler of thy Church; so at his intercession defend it with thy continual protection, through Jesus Christ thy Son our Lord, who liveth and reigneth with thee, in the unity of the Holy Spirit, one God, for ever and ever.

Common of Pastors: for a Bishop

ALMIGHTY God, the light of the faithful and shepherd of souls, who didst call thy servant *N.* to be a bishop in the Church, to feed thy sheep by the word of Christ and to guide them by his godly example: give us grace to abide by the faith of the Church and to follow in the footsteps of Jesus Christ thy Son our Lord; who liveth and reigneth with thee, in the unity of the Holy Spirit, one God, for ever and ever.

Common of Pastors: for other Pastors

ALMIGHTY and everlasting God, who didst call thy servant *N.* to proclaim thy glory by a life of prayer and the zeal of a true pastor: keep constant in faith the leaders of thy Church and so bless thy people through their ministry that the Church may grow into the full stature of thy Son Jesus Christ our Lord; who liveth and reigneth with thee, in the unity of the Holy Spirit, one God, for ever and ever.

Common of Pastors: for an Abbot or Abbess

O GOD, by whose grace the blessed *Abbot/Abbess N.*, enkindled with the fire of thy love, became a burning and shining light in thy Church: grant that, aided by *his/her* prayers we may be inflamed with the same spirit of discipline and love, and ever walk before thee as children of light; through Jesus Christ thy Son our Lord, who liveth and reigneth with thee, in the unity of the Holy Spirit, one God, for ever and ever.

Common of Pastors: for Missionaries

O EVERLASTING God, whose servant *N.* carried the gospel of thy Son to the people of ...: mercifully grant that we who commemorate *his/her* service may know the hope of the gospel in our hearts and manifest its light in all our ways; through Jesus Christ thy Son our Lord, who liveth and reigneth with thee, in the unity of the Holy Spirit, one God, for ever and ever.

Common of Doctors of the Church

O GOD, who hast enlightened thy Church by the teaching of thy servant *N.*: enrich it evermore, we beseech thee, with thy heavenly grace, and raise up faithful witnesses, who by their life and doctrine may set forth to all people the truth of thy salvation; through Jesus Christ thy Son our Lord, who liveth and reigneth with thee, in the unity of the Holy Spirit, one God, for ever and ever.

Common of Virgins

O GOD, who didst endue thy holy Virgin *N.* with grace to witness a good confession (*and to suffer gladly for thy sake*): grant that we, after her example, and assisted by her prayers, may be found ready when the Bridegroom cometh, and enter with him to the marriage feast; through the same thy Son Jesus Christ our Lord, who liveth and reigneth with thee, in the unity of the Holy Spirit, one God, for ever and ever.

Common of Saints: for Religious

ALMIGHTY God, by whose grace *N.*, enkindled with the fire of thy love, became a burning and a shining light in the Church: inflame us with the same spirit of discipline and love, that, assisted by *his/her* prayers, we may ever walk before thee as children of light; through Jesus Christ thy Son our Lord, who liveth and reigneth with thee, in the unity of the Holy Spirit, one God, for ever and ever.

Common of Saints: for a Saint Noted for Works of Mercy

O MERCIFUL God, who hast compassion on all that thou hast made, and hast enfolded thy whole creation in thy love: help us to stand firm for thy truth, to strive against poverty, and to share thy love with our neighbour, that with thy servant *N.* we may be instruments of thy peace; through Jesus Christ thy Son our Lord, who liveth and reigneth with thee, in the unity of the Holy Spirit, one God, for ever and ever.

Common of Saints: for an Educator

O GOD our Father, who gavest to thy servant *N.* wisdom and discernment that *he/she* might fathom the depths of thy love and understand thy design for the world that thou hast made: grant us the help of thy Holy Spirit, that we also may come to a full knowledge of thy purposes revealed in thy Son Jesus Christ, our wisdom and our life; who liveth and reigneth with thee, in the unity of the Holy Spirit, one God, for ever and ever.

Common of Saints: for Christian Rulers

SOVEREIGN God, who didst call *N.* to be a ruler among *his/her* people and gavest *him/her* grace to be their servant: help us to follow our Saviour Christ in the path of humble service, that we may see his kingdom set forward on earth and enjoy its fullness in heaven; through Jesus Christ thy Son our Lord, who liveth and reigneth with thee, in the unity of the Holy Spirit, one God, for ever and ever.

Common of Saints:
Holiness revealed in Marriage and Family Life

O ETERNAL God, whose love is revealed in the mystery of the Trinity: grant that we, like thy servant *N.*, may find in our human loving a mirror of thy divine love and discern in all thy children our brothers and sisters in Christ; who liveth and reigneth with thee, in the unity of the Holy Spirit, one God, for ever and ever.

Common of Saints: Any Saint

ALMIGHTY Father, who hast built up thy Church through the love and devotion of thy Saints: inspire us to follow the example of *N.* whom we commemorate this day, that, aided by *his/her* intercession, we in our generation may rejoice with *him/her* in the vision of thy glory; through Jesus Christ thy Son our Lord, who liveth and reigneth with thee, in the unity of the Holy Spirit, one God, for ever and ever.

Dedication

Evening Prayer *Vespers*

Urbs Ierusalem beata

1.Blessed city, heavenly Salem,
  vision dear of peace and love,
who of living stones upbuilded
  art the joy of heaven above,
and, with angel cohorts circled,
  as a bride to earth dost move!

2.From celestial realms descending,
  bridal glory round her shed,
meet for him whose love espoused her,
  to her Lord shall she be led;
all her streets and all her bulwarks
  of pure gold are fashionèd.

3.Bright with pearls her portal glitters,
  it is open evermore;
and by virtue of his merits
  thither faithful souls may soar,
who, for Christ's dear Name, in this world
  pain and tribulation bore.

4.Many a blow and biting sculpture
  polished well those stones elect,
in their places now compacted
  by the heavenly Architect,
who therewith hath willed for ever
  that his palace should be decked.

5.Laud and honour to the Father,
  laud and honour to the Son,
laud and honour to the Spirit,
  ever Three, and ever One,
consubstantial, Co-eternal,
  while unending ages run. Amen.

c.7th cent. Tr. J. M. Neale *and others*

666

Angularis fundamentum

1.Christ is made the sure Foundation,
  Christ the Head and Cornerstone;
chosen of the Lord, and precious,
  binding all the Church in one,
holy Zion's Help forever,
  and her Confidence alone.

2.All that dedicated city,
  dearly loved of God on high,
in exultant jubilation,
  pours perpetual melody,
God the One in Three adoring
  in glad hymns eternally.

3.To this temple, where we call thee,
  come, O Lord of Hosts, today;
with thy wonted loving-kindness
  hear thy servants as they pray.
And thy fullest benediction
  shed within its walls alway.

4.Here vouchsafe to all thy servants
  what they ask of thee to gain;
what they gain from thee forever
  with the blessèd to retain,
and hereafter in thy glory
  evermore with thee to reign.

5.Laud and honour to the Father,
  laud and honour to the Son,
laud and honour to the Spirit,
  ever Three and ever One;
consubstantial, co-eternal,
  while unending ages run.Amen.

c.7ᵗʰ cent. Tr. J. M. Neale

The Blessed Virgin Mary

O gloriosa Domina

1.O glorious Maid, exalted far
   beyond the light of burning star,
from him who made thee thou hast won
   grace to be Mother of his Son.

2.That which was lost in hapless Eve
   thy holy Scion did retrieve;
the tear-worn sons of Adam's race
   through thee have seen the heavenly place.

3.Thou wast the gate of heaven's high Lord,
   the door through which the light hath poured.
Christians rejoice, for through a Maid
   To all mankind is life conveyed!

4.All honour, laud and glory be,
   O Jesus, Virgin-born to thee!
all glory, as is ever meet,
   to Father and to Paraclete. Amen.

9th cent., Tr. Percy Dearmer

Tune I

or   Tune II

Ave maris stella

1.Hail, O Star that pointest
   towards the port of heaven,
thou to whom as maiden
   God for son was given.

2.When the salutation
   Gabriel had spoken,
peace was shed upon us,
   Eva's bonds were broken.

3.Bound by Satan's fetters,
   health and vision needing,
God will aid and light us
   at thy gentle pleading.

4.Jesu's tender Mother
   make thy supplication
unto him who chose thee
   at his Incarnation;

5.That, O matchless Maiden,
   passing meek and lowly,
thy dear Son may make us
   blameless, chaste and holy.

6.So, as now we journey,
   aid our weak endeavour.
till we gaze on Jesus,
   and rejoice for ever.

7.Father, Son and Spirit,
   Three in One confessing,
give we equal glory,
   equal praise and blessing. Amen.

9th cent., Tr. Athelstan Riley (1858-1945)

Apostles

Morning Prayer *Lauds (Easter)*

The hymns are sung to the same tune, given above. Both conclude with the verse **Maker of all,** *and the doxology, as given below.*

Claro paschali gaudio

1. On that fair day of Paschal joy
   the sunshine was without alloy,
   when to their very eyes restored
   they looked upon the risen Lord.

2. The wounds before their eyes displayed
   they see in living light arrayed,
   and that they see they testify
   in open witness fearlessly.

3. O Christ, the King of gentleness,
   our several hearts do thou possess,
   that we may render all our days
   due deeds of thankfulness and praise.

Evening Prayer *Vespers (Easter)*

Tristes erant Apostoli

1. The sad Apostles mourn him slain,
   nor hope to see their Lord again;
   their Lord, whom rebel thralls defy,
   arraign, accuse, and doom to die.

2. But now they put their grief away,
   the pains of hell are loosed to-day;
   for by the grave, with flashing eyes,
   'Your Lord is risen,' the angel cries.

Maker of all, to thee we pray,
  fulfil in us thy joy to-day;
when death assails, grant, Lord, that we
  may share thy Paschal victory.

To thee who, dead, again dost live,
  All glory, Lord, thy people give;
All glory, as is ever meet,
  To Father and to Paraclete. Amen.

4th or 5th cent., Tr. T. A. Lacey

670

or

Exsultet cælum laudibus

1.Let the round world with songs rejoice;
 let heaven return the joyful voice;
all mindful of the Apostles' fame,
 let heaven and earth their praise proclaim.

2.Ye servants who once bore the light
 of Gospel truth o'er heathen night,
still may your work that light impart
 to glad our eyes and cheer our heart.

3.O God, by whom to them was given
 the key that shuts and opens heaven,
our chains unbind, our loss repair,
 and grant us garce to enter there;

4.For at thy will they preached the word
 Which cured disease, which health
 conferred:
O may that healing power once more
 our souls to grace and health restore.

5.That when thy Son again shall come,
 and speak the world's unerring doom,
he may with them pronounce us blest,
 and place us in thy endless rest.

6.To thee, O Father; Son, to thee;
 to thee, blest Spirit, glory be!
so was it ay for ages past,
 so shall through endless ages last. Amen.

c.10ᵗʰ cent., Tr. R. Mant

671

Æterna Christi munera

1. The eternal gifts of Christ the King,
   the Apostles' glorious deed, we sing;
   and while due hymns of praise we pay,
   our thankful hearts cast grief away.

2. The Church in these her princes boasts,
   these victor chiefs of warrior hosts;
   the soldiers of the heavenly hall,
   the lights that rose on earth for all.

3. 'Twas thus the yearning faith of Saints,
   the unconquered hope that never faints,
   the love of Christ that knows not shame,
   the prince of this world overcame.

4. In these the Father's glory shone;
   in these the will of God the Son;
   in these exults the Holy Ghost;
   through these rejoice the heavenly host.

5. Redeemer, hear us of thy love,
   that, with this glorious band above,
   hereafter, of thine endless grace,
   thy servants also may have place. Amen.

Before 11th cent. Tr. J. M. Neale

or

Martyr Dei qui (quæ) unicum

1. Martyr of God, whose strength was steeled
   to follow close God's only Son,
   well didst thou brave thy battlefield,
   and well thy heavenly bliss was won!

2. Now join thy prayers with ours, who pray
   that God may pardon us and bless;
   for prayer keeps evil's plague away,
   and draws from life its weariness.

3. Long, long ago, were loosed the chains
   that held thy body once in thrall;
   for us how many a bond remains!
   O Love of God, release us all.

4. All praise to God the Father be,
   All praise to thee, eternal Son;
   all praise, O Holy Ghost, to thee,
   while never-ending ages run. Amen

c.10ᵗʰ cent., Tr. Percy Dearmer

673

Deus tuorum militum

1.O God, thy soldiers' crown and guard,
 and their exceeding great reward;
from all transgressions set us free,
 who sing thy martyr's victory.

2.The pleasures of the world he spurned,
 from sin's pernicious lures he turned;
he knew their joys imbued with gall,
 and thus he reached thy heavenly hall.

3.For thee through many a woe he ran,
 in many a fight he played the man;
for thee his blood he dared to pour,
 and thence hath joy for evermore.

4.We therefore pray thee, full of love,
 regard us from thy throne above;
on this thy martyr's triumph day,
 wash every stain of sin away.

5.O Christ, most loving King, to thee,
 with God the Father, glory be;
like glory, as is ever meet,
 to God the holy Paraclete. Amen.

6ᵗʰ cent., Tr. J. M. Neale

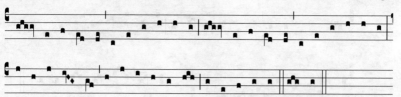

Virginis proles

1.Son of a Virgin, Maker of thy mother,
thou, Rod and Blossom from a Stem unstained,
now while a Virgin fair of fame we honour,
       hear our devotion!

2.Lo, on thy handmaid fell a twofold blessing,
who, in her body, vanquishing the weakness,
in that same body, grace from heaven obtaining,
       bore the world witness.

3.Death, nor the rending pains of death appalled her
bondage and torment found her undefeated:
so by the shedding of her life attained she
       heavenly guerdon.

4.Fountain of mercy, hear the prayers she offer;
purge our offences, pardon our transgressions,
so that hereafter we to thee may render
       praise with thanksgiving.

5.Thou, the All-Father, thou the One-Begotten,
thou, Holy Spirit, Three in One co-equal,
glory be henceforth thine through all the ages,
       world without ending. Amen.

8th cent., Tr. Laurence Housman.

Morning and Evening Prayer

Doctor æternus

1. Jesus, our Master and our only Saviour,
in adoration we acclaim your teaching,
you alone offer words of life eternal,
  laws of salvation.

2. Humbly we thank you, Shepherd through the ages,
for the protection to your Church extended,
constantly guiding, that all souls may find there
  light in the darkness.

3. Wisest of scholars were your eager servants,
stars of great splendour with but one intention,
deeper to ponder teachings that might show us
  life ever blessed.

4. All tongues should praise you, Jesus, Lord and Master,
who showers treasures through your Holy Spirit,
by words and writings of the Church's doctors,
  flame ever-fruitful.

5. May this day's patron whom we gladly honour,
ever be near us, leading on your people,
till we all praise you, faith and hope rewarded,
  in love eternal.

Tr. St Cecila's Abbey, Ryde

Iesu corona virginum

1. Jesu, the Virgins' Crown, do thou
   accept us as in prayer we bow,
born of that virgin whom alone
   the Mother and the Maid we own.

2. Amongst the lilies thou dost feed,
   with Virgin choirs accompanied –
with glory decked, the spotless bride
   whose bridal gifts thy love provides.

3. They, wheresoe'er thy footsteps bend,
   with hymn and praises still attent;
in blessed troops they follow thee,
   with dance, and song, and melody.

4. We pray thee therefore to bestow
   upon our senses here below
thy grace, that so we may endure
   from taint of all corruption pure.

5. All laud to God the Father be,
   all praise, eternal Son, to thee,
all glory, as is ever meet,
   yo God the holy Paraclete. Amen.

St Ambrose, *Tr.* J. M. Neale

Iesu redemptor omnium

1. O thou whose all-redeeming might
   crowns every chief in faith's true fight,
on this commemoration deay
   hear us, good Jesu, while we pray.

2. In faithful strife for thy dear name
   thy servant earned the saintly fame,
which pious hearts with praise revere
   in constant memory year by year.

3. Earth's fleeting joys he counted nought,
   for higher, truer joys he sought,
and now, with angels round thy throne,
   unfading treasures are his own.

4. O grant that we, most gracious God,
   may follow in the steps he trod;
and, freed from every stain of sin,
   as he hath won may also win.

5. To thee, O Christ, our loving King,
   all glory, praise, and thanks we bring;
whom with the Father we adore
   and Holy Ghost for evermore. Amen.

6ᵗʰ cent., Tr. Richard Meux Benson

Fortem virili pectore

1. The praises of that Saint we sing,
   to whom all lands their tribute bring,
who with indomitable heart
   bore throughout life true woman's part.

2. Restraining every froward sense
   by gentle bonds of abstinence,
with prayer her hungry soul she fed,
   and thus to heavenly joys hath sped.

3. King Christ, from whom all virtue springs,
   who only doest wondrous things,
as now to thee she kneels in prayer,
   in mercy our petitions hear.

4. All praise to God the Father be,
   all praise, eternal Son, to thee;
whom with the Spirit we adore
   for ever and for evermore. Amen.

Silvio Antoniano (1540-1603), *Tr.* Athelstan Riley.

Various Needs and Occasions

I.   Guidance of the Holy Spirit

II.   Harvest

III.   Ministry and Vocations

IV.   Mission and Evangelism

V.   Peace of the World

VI.   Remembrance and Time of Trouble

VII.   Social Justice and Responsibility

VIII.   Unity of the Church

I. Guidance of the Holy Spirit

Office

Opening Sentence
The love of God has been shed abroad in our hearts through the Holy Spirit which was given unto us.

Rom 5:5

Collect
GOD, who dost teach the hearts of thy faithful people by sending to them the light of thy Holy Spirit: grant us by the same Spirit to have a right judgment in all things and evermore to rejoice in his holy comfort; through the merits of Christ Jesus our Saviour, who liveth and reigneth with thee, in the unity of the same Spirit, one God, for ever and ever.

II. Harvest

Office

Opening Sentence
The earth is the Lord's, and the fullness thereof.

Ps 24:1

Collect
O ETERNAL God, who crownest the year with thy goodness and dost give us the fruits of the earth in their season: give us grace that we may use them to thy glory, for the relief of those in need and for our own well-being; through Jesus Christ thy Son our Lord, who liveth and reigneth with thee, in the unity of the Holy Spirit, one God, for ever and ever.

681

III. Ministry and Vocations

(and for Ember Days)

Office

Opening Sentence
You did not choose me but I chose you.
And I appointed you to go and bear fruit, fruit that will last.

Jn 15:16

Collects

ALMIGHTY and everlasting God, by whose Spirit the whole body of the Church is governed and sanctified: hear our prayer which we offer for all thy faithful people, that in their vocation and ministry each may serve thee in holiness and truth to the glory of thy name; through our Lord and Saviour Jesus Christ, who liveth and reigneth with thee, in the unity of the Holy Spirit, one God, for ever and ever.

or (for those to be ordained)

ALMIGHTY God, the giver of all good gifts, who by thy Holy Spirit hast appointed various orders of ministry in thy Church: look with mercy on thy servants now called to be deacons and priests, so maintain them in truth and renew them in holiness, that they may faithfully serve thee both in word and deed, to the glory of thy name and the benefit of thy holy Church; through the merits of our Saviour Jesus Christ, who liveth and reigneth with thee, in the unity of the Holy Spirit, one God, for ever and ever.

or (for vocations)

ALMIGHTY God, who hast entrusted to thy Church a share in the ministry of thy Son our great High Priest: we pray that by the inspiration of thy Holy Spirit the hearts of many may be moved to offer themselves for the ministry of thy Church, and that, strengthened by his power, they may work for the increase of thy kingdom and set forward the eternal praise of thy name; through Jesus Christ thy Son our Lord, who liveth and reigneth with thee, in the unity of the Holy Spirit, one God, for ever and ever.

IV. Mission and Evangelism

Office

Opening Sentence

Look around you, and see how the fields are ripe for harvesting.

Jn 4:35

Collect

ALMIGHTY God, who hast called thy Church to witness that thou wast in Christ reconciling the world to thyself: help us so to proclaim the good news of thy love that all who hear it may be drawn to thee; through him who was lifted up on the cross, and reigneth with thee and the Holy Spirit, one God, for ever and ever.

V. Peace of the World

Office

Opening Sentence

The wisdom from above is first pure, then peaceable, gentle, willing to yield, full of mercy and good fruits, without a trace of partiality or hypocrisy. And a harvest of righteousness is sown in peace for those who make peace.

Jas 3:17, 18

Collect

ALMIGHTY God, from whom all thoughts of truth and peace proceed: kindle, we pray thee, in every heart the true love of peace; and guide with thy pure and peaceable wisdom those who take counsel for the nations of the earth, that in tranquillity thy kingdom may go forward, till the earth is filled with the knowledge of thy love; through Jesus Christ thy Son our Lord, who liveth and reigneth with thee, in the unity of the Holy Spirit, one God, for ever and ever.

VI. Remembrance and Time of Trouble

Office

Opening Sentence

God is our hope and strength: a very present help in trouble.

Ps 46:1

Collect

SOVEREIGN God, who art the defence of those who trust in thee and the strength of those who suffer: mercifully look upon our affliction and deliver us through the might of our Saviour Jesus Christ, who liveth and reigneth with thee, in the unity of the Holy Spirit, one God, for ever and ever.

VII. Social Justice and Responsibility

Office

Opening Sentence

What does the Lord require of you but to do justice, and to love kindness, and to walk humbly with your God?

Mic 6:8

Collect

O ETERNAL God, in whose perfect realm no sword is drawn but the sword of righteousness, and no strength known but the strength of love: so guide and inspire the work of those who seek thy kingdom that all thy people may find their strength in that love which casteth out fear and in the fellowship revealed to us in Jesus Christ our Saviour, who liveth and reigneth with thee, in the unity of the Holy Spirit, one God, for ever and ever.

or

ALMIGHTY and eternal God, to whom we must all give account: guide with thy Spirit the ... of this *(city, society, &c.)*, that *we/they* may be faithful to the mind of Christ and seek in all *our/their* purposes to enrich our common life; through Jesus Christ thy Son our Lord, who liveth and reigneth with thee, in the unity of the Holy Spirit, one God, for ever and ever.

VIII. Unity of the Church

Office

Opening Sentence
There is one Body and one Spirit, one Lord, one faith, one baptism, one God and Father of all, who is above all and through all and in all.

Eph 4:4a, 5, 6

Collect
HEAVENLY Father, who hast called us in the Body of thy Son Jesus Christ to continue his work of reconciliation and reveal thee to the world: forgive us the sins which tear us apart; give us the courage to overcome our fears and to seek that unity which is thy gift and thy will; through Jesus Christ thy Son our Lord, who liveth and reigneth with thee, in the unity of the Holy Spirit, one God, for ever and ever.

or

LORD Jesus Christ, who didst say to thine apostles, Peace I leave with you, my peace I give unto you: look not on our sins but on the faith of thy Church and grant it the peace and unity of thy kingdom; where thou livest and reignest with the Father in the unity of the Holy Spirit, ever one God, world without end.

V.   The Psalter

Psalm 1	*Beatus vir, qui non abiit*

1   BLESSED is the man that hath not walked in the counsel of the
     ungodly, nor stood in the way of sinners :
     and hath not sat in the seat of the scornful.

2   But his delight is in the law of the Lord :
     and in his law will he exercise himself day and night.

3   And he shall be like a tree planted by the water-side :
     that will bring forth his fruit in due season.

4   His leaf also shall not wither :
     and look, whatsoever he doeth, it shall prosper.

6   As for the ungodly, it is not so with them :
     but they are like the chaff, which the wind scattereth away
      from the face of the earth.

6   Therefore the ungodly shall not be able to stand in the judgement :
     neither the sinners in the congregation of the righteous.

7   But the Lord knoweth the way of the righteous :
     and the way of the ungodly shall perish.

Psalm 2	*Quare fremuerunt gentes?*

1   WHY do the heathen so furiously rage together :
     and why do the people imagine a vain thing?

2   The kings of the earth stand up, and the rulers take counsel together :
     against the Lord, and against his Anointed.

3   Let us break their bonds asunder :
     and cast away their cords from us.

4   He that dwelleth in heaven shall laugh them to scorn :
     the Lord shall have them in derision.

5   Then shall he speak unto them in his wrath :
     and vex them in his sore displeasure.

6   Yet have I set my King :
     upon my holy hill of Sion.

7   I will preach the law, whereof the Lord hath said unto me :
     Thou art my Son, this day have I begotten thee.

8   Desire of me, and I shall give thee the heathen for thine inheritance :
     and the utmost parts of the earth for thy possession.

9   Thou shalt bruise them with a rod of iron :
     and break them in pieces like a potter's vessel.

10 Be wise now therefore, O ye kings :
be learned, ye that are judges of the earth.

11 Serve the Lord in fear :
and rejoice unto him with reverence.

12 Kiss the Son, lest he be angry, and so ye perish from the right way :
if his wrath be kindled, (yea, but a little,)
blessed are all they that put their trust in him.

Psalm 3   *Domine, quid multiplicati,*

1 LORD, how are they increased that trouble me :
many are they that rise against me.

2 Many one there be that say of my soul :
There is no help for him in his God.

3 But thou, O Lord, art my defender :
thou art my worship, and the lifter up of my head.

4 I did call upon the Lord with my voice :
and he heard me out of his holy hill.

5 I laid me down and slept, and rose up again :
for the Lord sustained me.

6 I will not be afraid for ten thousands of the people :
that have set themselves against me round about.

7 Up, Lord, and help me, O my God :
for thou smitest all mine enemies upon the cheekbone;
thou hast broken the teeth of the ungodly.

8 Salvation belongeth unto the Lord :
and thy blessing is upon thy people.

Psalm 4   *Cum invocarem*

1 HEAR me when I call, O God of my righteousness :
thou hast set me at liberty when I was in trouble;
have mercy upon me, and hearken unto my prayer.

2 O ye sons of men, how long will ye blaspheme mine honour :
and have such pleasure in vanity, and seek after leasing?

3 Know this also, that the Lord hath chosen to himself
the man that is godly :
when I call upon the Lord, he will hear me.

4 Stand in awe, and sin not :
commune with your own heart, and in your chamber, and be still.

5	Offer the sacrifice of righteousness :
	and put your trust in the Lord.
6	There be many that say :
	Who will shew us any good?
7	Lord, lift thou up :
	the light of thy countenance upon us.
8	Thou hast put gladness in my heart :
	since the time that their corn and wine and oil increased.
9	I will lay me down in peace, and take my rest :
	for it is thou, Lord, only, that makest me dwell in safety.

Psalm 5 *Verba mea auribus.*

1 PONDER my words, O Lord :
  consider my meditation

2 O hearken thou unto the voice of my calling, my King, and my God :
  for unto thee will I make my prayer.

3 My voice shalt thou hear betimes, O Lord :
  early in the morning will I direct my prayer unto thee,
    and will look up.

4 For thou art the God that hast no pleasure in wickedness :
  neither shall any evil dwell with thee.

5 Such as be foolish shall not stand in thy sight :
  for thou hatest all them that work vanity.

6 Thou shalt destroy them that speak leasing :
  the Lord will abhor both the blood-thirsty and deceitful man.

7 But as for me, I will come into thine house,
    even upon the multitude of thy mercy :
  and in thy fear will I worship toward thy holy temple.

8 Lead me, O Lord, in thy righteousness, because of mine enemies :
  make thy way plain before my face.

9 For there is no faithfulness in his mouth :
  their inward parts are very wickedness.

10 Their throat is an open sepulchre :
  they flatter with their tongue.

11 Destroy thou them, O God;
    let them perish through their own imaginations :
  cast them out in the multitude of their ungodliness;
    for they have rebelled against thee.

12	And let all them that put their trust in thee rejoice :
	they shall ever be giving of thanks, because thou defendest them;
	they that love thy Name shall be joyful in thee;
13	For thou, Lord, wilt give thy blessing unto the righteous :
	and with thy favourable kindness wilt thou defend him
	as with a shield.

Day 1. Evening Prayer.

Psalm 6   *Domine, ne in furore*

1   O LORD, rebuke me not in thine indignation :
     neither chasten me in thy displeasure.
2   Have mercy upon me, O Lord, for I am weak :
     O Lord, heal me, for my bones are vexed.
3   My soul also is sore troubled :
     but, Lord, how long wilt thou punish me?
4   Turn thee, O Lord, and deliver my soul :
     O save me for thy mercy's sake.
5   For in death no man remembereth thee :
     and who will give thee thanks in the pit?
6   I am weary of my groaning; every night wash I my bed :
     and water my couch with my tears.
7   My beauty is gone for very trouble :
     and worn away because of all mine enemies.
8   Away from me, all ye that work vanity :
     for the Lord hath heard the voice of my weeping.
9   The Lord hath heard my petition :
     the Lord will receive my prayer.
10   All mine enemies shall be confounded, and sore vexed :
     they shall be turned back, and put to shame suddenly.

Psalm 7   *Domine, Deus meus*

1   O LORD my God, in thee have I put my trust :
     save me from all them that persecute me, and deliver me;
2   Lest he devour my soul, like a lion, and tear it in pieces :
     while there is none to help.
3   O Lord my God, if I have done any such thing :
     or if there be any wickedness in my hands;
4   If I have rewarded evil unto him that dealt friendly with me :
     yea, I have delivered him that without any cause is mine enemy,

5   Then let mine enemy persecute my soul, and take me :
yea, let him tread my life down upon the earth,
  and lay mine honour in the dust.

6   Stand up, O Lord, in thy wrath, and lift up thyself,
  because of the indignation of mine enemies :
arise up for me in the judgement that thou hast commanded.

7   And so shall the congregation of the people come about thee :
for their sakes therefore lift up thyself again.

8   The Lord shall judge the people; give sentence with me, O Lord :
according to my righteousness,
  and according to the innocency that is in me.

9   O let the wickedness of the ungodly come to an end :
but guide thou the just.

10   For the righteous God :
trieth the very hearts and reins.

11   My help cometh of God :
who preserveth them that are true of heart.

12   God is a righteous Judge, strong and patient :
and God is provoked every day.

13   If a man will not turn, he will whet his sword :
he hath bent his bow, and made it ready

14   He hath prepared for him the instruments of death :
he ordaineth his arrows against the persecutors

15   Behold, he travaileth with mischief :
he hath conceived sorrow, and brought forth ungodliness.

16   He hath graven and digged up a pit :
and is fallen on himself into the destruction that he made for other.

17   For his travail shall come upon his own head :
and his wickedness shall fall on his own pate.

18   I will give thanks unto the Lord, according to his righteousness :
and I will praise the Name of the Lord most High.

Psalm 8   *Domine, Dominus noster*

1   O LORD our Governor, how excellent is thy Name in all the world :
thou that hast set thy glory above the heavens!

2   Out of the mouth of very babes and sucklings
  hast thou ordained strength, because of thine enemies :
that thou mightest still the enemy and the avenger.

3   For I will consider thy heavens, even the works of thy fingers :
the moon and the stars, which thou hast ordained.

4	What is man, that thou art mindful of him :
	and the son of man, that thou visitest him?
5	Thou madest him lower than the angels :
	to crown him with glory and worship.
6	Thou makest him to have dominion of the works of thy hands :
	and thou hast put all things in subjection under his feet;
7	All sheep and oxen :
	yea, and the beasts of the field;
8	The fowls of the air, and the fishes of the sea :
	and whatsoever walketh through the paths of the seas.
9	O Lord our Governor :
	how excellent is thy Name in all the world!

Day 2. Morning Prayer.

Psalm 9   *Confitebor tibi*

1	I WILL give thanks unto thee, O Lord, with my whole heart :
	I will speak of all thy marvellous works.
2	I will be glad and rejoice in thee :
	yea, my songs will I make of thy Name, O thou most Highest.
3	While mine enemies are driven back :
	they shall fall and perish at thy presence.
4	For thou hast maintained my right and my cause :
	thou art set in the throne that judgest right.
5	Thou hast rebuked the heathen, and destroyed the ungodly :
	thou hast put out their name for ever and ever.
6	O thou enemy, destructions are come to a perpetual end :
	even as the cities which thou hast destroyed,
	their memorial is perished with them.
7	But the Lord shall endure for ever :
	he hath also prepared his seat for judgement.
8	For he shall judge the world in righteousness :
	and minister true judgement unto the people.
9	The Lord also will be a defence for the oppressed :
	even a refuge in due time of trouble.
10	And they that know thy Name will put their trust in thee :
	for thou, Lord, hast never failed them that seek thee.
11	O praise the Lord which dwelleth in Sion :
	shew the people of his doings.
12	For when he maketh inquisition for blood, he remembereth them :
	and forgetteth not the complaint of the poor.

13	Have mercy upon me, O Lord;
	consider the trouble which I suffer of them that hate me :
	thou that liftest me up from the gates of death.
14	That I may shew all thy praises
	within the ports of the daughter of Sion :
	I will rejoice in thy salvation.
15	The heathen are sunk down in the pit that they made :
	in the same net which they hid privily, is their foot taken.
16	The Lord is known to execute judgement :
	the ungodly is trapped in the work of his own hands.
17	The wicked shall be turned into hell :
	and all the people that forget God.
18	For the poor shall not alway be forgotten :
	the patient abiding of the meek shall not perish for ever.
19	Up, Lord, and let not man have the upper hand :
	let the heathen be judged in thy sight.
20	Put them in fear, O Lord :
	that the heathen may know themselves to be but men.

Psalm 10   *Ut quid, Domine?*

1	WHY standest thou so far off, O Lord :
	and hidest thy face in the needful time of trouble?
2	The ungodly for his own lust doth persecute the poor :
	let them be taken in the crafty wiliness that they have imagined.
3	For the ungodly hath made boast of his own heart's desire :
	and speaketh good of the covetous, whom God abhorreth.
4	The ungodly is so proud, that he careth not for God :
	neither is God in all his thoughts.
5	His ways are alway grievous :
	thy judgements are far above out of his sight,
	and therefore defieth he all his enemies.
6	For he hath said in his heart, Tush, I shall never be cast down :
	there shall no harm happen unto me.
7	His mouth is full of cursing, deceit, and fraud :
	under his tongue is ungodliness and vanity.
8	He sitteth lurking in the thievish corners of the streets :
	and privily in his lurking dens doth he murder the innocent;
	his eyes are set against the poor.
9	For he lieth waiting secretly, even as a lion lurketh he in his den :
	that he may ravish the poor.

10	He doth ravish the poor :
	when he getteth him into his net.
11	He falleth down, and humbleth himself :
	that the congregation of the poor
	may fall into the hands of his captains.
12	He hath said in his heart, Tush, God hath forgotten :
	he hideth away his face, and he will never see it.
13	Arise, O Lord God, and lift up thine hand :
	forget not the poor.
14	Wherefore should the wicked blaspheme God :
	while he doth say in his heart, Tush, thou God carest not for it.
15	Surely thou hast seen it :
	for thou beholdest ungodliness and wrong.
16	That thou mayest take the matter into thy hand :
	the poor committeth himself unto thee;
	for thou art the helper of the friendless.
17	Break thou the power of the ungodly and malicious :
	take away his ungodliness, and thou shalt find none.
18	The Lord is King for ever and ever :
	and the heathen are perished out of the land.
19	Lord, thou hast heard the desire of the poor :
	thou preparest their heart, and thine ear hearkeneth thereto;
20	To help the fatherless and poor unto their right :
	that the man of the earth be no more exalted against them.

Psalm 11   *In Domino confido*

1	IN THE Lord put I my trust :
	how say ye then to my soul,
	that she should flee as a bird unto the hill?
2	For lo, the ungodly bend their bow,
	and make ready their arrows within the quiver :
	that they may privily shoot at them which are true of heart.
3	For the foundations will be cast down :
	and what hath the righteous done?
4	The Lord is in his holy temple :
	the Lord's seat is in heaven.
5	His eyes consider the poor :
	and his eye-lids try the children of men.

6   The Lord alloweth the righteous :
      but the ungodly, and him that delighteth in wickedness,
         doth his soul abhor.

7   Upon the ungodly he shall rain snares,
         fire and brimstone, storm and tempest :
      this shall be their portion to drink.

8   For the righteous Lord loveth righteousness :
      his countenance will behold the thing that is just.

Day 2. Evening Prayer.

Psalm 12   *Salvum me fac*

1   HELP me, Lord, for there is not one godly man left :
      for the faithful are minished from among the children of men,

2   They talk of vanity every one with his neighbour :
      they do but flatter with their lips, and dissemble in their double heart.

3   The Lord shall root out all deceitful lips :
      and the tongue that speaketh proud things;

4   Which have said, With our tongue will we prevail :
      we are they that ought to speak , who is lord over us?

5   Now for the comfortless trouble's sake of the needy :
      and because of the deep sighing of the poor,

6   I will up, saith the Lord :
      and will help every one from him that swelleth against him,
         and will set him at rest.

7   The words of the Lord are pure words :
       even as the silver, which from the earth is tried,
         and purified seven times in the fire.

8   Thou shalt keep them, O Lord :
      thou shalt preserve him from this generation for ever.

9   The ungodly walk on every side :
      when they are exalted, the children of men are put to rebuke.

Psalm 13   *Usque quo, Domine?*

1   HOW long wilt thou forget me, O Lord, for ever :
      how long wilt thou hide thy face from me?

2   How long shall I seek counsel in my soul,
         and be so vexed in my heart :
      how long shall mine enemies triumph over me?

3   Consider, and hear me, O Lord my God :
      lighten mine eyes, that I sleep not in death.

4   Lest mine enemy say, I have prevailed against him :
     for if I be cast down, they that trouble me will rejoice at it.
5   But my trust is in thy mercy :
     and my heart is joyful in thy salvation.
6   I will sing of the Lord, because he hath dealt so lovingly with me :
     yea, I will praise the Name of the Lord most Highest.

[Psalm 14   *Dixit insipiens*
1   THE fool hath said in his heart :
     There is no God.
2   They are corrupt, and become abominable in their doings :
     there is none that doeth good, no not one.
3   The Lord looked down from heaven upon the children of men :
     to see if there were any that would understand, and seek after God.
4   But they are all gone out of the way,
        they are altogether become abominable :
     there is none that doeth good, no not one.
5   Their throat is an open sepulchre,
        with their tongues have they deceived :
     the poison of asps is under their lips.
6   Their mouth is full of cursing and bitterness :
     their feet are swift to shed blood.
7   Destruction and unhappiness is in their ways,
        and the way of peace have they not known :
     there is no fear of God before their eyes.
8   Have they no knowledge, that they are all such workers of mischief :
     eating up my people as it were bread, and call not upon the Lord?
9   There were they brought in great fear, even where no fear was :
     for God is in the generation of the righteous.
10   As for you, ye have made a mock at the counsel of the poor :
     because he putteth his trust in the Lord.
11   Who shall give salvation unto Israel out of Sion?
        When the Lord turneth the captivity of his people :
     then shall Jacob rejoice, and Israel shall be glad.]

697

Psalm 15 *Domine, quis habitabit?*

1   LORD, who shall dwell in thy tabernacle :
    or who shall rest upon thy holy hill?

2   Even he that leadeth an uncorrupt life :
    and doeth the thing which is right,
    and speaketh the truth from his heart.

3   He that hath used no deceit in his tongue,
      nor done evil to his neighbour :
    and hath not slandered his neighbour.

4   He that setteth not by himself, but is lowly in his own eyes :
    and maketh much of them that fear the Lord.

5   He that sweareth unto his neighbour, and disappointeth him not :
    though it were to his own hindrance.

6   He that hath not given his money upon usury :
    nor taken reward against the innocent.

7   Whoso doeth these things :
    shall never fall.

Psalm 16 *Conserva me, Domine*

1   PRESERVE me, O God :
    for in thee have I put my trust.

2   O my soul, thou hast said unto the Lord :
    Thou art my God, my goods are nothing unto thee.

3   All my delight is upon the saints, that are in the earth :
    and upon such as excel in virtue.

4   But they that run after another god :
    shall have great trouble.

5   Their drink-offerings of blood will I not offer :
    neither make mention of their names within my lips.

6   The Lord himself is the portion of mine inheritance, and of my cup :
    thou shalt maintain my lot.

7   The lot is fallen unto me in a fair ground :
    yea, I have a goodly heritage.

8   I will thank the Lord for giving me warning :
    my reins also chasten me in the night-season.

9   I have set God always before me :
    for he is on my right hand, therefore I shall not fall.

10   Wherefore my heart was glad, and my glory rejoiced :
    my flesh also shall rest in hope.

11   For why? thou shalt not leave my soul in hell :
      neither shalt thou suffer thy Holy One to see corruption.

12   Thou shalt shew me the path of life;
      in thy presence is the fulness of joy :
    and at thy right hand there is pleasure for evermore.

Psalm 17   *Exaudi, Domine*

1   HEAR the right, O Lord, consider my complaint :
    and hearken unto my prayer, that goeth not out of feigned lips.

2   Let my sentence come forth from thy presence :
    and let thine eyes look upon the thing that is equal.

3   Thou hast proved and visited mine heart in the night-season :
    thou hast tried me, and shalt find no wickedness in me;
      for I am utterly purposed that my mouth shall not offend.

4   Because of men's works, that are done against the words of thy lips :
    I have kept me from the ways of the destroyer.

5   O hold thou up my goings in thy paths :
    that my footsteps slip not.

6   I have called upon thee, O God, for thou shalt hear me :
    incline thine ear to me, and hearken unto my words.

7   Shew thy marvellous loving-kindness,
      thou that art the Saviour of them which put their trust in thee :
    from such as resist thy right hand.

8   Keep me as the apple of an eye :
    hide me under the shadow of thy wings.

9   From the ungodly that trouble me :
    mine enemies compass me round about to take away my soul.

10   They are inclosed in their own fat :
    and their mouth speaketh proud things.

11   They lie waiting in our way on every side :
    turning their eyes down to the ground.

12   Like as a lion that is greedy of his prey :
    and as it were a lion's whelp, lurking in secret places.

13   Up, Lord, disappoint him, and cast him down :
    deliver my soul from the ungodly, which is a sword of thine;

14   From the men of thy hand, O Lord, from the men, I say,
      and from the evil world :
    which have their portion in this life,
      whose bellies thou fillest with thy hid treasure.

15	They have children at their desire :
	and leave the rest of their substance for their babes.
16	But as for me, I will behold thy presence in righteousness :
	and when I awake up after thy likeness, I shall be satisfied with it.

Day 3. Evening Prayer.

Psalm 18	*Diligam te, Domine*
1	I WILL love thee, O Lord, my strength;
	the Lord is my stony rock, and my defence :
	my saviour, my God, and my might, in whom I will trust,
	my buckler, the horn also of my salvation, and my refuge.
2	I will call upon the Lord, which is worthy to be praised :
	so shall I be safe from mine enemies.
3	The sorrows of death compassed me :
	and the overflowings of ungodliness made me afraid.
4	The pains of hell came about me :
	the snares of death overtook me.
5	In my trouble I will call upon the Lord :
	and complain unto my God.
6	So shall he hear my voice out of his holy temple :
	and my complaint shall come before him,
	it shall enter even into his ears.
7	The earth trembled and quaked :
	the very foundations also of the hills shook, and were removed,
	because he was wroth.
8	There went a smoke out in his presence :
	and a consuming fire out of his mouth,
	so that coals were kindled at it.
9	He bowed the heavens also, and came down :
	and it was dark under his feet.
10	He rode upon the cherubins, and did fly :
	he came flying upon the wings of the wind.
11	He made darkness his secret place :
	his pavilion round about him,
	with dark water and thick clouds to cover him.
12	At the brightness of his presence his clouds removed :
	hail-stones, and coals of fire.
13	The Lord also thundered out of heaven,
	and the Highest gave his thunder :
	hail-stones, and coals of fire.

14   He sent out his arrows, and scattered them :
he cast forth lightnings, and destroyed them.

15   The springs of water were seen,
    and the foundations of the round world were discovered,
    at thy chiding, O Lord :
at the blasting of the breath of thy displeasure.

16   He shall send down from on high to fetch me :
and shall take me out of many waters.

17   He shall deliver me from my strongest enemy,
    and from them which hate me :
for they are too mighty for me.

18   They prevented me in the day of my trouble :
but the Lord was my upholder.

19   He brought me forth also into a place of liberty :
he brought me forth, even because he had a favour unto me.

20   The Lord shall reward me after my righteous dealing :
according to the cleanness of my hands shall he recompense me.

21   Because I have kept the ways of the Lord :
and have not forsaken my God, as the wicked doth.

22   For I have an eye unto all his laws :
and will not cast out his commandments from me.

23   I was also uncorrupt before him :
and eschewed mine own wickedness.

24   Therefore shall the Lord reward me after my righteous dealing :
and according unto the cleanness of my hands in his eye-sight.

25   With the holy thou shalt be holy :
and with a perfect man thou shalt be perfect.

26   With the clean thou shalt be clean :
and with the froward thou shalt learn frowardness.

27   For thou shalt save the people that are in adversity :
and shalt bring down the high looks of the proud.

28   Thou also shalt light my candle :
the Lord my God shall make my darkness to be light.

29   For in thee I shall discomfit an host of men :
and with the help of my God I shall leap over the wall.

30   The way of God is an undefiled way :
the word of the Lord also is tried in the fire;
    he is the defender of all them that put their trust in him.

31   For who is God, but the Lord :
or who hath any strength, except our God?

32	It is God, that girdeth me with strength of war :
	and maketh my way perfect.
33	He maketh my feet like harts' feet :
	and setteth me up on high.
34	He teacheth mine hands to fight :
	and mine arms shall break even a bow of steel.
35	Thou hast given me the defence of thy salvation :
	thy right hand also shall hold me up,
	and thy loving correction shall make me great.
36	Thou shalt make room enough under me for to go :
	that my footsteps shall not slide.
37	I will follow upon mine enemies, and overtake them :
	neither will I turn again till I have destroyed them.
38	I will smite them, that they shall not be able to stand :
	but fall under my feet.
39	Thou hast girded me with strength unto the battle :
	thou shalt throw down mine enemies under me.
40	Thou hast made mine enemies also to turn their backs upon me :
	and I shall destroy them that hate me.
41	They shall cry, but there shall be none to help them :
	yea, even unto the Lord shall they cry, but he shall not hear them.
42	I will beat them as small as the dust before the wind :
	I will cast them out as the clay in the streets.
43	Thou shalt deliver me from the strivings of the people :
	and thou shalt make me the head of the heathen.
44	A people whom I have not known :
	shall serve me.
45	As soon as they hear of me, they shall obey me :
	but the strange children shall dissemble with me.
46	The strange children shall fail :
	and be afraid out of their prisons.
47	The Lord liveth, and blessed be my strong helper :
	and praised be the Lord of my salvation;
48	Even the God that seeth that I be avenged :
	and subdueth the people unto me.
49	It is he that delivereth me from my cruel enemies,
	and setteth me up above mine adversaries :
	thou shalt rid me from the wicked man.

50   For this cause will I give thanks unto thee, O Lord,
       among the Gentiles :
    and sing praises unto thy Name.

51   Great prosperity giveth he unto his King :
    and sheweth loving-kindness unto David his Anointed,
       and unto his seed for evermore.

Day 4. Morning Prayer.

Psalm 19   *Cæli enarrant*

1   THE heavens declare the glory of God :
    and the firmament sheweth his handywork.

2   One day telleth another :
    and one night certifieth another.

3   There is neither speech nor language :
    but their voices are heard among them.

4   Their sound is gone out into all lands :
    and their words into the ends of the world.

5   In them hath he set a tabernacle for the sun :
    which cometh forth as a bridegroom out of his chamber,
       and rejoiceth as a giant to run his course.

6   It goeth forth from the uttermost part of the heaven,
       and runneth about unto the end of it again :
    and there is nothing hid from the heat thereof.

7   The law of the Lord is an undefiled law, converting the soul :
    the testimony of the Lord is sure, and giveth wisdom unto the simple.

8   The statutes of the Lord are right, and rejoice the heart :
    the commandment of the Lord is pure, and giveth light unto the eyes.

9   The fear of the Lord is clean, and endureth for ever :
    the judgements of the Lord are true, and righteous altogether.

10   More to be desired are they than gold, yea, than much fine gold :
    sweeter also than honey, and the honey-comb.

11   Moreover, by them is thy servant taught :
    and in keeping of them there is great reward.

12   Who can tell how oft he offendeth :
    O cleanse thou me from my secret faults.

13   Keep thy servant also from presumptuous sins,
       lest they get the dominion over me :
    so shall I be undefiled, and innocent from the great offence.

14   Let the words of my mouth, and the meditation of my heart :
    be alway acceptable in thy sight,

15.   O Lord :
        my strength, and my redeemer.

Psalm 20   *Exaudiat te Dominus*

1   THE Lord hear thee in the day of trouble :
        the Name of the God of Jacob defend thee;
2   Send thee help from the sanctuary :
        and strengthen thee out of Sion;
3   Remember all thy offerings :
        and accept thy burnt-sacrifice;
4   Grant thee thy heart's desire :
        and fulfil all thy mind.
5   We will rejoice in thy salvation,
          and triumph in the Name of the Lord our God :
        the Lord perform all thy petitions.
6   Now know I that the Lord helpeth his Anointed,
          and will hear him from his holy heaven :
        even with the wholesome strength of his right hand.
7   Some put their trust in chariots, and some in horses :
        but we will remember the Name of the Lord our God.
8   They are brought down, and fallen :
        but we are risen, and stand upright.
9   Save, Lord, and hear us, O King of heaven :
        when we call upon thee.

Psalm 21   *Domine, in virtute tua*

1   THE King shall rejoice in thy strength, O Lord :
        exceeding glad shall he be of thy salvation.
2   Thou hast given him his heart's desire :
        and hast not denied him the request of his lips.
3   For thou shalt prevent him with the blessings of goodness :
        and shalt set a crown of pure gold upon his head.
4   He asked life of thee, and thou gavest him a long life :
        even for ever and ever.
5   His honour is great in thy salvation :
        glory and great worship shalt thou lay upon him.
6   For thou shalt give him everlasting felicity :
        and make him glad with the joy of thy countenance.
7   And why? because the King putteth his trust in the Lord :
        and in the mercy of the most Highest he shall not miscarry.

8	All thine enemies shall feel thine hand :
	thy right hand shall find out them that hate thee.
9	Thou shalt make them like a fiery oven in time of thy wrath :
	the Lord shall destroy them in his displeasure, and the fire shall consume them.
10	Their fruit shalt thou root out of the earth :
	and their seed from among the children of men.
11	For they intended mischief against thee :
	and imagined such a device as they are not able to perform.
12	Therefore shalt thou put them to flight :
	and the strings of thy bow shalt make ready against the face of them.
13	Be thou exalted, Lord, in thine own strength :
	so we will sing, and praise thy power.

Day 4. Evening Prayer.

Psalm 22   *Deus, Deus meus*

1	MY GOD, my God, look upon me; why hast thou forsaken me :
	and art so far from my health, and from the words of my complaint?
2	O my God, I cry in the day-time, but thou hearest not :
	and in the night-season also I take no rest.
3	And thou continuest holy :
	O thou worship of Israel.
4	Our fathers hoped in thee :
	they trusted in thee, and thou didst deliver them.
5	They called upon thee, and were holpen :
	they put their trust in thee, and were not confounded.
6	But as for me, I am a worm, and no man :
	a very scorn of men, and the outcast of the people.
7	All they that see me laugh me to scorn :
	they shoot out their lips, and shake their heads, saying,
8	He trusted in God, that he would deliver him :
	let him deliver him, if he will have him.
9	But thou art he that took me out of my mother's womb :
	thou wast my hope, when I hanged yet upon my mother's breasts.
10	I have been left unto thee ever since I was born :
	thou art my God, even from my mother's womb.
11	O go not from me, for trouble is hard at hand :
	and there is none to help me.

12	Many oxen are come about me :
	fat bulls of Basan close me in on every side.
13	They gape upon me with their mouths :
	as it were a ramping and a roaring lion.
14	I am poured out like water, and all my bones are out of joint :
	my heart also in the midst of my body is even like melting wax.
15	My strength is dried up like a potsherd,
	and my tongue cleaveth to my gums :
	and thou shalt bring me into the dust of death.
16	For many dogs are come about me :
	and the council of the wicked layeth siege against me.
17	They pierced my hands and my feet; I may tell all my bones :
	they stand staring and looking upon me.
18	They part my garments among them :
	and casts lots upon my vesture.
19	But be not thou far from me, O Lord :
	thou art my succour, haste thee to help me.
20	Deliver my soul from the sword :
	my darling from the power of the dog.
21	Save me from the lion's mouth :
	thou hast heard me also from among the horns of the unicorns.
22	I will declare thy Name unto my brethren :
	in the midst of the congregation will I praise thee.
23	O praise the Lord, ye that fear him :
	magnify him, all ye of the seed of Jacob, and fear him,
	all ye seed of Israel.
24	For he hath not despised, nor abhorred, the low estate of the poor :
	he hath not hid his face from him,
	but when he called unto him he heard him.
25	My praise is of thee in the great congregation :
	my vows will I perform in the sight of them that fear him.
26	The poor shall eat and be satisfied :
	they that seek after the Lord shall praise him;
	your heart shall live for ever.
27	All the ends of the world shall remember themselves,
	and be turned unto the Lord :
	and all the kindreds of the nations shall worship before him.
28	For the kingdom is the Lord's :
	and he is the Governor among the people.

29	All such as be fat upon earth :
	have eaten and worshipped.
30	All they that go down into the dust shall kneel before him :
	and no man hath quickened his own soul.
31	My seed shall serve him :
	they shall be counted unto the Lord for a generation.
32	They shall come, and the heavens shall declare his righteousness :
	unto a people that shall be born, whom the Lord hath made.

Psalm 23 *Dominus regit me.*

1	THE Lord is my shepherd :
	therefore can I lack nothing.
2	He shall feed me in a green pasture :
	and lead me forth beside the waters of comfort.
3	He shall convert my soul :
	and bring me forth in the paths of righteousness, for his Name's sake.
4	Yea, though I walk through the valley of the shadow of death,
	I will fear no evil :
	for thou art with me; thy rod and thy staff comfort me.
5	Thou shalt prepare a table before me against them that trouble me :
	thou hast anointed my head with oil, and my cup shall be full.
6	But thy loving-kindness and mercy shall follow me
	all the days of my life :
	and I will dwell in the house of the Lord for ever.

Day 5. Morning Prayer.

Psalm 24 *Domini est terra*

1	THE earth is the Lord's, and all that therein is :
	the compass of the world, and they that dwell therein.
2	For he hath founded it upon the seas :
	and prepared it upon the floods.
3	Who shall ascend into the hill of the Lord :
	or who shall rise up in his holy place?
4	Even he that hath clean hands, and a pure heart :
	and that hath not lift up his mind unto vanity,
	nor sworn to deceive his neighbour.
5	He shall receive the blessing from the Lord :
	and righteousness from the God of his salvation.
6	This is the generation of them that seek him :
	even of them that seek thy face, O Jacob.

7	Lift up your heads, O ye gates, and be ye lift up, ye everlasting doors :
	and the King of glory shall come in.
8	Who is the King of glory :
	it is the Lord strong and mighty, even the Lord mighty in battle.
9	Lift up your heads, O ye gates, and be ye lift up, ye everlasting doors :
	and the King of glory shall come in.
10	Who is the King of glory :
	even the Lord of hosts, he is the King of glory.

Psalm 25   *Ad te, Domine, levavi*

1   UNTO thee, O Lord, will I lift up my soul;
       my God, I have put my trust in thee :
     O let me not be confounded,
       neither let mine enemies triumph over me.

2   For all they that hope in thee shall not be ashamed :
     but such as transgress without a cause shall be put to confusion.

3   Shew me thy ways, O Lord :
     and teach me thy paths.

4   Lead me forth in thy truth, and learn me :
     for thou art the God of my salvation;
       in thee hath been my hope all the day long.

5   Call to remembrance, O Lord, thy tender mercies :
     and thy loving-kindnesses, which have been ever of old.

6   O remember not the sins and offences of my youth :
     but according to thy mercy think thou upon me, O Lord,
       for thy goodness.

7   Gracious and righteous is the Lord :
     therefore will he teach sinners in the way.

8   Them that are meek shall he guide in judgement :
     and such as are gentle, them shall he learn his way.

9   All the paths of the Lord are mercy and truth :
     unto such as keep his covenant and his testimonies.

10   For thy Name's sake, O Lord :
     be merciful unto my sin, for it is great.

11   What man is he that feareth the Lord :
     him shall he teach in the way that he shall choose.

12   His soul shall dwell at ease :
     and his seed shall inherit the land.

13   The secret of the Lord is among them that fear him :
     and he will shew them his covenant.

14	Mine eyes are ever looking unto the Lord :
	for he shall pluck my feet out of the net.
15	Turn thee unto me, and have mercy upon me :
	for I am desolate and in misery.
16	The sorrows of my heart are enlarged :
	O bring thou me out of my troubles.
17	Look upon my adversity and misery :
	and forgive me all my sin.
18	Consider mine enemies, how many they are :
	and they bear a tyrannous hate against me.
19	O keep my soul, and deliver me :
	let me not be confounded, for I have put my trust in thee.
20	Let perfectness and righteous dealing wait upon me :
	for my hope hath been in thee.
21	Deliver Israel, O God :
	out of all his troubles.

Psalm 26   *Judica me, Domine*

1   BE THOU my judge, O Lord, for I have walked innocently :
      my trust hath been also in the Lord, therefore shall I not fall.

2   Examine me, O Lord, and prove me :
      try out my reins and my heart.

3   For thy loving-kindness is ever before mine eyes :
      and I will walk in thy truth.

4   I have not dwelt with vain persons :
      neither will I have fellowship with the deceitful.

5   I have hated the congregation of the wicked :
      and will not sit among the ungodly.

6   I will wash my hands in innocency, O Lord :
      and so will I go to thine altar.

7   That I may shew the voice of thanksgiving :
      and tell of all thy wondrous works.

8   Lord, I have loved the habitation of thy house :
      and the place where thine honour dwelleth.

9   O shut not up my soul with the sinners :
      nor my life with the blood-thirsty.

10   In whose hands is wickedness :
      and their right hand is full of gifts.

11   But as for me, I will walk innocently :
         O deliver me, and be merciful unto me.

12   My foot standeth right :
         I will praise the Lord in the congregations.

Day 5. Evening Prayer.

Psalm 27   *Dominus illuminatio*

1   THE Lord is my light and my salvation; whom then shall I fear :
         the Lord is the strength of my life; of whom then shall I be afraid?

2   When the wicked, even mine enemies and my foes,
         came upon me to eat up my flesh :
         they stumbled and fell.

3   Though an host of men were laid against me,
         yet shall not my heart be afraid :
         and though there rose up war against me,
         yet will I put my trust in him.

4   One thing have I desired of the Lord, which I will require :
         even that I may dwell in the house of the Lord all the days of my life,
         to behold the fair beauty of the Lord, and to visit his temple.

5   For in the time of trouble he shall hide me in his tabernacle :
         yea, in the secret place of his dwelling shall he hide me,
         and set me up upon a rock of stone.

6   And now shall he lift up mine head :
         above mine enemies round about me.

7   Therefore will I offer in his dwelling an oblation with great gladness :
         I will sing, and speak praises unto the Lord.

8   Hearken unto my voice, O Lord, when I cry unto thee :
         have mercy upon me, and hear me.

9   My heart hath talked of thee, Seek ye my face :
         Thy face, Lord, will I seek.

10   O hide not thou thy face from me :
         nor cast thy servant away in displeasure.

11   Thou hast been my succour :
         leave me not, neither forsake me, O God of my salvation.

12   When my father and my mother forsake me :
         the Lord taketh me up.

13   Teach me thy way, O Lord :
         and lead me in the right way, because of mine enemies.

14	Deliver me not over into the will of mine adversaries :
	for there are false witnesses risen up against me,
	and such as speak wrong.
15	I should utterly have fainted :
	but that I believe verily to see the goodness of the Lord
	in the land of the living.
16	O tarry thou the Lord's leisure :
	be strong, and he shall comfort thine heart;
	and put thou thy trust in the Lord.

Psalm 28   *Ad te, Domine*

1 UNTO thee will I cry, O Lord my strength :
   think no scorn of me; lest, if thou make as though thou hearest not,
      I become like them that go down into the pit.
2 Hear the voice of my humble petitions, when I cry unto thee :
   when I hold up my hands towards the mercy-seat of thy holy temple.
3 O pluck me not away, neither destroy me,
      with the ungodly and wicked doers :
   which speak friendly to their neighbours,
      but imagine mischief in their hearts.
4 Reward them according to their deeds :
   and according to the wickedness of their own inventions.
5 Recompense them after the work of their hands :
   pay them that they have deserved.
6 For they regard not in their mind the works of the Lord,
      nor the operation of his hands :
   therefore shall he break them down, and not build them up.
7 Praised be the Lord :
   for he hath heard the voice of my humble petitions.
8 The Lord is my strength and my shield;
      my heart hath trusted in him, and I am helped :
   therefore my heart danceth for joy, and in my song will I praise him.
9 The Lord is my strength :
   and he is the wholesome defence of his Anointed.
10 O save thy people, and give thy blessing unto thine inheritance :
   feed them , and set them up for ever.

Afferte Domino

1   BRING unto the Lord, O ye mighty,
         bring young rams unto the Lord :
     ascribe unto the Lord worship and strength.

2   Give the Lord the honour due unto his Name :
     worship the Lord with holy worship.

3   It is the Lord that commandeth the waters :
     it is the glorious God that maketh the thunder.

4   It is the Lord that ruleth the sea;
         the voice of the Lord is mighty in operation :
     the voice of the Lord is a glorious voice.

5   The voice of the Lord breaketh the cedar-trees :
     yea, the Lord breaketh the cedars of Libanus.

6   He maketh them also to skip like a calf :
     Libanus also, and Sirion, like a young unicorn.

7   The voice of the Lord divideth the flames of fire;
         the voice of the Lord shaketh the wilderness :
     yea, the Lord shaketh the wilderness of Cades.

8   The voice of the Lord maketh the hinds to bring forth young,
         and discovereth the thick bushes :
     in his temple doth every man speak of his honour.

9   The Lord sitteth above the water-flood :
     and the Lord remaineth a King for ever.

10   The Lord shall give strength unto his people :
     the Lord shall give his people the blessing of peace.

Day 6. Morning Prayer.

Psalm 30   *Exaltabo te, Domine*

1   I WILL magnify thee, O Lord, for thou hast set me up :
     and not made my foes to triumph over me.

2   O Lord my God, I cried unto thee :
     and thou hast healed me.

3   Thou, Lord, hast brought my soul out of hell :
     thou hast kept my life from them that go down to the pit.

4   Sing praises unto the Lord, O ye saints of his :
     and give thanks unto him for a remembrance of his holiness.

5   For his wrath endureth but the twinkling of an eye,
         and in his pleasure is life :
     heaviness may endure for a night, but joy cometh in the morning.

6	And in my prosperity I said, I shall never be removed :
	thou, Lord, of thy goodness hast made my hill so strong.
7	Thou didst turn thy face from me :
	and I was troubled.
8	Then cried I unto thee, O Lord :
	and gat me to my Lord right humbly.
9	What profit is there in my blood :
	when I go down to the pit?
10	Shall the dust give thanks unto thee :
	or shall it declare thy truth?
11	Hear, O Lord, and have mercy upon me :
	Lord, be thou my helper.
12	Thou hast turned my heaviness into joy :
	thou hast put off my sackcloth, and girded me with gladness.
13	Therefore shall every good man sing of thy praise without ceasing :
	O my God, I will give thanks unto thee for ever.

Psalm 31   *In te, Domine, speravi*

1 IN THEE, O Lord, have I put my trust :
let me never be put to confusion, deliver me in thy righteousness.

2 Bow down thine ear to me :
make haste to deliver me.

3 And be thou my strong rock, and house of defence :
that thou mayest save me.

4 For thou art my strong rock, and my castle :
be thou also my guide, and lead me for thy Name's sake.

5 Draw me out of the net that they have laid privily for me :
for thou art my strength.

6 Into thy hands I commend my spirit :
for thou hast redeemed me, O Lord, thou God of truth.

7 I have hated them that hold of superstitious vanities :
and my trust hath been in the Lord.

8 I will be glad and rejoice in thy mercy :
for thou hast considered my trouble,
    and hast known my soul in adversities.

9 Thou hast not shut me up into the hand of the enemy :
but hast set my feet in a large room.

10 Have mercy upon me, O Lord, for I am in trouble :
and mine eye is consumed for very heaviness;
    yea, my soul and my body.

11	For my life is waxen old with heaviness :
	and my years with mourning.
12	My strength faileth me, because of mine iniquity :
	and my bones are consumed.
13	I became a reproof among all mine enemies,
	but especially among my neighbours :
	and they of mine acquaintance were afraid of me;
	and they that did see me without conveyed themselves from me
14	I am clean forgotten, as a dead man out of mind :
	I am become like a broken vessel.
15	For I have heard the blasphemy of the multitude :
	and fear is on every side, while they conspire together against me,
	and take their counsel to take away my life.
16	But my hope hath been in thee, O Lord :
	I have said, Thou art my God.
17	My time is in thy hand; deliver me from the hand of mine enemies :
	and from them that persecute me.
18	Shew thy servant the light of thy countenance :
	and save me for thy mercy's sake.
19	Let me not be confounded, O Lord, for I have called upon thee :
	let the ungodly be put to confusion, and be put to silence in the grave.
20	Let the lying lips be put to silence :
	which cruelly, disdainfully, and despitefully,
	speak against the righteous.
21	O how plentiful is thy goodness,
	which thou hast laid up for them that fear thee :
	and that thou hast prepared for them that put their trust in thee,
	even before the sons of men!
22	Thou shalt hide them privily by thine own presence
	from the provoking of all men :
	thou shalt keep them secretly in thy tabernacle
	from the strife of tongues.
23	Thanks be to the Lord :
	for he hath shewed me marvellous great kindness in a strong city.
24	And when I made haste, I said :
	I am cast out of the sight of thine eyes.
25	Nevertheless, thou heardest the voice of my prayer :
	when I cried unto thee.

26   O love the Lord, all ye his saints :
      for the Lord preserveth them that are faithful,
        and plenteously rewardeth the proud doer.

27   Be strong, and he shall establish your heart :
      all ye that put your trust in the Lord.

Day 6. Evening Prayer.

Psalm 32   *Beati, quorum*

1   BLESSED is he whose unrighteousness is forgiven :
      and whose sin is covered.

2   Blessed is the man unto whom the Lord imputeth no sin :
      and in whose spirit there is no guile.

3   For while I held my tongue :
      my bones consumed away through my daily complaining.

4   For thy hand is heavy upon me day and night :
      and my moisture is like the drought in summer.

5   I will acknowledge my sin unto thee :
      and mine unrighteousness have I not hid.

6   I said, I will confess my sins unto the Lord :
      and so thou forgavest the wickedness of my sin.

7   For this shall every one that is godly make his prayer unto thee,
        in a time when thou mayest be found :
      but in the great water-floods they shall not come nigh him.

8   Thou art a place to hide me in, thou shalt preserve me from trouble :
      thou shalt compass me about with songs of deliverance.

9   I will inform thee, and teach thee in the way wherein thou shalt go :
      and I will guide thee with mine eye.

10   Be ye not like to horse and mule, which have no understanding :
      whose mouths must be held with bit and bridle,
        lest they fall upon thee.

11   Great plagues remain for the ungodly :
      but whoso putteth his trust in the Lord,
        mercy embraceth him on every side.

12   Be glad, O ye righteous, and rejoice in the Lord :
      and be joyful, all ye that are true of heart.

1   REJOICE in the Lord, O ye righteous :
     for it becometh well the just to be thankful.

2   Praise the Lord with harp :
     sing praises unto him with the lute, and instrument of ten strings.

3   Sing unto the Lord a new song :
     sing praises lustily unto him with a good courage.

4   For the word of the Lord is true :
     and all his works are faithful.

5   He loveth righteousness and judgement :
     the earth is full of the goodness of the Lord.

6   By the word of the Lord were the heavens made :
     and all the hosts of them by the breath of his mouth.

7   He gathereth the waters of the sea together, as it were upon an heap :
     and layeth up the deep, as in a treasure-house.

8   Let all the earth fear the Lord :
     stand in awe of him, all ye that dwell in the world.

9   For he spake, and it was done :
     he commanded, and it stood fast.

10   The Lord bringeth the counsel of the heathen to nought :
     and maketh the devices of the people to be of none effect,
     and casteth out the counsels of princes.

11   The counsel of the Lord shall endure for ever :
     and the thoughts of his heart from generation to generation.

12   Blessed are the people, whose God is the LORD :
     and blessed are the folk,
     that he hath chosen to him to be his inheritance.

13.   The Lord looked down from heaven,
     and beheld all the children of men :
     from the habitation of his dwelling
     he considereth all them that dwell on the earth.

14   He fashioneth all the hearts of them :
     and understandeth all their works.

15   There is no king that can be saved by the multitude of an host :
     neither is any mighty man delivered by much strength.

16   A horse is counted but a vain thing to save a man :
     neither shall he deliver any man by his great strength.

17   Behold, the eye of the Lord is upon them that fear him :
     and upon them that put their trust in his mercy;

18	To deliver their soul from death :
	and to feed them in the time of dearth.
19	Our soul hath patiently tarried for the Lord :
	for he is our help and our shield.
20	For our heart shall rejoice in him :
	because we have hoped in his holy Name.
21	Let thy merciful kindness, O Lord, be upon us :
	like as we do put our trust in thee.

Psalm 34   *Benedicam Domino*

1	I WILL alway give thanks unto the Lord :
	his praise shall ever be in my mouth.
2	My soul shall make her boast in the Lord :
	the humble shall hear thereof, and be glad.
3	O praise the Lord with me :
	and let us magnify his Name together.
4	I sought the Lord, and he heard me :
	yea, he delivered me out of all my fear.
5	They had an eye unto him, and were lightened :
	and their faces were not ashamed.
6	Lo, the poor crieth, and the Lord heareth him :
	yea, and saveth him out of all his troubles.
7	The angel of the Lord tarrieth round about them that fear him :
	and delivereth them.
8	O taste, and see, how gracious the Lord is :
	blessed is the man that trusteth in him.
9	O fear the Lord, ye that are his saints :
	for they that fear him lack nothing.
10	The lions do lack, and suffer hunger :
	but they who seek the Lord
	shall want no manner of thing that is good.
11	Come, ye children, and hearken unto me :
	I will teach you the fear of the Lord.
12	What man is he that lusteth to live :
	and would fain see good days?
13	Keep thy tongue from evil :
	and thy lips, that they speak no guile.
14	Eschew evil, and do good :
	seek peace, and ensue it.

15	The eyes of the Lord are over the righteous :
	and his ears are open unto their prayers.
16	The countenance of the Lord is against them that do evil :
	to root out the remembrance of them from the earth.
17	The righteous cry, and the Lord heareth them :
	and delivereth them out of all their troubles.
18	The Lord is nigh unto them that are of a contrite heart :
	and will save such as be of an humble spirit.
19	Great are the troubles of the righteous :
	but the Lord delivereth him out of all.
20	He keepeth all his bones :
	so that not one of them is broken.
21	But misfortune shall slay the ungodly :
	and they that hate the righteous shall be desolate.
22	The Lord delivereth the souls of his servants :
	and all they that put their trust in him shall not be destitute.

Day 7. Morning Prayer.

Psalm 35   *Judica, Domine*

1	PLEAD thou my cause, O Lord, with them that strive with me :
	and fight thou against them that fight against me.
2	Lay hand upon the shield and buckler :
	and stand up to help me.
3	Bring forth the spear,
	and stop the way against them that persecute me :
	say unto my soul, I am thy salvation.
4	Let them be confounded and put to shame, that seek after my soul :
	let them be turned back and brought to confusion,
	that imagine mischief for me.
5	Let them be as the dust before the wind :
	and the angel of the Lord scattering them.
6	Let their way be dark and slippery :
	and let the angel of the Lord persecute them.
7	For they have privily laid their net to destroy me without a cause :
	yea, even without a cause have they made a pit for my soul.
8	Let a sudden destruction come upon him unawares,
	and his net, that he hath laid privily, catch himself :
	that he may fall into his own mischief.

9   And, my soul, be joyful in the Lord :
    it shall rejoice in his salvation.

10 All my bones shall say, Lord, who is like unto thee,
        who deliverest the poor from him that is too strong for him :
    yea, the poor, and him that is in misery, from him that spoileth him?

11 False witnesses did rise up :
    they laid to my charge things that I knew not.

12 They rewarded me evil for good :
    to the great discomfort of my soul.

13 Nevertheless, when they were sick, I put on sackcloth,
        and humbled my soul with fasting :
    and my prayer shall turn into mine own bosom.

14 I behaved myself as though it had been my friend or my brother :
    I went heavily, as one that mourneth for his mother.

15 But in mine adversity they rejoiced,
        and gathered themselves together :
    yea, the very abjects came together against me unawares,
        making mouths at me, and ceased not.

16 With the flatterers were busy mockers :
    who gnashed upon me with their teeth.

17 Lord, how long wilt thou look upon this :
    O deliver my soul from the calamities which they bring on me,
        and my darling from the lions.

18 So will I give thee thanks in the great congregation :
    I will praise thee among much people.

19 O let not them that are mine enemies triumph over me ungodly :
    neither let them wink with their eyes that hate me without a cause.

20 And why? their communing is not for peace :
    but they imagine deceitful words
        against them that are quiet in the land.

21 They gaped upon me with their mouths, and said :
    Fie on thee, fie on thee, we saw it with our eyes.

22 This thou hast seen, O Lord :
    hold not thy tongue then, go not far from me, O Lord.

23 Awake, and stand up to judge my quarrel :
    avenge thou my cause, my God, and my Lord.

24 Judge me, O Lord my God, according to thy righteousness :
    and let them not triumph over me.

25	Let them not say in their hearts, There, there, so would we have it :
	neither let them say, We have devoured him.
26	Let them be put to confusion and shame together,
	that rejoice at my trouble :
	let them be clothed with rebuke and dishonour,
	that boast themselves against me.
27	Let them be glad and rejoice, that favour my righteous dealing :
	yea, let them say alway, Blessed be the Lord,
	who hath pleasure in the prosperity of his servant.
28	And as for my tongue, it shall be talking of thy righteousness :
	and of thy praise all the day long.

Psalm 36   *Dixit injustus*

1	MY HEART sheweth me the wickedness of the ungodly :
	that there is no fear of God before his eyes.
2	For he flattereth himself in his own sight :
	until his abominable sin be found out.
3	The words of his mouth are unrighteous, and full of deceit :
	he hath left off to behave himself wisely, and to do good.
4	He imagineth mischief upon his bed,
	and hath set himself in no good way :
	neither doth he abhor any thing that is evil.
5	Thy mercy, O Lord, reacheth unto the heavens :
	and thy faithfulness unto the clouds.
6	Thy righteousness standeth like the strong mountains :
	thy judgements are like the great deep.
7	Thou, Lord, shalt save both man and beast;
	How excellent is thy mercy, O God :
	and the children of men shall put their trust
	under the shadow of thy wings.
8	They shall be satisfied with the plenteousness of thy house :
	and thou shalt give them drink of thy pleasures, as out of the river.
9	For with thee is the well of life :
	and in thy light shall we see light.
10	O continue forth thy loving-kindness unto them that know thee :
	and thy righteousness unto them that are true of heart.
11	O let not the foot of pride come against me :
	and let not the hand of the ungodly cast me down.
12	There are they fallen, all that work wickedness :
	they are cast down, and shall not be able to stand.

Psalm 37   *Noli æmulari*

1   FRET not thyself because of the ungodly :
    neither be thou envious against the evil-doers.

2   For they shall soon be cut down like the grass :
    and be withered even as the green herb.

3   Put thou thy trust in the Lord, and be doing good :
    dwell in the land, and verily thou shalt be fed.

4   Delight thou in the Lord :
    and he shall give thee thy heart's desire.

5   Commit thy way unto the Lord, and put thy trust in him :
    and he shall bring it to pass.

6   He shall make thy righteousness as clear as the light :
    and thy just dealing as the noon-day.

7   Hold thee still in the Lord, and abide patiently upon him :
    but grieve not thyself at him whose way doth prosper,
        against the man that doeth after evil counsels.

8   Leave off from wrath, and let go displeasure :
    fret not thyself, else shalt thou be moved to do evil.

9   Wicked doers shall be rooted out :
    and they that patiently abide the Lord, those shall inherit the land.

10 Yet a little while, and the ungodly shall be clean gone :
    thou shalt look after his place, and he shall be away.

11 But the meek-spirited shall possess the earth :
    and shall be refreshed in the multitude of peace.

12 The ungodly seeketh counsel against the just :
    and gnasheth upon him with his teeth.

13 The Lord shall laugh him to scorn :
    for he hath seen that his day is coming.

14 The ungodly have drawn out the sword, and have bent their bow :
    to cast down the poor and needy,
        and to slay such as are of a right conversation.

15 Their sword shall go through their own heart :
    and their bow shall be broken.

16 A small thing that the righteous hath :
    is better than great riches of the ungodly.

17 For the arms of the ungodly shall be broken :
    and the Lord upholdeth the righteous.

18	The Lord knoweth the days of the godly :
	and their inheritance shall endure for ever.
19	They shall not be confounded in the perilous time :
	and in the days of dearth they shall have enough.
20	As for the ungodly, they shall perish;
	and the enemies of the Lord shall consume as the fat of lambs :
	yea, even as the smoke shall they consume away.
21	The ungodly borroweth, and payeth not again :
	but the righteous is merciful and liberal.
22	Such as are blessed of God shall possess the land :
	and they that are cursed of him shall be rooted out.
23	The Lord ordereth a good man's going :
	and maketh his way acceptable to himself.
24	Though he fall, he shall not be cast away :
	for the Lord upholdeth him with his hand.
25	I have been young, and now am old :
	and yet saw I never the righteous forsaken,
	nor his seed begging their bread.
26	The righteous is ever merciful, and lendeth :
	and his seed is blessed.
27	Flee from evil, and do the thing that is good :
	and dwell for evermore.
28	For the Lord loveth the thing that is right :
	he forsaketh not his that be godly, but they are preserved for ever.
29	The unrighteous shall be punished :
	as for the seed of the ungodly, it shall be rooted out.
30	The righteous shall inherit the land :
	and dwell therein for ever.
31	The mouth of the righteous is exercised in wisdom :
	and his tongue will be talking of judgement.
32	The law of his God is in his heart :
	and his goings shall not slide.
33	The ungodly seeth the righteous :
	and seeketh occasion to slay him.
34	The Lord will not leave him in his hand :
	nor condemn him when he is judged.
35	Hope thou in the Lord, and keep his way,
	and he shall promote thee, that thou shalt possess the land :
	when the ungodly shall perish, thou shalt see it.

36	I myself have seen the ungodly in great power :
	and flourishing like a green bay-tree.
37	I went by, and lo, he was gone :
	I sought him, but his place could no where be found.
38	Keep innocency, and take heed unto the thing that is right :
	for that shall bring a man peace at the last.
39	As for the transgressors, they shall perish together :
	and the end of the ungodly is, they shall be rooted out at the last.
40	But the salvation of the righteous cometh of the Lord :
	who is also their strength in the time of trouble.
41	And the Lord shall stand by them, and save them :
	he shall deliver them from the ungodly, and shall save them,
	because they put their trust in him.

Day 8. Morning Prayer.

Psalm 38   *Domine, ne in furore*

1	PUT me not to rebuke, O Lord, in thine anger :
	neither chasten me in thy heavy displeasure.
2	For thine arrows stick fast in me :
	and thy hand presseth me sore.
3	There is no health in my flesh, because of thy displeasure :
	neither is there any rest in my bones, by reason of my sin.
4	For my wickednesses are gone over my head :
	and are like a sore burden, too heavy for me to bear.
5	My wounds stink, and are corrupt :
	through my foolishness.
6	I am brought into so great trouble and misery :
	that I go mourning all the day long.
7	For my loins are filled with a sore disease :
	and there is no whole part in my body.
8	I am feeble, and sore smitten :
	I have roared for the very disquietness of my heart.
9	Lord, thou knowest all my desire :
	and my groaning is not hid from thee.
10	My heart panteth, my strength hath failed me :
	and the sight of mine eyes is gone from me.
11	My lovers and my neighbours did stand looking upon my trouble :
	and my kinsmen stood afar off.

12   They also that sought after my life laid snares for me :
and they that went about to do me evil talked of wickedness,
    and imagined deceit all the day long.

13   As for me, I was like a deaf man, and heard not :
and as one that is dumb, who doth not open his mouth.

14   I became even as a man that heareth not :
and in whose mouth are no reproofs.

15   For in thee, O Lord, have I put my trust :
thou shalt answer for me, O Lord my God.

16   I have required that they, even mine enemies,
    should not triumph over me :
for when my foot slipped, they rejoiced greatly against me.

17   And I, truly, am set in the plague :
and my heaviness is ever in my sight.

18   For I will confess my wickedness :
and be sorry for my sin.

19   But mine enemies live, and are mighty :
and they that hate me wrongfully are many in number.

20   They also that reward evil for good are against me :
because I follow the thing that good is.

21   Forsake me not, O Lord my God :
be not thou far from me.

22   Haste thee to help me :
O Lord God of my salvation.

Psalm 39   *Dixi, Custodiam*

1   I SAID, I will take heed to my ways :
that I offend not in my tongue.

2   I will keep my mouth as it were with a bridle :
while the ungodly is in my sight.

3   I held my tongue, and spake nothing :
I kept silence, yea, even from good words;
    but it was pain and grief to me.

4   My heart was hot within me,
    and while I was thus musing the fire kindled :
and at the last I spake with my tongue;

5   Lord, let me know mine end, and the number of my days :
that I may be certified how long I have to live.

6	Behold, thou hast made my days as it were a span long :
	and mine age is even as nothing in respect of thee;
	and verily every man living is altogether vanity.
7	For man walketh in a vain shadow, and disquieteth himself in vain :
	he heapeth up riches, and cannot tell who shall gather them.
8	And now, Lord, what is my hope :
	truly my hope is even in thee.
9	Deliver me from all mine offences :
	and make me not a rebuke unto the foolish.
10	I became dumb, and opened not my mouth :
	for it was thy doing.
11	Take thy plague away from me :
	I am even consumed by the means of thy heavy hand.
12	When thou with rebukes dost chasten man for sin,
	thou makest his beauty to consume away,
	like as it were a moth fretting a garment :
	every man therefore is but vanity.
13	Hear my prayer, O Lord, and with thine ears consider my calling :
	hold not thy peace at my tears.
14	For I am a stranger with thee :
	and a sojourner, as all my fathers were.
15	O spare me a little, that I may recover my strength :
	before I go hence, and be no more seen.

Psalm 40 *Expectans expectavi*

1	I WAITED patiently for the Lord :
	and he inclined unto me, and heard my calling.
2	He brought me also out of the horrible pit, out of the mire and clay :
	and set my feet upon the rock, and ordered my goings.
3	And he hath put a new song in my mouth :
	even a thanksgiving unto our God.
4	Many shall see it, and fear :
	and shall put their trust in the Lord.
5	Blessed is the man that hath set his hope in the Lord :
	and turned not unto the proud, and to such as go about with lies.
6	O Lord my God, great are the wondrous works which thou hast done,
	like as be also thy thoughts which are to us-ward :
	and yet there is no man that ordereth them unto thee:

7	If I should declare them, and speak of them :
	they should be more than I am able to express.
8	Sacrifice and meat-offering thou wouldest not :
	but mine ears hast thou opened.
9	Burnt-offerings, and sacrifice for sin, hast thou not required :
	then said I, Lo, I come,
10	In the volume of the book it is written of me,
	that I should fulfil thy will, O my God :
	I am content to do it; yea, thy law is within my heart.
11	I have declared thy righteousness in the great congregation :
	lo, I will not refrain my lips, O Lord, and that thou knowest.
12	I have not hid thy righteousness within my heart :
	my talk hath been of thy truth and of thy salvation.
13	I have not kept back thy loving mercy and truth :
	from the great congregation.
14	Withdraw not thou thy mercy from me, O Lord :
	let thy loving-kindness and thy truth alway preserve me.
15	For innumerable troubles are come about me; my sins have taken
	such hold upon me that I am not able to look up :
	yea, they are more in number than the hairs of my head,
	and my heart hath failed me.
16	O Lord, let it be thy pleasure to deliver me :
	make haste, O Lord, to help me.
17	Let them be ashamed and confounded together,
	that seek after my soul to destroy it :
	let them be driven backward and put to rebuke, that wish me evil.
18	Let them be desolate, and rewarded with shame :
	that say unto me, Fie upon thee, fie upon thee.
19	Let all those that seek thee be joyful and glad in thee :
	and let such as love thy salvation say alway, The Lord be praised.
20	As for me, I am poor and needy :
	but the Lord careth for me.
21	Thou art my helper and redeemer :
	make no long tarrying, O my God.

Psalm 41   *Beatus qui intelligit*

1 BLESSED is he that considereth the poor and needy :
   the Lord shall deliver him in the time of trouble.

2 The Lord preserve him, and keep him alive,
       that he may be blessed upon earth :
   and deliver not thou him into the will of his enemies.

3 The Lord comfort him, when he lieth sick upon his bed :
   make thou all his bed in his sickness.

4 I said, Lord, be merciful unto me :
   heal my soul, for I have sinned against thee.

5 Mine enemies speak evil of me :
   When shall he die, and his name perish?

6 And if he come to see me, he speaketh vanity :
   and his heart conceiveth falsehood within himself,
       and when he cometh forth he telleth it.

7 All mine enemies whisper together against me :
   even against me do they imagine this evil.

8 Let the sentence of guiltiness proceed against him :
   and now that he lieth, let him rise up no more.

9 Yea, even mine own familiar friend, whom I trusted :
   who did also eat of my bread, hath laid great wait for me.

10 But be thou merciful unto me, O Lord :
    raise thou me up again, and I shall reward them.

11 By this I know thou favourest me :
    that mine enemy doth not triumph against me.

12 And when I am in my health, thou upholdest me :
    and shalt set me before thy face for ever.

13 Blessed be the Lord God of Israel :
    world without end. Amen.

Psalm 42   *Quemadmodum*

1 LIKE as the hart desireth the water-brooks :
   so longeth my soul after thee, O God.

2 My soul is athirst for God, yea, even for the living God :
   when shall I come to appear before the presence of God?

3 My tears have been my meat day and night :
   while they daily say unto me, Where is now thy God?

4   Now when I think thereupon, I pour out my heart by myself :
                for I went with the multitude,
                    and brought them forth into the house of God;

5   In the voice of praise and thanksgiving :
                among such as keep holy-day.

6   Why art thou so full of heaviness, O my soul :
                and why art thou so disquieted within me?

7   Put thy trust in God :
                  for I will yet give him thanks for the help of his countenance.

8   My God, my soul is vexed within me :
                therefore will I remember thee concerning the land of Jordan,
                    and the little hill of Hermon.

9   One deep calleth another, because of the noise of the water-pipes :
                all thy waves and storms are gone over me.

10   The Lord hath granted his loving-kindness in the day-time :
                and in the night-season did I sing of him,
                    and made my prayer unto the God of my life.

11   I will say unto the God of my strength, Why hast thou forgotten me :
                why go I thus heavily, while the enemy oppresseth me?

12   My bones are smitten asunder as with a sword :
                while mine enemies that trouble me cast me in the teeth;

13   Namely, while they say daily unto me :
                Where is now thy God?

14   Why art thou so vexed, O my soul :
                and why art thou so disquieted within me?

15   O put thy trust in God :
                for I will yet thank him,
                    which is the help of my countenance, and my God.

Psalm 43   *Judica me, Deus*

1   GIVE sentence with me, O God,
                  and defend my cause against the ungodly people :
                O deliver me from the deceitful and wicked man.

2   For thou art the God of my strength,
                  why hast thou put me from thee :
                and why go I so heavily, while the enemy oppresseth me?

3   O send out thy light and thy truth, that they may lead me :
                and bring me unto thy holy hill, and to thy dwelling.

4 And that I may go unto the altar of God,
  even unto the God of my joy and gladness :
 and upon the harp will I give thanks unto thee, O God, my God.

5 Why art thou so heavy, O my soul :
 and why art thou so disquieted within me?

6 O put thy trust in God :
 for I will yet give him thanks,
  which is the help of my countenance, and my God.

Day 9. Morning Prayer.

Psalm 44   *Deus, auribus*

1 WE HAVE heard with our ears, O God, our fathers have told us :
 what thou hast done in their time of old;

2 How thou hast driven out the heathen with thy hand,
  and planted them in :
 how thou hast destroyed the nations and cast them out.

3 For they gat not the land in possession through their own sword :
 neither was it their own arm that helped them;

4 But thy right hand, and thine arm, and the light of thy countenance :
 because thou hadst a favour unto them.

5 Thou art my King, O God :
 send help unto Jacob.

6 Through thee will we overthrow our enemies :
 and in thy Name will we tread them under, that rise up against us.

7 For I will not trust in my bow :
 it is not my sword that shall help me;

8 But it is thou that savest us from our enemies :
 and puttest them to confusion that hate us.

9 We make our boast of God all day long :
 and will praise thy Name for ever.

10 But now thou art far off, and puttest us to confusion :
 and goest not forth with our armies.

11 Thou makest us to turn our backs upon our enemies :
 so that they which hate us spoil our goods.

12 Thou lettest us be eaten up like sheep :
 and hast scattered us among the heathen.

13 Thou sellest thy people for nought :
 and takest no money for them.

14	Thou makest us to be rebuked of our neighbours :
	to be laughed to scorn,
	and had in derision of them that are round about us.
15	Thou makest us to be a by-word among the heathen :
	and that the people shake their heads at us.
16	My confusion is daily before me :
	and the shame of my face hath covered me;
17	For the voice of the slanderer and blasphemer :
	for the enemy and avenger.
18	And though all this be come upon us, yet do we not forget thee :
	nor behave ourselves frowardly in thy covenant.
19	Our heart is not turned back :
	neither our steps gone out of thy way;
20	No, not when thou hast smitten us into the place of dragons :
	and covered us with the shadow of death.
21	If we have forgotten the Name of our God,
	and holden up our hands to any strange god :
	shall not God search it out?
	for he knoweth the very secrets of the heart.
22	For thy sake also are we killed all the day long :
	and are counted as sheep appointed to be slain.
23	Up, Lord, why sleepest thou :
	awake, and be not absent from us for ever.
24	Wherefore hidest thou thy face :
	and forgettest our misery and trouble?
25	For our soul is brought low, even unto the dust :
	our belly cleaveth unto the ground.
26	Arise, and help us :
	and deliver us for thy mercy's sake.

Psalm 45   *Eructavit cor meum*

1	MY HEART is inditing of a good matter :
	I speak of the things which I have made unto the King.
2	My tongue is the pen :
	of a ready writer.
3	Thou art fairer than the children of men:
	full of grace are thy lips, because God hath blessed thee for ever.
4	Gird thee with thy sword upon thy thigh, O thou most Mighty :
	according to thy worship and renown.

5   Good luck have thou with thine honour :
     ride on, because of the word of truth, of meekness, and righteousness;
         and thy right hand shall teach thee terrible things.

6   Thy arrows are very sharp,
         and the people shall be subdued unto thee :
     even in the midst among the King's enemies.

7   Thy seat, O God, endureth for ever :
     the sceptre of thy kingdom is a right sceptre.

8   Thou hast loved righteousness, and hated iniquity :
     wherefore God, even thy God,
         hath anointed thee with the oil of gladness above thy fellows.

9   All thy garments smell of myrrh, aloes, and cassia :
     out of the ivory palaces, whereby they have made thee glad.

10   Kings' daughters were among thy honourable women :
     upon thy right hand did stand the queen in a vesture of gold,
         wrought about with divers colours.

11   Hearken, O daughter, and consider, incline thine ear :
     forget also thine own people, and thy father's house.

12   So shall the King have pleasure in thy beauty :
     for he is thy Lord God, and worship thou him.

13   And the daughter of Tyre shall be there with a gift :
     like as the rich also among the people
         shall make their supplication before thee.

14   The King's daughter is all glorious within :
     her clothing is of wrought gold.

15   She shall be brought unto the King in raiment of needle-work :
     the virgins that be her fellows shall bear her company,
         and shall be brought unto thee.

16   With joy and gladness shall they be brought :
     and shall enter into the King's palace.

17   Instead of thy fathers thou shalt have children :
     whom thou mayest make princes in all lands.

18   I will remember thy Name from one generation to another :
     therefore shall the people give thanks unto thee, world without end.

Psalm 46   *Deus noster refugium*

1   GOD is our hope and strength :
     a very present help in trouble.

2   Therefore will we not fear, though the earth be moved :
     and though the hills be carried into the midst of the sea;

731

3	Though the waters thereof rage and swell :
	and though the mountains shake at the tempest of the same.
4	The rivers of the flood thereof shall make glad the city of God :
	the holy place of the tabernacle of the most Highest.
5	God is in the midst of her, therefore shall she not be removed :
	God shall help her, and that right early.
6	The heathen make much ado, and the kingdoms are moved :
	but God hath shewed his voice, and the earth shall melt away.
7	The Lord of hosts is with us :
	the God of Jacob is our refuge.
8	O come hither, and behold the works of the Lord :
	what destruction he hath brought upon the earth.
9	He maketh wars to cease in all the world :
	he breaketh the bow, and knappeth the spear in sunder,
	and burneth the chariots in the fire.
10	Be still then, and know that I am God :
	I will be exalted among the heathen, and I will be exalted in the earth.
11	The Lord of hosts is with us :
	the God of Jacob is our refuge.

Day 9. Evening Prayer.

Psalm 47   *Omnes gentes, plaudite*

1	O CLAP your hands together, all ye people :
	O sing unto God with the voice of melody.
2	For the Lord is high, and to be feared :
	he is the great King upon all the earth.
3	He shall subdue the people under us :
	and the nations under our feet.
4	He shall choose out an heritage for us :
	even the worship of Jacob, whom he loved.
5	God is gone up with a merry noise :
	and the Lord with the sound of the trump.
6	O sing praises, sing praises unto our God :
	O sing praises, sing praises unto our King.
7	For God is the King of all the earth :
	sing ye praises with understanding.
8	God reigneth over the heathen :
	God sitteth upon his holy seat.

9   The princes of the people are joined
         unto the people of the God of Abraham:
     for God, which is very high exalted, doth defend the earth,
         as it were with a shield.

Psalm 48   *Magnus Dominus*

1   GREAT is the Lord, and highly to be praised :
     in the city of our God, even upon his holy hill.

2   The hill of Sion is a fair place, and the joy of the whole earth :
     upon the north-side lieth the city of the great King;
         God is well known in her palaces as a sure refuge.

3   For lo, the kings of the earth :
     are gathered, and gone by together.

4   They marvelled to see such things :
     they were astonished, and suddenly cast down.

5   Fear came there upon them, and sorrow :
     as upon a woman in her travail.

6   Thou shalt break the ships of the sea :
     through the east-wind.

7   Like as we have heard, so have we seen
         in the city of the Lord of hosts, in the city of our God :
     God upholdeth the same for ever.

8   We wait for thy loving-kindness, O God :
         in the midst of thy temple.

9   O God, according to thy Name, so is thy praise unto the world's end :
     thy right hand is full of righteousness.

10   Let the mount Sion rejoice, and the daughters of Judah be glad :
     because of thy judgements.

11   Walk about Sion, and go round about her :
     and tell the towers thereof.

12   Mark well her bulwarks, set up her houses :
     that ye may tell them that come after.

13   For this God is our God for ever and ever :
     he shall be our guide unto death.

Psalm 49   *Audite hæc, omnes*

1   O HEAR ye this, all ye people :
     ponder it with your ears, all ye that dwell in the world;

2   High and low, rich and poor :
     one with another.

3	My mouth shall speak of wisdom :
	and my heart shall muse of understanding.
4	I will incline mine ear to the parable :
	and shew my dark speech upon the harp.
5	Wherefore should I fear in the days of wickedness :
	and when the wickedness of my heels compasseth me round about?
6	There be some that put their trust in their goods :
	and boast themselves in the multitude of their riches.
7	But no man may deliver his brother :
	nor make agreement unto God for him;
8	For it cost more to redeem their souls :
	so that he must let that alone for ever;
9	Yea, though he live long :
	and see not the grave.
10	For he seeth that wise men also die, and perish together :
	as well as the ignorant and foolish, and leave their riches for other.
11	And yet they think that their houses shall continue for ever :
	and that their dwelling-places shall endure from one generation
	to another; and call the lands after their own names.
12	Nevertheless, man will not abide in honour :
	seeing he may be compared unto the beasts that perish;
	this is the way of them.
13	This is their foolishness :
	and their posterity praise their saying.
14	They lie in the hell like sheep, death gnaweth upon them,
	and the righteous shall have domination over them in the morning :
	their beauty shall consume in the sepulchre out of their dwelling.
15	But God hath delivered my soul from the place of hell :
	for he shall receive me.
16	Be not thou afraid, though one be made rich :
	or if the glory of his house be increased;
17	For he shall carry nothing away with him when he dieth :
	neither shall his pomp follow him.
18	For while he lived, he counted himself an happy man :
	and so long as thou doest well unto thyself,
	men will speak good of thee.
19	He shall follow the generation of his fathers :
	and shall never see light.
20	Man being in honour hath no understanding :
	but is compared unto the beasts that perish.

Psalm 50   *Deus deorum*

1   THE Lord, even the most mighty God, hath spoken :
     and called the world, from the rising up of the sun
          unto the going down thereof.

2   Out of Sion hath God appeared :
     in perfect beauty.

3   Our God shall come, and shall not keep silence :
     there shall go before him a consuming fire,
          and a mighty tempest shall be stirred up round about him.

4   He shall call the heaven from above :
     and the earth, that he may judge his people.

5   Gather my saints together unto me :
     those that have made a covenant with me with sacrifice.

6   And the heavens shall declare his righteousness :
     for God is Judge himself.

7   Hear, O my people, and I will speak :
     I myself will testify against thee, O Israel;
          for I am God, even thy God.

8   I will not reprove thee because of thy sacrifices,
          or for thy burnt-offerings :
     because they were not alway before me.

9   I will take no bullock out of thine house :
     nor he-goat out of thy folds.

10   For all the beasts of the forest are mine :
     and so are the cattle upon a thousand hills.

11   I know all the fowls upon the mountains :
     and the wild beasts of the field are in my sight.

12   If I be hungry, I will not tell thee :
     for the whole world is mine, and all that is therein.

13   Thinkest thou that I will eat bulls' flesh :
     and drink the blood of goats?

14   Offer unto God thanksgiving :
     and pay thy vows unto the most Highest.

15   And call upon me in the time of trouble :
     so will I hear thee, and thou shalt praise me.

16   But unto the ungodly said God :
     Why dost thou preach my laws, and takest my covenant in thy mouth;

17   Whereas thou hatest to be reformed :
     and has cast my words behind thee?

18	When thou sawest a thief, thou consentedst unto him :
	and hast been partaker with the adulterers.
19	Thou hast let thy mouth speak wickedness :
	and with thy tongue thou hast set forth deceit.
20	Thou satest, and spakest against thy brother :
	yea, and hast slandered thine own mother's son.
21	These things hast thou done, and I held my tongue,
	and thou thoughtest wickedly, that I am even such a one as thyself :
	but I will reprove thee,
	and set before thee the things that thou hast done.
22	O consider this, ye that forget God :
	lest I pluck you away, and there be none to deliver you.
23	Whoso offereth me thanks and praise, he honoureth me :
	and to him that ordereth his conversation right
	will I shew the salvation of God.

Psalm 51   *Miserere mei, Deus*

1	HAVE mercy upon me, O God, after thy great goodness :
	according to the multitude of thy mercies do away mine offences.
2	Wash me throughly from my wickedness :
	and cleanse me from my sin.
3	For I acknowledge my faults :
	and my sin is ever before me.
4	Against thee only have I sinned, and done this evil in thy sight :
	that thou mightest be justified in thy saying,
	and clear when thou art judged.
5	Behold, I was shapen in wickedness :
	and in sin hath my mother conceived me.
6	But lo, thou requirest truth in the inward parts:
	and shalt make me to understand wisdom secretly.
7	Thou shalt purge me with hyssop, and I shall be clean :
	thou shalt wash me, and I shall be whiter than snow.
8	Thou shalt make me hear of joy and gladness :
	that the bones which thou hast broken may rejoice.
9	Turn thy face from my sins :
	and put out all my misdeeds.
10	Make me a clean heart, O God :
	and renew a right spirit within me.
11	Cast me not away from thy presence :
	and take not thy holy Spirit from me.

12	O give me the comfort of thy help again :
	and stablish me with thy free Spirit.
13	Then shall I teach thy ways unto the wicked :
	and sinners shall be converted unto thee.
14	Deliver me from blood-guiltiness, O God,
	thou that art the God of my health :
	and my tongue shall sing of thy righteousness.
15	Thou shalt open my lips, O Lord :
	and my mouth shall shew thy praise.
16	For thou desirest no sacrifice, else would I give it thee :
	but thou delightest not in burnt-offerings.
17	The sacrifice of God is a troubled spirit :
	a broken and contrite heart, O God, shalt thou not despise.
18	O be favourable and gracious unto Sion :
	build thou the walls of Jerusalem.
19	Then shalt thou be pleased with the sacrifice of righteousness,
	with the burnt-offerings and oblations :
	then shall they offer young bullocks upon thine altar.

Psalm 52   *Quid gloriaris?*

1	WHY boastest thou thyself, thou tyrant :
	that thou canst do mischief;
2	Whereas the goodness of God :
	endureth yet daily?
3	Thy tongue imagineth wickedness :
	and with lies thou cuttest like a sharp rasor.
4	Thou hast loved unrighteousness more then goodness :
	and to talk of lies more than righteousness.
5	Thou hast loved to speak all words that may do hurt :
	O thou false tongue.
6	Therefore shall God destroy thee for ever :
	he shall take thee, and pluck thee out of thy dwelling,
	and root thee out of the land of the living.
7	The righteous also shall see this, and fear :
	and shall laugh him to scorn;
8	Lo, this is the man that took not God for his strength :
	but trusted unto the multitude of his riches,
	and strengthened himself in his wickedness.
9	As for me, I am like a green olive-tree in the house of God :
	my trust is in the tender mercy of God for ever and ever.

10   I will always give thanks unto thee for that thou hast done :
and I will hope in thy Name, for thy saints like it well.

Day 10. Evening Prayer.

Psalm 53   *Dixit insipiens*

1   THE foolish body hath said in his heart :
There is no God.

2   Corrupt are they, and become abominable in their wickedness :
there is none that doeth good.

3   God looked down from heaven upon the children of men :
to see if there were any that would understand, and seek after God.

4   But they are all gone out of the way,
    they are altogether become abominable :
there is also none that doeth good, no not one.

5   Are not they without understanding, that work wickedness :
eating up my people as if they would eat bread?
    they have not called upon God.

6   They were afraid where no fear was :
for God hath broken the bones of him that besieged thee;
    thou hast put them to confusion, because God hath despised them.

7   O that the salvation were given unto Israel out of Sion :
O that the Lord would deliver his people out of captivity!

8   Then should Jacob rejoice :
and Israel should be right glad.

Psalm 54   *Deus, in nomine*

1   SAVE me, O God, for thy Name's sake :
and avenge me in thy strength.

2   Hear my prayer, O God :
and hearken unto the words of my mouth.

3   For strangers are risen up against me :
and tyrants, which have not God before their eyes, seek after my soul.

4   Behold, God is my helper :
the Lord is with them that uphold my soul.

5   He shall reward evil unto mine enemies :
destroy thou them in thy truth.

6   An offering of a free heart will I give thee,
    and praise thy Name, O Lord :
because it is so comfortable.

7 For he hath delivered me out of all my trouble :
and mine eye hath seen his desire upon mine enemies.

Psalm 55   *Exaudi, Deus*

1 HEAR my prayer, O God :
and hide not thyself from my petition.

2 Take heed unto me, and hear me :
how I mourn in my prayer, and am vexed.

3 The enemy crieth so, and the ungodly cometh on so fast :
for they are minded to do me some mischief;
so maliciously are they set against me.

4 My heart is disquieted within me :
and the fear of death is fallen upon me.

5 Fearfulness and trembling are come upon me :
and an horrible dread hath overwhelmed me.

6 And I said, O that I had wings like a dove :
for then would I flee away, and be at rest.

7 Lo, then would I get me away far off :
and remain in the wilderness.

8 I would make haste to escape :
because of the stormy wind and tempest.

9 Destroy their tongues, O Lord, and divide them :
for I have spied unrighteousness and strife in the city.

10 Day and night they go about within the walls thereof :
mischief also and sorrow are in the midst of it.

11 Wickedness is therein :
deceit and guile go not out of their streets.

12 For it is not an open enemy, that hath done me this dishonour :
for then I could have borne it.

13 Neither was it mine adversary, that did magnify himself against me :
for then peradventure I would have hid myself from him.

14 But it was even thou, my companion :
my guide, and mine own familiar friend.

15 We took sweet counsel together :
and walked in the house of God as friends.

16 Let death come hastily upon them,
and let them go down quick into hell :
for wickedness is in their dwellings, and among them.

17 As for me, I will call upon God :
and the Lord shall save me.

18	In the evening, and morning, and at noonday will I pray,
	and that instantly :
	and he shall hear my voice.
19	It is he that hath delivered my soul in peace
	from the battle that was against me :
	for there were many with me.
20	Yea, even God, that endureth for ever,
	shall hear me, and bring them down :
	for they will not turn, nor fear God.
21	He laid his hands upon such as be at peace with him :
	and he brake his covenant.
22	The words of his mouth were softer than butter,
	having war in his heart :
	his words were smoother than oil, and yet be they very swords.
23	O cast thy burden upon the Lord, and he shall nourish thee :
	and shall not suffer the righteous to fall for ever.
24	And as for them :
	thou, O God, shalt bring them into the pit of destruction.
25	The blood-thirsty and deceitful men shall not live out half their days :
	nevertheless, my trust shall be in thee, O Lord.

Day 11. Morning Prayer.

Psalm 56   *Miserere mei, Deus*

1	BE MERCIFUL unto me, O God,
	for man goeth about to devour me :
	he is daily fighting, and troubling me.
2	Mine enemies are daily in hand to swallow me up :
	for they be many that fight against me, O thou most Highest.
3	Nevertheless, though I am sometime afraid :
	yet put I my trust in thee.
4	I will praise God, because of his word :
	I have put my trust in God,
	and will not fear what flesh can do unto me.
5	They daily mistake my words :
	all that they imagine is to do me evil.
6	They hold all together, and keep themselves close :
	and mark my steps, when they lay wait for my soul.
7	Shall they escape for their wickedness :
	thou, O God, in thy displeasure shalt cast them down.

8	Thou tellest my flittings; put my tears into thy bottle :
	are not these things noted in thy book?
9	Whensoever I call upon thee,
	then shall mine enemies be put to flight :
	this I know; for God is on my side.
10	In God's word I will rejoice :
	in the Lord's word will I comfort me.
11	Yea, in God have I put my trust :
	I will not be afraid what man can do unto me.
12	Unto thee, O God, will I pay my vows :
	unto thee will I give thanks.
13	For thou hast delivered my soul from death, and my feet from falling :
	that I may walk before God in the light of the living.

Psalm 57   *Miserere mei, Deus*

1	BE MERCIFUL unto me, O God, be merciful unto me,
	for my soul trusteth in thee :
	and under the shadow of thy wings shall be my refuge,
	until this tyranny be over-past.
2	I will call unto the most high God :
	even unto the God that shall perform the cause which I have in hand.
3	He shall send from heaven :
	and save me from the reproof of him that would eat me up.
4	God shall send forth his mercy and truth :
	my soul is among lions.
5	And I lie even among the children of men, that are set on fire :
	whose teeth are spears and arrows, and their tongue a sharp sword
6	Set up thyself, O God, above the heavens :
	and thy glory above all the earth.
7	They have laid a net for my feet, and pressed down my soul :
	they have digged a pit before me,
	and are fallen into the midst of it themselves.
8	My heart is fixed, O God, my heart is fixed :
	I will sing, and give praise.
9	Awake up, my glory; awake, lute and harp :
	I myself will awake right early.
10	I will give thanks unto thee, O Lord, among the people :
	and I will sing unto thee among the nations.
11	For the greatness of thy mercy reacheth unto the heavens :
	and thy truth unto the clouds.

12   Set up thyself, O God, above the heavens :
and thy glory above all the earth.

[Psalm 58   *Si vere utique*

1   ARE your minds set upon righteousness, O ye congregation :
and do ye judge the thing that is right, O ye sons of men?

2   Yea, ye imagine mischief in your heart upon the earth :
and your hands deal with wickedness.

3   The ungodly are froward, even from their mother's womb :
as soon as they are born, they go astray, and speak lies.

4   They are as venomous as the poison of a serpent :
even like the deaf adder that stoppeth her ears;

5   Which refuseth to hear the voice of the charmer :
charm he never so wisely.

6   Break their teeth, O God, in their mouths;
    smite the jaw-bones of the lions, O Lord :
let them fall away like water that runneth apace;
    and when they shoot their arrows let them be rooted out.

7   Let them consume away like a snail,
    and be like the untimely fruit of a woman :
and let them not see the sun.

8   Or ever your pots be made hot with thorns :
so let indignation vex him, even as a thing that is raw.

9   The righteous shall rejoice when he seeth the vengeance :
he shall wash his footsteps in the blood of the ungodly.

10   So that a man shall say, Verily there is a reward for the righteous :
doubtless there is a God that judgeth the earth.]

Day 11. Evening Prayer.

Psalm 59   *Eripe me de inimicis*

1   DELIVER me from mine enemies, O God :
defend me from them that rise up against me.

2   O deliver me from the wicked doers :
and save me from the blood-thirsty men.

3   For lo, they lie waiting for my soul :
the mighty men are gathered against me,
    without any offence or fault of me, O Lord.

4   They run and prepare themselves without my fault :
arise thou therefore to help me, and behold.

5	Stand up, O Lord God of hosts, thou God of Israel,
	to visit all the heathen :
	and be not merciful unto them that offend of malicious wickedness.
6	They go to and fro in the evening :
	they grin like a dog, and run about through the city.
7	Behold, they speak with their mouth, and swords are in their lips :
	for who doth hear?
8	But thou. O Lord, shalt have them in derision :
	and thou shalt laugh all the heathen to scorn.
9	My strength will I ascribe unto thee :
	for thou art the God of my refuge.
10	God sheweth me his goodness plenteously :
	and God shall let me see my desire upon mine enemies.
11	Slay them not, lest my people forget it :
	but scatter them abroad among the people,
	and put them down, O Lord, our defence.
12	For the sin of their mouth, and for the words of their lips,
	they shall be taken in their pride :
	and why? their preaching is of cursing and lies.
13	Consume them in thy wrath, consume them, that they may perish :
	and know that it is God that ruleth in Jacob,
	and unto the ends of the world.
14	And in the evening they will return :
	grin like a dog, and will go about the city.
15	They will run here and there for meat :
	and grudge if they be not satisfied.
16	As for me, I will sing of thy power, and will praise thy mercy betimes
	in the morning :
	for thou hast been my defence and refuge in the day of my trouble.
17	Unto thee, O my strength, will I sing :
	for thou, O God, art my refuge, and my merciful God.

Psalm 60   *Deus, repulisti nos*

1	O GOD, thou hast cast us out, and scattered us abroad :
	thou hast also been displeased; O turn thee unto us again.
2	Thou hast moved the land, and divided it :
	heal the sores thereof, for it shaketh.
3	Thou hast shewed thy people heavy things :
	thou hast given us a drink of deadly wine.

4	Thou hast given a token for such as fear thee :
	that they may triumph because of the truth.
5	Therefore were thy beloved delivered :
	help me with thy right hand, and hear me.
6	God hath spoken in his holiness, I will rejoice, and divide Sichem :
	and mete out the valley of Succoth.
7	Gilead is mine, and Manasses is mine :
	Ephraim also is the strength of my head; Judah is my law-giver;
8	Moab is my wash-pot; over Edom will I cast out my shoe :
	Philistia, be thou glad of me.
9	Who will lead me into the strong city :
	who will bring me into Edom?
10	Hast not thou cast us out, O God :
	wilt not thou, O God, go out with our hosts?
11	O be thou our help in trouble :
	for vain is the help of man.
12	Through God will we do great acts :
	for it is he that shall tread down our enemies.

Psalm 61   *Exaudi, Deus*

1   HEAR my crying, O God :
       give ear unto my prayer.
2   From the ends of the earth will I call upon thee :
       when my heart is in heaviness.
3   O set me up upon the rock that is higher than I :
       for thou hast been my hope,
          and a strong tower for me against the enemy.
4   I will dwell in thy tabernacle for ever :
       and my trust shall be under the covering of thy wings.
5   For thou, O Lord, hast heard my desires :
       and hast given an heritage unto those that fear thy Name.
6   Thou shalt grant the King a long life :
       that his years may endure throughout all generations.
7   He shall dwell before God for ever :
       O prepare thy loving mercy and faithfulness,
          that they may preserve him.
8   So will I always sing praise unto thy Name :
       that I may daily perform my vows.

Day 12. Morning Prayer.

Psalm 62   *Nonne Deo?*

1 MY SOUL truly waiteth still upon God :
    for of him cometh my salvation.

2 He verily is my strength and my salvation :
    he is my defence, so that I shall not greatly fall.

3 How long will ye imagine mischief against every man :
     ye shall be slain all the sort of you; yea, as a tottering wall shall ye be,
    and like a broken hedge.

4 Their device is only how to put him out whom God will exalt :
    their delight is in lies; they give good words with their mouth,
     but curse with their heart.

5 Nevertheless, my soul, wait thou still upon God :
    for my hope is in him.

6 He truly is my strength and my salvation :
    he is my defence, so that I shall not fall.

7 In God is my health, and my glory :
    the rock of my might, and in God is my trust.

8 O put your trust in him alway, ye people :
    pour out your hearts before him, for God is our hope.

9 As for the children of men, they are but vanity :
    the children of men are deceitful upon the weights,
     they are altogether lighter than vanity itself.

10 O trust not in wrong and robbery, give not yourselves unto vanity :
    if riches increase, set not your heart upon them.

11 God spake once, and twice I have also heard the same :
    that power belongeth unto God;

12 And that thou, Lord, art merciful :
    for thou rewardest every man according to his work.

Psalm 63   *Deus, Deus meus*

1 O GOD, thou art my God :
     early will I seek thee.

2 My soul thirsteth for thee, my flesh also longeth after thee :
    in a barren and dry land where no water is.

3 Thus have I looked for thee in holiness :
    that I might behold thy power and glory.

4 For thy loving-kindness is better than the life itself :
    my lips shall praise thee.

5	As long as I live will I magnify thee on this manner :
	and lift up my hands in thy Name.
6	My soul shall be satisfied, even as it were with marrow and fatness :
	when my mouth praiseth thee with joyful lips.
7	Have I not remembered thee in my bed :
	and thought upon thee when I was waking?
8	Because thou hast been my helper :
	therefore under the shadow of thy wings will I rejoice.
9	My soul hangeth upon thee :
	thy right hand hath upholden me.
10	These also that seek the hurt of my soul :
	they shall go under the earth.
11	Let them fall upon the edge of the sword :
	that they may be a portion for foxes.
12	But the King shall rejoice in God;
	all they also that swear by him shall be commended :
	for the mouth of them that speak lies shall be stopped.

Psalm 64　　　　　　*Exaudi, Deus*

1	HEAR my voice, O God, in my prayer :
	preserve my life from fear of the enemy.
2	Hide me from the gathering together of the froward :
	and from the insurrection of wicked doers;
3	Who have whet their tongue like a sword :
	and shoot out their arrows, even bitter words;
4	That they may privily shoot at him that is perfect :
	suddenly do they hit him, and fear not.
5	They encourage themselves in mischief :
	and commune among themselves how they may lay snares,
	and say that no man shall see them.
6	They imagine wickedness, and practise it :
	that they keep secret among themselves,
	every man in the deep of his heart.
7	But God shall suddenly shoot at them with a swift arrow :
	that they shall be wounded.
8	Yea, their own tongues shall make them fall :
	insomuch that whoso seeth them shall laugh them to scorn.
9	And all men that see it shall say, This hath God done :
	for they shall perceive that it is his work.

10   The righteous shall rejoice in the Lord, and put his trust in him :
and all they that are true of heart shall be glad.

Day 12. Evening Prayer.

Psalm 65   *Te decet hymnus*

1   THOU, O God, art praised in Sion :
and unto thee shall the vow be performed in Jerusalem.

2   Thou that hearest the prayer :
unto thee shall all flesh come.

3   My misdeeds prevail against me :
O be thou merciful unto our sins.

4   Blessed is the man whom thou choosest, and receivest unto thee :
he shall dwell in thy court, and shall be satisfied
with the pleasures of thy house, even of thy holy temple.

5   Thou shalt shew us wonderful things in thy righteousness,
    O God of our salvation :
thou that art the hope of all the ends of the earth,
and of them that remain in the broad sea.

6   Who in his strength setteth fast the mountains :
and is girded about with power.

7   Who stilleth the raging of the sea :
and the noise of his waves, and the madness of the people.

8   They also that dwell in the uttermost parts of the earth
    shall be afraid at thy tokens :
thou that makest the outgoings of the morning and evening
    to praise thee.

9   Thou visitest the earth, and blessest it :
thou makest it very plenteous.

10   The river of God is full of water :
thou preparest their corn, for so thou providest for the earth.

11   Thou waterest her furrows,
    thou sendest rain into the little valleys thereof :
thou makest it soft with the drops of rain,
    and blessest the increase of it.

12   Thou crownest the year with thy goodness :
and thy clouds drop fatness.

13   They shall drop upon the dwellings of the wilderness :
and the little hills shall rejoice on every side.

14   The folds shall be full of sheep :
    the valleys also shall stand so thick with corn,
     that they shall laugh and sing.

Psalm 66   *Jubilate Deo*

1   O BE joyful in God, all ye lands :
    sing praises unto the honour of his Name,
     make his praise to be glorious.

2   Say unto God, O how wonderful art thou in thy works :
    through the greatness of thy power
     shall thine enemies be found liars unto thee.

3   For all the world shall worship thee :
    sing of thee, and praise thy Name.

4   O come hither, and behold the works of God :
    how wonderful he is in his doing toward the children of men.

5   He turned the sea into dry land :
    so that they went through the water on foot;
     there did we rejoice thereof.

6   He ruleth with his power for ever; his eyes behold the people :
    and such as will not believe shall not be able to exalt themselves.

7   O praise our God, ye people :
    and make the voice of his praise to be heard;

8   Who holdeth our soul in life :
    and suffereth not our feet to slip.

9   For thou, O God, hast proved us :
    thou also hast tried us, like as silver is tried.

10   Thou broughtest us into the snare :
    and laidest trouble upon our loins.

11   Thou sufferedst men to ride over our heads :
    we went through fire and water,
     and thou broughtest us out into a wealthy place.

12   I will go into thine house with burnt-offerings :
    and will pay thee my vows, which I promised with my lips,
     and spake with my mouth, when I was in trouble.

13   I will offer unto thee fat burnt-sacrifices, with the incense of rams :
    I will offer bullocks and goats.

14   O come hither, and hearken, all ye that fear God :
    and I will tell you what he hath done for my soul.

15   I called unto him with my mouth :
    and gave him praises with my tongue.

16 If I incline unto wickedness with mine heart :
and the Lord will not hear me.

17 But God hath heard me :
and considered the voice of my prayer.

18 Praised be God, who hath not cast out my prayer :
nor turned his mercy from me.

Psalm 67   *Deus misereatur*

1 GOD be merciful unto us, and bless us :
and shew us the light of his countenance, and be merciful unto us:

2 That thy way may be known upon earth :
thy saving health among all nations.

3 Let the people praise thee, O God :
yea, let all the people praise thee.

4 O let the nations rejoice and be glad :
for thou shalt judge the folk righteously,
and govern the nations upon earth.

5 Let the people praise thee, O God :
let all the people praise thee.

6 Then shall the earth bring forth her increase :
and God, even our own God, shall give us his blessing.

7 God shall bless us :
and all the ends of the world shall fear him.

Day 13. Morning Prayer.

Psalm 68   *Exurgat Deus*

1 LET God arise, and let his enemies be scattered :
let them also that hate him flee before him.

2 Like as the smoke vanisheth, so shalt thou drive them away :
and like as wax melteth at the fire,
so let the ungodly perish at the presence of God.

3 But let the righteous be glad and rejoice before God :
let them also be merry and joyful.

4 O sing unto God, and sing praises unto his Name :
magnify him that rideth upon the heavens, as it were upon an horse;
praise him in his Name, and rejoice before him.

5 He is a father of the fatherless,
and defendeth the cause of the widows :
even God in his holy habitation.

749

6	He is the God that maketh men to be of one mind in an house,
	and bringeth the prisoners out of captivity :
	but letteth the runagates continue in scarceness.
7	O God, when thou wentest forth before the people :
	when thou wentest through the wilderness;
8	The earth shook, and the heavens dropped at the presence of God :
	even as Sinai also was moved at the presence of God,
	who is the God of Israel.
9	Thou, O God, sentest a gracious rain upon thine inheritance :
	and refreshedst it when it was weary.
10	Thy congregation shall dwell therein :
	for thou, O God, hast of thy goodness prepared for the poor.
11	The Lord gave the word :
	great was the company of the preachers.
12	Kings with their armies did flee, and were discomfited :
	and they of the household divided the spoil.
13	Though ye have lien among the pots,
	yet shall ye be as the wings of a dove :
	that is covered with silver wings, and her feathers like gold.
14	When the Almighty scattered kings for their sake :
	then were they as white as snow in Salmon.
15	As the hill of Basan, so is God's hill :
	even an high hill, as the hill of Basan.
16	Why hop ye so, ye high hills? this is God's hill,
	in the which it pleaseth him to dwell :
	yea, the Lord will abide in it for ever.
17	The chariots of God are twenty thousand, even thousands of angels :
	and the Lord is among them, as in the holy place of Sinai.
18	Thou art gone up on high, thou hast led captivity captive,
	and received gifts for men :
	yea, even for thine enemies,
	that the Lord God might dwell among them.
19	Praised be the Lord daily :
	even the God who helpeth us, and poureth his benefits upon us.
20	He is our God, even the God of whom cometh salvation :
	God is the Lord, by whom we escape death.
21	God shall wound the head of his enemies :
	and the hairy scalp of such a one as goeth on still in his wickedness.

22	The Lord hath said, I will bring my people again, as I did from Basan :
	mine own will I bring again,
	as I did sometime from the deep of the sea.
23	That thy foot may be dipped in the blood of thine enemies :
	and that the tongue of thy dogs may be red through the same.
24	It is well seen, O God, how thou goest :
	how thou, my God and King, goest in the sanctuary.
25	The singers go before, the minstrels follow after :
	in the midst are the damsels playing with the timbrels.
26	Give thanks, O Israel, unto God the Lord in the congregations :
	from the ground of the heart.
27	There is little Benjamin their ruler,
	and the princes of Judah their counsel :
	the princes of Zabulon, and the princes of Nephthali.
28	Thy God hath sent forth strength for thee :
	stablish the thing, O God, that thou hast wrought in us,
29	For thy temple's sake at Jerusalem :
	so shall kings bring presents unto thee.
30	When the company of the spear-men, and multitude of the mighty
	are scattered abroad among the beasts of the people,
	so that they humbly bring pieces of silver :
	and when he hath scattered the people that delight in war;
31	Then shall the princes come out of Egypt :
	the Morians' land shall soon stretch our her hands unto God.
32	Sing unto God, O ye kingdoms of the earth :
	O sing praises unto the Lord;
33	Who sitteth in the heavens over all from the beginning :
	lo, he doth send out his voice, yea, and that a mighty voice.
34	Ascribe ye the power to God over Israel :
	his worship and strength is in the clouds.
35	O God, wonderful art thou in thy holy places :
	even the God of Israel,
	he will give strength and power unto his people; blessed be God.

Day 13. Evening Prayer.

Psalm 69   *Salvum me fac*

1	SAVE me, O God :
	for the waters are come in, even unto my soul.
2	I stick fast in the deep mire, where no ground is :
	I am come into deep waters, so that the floods run over me.

3 I am weary of crying; my throat is dry :
my sight faileth me for waiting so long upon my God.

4 They that hate me without a cause
 are more than the hairs of my head :
they that are mine enemies, and would destroy me guiltless,
 are mighty.

5 I paid them the things that I never took :
God, thou knowest my simpleness,
 and my faults are not hid from thee.

6 Let not them that trust in thee, O Lord God of hosts,
 be ashamed for my cause :
let not those that seek thee be confounded through me,
 O Lord God of Israel.

7 And why? for thy sake have I suffered reproof :
shame hath covered my face.

8 I am become a stranger unto my brethren :
even an alien unto my mother's children.

9 For the zeal of thine house hath even eaten me :
and the rebukes of them that rebuked thee are fallen upon me.

10 I wept, and chastened myself with fasting :
and that was turned to my reproof.

11 I put on sackcloth also :
and they jested upon me.

12 They that sit in the gate speak against me :
and the drunkards make songs upon me.

13 But, Lord, I make my prayer unto thee :
in an acceptable time.

14 Hear me, O God, in the multitude of thy mercy :
even in the truth of thy salvation.

15 Take me out of the mire, that I sink not :
O let me be delivered from them that hate me,
 and out of the deep waters.

16 Let not the water-flood drown me,
 neither let the deep swallow me up :
and let not the pit shut her mouth upon me.

17 Hear me, O Lord, for thy loving-kindness is comfortable :
turn thee unto me according to the multitude of thy mercies.

18 And hide not thy face from thy servant, for I am in trouble :
O haste thee, and hear me.

19	Draw nigh unto my soul, and save it :
	O deliver me, because of mine enemies.
20	Thou hast known my reproof, my shame, and my dishonour :
	mine adversaries are all in thy sight
21	Thy rebuke hath broken my heart; I am full of heaviness :
	I looked for some to have pity on me, but there was no man,
	neither found I any to comfort me.
22	They gave me gall to eat :
	and when I was thirsty they gave me vinegar to drink.
23	Let their table be made a snare to take themselves withal :
	and let the things that should have been for their wealth
	be unto them an occasion of falling.
24	Let their eyes be blinded, that they see not :
	and ever bow thou down their backs.
25	Pour out thine indignation upon them :
	and let thy wrathful displeasure take hold of them.
26	Let their habitation be void :
	and no man to dwell in their tents.
27	For they persecute him whom thou hast smitten :
	and they talk how they may vex them whom thou hast wounded.
28	Let them fall from one wickedness to another :
	and not come into thy righteousness.
29	Let them be wiped out of the book of the living :
	and not be written among the righteous.
30	As for me, when I am poor and in heaviness :
	thy help, O God, shall lift me up.
31	I will praise the Name of God with a song :
	and magnify it with thanksgiving.
32	This also shall please the Lord :
	better than a bullock that hath horns and hoofs.
33	The humble shall consider this, and be glad :
	seek ye after God, and your soul shall live.
34	For the Lord heareth the poor :
	and despiseth not his prisoners.
35	Let heaven and earth praise him :
	the sea, and all that moveth therein.
36	For God will save Sion, and build the cities of Judah :
	that men may dwell there, and have it in possession.
37	The posterity also of his servants shall inherit it :
	and they that love his Name shall dwell therein.

Psalm 70 *Deus, in adjutorium*

1   HASTE thee, O God, to deliver me :
    make haste to help me, O Lord.

2   Let them be ashamed and confounded that seek after my soul :
    let them be turned backward and put to confusion that wish me evil.

3   Let them for their reward be soon brought to shame :
    that cry over me, There, there.

4   But let all those that seek thee be joyful and glad in thee :
    and let all such as delight in thy salvation say alway,
      The Lord be praised.

5   As for me, I am poor and in misery :
    haste thee unto me, O God.

6   Thou art my helper and my redeemer :
    O Lord, make no long tarrying.

Day 14. Morning Prayer.

Psalm 71 *In te, Domine, speravi*

1   IN THEE, O Lord, have I put my trust,
      let me never be put to confusion :
    but rid me and deliver me in thy righteousness,
      incline thine ear unto me, and save me.

2   Be thou my strong hold, whereunto I may alway resort :
    thou hast promised to help me,
      for thou art my house of defence and my castle.

3   Deliver me, O my God, out of the hand of the ungodly :
    out of the hand of the unrighteous and cruel man.

4   For thou, O Lord God, art the thing that I long for :
    thou art my hope, even from my youth.

5   Through thee have I been holden up ever since I was born :
    thou art he that took me out of my mother's womb;
      my praise shall be always of thee.

6   I am become as it were a monster unto many :
    but my sure trust is in thee.

7   O let my mouth be filled with thy praise :
    that I may sing of thy glory and honour all the day long.

8   Cast me not away in the time of age :
    forsake me not when my strength faileth me.

9   For mine enemies speak against me, and they that lay wait for my soul
      take their counsel together, saying :
    God hath forsaken him; persecute him, and take him,
      for there is none to deliver him.

10   Go not far from me, O God :
    my God, haste thee to help me.

11   Let them be confounded and perish that are against my soul :
    let them be covered with shame and dishonour
      that seek to do me evil.

12   As for me, I will patiently abide alway :
    and will praise thee more and more.

13   My mouth shall daily speak of thy righteousness and salvation :
    for I know no end thereof.

14   I will go forth in the strength of the Lord God :
    and will make mention of thy righteousness only.

15   Thou, O God, hast taught me from my youth up until now :
    therefore will I tell of thy wondrous works.

16   Forsake me not, O God, in mine old age, when I am gray-headed :
    until I have shewed thy strength unto this generation,
      and thy power to all them that are yet for to come.

17   Thy righteousness, O God, is very high :
    and great things are they that thou hast done;
      O God, who is like unto thee?

18   O what great troubles and adversities hast thou shewed me,
      and yet didst thou turn and refresh me :
    yea, and broughtest me from the deep of the earth again.

19   Thou hast brought me to great honour :
    and comforted me on every side.

20   Therefore will I praise thee and thy faithfulness, O God,
      playing upon an instrument of musick :
    unto thee will I sing upon the harp, O thou Holy One of Israel.

21   My lips will be fain when I sing unto thee :
    and so will my soul whom thou hast delivered.

22   My tongue also shall talk of thy righteousness all the day long :
    for they are confounded and brought unto shame
      that seek to do me evil.

755

Deus, judicium

1   GIVE the King thy judgements, O God :
     and thy righteousness unto the King's son.

2   Then shall he judge thy people according unto right :
     and defend the poor.

3   The mountains also shall bring peace :
     and the little hills righteousness unto the people.

4   He shall keep the simple folk by their right :
     defend the children of the poor, and punish the wrong-doer.

5   They shall fear thee, as long as the sun and moon endureth :
     from one generation to another.

6   He shall come down like the rain into a fleece of wool :
     even as the drops that water the earth.

7   In his time shall the righteous flourish :
     yea, and abundance of peace, so long as the moon endureth.

8   His dominion shall be also from the one sea to the other :
     and from the flood unto the world's end.

9   They that dwell in the wilderness shall kneel before him :
     his enemies shall lick the dust.

10   The kings of Tharsis and of the isles shall give presents :
     the kings of Arabia and Saba shall bring gifts.

11   All kings shall fall down before him :
     all nations shall do him service.

12   For he shall deliver the poor when he crieth :
     the needy also, and him that hath no helper.

13   He shall be favourable to the simple and needy :
     and shall preserve the souls of the poor.

14   He shall deliver their souls from falsehood and wrong :
     and dear shall their blood be in his sight.

15   He shall live, and unto him shall be given of the gold of Arabia :
     prayer shall be made ever unto him, and daily shall he be praised.

16   There shall be an heap of corn in the earth, high upon the hills :
     his fruit shall shake like Libanus,
        and shall be green in the city like grass upon the earth.

17   His Name shall endure for ever;
        his Name shall remain under the sun among the posterities :
     which shall be blessed through him;
     and all the heathen shall praise him.

18	Blessed be the Lord God, even the God of Israel :
	which only doeth wondrous things;
19	And blessed be the Name of his majesty for ever :
	and all the earth shall be filled with his majesty. *Amen, Amen.*

Day 14. Evening Prayer.

Psalm 73   *Quam bonus Israel!*

1	TRULY God is loving unto Israel :
	even unto such as are of a clean heart.
2	Nevertheless, my feet were almost gone :
	my treadings had well-nigh slipt.
3	And why? I was grieved at the wicked :
	I do also see the ungodly in such prosperity.
4	For they are in no peril of death :
	but are lusty and strong.
5	They come in no misfortune like other folk :
	neither are they plagued like other men.
6	And this is the cause that they are so holden with pride :
	and overwhelmed with cruelty.
7	Their eyes swell with fatness :
	and they do even what they lust.
8	They corrupt other, and speak of wicked blasphemy :
	their talking is against the most High.
9	For they stretch forth their mouth unto the heaven :
	and their tongue goeth through the world.
10	Therefore fall the people unto them :
	and thereout suck they no small advantage.
11	Tush, say they, how should God perceive it :
	is there knowledge in the most High?
12	Lo, these are the ungodly, these prosper in the world,
	and these have riches in possession :
	and I said, Then have I cleansed my heart in vain,
	and washed mine hands in innocency.
13	All the day long have I been punished :
	and chastened every morning.
14	Yea, and I had almost said even as they :
	but lo, then I should have condemned the generation of thy children.
15	Then thought I to understand this :
	but it was too hard for me,

16	Until I went into the sanctuary of God :
	then understood I the end of these men;
17	Namely, how thou dost set them in slippery places :
	and castest them down, and destroyest them.
18	O how suddenly do they consume :
	perish, and come to a fearful end!
19	Yea, even like as a dream when one awaketh :
	so shalt thou make their image to vanish out of the city.
20	Thus my heart was grieved :
	and it went even through my reins.
21	So foolish was I, and ignorant :
	even as it were a beast before thee.
22	Nevertheless, I am alway by thee :
	for thou hast holden me by my right hand.
23	Thou shalt guide me with thy counsel :
	and after that receive me with glory.
24	Whom have I in heaven but thee :
	and there is none upon earth that I desire in comparison of thee.
25	My flesh and my heart faileth :
	but God is the strength of my heart, and my portion for ever.
26	For lo, they that forsake thee shall perish :
	thou hast destroyed all them that commit fornication against thee.
27	But it is good for me to hold me fast by God,
	to put my trust in the Lord God :
	and to speak of all thy works in the gates of the daughter of Sion.

Psalm 74   *Ut quid, Deus?*

1	O GOD, wherefore art thou absent from us so long :
	why is thy wrath so hot against the sheep of thy pasture?
2	O think upon thy congregation :
	whom thou hast purchased and redeemed of old.
3	Think upon the tribe of thine inheritance :
	and mount Sion, wherein thou hast dwelt.
4	Lift up thy feet, that thou mayest utterly destroy every enemy :
	which hath done evil in thy sanctuary.
5	Thine adversaries roar in the midst of thy congregations :
	and set up their banners for tokens.
6	He that hewed timber afore out of the thick trees :
	was known to bring it to an excellent work.

7.	But now they break down all the carved work thereof :
	with axes and hammers.
8	They have set fire upon thy holy places :
	and have defiled the dwelling-place of thy Name,
	even unto the ground.
9	Yea, they said in their hearts, Let us make havock of them altogether :
	thus have they burnt up all the houses of God in the land.
10	We see not our tokens, there is not one prophet more :
	no, not one is there among us, that understandeth any more.
11	O God, how long shall the adversary do this dishonour :
	how long shall the enemy blaspheme thy Name, for ever?
12	Why withdrawest thou thy hand :
	why pluckest thou not thy right hand out of thy bosom
	to consume the enemy?
13	For God is my King of old :
	the help that is done upon earth he doeth it himself.
14	Thou didst divide the sea through thy power :
	thou brakest the heads of the dragons in the waters.
15	Thou smotest the heads of Leviathan in pieces :
	and gavest him to be meat for the people in the wilderness.
16	Thou broughtest out fountains and waters out of the hard rocks :
	thou driedst up mighty waters.
17	The day is thine, and the night is thine :
	thou hast prepared the light and the sun.
18	Thou hast set all the borders of the earth :
	thou hast made summer and winter.
19	Remember this, O Lord, how the enemy hath rebuked :
	and how the foolish people hath blasphemed thy Name.
20	O deliver not the soul of thy turtle-dove
	unto the multitude of the enemies :
	and forget not the congregation of the poor for ever.
21	Look upon the covenant :
	for all the earth is full of darkness and cruel habitations.
22	O let not the simple go away ashamed :
	but let the poor and needy give praise unto thy Name.
23	Arise, O God, maintain thine own cause :
	remember how the foolish man blasphemeth thee daily.
24	Forget not the voice of thine enemies :
	the presumption of them that hate thee
	increaseth ever more and more.

Psalm 75   *Confitebimur tibi*

1 UNTO thee, O God, do we give thanks :
yea, unto thee do we give thanks.

2 Thy Name also is so nigh :
and that do thy wondrous works declare.

3 When I receive the congregation :
I shall judge according unto right.

4 The earth is weak, and all the inhabiters thereof :
I bear up the pillars of it.

5 I said unto the fools, Deal not so madly :
and to the ungodly, Set not up your horn.

6 Set not up your horn on high :
and speak not with a stiff neck.

7 For promotion cometh neither from the east, nor from the west :
nor yet from the south.

8 And why? God is the Judge :
he putteth down one, and setteth up another.

9 For in the hand of the Lord there is a cup, and the wine is red :
it is full mixed, and he poureth out of the same.

10 As for the dregs thereof :
all the ungodly of the earth shall drink them, and suck them out.

11 But I will talk of the God of Jacob :
and praise him for ever.

12 All the horns of the ungodly also will I break :
and the horns of the righteous shall be exalted.

Psalm 76   *Notus in Judæa*

1 IN JEWRY is God known :
his Name is great in Israel.

2 At Salem is his tabernacle :
and his dwelling in Sion.

3 There brake he the arrows of the bow :
the shield, the sword, and the battle.

4 Thou art of more honour and might :
than the hills of the robbers.

5 The proud are robbed, they have slept their sleep :
and all the men whose hands were mighty have found nothing.

6 At thy rebuke, O God of Jacob :
both the chariot and horse are fallen.

7	Thou, even thou art to be feared :
	and who may stand in thy sight when thou art angry?
8	Thou didst cause thy judgement to be heard from heaven :
	the earth trembled, and was still;
9	When God arose to judgement :
	and to help all the meek upon earth.
10	The fierceness of man shall turn to thy praise :
	and the fierceness of them shalt thou refrain.
11	Promise unto the Lord your God, and keep it,
	all ye that are round about him :
	bring presents unto him that ought to be feared.
12	He shall refrain the spirit of princes :
	and is wonderful among the kings of the earth.

Psalm 77   *Voce mea ad Dominum*

1	I WILL cry unto God with my voice :
	even unto God will I cry with my voice, and he shall hearken unto me.
2	In the time of my trouble I sought the Lord :
	my sore ran and ceased not in the night-season;
	my soul refused comfort.
3	When I am in heaviness, I will think upon God :
	when my heart is vexed, I will complain.
4	Thou holdest mine eyes waking :
	I am so feeble, that I cannot speak.
5	I have considered the days of old :
	and the years that are past.
6	I call to remembrance my song :
	and in the night I commune with mine own heart,
	and search out my spirits.
7	Will the Lord absent himself for ever :
	and will he be no more intreated?
8	Is his mercy clean gone for ever :
	and is his promise come utterly to an end for evermore?
9	Hath God forgotten to be gracious :
	and will he shut up his loving-kindness in displeasure?
10	And I said, It is mine own infirmity :
	but I will remember the years of the right hand of the most Highest.
11	I will remember the works of the Lord :
	and call to mind thy wonders of old time.

12	I will think also of all thy works :
	and my talking shall be of thy doings.
13	Thy way, O God, is holy :
	who is so great a God as our God?
14	Thou art the God that doeth wonders :
	and hast declared thy power among the people.
15	Thou hast mightily delivered thy people :
	even the sons of Jacob and Joseph.
16	The waters saw thee, O God, the waters saw thee, and were afraid :
	the depths also were troubled.
17	The clouds poured out water, the air thundered :
	and thine arrows went abroad.
18	The voice of thy thunder was heard round about;
	the lightnings shone upon the ground :
	the earth was moved, and shook withal.
19	Thy way is in the sea, and thy paths in the great waters :
	and thy footsteps are not known.
20	Thou leddest thy people like sheep :
	by the hand of Moses and Aaron.

Day 15. Evening Prayer.

Psalm 78   *Attendite, popule*

1 HEAR my law, O my people :
and incline your ears unto the words of my mouth.

2 I will open my mouth in a parable :
I will declare hard sentences of old;

3 Which we have heard and known :
and such as our fathers have told us;

4 That we should not hide them
from the children of the generations to come :
but to shew the honour of the Lord,
his mighty and wonderful works that he hath done.

5 He made a covenant with Jacob, and gave Israel a law :
which he commanded our forefathers to teach their children;

6 That their posterity might know it :
and the children which were yet unborn;

7 To the intent that when they came up :
they might shew their children the same;

8 That they might put their trust in God :
and not to forget the works of God, but to keep his commandments;

762

9	And not to be as their forefathers,
	a faithless and stubborn generation :
	a generation that set not their heart aright,
	and whose spirit cleaveth not stedfastly unto God;
10	Like as the children of Ephraim :
	who being harnessed, and carrying bows,
	turned themselves back in the day of battle.
11	They kept not the covenant of God :
	and would not walk in his law;
12	But forgat what he had done :
	and the wonderful works that he had shewed for them.
13	Marvellous things did he in the sight of our forefathers,
	in the land of Egypt :
	even in the field of Zoan.
14	He divided the sea, and let them go through :
	he made the waters to stand on an heap.
15	In the day-time also he led them with a cloud :
	and all the night through with a light of fire.
16	He clave the hard rocks in the wilderness :
	and gave them drink thereof, as it had been out of the great depth.
17	He brought waters out of the stony rock :
	so that it gushed out like the rivers.
18	Yet for all this they sinned more against him :
	and provoked the most Highest in the wilderness.
19	They tempted God in their hearts :
	and required meat for their lust.
20	They spake against God also, saying :
	Shall God prepare a table in the wilderness?
21	He smote the stony rock indeed, that the waters gushed out,
	and the streams flowed withal :
	but can he give bread also, or provide flesh for his people?
22	When the Lord heard this, he was wroth :
	so the fire was kindled in Jacob,
	and there came up heavy displeasure against Israel;
23	Because they believed not in God :
	and put not their trust in his help.
24	So he commanded the clouds above :
	and opened the doors of heaven.
25	He rained down manna also upon them for to eat :
	and gave them food from heaven.

26	So man did eat angels' food :
	for he sent them meat enough.
27	He caused the east-wind to blow under heaven :
	and through his power he brought in the south-west-wind.
28	He rained flesh upon them as thick as dust :
	and feathered fowls like as the sand of the sea.
29	He let it fall among their tents :
	even round about their habitation.
30	So they did eat and were well filled,
	for he gave them their own desire :
	they were not disappointed of their lust.
31	But while the meat was yet in their mouths,
	the heavy wrath of God came upon them,
	and slew the wealthiest of them :
	yea, and smote down the chosen men that were in Israel.
32	But for all this they sinned yet more :
	and believed not his wondrous works.
33	Therefore their days did he consume in vanity :
	and their years in trouble.
34	When he slew them, they sought him :
	and turned them early, and inquired after God.
35	And they remembered that God was their strength :
	and that the high God was their redeemer.
36	Nevertheless, they did but flatter him with their mouth :
	and dissembled with him in their tongue.
37	For their heart was not whole with him :
	neither continued they stedfast in his covenant.
38	But he was so merciful, that he forgave their misdeeds :
	and destroyed them not.
39	Yea, many a time turned he his wrath away :
	and would not suffer his whole displeasure to arise.
40	For he considered that they were but flesh :
	and that they were even a wind that passeth away,
	and cometh not again.
41	Many a time did they provoke him in the wilderness :
	and grieved him in the desert.
42	They turned back, and tempted God :
	and moved the Holy One in Israel.
43	They thought not of his hand :
	and of the day when he delivered them from the hand of the enemy;

44	How he had wrought his miracles in Egypt :
	and his wonders in the field of Zoan.
45	He turned their waters into blood :
	so that they might not drink of the rivers.
46	He sent lice among them, and devoured them up :
	and frogs to destroy them.
47	He gave their fruit unto the caterpillar :
	and their labour unto the grasshopper.
48	He destroyed their vines with hail-stones :
	and their mulberry-trees with the frost.
49	He smote their cattle also with hail-stones :
	and their flocks with hot thunderbolts.
50	He cast upon them the furiousness of his wrath,
	anger, displeasure and trouble :
	and sent evil angels among them.
51	He made a way to his indignation,
	and spared not their soul from death :
	but gave their life over to the pestilence;
52	And smote all the first-born in Egypt :
	the most principal and mightiest in the dwellings of Ham.
53	But as for his own people, he led them forth like sheep :
	and carried them in the wilderness like a flock.
54	He brought them out safely, that they should not fear :
	and overwhelmed their enemies with the sea.
55	And brought them within the borders of his sanctuary :
	even to his mountain which he purchased with his right hand.
56	He cast out the heathen also before them :
	caused their land to be divided among them for an heritage,
	and made the tribes of Israel to dwell in their tents.
57	So they tempted and displeased the most high God :
	and kept not his testimonies;
58	But turned their backs, and fell away like their forefathers :
	starting aside like a broken bow.
59	For they grieved him with their hill-altars :
	and provoked him to displeasure with their images.
60	When God heard this, he was wroth :
	and took sore displeasure at Israel.
61	So that he forsook the tabernacle in Silo :
	even the tent that he had pitched among men.

62 He delivered their power into captivity :
and their beauty into the enemy's hand.

63 He gave his people over also unto the sword :
and was wroth with his inheritance.

64 The fire consumed their young men :
and their maidens were not given to marriage.

65 Their priests were slain with the sword :
and there were no widows to make lamentation.

66 So the Lord awaked as one out of sleep :
and like a giant refreshed with wine.

67 He smote his enemies in the hinder parts :
and put them to a perpetual shame.

68 He refused the tabernacle of Joseph :
and chose not the tribe of Ephraim;

69 But chose the tribe of Judah :
even the hill of Sion which he loved.

70 And there he built his temple on high :
and laid the foundation of it like the ground
which he hath made continually.

71 He chose David also his servant :
and took him away from the sheep-folds.

72 As he was following the ewes great with young ones he took him :
that he might feed Jacob his people, and Israel his inheritance.

73 So he fed them with a faithful and true heart :
and ruled them prudently with all his power.

Day 16. Morning Prayer.

Psalm 79   *Deus, venerunt*

1 O GOD, the heathen are come into thine inheritance :
thy holy temple have they defiled,
and made Jerusalem an heap of stones.

2 The dead bodies of thy servants have they given
to be meat unto the fowls of the air :
and the flesh of thy saints unto the beasts of the land.

3 Their blood have they shed like water on every side of Jerusalem :
and there was no man to bury them.

4 We are become an open shame to our enemies :
a very scorn and derision unto them that are round about us.

5 Lord, how long wilt thou be angry :
shall thy jealousy burn like fire for ever?

6   Pour out thine indignation
        upon the heathen that have not known thee :
    and upon the kingdoms that have not called upon thy Name.

7   For they have devoured Jacob :
    and laid waste his dwelling-place.

8   O remember not our old sins, but have mercy upon us,
        and that soon :
    for we are come to great misery.

9   Help us, O God of our salvation, for the glory of thy Name :
    O deliver us, and be merciful unto our sins, for thy Name's sake.

10   Wherefore do the heathen say :
    Where is now their God?

11   O let the vengeance of thy servants' blood that is shed :
    be openly shewed upon the heathen in our sight.

12   O let the sorrowful sighing of the prisoners come before thee :
    according to the greatness of thy power,
        preserve thou those that are appointed to die.

13   And for the blasphemy wherewith our neighbours
        have blasphemed thee :
    reward thou them, O Lord, seven-fold into their bosom.

14   So we, that are thy people, and sheep of thy pasture,
        shall give thee thanks for ever :
    and will alway be shewing forth thy praise
        from generation to generation.

Psalm 80   *Qui regis Israel*

1   HEAR, O thou Shepherd of Israel,
        thou that leadest Joseph like a sheep :
    shew thyself also, thou that sittest upon the cherubims.

2   Before Ephraim, Benjamin, and Manasses :
    stir up thy strength, and come, and help us.

3   Turn us again, O God :
    shew the light of thy countenance, and we shall be whole.

4   O Lord God of hosts :
    how long wilt thou be angry with thy people that prayeth?

5   Thou feedest them with the bread of tears :
    and givest them plenteousness of tears to drink.

6   Thou hast made us a very strife unto our neighbours :
    and our enemies laugh us to scorn.

7	Turn us again, thou God of hosts :
	shew the light of thy countenance, and we shall be whole.
8	Thou hast brought a vine out of Egypt :
	thou hast cast out the heathen, and planted it.
9	Thou madest room for it :
	and when it had taken root it filled the land.
10	The hills were covered with the shadow of it :
	and the boughs thereof were like the goodly cedar-trees.
11	She stretched out her branches unto the sea :
	and her boughs unto the river.
12	Why hast thou then broken down her hedge :
	that all they that go by pluck off her grapes?
13	The wild boar out of the wood doth root it up :
	and the wild beasts of the field devour it.
14	Turn thee again, thou God of hosts, look down from heaven :
	behold, and visit this vine;
15	And the place of the vineyard that thy right hand hath planted :
	and the branch that thou madest so strong for thyself.
16	It is burnt with fire, and cut down :
	and they shall perish at the rebuke of thy countenance.
17	Let thy hand be upon the man of thy right hand :
	and upon the son of man,
	whom thou madest so strong for thine own self.
18	And so will not we go back from thee :
	O let us live, and we shall call upon thy Name.
19	Turn us again, O Lord God of hosts :
	shew the light of thy countenance, and we shall be whole.

Psalm 81   *Exultate Deo*

1	SING we merrily unto God our strength :
	make a cheerful noise unto the God of Jacob.
2	Take the psalm, bring hither the tabret :
	the merry harp with the lute.
3	Blow up the trumpet in the new-moon :
	even in the time appointed, and upon our solemn feast-day.
4	For this was made a statute for Israel :
	and a law of the God of Jacob.
5	This he ordained in Joseph for a testimony :
	when he came out of the land of Egypt,
	and had heard a strange language.

6	I eased his shoulder from the burden :
	and his hands were delivered from making the pots.
7	Thou calledst upon me in troubles, and I delivered thee :
	and heard thee what time as the storm fell upon thee.
8	I proved thee also :
	at the waters of strife.
9	Hear, O my people, and I will assure thee, O Israel :
	if thou wilt hearken unto me,
10	There shall no strange god be in thee :
	neither shalt thou worship any other god.
11	I am the Lord thy God, who brought thee out of the land of Egypt :
	open thy mouth wide, and I shall fill it.
12	But my people would not hear my voice :
	and Israel would not obey me.
13	So I gave them up unto their own hearts' lusts :
	and let them follow their own imaginations.
14	O that my people would have hearkened unto me :
	for if Israel had walked in my ways,
15	I should soon have put down their enemies :
	and turned my hand against their adversaries.
16	The haters of the Lord should have been found liars :
	but their time should have endured for ever.
17	He should have fed them also with the finest wheat-flour :
	and with honey out of the stony rock should I have satisfied thee.

Day 16. Evening Prayer.

Psalm 82　　　　　　　*Deus stetit*

1	GOD standeth in the congregation of princes :
	he is a Judge among gods.
2	How long will ye give wrong judgement :
	and accept the persons of the ungodly?
3	Defend the poor and fatherless :
	see that such as are in need and necessity have right.
4	Deliver the outcast and poor :
	save them from the hand of the ungodly.
5	They will not be learned nor understand, but walk on still in darkness :
	all the foundations of the earth are out of course.
6	I have said, Ye are gods :
	and ye are all the children of the most Highest.

7	But ye shall die like men :
	and fall like one of the princes.
8	Arise, O God, and judge thou the earth :
	for thou shalt take all heathen to thine inheritance.

Psalm 83   *Deus, quis similis?*

1	HOLD not thy tongue, O God, keep not still silence :
	refrain not thyself, O God.
2	For lo, thine enemies make a murmuring :
	and they that hate thee have lift up their head.
3	They have imagined craftily against thy people :
	and taken counsel against thy secret ones.
4	They have said, Come, and let us root them out,
	that they be no more a people :
	and that the name of Israel may be no more in remembrance.
5	For they have cast their heads together with one consent :
	and are confederate against thee;
6	The tabernacles of the Edomites, and the Ismaelites :
	the Moabites and Hagarenes;
7	Gebal, and Ammon, and Amalek :
	the Philistines, with them that dwell at Tyre.
8	Assur also is joined with them :
	and have holpen the children of Lot.
9	But do thou to them as unto the Madianites :
	unto Sisera, and unto Jabin at the brook of Kison;
10	Who perished at Endor :
	and became as the dung of the earth.
11	Make them and their princes like Oreb and Zeb :
	yea, make all their princes like as Zeba and Salmana;
12	Who say, Let us take to ourselves :
	the houses of God in possession.
13	O my God, make them like unto a wheel :
	and as the stubble before the wind;
14	Like as the fire that burneth up the wood :
	and as the flame that consumeth the mountains.
15	Persecute them even so with thy tempest :
	and make them afraid with thy storm.
16	Make their faces ashamed, O Lord :
	that they may seek thy Name.

17   Let them be confounded and vexed ever more and more :
        let them be put to shame, and perish.
18   And they shall know that thou, whose Name is the LORD :
        art only the most Highest over all the earth.

Psalm 84   *Quam dilecta!*

1   O HOW amiable are thy dwellings :
        thou Lord of hosts!
2   My soul hath a desire and longing
        to enter into the courts of the Lord :
        my heart and my flesh rejoice in the living God.
3   Yea, the sparrow hath found her an house,
        and the swallow a nest where she may lay her young :
        even thy altars, O Lord of hosts, my King and my God.
4   Blessed are they that dwell in thy house :
        they will be alway praising thee.
5   Blessed is the man whose strength is in thee :
        in whose heart are thy ways.
6   Who going through the vale of misery use it for a well :
        and the pools are filled with water.
7   They will go from strength to strength :
        and unto the God of gods appeareth every one of them in Sion.
8   O Lord God of hosts, hear my prayer :
        hearken, O God of Jacob.
9   Behold, O God our defender :
        and look upon the face of thine Anointed.
10   For one day in thy courts :
        is better than a thousand.
11   I had rather be a door-keeper in the house of my God :
        than to dwell in the tents of ungodliness.
12   For the Lord God is a light and defence :
        the Lord will give grace and worship,
        and no good thing shall he withhold from them that live a godly life.
13   O Lord God of hosts :
        blessed is the man that putteth his trust in thee.

Psalm 85

1   LORD, thou art become gracious unto thy land :
     thou hast turned away the captivity of Jacob.

2   Thou hast forgiven the offence of thy people :
     and covered all their sins.

3   Thou hast taken away all thy displeasure :
     and turned thyself from thy wrathful indignation.

4   Turn us then, O God our Saviour :
     and let thine anger cease from us.

5   Wilt thou be displeased at us for ever :
     and wilt thou stretch out thy wrath from one generation to another?

6   Wilt thou not turn again, and quicken us :
     that thy people may rejoice in thee?

7   Shew us thy mercy, O Lord :
     and grant us thy salvation.

8   I will hearken what the Lord God will say concerning me :
     for he shall speak peace unto his people, and to his saints,
        that they turn not again.

9   For his salvation is nigh them that fear him :
     that glory may dwell in our land.

10   Mercy and truth are met together :
     righteousness and peace have kissed each other.

11   Truth shall flourish out of the earth :
     and righteousness hath looked down from heaven.

12   Yea, the Lord shall shew loving-kindness :
     and our land shall give her increase.

13   Righteousness shall go before him :
     and he shall direct his going in the way.

Day 17. Morning Prayer.

Psalm 86   *Inclina, Domine*

1   BOW down thine ear, O Lord, and hear me :
     for I am poor, and in misery.

2   Preserve thou my soul, for I am holy :
     my God, save thy servant that putteth his trust in thee.

3   Be merciful unto me, O Lord :
     for I will call daily upon thee.

4   Comfort the soul of thy servant :
     for unto thee, O Lord, do I lift up my soul.

5	For thou, Lord, art good and gracious :
	and of great mercy unto all them that call upon thee.
6	Give ear, Lord, unto my prayer :
	and ponder the voice of my humble desires.
7	In the time of my trouble I will call upon thee :
	for thou hearest me.
8	Among the gods there is none like unto thee, O Lord :
	there is not one that can do as thou doest.
9	All nations whom thou hadst made
	shall come and worship thee, O Lord :
	and shall glorify thy Name.
10	For thou art great, and doest wondrous things :
	thou art God alone.
11	Teach me thy way, O Lord, and I will walk in thy truth :
	O knit my heart unto thee, that I may fear thy Name.
12	I will thank thee, O Lord my God, with all my heart :
	and will praise thy Name for evermore.
13	For great is thy mercy toward me :
	and thou hast delivered my soul from the nethermost hell.
14	O God, the proud are risen against me :
	and the congregations of naughty men have sought after my soul,
	and have not set thee before their eyes.
15	But thou, O Lord God, art full of compassion and mercy :
	long-suffering, plenteous in goodness and truth.
16	O turn thee then unto me, and have mercy upon me :
	give thy strength unto thy servant,
	and help the son of thine handmaid.
17	Shew some token upon me for good,
	that they who hate me may see it and be ashamed :
	because thou, Lord, hast holpen me and comforted me.

Psalm 87   *Fundamenta ejus*

1	HER foundations are upon the holy hills :
	the Lord loveth the gates of Sion more than all the dwellings of Jacob.
2	Very excellent things are spoken of thee :
	thou city of God.
3	I will think upon Rahab and Babylon :
	with them that know me.

4	Behold ye the Philistines also :
	and they of Tyre, with the Morians; lo, there was he born.
5	And of Sion it shall be reported that he was born in her :
	and the most High shall stablish her.
6	The Lord shall rehearse it when he writeth up the people :
	that he was born there.
7	The singers also and trumpeters shall he rehearse :
	All my fresh springs shall be in thee.

Psalm 88   *Domine Deus*

1	O LORD God of my salvation,
	I have cried day and night before thee :
	O let my prayer enter into thy presence,
	incline thine ear unto my calling.
2	For my soul is full of trouble :
	and my life draweth nigh unto hell.
3	I am counted as one of them that go down into the pit :
	and I have been even as a man that hath no strength.
4	Free among the dead, like unto them that are wounded,
	and lie in the grave :
	who are out of remembrance, and are cut away from thy hand.
5	Thou hast laid me in the lowest pit :
	in a place of darkness, and in the deep.
6	Thine indignation lieth hard upon me :
	and thou hast vexed me with all thy storms.
7	Thou hast put away mine acquaintance far from me :
	and made me to be abhorred of them.
8	I am so fast in prison :
	that I cannot get forth.
9	My sight faileth for very trouble :
	Lord, I have called daily upon thee,
	I have stretched forth my hands unto thee.
10	Dost thou shew wonders among the dead :
	or shall the dead rise up again, and praise thee?
11	Shall thy loving-kindness be shewed in the grave :
	or thy faithfulness in destruction?
12	Shall thy wondrous works be known in the dark :
	and thy righteousness in the land where all things are forgotten?

13	Unto thee have I cried, O Lord :
	and early shall my prayer come before thee.
14	Lord, why abhorrest thou my soul :
	and hidest thou thy face from me?
15	I am in misery, and like unto him that is at the point to die :
	even from my youth up
	thy terrors have I suffered with a troubled mind.
16	Thy wrathful displeasure goeth over me :
	and the fear of thee hath undone me.
17	They came round about me daily like water :
	and compassed me together on every side.
18	My lovers and friends hast thou put away from me:
	and hid mine acquaintance out of my sight.

Day 17. Evening Prayer.

Psalm 89   *Misericordias Domini*

1	MY SONG shall be alway of the loving-kindness of the Lord :
	with my mouth will I ever be shewing thy truth
	from one generation to another.
2	For I have said, Mercy shall be set up for ever :
	thy truth shalt thou stablish in the heavens.
3	I have made a covenant with my chosen :
	I have sworn unto David my servant;
4	Thy seed will I stablish for ever :
	and set up thy throne from one generation to another.
5	O Lord, the very heavens shall praise thy wondrous works :
	and thy truth in the congregation of the saints.
6	For who is he among the clouds :
	that shall be compared unto the Lord?
7	And what is he among the gods :
	that shall be like unto the Lord?
8	God is very greatly to be feared in the council of the saints :
	and to be had in reverence of all them that are round about him.
9	O Lord God of hosts, who is like unto thee :
	thy truth, most mighty Lord, is on every side.
10	Thou rulest the raging of the sea :
	thou stillest the waves thereof when they arise.
11	Thou hast subdued Egypt, and destroyed it :
	thou hast scattered thine enemies abroad with thy mighty arm.

12   The heavens are thine, the earth also is thine :
thou hast laid the foundation of the round world,
   and all that therein is.

13   Thou hast made the north and the south :
 Tabor and Hermon shall rejoice in thy Name.

14   Thou hast a mighty arm :
strong is thy hand, and high is thy right hand.

15   Righteousness and equity are the habitation of thy seat :
mercy and truth shall go before thy face.

16   Blessed is the people, O Lord, that can rejoice in thee :
they shall walk in the light of thy countenance.

17   Their delight shall be daily in thy Name :
and in thy righteousness shall they make their boast.

18   For thou art the glory of their strength :
and in thy loving-kindness thou shalt lift up our horns.

19   For the Lord is our defence :
the Holy One of Israel is our King.

20   Thou spakest sometime in visions unto thy saints, and saidst :
I have laid help upon one that is mighty;
   I have exalted one chosen out of the people.

21   I have found David my servant :
with my holy oil have I anointed him.

22   My hand shall hold him fast :
and my arm shall strengthen him.

23   The enemy shall not be able to do him violence :
the son of wickedness shall not hurt him.

24   I will smite down his foes before his face :
and plague them that hate him.

25   My truth also and my mercy shall be with him :
and in my Name shall his horn be exalted.

26   I will set his dominion also in the sea :
and his right hand in the floods.

27   He shall call me, Thou art my Father :
my God, and my strong salvation.

28   And I will make him my first-born :
higher than the kings of the earth.

29   My mercy will I keep for him for evermore :
and my covenant shall stand fast with him.

30	His seed also will I make to endure for ever :
	and his throne as the days of heaven.
31	But if his children forsake my law :
	and walk not in my judgements;
32	If they break my statutes, and keep not my commandments :
	I will visit their offences with the rod, and their sin with scourges.
33	Nevertheless, my loving-kindness will I not utterly take from him :
	nor suffer my truth to fail.
34	My covenant I will not break,
	nor alter the thing that is gone out of my lips :
	I have sworn once by my holiness, that I will not fail David.
35	His seed shall endure for ever :
	and his seat is like as the sun before me.
36	He shall stand fast for evermore as the moon :
	and as the faithful witness in heaven.
37	But thou hast abhorred and forsaken thine Anointed :
	and art displeased at him.
38	Thou hast broken the covenant of thy servant :
	and cast his crown to the ground.
39	Thou hast overthrown all his hedges :
	and broken down his strong holds.
40	All they that go by spoil him :
	and he is become a reproach to his neighbours.
41	Thou hast set up the right hand of his enemies :
	and made all his adversaries to rejoice.
42	Thou hast taken away the edge of his sword :
	and givest him not victory in the battle.
43	Thou hast put out his glory :
	and cast his throne down to the ground.
44	The days of his youth hast thou shortened :
	and covered him with dishonour.
45	Lord, how long wilt thou hide thyself, for ever :
	and shall thy wrath burn like fire?
46	O remember how short my time is :
	wherefore hast thou made all men for nought?
47	What man is he that liveth, and shall not see death :
	and shall he deliver his soul from the hand of hell?
48	Lord, where are thy old loving-kindnesses :
	which thou swarest unto David in thy truth?

49   Remember, Lord, the rebuke that thy servants have :
        and how I do bear in my bosom the rebukes of many people.

50   Wherewith thine enemies have blasphemed thee,
         and slandered the footsteps of thine Anointed :
        Praised be the Lord for evermore. *Amen*, and *Amen*.

Day 18. Morning Prayer.

Psalm 90   *Domine, refugium*

1   LORD, thou hast been our refuge :
        from one generation to another.

2   Before the mountains were brought forth,
         or ever the earth and the world were made :
        thou art God from everlasting, and world without end.

3   Thou turnest man to destruction :
        again thou sayest, Come again, ye children of men.

4   For a thousand years in thy sight are but as yesterday :
        seeing that is past as a watch in the night.

5   As soon as thou scatterest them they are even as a sleep :
        and fade away suddenly like the grass.

6   In the morning it is green, and groweth up :
        but in the evening it is cut down, dried up, and withered.

7   For we consume away in thy displeasure :
        and are afraid at thy wrathful indignation.

8   Thou hast set our misdeeds before thee :
        and our secret sins in the light of thy countenance.

9   For when thou art angry all our days are gone :
        we bring our years to an end, as it were a tale that is told.

10   The days of our age are threescore years and ten;
         and though men be so strong that they come to fourscore years :
        yet is their strength then but labour and sorrow;
         so soon passeth it away, and we are gone.

11   But who regardeth the power of thy wrath :
        for even thereafter as a man feareth, so is thy displeasure.

12   So teach us to number our days :
        that we may apply our hearts unto wisdom.

13   Turn thee again, O Lord, at the last :
        and be gracious unto thy servants.

14   O satisfy us with thy mercy, and that soon :
        so shall we rejoice and be glad all the days of our life.

15 Comfort us again now after the time that thou hast plagued us :
and for the years wherein we have suffered adversity.

16 Shew thy servants thy work :
and their children thy glory.

17 And the glorious majesty of the Lord our God be upon us :
prosper thou the work of our hands upon us,
O prosper thou our handiwork.

Psalm 91   *Qui habitat*

1 WHOSO dwelleth under the defence of the most High :
shall abide under the shadow of the Almighty.

2 I will say unto the Lord, Thou art my hope, and my strong hold :
my God, in him will I trust.

3 For he shall deliver thee from the snare of the hunter :
and from the noisome pestilence.

4 He shall defend thee under his wings,
and thou shalt be safe under his feathers :
his faithfulness and truth shall be thy shield and buckler.

5 Thou shalt not be afraid for any terror by night :
nor for the arrow that flieth by day;

6 For the pestilence that walketh in darkness :
nor for the sickness that destroyeth in the noon-day.

7 A thousand shall fall beside thee, and ten thousand at thy right hand :
but it shall not come nigh thee.

8 Yea, with thine eyes shalt thou behold :
and see the reward of the ungodly.

9 For thou, Lord, art my hope :
thou hast set thine house of defence very high.

10 There shall no evil happen unto thee :
neither shall any plague come nigh thy dwelling.

11 For he shall give his angels charge over thee :
to keep thee in all thy ways.

12 They shall bear thee in their hands :
that thou hurt not thy foot against a stone.

13 Thou shalt go upon the lion and adder :
the young lion and the dragon shalt thou tread under thy feet.

14 Because he hath set his love upon me, therefore will I deliver him :
I will set him up, because he hath known my Name.

15	He shall call upon me, and I will hear him :
	yea, I am with him in trouble;
	I will deliver him, and bring him to honour.
16	With long life will I satisfy him :
	and shew him my salvation.

Psalm 92   *Bonum est confiteri*

1	IT IS a good thing to give thanks unto the Lord :
	and to sing praises unto thy Name, O most Highest;
2	To tell of thy loving-kindness early in the morning :
	and of thy truth in the night-season;
3	Upon an instrument of ten strings, and upon the lute :
	upon a loud instrument, and upon the harp.
4	For thou, Lord, hast made me glad through thy works :
	and I will rejoice in giving praise for the operations of thy hands.
5	O Lord, how glorious are thy works :
	thy thoughts are very deep.
6	An unwise man doth not well consider this :
	and a fool doth not understand it.
7	When the ungodly are green as the grass,
	and when all the workers of wickedness do flourish :
	then shall they be destroyed for ever;
	but thou, Lord, art the most Highest for evermore.
8	For lo, thine enemies, O Lord, lo, thine enemies shall perish :
	and all the workers of wickedness shall be destroyed.
9	But mine horn shall be exalted like the horn of an unicorn :
	for I am anointed with fresh oil.
10	Mine eye also shall see his lust of mine enemies :
	and mine ear shall hear his desire of the wicked
	that arise up against me.
11	The righteous shall flourish like a palm-tree :
	and shall spread abroad like a cedar in Libanus.
12	Such as are planted in the house of the Lord :
	shall flourish in the courts of the house of our God.
13	They also shall bring forth more fruit in their age :
	and shall be fat and well-liking.
14	That they may shew how true the Lord my strength is :
	and that there is no unrighteousness in him.

Psalm 93   *Dominus regnavit*

1   THE Lord is King, and hath put on glorious apparel :
     the Lord hath put on his apparel, and girded himself with strength.

2   He hath made the round world so sure :
     that it cannot be moved.

3   Ever since the world began hath thy seat been prepared :
     thou art from everlasting.

4   The floods are risen, O Lord, the floods have lift up their voice :
     the floods lift up their waves.

5   The waves of the sea are mighty, and rage horribly :
     but yet the Lord, who dwelleth on high, is mightier.

6   Thy testimonies, O Lord, are very sure :
     holiness becometh thine house for ever.

Psalm 94   *Deus ultionum*

1   O LORD God, to whom vengeance belongeth :
     thou God, to whom vengeance belongeth, shew thyself.

2   Arise, thou Judge of the world :
     and reward the proud after their deserving.

3   Lord, how long shall the ungodly :
     how long shall the ungodly triumph?

4   How long shall all wicked doers speak so disdainfully :
     and make such proud boasting?

5   They smite down thy people, O Lord :
     and trouble thine heritage.

6   They murder the widow and the stranger :
     and put the fatherless to death.

7   And yet they say, Tush, the Lord shall not see :
     neither shall the God of Jacob regard it.

8   Take heed, ye unwise among the people :
     O ye fools, when will ye understand?

9   He that planted the ear, shall he not hear :
     or he that made the eye, shall he not see?

10   Or he that nurtureth the heathen :
      it is he that teacheth man knowledge, shall not he punish?

11   The Lord knoweth the thoughts of man :
     that they are but vain.

12   Blessed is the man whom thou chastenest, O Lord :
     and teachest him in thy law;

13   That thou mayest give him patience in time of adversity :
             until the pit be digged up for the ungodly.

14   For the Lord will not fail his people :
             neither will he forsake his inheritance;

15   Until righteousness turn again unto judgement :
             all such as are true in heart shall follow it.

16   Who will rise up with me against the wicked :
             or who will take my part against the evil-doers?

17   If the Lord had not helped me :
             it had not failed but my soul had been put to silence.

18   But when I said, My foot hath slipt :
             thy mercy, O Lord, held me up.

19   In the multitude of the sorrows that I had in my heart :
             thy comforts have refreshed my soul.

20   Wilt thou have any thing to do with the stool of wickedness :
             which imagineth mischief as a law?

21   They gather them together against the soul of the righteous :
             and condemn the innocent blood.

22   But the Lord is my refuge :
             and my God is the strength of my confidence.

23   He shall recompense them their wickedness,
              and destroy them in their own malice :
             yea, the Lord our God shall destroy them.

Day 19. Morning Prayer.

Psalm 95   *Venite, exultemus*

1   O COME, let us sing unto the Lord :
             let us heartily rejoice in the strength of our salvation.

2   Let us come before his presence with thanksgiving :
             and shew ourselves glad in him with psalms.

3   For the Lord is a great God :
             and a great King above all gods.

4   In his hand are all the corners of the earth :
             and the strength of the hills is his also.

5   The sea is his, and he made it :
             and his hands prepared the dry land.

6   O come, let us worship and fall down :
             and kneel before the Lord our Maker.

7   For he is the Lord our God :
             and we are the people of his pasture, and the sheep of his hand.

8   To-day if ye will hear his voice, harden not your hearts :
          as in the provocation,
            and as in the day of temptation in the wilderness.

9   When your fathers tempted me :
          proved me, and saw my works.

10   Forty years long was I grieved with this generation, and said :
          It is a people that do err in their hearts,
            for they have not known my ways;

11   Unto whom I sware in my wrath :
          that they should not enter into my rest.

Psalm 96   *Cantate Domino*

1   O SING unto the Lord a new song :
          sing unto the Lord, all the whole earth.

2   Sing unto the Lord, and praise his Name :
          be telling of his salvation from day to day.

3   Declare his honour unto the heathen :
          and his wonders unto all people.

4   For the Lord is great, and cannot worthily be praised :
          he is more to be feared than all gods.

5   As for all the gods of the heathen, they are but idols :
          but it is the Lord that made the heavens.

6   Glory and worship are before him :
          power and honour are in his sanctuary.

7   Ascribe unto the Lord, O ye kindreds of the people :
          ascribe unto the Lord worship and power.

8   Ascribe unto the Lord the honour due unto his Name :
          bring presents, and come into his courts.

9   O worship the Lord in the beauty of holiness :
          let the whole earth stand in awe of him.

10   Tell it out among the heathen that the Lord is King :
          and that it is he who hath made the round world
            so fast that it cannot be moved;
          and how that he shall judge the people righteously.

11   Let the heavens rejoice, and let the earth be glad :
          let the sea make a noise, and all that therein is.

12   Let the field be joyful, and all that is in it :
          then shall all the trees of the wood rejoice before the Lord.

13   For he cometh, for he cometh to judge the earth :
      and with righteousness to judge the world,
          and the people with his truth.

Psalm 97   *Dominus regnavit*

1   THE Lord is King, the earth may be glad thereof :
      yea, the multitude of the isles may be glad thereof.
2   Clouds and darkness are round about him :
      righteousness and judgement are the habitation of his seat.
3   There shall go a fire before him :
      and burn up his enemies on every side.
4   His lightnings gave shine unto the world :
      the earth saw it, and was afraid.
5   The hills melted like wax at the presence of the Lord :
      at the presence of the Lord of the whole earth.
6   The heavens have declared his righteousness :
      and all the people have seen his glory.
7   Confounded be all they that worship carved images,
          and that delight in vain gods :
      worship him, all ye gods.
8   Sion heard of it, and rejoiced :
      and the daughters of Judah were glad,
          because of thy judgements, O Lord.
9   For thou, Lord, art higher than all that are in the earth :
      thou art exalted far above all gods.
10   O ye that love the Lord, see that ye hate the thing which is evil : t
      he Lord preserveth the souls of his saints;
          he shall deliver them from the hand of the ungodly.
11   There is sprung up a light for the righteous :
      and joyful gladness for such as are true-hearted.
12   Rejoice in the Lord, ye righteous :
      and give thanks for a remembrance of his holiness.

Day 19. Evening Prayer.

Psalm 98   *Cantate Domino*

1   O SING unto the Lord a new song :
      for he hath done marvellous things.
2   With his own right hand, and with his holy arm :
      hath he gotten himself the victory.

3	The Lord declared his salvation :

3   The Lord declared his salvation :
           his righteousness hath he openly shewed in the sight of the heathen.

4   He hath remembered his mercy and truth toward the house of Israel :
           and all the ends of the world have seen the salvation of our God.

5   Shew yourselves joyful unto the Lord, all ye lands :
           sing, rejoice, and give thanks.

6   Praise the Lord upon the harp :
           sing to the harp with a psalm of thanksgiving.

7   With trumpets also and shawms :
           O shew yourselves joyful before the Lord the King.

8   Let the sea make a noise, and all that therein is :
           the round world, and they that dwell therein.

9   Let the floods clap their hands,
           and let the hills be joyful together before the Lord :
           for he is come to judge the earth.

10   With righteousness shall he judge the world :
           and the people with equity.

Psalm 99   *Dominus regnavit*

1   THE Lord is King, be the people never so unpatient :
           he sitteth between the cherubims, be the earth never so unquiet.

2   The Lord is great in Sion :
           and high above all people.

3   They shall give thanks unto thy Name :
           which is great, wonderful, and holy.

4   The King's power loveth judgement; thou hast prepared equity:
           thou hast executed judgement and righteousness in Jacob.

5   O magnify the Lord our God :
           and fall down before his footstool, for he is holy.

6   Moses and Aaron among his priests,
           and Samuel among such as call upon his Name :
           these called upon the Lord, and he heard them.

7   He spake unto them out of the cloudy pillar :
           for they kept his testimonies, and the law that he gave them.

8   Thou heardest them, O Lord our God :
           thou forgavest them, O God, and punishedst their own inventions.

9   O magnify the Lord our God, and worship him upon his holy hill :
           for the Lord our God is holy.

Psalm 100 *Jubilate Deo*

1 O BE joyful in the Lord, all ye lands :
serve the Lord with gladness,
    and come before his presence with a song.

2 Be ye sure that the Lord he is God :
it is he that hath made us, and not we ourselves;
    we are his people, and the sheep of his pasture.

3 O go your way into his gates with thanksgiving,
    and into his courts with praise :
be thankful unto him, and speak good of his Name.

4 For the Lord is gracious, his mercy is everlasting :
and his truth endureth from generation to generation.

Psalm 101 *Misericordiam et judicium*

1 MY SONG shall be of mercy and judgement :
unto thee, O Lord, will I sing.

2 O let me have understanding :
in the way of godliness.

3 When wilt thou come unto me :
I will walk in my house with a perfect heart.

4 I will take no wicked thing in hand; I hate the sins of unfaithfulness :
there shall no such cleave unto me.

5 A froward heart shall depart from me :
I will not know a wicked person.

6 Whoso privily slandereth his neighbour :
him will I destroy.

7 Whoso hath also a proud look and high stomach :
I will not suffer him.

8 Mine eyes look upon such as are faithful in the land :
that they may dwell with me.

9 Whoso leadeth a godly life :
he shall be my servant.

10 There shall no deceitful person dwell in my house :
he that telleth lies shall not tarry in my sight.

11 I shall soon destroy all the ungodly that are in the land :
that I may root out all wicked doers from the city of the Lord.

Psalm 102   *Domine, exaudi*

1 HEAR my prayer, O Lord :
   and let my crying come unto thee.

2 Hide not thy face from me in the time of my trouble :
   incline thine ear unto me when I call; O hear me, and that right soon.

3 For my days are consumed away like smoke :
   and my bones are burnt up as it were a firebrand.

4 My heart is smitten down, and withered liked grass :
   so that I forget to eat my bread.

5 For the voice of my groaning :
   my bones will scarce cleave to my flesh.

6 I am become like a pelican in the wilderness :
   and like an owl that is in the desert.

7 I have watched, and am even as it were a sparrow :
   that sitteth alone upon the house-top.

8 Mine enemies revile me all the day long :
   and they that are mad upon me are sworn together against me.

9 For I have eaten ashes as it were bread :
   and mingled my drink with weeping;

10 And that because of thine indignation and wrath :
    for thou hast taken me up, and cast me down.

11 My days are gone like a shadow :
    and I am withered like grass.

12 But thou, O Lord, shalt endure for ever :
    and thy remembrance throughout all generations.

13 Thou shalt arise, and have mercy upon Sion :
    for it is time that thou have mercy upon her, yea, the time is come.

14 And why? thy servants think upon her stones :
    and it pitieth them to see her in the dust.

15 The heathen shall fear thy Name, O Lord :
    and all the kings of the earth thy majesty;

16 When the Lord shall build up Sion :
    and when his glory shall appear;

17 When he turneth him unto the prayer of the poor destitute :
    and despiseth not their desire.

18 This shall be written for those that come after :
    and the people which shall be born shall praise the Lord.

19 For he hath looked down from his sanctuary :
    out of the heaven did the Lord behold the earth;

20	That he might hear the mournings of such as are in captivity :
	and deliver the children appointed unto death;
21	That they may declare the Name of the Lord in Sion :
	and his worship at Jerusalem;
22	When the people are gathered together :
	and the kingdoms also, to serve the Lord.
23	He brought down my strength in my journey :
	and shortened my days.
24	But I said, O my God, take me not away in the midst of mine age :
	as for thy years, they endure throughout all generations.
25	Thou, Lord, in the beginning hast laid the foundation of the earth :
	and the heavens are the work of thy hands.
26	They shall perish, but thou shalt endure :
	they all shall wax old as doth a garment;
27	And as a vesture shalt thou change them, and they shall be changed :
	but thou art the same, and thy years shall not fail.
28	The children of thy servants shall continue :
	and their seed shall stand fast in thy sight.

Psalm 103   *Benedic, anima mea*

1	PRAISE the Lord, O my soul :
	and all that is within me praise his holy Name.
2	Praise the Lord, O my soul :
	and forget not all his benefits;
3	Who forgiveth all thy sin :
	and healeth all thine infirmities;
4	Who saveth thy life from destruction :
	and crowneth thee with mercy and loving-kindness;
5	Who satisfieth thy mouth with good things :
	making thee young and lusty as an eagle.
6	The Lord executeth righteousness and judgement :
	for all them that are oppressed with wrong.
7	He shewed his ways unto Moses :
	his works unto the children of Israel.
8	The Lord is full of compassion and mercy :
	long-suffering, and of great goodness.
9	He will not alway be chiding :
	neither keepeth he his anger for ever.
10	He hath not dealt with us after our sins :
	nor rewarded us according to our wickednesses.

11 For look how high the heaven is in comparison of the earth :
so great is his mercy also toward them that fear him.

12 Look how wide also the east is from the west :
so far hath he set our sins from us.

13 Yea, like as a father pitieth his own children :
even so is the Lord merciful unto them that fear him.

14 For he knoweth whereof we are made :
he remembereth that we are but dust.

15 The days of man are but as grass :
for he flourisheth as a flower of the field.

16 For as soon as the wind goeth over it, it is gone :
and the place thereof shall know it no more.

17 But the merciful goodness of the Lord endureth for ever and ever
upon them that fear him :
and his righteousness upon children's children;

18 Even upon such as keep his covenant :
and think upon his commandments to do them.

19 The Lord hath prepared his seat in heaven :
and his kingdom ruleth over all.

20 O praise the Lord, ye angels of his, ye that excel in strength :
ye that fulfil his commandment,
and hearken unto the voice of his words.

21 O praise the Lord, all ye his hosts :
ye servants of his that do his pleasure.

22 O speak good of the Lord, all ye works of his,
in all places of his dominion :
praise thou the Lord, O my soul.

Day 20. Evening Prayer.

Psalm 104   *Benedic, anima mea*

1 PRAISE the Lord, O my soul :
O Lord my God, thou art become exceeding glorious;
thou art clothed with majesty and honour.

2 Thou deckest thyself with light as it were with a garment :
and spreadest out the heavens like a curtain.

3 Who layeth the beams of his chambers in the waters :
and maketh the clouds his chariot,
and walketh upon the wings of the wind.

4 He maketh his angels spirits :
and his ministers a flaming fire.

5	He laid the foundations of the earth :
	that it never should move at any time.
6	Thou coveredst it with the deep like as with a garment :
	the waters stand in the hills.
7	At thy rebuke they flee :
	at the voice of thy thunder they are afraid.
8	They go up as high as the hills, and down to the valleys beneath :
	even unto the place which thou hast appointed for them.
9	Thou hast set them their bounds which they shall not pass :
	neither turn again to cover the earth.
10	He sendeth the springs into the rivers :
	which run among the hills.
11	All beasts of the field drink thereof :
	and the wild asses quench their thirst.
12	Beside them shall the fowls of the air have their habitation :
	and sing among the branches.
13	He watereth the hills from above :
	the earth is filled with the fruit of thy works.
14	He bringeth forth grass for the cattle :
	and green herb for the service of men;
15	That he may bring food out of the earth,
	and wine that maketh glad the heart of man :
	and oil to make him a cheerful countenance,
	and bread to strengthen man's heart.
16	The trees of the Lord also are full of sap :
	even the cedars of Libanus which he hath planted;
17	Wherein the birds make their nests :
	and the fir-trees are a dwelling for the stork.
18	The high hills are a refuge for the wild goats :
	and so are the stony rocks for the conies.
19	He appointed the moon for certain seasons :
	and the sun knoweth his going down.
20	Thou makest darkness that it may be night :
	wherein all the beasts of the forest do move.
21	The lions roaring after their prey :
	do seek their meat from God.
22	The sun ariseth, and they get them away together :
	and lay them down in their dens.
23	Man goeth forth to his work, and to his labour :
	until the evening.

24	O Lord, how manifold are thy works :
	in wisdom hast thou made them all; the earth is full of thy riches.
25	So is the great and wide sea also :
	wherein are things creeping innumerable, both small and great beasts.
26	There go the ships, and there is that Leviathan :
	whom thou hast made to take his pastime therein.
27	These wait all upon thee :
	that thou mayest give them meat in due season.
28	When thou givest it them they gather it :
	and when thou openest thy hand they are filled with good.
29	When thou hidest thy face they are troubled :
	when thou takest away their breath they die,
	and are turned again to their dust.
30	When thou lettest thy breath go forth they shall be made :
	and thou shalt renew the face of the earth.
31	The glorious majesty of the Lord shall endure for ever :
	the Lord shall rejoice in his works.
32	The earth shall tremble at the look of him :
	if he do but touch the hills, they shall smoke.
33	I will sing unto the Lord as long as I live :
	I will praise my God while I have my being.
34	And so shall my words please him :
	my joy shall be in the Lord.
35	As for sinners, they shall be consumed out of the earth,
	and the ungodly shall come to an end :
	praise thou the Lord, O my soul, praise the Lord.

Day 21. Morning Prayer.

Psalm 105 *Confitemini Domino*

1	O GIVE thanks unto the Lord, and call upon his Name :
	tell the people what things he hath done.
2	O let your songs be of him, and praise him :
	and let your talking be of all his wondrous works.
3	Rejoice in his holy Name :
	let the heart of them rejoice that seek the Lord.
4	Seek the Lord and his strength :
	seek his face evermore.
5	Remember the marvellous works that he hath done :
	his wonders, and the judgements of his mouth.

6	O ye seed of Abraham his servant :
	ye children of Jacob his chosen.
7	He is the Lord our God :
	his judgements are in all the world.
8	He hath been alway mindful of his covenant and promise :
	that he made to a thousand generations;
9	Even the covenant that he made with Abraham :
	and the oath that he sware unto Isaac;
10	And appointed the same unto Jacob for a law :
	and to Israel for an everlasting testament;
11	Saying, Unto thee will I give the land of Canaan :
	the lot of your inheritance;
12	When there were yet but a few of them :
	and they strangers in the land;
13	What time as they went from one nation to another :
	from one kingdom to another people;
14	He suffered no man to do them wrong :
	but reproved even kings for their sakes;
15	Touch not mine Anointed :
	and do my prophets no harm.
16	Moreover, he called for a dearth upon the land :
	and destroyed all the provision of bread.
17	But he had sent a man before them :
	even Joseph, who was sold to be a bond-servant;
18	Whose feet they hurt in the stocks :
	the iron entered into his soul;
19	Until the time came that his cause was known :
	the word of the Lord tried him.
20	The king sent, and delivered him :
	the prince of the people let him go free.
21	He made him lord also of his house :
	and ruler of all his substance;
22	That he might inform his princes after his will :
	and teach his senators wisdom.
23	Israel also came into Egypt :
	and Jacob was a stranger in the land of Ham.
24	And he increased his people exceedingly :
	and made them stronger than their enemies;
25	Whose heart turned, so that they hated his people :
	and dealt untruly with his servants.

26	Then sent he Moses his servant :
	and Aaron whom he had chosen.
27	And these shewed his tokens among them :
	and wonders in the land of Ham.
28	He sent darkness, and it was dark :
	and they were not obedient unto his word.
29	He turned their waters into blood :
	and slew their fish.
30	Their land brought forth frogs :
	yea, even in their kings' chambers.
31	He spake the word, and there came all manner of flies :
	and lice in all their quarters.
32	He gave them hail-stones for rain :
	and flames of fire in their land.
33	He smote their vines also and fig-trees :
	and destroyed the trees that were in their coasts.
34	He spake the word, and the grasshoppers came,
	and caterpillars innumerable :
	and did eat up all the grass in their land,
	and devoured the fruit of their ground.
35	He smote all the first-born in their land :
	even the chief of all their strength.
36	He brought them forth also with silver and gold :
	there was not one feeble person among their tribes.
37	Egypt was glad at their departing :
	for they were afraid of them.
38	He spread out a cloud to be a covering :
	and fire to give light in the night-season.
39	At their desire he brought quails :
	and he filled them with the bread of heaven.
40	He opened the rock of stone, and the waters flowed out :
	so that rivers ran in the dry places.
41	For why? he remembered his holy promise :
	and Abraham his servant.
42	And he brought forth his people with joy:
	and his chosen with gladness;
43	And gave them the lands of the heathen :
	and they took the labours of the people in possession;
44	That they might keep his statutes :
	and observe his laws.

Psalm 106   *Confitemini Domino*

1   O GIVE thanks unto the Lord, for he is gracious :
and his mercy endureth for ever.

2   Who can express the noble acts of the Lord :
or shew forth all his praise?

3   Blessed are they that alway keep judgement :
and do righteousness.

4   Remember me, O Lord,
according to the favour that thou bearest unto thy people :
O visit me with thy salvation;

5   That I may see the felicity of thy chosen :
and rejoice in the gladness of thy people,
and give thanks with thine inheritance.

6   We have sinned with our fathers :
we have done amiss, and dealt wickedly.

7   Our fathers regarded not thy wonders in Egypt,
neither kept they thy great goodness in remembrance :
but were disobedient at the sea, even at the Red sea.

8   Nevertheless, he helped them for his Name's sake :
that he might make his power to be known.

9   He rebuked the Red sea also, and it was dried up :
so he led them through the deep, as through a wilderness.

10   And he saved them from the adversaries' hand :
and delivered them from the hand of the enemy.

11   As for those that troubled them, the waters overwhelmed them :
there was not one of them left.

12   Then believed they his words :
and sang praise unto him.

13   But within a while they forgat his works :
and would not abide his counsel.

14   But lust came upon them in the wilderness :
and they tempted God in the desert.

15   And he gave them their desire :
and sent leanness withal into their soul.

16   They angered Moses also in the tents :
and Aaron the saint of the Lord.

17   So the earth opened, and swallowed up Dathan :
and covered the congregation of Abiram.

18	And the fire was kindled in their company :
	the flame burnt up the ungodly.
19	They made a calf in Horeb :
	and worshipped the molten image.
20	Thus they turned their glory :
	into the similitude of a calf that eateth hay.
21	And they forgat God their Saviour :
	who had done so great things in Egypt;
22	Wondrous works in the land of Ham :
	and fearful things by the Red sea.
23	So he said, he would have destroyed them,
	had not Moses his chosen stood before him in the gap :
	to turn away his wrathful indignation, lest he should destroy them.
24	Yea, they thought scorn of that pleasant land :
	and gave no credence unto his word;
25	But murmured in their tents :
	and hearkened not unto the voice of the lord.
26	Then lift he up his hand against them :
	to overthrow them in the wilderness;
27	To cast out their seed among the nations :
	and to scatter them in the lands.
28	They joined themselves unto Baal-peor :
	and ate the offerings of the dead.
29	Thus they provoked him to anger with their own inventions :
	and the plague was great among them.
30	Then stood up Phinees and prayed :
	and so the plague ceased.
31	And that was counted unto him for righteousness :
	among all posterities for evermore.
32	They angered him also at the waters of strife :
	so that he punished Moses for their sakes;
33	Because they provoked his spirit :
	so that he spake unadvisedly with his lips.
34	Neither destroyed they the heathen :
	as the Lord commanded them;
35	But were mingled among the heathen :
	and learned their works.
36	Insomuch that they worshipped their idols,
	which turned to their own decay :
	yea, they offered their sons and their daughters unto devils;

37 And shed innocent blood,
    even the blood of their sons and of their daughters :
  whom they had offered unto the idols of Canaan;
    and the land was defiled with blood.

38 Thus were they stained with their own works :
  and went a whoring with their own inventions.

39 Therefore was the wrath of the Lord kindled against his people :
    insomuch that he abhorred his own inheritance.

40 And he gave them over into the hands of the heathen :
  and they that hated them were lords over them.

41 Their enemies oppressed them :
  and had them in subjection.

42 Many a time did he deliver them :
  but they rebelled against him with their own inventions,
    and were brought down in their wickedness.

43 Nevertheless, when he saw their adversity :
  he heard their complaint.

44 He thought upon his covenant,
    and pitied them according unto the multitude of his mercies :
  yea, he made all those that led them away captive to pity them.

45 Deliver us, O Lord our God, and gather us from among the heathen :
  that we may give thanks unto thy holy Name,
    and make our boast of thy praise.

46 Blessed be the Lord God of Israel
    from everlasting and world without end :
  and let all the people say, *Amen.*

Day 22. Morning Prayer.

Psalm 107   *Confitemini Domino*

1 O GIVE thanks unto the Lord, for he is gracious :
  and his mercy endureth for ever.

2 Let them give thanks whom the Lord hath redeemed :
  and delivered from the hand of the enemy;

3 And gathered them out of the lands, from the east and from the west :
  from the north and from the south.

4 They went astray in the wilderness out of the way :
  and found no city to dwell in;

5 Hungry and thirsty :
  their soul fainted in them.

6	So they cried unto the Lord in their trouble :
	and he delivered them from their distress.
7	He led them forth by the right way :
	that they might go to the city where they dwelt.
8	O that men would therefore praise the Lord for his goodness :
	and declare the wonders that he doeth for the children of men!
9	For he satisfieth the empty soul :
	and filleth the hungry soul with goodness.
10	Such as sit in darkness, and in the shadow of death :
	being fast bound in misery and iron ;
11	Because they rebelled against the words of the Lord :
	and lightly regarded the counsel of the most Highest;
12	He also brought down their heart through heaviness :
	they fell down, and there was none to help them.
13	So when they cried unto the Lord in their trouble :
	he delivered them out of their distress.
14	For he brought them out of darkness,
	and out of the shadow of death :
	and brake their bonds in sunder.
15	O that men would therefore praise the Lord for his goodness :
	and declare the wonders that he doeth for the children of men!
16	For he hath broken the gates of brass :
	and smitten the bars of iron in sunder.
17	Foolish men are plagued for their offence :
	and because of their wickedness.
18	Their soul abhorred all manner of meat :
	and they were even hard at death's door.
19	So when they cried unto the Lord in their trouble :
	he delivered them out of their distress.
20	He sent his word, and healed them :
	and they were saved from their destruction.
21	O that men would therefore praise the Lord for his goodness :
	and declare the wonders that he doeth for the children of men!
22	That they would offer unto him the sacrifice of thanksgiving :
	and tell out his works with gladness!
23	They that go down to the sea in ships :
	and occupy their business in great waters;
24	These men see the works of the Lord :
	and his wonders in the deep.

25	For at his word the stormy wind ariseth :
	which lifteth up the waves thereof.
26	They are carried up to the heaven, and down again to the deep :
	their soul melteth away because of the trouble.
27	They reel to and fro, and stagger like a drunken man :
	and are at their wits' end.
28	So when they cry unto the Lord in their trouble :
	he delivereth them out of their distress.
29	For he maketh the storm to cease :
	so that the waves thereof are still.
30	Then are they glad, because they are at rest :
	and so he bringeth them unto the haven where they would be.
31	O that men would therefore praise the Lord for his goodness :
	and declare the wonders that he doeth for the children of men!
32	That they would exalt him also in the congregation of the people :
	and praise him in the seat of the elders!
33	Who turneth the floods into a wilderness :
	and drieth up the water-springs.
34	A fruitful land maketh he barren :
	for the wickedness of them that dwell therein.
35	Again, he maketh the wilderness a standing water :
	and water-springs of a dry ground.
36	And there he setteth the hungry :
	that they may build them a city to dwell in;
37	That they may sow their land, and plant vineyards :
	to yield them fruits of increase.
38	He blesseth them so that they multiply exceedingly :
	and suffereth not their cattle to decrease.
39	And again, when they are minished and brought low :
	through oppression, through any plague or trouble;
40	Though he suffer them to be evil intreated through tyrants :
	and let them wander out of the way in the wilderness;
41	Yet helpeth he the poor out of misery :
	and maketh him households like a flock of sheep.
42	The righteous will consider this, and rejoice :
	and the mouth of all wickedness shall be stopped.
43	Whoso is wise will ponder these things :
	and they shall understand the loving-kindness of the Lord.

Day 22. Evening Prayer.

Psalm 108   *Paratum cor meum*

1   O GOD, my heart is ready, my heart is ready :
       I will sing and give praise with the best member that I have.

2   Awake, thou lute, and harp :
       I myself will awake right early.

3   I will give thanks unto thee, O Lord, among the people :
       I will sing praises unto thee among the nations.

4   For thy mercy is greater than the heavens :
       and thy truth reacheth unto the clouds.

5   Set up thyself, O God, above the heavens :
       and thy glory above all the earth.

6   That thy beloved may be delivered :
       let thy right hand save them, and hear thou me.

7   God hath spoken in his holiness :
       I will rejoice therefore, and divide Sichem,
          and mete out the valley of Succoth.

8   Gilead is mine, and Manasses is mine :
       Ephraim also is the strength of my head.

9   Judah is my law-giver, Moab is my wash-pot :
       over Edom will I cast out my shoe, upon Philistia will I triumph.

10   Who will lead me into the strong city :
       and who will bring me into Edom?

11   Hast not thou forsaken us, O God :
       and wilt not thou, O God, go forth with our hosts?

12   O help us against the enemy :
       for vain is the help of man.

13   Through God we shall do great acts :
       and it is he that shall tread down our enemies.

Psalm 109   *Deus, laudem*

1   HOLD not thy tongue, O God of my praise :
       for the mouth of the ungodly,
          yea, the mouth of the deceitful is opened upon me.

2   And they have spoken against me with false tongues :
       they compassed me about also with words of hatred,
          and fought against me without a cause.

3   For the love that I had unto them,
       lo, they take now my contrary part :
       but I give myself unto prayer.

4   Thus have they rewarded me evil for good :
           and hatred for my good will.

5   Set thou an ungodly man to be ruler over him :
           and let Satan stand at his right hand.

6   When sentence is given upon him, let him be condemned :
           and let his prayer be turned into sin.

7   Let his days be few :
           and let another take his office.

8   Let his children be fatherless :
           and his wife a widow.

9   Let his children be vagabonds, and beg their bread :
           let them seek it also out of desolate places.

10   Let the extortioner consume all that he hath :
           and let the stranger spoil his labour.

11   Let there be no man to pity him :
           nor to have compassion upon his fatherless children.

12   Let his posterity be destroyed :
           and in the next generation let his name be clean put out.

13   Let the wickedness of his fathers be had in remembrance
             in the sight of the Lord :
           and let not the sin of his mother be done away.

14   Let them alway be before the Lord :
           that he may root out the memorial of them from off the earth.

15   And that, because his mind was not to do good :
           but persecuted the poor helpless man,
             that he might slay him that was vexed at the heart.

16   His delight was in cursing, and it shall happen unto him :
           he loved not blessing, therefore shall it be far from him.

17   He clothed himself with cursing, like as with a raiment :
           and it shall come into his bowels like water, and like oil into his bones.

18   Let it be unto him as the cloke that he hath upon him :
           and as the girdle that he is alway girded withal.

19   Let it thus happen from the Lord unto mine enemies :
           and to those that speak evil against my soul.

20   But deal thou with me, O Lord God, according unto thy Name :
           for sweet is thy mercy.

21   O deliver me, for I am helpless and poor :
           and my heart is wounded within me.

22   I go hence like the shadow that departeth :
           and am driven away as the grasshopper.

23	My knees are weak through fasting :
	my flesh is dried up for want of fatness.
24	I became also a reproach unto them :
	they that looked upon me shaked their heads.
25	Help me, O Lord my God :
	O save me according to thy mercy.
26	And they shall know, how that this is thy hand :
	and that thou, Lord, hast done it.
27	Though they curse, yet bless thou :
	and let them be confounded that rise up against me;
	but let thy servant rejoice.
28	Let mine adversaries be clothed with shame :
	and let them cover themselves with their own confusion,
	as with a cloke.
29	As for me, I will give great thanks unto the Lord with my mouth :
	and praise him among the multitude.
30	For he shall stand at the right hand of the poor :
	to save his soul from the unrighteous judges.

Day 23. Morning Prayer.

Psalm 110   *Dixit Dominus*

1	THE Lord said unto my Lord :
	Sit thou on my right hand, until I make thine enemies thy footstool.
2	The Lord shall send the rod of thy power out of Sion :
	be thou ruler, even in the midst among thine enemies.
3	In the day of thy power shall the people offer thee free-will offerings
	with an holy worship :
	the dew of thy birth is of the womb of the morning.
4	The Lord sware, and will not repent :
	Thou art a priest for ever after the order of Melchisedech.
5	The Lord upon thy right hand :
	shall wound even kings in the day of his wrath.
6	He shall judge among the heathen;
	he shall fill the places with the dead bodies :
	and smite in sunder the heads over divers countries.
7	He shall drink of the brook in the way :
	therefore shall he lift up his head.

Psalm 111

Confitebor tibi

1   I WILL give thanks unto the Lord with my whole heart :
    secretly among the faithful, and in the congregation.

2   The works of the Lord are great :
    sought out of all them that have pleasure therein.

3   His work is worthy to be praised and had in honour :
    and his righteousness endureth for ever.

4   The merciful and gracious Lord hath so done his marvellous works :
    that they ought to be had in remembrance.

5   He hath given meat unto them that fear him :
    he shall ever be mindful of his covenant.

6   He hath shewed his people the power of his works :
    that he may give them the heritage of the heathen.

7   The works of his hands are verity and judgement :
    all his commandments are true.

8   They stand fast for ever and ever :
    and are done in truth and equity.

9   He sent redemption unto his people :
    he hath commanded his covenant for ever;
      holy and reverend is his Name.

10   The fear of the Lord is the beginning of wisdom :
    a good understanding have all they that do thereafter;
      the praise of it endureth for ever.

Psalm 112

Beatus vir

1   BLESSED is the man that feareth the Lord :
    he hath great delight in his commandments.

2   His seed shall be mighty upon earth :
    the generation of the faithful shall be blessed.

3   Riches and plenteousness shall be in his house :
    and his righteousness endureth for ever.

4   Unto the godly there ariseth up light in the darkness :
    he is merciful, loving, and righteous.

5   A good man is merciful, and lendeth :
    and will guide his words with discretion.

6   For he shall never be moved :
    and the righteous shall be had in everlasting remembrance.

7   He will not be afraid of any evil tidings :
    for his heart standeth fast, and believeth in the Lord.

8	His heart is established, and will not shrink :
	until he see his desire upon his enemies.
9	He hath dispersed abroad, and given to the poor :
	and his righteousness remaineth for ever;
	his horn shall be exalted with honour.
10	The ungodly shall see it, and it shall grieve him :
	he shall gnash with his teeth, and consume away;
	the desire of the ungodly shall perish.

Day 23. Evening Prayer.

Psalm 113   *Laudate, pueri*

1	PRAISE the Lord, ye servants :
	O praise the Name of the Lord.
2	Blessed be the Name of the Lord :
	from this time forth for evermore.
3	The Lord's Name is praised :
	from the rising up of the sun unto the going down of the same.
4	The Lord is high above all heathen :
	and his glory above the heavens.
5	Who is like unto the Lord our God, that hath his dwelling so high :
	and yet humbleth himself
	to behold the things that are in heaven and earth?
6	He taketh up the simple out of the dust :
	and lifteth the poor out of the mire;
7	That he may set him with the princes :
	even with the princes of his people.
8	He maketh the barren woman to keep house :
	and to be a joyful mother of children.

Psalm 114   *In exitu Israel*

1	WHEN Israel came out of Egypt :
	and the house of Jacob from among the strange people,
2	Judah was his sanctuary :
	and Israel his dominion.
3	The sea saw that, and fled :
	Jordan was driven back.
4	The mountains skipped like rams :
	and the little hills like young sheep.
5	What aileth thee, O thou sea, that thou fleddest :
	and thou Jordan, that thou wast driven back?

6   Ye mountains, that ye skipped like rams :
           and ye little hills, like young sheep?

7   Tremble, thou earth, at the presence of the Lord :
           at the presence of the God of Jacob;

8   Who turned the hard rock into a standing water :
           and the flint-stone into a springing well.

Psalm 115   *Non nobis, Domine*

1   NOT unto us, O Lord, not unto us,
           but unto thy Name give the praise :
           for thy loving mercy and for thy truth's sake.

2   Wherefore shall the heathen say :
           Where is now their God?

3   As for our God, he is in heaven :
           he hath done whatsoever pleased him.

4   Their idols are silver and gold :
           even the work of men's hands.

5   They have mouths, and speak not :
           eyes have they, and see not.

6   They have ears, and hear not :
           noses have they, and smell not.

7   They have hands, and handle not; feet have they, and walk not :
           neither speak they through their throat.

8   They that make them are like unto them :
           and so are all such as put their trust in them.

9   But thou, house of Israel, trust thou in the Lord :
           he is their succour and defence.

10   Ye house of Aaron, put your trust in the Lord :
           he is their helper and defender.

11   Ye that fear the Lord, put your trust in the Lord :
           he is their helper and defender.

12   The Lord hath been mindful of us, and he shall bless us :
           even he shall bless the house of Israel,
           he shall bless the house of Aaron.

13   He shall bless them that fear the Lord :
           both small and great.

14   The Lord shall increase you more and more :
           you and your children.

15   Ye are the blessed of the Lord :
           who made heaven and earth.

16	All the whole heavens are the Lord's :
	the earth hath he given to the children of men.
17	The dead praise not thee, O Lord :
	neither all they that go down into silence.
18	But we will praise the Lord :
	from this time forth for evermore. Praise the Lord.

Day 24. Morning Prayer.

Psalm 116   *Dilexi, quoniam*

1	I AM well pleased :
	that the Lord hath heard the voice of my prayer;
2	That he hath inclined his ear unto me :
	therefore will I call upon him as long as I live.
3	The snares of death compassed me round about :
	and the pains of hell gat hold upon me.
4	I shall find trouble and heaviness,
	and I will call upon the Name of the Lord :
	O Lord, I beseech thee, deliver my soul.
5	Gracious is the Lord, and righteous :
	yea, our God is merciful.
6	The Lord preserveth the simple :
	I was in misery, and he helped me.
7	Turn again then unto thy rest, O my soul :
	for the Lord hath rewarded thee.
8	And why? thou hast delivered my soul from death :
	mine eyes from tears, and my feet from falling.
9	I will walk before the Lord :
	in the land of the living.
10	I believed, and therefore will I speak; but I was sore troubled :
	I said in my haste, All men are liars.
11	What reward shall I give unto the Lord :
	for all the benefits that he hath done unto me?
12	I will receive the cup of salvation :
	and call upon the Name of the Lord.
13	I will pay my vows now in the presence of all his people :
	right dear in the sight of the Lord is the death of his saints.
14	Behold, O Lord, how that I am thy servant :
	I am thy servant, and the son of thine handmaid;
	thou hast broken my bonds in sunder.

15 I will offer to thee the sacrifice of thanksgiving :
    and will call upon the Name of the Lord.
16 I will pay my vows unto the Lord, in the sight of all his people :
    in the courts of the Lord's house,
        even in the midst of thee, O Jerusalem. Praise the Lord.

Psalm 117   *Laudate Dominum*
1   O PRAISE the Lord, all ye heathen :
    praise him, all ye nations.
2   For his merciful kindness is ever more and more towards us :
    and the truth of the Lord endureth for ever. Praise the Lord.

Psalm 118   *Confitemini Domino*
1   O GIVE thanks unto the Lord, for he is gracious :
    because his mercy endureth for ever.
2   Let Israel now confess that he is gracious :
    and that his mercy endureth for ever.
3   Let the house of Aaron now confess :
    that his mercy endureth for ever.
4   Yea, let them now that fear the Lord confess :
    that his mercy endureth for ever.
5   I called upon the Lord in trouble :
    and the Lord heard me at large.
6   The Lord is on my side :
    I will not fear what man doeth unto me.
7   The Lord taketh my part with them that help me :
    therefore shall I see my desire upon mine enemies.
8   It is better to trust in the Lord :
    than to put any confidence in man.
9   It is better to trust in the Lord :
    than to put any confidence in princes.
10 All nations compassed me round about :
    but in the Name of the Lord will I destroy them.
11 They kept me in on every side, they kept me in, I say, on every side :
    but in the Name of the Lord will I destroy them.
12 They came about me like bees,
        and are extinct even as the fire among the thorns :
    for in the Name of the Lord I will destroy them.
13 Thou hast thrust sore at me, that I might fall :
    but the Lord was my help.

14	The Lord is my strength, and my song :
	and is become my salvation.
15	The voice of joy and health is in the dwellings of the righteous :
	the right hand of the Lord bringeth mighty things to pass.
16	The right hand of the Lord hath the pre-eminence :
	the right hand of the Lord bringeth mighty things to pass.
17	I shall not die, but live :
	and declare the works of the Lord.
18	The Lord hath chastened and corrected me :
	but he hath not given me over unto death.
19	Open me the gates of righteousness :
	that I may go into them, and give thanks unto the Lord.
20	This is the gate of the Lord :
	the righteous shall enter into it.
21	I will thank thee, for thou hast heard me :
	and art become my salvation.
22	The same stone which the builders refused :
	is become the head-stone in the corner.
23	This is the Lord's doing :
	and it is marvellous in our eyes.
24	This is the day which the Lord hath made :
	we will rejoice and be glad in it.
25	Help me now, O Lord :
	O Lord, send us now prosperity.
26	Blessed be he that cometh in the Name of the Lord :
	we have wished you good luck , ye that are of the house of the Lord.
27	God is the Lord who hath shewed us light :
	bind the sacrifice with cords, yea, even unto the horns of the altar.
28	Thou art my God, and I will thank thee :
	thou art my God, and I will praise thee.29. O give thanks unto the Lord, for he is gracious :
	and his mercy endureth for ever.

Day 24. Evening Prayer.

Psalm 119   *Beati immaculati*

1	BLESSED are those that are undefiled in the way :
	and walk in the law of the Lord.
2	Blessed are they that keep his testimonies :
	and seek him with their whole heart.

3	For they who do no wickedness :
	walk in his ways.
4	Thou hast charged :
	that we shall diligently keep thy commandments.
5	O that my ways were made so direct :
	that I might keep thy statutes!
6	So shall I not be confounded :
	while I have respect unto all thy commandments.
7	I will thank thee with an unfeigned heart :
	when I shall have learned the judgements of thy righteousness.
8	I will keep thy ceremonies :
	O forsake me not utterly.

In quo corriget?

9	WHEREWITHAL shall a young man cleanse his way :
	even by ruling himself after thy word.
10	With my whole heart have I sought thee :
	O let me not go wrong out of thy commandments.
11	Thy words have I hid within my heart :
	that I should not sin against thee.
12	Blessed art thou, O Lord :
	O teach me thy statutes.
13	With my lips have I been telling :
	of all the judgements of thy mouth.
14	I have had as great delight in the way of thy testimonies :
	as in all manner of riches.
15	I will talk of thy commandments :
	and have respect unto thy ways.
16	My delight shall be in thy statutes :
	and I will not forget thy word.

Retribue servo tuo

17	O DO well unto thy servant :
	that I may live, and keep thy word.
18	Open thou mine eyes :
	that I may see the wondrous things of thy law.
19	I am a stranger upon earth :
	O hide not thy commandments from me.
20	My soul breaketh out for the very fervent desire :
	that it hath alway unto thy judgements.

21   Thou hast rebuked the proud :
and cursed are they that do err from thy commandments.

22   O turn from me shame and rebuke :
for I have kept thy testimonies.

23   Princes also did sit and speak against me :
but thy servant is occupied in thy statutes.

24   For thy testimonies are my delight :
and my counsellors.

Adhæsit pavimento

25   MY SOUL cleaveth to the dust :
O quicken thou me, according to thy word.

26   I have acknowledged my ways, and thou heardest me :
O teach me thy statutes.

27   Make me to understand the way of thy commandments :
and so shall I talk of thy wondrous works.

28   My soul melteth away for very heaviness :
comfort thou me according unto thy word.

29   Take from me the way of lying :
and cause thou me to make much of thy law.

30   I have chosen the way of truth :
and thy judgements have I laid before me.

31   I have stuck unto thy testimonies :
O Lord, confound me not.

32   I will run the way of thy commandments :
when thou hast set my heart at liberty.

Day 25. Morning Prayer.
Legem pone

33   TEACH me, O Lord, the way of thy statutes :
and I shall keep it unto the end.

34   Give me understanding, and I shall keep thy law :
yea, I shall keep it with my whole heart.

35   Make me to go in the path of thy commandments :
for therein is my desire.

36   Incline my heart unto thy testimonies :
and not to covetousness.

37   O turn away mine eyes, lest they behold vanity :
and quicken thou me in thy way.

38 O stablish thy word in thy servant :
  that I may fear thee.

39 Take away the rebuke that I am afraid of :
  for thy judgements are good.

40 Behold, my delight is in thy commandments :
  O quicken me in thy righteousness.

Et veniat super me

41 LET thy loving mercy come also unto me, O Lord :
  even thy salvation, according unto thy word.

42 So shall I make answer unto my blasphemers :
  for my trust is in thy word.

43 O take not the word of thy truth utterly out of my mouth :
  for my hope is in thy judgements.

44 So shall I alway keep thy law :
  yea, for ever and ever.

45 And I will walk at liberty :
  for I seek thy commandments.

46 I will speak of thy testimonies also, even before kings :
  and will not be ashamed.

47 And my delight shall be in thy commandments :
  which I have loved.

48 My hands also will I lift up unto thy commandments,
    which I have loved :
  and my study shall be in thy statutes.

Memor esto servi tui

49 O THINK upon thy servant, as concerning thy word :
  wherein thou hast caused me to put my trust.

50 The same is my comfort in my trouble :
  for thy word hath quickened me.

51 The proud have had me exceedingly in derision :
  yet have I not shrinked from thy law.

52 For I remembered thine everlasting judgements, O Lord :
  and received comfort.

53 I am horribly afraid :
  for the ungodly that forsake thy law.

54 Thy statutes have been my songs :
  in the house of my pilgrimage.

55	I have thought upon thy Name, O Lord, in the night-season :
	and have kept thy law.
56	This I had :
	because I kept thy commandments.

Portio mea, Domine

57	THOU art my portion, O Lord :
	I have promised to keep thy law.
58	I made my humble petition in thy presence with my whole heart :
	O be merciful unto me, according to thy word.
59	I called mine own ways to remembrance :
	and turned my feet unto thy testimonies.
60	I made haste, and prolonged not the time :
	to keep thy commandments.
61	The congregations of the ungodly have robbed me :
	but I have not forgotten thy law.
62	At midnight I will rise to give thanks unto thee :
	because of thy righteous judgements.
63	I am a companion of all them that fear thee :
	and keep thy commandments.
64	The earth, O Lord, is full of thy mercy :
	O teach me thy statutes.

Bonitatem fecisti

65	O LORD, thou hast dealt graciously with thy servant :
	according unto thy word.
66	O learn me true understanding and knowledge :
	for I have believed thy commandments.
67	Before I was troubled, I went wrong :
	but now have I kept thy word.
68	Thou art good and gracious :
	O teach me thy statutes.
69	The proud have imagined a lie against me :
	but I will keep thy commandments with my whole heart.
70	Their heart is as fat as brawn :
	but my delight hath been in thy law.
71	It is good for me that I have been in trouble :
	that I may learn thy statutes.
72	The law of thy mouth is dearer unto me :
	than thousands of gold and silver.

Manus tuæ fecerunt me

73   THY hands have made me and fashioned me :
     O give me understanding, that I may learn thy commandments.

74   They that fear thee will be glad when they see me :
     because I have put my trust in thy word.

75   I know, O Lord, that thy judgements are right :
     and that thou of very faithfulness hast caused me to be troubled.

76   O let thy merciful kindness be my comfort :
     according to thy word unto thy servant.

77   O let thy loving mercies come unto me, that I may live :
     for thy law is my delight.

78   Let the proud be confounded,
       for they go wickedly about to destroy me :
     but I will be occupied in thy commandments.

79   Let such as fear thee, and have known thy testimonies :
     be turned unto me.

80   O let my heart be sound in thy statutes :
     that I be not ashamed.

Defecit anima mea

81   MY SOUL hath longed for thy salvation :
     and I have a good hope because of thy word.

82   Mine eyes long sore for thy word :
     saying, O when wilt thou comfort me?

83   For I am become like a bottle in the smoke :
     yet do I not forget thy statutes.

84   How many are the days of thy servant :
     when wilt thou be avenged of them that persecute me?

85   The proud have digged pits for me :
     which are not after thy law.

86   All thy commandments are true :
     they persecute me falsely; O be thou my help.

87   They had almost made an end of me upon earth :
     but I forsook not thy commandments.

88   O quicken me after thy loving-kindness :
     and so shall I keep the testimonies of thy mouth.

89 O LORD, thy word :
    endureth for ever in heaven.

90 Thy truth also remaineth from one generation to another :
    thou hast laid the foundation of the earth, and it abideth.

91 They continue this day according to thine ordinance :
    for all things serve thee.

92 If my delight had not been in thy law :
    I should have perished in my trouble.

93 I will never forget thy commandments :
    for with them thou hast quickened me.

94 I am thine, O save me :
    for I have sought thy commandments.

95 The ungodly laid wait for me to destroy me :
    but I will consider thy testimonies.

96 I see that all things come to an end :
    but thy commandment is exceeding broad.

Quomodo dilexi!

97 LORD, what love have I unto thy law :
    all the day long is my study in it.

98 Thou through thy commandments
       hast made me wiser than mine enemies :
    for they are ever with me.

99 I have more understanding than my teachers :
    for thy testimonies are my study.

100 I am wiser than the aged :
    because I keep thy commandments.

101 I have refrained my feet from every evil way :
    that I may keep thy word.

102 I have not shrunk from thy judgements :
     for thou teachest me.

103 O how sweet are thy words unto my throat :
    yea, sweeter than honey unto my mouth.

104 Through thy commandments I get understanding :
    therefore I hate all evil ways.

Day 26. Morning Prayer.

Lucerna pedibus meis

105 THY word is a lantern unto my feet :
and a light unto my paths.

106 I have sworn, and am stedfastly purposed :
to keep thy righteous judgements.

107 I am troubled above measure :
quicken me, O Lord, according to thy word.

108 Let the free-will offerings of my mouth please thee, O Lord :
and teach me thy judgements.

109 My soul is alway in my hand :
yet do I not forget thy law.

110 The ungodly have laid a snare for me :
but yet I swerved not from thy commandments.

111 Thy testimonies have I claimed as mine heritage for ever :
and why? they are the very joy of my heart.

112 I have applied my heart to fulfil thy statutes alway :
even unto the end.

Iniquos odio habui

113 I HATE them that imagine evil things :
but thy law do I love.

114 Thou art my defence and shield :
and my trust is in thy word.

115 Away from me, ye wicked :
I will keep the commandments of my God.

116 O stablish me according to thy word, that I may live :
and let me not be disappointed of my hope.

117 Hold thou me up, and I shall be safe :
yea, my delight shall be ever in thy statutes.

118 Thou hast trodden down all them that depart from thy statutes :
for they imagine but deceit.

119 Thou puttest away all the ungodly of the earth like dross :
therefore I love thy testimonies.

120 My flesh trembleth for fear of thee :
and I am afraid of thy judgements.

121   I DEAL with the thing that is lawful and right :
O give me not over unto mine oppressors.

122   Make thou thy servant to delight in that which is good :
that the proud do me no wrong.

123   Mine eyes are wasted away with looking for thy health :
and for the word of thy righteousness.

124   O deal with thy servant according unto thy loving mercy :
and teach me thy statutes.

125   I am thy servant, O grant me understanding :
that I may know thy testimonies.

126   It is time for thee, Lord, to lay to thine hand :
for they have destroyed thy law.

127   For I love thy commandments :
above gold and precious stone.

128   Therefore hold I straight all thy commandments :
and all false ways I utterly abhor.

Mirabilia

129   THY testimonies are wonderful :
therefore doth my soul keep them.

130   When thy word goeth forth :
it giveth light and understanding unto the simple.

131   I opened my mouth, and drew in my breath :
for my delight was in thy commandments.

132   O look thou upon me, and be merciful unto me :
as thou usest to do unto those that love thy Name.

133   Order my steps in thy word :
and so shall no wickedness have dominion over me.

134   O deliver me from the wrongful dealings of men :
and so shall I keep thy commandments.

135   Shew the light of thy countenance upon thy servant :
and teach me thy statutes.

136   Mine eyes gush out with water :
because men keep not thy law.

137	RIGHTEOUS art thou, O Lord :
	and true is thy judgement.
138	The testimonies that thou hast commanded :
	are exceeding righteous and true.
139	My zeal hath even consumed me :
	because mine enemies have forgotten thy words.
140	Thy word is tried to the uttermost :
	and thy servant loveth it.
141	I am small, and of no reputation :
	yet do I not forget thy commandments.
142	Thy righteousness is an everlasting righteousness :
	and thy law is the truth.
143	Trouble and heaviness have taken hold upon me :
	yet is my delight in thy commandments.
144	The righteousness of thy testimonies is everlasting :
	O grant me understanding, and I shall live.

Day 26. Evening Prayer.

Clamavi in toto corde meo

145	I CALL with my whole heart :
	hear me, O Lord, I will keep thy statutes.
146	Yea, even unto thee do I call :
	help me, and I shall keep thy testimonies.
147	Early in the morning do I cry unto thee :
	for in thy word is my trust.
148	Mine eyes prevent the night-watches :
	that I might be occupied in thy words.
149	Hear my voice, O Lord, according unto thy loving-kindness :
	quicken me, according as thou art wont.
150	They draw nigh that of malice persecute me :
	and are far from thy law.
151	Be thou nigh at hand, O Lord :
	for all thy commandments are true.
152	As concerning thy testimonies, I have known long since :
	that thou hast grounded them for ever.

Vide humilitatem

153   O CONSIDER mine adversity, and deliver me :
             for I do not forget thy law.

154   Avenge thou my cause, and deliver me :
             quicken me, according to thy word.

155   Health is far from the ungodly :
             for they regard not thy statutes.

156   Great is thy mercy, O Lord :
             quicken me, as thou art wont.

157   Many there are that trouble me, and persecute me :
             yet do I not swerve from thy testimonies.

158   It grieveth me when I see the transgressors :
             because they keep not thy law.

159   Consider, O Lord, how I love thy commandments :
             O quicken me, according to thy loving-kindness.

160   Thy word is true from everlasting :
             all the judgements of thy righteousness endure for evermore.

Principes persecuti sunt

161   PRINCES have persecuted me without a cause :
             but my heart standeth in awe of thy word.

162   I am as glad of thy word :
             as one that findeth great spoils.

163   As for lies, I hate and abhor them :
             but thy law do I love.

164   Seven times a day do I praise thee :
             because of thy righteous judgements.

165   Great is the peace that they have who love thy law :
             and they are not offended at it.

166   Lord, I have looked for thy saving health :
             and done after thy commandments.

167   My soul hath kept thy testimonies :
             and loved them exceedingly.

168   I have kept thy commandments and testimonies :
             for all my ways are before thee.

169 LET my complaint come before thee, O Lord :
give me understanding, according to thy word.

170 Let my supplication come before thee :
deliver me, according to thy word.

171 My lips shall speak of thy praise :
when thou hast taught me thy statutes.

172 Yea, my tongue shall sing of thy word :
for all thy commandments are righteous.

173 Let thine hand help me :
for I have chosen thy commandments.

174 I have longed for thy saving health, O Lord :
and in thy law is my delight.

175 O let my soul live, and it shall praise thee :
and thy judgements shall help me.

176 I have gone astray like a sheep that is lost :
O seek thy servant, for I do not forget thy commandments.

Day 27. Morning Prayer.

Psalm 120 *Ad Dominum*

1 WHEN I was in trouble I called upon the Lord :
and he heard me.

2 Deliver my soul, O Lord, from lying lips :
and from a deceitful tongue.

3 What reward shall be given or done unto thee, thou false tongue :
even mighty and sharp arrows, with hot burning coals.

4 Woe is me, that I am constrained to dwell with Mesech :
and to have my habitation among the tents of Kedar.

5 My soul hath long dwelt among them :
that are enemies unto peace.

6 I labour for peace, but when I speak unto them thereof :
they make them ready to battle.

Psalm 121 *Levavi oculus*

1 I WILL lift up mine eyes unto the hills :
from whence cometh my help.

2 My help cometh even from the Lord :
who hath made heaven and earth.

3   He will not suffer thy foot to be moved :
    and he that keepeth thee will not sleep.

4   Behold, he that keepeth Israel :
    shall neither slumber nor sleep.

5   The Lord himself is thy keeper :
    the Lord is thy defence upon thy right hand;

6   So that the sun shall not burn thee by day :
    neither the moon by night.

7   The Lord shall preserve thee from all evil :
    yea, it is even he that shall keep thy soul.

8   The Lord shall preserve thy going out, and thy coming in :
    from this time forth for evermore.

Psalm 122   *Lætatus sum*

1   I WAS glad when they said unto me :
    We will go into the house of the Lord.

2   Our feet shall stand in thy gates :
    O Jerusalem.

3   Jerusalem is built as a city :
    that is at unity in itself.

4   For thither the tribes go up, even the tribes of the Lord :
    to testify unto Israel, to give thanks unto the Name of the Lord.

5   For there is the seat of judgement :
    even the seat of the house of David.

6   O pray for the peace of Jerusalem :
    they shall prosper that love thee.

7   Peace be within thy walls :
    and plenteousness within thy palaces.

8   For my brethren and companions' sakes :
    I will wish thee prosperity.

9   Yea, because of the house of the Lord our God :
    I will seek to do thee good.

Psalm 123 *Ad te levavi oculos meos*

1 UNTO thee lift I up mine eyes :
O thou that dwellest in the heavens.

2 Behold, even as the eyes of servants
look unto the hand of their masters,
and as the eyes of a maiden unto the hand of her mistress :
even so our eyes wait upon the Lord our God,
until he have mercy upon us.

3 Have mercy upon us, O Lord, have mercy upon us :
for we are utterly despised.

4 Our soul is filled with the scornful reproof of the wealthy :
and with the despitefulness of the proud.

Psalm 124 *Nisi quia Dominus*

1 IF THE Lord himself had not been on our side, now may Israel say :
if the Lord himself had not been on our side,
when men rose up against us;

2 They had swallowed us up quick :
when thy were so wrathfully displeased at us.

3 Yea, the waters had drowned us :
and the stream had gone over our soul.

4 The deep waters of the proud :
had gone even over our soul.

5 But praised be the Lord :
who hath not given us over for a prey unto their teeth.

6 Our soul is escaped even as a bird out of the snare of the fowler :
the snare is broken, and we are delivered.

7 Our help standeth in the Name of the Lord :
who hath made heaven and earth.

Psalm 125 *Qui confidunt*

1 THEY that put their trust in the Lord
shall be even as the mount Sion :
which may not be removed, but standeth fast for ever.

2 The hills stand about Jerusalem :
even so standeth the Lord round about his people,
from this time forth for evermore.

3 For the rod of the ungodly cometh not into the lot of the righteous :
lest the righteous put their hand unto wickedness.

4	Do well, O Lord :
	unto those that are good and true of heart.
5	As for such as turn back unto their own wickedness :
	the Lord shall lead them forth with the evil-doers;
	but peace shall be upon Israel.

Day 27. Evening Prayer.

Psalm 126	*In convertendo*
1	WHEN the Lord turned again the captivity of Sion :
	then were we like unto them that dream.
2	Then was our mouth filled with laughter :
	and our tongue with joy.
3	Then said they among the heathen :
	The Lord hath done great things for them.
4	Yea, the Lord hath done great things for us already :
	whereof we rejoice.
5	Turn our captivity, O Lord :
	as the rivers in the south.
6	They that sow in tears :
	shall reap in joy.
7	He that now goeth on his way weeping, and beareth forth good seed :
	shall doubtless come again with joy, and bring his sheaves with him.

Psalm 127	*Nisi Dominus*
1	EXCEPT the Lord build the house :
	their labour is but lost that build it.
2	Except the Lord keep the city :
	the watchman waketh but in vain.
3	It is but lost labour that ye haste to rise up early,
	and so late take rest, and eat the bread of carefulness :
	for so he giveth his beloved sleep.
4	Lo, children and the fruit of the womb :
	are an heritage and gift that cometh of the Lord.
5	Like as the arrows in the hand of the giant :
	even so are the young children.
6	Happy is the man that hath his quiver full of them :
	they shall not be ashamed
	when they speak with their enemies in the gate.

Psalm 128 *Beati omnes*

1 BLESSED are all they that fear the Lord :
and walk in his ways.

2 For thou shalt eat the labours of thine hands :
O well is thee, and happy shalt thou be.

3 Thy wife shall be as the fruitful vine :
upon the walls of thine house.

4 Thy children like the olive-branches :
round about thy table.

5 Lo, thus shall the man be blessed :
that feareth the Lord.

6 The Lord from out of Sion shall so bless thee :
that thou shalt see Jerusalem in prosperity all thy life long.

7 Yea, that thou shalt see thy children's children :
and peace upon Israel.

Psalm 129 *Sæpe expugnaverunt*

1 MANY a time have they fought against me from my youth up :
may Israel now say.

2 Yea, many a time have they vexed me from my youth up :
but they have not prevailed against me.

3 The plowers plowed upon my back :
and made long furrows.

4 But the righteous Lord :
hath hewn the snares of the ungodly in pieces.

5 Let them be confounded and turned backward :
as many as have evil will at Sion.

6 Let them be even as the grass growing upon the house-tops :
which withereth afore it be plucked up;

7 Whereof the mower filleth not his hand :
neither he that bindeth up the sheaves his bosom.

8 So that they who go by say not so much as, The Lord prosper you :
we wish you good luck in the Name of the Lord.

Psalm 130 *De profundis*

1 OUT of the deep have I called unto thee, O Lord :
Lord, hear my voice.

2 O let thine ears consider well :
the voice of my complaint.

3   If thou, Lord, wilt be extreme to mark what is done amiss :
O Lord, who may abide it?

4   For there is mercy with thee :
therefore shalt thou be feared.

5   I look for the Lord; my soul doth wait for him :
in his word is my trust.

6   My soul fleeth unto the Lord :
before the morning watch, I say, before the morning watch.

7   O Israel, trust in the Lord, for with the Lord there is mercy :
and with him is plenteous redemption.

8   And he shall redeem Israel :
from all his sins.

Psalm 131   *Domine, non est*

1   LORD, I am not high-minded :
I have no proud looks.

2   I do not exercise myself in great matters :
which are too high for me.

3   But I refrain my soul, and keep it low,
like as a child that is weaned from his mother :
yea, my soul is even as a weaned child.

4   O Israel, trust in the Lord :
from this time forth for evermore.

Day 28. Morning Prayer.

Psalm 132   *Memento, Domine*

1   LORD, remember David :
and all his trouble;

2   How he sware unto the Lord :
and vowed a vow unto the Almighty God of Jacob;

3   I will not come within the tabernacle of mine house :
nor climb up into my bed;

4   I will not suffer mine eyes to sleep, nor mine eye-lids to slumber :
neither the temples of my head to take any rest;

5   Until I find out a place for the temple of the Lord :
an habitation for the mighty God of Jacob.

6   Lo, we heard of the same at Ephrata :
and found it in the wood.

7	We will go into his tabernacle :
	and fall low on our knees before his footstool.
8	Arise, O Lord, into thy resting-place :
	thou, and the ark of thy strength.
9	Let thy priests be clothed with righteousness :
	and let thy saints sing with joyfulness.
10	For thy servant David's sake :
	turn not away the presence of thine Anointed.
11	The Lord hath made a faithful oath unto David :
	and he shall not shrink from it;
12	Of the fruit of thy body :
	shall I set upon thy seat.
13	If thy children will keep my covenant,
	and my testimonies that I shall learn them :
	their children also shall sit upon thy seat for evermore.
14	For the Lord hath chosen Sion to be an habitation for himself :
	he hath longed for her.
15	This shall be my rest for ever :
	here will I dwell, for I have a delight therein.
16	I will bless her victuals with increase :
	and will satisfy her poor with bread.
17	I will deck her priests with health :
	and her saints shall rejoice and sing.
18	There shall I make the horn of David to flourish :
	I have ordained a lantern for mine Anointed.
19	As for his enemies, I shall clothe them with shame :
	but upon himself shall his crown flourish.

Psalm 133   *Ecce, quam bonum!*

1	BEHOLD, how good and joyful a thing it is :
	brethren, to dwell together in unity!
2	It is like the precious ointment upon the head,
	that ran down unto the beard :
	even unto Aaron's beard, and went down to the skirts of his clothing.
3	Like as the dew of Hermon :
	which fell upon the hill of Sion.
4	For there the Lord promised his blessing :
	and life for evermore.

Psalm 134 *Ecce nunc*

1 BEHOLD now, praise the Lord :
  all ye servants of the Lord;

2 Ye that by night stand in the house of the Lord :
  even in the courts of the house of our God.

3 Lift up your hands in the sanctuary :
  and praise the Lord.

4 The Lord that made heaven and earth :
  give thee blessing out of Sion.

Psalm 135 *Laudate Nomen*

1 O PRAISE the Lord, laud ye the Name of the Lord :
  praise it, O ye servants of the Lord;

2 Ye that stand in the house of the Lord :
  in the courts of the house of our God.

3 O praise the Lord, for the Lord is gracious :
  O sing praises unto his Name, for it is lovely.

4 For why? the Lord hath chosen Jacob unto himself :
  and Israel for his own possession.

5 For I know that the Lord is great :
  and that our Lord is above all gods.

6 Whatsoever the Lord pleased, that did he in heaven and in earth :
  and in the sea, and in all deep places.

7 He bringeth forth the clouds from the ends of the world :
   and sendeth forth lightnings with the rain,
   bringing the winds out of his treasures.

8 He smote the first-born of Egypt :
  both of man and beast.

9 He hath sent tokens and wonders into the midst of thee,
   O thou land of Egypt :
  upon Pharaoh, and all his servants.

10 He smote divers nations :
  and slew mighty kings;

11 Sehon king of the Amorites, and Og the king of Basan :
  and all the kingdoms of Canaan;

12 And gave their land to be an heritage :
  even an heritage unto Israel his people.

13 Thy Name, O Lord, endureth for ever :
  so doth thy memorial, O Lord, from one generation to another.

14	For the Lord will avenge his people :
	and be gracious unto his servants.
15	As for the images of the heathen, they are but silver and gold :
	the work of men's hands.
16	They have mouths, and speak not :
	eyes have they, but they see not.
17	They have ears, and yet they hear not :
	neither is there any breath in their mouths.
18	They that make them are like unto them :
	and so are all they that put their trust in them.
19	Praise the Lord, ye house of Israel :
	praise the Lord, ye house of Aaron.
20	Praise the Lord, ye house of Levi :
	ye that fear the Lord, praise the Lord.
21	Praised be the Lord out of Sion :
	who dwelleth at Jerusalem.

Day 28. Evening Prayer.

Psalm 136　　　　*Confitemini*

1	O GIVE thanks unto the LORD, for he is gracious :
	and his mercy endureth for ever.
2	O give thanks unto the God of all gods :
	for his mercy endureth for ever.
3	O thank the Lord of all lords :
	for his mercy endureth for ever.
4	Who only doeth great wonders :
	for his mercy endureth for ever.
5	Who by his excellent wisdom made the heavens :
	for his mercy endureth for ever.
6	Who laid out the earth above the waters :
	for his mercy endureth for ever.
7	Who hath made great lights :
	for his mercy endureth for ever;
8	The sun to rule the day :
	for his mercy endureth for ever;
9	The moon and the stars to govern the night :
	for his mercy endureth for ever.
10	Who smote Egypt with their first-born :
	for his mercy endureth for ever;

11	And brought out Israel from among them :
	for his mercy endureth for ever;
12	With a mighty hand, and stretched out arm :
	for his mercy endureth for ever.
13	Who divided the Red sea in two parts :
	for his mercy endureth for ever;
14	And made Israel to go through the midst of it :
	for his mercy endureth for ever.
15	But as for Pharaoh and his host, he overthrew them in the Red sea :
	for his mercy endureth for ever.
16	Who led his people through the wilderness :
	for his mercy endureth for ever.
17	Who smote great kings :
	for his mercy endureth for ever;
18	Yea, and slew mighty kings :
	for his mercy endureth for ever;
19	Sehon king of the Amorites :
	for his mercy endureth for ever;
20	And Og the king of Basan :
	for his mercy endureth for ever;
21	And gave away their land for an heritage :
	for his mercy endureth for ever;
22	Even for an heritage unto Israel his servant :
	for his mercy endureth for ever.
23	Who remembered us when we were in trouble :
	for his mercy endureth for ever;
24	And hath delivered us from our enemies :
	for his mercy endureth for ever.
25	Who giveth food to all flesh :
	for his mercy endureth for ever.
26	O give thanks unto the God of heaven :
	for his mercy endureth for ever.
27	O give thanks unto the Lord of lords :
	for his mercy endureth for ever.

Psalm 137 *Super flumina*

1	BY THE waters of Babylon we sat down and wept :
	when we remembered thee, O Sion.
2	As for our harps, we hanged them up :
	upon the trees that are therein.

3   For they that led us away captive required of us then a song,
         and melody in our heaviness :
      Sing us one of the songs of Sion.

4   How shall we sing the Lord's song :
         in a strange land?

5   If I forget thee, O Jerusalem :
      let my right hand forget her cunning.

6   If I do not remember thee,
         let my tongue cleave to the roof of my mouth :
      yea, if I prefer not Jerusalem in my mirth.

7   Remember the children of Edom, O Lord, in the day of Jerusalem :
      how they said, Down with it, down with it, even to the ground.

8   O daughter of Babylon , wasted with misery :
      yea, happy shall he be that rewardeth thee, as thou hast served us.

9   Blessed shall he be that taketh thy children :
      and throweth them against the stones.

Psalm 138   *Confitebor tibi*

1   I WILL give thanks unto thee, O Lord, with my whole heart :
      even before the gods will I sing praise unto thee.

2   I will worship toward thy holy temple, and praise thy Name,
         because of thy loving-kindness and truth :
      for thou hast magnified thy Name and thy word above all things.

3   When I called upon thee, thou heardest me :
      and enduedst my soul with much strength.

4   All the kings of the earth shall praise thee, O Lord :
      for they have heard the words of thy mouth.

5   Yea, they shall sing in the ways of the Lord :
      that great is the glory of the Lord.

6   For though the Lord be high, yet hath he respect unto the lowly :
      as for the proud, he beholdeth them afar off.

7   Though I walk in the midst of trouble, yet shalt thou refresh me :
      thou shalt stretch forth thy hand
         upon the furiousness of mine enemies,
          and thy right hand shall save me.

8   The Lord shall make good his loving-kindness toward me :
      yea, thy mercy, O Lord, endureth for ever;
         despise not then the works of thine own hands.

Psalm 139   *Domine, probasti*

1   O LORD, thou hast searched me out and known me :
     thou knowest my down-sitting and mine up-rising,
      thou understandest my thoughts long before.

2   Thou art about my path, and about my bed :
     and spiest out all my ways.

3   For lo, there is not a word in my tongue :
     but thou, O Lord, knowest it altogether.

4   Thou hast fashioned me behind and before :
     and laid thine hand upon me.

5   Such knowledge is too wonderful and excellent for me :
     I cannot attain unto it.

6   Whither shall I go then from thy Spirit :
     or whither shall I go then from thy presence?

7   If I climb up into heaven, thou art there :
     if I go down to hell, thou art there also.

8   If I take the wings of the morning :
     and remain in the uttermost parts of the sea;

9   Even there also shall thy hand lead me :
     and thy right hand shall hold me.

10   If I say, Peradventure the darkness shall cover me :
     then shall my night be turned to day.

11   Yea, the darkness is no darkness with thee,
     but the night is as clear as the day :
     the darkness and light to thee are both alike.

12   For my reins are thine :
     thou hast covered me in my mother's womb.

13   I will give thanks unto thee, for I am fearfully and wonderfully made :
     marvellous are thy works, and that my soul knoweth right well.

14   My bones are not hid from thee :
     though I be made secretly, and fashioned beneath in the earth.

15   Thine eyes did see my substance, yet being unperfect :
     and in thy book were all my members written;

16   Which day by day were fashioned :
     when as yet there was none of them.

17   How dear are thy counsels unto me, O God :
     O how great is the sum of them!

18   If I tell them, they are more in number than the sand :
     when I wake up I am present with thee.

19	Wilt thou not slay the wicked, O God : depart from me, ye blood-thirsty men.
20	For they speak unrighteously against thee : and thine enemies take thy Name in vain.
21	Do not I hate them, O Lord, that hate thee : and am not I grieved with those that rise up against thee?
22	Yea, I hate them right sore : even as though they were mine enemies.
23	Try me, O God, and seek the ground of my heart : prove me, and examine my thoughts.
24	Look well if there be any way of wickedness in me : and lead me in the way everlasting.

Psalm 140 *Eripe me, Domine*

1	DELIVER me, O Lord, from the evil man : and preserve me from the wicked man.
2	Who imagine mischief in their hearts : and stir up strife all the day long.
3	They have sharpened their tongues like a serpent : adders' poison is under their lips.
4	Keep me, O Lord, from the hands of the ungodly : preserve me from the wicked men, who are purposed to overthrow my goings.
5	The proud have laid a snare for me, and spread a net abroad with cords : yea, and set traps in my way.
6	I said unto the Lord, Thou art my God : hear the voice of my prayers, O Lord.
7	O Lord God, thou strength of my health : thou hast covered my head in the day of the battle.
8	Let not the ungodly have his desire, O Lord : let not his mischievous imagination prosper, lest they be too proud.
9	Let the mischief of their own lips fall upon the head of them : that compass me about.
10	Let hot burning coals fall upon them : let them be cast into the fire and into the pit, that they never rise up again.
11	A man full of words shall not prosper upon the earth : evil shall hunt the wicked person to overthrow him.

12   Sure I am that the Lord will avenge the poor :
        and maintain the cause of the helpless.

13   The righteous also shall give thanks unto thy Name :
        and the just shall continue in thy sight.

Day 29. Evening Prayer.

Psalm 141   *Domine, clamavi*

1   LORD, I call upon thee, haste thee unto me :
        and consider my voice when I cry unto thee.

2   Let my prayer be set forth in thy sight as the incense :
        and let the lifting up of my hands be an evening sacrifice.

3   Set a watch, O Lord, before my mouth :
        and keep the door of my lips.

4   O let not mine heart be inclined to any evil thing :
        let me not be occupied in ungodly works
            with the men that work wickedness,
            lest I eat of such things as please them.

5   Let the righteous rather smite me friendly :
        and reprove me.

6   But let not their precious balms break my head :
        yea, I will pray yet against their wickedness.

7   Let their judges be overthrown in stony places :
        that they may hear my words, for they are sweet.

8   Our bones lie scattered before the pit :
        like as when one breaketh and heweth wood upon the earth.

9   But mine eyes look unto thee, O Lord God :
        in thee is my trust , O cast not out my soul.

10   Keep me from the snare that they have laid for me :
        and from the traps of the wicked doers.

11   Let the ungodly fall into their own nets together :
        and let me ever escape them.

Psalm 142   *Voce mea ad Dominum*

1   I CRIED unto the Lord with my voice :
        yea, even unto the Lord did I make my supplication.

2   I poured out my complaints before him :
        and shewed him of my trouble.

3   When my spirit was in heaviness thou knewest my path :
        in the way wherein I walked have they privily laid a snare for me.

| 4 | I looked also upon my right hand : |
| | and saw there was no man that would know me. |

| 5 | I had no place to flee unto : |
| | and no man cared for my soul. |

| 6 | I cried unto thee, O Lord, and said : |
| | Thou art my hope, and my portion in the land of the living. |

| 7 | Consider my complaint : |
| | for I am brought very low. |

| 8 | O deliver me from my persecutors : |
| | for they are too strong for me. |

9	Bring my soul out of prison, that I may give thanks unto thy Name :
	which thing if thou wilt grant me,
	then shall the righteous resort unto my company.

Psalm 143   *Domine, exaudi*

| 1 | HEAR my prayer, O Lord, and consider my desire : |
| | hearken unto me for thy truth and righteousness' sake. |

| 2 | And enter not into judgement with thy servant : |
| | for in thy sight shall no man living be justified. |

3	For the enemy hath persecuted my soul;
	he hath smitten my life down to the ground :
	he hath laid me in the darkness, as the men that have been long dead.

| 4 | Therefore is my spirit vexed within me : |
| | and my heart within me is desolate. |

| 5 | Yet do I remember the time past; I muse upon all thy works : |
| | yea, I exercise myself in the works of thy hands. |

| 6 | I stretch forth my hands unto thee : |
| | my soul gaspeth unto thee as a thirsty land. |

7	Hear me, O Lord, and that soon, for my spirit waxeth faint :
	hide not thy face from me,
	lest I be like unto them that go down into the pit.

8	O let me hear thy loving-kindness betimes in the morning,
	for in thee is my trust :
	shew thou me the way that I should walk in,
	for I lift up my soul unto thee.

| 9 | Deliver me, O Lord, from mine enemies : |
| | for I flee unto thee to hide me. |

| 10 | Teach me to do the thing that pleaseth thee, for thou art my God : |
| | let thy loving Spirit lead me forth into the land of righteousness. |

11   Quicken me, O Lord, for thy Name's sake :
        and for thy righteousness' sake bring my soul out of trouble.

12   And of thy goodness slay mine enemies :
        and destroy all them that vex my soul ; for I am thy servant.

Day 30 (and 31). Morning Prayer.

Psalm 144   *Benedictus Dominus*

1   BLESSED be the Lord my strength :
        who teacheth my hands to war, and my fingers to fight;

2   My hope and my fortress, my castle and deliverer,
         my defender in whom I trust :
        who subdueth my people that is under me.

3   Lord, what is man, that thou hast such respect unto him :
        or the son of man, that thou so regardest him?

4   Man is like a thing of nought :
        his time passeth away like a shadow.

5   Bow thy heavens, O Lord, and come down :
        touch the mountains, and they shall smoke.

6   Cast forth thy lightning, and tear them :
        shoot out thine arrows, and consume them.

7   Send down thine hand from above :
        deliver me, and take me out of the great waters,
         from the hand of strange children;

8   Whose mouth talketh of vanity :
        and their right hand is a right hand of wickedness.

9   I will sing a new song unto thee, O God :
        and sing praises unto thee upon a ten-stringed lute.

10   Thou hast given victory unto kings :
        and hast delivered David thy servant from the peril of the sword.

11   Save me, and deliver me from the hand of strange children :
        whose mouth talketh of vanity,
         and their right hand is a right hand of iniquity.

12   That our sons may grow up as the young plants :
        and that our daughters may be as the polished corners of the temple.

13   That our garners may be full and plenteous with all manner of store :
        that our sheep may bring forth thousands
         and ten thousands in our streets.

14   That our oxen may be strong to labour, that there be no decay :
        no leading into captivity, and no complaining in our streets.

15   Happy are the people that are in such a case :
          yea, blessed are the people who have the Lord for their God.

Psalm 145   *Exaltabo te, Deus*

1   I WILL magnify thee, O God, my King :
         and I will praise thy Name for ever and ever.

2   Every day will I give thanks unto thee :
         and praise thy Name for ever and ever.

3   Great is the Lord, and marvellous worthy to be praised :
         there is no end of his greatness.

4   One generation shall praise thy works unto another :
         and declare thy power.

5   As for me, I will be talking of thy worship :
         thy glory, thy praise, and wondrous works;

6   So that men shall speak of the might of thy marvellous acts :
         and I will also tell of thy greatness.

7   The memorial of thine abundant kindness shall be shewed :
         and men shall sing of thy righteousness.

8   The Lord is gracious and merciful :
         long-suffering and of great goodness.

9   The Lord is loving unto every man :
         and his mercy is over all his works.

10   All thy works praise thee, O Lord :
         and thy saints give thanks unto thee.

11   They shew the glory of thy kingdom :
         and talk of thy power;

12   That thy power, thy glory, and mightiness of thy kingdom :
         might be known unto men.

13   Thy kingdom is an everlasting kingdom :
         and thy dominion endureth throughout all ages.

14   The Lord upholdeth all such as fall :
         and lifteth up all those that are down.

15   The eyes of all wait upon thee, O Lord :
         and thou givest them their meat in due season.

16   Thou openest thine hand :
         and fillest all things living with plenteousness.

17   The Lord is righteous in all his ways :
         and holy in all his works.

18   The Lord is nigh unto all them that call upon him :
         yea, all such as call upon him faithfully.

19   He will fulfil the desire of them that fear him :
        he also will hear their cry, and will help them.

20   The Lord preserveth all them that love him :
        but scattereth abroad all the ungodly.

21   My mouth shall speak the praise of the Lord :
        and let all flesh give thanks unto his holy Name for ever and ever.

Psalm 146   *Lauda, anima mea*

1   PRAISE the Lord, O my soul; while I live will I praise the Lord :
        yea, as long as I have any being, I will sing praises unto my God.

2   O put not your trust in princes, nor in any child of man :
        for there is no help in them.

3   For when the breath of man goeth forth
        he shall turn again to his earth :
        and then all his thoughts perish.

4   Blessed is he that hath the God of Jacob for his help :
        and whose hope is in the Lord his God;

5   Who made heaven and earth, the sea, and all that therein is :
        who keepeth his promise for ever;

6   Who helpeth them to right that suffer wrong :
        who feedeth the hungry.

7   The Lord looseth men out of prison :
        the Lord giveth sight to the blind.

8   The Lord helpeth them that are fallen :
        the Lord careth for the righteous.

9   The Lord careth for the strangers,
        he defendeth the fatherless and widow :
        as for the way of the ungodly, he turneth it upside down.

10   The Lord thy God, O Sion, shall be King for evermore :
        and throughout all generations.

Day 30 (and 31). Evening Prayer.

Psalm 147   *Laudate Dominum*

1   O PRAISE the Lord,
        for it is a good thing to sing praises unto our God :
        yea, a joyful and pleasant thing it is to be thankful.

2   The Lord doth build up Jerusalem :
        and gather together the out-casts of Israel.

3   He healeth those that are broken in heart :
        and giveth medicine to heal their sickness.

4   He telleth the number of the stars :
          and calleth them all by their names.

5   Great is our Lord, and great is his power :
          yea, and his wisdom is infinite.

6   The Lord setteth up the meek :
          and bringeth the ungodly down to the ground.

7   O sing unto the Lord with thanksgiving :
          sing praises upon the harp unto our God;

8   Who covereth the heaven with clouds,
          and prepareth rain for the earth :
          and maketh the grass to grow upon the mountains,
          and herb for the use of men;

9   Who giveth fodder unto the cattle :
          and feedeth the young ravens that call upon him.

10   He hath no pleasure in the strength of an horse :
          neither delighteth he in any man's legs.

11   But the Lord's delight is in them that fear him :
          and put their trust in his mercy.

12   Praise the Lord, O Jerusalem :
          praise thy God, O Sion.

13   For he hath made fast the bars of thy gates :
          and hath blessed thy children within thee.

14   He maketh peace in thy borders :
          and filleth thee with the flour of wheat.

15   He sendeth forth his commandment upon earth :
          and his word runneth very swiftly.

16   He giveth snow like wool :
          and scattereth the hoar-frost like ashes.

17   He casteth forth his ice like morsels :
          who is able to abide his frost?

18   He sendeth out his word, and melteth them :
          he bloweth with his wind, and the waters flow.

19   He sheweth his word unto Jacob :
          his statutes and ordinances unto Israel.

20   He hath not dealt so with any nation :
          neither have the heathen knowledge of his laws.

Psalm 148   *Laudate Dominum*

1 O PRAISE the Lord of heaven :
  praise him in the height.

2 Praise him, all ye angels of his :
  praise him, all his host.

3 Praise him, sun and moon :
  praise him, all ye stars and light.

4 Praise him, all ye heavens :
  and ye waters that are above the heavens.

5 Let them praise the Name of the Lord :
  for he spake the word, and they were made;
    he commanded, and they were created.

6 He hath made them fast for ever and ever :
  he hath given them a law which shall not be broken.

7 Praise the Lord upon earth :
  ye dragons, and all deeps;

8 Fire and hail, snow and vapours :
  wind and storm, fulfilling his word;

9 Mountains and all hills :
  fruitful trees and all cedars;

10 Beasts and all cattle :
  worms and feathered fowls;

11 Kings of the earth and all people :
  princes and all judges of the world;

12 Young men and maidens, old men and children,
    praise the Name of the Lord :
  for his Name only is excellent, and his praise above heaven and earth.

13 He shall exalt the horn of his people; all his saints shall praise him :
  even the children of Israel, even the people that serveth him.

Psalm 149   *Cantate Domino*

1 O SING unto the Lord a new song :
  let the congregation of saints praise him.

2 Let Israel rejoice in him that made him :
  and let the children of Sion be joyful in their King.

3 Let them praise his Name in the dance :
  let them sing praises unto him with tabret and harp.

4 For the Lord hath pleasure in his people :
  and helpeth the meek-hearted.

5	Let the saints be joyful with glory :
	let them rejoice in their beds.
6	Let the praises of God be in their mouth :
	and a two-edged sword in their hands;
7	To be avenged of the heathen :
	and to rebuke the people;
8	To bind their kings in chains :
	and their nobles with links of iron.
9	That they may be avenged of them, as it is written :
	Such honour have all his saints.

Psalm 150   *Laudate Dominum*

1	O PRAISE God in his holiness :
	praise him in the firmament of his power.
2	Praise him in his noble acts :
	praise him according to his excellent greatness.
3	Praise him in the sound of the trumpet :
	praise him upon the lute and harp.
4	Praise him in the cymbals and dances :
	praise him upon the strings and pipe.
5	Praise him upon the well-tuned cymbals :
	praise him upon the loud cymbals.
6	Let every thing that hath breath :
	praise the Lord.

VI. The Lectionary

General Note

The psalms are read in course (see below). Proper Psalms, where these occur, are noted in the Lectionary. The numbering of psalms given in the Lectionary tables is as in the Hebrew sequence. The order of psalms in the Divine Office is also given for reference. At Morning Prayer, when not already prescribed, any or all of Psalms 148-150, without intervening Glory be, &c., may conclude the psalmody. The scheme may be as follows: Sundays, solemnities, and feasts, Pss 148-150, Mondays and Thursdays, Ps 148, Tuesdays and Fridays, Ps 149, Wednesdays and Saturdays, Ps 150.

On all days, at least one lesson from Holy Scripture must be read from the Office of Readings Lectionary, following the sequence of the One-Year Cycle or the appropriate year of the Two-Year Cycle in the Liturgy of the Hours. The second reading at Morning Prayer may be from an approved anthology of Patristic and Hagiographical readings in the Liturgy of the Hours or from Holy Scripture as prescribed here.

The readings at Evening Prayer should normally be from Holy Scripture, the first lesson from the Old Testament and the second lesson from the New Testament. Where further use is made of the One-Year or Two-Year Cycle of the Office of Readings Lectionary, care should be taken not to repeat the morning reading.

For pastoral reasons, in particular communities and on particular occasions, the first reading at Evening Prayer may be from the New Testament and the second reading from the Patristic and Hagiographical resources. If this pattern is prevalent, the convention at Morning Prayer should be to read two readings from Holy Scripture, one from the Old Testament and the other from the New Testament.

The Gospel readings, where they occur, generally follow the conventions of the reading of the Gospel at an extended Vigil in the Liturgy of the Hours. It is often appropriate to replace the convention of a 'Gospel of the Resurrection' with the reading of the Gospel of the Day. At Solemn Evening Prayer, the Gospel may be sung, with incense and lights, and the people standing. Only those in holy orders may read the Gospel in a public liturgical celebration.

Psalter

Proper Psalms

See Lectionary. On solemnities, except Easter Sunday, the Office of Readings psalmody as well as the Lauds psalms may be used at Morning Prayer. On feast days, the Office of Readings psalmody may be used instead of the Lauds psalmody at Morning Prayer. The Office of Readings psalmody is noted, where appropriate, in the lectionary, with the shorthand 'Matins'. The Lauds psalms are always used on Sundays.

Sundays *Per Annum*

Evening Prayer I	Morning Prayer[1]	Evening Prayer II
Either: **Scheme A**[2]		
Week 1[3] 144; 145	93; 63; 118; 148-150	110; 111; 112; 113
Week 2 146; 147	148-150	114; 115
Or: **Scheme B**[4]		
Week 1 141; 142	63:1-9; 149	110; 114
Week 2 119:105-112; 16	118; 150	110; 115
Week 3 113; 116	93; 148	110; 111
Week 4 122; 130	118; 150	110; 112

---

[1] Since the Office of Readings Psalms of the Liturgy of Hours are included in the scheme for the Psalter in Course, only the Lauds psalms are listed here.

[2] 'Scheme A and Scheme B' are not here references to 'Schema A and Schema B' of the Benedictine Thesaurus. 'Scheme A' is the pre-conciliar scheme which, however, is very similar to the Sunday provision of Benedictine 'Schema A.'

[3] This is a convenient division of Sunday psalms into a two-week pattern. Where desired there may be no such division and the psalms of both Week 1 and Week 2 may be used each Sunday.

[4] 'Scheme B' is as prescribed in the Liturgy of the Hours (hereafter LH).

Psalter in Course[5]

	Morning Prayer	Evening Prayer
Day 1	1; 2; 3; *(4)*[6] 5	6; 7; 8
Day 2	9; 10; 11	12; 13; *(14)*[7]
Day 3	15; 16; 17	18
Day 4	19; 20; 21	22; 23
Day 5	24;[8] 25; 26	27; 28; 29
Day 6	30; 31	32; 33; 34
Day 7	35; 36	37
Day 8	38; 39; 40	41; 42; 43
Day 9	44; 45; 46	47; 48; 49
Day 10	50; 51; 52	53; 54; 55
Day 11	56; 57; *(58)*[9]	59; 60; 61
Day 12	62; 63; 64	65; 66; 67[10]
Day 13	68	69; 70
Day 14	71; 72	73; 74

---

[5] Psalms regularly used on Sunday may be omitted from the Psalter in Course. Since there is a variety of schemes and weeks, no note is made here of which these psalms are.

[6] Pss 4; 91; 134 are used daily at Compline and may be omitted from the Psalter in Course.

[7] Ps 14 is very similar to Ps 53 and may be omitted from the Psalter in Course.

[8] When Ps 24 is used as the Invitatory at Morning Prayer (hereafter MP), it is not here repeated.

[9] Ps 58 - one of the so-called 'cursing psalms' - may be omitted from the Psalter in Course.

[10] When Ps 67 is used as the Invitatory at MP, it is not repeated that day.

Day 15	75; 76; 77	78
Day 16	79; 80; 81	82; 83; 84; 85
Day 17	86; 87; 88	89
Day 18	90; *(91)* 92	93; 94
Day 19	*(95)*[11] 96; 97	98; 99; 100 ;[12] 101
Day 20	102; 103	104
Day 21	105	106
Day 22	107	108; 109
Day 23	110; 111; 112	113; 114; 115
Day 24	116; 117; 118	119:1-32
Day 25	119:33-72	119:73-104
Day 26	119:105-144	119:145-176
Day 27	120; 121; 122; 123; 124; 125	126; 127; 128; 129; 130; 131
Day 28	132; 133; *(134)* 135	136; 137; 138
Day 29	139; 140	141; 142; 143
Day 30-31[13]	144; 145; 146	147; 148; 149; 150

---

[11] When Ps 95 is used as the Invitatory at MP, it is not here repeated.
[12] When Ps 100 is used as the Invitatory at MP, it is not here repeated.
[13] When Saturday falls on the 30th or 31st of the month, Pss 139 and 140, as prescribed for the 29th morning, are used for Saturday MP in place of Pss 144, 145 and 146.

Office of Readings

	Week 1	Week 2	Week 3	Week 4
Monday	5	42	84	90
Tuesday	24	43	85	101
Wednesday	36	77	86	108
Thursday	57	80	87	143
Friday	51	51	51	51
Saturday	119:145-152	92	119:145-152	92

Morning Prayer

	Week 1	Week 2	Week 3	Week 4
Monday	29	19:1-6	96	135
Tuesday	33	65	67	144:1-10
Wednesday	47	97	98	146
Thursday	48	81	99	147:1-12
Friday	100	147:13-21	100	147:13-21
Saturday	117	8	117	8

Evening Prayer

	Week 1	Week 2	Week 3	Week 4
Monday	11; 15	45	123; 124	136
Tuesday	20; 21	49	125; 131	137; 138
Wednesday	27	62; 67	126; 127	139
Thursday	30; 32	71	132	144
Friday	41; 46	116; 121	135	145

Temporale

Advent

First Sunday of Advent

Evening Prayer I
First Reading Is 40:1-11[1]
Second Reading 1 Thess 5:12-24
or Gospel Reading Lk 24:1-12
Morning Prayer
OT (Yr 1) Is 6:1-13
OT 1-Yr[2] (& Yr 2) Is 1:1-18
Second Reading Rom 13:8-14
Evening Prayer II
OT (Yr 2 & 1-Yr) Is 1:1-18
or OT (Yr 1) Is 6:1-13
Second Reading Phil 4:4-9

Monday of Advent Week 1
Morning Prayer
OT (Yr 2 & 1-Yr)Is 1:21-27; 2:1-5
Second Reading 1 Thess 3:(7b-10), 11-13
Evening Prayer
OT (Yr 1) Is 7:1-17
Second Reading Phil 3: (17-19), 20b-21

Tuesday of Advent Week 1
Morning Prayer
OT (Yr 2 & 1-Yr) Is 2:6-22; 4:2-6
Second Reading 2 Thess 1:5-12
Evening Prayer
OT (Yr 1) Is 8: 1-18
Second Reading1 Cor 1:3-9

Wednesday of Advent Week 1
Morning Prayer
OT (Yr 2 & 1-Yr) Is 5:1-7
Second Reading Rev 21:1-4

---

[1] In Year B Is 40:1-5, 9-11 is the First Reading at Mass.
[2] 1-Yr means One-Year Cycle, as found in the Breviary.

Evening Prayer
OT (Yr 1) Is 9:1-6
Second Reading 1 Cor 4:1-5

Thursday of Advent Week 1
Morning Prayer
OT (Yr 2 & 1-Yr)Is 16:1-5; 17:4-8
Second Reading Acts 28:26-28
Evening Prayer
OT (Yr 1) Is 10:5-21
Second Reading Jas 5:7-11

Friday of Advent Week 1
Morning Prayer
OT (Yr 2 & 1-Yr) Is 19:16-25
Second Reading2 Pet 3:3-7
Evening Prayer
OT (Yr 1)Is 11:10-16
Second Reading 2 Pet 3:8b-11

Saturday of Advent Week 1
Morning Prayer
OT (Yr 2 & 1-Yr)Is 21:6-12
Second Reading Rev 18:2-5

Second Sunday of Advent
Evening Prayer I
OT (Yr 2 & 1-Yr) Is 21:6-12
or OT (Yr 1) Is 13:1-22
Second Reading 1 Thess 5:12-24
or Gospel Reading Lk 24:13-35
Morning Prayer
OT (Yr 1)Is 14:1-21
or OT (Yr 2 & 1-Yr) Is 22:8b-23
Second Reading Rom 13:8-14
Evening Prayer II
OT (Yr 2 & 1-Yr) Is 22:8b-23
or OT (Yr 1) Is 14:1-21
Second Reading Phil 4:4-9

Monday of Advent Week 2
Morning Prayer
OT (Yr 2 & 1-Yr) Is 24:1-18
Second Reading 1 Thess 3: (7b-10),
11-13
Evening Prayer
OT (Yr 1) Is 34:1-17
Second Reading Phil 3: (17-19), 20b-21
Tuesday of Advent Week 2
Morning Prayer
OT (Yr 2 & 1-Yr) Is 24:19 - 25:5
Second Reading 2 Thess 1:5-12
Evening Prayer
OT (Yr 1) Is 35:1-10
Second Reading 1 Cor 1:3-9
Wednesday of Advent Week 2
Morning Prayer
OT (Yr 2 & 1-Yr) Is 25:6 – 26:6
Second Reading Rev 21:1-4
Evening Prayer
OT (Yr 1) Ruth 1:1-22
Second Reading 1 Cor 4:1-5
Thursday of Advent Week 2
Morning Prayer
OT (Yr 2 & 1-Yr) Is 26:7-21
Second Reading Acts 28:26-28
Evening Prayer
OT (Yr 1) Ruth 2:1-13
Second Reading Jas 5:7-11
Friday of Advent Week 2
Morning Prayer
OT (Yr 2 & 1-Yr) Is 27:1-13
Second Reading 2 Pet 3:3-7
Evening Prayer
OT (Yr 1) Ruth 2:14-23
Second Reading 2 Pet 3:8b-11
Saturday of Advent Week 2
Morning Prayer
OT (Yr 2 & 1-Yr) Is 29:1-8
Second Reading Rev 18:2-5

Third Sunday of Advent
Evening Prayer I
OT (Yr 2 & 1-Yr) Is 29:1-8
or OT (Yr 1) Ruth 3:1-18
Second Reading 1 Thess 5:12-24
or Gospel Reading Lk 24:35-53
Morning Prayer
OT (Yr 1) Ruth 4:1-22
or OT (Yr 2 & 1-Yr) Is 29:13-24
Second Reading Rom 13:8-14
Evening Prayer II
OT (Yr 2 & 1-Yr) Is 29:13-24
or OT (Yr 1) Ruth 4:1-22
Second Reading Phil 4:4-9
Readings as for 17-24 December (see below)
Monday of Advent Week 3
Morning Prayer
OT (Yr 2 & 1-Yr) Is 30:18-26
Second Reading 1 Thess 3: (7b-10),
11-13
Evening Prayer
OT (Yr 1) 1 Chron 17:1-15
Second Reading Phil 3: (17-19), 20b-21
Readings as for 17-24 December (see below)
Tuesday of Advent Week 3
Morning Prayer
OT (Yr 2 & 1-Yr) Is 30:27-33; 31:4-9
Second Reading 2 Thess 1:5-12
Evening Prayer
OT (Yr 1) Mic 4:1-7
Second Reading 1 Cor 1:3-9
Readings as for 17-24 December (see below)
Wednesday of Advent Week 3
Morning Prayer
OT (Yr 2 & 1-Yr) Is 31:1-3; 32:1-8
Second Reading Rev 21:1-4
Evening Prayer
OT (Yr 1) Mic 5:1-8
Second Reading 1 Cor 4:1-5
Readings as for 17-24 December (see below)

Thursday of Advent Week 3
Morning Prayer
OT (Yr 2 & 1-Yr) Is 32:15 – 33:6
Second Reading Acts 28:26-28
Evening Prayer
OT (Yr 1) Mic 7:7-13
Second Reading Jas 5:7-11
Readings as for 17-24 December (see below)
Friday of Advent Week 3
Morning Prayer
OT (Yr 2 & 1-Yr) Is 33:7-24
Second Reading 2 Pet 3:3-7
Evening Prayer
OT (Yr 1) Mic 7:14-20
Second Reading 2 Pet 3:8b-11
Readings as for 17-24 December (see below)
Saturday of Advent Week 3
Morning Prayer
Readings as for 17-24 December (see below)

Fourth Sunday of Advent
Evening Prayer I
Readings as for 17-24 December (see below)
Gospel Reading Jn 20:1-18
Morning Prayer
Readings as for 17-24 December (see below)
Evening Prayer II
Readings as for 17-24 December (see below)

Weekdays of Advent Week 4
Readings as for 17-24 December (see below)

---

17 December *(O Sapientia)*
Morning Prayer
OT (Yr 1) Is 40:1-11
or OT (Yr 2 & 1-Yr) Is 45:1-13
Second Reading Rev 18:2-5
Evening Prayer
OT (Yr 2 & 1-Yr) Is 45:1-13
or OT (Yr 1) Is 40:1-11

Second Reading 1 Thess 5:12-24
18 December *(O Adonai)*
Morning Prayer
OT (Yr 1) Is 40:12-18, 21-31
or OT (Yr 2 & 1-Yr) Is 46:1-13
Second Reading Rom 13:8-14
Evening Prayer
OT (Yr 2 & 1-Yr) Is 46:1-13
or OT (Yr 1) Is 40:12-18, 21-31
Second Reading Phil 4:4-9
19 December *(O Radix Jesse)*
Morning Prayer
OT (Yr 1) Is 41:8-20
or OT (Yr 2 & 1-Yr) Is 47:1, 3b-15
(or Is 47:1-15)[3]
Second Reading 1 Thess 3: (7b-10),
11-13
Evening Prayer
OT (Yr 2 & 1-Yr) Is 47:1, 3b-15 (*or* Is
47:1-15)[4]
or OT (Yr 1)Is 41:8-20
Second Reading Phil 3: (17-19), 20b-21
20 December *(O Clavis David)*
Morning Prayer
OT (Yr 1) Is 41:21-29
or OT (Yr 2 & 1-Yr) Is 48:1-11
Second Reading 2 Thess 1:5-12
Evening Prayer
OT (Yr 2 & 1-Yr) Is 48:1-11
or OT (Yr 1) Is 41:21-29
Second Reading 1 Cor 1:3-9
21 December *(O Oriens)*
Morning Prayer
OT (Yr 1) Is 42:10-25

---

[3] The longer version is more convenient when reading direct from the Bible.
[4] The longer version is more convenient when reading direct from the Bible.

or OT (Yr 2 & 1-Yr) Is 48:12-21;
49:9b-13 (*or* Is 48:12-22; 49:8-13)[5]
Second Reading Rev 21:1-4
Evening Prayer
OT (Yr 2 & 1-Yr) Is 48:12-21; 49:9b-
13 (*or* Is 48:12-22; 49:8-13)[6]
or OT (Yr 1) Is 42:10-25
Second Reading 1 Cor 4:1-5
22 December *(O Rex Gentium)*
Morning Prayer
OT (Yr 1) Is 43:1-13
or OT (Yr 2 & 1-Yr) Is 49:14 – 50:1
Second Reading Acts 28:26-28
Evening Prayer
OT (Yr 2 & 1-Yr) Is 49:14 – 50:1
or OT (Yr 1) Is 43:1-13
Second Reading Jas 5:7-11
23 December *(O Emmanuel)*
Morning Prayer
OT (Yr 1) Is 43:18-28
or OT (Yr 2 & 1-Yr) Is 51:1-1
Second Reading 2 Pet 3:3-7
Evening Prayer
OT (Yr 2 & 1-Yr) Is 51:1-11
or OT (Yr 1) Is 43:18-28
Second Reading 2 Pet 3:8b-11
24 December
Morning Prayer
OT (Yr 2 & 1-Yr) Is 51:17 – 52:2, 7-
10 *or* OT (Yr 1)Is 44:1-8, 21-23
Second ReadingRev 18:2-5

---

[5] The longer version is more
convenient when reading direct
from the Bible.
[6] The longer version is more
convenient when reading direct
from the Bible.

CHRISTMAS DAY
Evening Prayer I
Vespers I Pss 113; 147:12-20
OT (Yrs 1 & 2)[1] Is 9:1-6
Second Reading Gal 4:1-7
or Gospel Reading Mt 1: (1-17), 18-25
Morning Prayer
Matins Pss 2; 19:1-6; 45
Lauds Pss 63:1-9; 148-150
OT (Yrs 1 & 2 & 1-Yr)[2] Is 11:1-10
Second Reading Heb 1:1-9
Evening Prayer II
Vespers II Pss 110; 130
OT (Yrs 1 & 2) Is 52:1-6
Second Reading 1 Jn 1:1-5

First Sunday of Christmas (Holy Family)
Evening Prayer I
Vespers I Pss 113; 147:12-20
First Reading *The First Reading of the Feast for a different year in the Three-Year Cycle is chosen.*
(A) Sir 3:2-6, 12-14
(B) Gen 15:1-6; 21:1-3
(C) 1 Sam 1:20-22, 24-28

---

[1] Years 1 and 2 give Is 9:1-6; Is 40:1-8 and Is 52:1-5 as additional readings for the Office of Readings. Pastoral considerations may suggest the rearrangement of the order of the readings, for instance using Is 40:1-8 at EP I.
[2] Years 1 and 2 give Is 9:1-6; Is 40:1-8; Is 52:1-5 as additional readings for the Office of Readings. Pastoral considerations may suggest the rearrangement of the order of the readings.

NT (Yrs 1 & 2 and 1-Yr) Eph 5:21 - 6:4
or Gospel Reading *The Gospel of the Feast for a different year in the Three-Year Cycle is chosen.*
(A) Mt 2:13-15, 19-23
(B) Lk 2:22-20
(C) Lk 2:41-52
Morning Prayer
Matins Pss 24; 46; 87
Lauds Pss 63:1-9; 148-150
First Reading Is 63:7-9
Second Reading Col 3:12-17
or NT (Yrs 1 & 2 and 1-Yr) Eph 5:21 - 6:4
Evening Prayer II
Vespers II Pss 122; 127
First Reading *The First Reading of the Feast for a different year in the Three-Year Cycle is chosen.*
(A) Sir 3:2-6, 12-14
(B) Gen 15:1-6; 21:1-3
(C) 1 Sam 1:20-22, 24-28
Second Reading Phil 2:5-16
Saint Stephen, Deacon, First Martyr (26 December)
Morning Prayer
Matins Pss 2; 11; 17; 148-150
First Reading 2 Chron 24:20-24
NT (Yrs 1 & 2 and 1-Yr)Acts 6:8 - 7:2, 44-60
Evening Prayer of Christmas
Vespers Pss 110; 130
First Reading Is 11:1-10
Second Reading 1 Jn 1:5b-10

Saint John, Apostle and Evangelist
(27 December)
Morning Prayer
Matins Pss 19:1-6; 64; 99; 148-150
First Reading Exodus 33:7-11a
NT (Yrs 1 & 2 and 1-Yr) 1 Jn 1:1 - 2:3
Evening Prayer of Christmas
Vespers Pss 110; 130
First Reading Is 9:1-6
Second Reading Rom 8:1-4
Holy Innocents (28 December)
Morning Prayer
Matins Pss 2; 33; 148-150
OT (Yrs 1 & 2 & 1-Yr)Ex 1:8-16, 22
Second Reading Rev 14:1-5
Evening Prayer of Christmas
Vespers Pss 110; 130
First Reading Is 40:1-8
Second Reading Eph 2:3b-10
Fifth Day within the Octave of
Christmas
Saint Thomas of Canterbury
(29 December)
Morning Prayer
Matins Pss 46; 72; 148-150
OT (Yr 2) Song 1:1-8
NT (Yr 1 and 1-Yr) Col 1:1-14
Evening Prayer of Christmas
Vespers Pss 110; 130
First Reading Is 52:1-6
Second Reading Heb 1:1-9
Sixth Day within the Octave of
Christmas
(30 December)
Morning Prayer
Matins Pss 85; 89
OT (Yr 2) Song 2:1-7, 1:9-17
NT (Yr 1 and 1-Yr) Col 1:15 – 2:3

Evening Prayer of Christmas
Vespers Pss 110; 130
First Reading Tob 14:3-9
Second Reading 2 Pet 1:1-11
Seventh Day within the Octave of
Christmas
(31 December)
Morning Prayer
Matins Pss 96; 97; 98
OT (Yr 2) Song 2:8 – 3:5
NT (Yr 1 and 1-Yr) Col 2:4-15

SOLEMNITY OF MARY,
MOTHER OF GOD (1 January)
Evening Prayer I
Vespers I Pss 113; 147:12-20
First Reading Is 61:10-11
Second Reading Gal 4:1-7
or Heb 2:9-17
or Gospel Reading   Mt 2:13-15, 19-23
Morning Prayer
Matins Pss 24; 87; 99
Lauds Pss 63:1-9; 148-150
First Reading Micah 5:3-4, 5a
Second Reading Gal 4:1-7
Evening Prayer II
Vespers II Pss 122; 127;
First Reading Zeph 3:14-15
NT (Yrs 1 & 2 and 1-Yr) Heb 2:9-17[3]

---

[3] The long reading is read at one of
the offices of the day. If long
readings are required at other
offices, readings set for the first or
second reading in the Order of
Readings for Mass are used.

Second Sunday of Christmas
(between 2 and 5 January)
Evening Prayer I
Vespers I Pss 16; 23; 76
First Reading Is 26:1-4
or according to date: 2 – 5 January (below)
Second Reading 1 Jn 5:13-21
or according to date: 2 – 5 January (below)
or Gospel Reading   Jn 21:1-14
Morning Prayer
Matins Ps 104
Lauds Pss Ps 118; 148-150
First Reading Is 40:1-5
Second Reading Heb 1:1-9
Evening Prayer II
Vespers II Pss 110; 115;
First Reading Is 66:10-14a
or according to date: 2 – 5 January (below)
Second Reading 1 Jn 4:9-12
or according to date: 2 – 5 January (below)

**Psalms for Weekdays before the
Epiphany of the Lord** *(Week 2)*
Monday of Week 2
Morning Prayer
Matins Ps 31
Evening Prayer
Vespers Pss 40; 45
Tuesday of Week 2
Morning Prayer
Matins Pss 37
Evening Prayer
Vespers Pss 49; 53; 54
Wednesday of Week 2
Morning Prayer
Matins Pss 39; 52
Evening Prayer
Vespers Pss 62; 67

Thursday of Week 2
Morning Prayer
Matins Ps 44
Evening Prayer
Vespers Pss 56
Friday of Week 2
Morning Prayer
Matins Ps 38
Evening Prayer
Vespers Pss 59; 60; 116; 121
Saturday of Week 2
Morning Prayer
Matins Ps 106
**Readings for Weekdays before the
Epiphany of the Lord** *(Week 2)*
**SS Basil and Gregory Nazianzen (2
January)**
Morning Prayer
OT (Yr 2) Song 4:1 – 5:1
Second Reading Col 1:13-15
Evening Prayer
First Reading Is 49:8-9
NT (Yr 1 and 1-Yr) Col 2:16 – 3:4
**Most Holy Name of Jesus (3
January)**
Morning Prayer
OT (Yr 2) Song 5:2 – 6:1
Second Reading Acts 3:1-16
Evening Prayer
First Reading Is 29:22-24
NT (Yr 1 and 1-Yr) Col 3:5-16
4 January
Morning Prayer
OT (Yr 2) Song 6:2 – 7:10
Second Reading Rom 8:3-4
Evening Prayer
First Reading Is 45:22-24
NT (Yr 1 and 1-Yr) Col 3:17 – 4:1

5 January
Morning Prayer
OT (Yr 2) Song 7:11 – 8:7
Second Reading 1 Jn 5:11-14
Evening Prayer
First Reading Wis 7:26-27
NT (Yr 1 and 1-Yr) Col 4:2-18
6 January (before Epiphany)
Morning Prayer
OT (Yr 2) Is 49:1-9
Second Reading 1 Jn 5:20
Evening Prayer
OT (Yr 1 and 1-Yr) Is 42:1-8
Second Reading Acts 10:37-38
7 January or Monday (before Epiphany)
Morning Prayer
OT (Yr 1 & 1-Yr) Is 61:1-11
Second Reading 1 Jn 4:14-17
Evening Prayer
OT (Yr 2) Is 54:1-17
Second Reading 2 Pet 1:3-4
8 January or Tuesday (before Epiphany)
Morning Prayer
OT (Yr 1 & 1-Yr) Is 62:1-12
Second Reading Eph 2:1-7
Evening Prayer
OT (Yr 2) Is 55:1-13
Second Reading Eph 2:8-10
9 January or Wednesday (before Epiphany)
Morning Prayer
OT (Yr 1 & 1-Yr) Is 63:7-19
Second Reading Rev 21:22-27
Evening Prayer
OT (Yr 2) Is 56:1-8
Second Reading Col 1:13-15

10 January or Thursday (before Epiphany)
Morning Prayer
OT (Yr 1 & 1-Yr) Is 63:19b – 64:11
Second Reading 1 Jn 1:5-7
Evening Prayer
OT (Yr 2) Is 59:15-21
Second Reading 1 Jn 1:8-10
11 January or Friday (before Epiphany)
Morning Prayer
OT (Yr 1 & 1-Yr) Is 65:13-25
Second Reading 1 Jn 5:1-4
Evening Prayer
OT (Yr 2) Bar 4:5-29
Second Reading Rom 8:1-4

EPIPHANY OF THE LORD
Evening Prayer I
Vespers I Pss 22; 135
OT (Yr 1 & 1-Yr)   Is 66:10-14, 18-23
or OT (Yr 2) Bar 4:30 – 5:9
Second Reading 2 Tim 1:8-10
or Gospel Reading John 1:1-18
or John 2:1-12
Morning Prayer
Matins Pss 72; 96; 97
Lauds Pss 63:1-9; 148-150
First Reading Is 52:7-10
Second Reading Rev 15:1-4
Evening Prayer II
Vespers II Pss 110; 112
OT (Yrs 1 & 2 & 1-Yr) Is 60:1-22
Second Reading Tit 3:4-7

Readings for Weekdays after the Epiphany of the Lord (Week 2)
Monday after the Sunday of the Epiphany (or 7 January)
Morning Prayer
OT (Yr 1 & 1-Yr) Is 61:1-11
Second Reading 1 Jn 4:14-17
Evening Prayer
OT (Yr 2) Is 54:1-17
Second Reading 2 Pet 1:3-4
Tuesday after the Sunday of the Epiphany (or 8 January)
Morning Prayer
OT (Yr 1 & 1-Yr) Is 62:1-12
Second Reading Eph 2:1-7
Evening Prayer
OT (Yr 2) Is 55:1-13
Second Reading Eph 2:8-10
Wednesday after the Sunday of the Epiphany (or 9 January)
Morning Prayer
OT (Yr 1 & 1-Yr) Is 63:7-19
Second Reading Rev 21:22-27
Evening Prayer
OT (Yr 2) Is 56:1-8
Second Reading Col 1:13-15
Thursday after the Sunday of the Epiphany (or 10 January)
Morning Prayer
OT (Yr 1 & 1-Yr) Is 63:19b – 64:11
Second Reading 1 Jn 1:5-7
Evening Prayer
OT (Yr 2) Is 59:15-21
Second Reading 1 Jn 1:8-10
Friday after the Sunday of the Epiphany (or 11 January)
Morning Prayer
OT (Yr 1 & 1-Yr) Is 65:13-25
Second Reading 1 Jn 5:1-4

Evening Prayer
OT (Yr 2) Bar 4:5-29
Second Reading Rom 8:1-4
Saturday after the Sunday of the Epiphany (or 12 January)
Morning Prayer
OT (Yr 1 & 1-Yr) Is 66:10-14, 18-23
Second Reading 1 Jn 5:13-15

Baptism of the Lord
Evening Prayer I
Vespers I Pss 22; 135
OT (Yr 2) Bar 4:30 – 5:9[4]
Second Reading Acts 10:34-43[5]
or Gospel Reading *The Gospel of the Feast in the Three-Year Cycle.*
(A) Mt 3:13-17
(B) Mk 1:7-11
(C) Lk 3:15-16, 21-22
Morning Prayer
Lauds Pss 63:1-9; 148-150
First Reading Is 61:1-2a
Second Reading 1 Jn 5:1-9
Evening Prayer
Vespers II Pss 110; 112
OT (Yrs 1 & 2 & 1-Yr) Is 42:1-9, 49:1-9
Second Reading Acts 10:34-43[6]

---

[4] Set for Saturday after the Sunday after Epiphany but suitable for EP I and II of the Baptism of the Lord
[5] The Second Reading for EPs I and II of the Baptism of the Lord are identical.
[6] Provision for EP I and II of the Baptism of the Lord is identical.

Presentation of Christ in the Temple (Candlemas) (2 February)

Evening Prayer I
Vespers Pss 113; 147:12-20
OT (Yrs 1 & 2 & 1-Yr) Ex 13:1-3a, 11-16
Second Reading Heb 10:5-7
or Gospel Reading Jn 1:1-18

Morning Prayer
Lauds Pss 63:1-9; 148-150
First Reading Mal 3:1-4
Second Reading 1 Jn 1:5b-10

Evening Prayer (II)
Vespers (II) Pss 110; 130
OT (Yrs 1 & 2 & 1-Yr) Ex 13:1-3a, 11-16[7]
Second Reading Heb 4:14-16

---

[7] The long reading is read at EP. If a long reading is required for MP, a reading set for the first or second reading in the Order of Readings for Mass is used.

Time *per annum*

Time per annum *begins with Monday of Week 1 on the day following the Baptism of the Lord.*
The Sunday after the Baptism of the Lord, for the purposes of the Office lectionary, is Sunday 2 and the
Sundays thereafter Sundays 3, 4, 5 &c. until Lent begins.

The Sunday sequence before Lent, and served by the Office lectionary, may be known as follows:

Second Sunday after Epiphany
* Third Sunday after Epiphany
* Fourth Sunday after Epiphany
* Fifth Sunday after Epiphany
* Sixth Sunday after Epiphany

Third Sunday before Lent *(Septuagesima)*
Second Sunday before Lent *(Sexagesima)*
Sunday next before Lent *(Quinquagesima)*

LENT, PASSIONTIDE, HOLY WEEK

Ash Wednesday
Morning Prayer
Lauds Pss 51; 100
OT (Yrs 1 & 2 & 1-Yr) Is 58:1-12[1]
*or*First Reading Deut 7:6-9
Second Reading Phil 2:12-18
Evening Prayer
Vespers Ps 94; 139
First Reading Deut 7:6-9
or OT (Yrs 1 & 2 & 1-Yr) Is 58:1-12[2]

Second Reading 1 Tim 6:6-19
Thursday after Ash Wednesday
Morning Prayer
OT (Yr 2 & 1-Yr) Ex 1:1-22
Second Reading Heb 10:32-36
Evening Prayer
OT (Yr 1)[3] Deut 1:6-18
Second Reading Jas 4:7-10
Friday after Ash Wednesday
Morning Prayer
OT (Yr 2 & 1-Yr) Ex 2:1-22
Second Reading Eph 5:1-4
Evening Prayer
OT (Yr 1) Deut 4:1-8, 32-40

---

[1] The long reading here is read at one of the offices of the day. If a long reading is required at the other office, the reading set for the first or second reading in the Order of Readings for Mass are used.
[2] The long reading is read at one of the offices of the day. If a long reading is required at the other office, the reading set for the first or second reading in the Order of Readings for Mass are used.
[3] During Lent, OT (Yr 1) is set for EP because the Year 2 series is mostly the same as LH.

Second Reading Jas 5:16-20
Saturday after Ash Wednesday
Morning Prayer
OT (Yr 2 & 1-Yr) Ex 3:1-20
Second Reading Rev 3:14-22

First Sunday in Lent
Evening Prayer I
OT (Yr 2 & 1-Yr) Ex 3:1-20
or OT (Yr 1) Deut 5:1-22
Second Reading 2 Cor 6:1-4a
or Gospel Reading Lk 13:22-33
Morning Prayer
Lauds Pss 51; 118; 63; 148-150
OT (Yr 1) Deut 6:4-25
or OT (Yr 2 & 1-Yr) Ex 5:1 – 6:1
Second Reading 1 Thess 4:1-8
Evening Prayer II
OT (Yr 2 & 1-Yr) Ex 5:1 – 6:1
or OT (Yr 1) Deut 6:4-25
Second Reading 1 Cor 9:19-27
Monday of Lent Week 1
Morning Prayer
OT (Yr 2 & 1-Yr)   Ex 6:2-13
Second Reading Jas 1:22-27
Evening Prayer
OT (Yr 1) Deut 7:6-14; 8:1-6
Second Reading Rom 12:1-8
Tuesday of Lent Week 1
Morning Prayer
OT (Yr 2 & 1-Yr) Ex 6:29 – 7:25
Second Reading Rom 12:9-12
Evening Prayer
OT (Yr 1) Deut 9:7-21, 25-29
Second Reading Jas 2:14-18
Wednesday of Lent Week 1
Morning Prayer
OT (Yr 2 & 1-Yr) Ex 10:21 – 11:10
Second Reading 2 Cor 6:4-10
Evening Prayer

OT (Yr 1) Deut 10:12 – 11:7, 26-28
Second Reading Phil 2:12-18
Thursday of Lent Week 1
Morning Prayer
OT (Yr 2 & 1-Yr) Ex 12:1-20
Second Reading Heb 10:32-36
Evening Prayer
OT (Yr 1) Deut 12:1-14
Second Reading Jas 4:7-10
Friday of Lent Week 1
Morning Prayer
OT (Yr 2 & 1-Yr) Ex 12:21-36
Second Reading Eph 5:1-4
Evening Prayer
OT (Yr 1) Deut 15:1-18
Second Reading Jas 5:16-20
Saturday of Lent Week 1
Morning Prayer
OT (Yr 2 & 1-Yr) Ex 12:37-49; 13:11-16
Second Reading Rev 3:14-22

Second Sunday in Lent
Evening Prayer I
OT (Yr 2 & 1-Yr) Ex 12:37-49; 13:11-16
or OT (Yr 1) Deut 16:1-17
First Reading 2 Cor 6:1-4a
or Gospel Reading Mk 8:27-38
Morning Prayer
Lauds Pss 51; 118; 63; 148-150
OT (Yr 1) Deut 18:1-22
or OT (Yr 2 & 1-Yr) Ex 13:17 – 14:9
Second Reading 1 Thess 4:1-8
Evening Prayer II
OT (Yr 2 & 1-Yr) Ex 13:17 – 14:9
or OT (Yr 1) Deut 18:1-22
Second Reading 1 Cor 9:19-27

Monday of Lent Week 2
Morning Prayer
OT (Yr 2 & 1-Yr) Ex 14:10-31
Second Reading Jas 1:22-27
Evening Prayer
OT (Yr 1) Deut 24:1 – 25:4
Second Reading Rom 12:1-8
Tuesday of Lent Week 2
Morning Prayer
OT (Yr 2 & 1-Yr) Ex 16:1-18, 35
Second Reading Rom 12:9-12
Evening Prayer
OT (Yr 1) Deut 26:1-19
Second Reading Jas 2:14-18
Wednesday of Lent Week 2
Morning Prayer
OT (Yr 2 & 1-Yr) Ex 17:1-16
Second Reading 2 Cor 6:4-10
Evening Prayer
OT (Yr 1) Deut 29:1-5, 9-28
Second Reading Phil 2:12-18
Thursday of Lent Week 2
Morning Prayer
OT (Yr 2 & 1-Yr) Ex 18:13-27
Second Reading Heb 10:32-36
Evening Prayer
OT (Yr 1) Deut 30:1-20
Second Reading Jas 4:7-10
Friday of Lent Week 2
Morning Prayer
OT (Yr 2 & 1-Yr) Ex 19:1-19;
20:18-21
Second Reading Eph 5:1-4
Evening Prayer
OT (Yr 1) Deut 31:1-15, 23
Second Reading Jas 5:16-20
Saturday of Lent Week 2
Morning Prayer
OT (Yr 2 & 1-Yr) Ex 20:1-17
Second Reading Rev 3:14-22

Third Sunday in Lent
Evening Prayer I
OT (Yr 2 & 1-Yr) Ex 20:1-17
or OT (Yr 1) Deut 32:48-52; 34:1-12
Second Reading 2 Cor 6:1-4a
or Gospel Reading Mk 9:30-48
Morning Prayer
Lauds Pss 51; 118; 63; 148-150
First Reading Neh 8:9-10
or OT (Yr 2 & 1-Yr) Ex 22:20 – 23:9
NT (Yr 1) Heb 1:1-9
or Second Reading 1 Thess 4:1-8
Evening Prayer II
OT (Yr 2 & 1-Yr) Ex 22:20 – 23:9
or First Reading Deut 4:29-31
Second Reading 1 Cor 9:19-27
or NT (Yr 1) Heb 1:1-9
Monday of Lent Week 3
Morning Prayer
OT (Yr 2 & 1-Yr) Ex 24:1-18
Second Reading Jas 1:22-27
Evening Prayer
First Reading Ex 19:4-6a
NT (Yr 1) Heb 2:5-18
Tuesday of Lent Week 3
Morning Prayer
OT (Yr 2 & 1-Yr) Ex 32:1-20
Second Reading Rom 12:9-12
Evening Prayer
First Reading Joel 2:12-17
NT (Yr 1) Heb 3:1-19
Wednesday of Lent Week 3
Morning Prayer
OT (Yr 2 & 1-Yr) Ex 33:7-11, 18-23;
34:5-9, 29-35
Second Reading 2 Cor 6:4-10
Evening Prayer
First Reading Deut 7:6-9
NT (Yr 1) Heb 4:1-13

Thursday of Lent Week 3
Morning Prayer
OT (Yr 2 & 1-Yr) Ex 34:10-28
Second Reading Heb 10:32-36
Evening Prayer
First Reading1 Kings 8:51-53a
NT (Yr 1) Heb 4:14 - 5:10
Friday of Lent Week 3
Morning Prayer
OT (Yr 2 & 1-Yr) Ex 35:30 - 36:1;
37:1-9
Second Reading Eph 5:1-4
Evening Prayer
First Reading Is 53:11b-12
NT (Yr 1) Heb 5:11 – 6:8
Saturday of Lent Week 3
Morning Prayer
OT (Yr 2 & 1-Yr) Ex 40:16-38
Second Reading Rev 3:14-22

Fourth Sunday in Lent
(Mothering Sunday)
Evening Prayer I
OT (Yr 2 & 1-Yr) Ex 40:16-38
NT (Yr 1) Heb 6:9-20
or Gospel Reading Mk 10:32-45
Morning Prayer
Lauds Pss 51; 118; 63; 148-150
First Reading Is 1:16-18
Second Reading 1 Thess 4:1-8
Evening Prayer II
OT (Yr 2 & 1-Yr) Lev 8:1-17; 9:22-24
NT (Yr 1) Heb 7:1-11
Monday of Lent Week 4
Morning Prayer
OT (Yr 2 & 1-Yr) Lev 16:2-28
Second Reading Jas 1:22-27
Evening Prayer
First Reading Ex 19:4-6a
NT (Yr 1) Heb 7:11-28

Tuesday of Lent Week 4
Morning Prayer
OT (Yr 2 & 1-Yr) Lev 19:1-18, 31-37
Second Reading Rom 12:9-12
Evening Prayer
First Reading Joel 2:12-17
NT (Yr 1) Heb 8:1-13
Wednesday of Lent Week 4
Morning Prayer
OT (1-Yr)Num 11:4-6, 10-30
or OT (Yr 2)[4]Lev 26:3-17, 38-45
Second Reading Phil 2:12-18
Evening Prayer
First Reading Deut 7:6-9
NT (Yr 1) Heb 9:1-10
Thursday of Lent Week 4
Morning Prayer
OT (1-Yr) Num 12:16 – 13:3, 17-33
or OT (Yr 2) Num 3:1-13; 8:5-11
Second Reading Heb 10:32-36
Evening Prayer
First Reading 1 Kings 8:51-53a
NT (Yr 1)Heb 9:11-28
Friday of Lent Week 4
Morning Prayer
OT (1-Yr) Num 14:1-25
or OT (Yr 2) Num 9:15 – 10:10, 33-36
Second Reading Eph 5:1-4
Evening Prayer
First Reading Is 53:11b-12
NT (Yr 1) Heb 10:1-10
Saturday of Lent Week 4
Morning Prayer
OT (1-Yr) Num 20:1-13; 21:4-9
or OT (Yr 2) Num 11:4-6, 10-30
Second Reading Rev 3:14-22

---

[4] Here LH and Year 2 diverge. One of the cycles should be maintained until the end of Lent Week 4.

PASSIONTIDE

Fifth Sunday in Lent
Evening Prayer I
OT (1-Yr) Num 20:1-13; 21:4-9
or OT (Yr 2) Num 11:4-6, 10-30
NT (Yr 1) Heb 10:11-25
or Gospel Reading Mt 21:33-46
Morning Prayer
Lauds Pss 51; 118; 63; 148-150
First Reading Lev 23:4-7
Second Reading Acts 13:26-30
Evening Prayer II
OT (Yr 2) Num 12:1-15
NT (Yr 1 and 1-Yr) Heb 1:1 - 2:4
Monday of Lent Week 5
Morning Prayer
First Reading Jer 11:19-20
NT (1-Yr) Heb 2:5-18
or Second Reading Rom 5:8-11
Evening Prayer
OT (Yr 2) Num 13:1-3, 17-33
NT (Yr 1) Heb 11:1-19
Tuesday of Lent Week 5
Morning Prayer
First Reading Zech 12:10-11a
NT (1-Yr) Heb 3:1-19
or Second Reading 1 Cor 1:18-30
Evening Prayer
OT (Yr 2) Num 14:1-25
NT (Yr 1) Heb 11:20-31
Wednesday of Lent Week 5
Morning Prayer
First Reading Is 50:5-7
NT (1-Yr) Heb 6:9-20
or Second Reading Eph 4:32 – 5:2
Evening Prayer
OT (Yr 2) Num 16:1-11, 16-24, 28-35
NT (Yr 1) Heb 11:32-40

Thursday of Lent Week 5
Morning Prayer
First Reading 1 Kings 8:51-53a
NT (1-Yr) Heb 7:1-10
or Second Reading Heb 2:9b-10
Evening Prayer
OT (Yr 2) Num 20:1-13; 21:4-9
NT (Yr 1) Heb 12:1-13
Friday of Lent Week 5
Morning Prayer
First Reading Is 52:13-15
NT (1-Yr) Heb 7:11-18
or Second Reading1 Pet 2:21-24
Evening Prayer
OT (Yr 2) Num 22:1-8, 20-35
NT (Yr 1) Heb 12:14-29
Saturday of Lent Week 5
Morning Prayer
First Reading Is 65:1b-3a
NT (1-Yr) Heb 8:1-13
or Second Reading 1 Pet 1:18-21

PALM SUNDAY
Evening Prayer I
OT (Yr 2) Num 24:1-19
NT (1-Yr)Heb 8:1-13
or NT (Yr 1) Heb 13:1-25
or Gospel Reading Jn 8:21-30
Morning Prayer
Lauds Pss 51; 118; 63; 148-150
OT (Yr 1) Is 50:4 – 51:3
or OT (Yr 2) Jer 22:1-9; 23:1-8
Second Reading 2 Cor 4:10-12
Evening Prayer II
OT (Yr 2) Jer 22:1-9; 23:1-8
or OT (Yr 1) Is 50:4 – 51:3
NT (1-Yr) Heb 10:1-18
or Second Reading Acts 13:26-30

Monday of Holy Week
Morning Prayer
First Reading Jer 11:19-20
NT (1-Yr) Heb 10:19-39
or Second Reading Heb 10:35-39
Evening Prayer
OT (Yr 1) Is 52:13 – 53:12
or OT (Yr 2) Jer 26:1-15
Second Reading Rom 5:8-9
Tuesday of Holy Week
Morning Prayer
First Reading Zech 12:10-11a
NT (1-Yr) Heb 12:1-13
or Second Reading Rom 6:3-5
Evening Prayer
*If Lamentations is to be read from Maundy
Thursday on according to the* **Tenebræ**
scheme for Morning Prayer:
First Reading Jer 8: 13 – 9:9
Otherwise:
OT (Yr 1) Lam 1:1-12, 18-20
or OT (Yr 2) Jer 8:13 – 9:9
Second Reading 1 Cor 1:18-30
Wednesday of Holy Week
Morning Prayer
First Reading Is 50:5-7
NT (1-Yr) Heb 12:14-29
or Second Reading 1 Jn 4:9-11
Evening Prayer
*If Lamentations is to be read from Maundy
Thursday on according to the* **Tenebræ**
scheme for Morning Prayer:
OT Jer 11:18 – 12:13
Otherwise: OT (Yr 1) Lam 2:1-10
or OT (Yr 2) Jer 11:18 – 12:13
Second Reading Eph 4:32 – 5:2

Maundy Thursday
Morning Prayer
Matins Ps 69[5]
Lauds Pss 80; 81
If the lessons are read according to the
Tenebræ *scheme for Morning Prayer:*
First Reading Lam 1:1-9 (see *Times and
Seasons* page 301)
Second Reading1 Cor 11:17-34 (see
Times and Seasons page 303)
Otherwise:
OT (Yr 1) Lam 2:10-22
or OT (Yr 2) Jer 15:10-21
NT (1-Yr) Heb 4:14 – 5:10
or Second Reading Heb 2:9-10
Prayer During the Day
Ps 119:65-72; 56; 57
Terce Heb 4:14-15
Sext Heb 7:26-27
None Heb 9:11-12

Easter Triduum
MAUNDY THURSDAY
Evening Prayer[6]
Vespers Pss 56; 72
First Reading Ex 12:1-8, 11-14
Second Reading Heb 13:12-13
or Second Reading 1 Cor 11:23-26

---

[5] The psalm for Thursday Week 2
(Ps 44) may be used instead.
[6] EP is said only by those who do
not attend the Evening Mass of
the Lord's Supper. The readings
(OT & NT) are accordingly drawn
from the Order of Readings for
Mass.

GOOD FRIDAY

Morning Prayer

Matins (No Invitatory); Pss 2; 22; 38

Lauds Pss 51; 147:12-20

If the lessons are read according to the

Tenebræ *scheme for Morning Prayer:*

First Reading Lam 2:8-15; 3:1-9 (see

Times and Seasons page 306)

Second Reading Heb 4:9 – 5:10 (see

Times and Seasons page 309)

Otherwise:

First Reading Is 52:13-15

or OT (Yr 1) Lam 3:1-33

NT (Yr 2 & 1-Yr) Heb 9:11-28

Prayer During the Day

Pss 40; 54; 88

Terce Is 53:2-3

Sext Is 53:4-5

None Is 53:6-7

Evening Prayer[7]

Vespers Pss 116; 143

First Reading Is 52:13 – 53:12

Second Reading Heb 4:14-16; 5:7-9

or Gospel Reading Mt 27:1-2, 11-56

or Mk 15:1-41

or Lk 23:1-49

Easter Eve (or Holy Saturday)

Morning Prayer

Matins (No Invitatory); Pss 4; 16; 24; 95

Lauds Pss 64; 150

If the lessons are read according to the

Tenebræ *scheme for Morning Prayer:*

First Reading Lam 3:22-31; 4:1-6; 5:1-11 (see *Times and Seasons* page 311)

Second Reading Heb 9:11–22 (see

Times and Seasons page 314)

Otherwise:

OT (Yr 1) Lam 5:1-22

or OT (Yr 2) Jer 20:7-18

NT (1-Yr) Heb 4:1-13

or Second Reading 1 Jn 1:8 – 1 Jn 2:10

Evening Prayer

Pss 27; 30

Vespers Pss 116; 143;

OT (Yr 2) Jer 20:7-18

or OT (Yr 1) Lam 5:1-22

Second Reading 1 Pet 1:18-21

or Gospel Reading Mt 27:57-66

or Mk 15:42-47

or Lk 23:50-56

---

[7] EP is said only by those who do not attend the Afternoon Liturgy of the Passion.

861

EASTERTIDE

EASTER SUNDAY

Morning Prayer

Lauds Pss 93; 63; 118; 148-150

OT (1-Yr) Ex 14:15 – 15:1[1]

or First Reading Ex 15:1b-2

Second Reading Acts 10:40-43

or Rom 6:3-11[2]

Evening Prayer

Vespers Pss 110; 111; 112; 113; 114; 115

First Reading Is 43:1-21

Second Reading Heb 10:12-14

or Easter Evening Gospel Lk 24:13-35

Monday of Easter Week

Morning Prayer

Lauds Pss 63:1-9; 148-150

First Reading Ex 15:1b-2

or Gen 22:1-18

NT (Yr 1 and 1-Yr) 1 Pet 1:1-21

or NT (Yr 2) Acts 1:1-26

Evening Prayer

Vespers Pss 110; 114

First Reading Song 1:9 – 2:7

NT (Yr 2) Acts 1:1-26

or NT (Yr 1 and 1-Yr) 1 Pet 1:1-21

---

[1] The First Reading set for the Office of Readings on Easter Sunday (to be used by those unable to attend the Easter Vigil). This is the Third Reading at the Easter Vigil.

[2] The Third Reading set for the Office of Readings on Easter Sunday (to be used by those unable to attend the Easter Vigil). This is the New Testament Reading at the Easter Vigil.

Tuesday of Easter Week

Morning Prayer

Lauds Pss 63:1-9; 148-150

First Reading Ex 15:1b-2

or Is 54:5-14

NT (Yr 1 and 1-Yr) 1 Pet 1:22 – 2:10

or NT (Yr 2) Acts 2:1-21

Evening Prayer

Vespers Pss 110; 114

First Reading Song 2:8-17

NT (Yr 2) Acts 2:1-21

or NT (Yr 1 and 1-Yr) 1 Pet 1:22 – 2:10

Wednesday of Easter Week

Morning Prayer

Lauds Pss 63:1-9; 148-150

First Reading Ex 15:1b-2

or Is 55:1-11

NT (Yr 1 and 1-Yr) 1 Pet 2:11-25

or NT (Yr 2) Acts 2:22-41

Evening Prayer

Vespers Pss 110; 114

First Reading Song 3

NT (Yr 2) Acts 2:22-41

or NT (Yr 1 and 1-Yr) 1 Pet 2:11-25

Thursday of Easter Week

Morning Prayer

Lauds Pss 63:1-9; 148-150

First Reading Ex 15:1b-2

or Bar 3:9-15, 32 – 4:4

NT (Yr 1 and 1-Yr) 1 Pet 3:1-17

or NT (Yr 2) Acts 2:42 – 3:11

Evening Prayer

Vespers Pss 110; 114

First Reading Song 5:2 – 6:3

NT (Yr 2) Acts 2:42 – 3:11

or NT (Yr 1 and 1-Yr) 1 Pet 3:1-17

Friday of Easter Week
Morning Prayer
Lauds Pss 63:1-9; 148-150
First Reading Ex 15:1b-2
or First Reading Ezek 36:16-28
NT (Yr 1 and 1-Yr) 1 Pet 3:18 – 4:11
or NT (Yr 2) Acts 3:12 – 4:4
Evening Prayer
Vespers Pss 110; 114
First Reading Song 7:10 – 8:4
NT (Yr 2) Acts 3:12 – 4:4
or NT (Yr 1 and 1-Yr) 1 Pet 3:18 –
4:11
Saturday of Easter Week
Morning Prayer
Lauds Pss 63:1-9; 148-150
First Reading Ex 15:1b-2
NT (Yr 1 and 1-Yr) 1 Pet 4:12 – 5:14
or NT (Yr 2) Acts 4:5-31

Second Sunday of Easter
Evening Prayer I
Vespers I Pss 110; 114
First Reading Song 8:5-7
NT (Yr 2) Acts 4:5-31
or NT (Yr 1 and 1-Yr) 1 Pet 4:12 –
5:14
or Gospel Reading   Mk 16:1-20
Morning Prayer
Lauds Pss 63:1-9; 148-150
First Reading Hos 6:1-2
or Ex 14:10-31; 15:20-21
Second Reading Acts 10:40-43
Evening Prayer II
Vespers II Pss 110; 114
First Reading Is 52:13 – 53:12
NT (1-Yr & Yrs 1 & 2)Col 3:1-17
or Second ReadingHeb 10:12-14

Monday of Easter Week 2
Morning Prayer
First Reading Hos 6:1-2
NT (Yr 1 and 1-Yr) Rev 1:1-20
Evening Prayer
First Reading Gen 7:1-5
NT (Yr 2) Acts 4:32 – 5:16
Tuesday of Easter Week 2
Morning Prayer
First Reading Hos 6:1-2
NT (Yr 1 and 1-Yr) Rev 2:1-11
Evening Prayer
First Reading Gen 7:11-18
NT (Yr 2) Acts 5:17-42
Wednesday of Easter Week 2
Morning Prayer
First Reading Hos 6:1-2
NT (Yr 1 and 1-Yr) Rev 2:12-29
Evening Prayer
First Reading Gen 8:6-19
NT (Yr 2) Acts 6:1-15
Thursday of Easter Week 2
Morning Prayer
First Reading Hos 6:1-2
NT (Yr 1 and 1-Yr) Rev 3:1-22
Evening Prayer
First Reading Gen 9:8-13
NT (Yr 2) Acts 7:1-16
Friday of Easter Week 2
Morning Prayer
First Reading Hos 6:1-2
NT (Yr 1 and 1-Yr) Rev 4:1-11
Evening Prayer
First Reading Gen 9:13-17
NT (Yr 2) Acts 7:17-43
Saturday of Easter Week 2
Morning Prayer
First Reading Hos 6:1-2
NT (Yr 1 and 1-Yr) Rev 5:1-14

Third Sunday of Easter

Evening Prayer I

First Reading Zeph 3:14-20

NT (Yr 2) Acts 7:44 – 8:4

or NT (Yr 1 and 1-Yr) Rev 5:1-14

or Gospel Reading Lk 24:1-12

Morning Prayer

First Reading Zeph 3:11-12

NT (Yr 1 and 1-Yr) Rev 6:1-17

or NT (Yr 2) Acts 8:4-25

or Second Reading Acts 10:40-43

Evening Prayer II

First Reading Is 38:9-20

NT (Yr 2) Acts 8:4-25

or NT (Yr 1 and 1-Yr) Rev 6:1-17

Monday of Easter Week 3

Morning Prayer

First Reading Zeph 3:11-12

NT (Yr 1 and 1-Yr) Rev 7:1-17

Evening Prayer

First Reading Jon 1:1-10

NT (Yr 2) Acts 8:26-40

Tuesday of Easter Week 3

Morning Prayer

First Reading Zeph 3:11-12

NT (Yr 1 and 1-Yr) Rev 8:1-13

Evening Prayer

First Reading Jon 1:11-17

NT (Yr 2) Acts 9:1-22

Wednesday of Easter Week 3

Morning Prayer

First Reading Zeph 3:11-12

NT (Yr 1 and 1-Yr) Rev 9:1-12

Evening Prayer

First Reading Jon 2:1-10

NT (Yr 2) Acts 9:23-43

Thursday of Easter Week 3

Morning Prayer

First Reading Zeph 3:11-12

NT (Yr 1 and 1-Yr) Rev 9:13-21

Evening Prayer

First Reading Jon 3:1-10

NT (Yr 2) Acts 10:1-33

Friday of Easter Week 3

Morning Prayer

First Reading Zeph 3:11-12

NT (Yr 1 and 1-Yr) Rev 10:1-11

Evening Prayer

First Reading Jon 4:1-11

NT (Yr 2) Acts 10:34 – 11:4, 18

Saturday of Easter Week 3

Morning Prayer

First Reading Zeph 3:11-12

NT (Yr 1 and 1-Yr) Rev 11:1-19

Fourth Sunday of Easter

Evening Prayer I

First Reading Gen 7:1-24

NT (Yr 2) Acts 11:19-30

or NT (Yr 1 and 1-Yr) Rev 11:1-19

or Gospel Reading Lk 24:13-35

Morning Prayer

First Reading Is 63:1-6

NT (Yr 1 and 1-Yr) Rev 12:1-18

or NT (Yr 2) Acts 12:1-23

or Second Reading Acts 10:40-43

Evening Prayer II

First Reading Wis 1:1-15

NT (Yr 2) Acts 12:1-23

or NT (Yr 1 and 1-Yr) Rev 12:1-18

Monday of Easter Week 4

Morning Prayer

First Reading Is 63:1-6

NT (Yr 1 and 1-Yr) Rev 13:1-18

Evening Prayer
First Reading Wis 1:16 – 2:11, 21-24
NT (Yr 2) Acts 12:24 – 13:4
Tuesday of Easter Week 4
Morning Prayer
First Reading Is 63:1-6
NT (Yr 1 and 1-Yr) Rev 14:1-13
Evening Prayer
First Reading Wis 3:1-9
NT (Yr 2) Acts 13:14-43
Wednesday of Easter Week 4
Morning Prayer
First Reading Is 63:1-6
NT (Yr 1 and 1-Yr) Rev 14:14 -15:4
Evening Prayer
First Reading Wis 4:16 – 5:8
NT (Yr 2) Acts 13:44 – 14:7
Thursday of Easter Week 4
Morning Prayer
First Reading Is 63:1-6
NT (Yr 1 and 1-Yr) Rev 15:5 – 16:21
Evening Prayer
First Reading Wis 5:9-23
NT (Yr 2) Acts 14:8 – 15:4
Friday of Easter Week 4
Morning Prayer
First Reading Is 63:1-6
NT (Yr 1 and 1-Yr) Rev 17:1-18
Evening Prayer
First Reading Wis 6:12-23
NT (Yr 2) Acts 15:5-35
Saturday of Easter Week 4
Morning Prayer
First Reading Is 63:1-6
NT (Yr 1 and 1-Yr) Rev 18:1-20

Fifth Sunday of Easter
Evening Prayer I
First Reading
(A) Gen 8:1-19

(B) and (C) Bar 3:9-15, 32-36; 4:1-4
or Wis 7:1-14
NT (Yr 2) Acts 15:36 – 16:15
or NT (Yr 1 and 1-Yr) Rev 18:1-20
or Gospel Reading Lk 24:35-53
Morning Prayer
First Reading Is 12:1-6
NT (Yr 1 and 1-Yr) Rev 18:21 – 19:10
or NT (Yr 2) Acts 16:16-40
or Second Reading Acts 10:40-43
Evening Prayer II
First Reading Wis 7:21 – 8:1
NT (Yr 2) Acts 16:16-40
or NT (Yr 1 and 1-Yr) Rev 18:21 –
19:10
Monday of Easter Week 5
Morning Prayer
First Reading Is 12:1-6
NT (Yr 1 and 1-Yr) Rev 19:11-21
Evening Prayer
First Reading Wis 9:1, 7-18
NT (Yr 2) Acts 17:1-18
Tuesday of Easter Week 5
Morning Prayer
First Reading Is 12:1-6
NT (Yr 1 and 1-Yr) Rev 20:1-15
Evening Prayer
First Reading Wis 10:1-4, (5-12), 13-21
NT (Yr 2) Acts 17:19-34
Wednesday of Easter Week 5
Morning Prayer
First Reading Is 12:1-6
NT (Yr 1 and 1-Yr) Rev 21:1-8
Evening Prayer
First Reading Wis 13:1-9
NT (Yr 2) Acts 18:1-28
Thursday of Easter Week 5
Morning Prayer
First Reading Is 12:1-6
NT (Yr 1 and 1-Yr) Rev 21:9-27

Evening Prayer
First Reading Wis 14:27 – 15:3
NT (Yr 2) Acts 19:1-20
Friday of Easter Week 5
Morning Prayer
First Reading Is 12:1-6
NT (Yr 1 and 1-Yr) Rev 22:1-9
Evening Prayer
First Reading Wis 16:15 – 17:1
NT (Yr 2) Acts 19:21-40
Saturday of Easter Week 5
Morning Prayer
First Reading Is 12:1-6
NT (Yr 1 and 1-Yr) Rev 22:10-21

Sixth Sunday of Easter
Evening Prayer I
First Reading Wis 19:1-8, 18-22
NT (Yr 2) Acts 20:1-16
or NT (Yr 1 and 1-Yr) Rev 22:10-21
or Gospel Reading Jn 20:1-18
Morning Prayer
First Reading Is 55:6-9
NT (Yr 1 and 1-Yr) 1 Jn 1:1-10
or NT (Yr 2) Acts 20:17-38
or Second Reading Acts 10:40-43
Evening Prayer II
First Reading Sir 43:1-12, 27-32
NT (Yr 2) Acts 20:17-38
or NT (Yr 1 and 1-Yr) 1 Jn 1:1-10
Monday of Easter Week 6
Morning Prayer
First Reading Is 55:6-9
NT (Yr 1 and 1-Yr) 1 Jn 2:1-11
Evening Prayer
First Reading Dan 6:1-9
NT (Yr 2) Acts 21:1-26
Tuesday of Easter Week 6
Morning Prayer
First Reading Is 55:6-9

NT (Yr 1 and 1-Yr) 1 Jn 2:12-17
Evening Prayer
First Reading *(when Ascension is to be celebrated on Thursday)* Dan 6:10-18
(when Ascension is to be celebrated on Sunday) Dan 6:10-14
NT (Yr 2) Acts 21:27-39
Wednesday of Easter Week 6
Morning Prayer
First Reading Is 55:6-9
NT (Yr 1 and 1-Yr) 1 Jn 2:18-29
Evening Prayer (when Ascension is to be celebrated on Sunday)
First Reading Dan 6:15-18
NT (Yr 2) Acts 21:40 - 22:21

Scheme A

ASCENSION DAY
Evening Prayer I
Vespers I Pss 113; 117
First Reading 2 Kings 2:1-15
Second Reading Eph 2:4-6
or NT (Yrs 1 & 2 and 1-Yr) Eph 4:1-24[3]
or Gospel Reading *The Gospel of the Feast in the Three-Year Cycle.*
(A) Mt 28:16-20
(B) Mk 16:15-20
(C) Lk 24:46-53
Morning Prayer
Lauds Pss 63:1-9; 148-150
First Reading Dan 7:9-14

---

[3] The long reading is read at one of the offices of the day. If long readings are required at other offices, readings set for the first or second reading in the Order of Readings for Mass are used.

Second Reading Heb 9:24-28; 10:19-23
or Heb 10:12-14
Evening Prayer II
Vespers II Pss 110; 47
First Reading 2 Kings 2:1-15
NT (Yrs 1 & 2 and 1-Yr) Eph 4:1-24
or Second Reading1 Pet 3:18-22
or Heb 9:24-28; 10:19-23
Friday after the Ascension
Morning Prayer
First Reading Is 55:6-9
NT (Yr 1 and 1-Yr) 1 Jn 3:11-17
Evening Prayer
First Reading *(after Ascension)*
Dan 6:19-28
(before Ascension) Dan 6:24-28
NT (Yr 2) Acts 23:12-35
Saturday after the Ascension
Morning Prayer
First Reading Is 55:6-9
NT (Yr 1 and 1-Yr) 1 Jn 3:18-24
**Seventh Sunday of Easter (Sunday
after the Ascension)**
Evening Prayer I
First Reading Ezek 3:16-27
NT (Yr 2) Acts 24:1-27
or Gospel Reading Jn 20:19-31
Morning Prayer
First Reading Ezek 37:4-7
Second Reading Acts 10:40-43
Evening Prayer II
First Reading Ezek 36:24-28
NT (1-Yr) (Yrs 1 & 2)1 Jn 3:18-24

or
Scheme B

**Thursday of Easter Week 6
(before Ascension)**
Morning Prayer
First Reading Is 55:6-9
NT (Yr 1 and 1-Yr) 1 Jn 3:1-10
Evening Prayer
First Reading Dan 6:19-23
NT (Yr 2) Acts 22:22 – 23:11
**Friday of Easter Week 6
(before Ascension)**
Morning Prayer
First Reading Is 55:6-9
NT (Yr 1 and 1-Yr) 1 Jn 3:11-17
Evening Prayer
First Reading *(after Ascension)*
Dan 6:19-28
(before Ascension) Dan 6:24-28
NT (Yr 2) Acts 23:12-35
**Saturday of Easter Week 6 (before
Ascension)**
Morning Prayer
First Reading Is 55:6-9
NT (Yr 1 and 1-Yr) 1 Jn 3:18-24

ASCENSION SUNDAY
Evening Prayer I
Vespers I Pss 113; 117
First Reading 2 Kings 2:1-15
Second Reading Eph 2:4-6
or NT (Yrs 1 & 2 and 1-Yr) Eph 4:1-24
or Gospel Reading*The Gospel of the Feast
in the Three-Year Cycle:*
(A) Mt 28:16-20
(B) Mk 16:15-20
(C) Lk 24:46-53
Morning Prayer
Lauds Pss 63:1-9; 148-150

First Reading Dan 7:9-14
Second Reading Heb 9:24-28; 10:19-23
or Heb 10:12-14
Evening Prayer II
Vespers II Pss 110; 47
First Reading 2 Kings 2:1-15
NT (Yrs 1 & 2 and 1-Yr) Eph 4:1-24
or Second Reading 1 Pet 3:18-22
or Heb 9:24 28; 10:19 23

Monday of Easter Week 7
Morning Prayer
First Reading Ezek 37:4-7
NT (Yr 1 and 1-Yr) 1 Jn 4:1-10
Evening Prayer
First Reading Gen 11:1-9
NT (Yr 2) Acts 25:1-27
Tuesday of Easter Week 7
Morning Prayer
First Reading Ezek 37:4-7
NT (Yr 1 and 1-Yr) 1 Jn 4:11-21
Evening Prayer
First Reading Ex 19:1-20
NT (Yr 2) Acts 26:1-32
Wednesday of Easter Week 7
Morning Prayer
First Reading Ezek 37:4-7
NT (Yr 1 and 1-Yr) 1 Jn 5:1-12
Evening Prayer
First Reading Ezek 37:1-14
NT (Yr 2) Acts 27:1-20
Thursday of Easter Week 7
Morning Prayer
First Reading Ezek 37:4-7
NT (Yr 1 and 1-Yr) 1 Jn 5:13-21
Evening Prayer
First Reading Joel 3:1-5
NT (Yr 2) Acts 27:21-44

Friday of Easter Week 7
Morning Prayer
First Reading Ezek 37:4-7
NT (Yr 1 and 1-Yr) 2 Jn
Evening Prayer
First Reading Dan 3:8-13, 19b-23,
24-30[4]
NT (Yr 2) Acts 28:1-14
Saturday of Easter Week 7
Morning Prayer
First Reading Ezek 37:4-7
NT (Yr 1 and 1-Yr) 3 Jn

---

[4] RSV (Second Catholic Edition) verses

868

PENTECOST (WHIT SUNDAY) AND WHITSUN WEEK, TRINITY SUNDAY, CORPUS CHRISTI, SACRED HEART OF JESUS

Evening Prayer I
Vespers I Pss 113; 147:1-11
First Reading Ezek 36:16-28
NT (Yr 2) Acts 28:15-31
or NT (Yr 1 and 1-Yr) 3 Jn
or Gospel Reading Mt 28:16-20
Morning Prayer
Lauds Pss 63:1-9; 148-150
First Reading Joel 3:1-5
NT (Yrs 1 & 2 and 1-Yr) Rom 8:5-27
or Second Reading Eph 4:3-6
Evening Prayer II
Vespers II Pss 110; 114
First Reading Num 11:24-30
Second Reading Eph 4:3-6
or NT (Yrs 1 & 2 and 1-Yr) Rom 8:5-27

Weekdays following Pentecost

*Psalms and canticles are from the occurring weekday in **Time per annum**, the week in which **Time per annum** is resumed is as indicated in the current **Ordo**. Readings may be from the occurring weekday or as follows:*

Monday in Whitsun Week
Morning Prayer
First Reading Ezek 11:14-20
Second Reading Acts 2:12-36
Evening Prayer
First Reading Wis 1:1-7
Second Reading Acts 2:37-47

Tuesday in Whitsun Week
Morning Prayer
First Reading Ezek 37:1-14
Second Reading 1 Cor 12:1-13
Evening Prayer
First Reading Wis 7:15 – 8:1
Second Reading 1 Cor 12:27 – 13:13
Wednesday in Whitsun Week
(Ember Day)
Morning Prayer
First Reading 1 Kings 19:1-18
Second Reading 1 Cor 2:1-16
Evening Prayer
First Reading Wis 9:1-18
Second Reading 1 Cor 3:1-23
Thursday in Whitsun Week
Morning Prayer
First Reading 2 Sam 23:1-5
Second Reading Eph 6:10-20
Evening Prayer
First Reading Ex 35:30 – 36:1
Second Reading Acts 18:24 – 19:7
Friday in Whitsun Week
(Ember Day)
Morning Prayer
First Reading Num 11:16-17, 24-29
Second Reading 2 Cor 5:14 – 6:10
Evening Prayer
First Reading Jer 31:31-34
Second Reading 2 Cor 3:1-18
Saturday in Whitsun Week
(Ember Day)
Morning Prayer
First Reading Num 27:15-end
Second Reading Mt 9:35 – 10:20

TRINITY SUNDAY

Evening Prayer I
Vespers I Pss 113; 147:12-20
First Reading Is 6:1-8 (9-13)
Second Reading Rom 11:33-36
or Gospel Reading *The Gospel of the Feast in the Three-Year Cycle.*
(A) Jn 3:16-18
(B) Mt 28:16-20
(C) Jn 16:12-15

Morning Prayer
Lauds Pss 63:1-9; 148-150
First Reading Gen 1:1-5
Second Reading 1 Cor 12:4-6

Evening Prayer II
Vespers II Pss 110; 114
First Reading Is 40:12-17, 27-31
NT (Yrs 1 & 2 and 1-Yr) 1 Cor 2:1-16

CORPUS CHRISTI

Evening Prayer I
Vespers I Pss 111; 147:12-20
First Reading Ex 24:1-11
or Prov 9:1-6, 10-12
Second Reading 1 Cor 10:16-17
or Gospel Reading
The Gospel of the Feast in the Three-Year Cycle.
(A) Jn 6:51-58
(B) Mk 14:12-16, 22-26
(C) Lk 9:11-17

Morning Prayer
Lauds Pss 63:1-9; 148-150
First Reading Gen 14:18-20
Second Reading Acts 2:42-47

Evening Prayer II
Vespers II Pss 110; 116;
OT (Yrs 1 & 2 & 1-Yr)Ex 24:1-11
Second Reading 1 Cor 11:23-25

SACRED HEART

Evening Prayer I
Vespers I Pss 113; 146
First Reading Jer 31:2-4
NT (Yrs 1 & 2 and 1-Yr) Rom 8:28-39[1]
or Second Reading Eph 5:25b-27
or Gospel Reading *The Gospel of the Feast in the Three-Year Cycle.*
(A) Mt 11:25-30
(B) Jn 19:31-37
(C) Lk 15:3-7

Morning Prayer
Lauds Pss 63:1-9; 148-150
First Reading Jer 31:31-34
Second Reading Rom 5:8-10

Evening Prayer II
Vespers II Pss 110; 111
First Reading Jer 32:37-41
Second Reading Eph 2:4-7
or NT (Yrs 1 & 2 and 1-Yr) Rom 8:28-39

---

[1] The long reading is read at one of the offices of the day. If long readings are required at other offices, readings set for the first or second reading in the Order of Readings for Mass are used.

870

*The week in which **Time per annum** is resumed is as indicated in the current **Ordo**. **Time per annum** is counted as resuming on the Monday after Pentecost Sunday though, as indicated above, the Octave of Pentecost, ending with Trinity Sunday, may be observed and **Time per annum** resumed on the Monday following Trinity Sunday.*

The Sunday sequence after Trinity, and served by the Office lectionary, may be known as follows:

First Sunday after Trinity
Second Sunday after Trinity
Third Sunday after Trinity
&c.

The Sunday next before Advent is kept as **the solemnity of CHRIST THE KING** *and the final weekdays before Advent are from Week 34*

Week after Epiphany
Monday of Week 1
Morning Prayer
OT (1-Yr) Sir 1:1-20
or First Reading 1 Chron 29:10-13
Second Reading 2 Thess 3:6-13
Evening Prayer
First Reading Jer 17:7-10
or OT (Yr 2) Gen 1:1 – 2:4
Second Reading Col 1:9b-14
or NT (Yr 1) Rom 1:1-17
Tuesday of Week 1
Morning Prayer
OT (1-Yr) Sir 11:11-28
or First Reading Tob 13:1b-8
Second Reading Rom 13:8-14
Evening Prayer
First Reading Job 5:17-18
or OT (Yr 2) Gen 2:4-25
Second Reading 1 Jn 3:1-3
or NT (Yr 1) Rom 1:18-32

Wednesday of Week 1
Morning Prayer
OT (1-Yr) Sir 24:1-23
or First Reading Judith 16:2-3a, 13-15
Second Reading 1 Pet 1:13-16
Evening Prayer
First Reading Tob 4:16-20
or OT (Yr 2) Gen 3:1-24
Second Reading Jas 1:22-25
or NT (Yr 1) Rom 2:1-16
Thursday of Week 1
Morning Prayer
OT (1-Yr) Sir 42:15 - 43:12
or First Reading Jer 31:10-14
Second Reading Rom 2:14-16
Evening Prayer
First Reading Is 66:1-2
or OT (Yr 2) Gen 4:1-24
Second Reading 1 Pet 1:6-9
or NT (Yr 1) Rom 2:17-29

Friday of Week 1
Morning Prayer
OT (1-Yr) Sir 43:13-33
or First Reading Is 45:15-22
Second Reading Eph 4:29-32
Evening Prayer
First Reading Is 45:22-25
or OT (Yr 2) Gen 6:5-22; 7:17-24
Second Reading Rom 15:1-3
or NT (Yr 1) Rom 3:1-20
Saturday of Week 1
Morning Prayer
OT (1-Yr) Sir 44:1-2, 16 – 45:5
or First Reading Ex 15:1-4a, 8-13, 17-18 (*or* Ex 15:1-18)
Second Reading 2 Pet 1:5b-11

Sunday 2
Evening Prayer I
First Reading Wis 7:27a - 8:1
or OT (Yr 2) Gen 8:1-22
Second Reading Col 1:3-6a
or NT (Yr 1) Rom 3:21-31
or Gospel Reading Mk 16:1-20
Morning Prayer
OT (1-Yr) Deut 1:1, 6-18
or First Reading Ezek 36:25-27
Second Reading Rom 5:1-5
Evening Prayer II
First Reading Deut 15:7-8, 10-11
or OT (Yr 2) Gen 9:1-17
Second Reading 2 Thess 2:13-14
or NT (Yr 1) Rom 4:1-25
Monday of Week 2
Morning Prayer
OT (1-Yr)Deut 4:1-8, 32-40
or First Reading Sir 36:1-7, 13-16
or First Reading Jer 15:15-21
Second Reading Eph 1:3-10

Evening Prayer
First Reading Is 55:1-5
or OT (Yr 2) Gen 11:1-26
Second Reading 1 Thess 2:9-13
or NT (Yr 1) Rom 5:1-11
Tuesday of Week 2
Morning Prayer
OT (1-Yr) Deut 6:4-25
or First Reading Is 38:10-14, 17-20
Second Reading 1 Thess 5:4-11
Evening Prayer
First Reading Is 55:6-9
or OT (Yr 2) Gen 12:1-9; 13:2-18
Second Reading Rom 3:21-26
or NT (Yr 1) Rom 5:12-21
Wednesday of Week 2
Morning Prayer
OT (1-Yr) Deut 7:6-14; 8:1-6
or First Reading 1 Sam 2:1-10
Second Reading Rom 8:35-39
Evening Prayer
First Reading Is 55:10-12
or OT (Yr 2) Gen 14:1-24
Second Reading 1 Pet 5:5b-7
or NT (Yr 1) Rom 6:1-11
Thursday of Week 2
Morning Prayer
OT (1-Yr) Deut 9:7-21, 25-29
or First Reading Is 12:1-6
Second Reading Rom 14:17-19
Evening Prayer
First Reading Deut 1:16-18
or OT (Yr 2) Gen 15:1-21
Second Reading 1 Pet 1:22-25
or NT (Yr 1) Rom 6:12-23
Friday of Week 2
Morning Prayer
OT (1-Yr) Deut 10:12 – 11:9, 26-28
or First ReadingHab 3:2-19
Second Reading Eph 2:13-16

Evening Prayer
First Reading Is 57:15-19
or OT (Yr 2) Gen 16:1-16
Second Reading 1 Cor 2:7-10a
or NT (Yr 1) Rom 7:1-13
Saturday of Week 2
Morning Prayer
OT (1-Yr) Deut 16:1-17
or First Reading Deut 32:1-12
Second Reading Rom 12:14-16a

Sunday 3
Evening Prayer I
First Reading Deut 8:5-10
or OT (Yr 2) Gen 17:1-27
Second Reading Heb 13:20-21
or NT (Yr 1) Rom 7:14-25
or Gospel Reading Lk 24:1-12
Morning Prayer
OT (1-Yr) Deut 18:1-22
or First Reading 1 Kings 2:1-4
Second Reading Rom 8:9-11
Evening Prayer II
First Reading Ezek 37:12b-14
or OT (Yr 2) Gen 18:1–33
Second Reading 1 Pet 1:3-9
or NT (Yr 1) Rom 8:1-17
Monday of Week 3
Morning Prayer
OT (1-Yr) Deut 24:1 – 25:4
or First Reading Is 2:2-5
Second Reading Jas 2:12-13
Evening Prayer
First Reading Jer 22:1-4
or OT (Yr 2) Gen 19:1-17, 23-29
Second Reading Jas 4:11-12
or NT (Yr 1) Rom 8:18-39
Tuesday of Week 3
Morning Prayer
OT (1-Yr) Deut 26:1-19

or First Reading Is 26:1b-4
Second Reading 1 Jn 4:13-17
Evening Prayer
First Reading Is 26:7-12
or OT (Yr 2) Gen 21:1-21
Second Reading Rom 12:9-12
or NT (Yr 1) Rom 9:1-18
Wednesday of Week 3
Morning Prayer
OT (1-Yr) Deut 29:1-5, 9-28
or First Reading Is 33:13-16
Second Reading 1 Cor 13:4-13
Evening Prayer
First Reading Job 1:20-22; 2:9-10
or OT (Yr 2) Gen 22:1-19
Second Reading Eph 3:14-21
or NT (Yr 1) Rom 9:19-33
Thursday of Week 3
Morning Prayer
OT (1-Yr) Deut 30:1-20
or First Reading Is 40:10-17
Second Reading 1 Pet 4:7-11
Evening Prayer
First Reading Deut 4:7-8
or OT (Yr 2) Gen 24:1-27
Second Reading 1 Pet 3:8-12
or NT (Yr 1) Rom 10:1-21
Friday of Week 3
Morning Prayer
OT (1-Yr) Deut 31:1-15, 23
or First Reading Jer 14:17-21
Second Reading 2 Cor 12:9b-10
Evening Prayer
First Reading Jer 18:1-6
or OT (Yr 2) Gen 24:33-41, 49-67
Second Reading Jas 1:2-6
or NT (Yr 1) Rom 11:1-12
Saturday of Week 3
Morning Prayer
OT (1-Yr)Deut 32:48-52; 34:1-12

or First Reading Wis 9:1-6, 9-11
Second Reading Phil 2:14-15

Sunday 4
Evening Prayer I
First Reading Is 25:6-10a
or OT (Yr 2) Gen 25:7-11, 19-34
Second Reading 2 Pet 1:16-21
or NT (Yr 1) Rom 11:13-24
or Gospel Reading Lk 24:13-35
Morning Prayer
First Reading Deut 10:12-15
NT (1-Yr) 1 Thess 1:1 – 2:11
or Second Reading 2 Tim 2:8-13
Evening Prayer II
First Reading Song 8:5-7
or OT (Yr 2) Gen 27:1–29
Second Reading Heb 12:22-34
or NT (Yr 1) Rom 11:25-36
Monday of Week 4
Morning Prayer
First Reading Judith 8:24-27
or First Reading Is 42:10-16
NT (1-Yr)1 Thess 2:13 – 3:13
or Second Reading Rom 12:3-8
Evening Prayer
First Reading Bar 4:21-22
or OT (Yr 2) Gen 27:30-45
Second Reading1 Thess 3:(7b-10),
11-13
or NT (Yr 1) Rom 12:1-21
Tuesday of Week 4
Morning Prayer
First Reading Is 55:1-5
or First Reading Dan 3:3-6, (7-10),
11-18
NT (1-Yr)1 Thess 4:1-18
or Second Reading 1 Jn 3:17-18
Evening Prayer
First Reading Deut 30:11-14

or OT (Yr 2) Gen 28:10 – 29:14
Second Reading Col 3:12-16
or NT (Yr 1) Rom 13:1-14
Wednesday of Week 4
Morning Prayer
First Reading Deut 4:39-40
or First Reading Is 61:10 – 62:5
or First Reading Is 55:10-12
NT (1-Yr) 1 Thess 5:1-28
or Second Reading Col 3:17, 23-24
Evening Prayer
First Reading Is 55:10-12
or OT (Yr 2) Gen 31:1-18
Second Reading 1 Jn 2:3-6
or NT (Yr 1) Rom 14:1-23
Thursday of Week 4
Morning Prayer
First Reading Is 66:10-14a
NT (1-Yr) 2 Thess 1:1-12
or Second Reading Rom 8:18-21
Evening Prayer
First Reading Wis 1:1-5
or OT (Yr 2) Gen 32:3-30
Second Reading Col 1:21-23
or NT (Yr 1) Rom 15:1-13
Friday of Week 4
Morning Prayer
First Reading Tob 13:8-15
NT (1-Yr) 2 Thess 2:1-17
or Second Reading Gal 2:19-20
Evening Prayer
First Reading Wis 1:6-11
or OT (Yr 2) Gen 35:1-29
Second Reading Rom 8:1-6
or NT (Yr 1) Rom 15:14-32
Saturday of Week 4
Morning Prayer
First Reading Ezek 36:24-28
NT (1-Yr) 2 Thess 3:1-18
or Second Reading 2 Pet 3:8b-15a

Sunday 5

Evening Prayer I

First Reading Dan 6:26b-27

or OT (Yr 2) Gen 37:2-4, 12-36

Second Reading Rom 11:33-36

or NT (Yr 1) Rom 16:1-27

or Gospel Reading Lk 24:35-53

Morning Prayer

First Reading Ex 20:1-17

NT (1-Yr) Gal 1:1-12

or Second Reading Rev 7:9-12

Evening Prayer II

First Reading Is 43:16-21

or OT (Yr 2) Gen 39:1-23

Second Reading 2 Cor 1:3-7

or NT (Yr 1) 1 Cor 1:1-17

Monday of Week 5

Morning Prayer

First Reading Deut 28:1-6

or First Reading1 Chron 29:10-13

NT (1-Yr)Gal 1:13 – 2:10

or Second Reading 2 Thess 3:6-13

Evening Prayer

First Reading Jer 17:7-10

or OT (Yr 2) Gen 41:1-17, 25-43

Second Reading Col 1:9b-14

or NT (Yr 1) 1 Cor 1:18-31

Tuesday of Week 5

Morning Prayer

First Reading Prov 3:13-15

or First Reading Tob 13:1b-8

NT (1-Yr)Gal 2:11 – 3:14

or Second Reading Rom 13:8-14

Evening Prayer

First Reading Job 5:17-18

or OT (Yr 2) Gen 41:56 – 42:26

Second Reading 1 Jn 3:1-3

or NT (Yr 1) 1 Cor 2:1-16

Wednesday of Week 5

Morning Prayer

First Reading Judith 16:2-3a, 13-15

NT (1-Yr) Gal 3:15 – 4:7

or Second Reading 1 Pet 1:13-16

Evening Prayer

First Reading Tob 4:16-20

or OT (Yr 2) Gen 43:1-11, 13-17,
26-34

or Gen 43:1-34

Second Reading Jas 1:22-25

or NT (Yr 1) 1 Cor 3:1-23

Thursday of Week 5

Morning Prayer

First Reading Is 66:1-2

or First Reading Jer 31:10-14

NT (1-Yr) Gal 4:8-31

or Second Reading Rom 2:14-16

Evening Prayer

First Reading Amos 4:13; 5:8; 9:6[1]

or OT (Yr 2) Gen 44:1-20, 30-34

or Gen 44:1-34

Second Reading 1 Pet 1:6-9

or NT (Yr 1) 1 Cor 4:1-21

Friday of Week 5

Morning Prayer

First Reading Is 45:15-22

NT (1-Yr) Gal 5:1-25

or Second Reading Eph 4:29-32

Evening Prayer

First Reading Is 45:22-25

or OT (Yr 2) Gen 45:1-15, 21-28;
46:1-7

or Gen 45:1 – 46:7

Second Reading Rom 15:1-3

or NT (Yr 1) 1 Cor 5:1-13

---

[1] Terce, Sext, and None readings, any of which may be read or all combined to form one reading.

875

Saturday of Week 5
Morning Prayer
First Reading Wis 7:27a - 8:1
or First Reading Ex 15:1-4a, 8-13, 17-18
or Ex 15:1-18
NT (1-Yr) Gal 5:26 – 6:18
or Second Reading 2 Pet 1:5b-11

Sunday 6
Evening Prayer I
First Reading Wis 7:27a - 8:1
or OT (Yr 2) Gen 49:1-29, 33
or Gen 49:1-33
Second Reading 2 Pet 1:5b-11
or NT (Yr 1) 1 Cor 6:1-11
or Gospel Reading Jn 20:1-18
Morning Prayer
OT (1-Yr)Prov 1:1-7, 20-33
or First Reading Ezek 36:25-27
Second Reading Rom 5:1-5
Evening Prayer II
First Reading Deut 15:7-8, 10-11
Second Reading 2 Thess 2:13-14
or NT (Yr 1) 1 Cor 6:12-20
or NT (Yr 2) 1 Thess 1:1 – 2:12
Monday of Week 6
Morning Prayer
OT (1-Yr) Prov 3:1-20
or First Reading Sir 36:1-7, 13-16
or First Reading Jer 15:15-21
Second Reading Eph 1:3-10
Evening Prayer
First Reading Is 55:1-5
Second Reading 1 Thess 2:9-13
or NT (Yr 1) 1 Cor 7:1-24
or NT (Yr 2) 1 Thess 2:13 – 3:13

Tuesday of Week 6
Morning Prayer
OT (1-Yr)Prov 8:1-5, 12-36
or First Reading Is 38:10-14, 17-20
Second Reading 1 Thess 5:4-11
Evening Prayer
First Reading Is 55:6-9
Second Reading Rom 3:21-26
or NT (Yr 1) 1 Cor 7:25-40
or NT (Yr 2) 1 Thess 4:1-18
Wednesday of Week 6
Morning Prayer
OT (1-Yr) Prov 9:1-18
or First Reading 1 Sam 2:1-10
Second Reading Rom 8:35-39
Evening Prayer
First Reading Is 55:10-12
Second Reading 1 Pet 5:5b-7
or NT (Yr 1) 1 Cor 8:1-13
or NT (Yr 2) 1 Thess 5:1-28
Thursday of Week 6
Morning Prayer
OT (1-Yr) Prov 10:6-32
or First Reading Is 12:1-6
Second Reading Rom 14:17-19
Evening Prayer
First Reading Deut 1:16-18
Second Reading 1 Pet 1:22-25
or NT (Yr 1) 1 Cor 9:1-18
or NT (Yr 2) 2 Thess 1:1-12
Friday of Week 6
Morning Prayer
OT (1-Yr)Prov (15:8-9, 16-17, 25, 26, 29, 33); 16:1-9; (17:5)
or First Reading Hab 3:2-19
Second Reading Eph 2:13-16
Evening Prayer
First Reading Is 57:15-19
Second Reading 1 Cor 2:7-10a
or NT (Yr 1) 1 Cor 9:19-27

or NT (Yr 2) 2 Thess 2:1-17
Saturday of Week 6
Morning Prayer
OT (1-Yr) Prov 31:10-31
or First Reading Deut 32:1-12
Second Reading Rom 12:14-16a

Sunday 7
Evening Prayer I
First Reading Deut 8:5-10
Second Reading Heb 13:20-21
or NT (Yr 1) 1 Cor 10:1-14
or NT (Yr 2) 2 Thess 3:1-18
or Gospel Reading Jn 20:19-31
Morning Prayer
OT (1-Yr) Eccles 1:1-18
or First Reading 1 Kings 2:1-4
Second Reading 1 Cor 10:16-17
Evening Prayer II
First Reading Ezek 37:12b-14
Second Reading 1 Pet 1:3-9
or NT (Yr 1) 1 Cor 10:14 – 11:1
or NT (Yr 2) 2 Cor 1:1–14
Monday of Week 7
Morning Prayer
OT (1-Yr) Eccles 2:1-3, 12-26
or First Reading Is 2:2-5
Second Reading Jas 2:12-13
Evening Prayer
First Reading Jer 22:1-4
Second Reading Jas 4:11-12
or NT (Yr 1) 1 Cor 11:2-16
or NT (Yr 2) 2 Cor 1:14 – 2:11
Tuesday of Week 7
Morning Prayer
OT (1-Yr) Eccles 3:1-22
or First Reading Is 26:1b-4
Second Reading 1 Jn 4:13-17
Evening Prayer
First Reading Is 26:7-12

Second Reading Rom 12:9-12
or NT (Yr 1) 1 Cor 11:17-34
or NT (Yr 2) 2 Cor 12:3-6
Wednesday of Week 7
Morning Prayer
OT (1-Yr) Eccles 5:9 – 6:8
or First Reading Is 33:13-16
Second Reading 1 Cor 13:4-13
Evening Prayer
First Reading Job 1:20-22; 2:9-10
Second Reading Eph 3:14-21
or NT (Yr 1) 1 Cor 12:1-11
or NT (Yr 2) 2 Cor 3:7 – 4:4
Thursday of Week 7
Morning Prayer
OT (1-Yr) Eccles 6:12 – 7:28
or First Reading Is 40:10-17
Second Reading 1 Pet 4:7-11
Evening Prayer
First Reading Deut 4:7-8
Second Reading 1 Pet 3:8-12
or NT (Yr 1) 1 Cor 12:12-31
or NT (Yr 2) 2 Cor 4:5-18
Friday of Week 7
Morning Prayer
OT (1-Yr) Eccles 8:5 – 9:10
or First Reading Jer 14:17-21
Second Reading 2 Cor 12:9b-10
Evening Prayer
First Reading Jer 18:1-6
Second Reading Jas 1:2-6
or NT (Yr 1) 1 Cor 12:31 – 13:13
or NT (Yr 2) 2 Cor 5:1-21
Saturday of Week 7
Morning Prayer
OT (1-Yr) Eccles 11:7 – 12:14
or First Reading Wis 9:1-6, 9-11
Second Reading Phil 2:14-15

Sunday 8

Evening Prayer I
First Reading Is 25:6-10a
Second Reading 2 Pet 1:16-21
or NT (Yr 1) 1 Cor 14:1-19
or NT (Yr 2) 2 Cor 6:1 – 7:1
or Gospel Reading Jn 21:1-14

Morning Prayer
OT (1-Yr) Job 1:1-22
or First Reading Deut 10:12-15
Second Reading 2 Tim 2:8-13

Evening Prayer II
First Reading Deut 10:12-15
Second Reading Heb 12:18-24
or NT (Yr 1) 1 Cor 14:20-40
or NT (Yr 2) 2 Cor 7:2-16

Monday of Week 8

Morning Prayer
OT (1-Yr) Job 2:1-13
or First Reading Is 42:10-16
Second Reading Rom 12:1-8

Evening Prayer
First Reading Bar 4:21-22
or First Reading Is 42:10-16
Second Reading 1 Thess 3: (7b-10),
11-13
or NT (Yr 1) 1 Cor 15:1-19
or NT (Yr 2) 2 Cor 8:1-24

Tuesday of Week 8

Morning Prayer
OT (1-Yr) Job 3:1-26
or First Reading Dan 3:3-6, (7-10), 11-18
or First Reading Is 55:1-5
Second Reading 1 Jn 3:17-18

Evening Prayer
First Reading Deut 4:39-40
Second Reading Col 3:12-16
or NT (Yr 1) 1 Cor 15:20-34
or NT (Yr 2) 2 Cor 9:1-15

Wednesday of Week 8

Morning Prayer
OT (1-Yr) Job 7:1-21
or First Reading Is 61:10 – 62:5
or First Reading Deut 4:39-40
Second Reading Col 3:17, 23-24

Evening Prayer
First Reading Is 55:10-12
Second Reading 1 Jn 2:3-6
or NT (Yr 1) 1 Cor 15:35-58
or NT (Yr 2) 2 Cor 10:1 – 11:6

Thursday of Week 8

Morning Prayer
OT (1-Yr) Job 11:1-20
or First Reading Is 66:10-14a
Second Reading Rom 8:18-21

Evening Prayer
First Reading Wis 1:1-5
Second Reading Col 1:21-23
or NT (Yr 1) 1 Cor 16:1-24
or NT (Yr 2) 2 Cor 11:7-29

Friday of Week 8

Morning Prayer
OT (1-Yr) Job 12:1-25
or First Reading Tob 13:8-15
Second Reading Gal 2:19-20

Evening Prayer
First Reading Wis 1:6-11
Second Reading Rom 8:1-6
or NT (Yr 1) Jas 1:1-18
or NT (Yr 2) 2 Cor 11:30 – 12:13

Saturday of Week 8

Morning Prayer
OT (1-Yr) Job 13:12 – 14:6
or First Reading Ezek 36:24-28
Second Reading 2 Pet 3:8b-15a

Sunday 9

Evening Prayer I

First Reading Dan 6:26b-27

Second Reading Rom 11:33-36

or NT (Yr 1)Jas 1:19-27

or NT (Yr 2) 2 Cor 12:14 – 13:13

or Gospel Reading Mt 28:1-10, 16-20

Morning Prayer

OT (1-Yr) Job 28:1-28

or First Reading Ex 20:1-17

Second Reading Rev 7:9-12

Evening Prayer II

First Reading Is 43:16-21

Second Reading 2 Cor 1:3-7

or NT (Yr 1) Jas 2:1-13

or NT (Yr 2) Gal 1:1-12

Monday of Week 9

Morning Prayer

OT (1-Yr) Job 29:1-10; 30:1, 9-23

or First Reading 1 Chron 29:10-13

Second Reading 2 Thess 3:6-13

Evening Prayer

First Reading Jer 17:7-10

or First Reading Deut 28:1-6

Second Reading Col 1:9b-14

or NT (Yr 1) Jas 2:14-26

or NT (Yr 2) Gal 1:13 – 2:10

Tuesday of Week 9

Morning Prayer

OT (1-Yr) Job 31:1-8, (9-12), 13-23, 35-37

or First Reading Tob 13:1b-8

Second Reading Rom 13:8-14

Evening Prayer

First Reading Job 5:17-18

Second Reading 1 Jn 3:1-3

or NT (Yr 1) Jas 3:1-12

or NT (Yr 2) Gal 2:11 – 3:14

Wednesday of Week 9

Morning Prayer

OT (1-Yr) Job 32:1-6; 33:1-22

or First Reading Judith 16:2-3a, 13-15

Second Reading 1 Pet 1:13-16

Evening Prayer

First Reading Tob 4:16-20

Second Reading Jas 1:22-25

or NT (Yr 1) Jas 3:13-18

or NT (Yr 2) Gal 3:15 – 4:7

Thursday of Week 9

Morning Prayer

OT (1-Yr) Job 38:1-30

or First Reading Jer 31:10-14

Second Reading Rom 2:14-16

Evening Prayer

First Reading Is 66:1-2

Second Reading 1 Pet 1:6-9

or NT (Yr 1) Jas 4:1-12

or NT (Yr 2) Gal 4:8-31

Friday of Week 9

Morning Prayer

OT (1-Yr) Job 40:1-14; 42:1-6

or First Reading Is 45:15-22

Second Reading Eph 4:29-32

Evening Prayer

First Reading Is 45:22-25

Second Reading Rom 15:1-3

or NT (Yr 1) Jas 4:13 – 5:11

or NT (Yr 2) Gal 5:1-25

Saturday of Week 9

Morning Prayer

OT (1-Yr) Job 42:7-17

or First Reading Ex 15:1-4a, 8-13, 17-18

or Ex 15:1-18

Second Reading 2 Pet 1:5b-11

Sunday 10

Evening Prayer I
First Reading Wis 7:27a - 8:1
Second Reading Col 1:3-6a
or NT (Yr 1) Jas 5:12-20
or NT (Yr 2) Gal 5:25 – 6:18
or Gospel Reading Mk 16:1-20

Morning Prayer
OT (Yr 1 & 1-Yr) ir 46:1-12
or First Reading Ezek 36:25-27
Second Reading Rom 5:1-5

Evening Prayer II
First Reading Deut 15:7-8, 10-11
or OT (Yr 1 & 1-Yr) Sir 46:1-12
Second Reading 2 Thess 2:13-14
or NT (Yr 2) Phil 1:1-11

Monday of Week 10
Morning Prayer
OT (Yr 1 & 1-Yr) Josh 1:1-18
or First Reading Sir 36:1-7, 13-16
or First Reading Jer 15:15-21
Second Reading Eph 1:3-10

Evening Prayer
First Reading Is 55:1-5
or OT (Yr 1 & 1-Yr) Josh 1:1-18
Second Reading 1 Thess 2:9-13
or NT (Yr 2) Phil 1:12-26

Tuesday of Week 10
Morning Prayer
OT (Yr 1 & 1-Yr) Josh 2:1-24
or First Reading Is 38:10-14, 17-20
Second Reading 1 Thess 5:4-11

Evening Prayer
First Reading Is 55:6-9
or OT (Yr 1 & 1-Yr) Josh 2:1-24
Second Reading Rom 3:21-26
or NT (Yr 2) Phil 1:27 – 2:11

Wednesday of Week 10
Morning Prayer
OT (Yr 1 & 1-Yr) Josh 3:1-17; 4:14-19;
5:10-12
or OT (Yr 1 & 1-Yr) [pt 1] Josh 3:1-17[2]
or First Reading 1 Sam 2:1-10
Second Reading Rom 8:35-39

Evening Prayer
First Reading Is 55:10-12
or OT (Yr 1 & 1-Yr) [pt 2] Josh 4:14-
19; 5:10-12[3]
Second Reading 1 Pet 5:5b-7
or NT (Yr 2) Phil 2:12-30

Thursday of Week 10
Morning Prayer
OT (Yr 1 & 1-Yr) Josh 5:13 – 6:21
or First Reading Is 12:1-6
Second Reading Rom 14:17-19

Evening Prayer
First Reading Deut 1:16-18
or OT (Yr 1 & 1-Yr) Josh 5:13 – 6:21
Second Reading 1 Pet 1:22-25
or NT (Yr 2) Phil 3:1-16

Friday of Week 10
Morning Prayer
OT (1-Yr) Josh 10:1-14; 11:15-17
or First Reading Hab 3:2-19
Second Reading Eph 2:13-16

Evening Prayer
First Reading Is 57:15-19
or OT (Yr 1) Josh 7:4-26
Second Reading 1 Cor 2:7-10a
or NT (Yr 2) Phil 3:17 – 4:9

---

[2] The first section of the long reading: both sections should be read within the day.
[3] The second section of the long reading: both sections should be read within the day.

Saturday of Week 10
Morning Prayer
OT (1-Yr) Josh 24:1-7, 13-28
or First Reading Deut 32:1-12
Second Reading Rom 12:14-16a

Sunday 11
Evening Prayer I
First Reading Deut 8:5-10
or OT (Yr 1) Josh 10:1-14; 11:15-17
Second Reading Heb 13:20-21
or NT (Yr 2) Phil 4:10-23
or Gospel Reading Lk 24:1-12
Morning Prayer
OT (1-Yr) Judg 2:6 – 3:4
or First Reading 1 Kings 2:1-4
Second Reading Rom 8:14-23
Evening Prayer II
First Reading Ezek 37:12b-14
or OT (Yr 1)Josh 24:1-7, 13-28
or OT (Yr 2) Is 44:21 – 45:3
Second Reading 1 Pet 1:3-9
Monday of Week 11
Morning Prayer
OT (1-Yr) Judg 4:1-24
or First Reading Is 2:2-5
Second Reading Jas 2:12-13
Evening Prayer
First Reading Jer 22:1-4
or OT (Yr 1) Judg 2:6 – 3:4
or OT (Yr 2) Ezra 1:1-8; 2:68 – 3:8
Second Reading Jas 4:11-12
Tuesday of Week 11
Morning Prayer
OT (1-Yr) Judg 6:1-6, 11-24a
or First Reading Is 26:1b-4
Second Reading 1 Jn 4:13-17
Evening Prayer
First Reading Is 26:7-12
or OT (Yr 1) Judg 4:1-24

or OT (Yr 2) Ezra 4:1-5, 24; 5:1-5
Second Reading Rom 12:9-12
Wednesday of Week 11
Morning Prayer
OT (1-Yr) Judg 6:33-40; 7:1-8; 7:16-22
or First Reading Is 33:13-16
Second Reading 1 Cor 13:4-13
Evening Prayer
First Reading Job 1:20-22; 2:9-10
or OT (Yr 1) Judg 6:1-6, 11-24
or OT (Yr 2) Hag 1:1 – 2:9
Second Reading Eph 3:14-21
Thursday of Week 11
Morning Prayer
OT (1-Yr) Judg 8:22-23, 30-32; 9:1-15, 19-20
or Judg 9:1-20
or First Reading Is 40:10-17
Second Reading 1 Pet 4:7-11
Evening Prayer
First Reading Deut 4:7-8
or OT (Yr 1) Judg 6:33 – 7:8, 16-22
or OT (Yr 2) Hag 2:11-23
Second Reading 1 Pet 3:8-12
Friday of Week 11
Morning Prayer
OT (1-Yr) Judg 13:1-25
or First Reading Jer 14:17-21
Second Reading 2 Cor 12:9b-10
Evening Prayer
First Reading Jer 18:1-6
or OT (Yr 1) Judg 8:22-24, 32; 9:1-15, 19-20
or OT (Yr 2) Zech 1:1 – 2:4
Second Reading Jas 1:2-6
Saturday of Week 11
Morning Prayer
OT (1-Yr) Judg 16:4-6, 16-31
or First Reading Wis 9:1-6, 9-11
Second Reading Phil 2:14-15

Sunday 12

Evening Prayer I
First Reading Is 25:6-10a
or OT (Yr 1) Judg 11:1-9, 29-40
or OT (Yr 2) Zech 2:5-17
Second Reading 2 Pet 1:16-21
or Gospel Reading Lk 24:13-35
Morning Prayer
OT (1-Yr) 1 Sam 16:1-13
or First Reading Deut 10:12-15
Second Reading 2 Tim 2:8-13
Evening Prayer II
OT (Yr 1) Judg13:1-25
or OT (Yr 2) Zech 3:1 – 4:14
Second Reading Heb 12:18-24

Monday of Week 12

Morning Prayer
OT (1-Yr) 1 Sam 17:1-10, 32, 38-51a
or 1 Sam 17:1-51a
or First Reading Is 42:10-16
Second Reading Rom 12:1-8
Evening Prayer
First Reading Bar 4:21-22
or OT (Yr 1) Judg 16:4-6, 16-31
or OT (Yr 2) Zech 8:1-17, 20-23
Second Reading 1 Thess 3: (7b-10),
11-13

Tuesday of Week 12

Morning Prayer
First Reading Is 55:1-5
or First Reading Dan 3:3-6, (7-10), 11-
18
or OT (1-Yr)1 Sam 17:57 – 18:9, 20-30
Second Reading 1 Jn 3:17-18
Evening Prayer
First Reading Deut 4:39-40
or OT (Yr 1) 1 Sam 1:1-19
or OT (Yr 2) Ezra 6:1-5, 14-22
Second Reading Col 3:12-16

Wednesday of Week 12

Morning Prayer
OT (1-Yr)1 Sam 19:8-10; 20:1-17
or First Reading Is 61:10 – 62:5
or First Reading Deut 4:39-40
Second Reading Col 3:17, 23-24
Evening Prayer
First Reading Is 55:10-12
or OT (Yr 1) 1 Sam 1:20-28; 2:11-21
or OT (Yr 2) Ezra 7:6-28
Second Reading 1 Jn 2:3-6

Thursday of Week 12

Morning Prayer
OT (1-Yr)1 Sam 21:1-9; 22:1-5
or First Reading Is 66:10-14a
Second Reading Rom 8:18-21
Evening Prayer
First Reading Wis 1:1-5
or OT (Yr 1) 1 Sam 2:22-36
or OT (Yr 2) Ezra 9:1-9, 15; 10:1-5
Second Reading Col 1:21-23

Friday of Week 12

Morning Prayer
OT (1-Yr)1 Sam 25:14-24a, 28-39a
or First Reading Tob 13:8-15
Second Reading Gal 2:19-20
Evening Prayer
First Reading Wis 1:6-11
or OT (Yr 1) 1 Sam 3:1-21
or OT (Yr 2) Neh 1:1 – 2:8
Second Reading Rom 8:1-6

Saturday of Week 12

Morning Prayer
OT (1-Yr) 1 Sam 26:5-25
or First Reading Ezek 36:24-28
Second Reading 2 Pet 3:8b-15a

Sunday 13

Evening Prayer I

First Reading Dan 6:26b-27

or OT (Yr 1) 1 Sam 4:1-18

or OT (Yr 2) Neh 2:9-20

Second Reading Rom 11:33-36

or Gospel Reading Lk 24:35-53

Morning Prayer

OT (1-Yr) 1 Sam 28:3-25

or First Reading Ex 20:1-17

Second Reading Rev 7:9-12

Evening Prayer II

First Reading Is 43:16-21

or OT (Yr 1) 1 Sam 5:6 – 6:5, 10-12, 19-21; 7:1

or 1 Sam 6:1-5, 10-12, 19-21; 7:1

or OT (Yr 2) Neh 3:33 – 4:17

Second Reading 2 Cor 1:3-7

Monday of Week 13

Morning Prayer

OT (1-Yr) 1 Sam 31:1-4; 2 Sam 1:1-16

or First Reading 1 Chron 29:10-13

Second Reading 2 Thess 3:6-13

Evening Prayer

First Reading Jer 17:7-10

or OT (Yr 1) 1 Sam 7:15 – 8:22

or OT (Yr 2) Neh 5:1-19

Second Reading Col 1:9b-14

Tuesday of Week 13

Morning Prayer

OT (1-Yr) 2 Sam 2:1-11; 3:1-5

or First Reading Tob 13:1b-8

Second Reading Rom 13:8-14

Evening Prayer

First Reading Job 5:17-18

or OT (Yr 1) 1 Sam 9:1-6, 14-27; 10:1

or OT (Yr 2) Neh 8:1-18

Second Reading 1 Jn 3:1-3

Wednesday of Week 13

Morning Prayer

OT (1-Yr) 2 Sam 4:2 – 5:7

or First Reading Judith 16:2-3a, 13-15

Second Reading 1 Pet 1:13-16

Evening Prayer

First Reading Tob 4:16-20

or OT (Yr 1) 1 Sam 11:1-15

or OT (Yr 2) Neh 9:1-2, 5-21

Second Reading Jas 1:22-25

Thursday of Week 13

Morning Prayer

OT (1-Yr) 2 Sam 6:1-23

or First Reading Jer 31:10-14

Second Reading Rom 2:14-16

Evening Prayer

First Reading Is 66:1-2

or OT (Yr 1) 1 Sam 12:1-25

or OT (Yr 2) Neh 9:22-36

Second Reading 1 Pet 1:6-9

Friday of Week 13

Morning Prayer

OT (1-Yr) 2 Sam 7:1-25

or First Reading Is 45:15-22

Second Reading Eph 4:29-32

Evening Prayer

First Reading Is 45:22-25

or OT (Yr 1) 1 Sam 15:1-23

or OT (Yr 2) Neh 12:27-47

Second Reading Rom 15:1-3

Saturday of Week 13

Morning Prayer

OT (1-Yr) 2 Sam 11:1-17, 26-27

or First Reading Ex 15:1-4a, 8-13, 17-18

or Ex 15:1-18

Second Reading 2 Pet 1:5b-11

Sunday 14

Evening Prayer I

First Reading Wis 7:27a - 8:1

or OT (Yr 1) 1 Sam 16:1-13

or OT (Yr 2) Is 59:1-14
Second Reading Col 1:3-6a
or Gospel Reading Jn 20:1-18
Morning Prayer
OT (1-Yr) 2 Sam 12:1-25
or First Reading Ezek 36:25-27
Second Reading Rom 5:1-5
Evening Prayer II
First Reading Deut 15:7-8, 10-11
or OT (Yr 1) 1 Sam 17:1-10, 23-26, 40-51
or OT (Yr 2) Prov 1:1-7, 20-33
Second Reading 2 Thess 2:13-14

Monday of Week 14
Morning Prayer
OT (1-Yr) 2 Sam 15:7-14, 24-30; 16:5-13
or First Reading Sir 36:1-7, 13-16
or First Reading Jer 15:15-21
Second Reading Eph 1:3-10
Evening Prayer
First Reading Is 55:1-5
or OT (Yr 1) 1 Sam 17:57 – 18:9, 20-23
or OT (Yr 2) Prov 3:1-20
Second Reading 1 Thess 2:9-13

Tuesday of Week 14
Morning Prayer
OT (1-Yr) 2 Sam 18:6-17, 24 – 19:4
or First Reading Is 38:10-14, 17-20
Second Reading 1 Thess 5:4-11
Evening Prayer
First Reading Is 55:6-9
or OT (Yr 1) 1 Sam 19:8-10; 20:1-17
or OT (Yr 2) Prov 8:1-5, 12-36
Second Reading Rom 3:21-26

Wednesday of Week 14
Morning Prayer
OT (1-Yr) 2 Sam 24:1-4, 10-18, 24b-25
or First Reading 1 Sam 2:1-10
or First Reading Jer 15:15-21

Second Reading Rom 8:35-39
Evening Prayer
First Reading Is 55:10-12
or OT (Yr 1) 1 Sam 21:1-10; 22:1-5
or OT (Yr 2) Prov 9:1-18
Second Reading 1 Pet 5:5b-7

Thursday of Week 14
Morning Prayer
OT (1-Yr) 1 Chron 22:5-19
or First Reading Is 12:1-6
Second Reading Rom 14:17-19
Evening Prayer
First Reading Deut 1:16-18
or OT (Yr 1) 1 Sam 25:14-24, 28-39
or OT (Yr 2) Prov 10:6-32
Second Reading 1 Pet 1:22-25

Friday of Week 14
Morning Prayer
OT (1-Yr)1 Kings 1:11-35; 2:10-12
or First Reading Hab 3:2-19
Second Reading Eph 2:13-16
Evening Prayer
First Reading Is 57:15-19
or OT (Yr 1) 1 Sam 26:5-25
or OT (Yr 2) Prov (15:8-9, 16-17, 25-26, 29, 33); 16:1-9; 17:5
Second Reading 1 Cor 2:7-10a

Saturday of Week 14
Morning Prayer
OT (1-Yr) Sir 47:12-25
or First Reading Deut 32:1-12
Second Reading Rom 12:14-16a

Sunday 15
Evening Prayer I
First Reading Deut 8:5-10
or OT (Yr 1) 1 Sam 28:3-25
or OT (Yr 2) Prov 31:10-31
Second Reading Heb 13:20-21
or Gospel Reading Jn 20:19-31

Morning Prayer
OT (1-Yr) 1 Kings 16:29 – 17:16
or First Reading 1 Kings 2:1-4
Second Reading Rom 8:14-23
Evening Prayer II
First Reading Ezek 37:12b-14
or OT (Yr 1) 1 Sam 3:1:1-4; 2 Sam 1:1-16
or OT (Yr 2) Job 1:1–22
Second Reading 1 Pet 1:3-9
Monday of Week 15
Morning Prayer
OT (1-Yr) 1 Kings 18:16b-40
or First Reading Is 2:2-5
Second Reading Jas 2:12-13
Evening Prayer
First Reading Jer 22:1-4
or OT (Yr 1) 2 Sam 2:1-11; 3:1-5
or OT (Yr 2) Job 2:1-13
Second Reading Jas 4:11-12
Tuesday of Week 15
Morning Prayer
OT (1-Yr) 1 Kings 19:1-9a, 11-21
or First Reading Is 26:1b-4
Second Reading 1 Jn 4:13-17
Evening Prayer
First Reading Is 26:7-12
or OT (Yr 1) 2 Sam 4:2 – 5:7
or OT (Yr 2) Job 3:1-26
Second Reading Rom 12:9-12
Wednesday of Week 15
Morning Prayer
OT (1-Yr) 1 Kings 21:1-21, 27-29
or First Reading Is 33:13-16
Second Reading 1 Cor 13:4-13
Evening Prayer
First Reading Job 1:20-22; 2:9-10
or OT (Yr 1) 2 Sam 6:1-23
or OT (Yr 2) Job 4:1-21
Second Reading Eph 3:14-21

Thursday of Week 15
Morning Prayer
OT (1-Yr) 1 Kings 22:1-9, 15-23, 29, 34-38
or First Reading Is 40:10-17
Second Reading 1 Pet 4:7-11
Evening Prayer
First Reading Deut 4:7-8
or OT (Yr 1) 2 Sam 7:1-25
or OT (Yr 2) Job 5:1-27
Second Reading 1 Pet 3:8-12
Friday of Week 15
Morning Prayer
OT (1-Yr) 2 Chron 20:1-9, 13-24
or First Reading Jer 14:17-21
Second Reading 2 Cor 12:9b-10
Evening Prayer
First Reading Jer 18:1-6
or OT (Yr 1) 2 Sam 11:1–17, 26-27
or OT (Yr 2) Job 6:1-30
Second Reading Jas 1:2-6
Saturday of Week 15
Morning Prayer
OT (1-Yr) 2 Kings 2:1-15
or First Reading Wis 9:1-6, 9-11
Second Reading Phil 2:14-15

Sunday 16
Evening Prayer I
First Reading Is 25:6-10a
or OT (Yr 1) 2 Sam 12:1-25
or OT (Yr 2) Job 7:1-21
Second Reading 2 Pet 1:16-21
or Gospel Reading Jn 21:1-14
Morning Prayer
First Reading Deut 10:12-15
NT (1-Yr) 2 Cor 1:1-14
or Second Reading 2 Tim 2:8-13
Evening Prayer II
First Reading Song 8:5-7

or OT (Yr 1) 2 Sam 15:7-14, 24-30; 16:5-13

or OT (Yr 2) Job 11:1–20

Second Reading 2 Tim 2:8-13

Monday of Week 16

Morning Prayer

First Reading Judith 8:24-27

or First Reading Is 42:10-16

NT (1-Yr) 2 Cor 1:15 – 2:11

or Second Reading Rom 12:1-8

Evening Prayer

First Reading Bar 4:21-22

or OT (Yr 1) 2 Sam 18:6-17, 24 - 19:4

or OT (Yr 2) Job 12:1-25

Second Reading 1 Thess 3:11-13

Tuesday of Week 16

Morning Prayer

First Reading Is 55:1-5

or First Reading Dan 3:3-6, (7-10), 11-18

NT (1-Yr) 2 Cor 2:12 – 3:6

or Second Reading 1 Jn 3:17-18

Evening Prayer

First Reading Deut 4:39-40

or OT (Yr 1) 2 Sam 24:1-4, 10-18, 24-25

or 2 Sam 24:1-25

or OT (Yr 2) Job 13:12 – 14:6

Second Reading Col 3:12-16

Wednesday of Week 16

Morning Prayer

First Reading Deut 4:39-40

or First Reading Is 61:10 – 62:5

or NT (1-Yr) 2 Cor 3:7 – 4:4

or Second Reading Col 3:17, 23-24

Evening Prayer

First Reading Is 55:10-12

or OT (Yr 1) 1 Chron 22:5-19

or OT (Yr 2) Job 18:1-21

Second Reading 1 Jn 2:3-6

Thursday of Week 16

Morning Prayer

First Reading Is 66:10-14a

NT (1-Yr) 2 Cor 4:5-18

or Second Reading Rom 8:18-21

Evening Prayer

First Reading Wis 1:1-5

or OT (Yr 1) 1 Kings 1:11-35; 2:10-12

or OT (Yr 2) Job 19:1-29

Second Reading Col 1:21-23

Friday of Week 16

Morning Prayer

First Reading Tob 13:8-15

NT (1-Yr) 2 Cor 5:1-21

or Second Reading Gal 2:19-20

Evening Prayer

First Reading Wis 1:6-11

or OT (Yr 1) 1 Kings 3:5-28

or OT (Yr 2) Job 22:1-30

Second Reading Rom 8:1-6

Saturday of Week 16

Morning Prayer

First Reading Ezek 36:24-28

NT (1-Yr) 2 Cor 6:1 – 7:1

or Second Reading 2 Pet 3:8b-15a

Sunday 17

Evening Prayer I

First Reading Dan 6:26b-27

or OT (Yr 1) 1 Kings 8:1-21

or OT (Yr 2) Job 23:1 – 24:12

Second Reading 2 Pet 3:8b-15a

or Gospel Reading Mt 28:1-10, 16-20

Morning Prayer

First Reading Ex 20:1-17

NT (1-Yr) 2 Cor 7:2-16

or Second Reading Rev 7:9-12

Evening Prayer II

First Reading Is 43:16-21

or OT (Yr 1) 1 Kings 8:22-34, 54-61

or OT (Yr 2) Job 28:1-28
Second Reading 2 Cor 1:3-7
Monday of Week 17
Morning Prayer
First Reading Deut 28:1-6
NT (1-Yr) 2 Cor 8:1-24
or First Reading 1 Chron 29:10-13
Second Reading 2 Thess 3:6-13
Evening Prayer
First Reading Jer 17:7-10
or OT (Yr 1) 1 Kings 10:1-13
or OT (Yr 2) Job 29:1-10; 30:1, 9-23
Second Reading Col 1:9b-14
Tuesday of Week 17
Morning Prayer
First Reading Prov 3:13-15
or First Reading Tob 13:1b-8
NT (1-Yr) 2 Cor 9:1-15
or Second Reading Rom 13:8-14
Evening Prayer
First Reading Job 5:17-18
or OT (Yr 1) 1 Kings 11:1-4, 26-43
or OT (Yr 2) Job 31:1-8, 13-23, 35-37
Second Reading 1 Jn 3:1-3
Wednesday of Week 17
Morning Prayer
First Reading Judith 16:2-3a, 13-15
NT (1-Yr) 2 Cor 10:1 – 11:6
or Second Reading 1 Pet 1:13-16
Evening Prayer
First Reading Tob 4:16-20
or OT (Yr 1) 1 Kings 12:1-19
or OT (Yr 2) Job 32:1-6; 33:1-22
Second Reading Jas 1:22-25
Thursday of Week 17
Morning Prayer
First Reading Is 66:1-2
or First Reading Jer 31:10-14
NT (1-Yr) 2 Cor 11:7-29
or Second Reading Rom 2:14-16

Evening Prayer
First Reading Amos 4:13; 5:8; 9:6 [4]
or OT (Yr 1) 1 Kings 12:20-33
or OT (Yr 2) Job 38:1-30
Second Reading 1 Pet 1:6-9
Friday of Week 17
Morning Prayer
First Reading Is 45:15-22
NT (1-Yr) 2 Cor 11:30 – 12:13
or Second Reading Eph 4:29-32
Evening Prayer
First Reading Is 45:22-25
or OT (Yr 1) 1 Kings 16:29 – 17.16
or OT (Yr 2) Job 40:1-14; 42:1-6
Second Reading Rom 15:1-3
Saturday of Week 17
Morning Prayer
First Reading Wis 7:27a - 8:1
or First Reading Ex 15:1-4a, 8-13, 17-18
or Ex 15:1-18
NT (1-Yr) 2 Cor 12:14 – 13:13
or Second Reading 2 Pet 1:5b-11

Sunday 18
Evening Prayer I
First Reading Wis 7:27a - 8:1
or OT (Yr 1) 1 Kings 18:16-40
or OT (Yr 2) Job 42:7-14
Second Reading 2 Pet 1:5b-11
or Gospel Reading Mk 16:1-20
Morning Prayer
OT (1-Yr) Amos 1:1 – 2:3
or First Reading Ezek 36:25-27
Second Reading Rom 5:1-5

---

[4] Terce, Sext, and None readings, any of which may be read or all combined to form one reading

Evening Prayer II
First Reading Deut 15:7-8, 10-11
or OT (Yr 1) 1 Kings 19:1-9, 11-21
or OT (Yr 2) Obad 1:1–21
Second Reading 2 Thess 2:13-14
Monday of Week 18
Morning Prayer
OT (1-Yr) Amos   2:4-16
or First Reading Sir 36:1-7, 13-16
or First Reading Jer 15:15-21
Second Reading Eph 1:3-10
Evening Prayer First Reading
Is 55:1-5
or OT (Yr 1) 1 Kings 21:1-21, 27-29
or OT (Yr 2) Joel 1:1, 13-20; 2:1-11
Second Reading 1 Thess 2:9-13
Tuesday of Week 18
Morning Prayer
OT (1-Yr) Amos 7:1-17
or First Reading Is 38:10-14, 17-20
Second Reading 1 Thess 5:4-11
Evening Prayer
First Reading Is 55:6-9
or OT (Yr 1) 1 Kings 22:1-9, 15-23, 29, 34-38
or OT (Yr 2) Joel 2:12-27
Second Reading Rom 3:21-26
Wednesday of Week 18
Morning Prayer
OT (1-Yr) Amos 9:1-15
or First Reading 1 Sam 2:1-10
Second Reading Rom 8:35-39
Evening Prayer
First Reading Is 55:10-12
or OT (Yr 1) 2 Chron 20:1-9, 13-24
or OT (Yr 2) Joel 3:1 – 4:8
Second Reading 1 Pet 5:5b-7
Thursday of Week 18
Morning Prayer
OT (1-Yr) Hos 1:1-9; 3:1-5
or First Reading Is 12:1-6

Second Reading Rom 14:17-19

Evening Prayer
First Reading Deut 1:16-18
or OT (Yr 1) 2 Kings 2:1-15
or OT (Yr 2) Joel 4:9-21
Second Reading 1 Pet 1:22-25
Friday of Week 18
Morning Prayer
OT (1-Yr) Hos 2:4a, 10-25
or First Reading Hab 3:2-19
Second Reading Eph 2:13-16
Evening Prayer
First Reading Is 57:15-19
or OT (Yr 1) 2 Kings 3:5-27
or OT (Yr 2) Mal 1:1-14; 2:13-16
Second Reading 1 Cor 2:7-10a
Saturday of Week 18
Morning Prayer
OT (1-Yr) Hos 5:15b – 7:2
or First Reading Deut 32:1-12
Second Reading Rom 12:14-16a

Sunday 19
Evening Prayer I
First Reading Deut 8:5-10
or OT (Yr 1) 2 Kings 4:8-37
or OT (Yr 2) Mal 3:1-24
Second Reading Heb 13:20-21
or Gospel Reading Lk 24:1-12
Morning Prayer
OT (1-Yr) Hos 11:1-11
or First Reading 1 Kings 2:1-4
Second Reading Rom 8:14-23
Evening Prayer II
First Reading Ezek 37:12b-14
or OT (Yr 1) 2 Kings 4:38-44; 6:1-7
or OT (Yr 2) Jon 1:1 - 2:1, 11
Second Reading 1 Pet 1:3-9

Monday of Week 19
Morning Prayer
OT (1-Yr)Hos 14:2-10
or First Reading Is 2:2-5
Second Reading Jas 2:12-13
Evening Prayer
First Reading Jer 22:1-4
or OT (Yr 1) 2 Kings 5:1-19
or OT (Yr 2) Jon 3:1 – 4:11
Second Reading Jas 4:11-12
Tuesday of Week 19
Morning Prayer
OT (1-Yr)Mic 3:1-12
or First Reading Is 26:1b-4
Second Reading 1 Jn 4:13-17
Evening Prayer
First Reading Is 26:7-12
or OT (Yr 1) 2 Kings 6:8-23
or OT (Yr 2) Zech 9:1 – 10:2
Second Reading Rom 12:9-12
Wednesday of Week 19
Morning Prayer
OT (1-Yr) Mic 4:1-7
or First Reading Is 33:13-16
Second Reading 1 Cor 13:4-13
Evening Prayer
First Reading Job 1:20-22; 2:9-10
or OT (Yr 1) 2 Kings 6:24-25, 32-33;
7:1-16
or OT (Yr 2) Zech 10:3 – 11:3
Second Reading Eph 3:14-21
Thursday of Week 19
Morning Prayer
OT (1-Yr) Mic 4:14 – 5:7
or First Reading Is 40:10-17
Second Reading 1 Pet 4:7-11
Evening Prayer
First Reading Deut 4:7-8
or OT (Yr 1) 2 Kings 9:1-16, 22-27
or OT (Yr 2) Zech 11:4 – 12:8

Second Reading 1 Pet 3:8-12
Friday of Week 19
Morning Prayer
OT (1-Yr) Mic 6:1-4, 6-15
or First Reading Jer 14:17-21
Second Reading 2 Cor 12:9b-10
Evening Prayer
First Reading Jer 18:1-6
or OT (Yr 1) 2 Kings 11:1-21
or OT (Yr 2) Zech 12:9-12; 13:1-9
Second Reading Jas 1:2-6
Saturday of Week 19
Morning Prayer
OT (1-Yr) Mic 7:7-20
or First Reading Wis 9:1-6, 9-11
Second Reading Phil 2:14-15

Sunday 20
Evening Prayer I
First Reading Is 25:6-10a
or OT (Yr 1) 2 Kings 13:10-25
or OT (Yr 2) Zech 14:1-21
Second Reading 2 Pet 1:16-21
or Gospel Reading Lk 24:13-35
Morning Prayer
OT (1-Yr) Is 6:1-13
or First Reading Deut 10:12-15
Second Reading 2 Tim 2:8-13
Evening Prayer II
First Reading Deut 10:12-15
or OT (Yr 2) Eccles 1:1-18
Second Reading Heb 12:18-24
or NT (Yr 1) Eph 1:1-14
Monday of Week 20
Morning Prayer
OT (1-Yr) Is 3:1-15
or First Reading Is 42:10-16
Second Reading Rom 12:1-8
Evening Prayer
First Reading Bar 4:21-22

or First Reading Is 42:10-16
or OT (Yr 2) Eccles 2:1-3, 12-26
Second Reading 1 Thess 3: (7b-10),
11-13
or NT (Yr 1) Eph 1:15-23
Tuesday of Week 20
Morning Prayer
OT (1-Yr) Is 7:1-17
or First Reading Is 55:1-5
or First Reading Dan 3:3-6, (7-10), 11-
18
Second Reading 1 Jn 3:17-18
Evening Prayer
First Reading Deut 4:39-40
or OT (Yr 2) Eccles 3:1-22
Second Reading Col 3:12-16
or NT (Yr 1) Eph 2:1-10
Wednesday of Week 20
Morning Prayer
OT (1-Yr) Is 9:8 – 10:4
or First Reading Deut 4:39-40
Second Reading Col 3:17, 23-24
Evening Prayer
First Reading Is 55:10-12
or OT (Yr 2) Eccles 5:9 – 6:8
Second Reading 1 Jn 2:3-6
or NT (Yr 1) Eph 2:11-22
Thursday of Week 20
Morning Prayer
OT (1-Yr) Is 11:1-16
or First Reading Is 66:10–14a
Second Reading Rom 8:18-21
Evening Prayer
First Reading Wis 1:1-5
or OT (Yr 2) Eccles 7:1-29
Second Reading Col 1:21-23
or NT (Yr 1) Eph 3:1-13
Friday of Week 20
Morning Prayer
OT (1-Yr) Is 30:1-18

or First Reading Tob 13:8-15
Second Reading Gal 2:19-20
Evening Prayer
First Reading Wis 1:6-11
or OT (Yr 2) Eccles 8:5 – 9:10
Second Reading Rom 8:1-6
or NT (Yr 1) Eph 3:14-21
Saturday of Week 20
Morning Prayer
OT (1-Yr) Is 37:21-35
or First Reading Ezek 36:24-28
Second Reading 2 Pet 3:8b-15a

Sunday 21
Evening Prayer I
First Reading Dan 6:26b-27
or OT (Yr 2) Eccles 11:7 – 12:14
Second Reading Rom 11:33-36
or NT (Yr 1) Eph 4:1-16
or Gospel Reading Lk 24:35-53
Morning Prayer
OT (1-Yr)Zeph 1:1-7, 14 – 2:3
or First Reading Ex 20:1-17
Second Reading Rev 7:9-12
Evening Prayer II
First Reading Is 43:16-21
Second Reading 2 Cor 1:3-7
or NT (Yr 1) Eph 4:17-24
or NT (Yr 2) Tit 1:1-16
Monday of Week 21
Morning Prayer
OT (1-Yr) Zeph 3:8-20
or First Reading 1 Chron 29:10-13
Second Reading 2 Thess 3:6-13
Evening Prayer
First Reading Jer 17:7-10
or First Reading Deut 28:1-6
Second Reading Col 1:9b-14
or NT (Yr 1)Eph 4:25 – 5:7
or NT (Yr 2) Tit 2:1 – 3:2

Tuesday of Week 21
Morning Prayer
OT (1-Yr) Jer 1:1-19
or First Reading Tob 13:1b-8
Second Reading Rom 13:8-14
Evening Prayer
First Reading Job 5:17-18
Second Reading 1 Jn 3:1-3
or NT (Yr 1) Eph 5:8-21
or NT (Yr 2) Tit 3:1-15
Wednesday of Week 21
Morning Prayer
OT (1-Yr) Jer 2:1-13, 20-25
or First Reading Judith 16:2-3a, 13-15
Second Reading 1 Pet 1:13-16
Evening Prayer
First Reading Tob 4:16-20
Second Reading Jas 1:22-25
or NT (Yr 1) Eph 5:22-33
or NT (Yr 2) 1 Tim 1-20
Thursday of Week 21
Morning Prayer
OT (1-Yr) Jer 3:1-5, 19 – 4:4
or First Reading Jer 31:10-14
Second Reading Rom 2:14-16
Evening Prayer
First Reading Is 66:1-2
Second Reading 1 Pet 1:6-9
or NT (Yr 1) Eph 6:1-9
or NT (Yr 2) 1 Tim 2:1-15
Friday of Week 21
Morning Prayer
OT (1-Yr) Jer 4:5-8, 13-28
or First Reading Is 45:15-22
Second Reading Eph 4:29-32
Evening Prayer
First Reading Is 45:22-25
Second Reading Rom 15:1-3
or NT (Yr 1)Eph 6:10-24

or NT (Yr 2) 1 Tim 3:1-16
Saturday of Week 21
Morning Prayer
OT (1-Yr) Jer 7:1-20
or First Reading Ex 15:1-4a, 8-13, 17-18
or Ex 15:1-18
Second Reading 2 Pet 1:5b-11

Sunday 22
Evening Prayer I
First Reading Wis 7:27a - 8:1
Second Reading Col 1:3-6a
or NT (Yr 1) Philem 13:1-25
or NT (Yr 2)1 Tim 4:1 – 5:2
or Gospel Reading Jn 20:1-18
Morning Prayer
OT (1-Yr) Jer 11:18-20; 12:1-13
or First Reading Ezek 36:25-27
Second Reading Rom 5:1-5
Evening Prayer II
First Reading Deut 15:7-8, 10-11
or OT (Yr 1) 2 Kings 14:1-27
Second Reading 2 Thess 2:13-14
or NT (Yr 2) 1 Tim 5:3-25
Monday of Week 22
Morning Prayer
OT (1-Yr) Jer 19:1-5, 10 – 20:6
or Jer 19: 1 – 20:6
or First Reading Jer 15:15-21
or First Reading Sir 36:1-7, 13-16
Second Reading Eph 1:3-10
Evening Prayer
First Reading Is 55:1-5
or OT (Yr 1) Amos 1:1–3
Second Reading 1 Thess 2:9-13
or NT (Yr 2) 1 Tim 6:1-10
Tuesday of Week 22
Morning Prayer
OT (1-Yr) Jer 20:7-18

or First Reading Is 38:10-14, 17-20
Second Reading 1 Thess 5:4-11
Evening Prayer
First Reading Is 55:6-9
or OT (Yr 1) Amos 2:4-16
Second Reading Rom 3:21-26
or NT (Yr 2) 1 Tim 6:11-21
Wednesday of Week 22
Morning Prayer
OT (1-Yr) Jer 26:1-15
or First Reading 1 Sam 2:1-10
Second Reading Rom 8:35-39
Evening Prayer
First Reading Is 55:10-12
or OT (Yr 1) Amos 3:1-15
Second Reading 1 Pet 5:5b-7
or NT (Yr 2) 2 Tim 1:1-18
Thursday of Week 22
Morning Prayer
OT (1-Yr) Jer 29:1-14
or First Reading Is 12:1-6
Second Reading Rom 14:17-19
Evening Prayer
First Reading Deut 1:16-18
or OT (Yr 1) Amos 4:1-13
Second Reading 1 Pet 1:22-25
or NT (Yr 2) 2 Tim 2:1-21
Friday of Week 22
Morning Prayer
OT (1-Yr) Jer 30:18 – 31:9
or First Reading Hab 3:2-19
Second Reading Eph 2:13-16
Evening Prayer
First Reading Is 57:15-19
or OT (Yr 1) Amos 5:1-17
Second Reading 1 Cor 2:7-10a
or NT (Yr 2) 2 Tim 2:22 – 3:17
Saturday of Week 22
Morning Prayer
OT (1-Yr) Jer 31:15-22, 27-34

or First Reading Deut 32:1-12
Second Reading Rom 12:14-16a

Sunday 23
Evening Prayer I
First Reading Deut 8:5-10
or OT (Yr 1) Amos 5:18 – 6:15
Second Reading Heb 13:20-21
or NT (Yr 2) 2 Tim 4:1-22
or Second Reading Heb 13:20-21
or Gospel Reading Jn 20:19-31
Morning Prayer
OT (1-Yr) Jer 37:21; 38:14-28
or First Reading 1 Kings 2:1-4
Second Reading Rom 8:14-23
Evening Prayer
First Reading Ezek 37:12b-14
or OT (Yr 1) Amos 7:1-17
Second Reading 1 Pet 1:3-9
or NT (Yr 2) 2 Pet 1:1-11
Monday of Week 23
Morning Prayer
OT (1-Yr) Jer 42:1-16; 43:4-7
or First Reading Is 2:2-5
Second Reading Jas 2:12-13
Evening Prayer
First Reading Jer 22:1-4
or OT (Yr 1) Amos 8:1-14
Second Reading Jas 4:11-12
or NT (Yr 2) 2 Pet 1: (5-7), 12-21
Tuesday of Week 23
Morning Prayer
OT (1-Yr) Hab 1:1-2, 4
or First Reading Is 26:1b-4
Second Reading 1 Jn 4:13-17
Evening Prayer
First Reading Is 26:7-12
or OT (Yr 1) Amos 9:1-15
Second Reading Rom 12:9-12
or NT (Yr 2) 2 Pet 2:1-9

Wednesday of Week 23
Morning Prayer
OT (1-Yr) Hab 2:5-20
or First Reading Is 33:13-16
Second Reading 1 Cor 13:4-13
Evening Prayer
First Reading Job 1:20-22; 2:9-10
or OT (Yr 1) Hos 1:1-9; 3:1-5
Second Reading Eph 3:14-21
or NT (Yr 2) 2 Pet 2:9-22
Thursday of Week 23
Morning Prayer
OT (1-Yr) Lam 1:1-12, 18-20
or First Reading Is 40:10-17
Second Reading 1 Pet 4:7-11
Evening Prayer
First Reading Deut 4:7-8
or OT (Yr 1) Hos 2:4, 8-25
Second Reading 1 Pet 3:8-12
or NT (Yr 2) 2 Pet 3:1-10
Friday of Week 23
Morning Prayer
OT (1-Yr)Lam 3:1-33
or First Reading Jer 14:17-21
Second Reading 2 Cor 12:9b-10
Evening Prayer
First Reading Jer 18:1-6
or OT (Yr 1) Hos 4:1–10; 5:1-7
Second Reading Jas 1:2-6
or NT (Yr 2) 2 Pet 3:11-18
Saturday of Week 23
Morning Prayer
OT (1-Yr) Lam 5:1-22
or First Reading Wis 9:1-6, 9-11
Second Reading Phil 2:14-15

Sunday 24
Evening Prayer I
First Reading Is 25:6-10a

or OT (Yr 1) Hos 5:15 – 7:2
Second Reading 2 Pet 1:16-21
or NT (Yr 2) Jude1-8, 12-13, 17-25
or Jude 1-25
or Gospel Reading Jn 21:1-14
Morning Prayer
OT (1-Yr) Ezek 1:3-14, 22 – 2:1a
or First Reading Deut 10:12-15
Second Reading 2 Tim 2:8-13
Evening Prayer II
First Reading Deut 10:12-15
or OT (Yr 1) Hos 8:1-14
or OT (Yr 2) Esther 1:1-3, 9-13, 15-16, 19; 2:5-10, 16-17
Second Reading Heb 12:18-24
Monday of Week 24
Morning Prayer
OT (1-Yr) Ezek 2:8 – 3:11, 16-21
or Ezek 2:8 – 3:21
or First Reading Is 42:10-16
Second Reading Rom 12:1-8
Evening Prayer
First Reading Bar 4:21-22
or First Reading Is 42:10-16
or OT (Yr 1) Hos 9:1-14
or OT (Yr 2) Esther 3:1-15
Second Reading 1 Thess 3: (7b-10), 11-13
Tuesday of Week 24
Morning Prayer
OT (1-Yr) Ezek 8:1-6, 16 – 9:11
or First Reading Dan 3:3-6, (7-10), 11-18
or First Reading Is 55:1-5
Second Reading 1 Jn 3:17-18
Evening Prayer
First Reading Deut 4:39-40
or OT (Yr 1) Hos 10:1-15
or OT (Yr 2) Esther 4:1-17
Second Reading Col 3:12-16

Wednesday of Week 24
Morning Prayer
OT (1-Yr) Ezek 10:18-22; 11:14-25
or First Reading Deut 4:39-40
or First Reading Is 61:10 – 62:5
Second Reading Col 3:17, 23-24
Evening Prayer
First Reading Is 55:10-12
or OT (Yr 1) Hos 11:1-9
or OT (Yr 2) Esther 4:17k-17z
Second Reading 1 Jn 2:3-6
Thursday of Week 24
Morning Prayer
OT (1-Yr) Ezek 12:1-16
or First Reading Is 66:10–14a
Second Reading Rom 8:18-21
Evening Prayer
First Reading Wis 1:1-5
or OT (Yr 1) Hos 13:1 – 14:1
or OT (Yr 2) Esther 5:1-5; 7:2-10
Second Reading Col 1:21-23
Friday of Week 24
Morning Prayer
OT (1-Yr) Ezek 16:3, 5b, 6-7a, 8-15,
35, 37a, 40-43, 59-63
or OT (1-Yr [*morning*]) Ezek 16:3-15,
35-43 [5]
or First Reading Tob 13:8-15
Second Reading Gal 2:19-20
Evening Prayer
OT (1-Yr [*evening*])   Ezek 16:59-63 [6]
or First Reading Wis 1:6-11
or OT (Yr 1) Hos 14:2-10

---

[5] The first section of the long reading: both sections should be read within the day.
[6] The second section of the long reading: both sections should be read within the day.

or OT (Yr 2) Bar 1:14 – 2:5; 3:1-8
Second Reading Rom 8:1-6
Saturday of Week 24
Morning Prayer
OT (1-Yr) Ezek 18:1-13, 20-32
or First Reading Ezek 36:24-28
Second Reading 2 Pet 3:8b-15a

Sunday 25
Evening Prayer I
First Reading Dan 6:26b-27
or OT (Yr 1) 2 Kings 15:1-5, 32-35;
16:1-8
or OT (Yr 2) Bar 3:9-15, 24-38; 4:1-4
Second Reading Rom 11:33-36
or Gospel Reading Mt 28:1-10, 16-20
Morning Prayer
OT (1-Yr) Ezek 24:15-27
or First Reading Ex 20:1-17
Second Reading Rev 7:9-12
Evening Prayer
First Reading Is 43:16-21
or OT (Yr 1) Is 6:1-13
or OT (Yr 2) Tob 1:1 – 2:1
Second Reading 2 Cor 1:3-7
Monday of Week 25
Morning Prayer
OT (1-Yr) Ezek 34:1-6, 11-16, 23-31
or First Reading 1 Chron 29:10-13
Second Reading 2 Thess 3:6-13
Evening Prayer
First Reading Jer 17:7-10
or OT (Yr 1) Is 3:1-15
or OT (Yr 2) Tob 2:1 – 3:6
Second Reading Col 1:9b-14
Tuesday of Week 25
Morning Prayer
OT (1-Yr) Ezek 36:16-36
or First Reading Tob 13:1b-8
Second Reading Rom 13:8-14

Evening Prayer
First Reading Job 5:17-18
or OT (Yr 1) Is 5:8-13, 17-24
or OT (Yr 2) Tob 3:7-17
Second Reading 1 Jn 3:1-3
Wednesday of Week 25
Morning Prayer
OT (1-Yr) Ezek 37:1-14
or First Reading Judith 16:2-3a, 13-15
Second Reading 1 Pet 1:13-16
Evening Prayer
First Reading Tob 4:16-20
or OT (Yr 1) Is 7:1–17
or OT (Yr 2) Tob 4:1–6, 19-21; 5:1-18
Second Reading Jas 1:22-25
Thursday of Week 25
Morning Prayer
OT (1-Yr) Ezek 37:15-28
or First Reading Jer 31:10-14
Second Reading Rom 2:14-16
Evening Prayer
First Reading Is 66:1-2
or OT (Yr 1) Is 9:7 – 10:4
or OT (Yr 2) Tob 6:1-19
Second Reading 1 Pet 1:6-9
Friday of Week 25
Morning Prayer
OT (1-Yr) Ezek 40:1-4; 43:1-12; 44:6-9
or First Reading Is 45:15-22
Second Reading Eph 4:29-32
Evening Prayer
First Reading Is 45:22-25
or OT (Yr 1) Is 28:1-6, 14-22
or OT (Yr 2) Tob 7:1, 8-17; 8:4-16
Second Reading Rom 15:1-3
Saturday of Week 25
Morning Prayer
OT (1-Yr) Ezek 47:1-12
or First Reading Ex 15:1-4a, 8-13, 17-18

or Ex 15:1-18
Second Reading 2 Pet 1:5b-11

Sunday 26
Evening Prayer I
First Reading Wis 7:27a - 8:1
or OT (Yr 1) Mic 1:1-9; 2:1-11
or OT (Yr 2) Tob 10:8 – 11:17
Second Reading Col 1:3-6a
or Gospel Reading Mk 16:1-20
Morning Prayer
First Reading Ezek 36:25-27
NT (1-Yr) Phil 1:1-11
or Second Reading Rom 5:1-5
Evening Prayer II
First Reading Deut 15:7-8, 10-11
or OT (Yr 1) Mic 3:1-12
or OT (Yr 2) Judith 2:1-6; 3:6; 4:1-2, 9-15
Second Reading 2 Thess 2:13-14
Monday of Week 26
Morning Prayer
First Reading Sir 36:1-7, 13-16
or First Reading Jer 15:15-21
NT (1-Yr) Phil 1:12-26
or Second Reading Eph 1:3-10
Evening Prayer
First Reading Is 55:1-5
or OT (Yr 1) Mic 6:1–15
or OT (Yr 2) Judith 5:1-21
Second Reading 1 Thess 2:9-13
Tuesday of Week 26
Morning Prayer
First Reading Is 38:10-14, 17-20
NT (1-Yr) Phil 1:27 – 2:11
or Second Reading 1 Thess 5:4-11
Evening Prayer
First Reading Is 55:6-9
or OT (Yr 1) 2 Kings 17:1-18

or OT (Yr 2) Judith 6:1-10, 14-16; 7:1, 4-5
Second Reading Rom 3:21-26

Wednesday of Week 26
Morning Prayer
First Reading 1 Sam 2:1-10
NT (1-Yr) Phil 2:12-30
or Second Reading Rom 8:35-39
Evening Prayer
First Reading Is 55:10-12
or OT (Yr 1) 2 Kings 17:24-41
or OT (Yr 2) Judith 8:1, 10-14, 28-33; 9:1-6, 14
Second Reading 1 Pet 5:5b-7

Thursday of Week 26
Morning Prayer
First Reading Wis 1:12-15
or First Reading Is 12:1-6
NT (1-Yr) Phil 3:1-16
or Second Reading Rom 14:17-19
Evening Prayer
First Reading Deut 1:16-18
or OT (Yr 1) 2 Chron 29:1-2; 30:1-16
or OT (Yr 2) Judith 10:1-5, 11-17; 11:1-8
Second Reading 1 Pet 1:22-25

Friday of Week 26
Morning Prayer
First Reading Is 57:15-19
or First Reading Hab 3:2-19
NT (1-Yr) Phil 3:17 – 4:9
or Second Reading Eph 2:13-16
Evening Prayer
First Reading Is 57:15-19
or OT (Yr 1) Is 20:1-6
or OT (Yr 2) Judith 12:1 – 13:3
Second Reading Eph 2:13-16

Saturday of Week 26
Morning Prayer
First Reading Deut 32:1-12

NT (1-Yr) Phil 4:10-23
or Second Reading Rom 12:14-16a

Evening Prayer I
First Reading Deut 8:5-10
or OT (Yr 1) 2 Kings 20:1-19
or OT (Yr 2) Judith 13:4-20
Second Reading Rom 12:14-16a
or Gospel Reading Lk 24:1-12
Morning Prayer
First Reading 1 Kings 2:1-4
NT (1-Yr) 1 Tim 1:1-20
or Second Reading Rom 8:9-11
Evening Prayer II
First Reading Ezek 37:12b-14
or OT (Yr 1) Is 22:1-14
or OT (Yr 2) Sir 1:1–18
Second Reading Rom 8:14-23

Monday of Week 27
Morning Prayer
First Reading Deut 28:1-6
or First Reading Is 2:2-5
NT (1-Yr) 1 Tim 2:1-15
or Second Reading Jas 2:12-13
Evening Prayer
First Reading Jer 22:1-4
or OT (Yr 1) Is 30:1-18
or OT (Yr 2) Sir 2:1-18
Second Reading Jas 2:12-13

Tuesday of Week 27
Morning Prayer
First Reading Is 26:1b-4
NT (1-Yr) 1 Tim 3:1-16
or Second Reading 1 Jn 4:13-17
Evening Prayer
First Reading Is 26:7-12
or OT (Yr 1) 2 Kings 18:17-36
or OT (Yr 2) Sir 3:1-26
Second Reading 1 Jn 4:13-17

Wednesday of Week 27

Morning Prayer
First Reading Is 33:13-16
NT (1-Yr) 1 Tim 4:1 – 5:2
or Second Reading1 Cor 13:4-13
Evening Prayer
First Reading Job 1:20-22; 2:9-10
or OT (Yr 1) 2 Kings 18:37 – 19:19, 35-37
or OT (Yr 2) Sir 3:17 – 4:10
Second Reading Eph 3:14-21
Thursday of Week 27
Morning Prayer
First Reading Is 66:1-2
or First Reading Is 40:10-17
NT (1-Yr) 1 Tim 5:3-25
or Second Reading 1 Pet 4:7-11
Evening Prayer
First Reading Deut 4:7-8
or OT (Yr 1) Is 37:21-35
or OT (Yr 2) Sir 5:1 – 6:4
Second Reading 1 Pet 4:7-11
Friday of Week 27
Morning Prayer
First Reading 1 Sam 15:22
or First Reading Jer 14:17-21
NT (1-Yr) 1 Tim 6:1-10
or Second Reading 2 Cor 12:9b-10
Evening Prayer
First Reading Jer 18:1-6
or OT (Yr 1) 2 Kings 21:1–18, 23-26, 22:1
or OT (Yr 2) Sir 6:5-37
Second Reading Jas 1:2-6
Saturday of Week 27
Morning Prayer
First Reading Wis 9:1-6, 9-11
NT (1-Yr)1 Tim 6:11-21
or Second Reading Phil 2:14-15

Sunday 28
Evening Prayer I
First Reading Is 25:6-10a[7]
or OT (Yr 1) Zeph 1:2-7, 14-18; 2:1-3
or OT (Yr 2) Sir 7:22-36
Second Reading 2 Pet 1:16-21
or Gospel Reading Lk 24:13-35
Morning Prayer
OT (1-Yr) Hag 1:1 – 2:9
or First Reading Deut 10:12-15
Second Reading 2 Tim 2:8-13
Evening Prayer II
First Reading Song 8:5-7
or OT (Yr 1) Zeph 3:8-20
or OT (Yr 2) Sir 10:6-18
Second Reading Heb 12:18-24
Monday of Week 28
Morning Prayer
OT (1-Yr) Hag 2:10-23
or First Reading Is 42:10-16
Second Reading Rom 12:1-8
Evening Prayer
First Reading Bar 4:21-24
or OT (Yr 1) Jer 1:1-19
or OT (Yr 2) Sir 11:12-28
Second Reading 1 Thess 3: (7b-10), 11-13
Tuesday of Week 28
Morning Prayer
OT (1-Yr) Zech 1:1 – 2:4
or First Reading Dan 3:3-6, (7-10), 11-18
or First Reading Is 55:1-5
Second Reading 1 Jn 3:17-18

Evening Prayer
First Reading Deut 30:11-14

---

[7] Also the first reading at Mass on Sunday 28, Year A

897

or OT (Yr 1) Jer 2:1-13, 20-25
or OT (Yr 2) Sir 14:20 – 15:10
Second Reading Col 3:12-16
Wednesday of Week 28
Morning Prayer
OT (1-Yr) Zech 3:1- 4:14
or First Reading Deut 4:39-40
or First Reading Is 61:10 – 62:5
Second Reading Col 3:17, 23-24
Evening Prayer
First Reading Is 55:10-12
or OT (Yr 1) Jer 3:1-5, 9-25; 4:1-4
or OT (Yr 2) Sir 15:11-20
Second Reading 1 Jn 2:3-6
Thursday of Week 28
Morning Prayer
OT (1-Yr) Zech 8:1-17, 20-23
or First Reading Is 66:10–14a
Second Reading Rom 8:18-21
Evening Prayer
First Reading Wis 1:1-5
or OT (Yr 1) Jer 4:5-8, 13-28
or OT (Yr 2) Sir 16:24 – 17:12
Second Reading Col 1:21-23
Friday of Week 28
Morning Prayer
OT (1-Yr) Mal 1:1-14: 2:13-16
or First Reading Tob 13:8-15
Second Reading Gal 2:19-20
Evening Prayer
First Reading Wis 1:6-11
or OT (Yr 1) Jer 7:1-20
or OT (Yr 2) Sir 17:13-27
Second Reading Rom 8:1-6
Saturday of Week 28
Morning Prayer
OT (1-Yr) Mal 3:1-24
or First Reading Ezek 36:24-28
Second Reading 2 Pet 3:8b-15a

Sunday 29
Evening Prayer I
First Reading Dan 6:26b-27
or OT (Yr 1) Jer 9:1-11, 16-21
or OT (Yr 2) Sir 24:1-22
Second Reading Rom 11:33-36
or Gospel Reading Lk 24:35-53
Morning Prayer
OT (1-Yr) Esther 1:1-3, 9-14, 16, 19;
2:5-10, 16-17
or First Reading Ex 20:1-17
Second Reading Rev 7:9-12
Evening Prayer II
First Reading Is 43:16-21
or OT (Yr 1) 2 Kings 22:8, 10 - 23:4,
21-23
or OT (Yr 2) Sir 26:1-4, 9-18
Second Reading 2 Cor 1:3-7
Monday of Week 29
Morning Prayer
OT (1-Yr) Esther 3:1-15
or First Reading 1 Chron 29:10-13
Second Reading 2 Thess 3:6-13
Evening Prayer
First Reading Jer 17:7-10
or OT (Yr 1) Nahum 1:1-8; 3:1-7, 12-
15
or OT (Yr 2) Sir 27:22 – 28:7
Second Reading Col 1:9b-14
Tuesday of Week 29
Morning Prayer
OT (1-Yr) Esther 4:1-17
or First Reading Tob 13:1b-8
Second Reading Rom 13:8-14
Evening Prayer
First Reading Job 5:17-18
or OT (Yr 1) 2 Chron 35:20 – 36:12
or OT (Yr 2) Sir 29:1-13; 31:1-4
Second Reading 1 Jn 3:1-3

Wednesday of Week 29
Morning Prayer
OT (1-Yr) Esther 4:17k-17z
or First Reading Judith 16:2-3a, 13-15
Second Reading 1 Pet 1:13-16
Evening Prayer
First Reading Tob 4:16-20
or OT (Yr 1) Hab 1:1-2, 4
or OT (Yr 2) Sir 35:1-18
Second Reading Jas 1:22-25
Thursday of Week 29
Morning Prayer
OT (1-Yr) Esther 5:1-8; 7:1-10
or First Reading Jer 31:10-14
Second Reading Rom 2:14-16
Evening Prayer
First Reading Is 66:1-2
or OT (Yr 1) Hab 2:5-20
or OT (Yr 2) Sir 38:24 – 39:11
Second Reading 1 Pet 1:6-9
Friday of Week 29
Morning Prayer
OT (1-Yr) Bar 1:14 – 2:5; 3:1-8
or First Reading Is 45:15-22
Second Reading Eph 4:29-32
Evening Prayer
First Reading Is 45:22-25
or OT (Yr 1) Jer 22:10-30
or OT (Yr 2) Sir 42:15-25; 43:29-33
Second Reading Rom 15:1-3
Saturday of Week 29
Morning Prayer
OT (1-Yr) Bar 3:9-15, 24 – 4:4
or First Reading Ex 15:1-4a, 8-13, 17-18
or Ex 15:1-18
Second Reading 2 Pet 1:5b-11

Sunday 30
Evening Prayer I
First Reading Wis 7:27a - 8:1
or OT (Yr 1) Jer 19:1-5, 10-15; 20:1-6
or OT (Yr 2) Sir 51:1-12
Second Reading Col 1:3-6a
or Gospel Reading Jn 20:1-18
Morning Prayer
OT (1-Yr) Wis 1:1-15
or First Reading Ezek 36:25-27
Second Reading Rom 5:1-5
Evening Prayer II
First Reading Deut 15:7-8, 10-11
or OT (Yr 1) Jer 23:9-17, 21-29
or OT (Yr 2) Wis 1:1-15
Second Reading 2 Thess 2:13-14
Monday of Week 30
Morning Prayer
OT (1-Yr)Wis 1:16 – 2:1a, 10-25
or First Reading Sir 36:1-7, 13-16
or First Reading Jer 15:15-21
Second Reading Eph 1:3-10
Evening Prayer
First Reading Is 55:1-5
or OT (Yr 1) Jer 25:15-17, 27-38
or OT (Yr 2) Wis 1:16 – 2:1a, 10-25
Second Reading 1 Thess 2:9-13
Tuesday of Week 30
Morning Prayer
OT (1-Yr)Wis 3:1-19
or First Reading Is 38:10-14, 17-20
Second Reading 1 Thess 5:4-11
Evening Prayer
First Reading Is 55:6-9
or OT (Yr 1) Jer 36:1-10, 21-32
or OT (Yr 2) Wis 3:1-19
Second Reading Rom 3:21-26

Wednesday of Week 30
Morning Prayer
OT (1-Yr)Wis 6:1-27
or First Reading 1 Sam 2:1-10
Second Reading Rom 8:35-39
Evening Prayer
First Reading Is 55:10-12
or OT (Yr 1) Jer 24:1-10
or OT (Yr 2) Wis 4:1-20
Second Reading 1 Pet 5:5b-7
Thursday of Week 30
Morning Prayer
OT (1-Yr) Wis 7:15-30
or First Reading Is 12:1-6
Second Reading Rom 14:17-19
Evening Prayer
First Reading Deut 1:16-18
or OT (Yr 1) Jer 27:1-15
or OT (Yr 2) Wis 5:1-23
Second Reading 1 Pet 1:22-25
Friday of Week 30
Morning Prayer
OT (1-Yr) Wis 8:1-21b
or First Reading Hab 3:2-19
Second Reading Eph 2:13-16
Evening Prayer
First Reading Is 57:15-19
or OT (Yr 1) Jer 28:1-17
or OT (Yr 2) Wis 6:1-27
Second Reading 1 Cor 2:7-10a
Saturday of Week 30
Morning Prayer
OT (1-Yr) Wis 11:21b – 12:2, 11b-19
or First Reading Deut 32:1-12
Second Reading Rom 12:14-16a

Sunday 31
Evening Prayer I
First Reading Deut 8:5-10
or OT (Yr 1) Jer 29:1-14

or OT (Yr 2) Wis 7:15-30
Second Reading Heb 13:20-21
or Gospel Reading Jn 20:19-31
Morning Prayer
OT (1-Yr) 1 Mac 1:1-24
or First Reading 1 Kings 2:1-4
Second Reading Rom 8:14-23
Evening Prayer II
First Reading Ezek 37:12b-14
or OT (Yr 1) 2 Kings 24:20; 25:1-13, 18-21
or OT (Yr 2) Wis 8:1-21
Second Reading 1 Pet 1:3-9
Monday of Week 31
Morning Prayer
OT (1-Yr) 1 Mac 1:41-64
or First Reading Is 2:2-5
First Reading1 Chron 29:10-13
Second Reading Jas 2:12-13
Evening Prayer
First Reading Jer 22:1-4
or OT (Yr 1) Jer 37:21; 38:14-28
or OT (Yr 2) Wis 9:1-18
Second Reading Jas 4:11-12
Tuesday of Week 31
Morning Prayer
OT (1-Yr) 1 Mac 2:1, 15-28, 42-50, 65-70
or First Reading Is 26:1b-4
Second Reading 1 Jn 4:13-17
Evening Prayer
First Reading Is 26:7-12
or OT (Yr 1) Jer 32:6-10, 16, 24-40
or OT (Yr 2) Wis 10:1 – 11:4
Second Reading Rom 12:9-12
Wednesday of Week 31
Morning Prayer
OT (1-Yr) 2 Mac 3:1-26
or First Reading Is 33:13-16
Second Reading 1 Cor 13:4-13

Evening Prayer
First Reading Job 1:20-22; 2:9-10
or OT (Yr 1) Jer 30:18 – 31:9
or OT (Yr 2) Wis 11:20-26; 12:1-2, 11-19
Second Reading Eph 3:14-21
Thursday of Week 31
Morning Prayer
OT (1-Yr) 1 Mac 4:36-59
or First Reading Is 40:10-17
Second Reading 1 Pet 4:7-11
Evening Prayer
First Reading Deut 4:7-8
or OT (Yr 1) Jer 31:15-22, 27-34
or OT (Yr 2) Wis 13:1-10; 14:15-21; 15:1-6
Second Reading 1 Pet 3:8-12
Friday of Week 31
Morning Prayer
OT (1-Yr) 2 Mac 12:32-45
or First Reading Jer 14:17-21
Second Reading 2 Cor 12:9b-10
Evening Prayer
First Reading Jer 18:1-6
or OT (Yr 1) Jer 42:1–16; 43:4-7
or OT (Yr 2) Wis 16:2-13, 20-26
Second Reading Jas 1:2-6
Saturday of Week 31
Morning Prayer
OT (1-Yr) 1 Mac 9:1-22
or First Reading Wis 9:1-6, 9-11
Second Reading Phil 2:14-15

Sunday 32
Evening Prayer I
First Reading Is 25:6-10a
or OT (Yr 1) Ezek 1:3-14, 22-28
or
OT (Yr 2) Wis 18:1-16; 19:3-9
Second Reading 2 Pet 1:16-21

or Gospel Reading Jn 21:1-14
Morning Prayer
OT (1-Yr)Dan 1:1-21
or First Reading Deut 10:12-15
Second Reading 2 Tim 2:8-13
Evening Prayer II
First Reading Song 8:5-7
or OT (Yr 1) Ezek 2:8-10; 3:1-11, 15-21
or OT (Yr 2) 1 Mac 1:1-24
Second Reading Heb 12:18-24
Monday of Week 32
Morning Prayer
OT (1-Yr) Dan 2:26-47
or First Reading Is 42:10-16
Second Reading Rom 12:1-8
Evening Prayer
First Reading Bar 4:21-24
or OT (Yr 1) Ezek 5:1-17
or OT (Yr 2) 1 Mac 1:41-64
Second Reading1 Thess 3: (7b-10), 11-13
Tuesday of Week 32
Morning Prayer
OT (1-Yr) Dan 3:8-13, 19b-23 (*or 24*), 24-30[8]
or First Reading Dan 3:3-6, (7-10), 11-18
or First Reading Is 55:1-5
Second Reading 1 Jn 3:17-18
Evening Prayer
First Reading Deut 4:39-40
or OT (Yr 1) Ezek 8:1-6, 16-18; 9:1-11
or OT (Yr 2) 2 Mac 6:12-31

---

[8] i.e. Daniel 3 without the insertion of the Prayer of Azariah, certainly beyond its first verse (*24*). The Vulgate numbering of vv.24-30 is vv. 91-97.

Second Reading Col 3:12-16
Wednesday of Week 32
Morning Prayer
OT (1-Yr) Dan 5:1-2, 5-9, 13-17, 25-31
or First Reading Deut 4:39-40
or First Reading Is 61:10 – 62:5
Second Reading Col 3:17, 23-24
Evening Prayer
First Reading Is 55:10-12
or OT (Yr 1) Ezek 10:18-22; 11:14-25
or OT (Yr 2) 2 Mac 7:1-19
Second Reading 1 Jn 2:3-6
Thursday of Week 32
Morning Prayer
OT (1-Yr) Dan 9:1-4a, 18-27
or First Reading Is 66:10–14a
Second Reading Rom 8:18-21
Evening Prayer
First Reading Wis 1:1-5
or OT (Yr 1) Ezek 12:1-16
or OT (Yr 2) 2 Mac 7:20-41
Second Reading Col 1:21-23
Friday of Week 32
Morning Prayer
OT (1-Yr) Dan 10:1-21
or First Reading Tob 13:8-15
Second Reading Gal 2:19-20
Evening Prayer
First Reading Wis 1:6-11
or OT (Yr 1) Ezek 13:1-16
or OT (Yr 2) 1 Mac 2:1, 15-28, 42-50, 65-70
Second Reading Rom 8:1-6
Saturday of Week 32
Morning Prayer
OT (1-Yr)Dan 12:1-13
or First Reading Ezek 36:24-28
Second Reading 2 Pet 3:8b-15a

Sunday 33
Evening Prayer I
First Reading Dan 6:26b-27
or OT (Yr 1) Ezek 14:12-23
or OT (Yr 2) 1 Mac 3:1-26
Second Reading Rom 11:33-36
or Gospel Reading Mt 28:1-10, 16-20
Morning Prayer
OT (1-Yr) Joel 2:21-32
or First Reading Ex 20:1-17
Second Reading Rev 7:9-12
Evening Prayer II
First Reading Is 43:16-21
or OT (Yr 1) Ezek 16:3, 5-15, 37, 40-43, 59-63
or OT (Yr 2) 1 Mac 4:36-59
Second Reading 2 Cor 1:3-7
Monday of Week 33
Morning Prayer
OT (1-Yr) Joel 3:1-3, 9-21
or First Reading 1 Chron 29:10-13
Second Reading 2 Thess 3:6-13
Evening Prayer
First Reading Jer 17:7-10
or OT (Yr 1) Ezek 17:3-15, 19-24
or OT (Yr 2) 2 Mac 12:32-46
Second Reading Col 1:9b-14
Tuesday of Week 33
Morning Prayer
OT (1-Yr) Zech 9:1 – 10:2
or First Reading Tob 13:1b-8
Second Reading Rom 13:8-14
Evening Prayer
First Reading Job 5:17-18
or OT (Yr 1) Ezek 18:1-13, 20-32
or OT (Yr 2) 1 Mac 6:1-17
Second Reading 1 Jn 3:1-3
Wednesday of Week 33
Morning Prayer
OT (1-Yr) Zech 10:3 –11:3

or First Reading Judith 16:2-3a, 13-15
Second Reading 1 Pet 1:13-16
Evening Prayer
First Reading Tob 4:16-20
or OT (Yr 1) Ezek 20:27-44
or OT (Yr 2) 1 Mac 9:1-22
Second Reading Jas 1:22-25
Thursday of Week 33
Morning Prayer
OT (1-Yr) Zech 11:4 – 12:8
or First Reading Jer 31:10-14
Second Reading Rom 2:14-16
Evening Prayer
First Reading Is 66:1-2
or OT (Yr 1) Ezek 24:15-27
or OT (Yr 2) Dan 1:1-21
Second Reading 1 Pet 1:6-9
Friday of Week 33
Morning Prayer
OT (1-Yr) Zech 12:9-12a; 13:1-9
or First Reading Is 45:15-22
Second Reading Eph 4:29-32
Evening Prayer
First Reading Is 45:22-25
or OT (Yr 1) Ezek 28:1-19
or OT (Yr 2) Dan 2:26-47
Second Reading Rom 15:1-3
Saturday of Week 33
Morning Prayer
OT (1-Yr)Zech 14:1-21
or First Reading Ex 15:1-4a, 8-13, 17-18
or Ex 15:1-18
Second Reading 2 Pet 1:5b-11

CHRIST THE KING (The Sunday next before Advent)
Evening Prayer I
First Reading Sir 36:1-7, 13-16
or OT (Yr 1) Ezek 34:1-6, 11-16, 23-31

or OT (Yr 2) Dan 3:8-12, 19-24, 91-97
Second Reading Eph 1:15-23
or Gospel Reading *The Gospel of the Feast in the Three-Year Cycle:*
(A) Mt 25:31-46
(B) Jn 18:33-37
(C) Lk 23:35-43
Morning Prayer
First Reading 2 Sam 23:1-7
NT (1-Yr) Rev 1:4-6, 10, 12-18; 2:26, 28; 3:5, 12, 20-21
or Second Reading Rev 1:5-8[9]
Evening Prayer II
OT (Yrs 1 & 2) Dan 7:1-27
Second Reading 1 Cor 15:20-28[10]
Monday of Week 34
Morning Prayer
First Reading Sir 36:1-7, 13-16
or First Reading Jer 15:15-21
NT (1-Yr)2 Pet 1:1-11
or Second Reading Eph 1:3-10
Evening Prayer
First Reading Is 55:1-5
or OT (Yr 1) Ezek 36:16-36
or OT (Yr 2) Dan 5:1-2, 5-9, 13-17, 25-31
Second Reading 1 Thess 2:9-13
Tuesday of Week 34
Morning Prayer
First Reading Is 38:10-14, 17-20
NT (1-Yr) 2 Pet 1:12-21
or Second Reading 1 Thess 5:4-11
Evening Prayer
First Reading Is 55:6-9

---

[9] The second reading for Christ the King, Year B, in the Mass Lectionary
[10] The second reading for Christ the King, Year A, in the Mass Lectionary is 1 Cor 15:20-26, 28.

or OT (Yr 1) Ezek 37:1-14
or OT (Yr 2) Dan 6:3-27
Second Reading Rom 3:21-26

Wednesday of Week 34
Morning Prayer
First Reading Is 55:10-12
or First Reading 1 Sam 2:1-10
NT (1-Yr)2 Pet 2:1-9
or Second Reading Rom 8:35-39
Evening Prayer
First Reading Is 55:10-12
or OT (Yr 1) Ezek 37:15-28
or OT (Yr 2) Dan 8:1-26
Second Reading 1 Pet 5:5b-7

Thursday of Week 34
Morning Prayer
First Reading Wis 1:12-15
or First Reading Is 12:1-6
NT (1-Yr)2 Pet 2:9-22
or Second Reading Rom 14:17-19
Evening Prayer
First Reading Deut 1:16-18
or OT (Yr 1) Ezek 38:14 – 39:10
or OT (Yr 2) Dan 9:1-4, 18-27
Second Reading 1 Pet 1:22-25

Friday of Week 34
Morning Prayer
First Reading Is 57:15-19
or First Reading Hab 3:2-19
NT (1-Yr) 2 Pet 3:1-18
or Second Reading Eph 2:13-16
Evening Prayer
First Reading Is 57:15-19
or OT (Yr 1) Ezek 40:1-4; 43:1-12;
44:6-9
or OT (Yr 2) Dan 10:1-21
Second Reading 1 Cor 2:7-10a

Saturday of Week 34
Morning Prayer[1]
First Reading Deut 32:1-12
or OT (Yr 1) Ezek 47:1-12
or OT (Yr 2) Dan 12:1-13
NT (1-Yr)Jude 1-8, 12-13, 17-25
or Second Reading Rom 12:14-16a

---

[1] Readings from the Two-Year Cycle are allocated to MP because there is no EP of Saturday of Week 34.

IMMACULATE CONCEPTION OF THE BLESSED VIRGIN MARY
(8 December)
Evening Prayer I
Vespers I Pss 113; 147:12-20
First Reading Mic 5:2-4
Second Reading Gal 4:1-7
or Gospel Matt 1:18-23
or other reading from the Common of the BVM
Morning Prayer
Matins Pss 24; 46; 87
Lauds Pss 63:1-9; 148-150
First Reading Is 61:9-11
NT (Yrs 1 & 2 and 1-Yr) Rom 5:12-21
or Second Reading Rom 8:28-30
Evening Prayer II
Vespers II Pss 122; 127
First Reading 1 Chron 15:3-4, 15-16; 16:1-2
Second Reading Rom 8:28-30
or NT (Yrs 1 & 2 and 1-Yr) Rom 5:12-21

Saint Stephen, Deacon, First Martyr (26 December)
Morning Prayer
Matins Pss 2; 11; 17
First Reading 2 Chron 24:20-2
NT (Yrs 1 & 2 and 1-Yr) Acts 6:8 - 7:2, 44-60
Evening Prayer of Christmas
Vespers Pss 110; 130
First Reading Is 11:1-10
Second Reading 1 Jn 1:5b-10

Saint John, Apostle and Evangelist (27 December)
Morning Prayer
Matins Pss 19:1-6; 64; 99; 148-150
First Reading Exodus 33:7-11a
NT (Yrs 1 & 2 and 1-Yr) 1 Jn 1:1 - 2:3
Evening Prayer of Christmas
Vespers Pss 110; 130
First Reading Is 9:1-6
Second Reading Rom 8:1-4

Holy Innocents (28 December)
Morning Prayer
Matins Pss 2; 33; 148-150
OT (Yrs 1 & 2 & 1-Yr) Ex 1:8-16, 22
Second Reading Rev 14:1-5
Evening Prayer of Christmas
Vespers Pss 110; 130
First Reading Is 40:1-8
Second Reading Eph 2:3b-10

Saint Thomas of Canterbury, Martyr (29 December)[1]
Morning Prayer
Matins Pss 21:1-7, 13; 148-150
First Reading Sir 51:1-12
NT (Yrs 1 & 2 and 1-Yr) 1 Thess 2:1-13, 19-20
Evening Prayer of Christmas
Vespers Pss 110; 130
First Reading Is 52:1-6
Second Reading 1 Jn 1:1-5

---

[1] Patron of Parish Clergy and National feast in England and Wales

Conversion of Saint Paul
(25 January)
Morning Prayer
Matins Pss 19:1-6; 64; 97; 148-150
First Reading Is 45:18-25
NT (Yrs 1 & 2 and 1-Yr) Gal 1:11-24
Evening Prayer
Vespers Pss 116, 126,
First Reading Sir 39:1-10
Second Reading 1 Cor 15:1-11

Presentation of Christ in the
Temple (Candlemas) (2 February)
Evening Prayer I (*on a Sunday*)
Vespers I Pss 113; 147:12-20
OT (Yrs 1 & 2 & 1-Yr) Ex 13:1-3a, 11-16[2]
or First Reading 1 Sam 1:19b-28
Second Reading Heb 10:5-7
or Gospel Reading Jn 1:1-18
Morning Prayer
Matins Pss 2; 19:1-6; 45
Lauds Pss 63:1-9; 148-150
OT (Yrs 1 & 2 & 1-Yr) Ex 13:1-3a, 11-16
or First Reading Hag 2:1-9
Second Reading 1 Jn 1:5b-10
Evening Prayer (II)
Vespers II Pss 110; 130
First Reading Ex 13:1-16
or OT (Yrs 1 & 2 & 1-Yr) Ex 13:1-3a, 11-16[3]

Second Reading Heb 4:15-16

Saints Cyril, Monk, and Methodius,
Bishop (14 February)[4]
Morning Prayer
Matins Pss 21; 92
First Reading Wis 5:15-16
NT (Yrs 1 & 2 and 1-Yr) Tit 1:7-11; 2:1-8
or Second Reading Heb 13:7-9a
Evening Prayer
Vespers Pss 15; 112
First Reading Wis 5:1-16
Second Reading 1 Pet 5:1-4
or NT (Yrs 1 & 2 and 1-Yr) Tit 1:7-11; 2:1-8

Chair of Saint Peter the Apostle
(22 February)
Morning Prayer
Matins Pss 19:1-6; 64; 97; 148-150
First Reading Ezek 3:4-11
NT (Yrs 1 & 2 and 1-Yr) Acts 11:1-18
or Second Reading 1 Pet 1:3-5
Evening Prayer
Vespers Pss 116; 126;
First Reading Ezek 34:11-16
Second Reading 1 Pet 1:3-5
or NT (Yrs 1 & 2 and 1-Yr) Acts 11:1-18

Saint David, Bishop (1 March)[5]
Morning Prayer
Matins Pss 21; 92; 148-150

---

[2] The long reading from the Office of Readings is read at one of the offices of the day.
[3] The long reading is read at one of the offices of the day. If long readings are required at other offices, readings set for the first or second reading in the Order of Readings for Mass are used.
[4] Patrons of Europe, Feast in Europe
[5] Feast in England, Solemnity in Wales

906

First Reading Wis 5:15-16
NT (Yrs 1 & 2 and 1-Yr) Phil 3:7 –
4:1, 4-9 *(Time per annum)*
or Eph 4:1-24 *(Lent)*
or Second Reading 8:28-30
Evening Prayer
Vespers Pss 15; 112
First Reading Wis 5:1-16
Second Reading Rom 8:28-30
or NT (Yrs 1 & 2 and 1-Yr) Phil 3:7 –
4:1, 4-9 *(Time per annum)*
or Eph 4:1-24 *(Lent)*

Saint Patrick, Bishop (17 March)[6]
Morning Prayer
Matins Pss 21; 92
First Reading Wis 5:15-16
NT (Yrs 1 & 2 and 1-Yr) 1 Thess 2:1-
13, 19-20
or Second Reading 1 Pet 5:1-4
Evening Prayer
Vespers Pss 15; 112
First Reading Wis 5:1-16
Second Reading 1 Pet 5:1-4
or NT (Yrs 1 & 2 and 1-Yr) 1 Thess
2:1-13, 19-20

SAINT JOSEPH (19 March)
Evening Prayer I
Vespers I Pss 113; 146
First Reading Wis 10:1-21 (or Wis
10:1-2, 9-21)
Second Reading Col 3:23-24
or Gospel Reading *The Gospel read at
Mass* Mt 1:16, 18-21, 24a
or Lk 2:41-51a
Morning Prayer
Matins Pss 21:1-7, 13

Lauds Pss 63:1-9; 148-150
First Reading Is 63:7-16
NT (Yrs 1 & 2 and 1-Yr) Heb 11:1-16
or Second Reading Eph 3:14-21
Evening Prayer II
Vespers II Pss 15; 112
First Reading 2 Chron 6:12-17
Second Reading Eph 3:14-21
or NT (Yrs 1 & 2 and 1-Yr) Heb 11:1-
16

**ANNUNCIATION OF THE
LORD (Lady Day) (25 March)**
Evening Prayer I
Vespers I Pss 113; 147:12-20
First Reading Gen 3:1-15
Second Reading Rom 5:12-21
or Gospel Matt 1:18-24
Morning Prayer
Matins Pss 2; 19:1-6; 45
Lauds Pss 63:1-9; 148-150
OT (Yrs 1 & 2 & 1-Yr) 1 Chron 17:1-
15
or First Reading Wis 9:1-12
Second Reading Heb 2:5-10
Evening Prayer II
Vespers II Pss 110; 130
First Reading Wis 9:1-12
or OT (Yrs 1 & 2 & 1-Yr)1 Chron
17:1-15
Second Reading Gal 4:1-7
Saint George, Martyr (23 April)[7]
Evening Prayer I
Vespers I Ps 118
First Reading 1 Macc 2:59-64
Second Reading Rev 3:10-12
or Gospel Reading *The Gospel read at
Mass* John 15:1-8

---

[6] Solemnity in Ireland

[7] Solemnity in England

or John 15:18-21
Morning Prayer
Matins Pss 2; 11; 17
Lauds Pss 63:1-9; 148-150
First Reading Josh 1:1-9
Second Reading Eph 6:10-20
Evening Prayer II
Vespers II Pss 116
First Reading Is 43:1-7
NT (Yrs 1 & 2 and 1-Yr) Rev 7:9-17

Saint Mark the Evangelist
(25 April)
Morning Prayer
Matins Pss 19:1-6; 64; 97; 148-150
First Reading Sir 2:1-11
NT (Yrs 1 & 2 and 1-Yr) Eph 4:1-16
Evening Prayer
Vespers Pss 116; 126
First Reading Is 62:6-12
Second Reading 2 Tim 4:1-11

**Saint Catherine of Siena, Virgin,
Doctor (29 April)** [8]
Morning Prayer
Matins Pss 21:1-7, 13; 92
First Reading Song 8:5-7
NT (Yrs 1 & 2 and 1-Yr) 1 Cor 7:25-40
Evening Prayer
Vespers Pss 122; 127
First Reading Wis 7:7-16, 22-30
Second Reading 1 Cor 2:1-16

Saints Philip and James, Apostles
(3 May)
Morning Prayer
Matins Pss 19:1-6; 64; 97
First Reading Job 23:1-12
NT (Yrs 1 & 2 and 1-Yr) Acts 5:12-32
or Second Reading Eph 4:11-16
Evening Prayer
Vespers Pss 116; 126
First Reading Prov 4:7-18
Second Reading Eph 4:11-16
or NT (Yrs 1 & 2 and 1-Yr) Acts 5:12-32

Holy English Martyrs (4 May) [9]
Morning Prayer
Matins Pss 2; 33
First Reading Wis 3:1-15
NT (Yrs 1 & 2 and 1-Yr) Rev 7:9-17
Evening Prayer
Vespers Pss 116; 126
First Reading Wis 5:1-16
Second Reading Rom 8:18-39

Saint Matthias the Apostle (14 May)
Morning Prayer
Matins Pss 19:1-6; 64; 97; 148-150
First Reading 1 Sam 16:1-13
NT (Yrs 1 & 2 and 1-Yr) Acts 5:12-32
Evening Prayer
Vespers Pss 116; 126
First Reading 1 Sam 12:1-5
Second Reading Acts 20:17-35

**Venerable Bede, Religious
(25 May)**
Morning Prayer
Matins Pss 21:1-7, 13; 92

---

[8] Patron of Europe, Feast in Europe

[9] Feast in England

OT (Yrs 1 & 2 & 1-Yr) Sir 39:1-10
or First Reading Wis 7:13-14
Second Reading 1 Pet 5:1-4
or NT (Yrs 1 & 2 and 1-Yr) 1 Cor 2:1-16
Evening Prayer
Vespers Pss 15; 112
First Reading Wis 7:22-30
or OT (Yrs 1 & 2 & 1-Yr) Sir 39:1-10
NT (Yrs 1 & 2 and 1-Yr) 1 Cor 2:1-16
or Second Reading 1 Pet 5:1-4

**Saint Augustine of Canterbury,
Bishop (27 May)**[10]
Morning Prayer
Matins Pss 21:1-7, 13; 92
First Reading Is 6:1-6
Second Reading 1 Thess 2:2b-8
or NT (Yrs 1 & 2 and 1-Yr) Acts
20:17-36 *(Eastertide)*
or Tit 1:7-11; 2:1-8 *(Time per annum)*
Evening Prayer
Vespers Pss 15; 112
First Reading Jer 1:4-9
NT (Yrs 1 & 2 and 1-Yr) Acts 20:17-36 *(Eastertide)*
or Tit 1:7-11; 2:1-8 *(Time per annum)*
or **Second Reading 1 Thess 2:2b-8**

Visitation of the Blessed Virgin
Mary (31 May)
Morning Prayer
Matins Pss 24; 46; 87; 148-150
OT (Yrs 1 & 2 & 1-Yr) Song 2:8-14; 8:6-7
or First Reading Zech 2:10-13
or Joel 2:27 – 3:1a
Second Reading 1 Pet 5:5b-7

or Heb 3:1-6
Evening Prayer
Vespers Pss 122; 127
First Reading Zech 2:10-13
or Joel 2:27 – 3:1a
or OT (Yrs 1 & 2 & 1-Yr) Song 2:8-14; 8:6-7
Second Reading Heb 2:11-18

**Saint Barnabas the Apostle
(11 June)**
Morning Prayer
Matins Pss 19:1-6; 64; 97
First Reading Sir 31:1-11
NT (Yrs 1 & 2 and 1-Yr) 1 Cor 4:1-16
or Second Reading Col 1:3-14
Evening Prayer
Vespers Pss 116; 126
First Reading Job 29:1-16
Second Reading Col 1:3-14
or NT (Yrs 1 & 2 and 1-Yr) 1 Cor 4:1-16

Saints John Fisher and Thomas
More, Martyrs (22 June)[11]
Morning Prayer
Matins Pss 2; 33; 148-150
First Reading 2 Chron 24:17-21
NT (Yrs 1 & 2 and 1-Yr) Rom 8:18-39
or Second Reading 1 Pet 4:12-19
Evening Prayer
Vespers Pss 116
First Reading Wis 3:1-9
Second Reading 1 Pet 4:12-19
or NT (Yrs 1 & 2 and 1-Yr) Rom 8:18-39

---

[10] Feast in England and Wales

[11] Feast in England and Wales

NATIVITY OF SAINT JOHN THE BAPTIST (24 June)
Evening Prayer I
Vespers I Pss 113; 146;
First Reading Mal 3:1-5
Second Reading 1 Pet 1:8-12
or Gospel Lk 1:5-17
or Jn 1:29-34a
or Jn 3:22-30
Morning Prayer
Matins Pss 21:1-7, 13; 92
Lauds Pss 63:1-9; 148-150
OT (Yrs 1 & 2 & 1-Yr) Jer 1:4-10, 17-19
or First Reading Mal 4:1-6
Second Reading Acts 13:14b-26
Evening Prayer II
Vespers II Pss 15; 112
First Reading Mal 4:1-6
Second Reading Acts 13:16-26
or OT (Yrs 1 & 2 & 1-Yr) Jer 1:4-10, 17-19

SAINTS PETER AND PAUL, Apostles (29 June)
Evening Prayer I
Vespers I Pss 117 147:12-20
First Reading Is 61:6-9
Second Reading Acts 11:1-18
or Gospel Jn 21:15-19
or Lk 5:1-11
or Jn 6:61-70

Morning Prayer
Matins Pss 19:1-6; 64; 97
Lauds Pss 63:1-9; 148-150
First Reading Ezek 2:1-7
NT (Yrs 1 & 2 and 1-Yr) Gal 1:15 – 2:10
or Second Reading Gal 2:1-9

Evening Prayer II
Vespers II Pss 116; 126
First Reading Is 49:1-6
Second Reading Gal 2:1-9
or NT (Yrs 1 & 2 and 1-Yr) Gal 1:15 – 2:10

Saint Thomas the Apostle (3 July)
Morning Prayer
Matins Pss 19:1-6; 64; 97
First Reading Job 42:1-6
NT (Yrs 1 & 2 and 1-Yr) 1 Cor 4:1-16
or Second Reading Eph 4:11-16
Evening Prayer
Vespers Pss 116; 126
First Reading Is 43:8-13
Second Reading Eph 4:11-16
or NT (Yrs 1 & 2 and 1-Yr) 1 Cor 4:1-16

Saint Benedict, Abbot (11 July)[12]
Morning Prayer
Matins Pss 21:1-7, 13; 92
First Reading Sir 45:1-5; 47:8-10
NT (Yrs 1 & 2 and 1-Yr) Phil 3:7 – 4:1, 4-9
or Second Reading Rom 12:1-21
Evening Prayer
Vespers Pss 122; 127
First Reading Sir 50:1-13
Second Reading Rom 12:1-21
or NT (Yrs 1 & 2 and 1-Yr) Phil 3:7 – 4:1, 4-9

Saint Mary Magdalen (22 July)
Morning Prayer
Matins Pss 19:1-6; 45
First Reading 1 Sam 16:14-23

---

[12] Patron of Europe

NT (Yrs 1 & 2 and 1-Yr) Rom 12:1-21
or Second Reading 2 Cor 5:14-17 [13]
Evening Prayer
Vespers Pss 122; 127
First Reading Zeph 3:14-20
Second Reading Rom 8:28-30
or NT (Yrs 1 & 2 and 1-Yr) Rom 12:1-21

**Saint Bridget of Sweden, Abbess
(23 July)** [14]
Morning Prayer
Matins Pss 19:1-6; 45
First Reading Song 8:5-7
NT (Yrs 1 & 2 and 1-Yr) Phil 3:7 –
4:1, 4-9
or Second Reading Rom 8:28-30
Evening Prayer
Vespers Pss 122; 127
First Reading Wis 8:17-21a
Second Reading Rom 8:28-30
or NT (Yrs 1 & 2 and 1-Yr) Phil 3:7 –
4:1, 4-9

Saint James the Apostle (25 July)
Morning Prayer
Matins Pss 19:1-6; 64; 97
First Reading Jer 16:14-21
NT (Yrs 1 & 2 and 1-Yr) 1 Cor 4:1-16
or Second Reading Eph 4:11-16
Evening Prayer
Vespers Pss 116; 126
First Reading Jer 26:1-15
Second Reading Eph 4:11-16

or NT (Yrs 1 & 2 and 1-Yr) 1 Cor 4:1-16

**Transfiguration of the Lord
(6 August)**
Evening Prayer I *(on a Sunday)*
Vespers I Pss 113; 117
First Reading 1 Kings 19:1-12
Second Reading 2 Cor 3:1-9, 18
or Phil 3:20 -21
or Gospel Reading *The Gospel read at
Mass*
Morning Prayer
Matins Pss 84; 97; 99
Lauds Pss 63:1-9; 148-150
First Reading Ex 24:12-18
NT (Yrs 1 & 2 and 1-Yr) 2 Cor 3:7 –
4:6
or Second Reading 2 Cor 4:1-6
Evening Prayer (II)
Vespers II Pss 110; 121
First Reading Dan 7:9-10, 13-14
Second Reading Rom 8:15b-21
or NT (Yrs 1 & 2 and 1-Yr) 2 Cor 3:7
– 4:6

**Saint Teresa Benedicta of the Cross
(Edith Stein), Virgin, Martyr
(9 August)** [15]
Morning Prayer
Matins Pss 19:1-6; 45
First Reading Song 8:5-7
NT (Yrs 1 & 2 and 1-Yr) 2 Cor 4:7 –
5:8
or Second Reading Gal 6:14-16
Evening Prayer
Vespers Pss 122; 127

---

[13] Alternative First Reading in the
Mass Lectionary
[14] Patron of Europe, Feast in
Europe

[15] Patron of Europe, Feast in
Europe

First Reading Wis 3:1-9
Second Reading Rom 8:31-39
or NT (Yrs 1 & 2 and 1-Yr) 2 Cor 4:7 – 5:8

Saint Laurence, Deacon, Martyr (10 August)
Morning Prayer
Matins Pss 2; 11; 17
First Reading 2 Macc 6:18-31
NT (Yrs 1 & 2 and 1-Yr) Acts 6:1-6; 8:1b, 4, 8
or Second Reading 2 Cor 1:3-5
Evening Prayer
Vespers Pss 116
First Reading Sir 51:1-8
Second Reading 1 Pet 4:12-19
or NT (Yrs 1 & 2 and 1-Yr) Acts 6:1-6; 8:1b, 4, 8

ASSUMPTION OF THE BLESSED VIRGIN MARY (15 August)
Evening Prayer I
Vespers I Pss 113; 147:12-20
First Reading Jer 31:1-14
Second Reading Rom 8:28-30
or Gospel Lk 11:27-28
Morning Prayer
Matins Pss 24; 46; 87
Lauds Pss 63:1-9; 148-150
First Reading 1 Sam 2:1-10
or Is 61:10-11
NT (Yrs 1 & 2 and 1-Yr) Eph 1:16 – 2:10
or Second Reading Acts 1:6-14
Evening Prayer II
Vespers II Pss 122; 127
First Reading Zech 2:10-13
Second Reading Acts 1:6-14

or NT (Yrs 1 & 2 and 1-Yr) Eph 1:16 – 2:10

Saint Bartholomew the Apostle (24 August)
Morning Prayer
Matins Pss 19:1-6; 64; 97
First Reading Gen 28:10-17
NT (Yrs 1 & 2 and 1-Yr) 1 Cor 1:18 – 2:5
or Second Reading Eph 4:11-16
Evening Prayer
Vespers Pss 116; 126
First Reading Is 66:1-2, 18-23
Second Reading Eph 4:11-16
or NT (Yrs 1 & 2 and 1-Yr) 1 Cor 1:18 – 2:5

Saint Gregory the Great, Pope, Doctor (3 September)[16]
Morning Prayer
Matins Pss 21:1-7, 13; 92
First Reading Ezek 34:11-16
NT (Yrs 1 & 2 and 1-Yr) Tit 1:7-11; 2:1-8
or Second Reading 1 Thess 2:2b-8
Evening Prayer
Vespers Pss 15; 112
First Reading Is 52:7-10
Second Reading 1 Thess 2:2b-8
or NT (Yrs 1 & 2 and 1-Yr) Tit 1:7-11; 2:1-8

---

[16] Feast in England and Wales

Nativity of the Blessed Virgin Mary (8 September)

Morning Prayer

Matins Pss 24; 46; 87

OT (Yrs 1 & 2 & 1-Yr) Gen 3:9-20

or First Reading Zech 2:10-13

Second Reading Rom 5:12, 17-19

Evening Prayer

Vespers Pss 122; 127

First Reading Is 11:1-5

or OT (Yrs 1 & 2 & 1-Yr) Gen 3:9-20

Second Reading Gal 4:1-7

or Rom 9:4-5

Holy Cross Day (14 September)

Evening Prayer I (on a Sunday)

Vespers I Ps 147

First Reading 1 Kings 8:22-30

Second Reading Eph 2:11-22

or Gospel Jn 12:31-36a

Morning Prayer

Matins Pss 2; 8; 96

Lauds Pss 63:1-9; 148-150

First Reading Num 21:4-9

NT (Yrs 1 & 2 and 1-Yr) Gal 2:19 – 3:7, 13-14; 6:14-16

or Second Reading 1 Pet 3:17-22

Evening Prayer (II)

Vespers II Pss 110; 116:10-19

First Reading Gen 3:1-15

Second Reading 1 Cor 1:23-24

or NT (Yrs 1 & 2 and 1-Yr) Gal 2:19 – 3:7, 13-14; 6:14-16

Saint Matthew the Apostle (21 September)

Morning Prayer

Matins Pss 19:1-6; 64; 97

First Reading Is 8:11-20

NT (Yrs 1 & 2 and 1-Yr) Eph 4:1-16

or Second Reading Acts 2:42-47

Evening Prayer

Vespers Pss 116; 126;

First Reading Job 28:12-28

Second Reading Acts 2:42-47

or NT (Yrs 1 & 2 and 1-Yr) Eph 4:1-16

Our Lady of Walsingham (24 September) [17]

Evening Prayer I

Vespers I Pss 113; 147:12-20

First Reading Zeph 3:14-20

Second Reading Gal 3:22 – 4:7 *(Time per annum)*

or Gospel Reading *The Gospel from the Common read at Mass*

Morning Prayer

Matins Pss 24; 46; 87

Lauds Pss 63:1-9; 148-150

OT (Yrs 1 & 2 & 1-Yr) Is 7:10-14; 8:10; 11:1-9

or First Reading Is 61:10-11

NT (Yrs 1 & 2 and 1-Yr) Gal 3:22 – 4:7

or Second Reading Gal 4:4-5

Evening Prayer II

Vespers Pss 122; 127

First Reading Judith 13:31 [18]

or OT (Yrs 1 & 2 & 1-Yr) Is 7:10-14; 8:10; 11:1-9

Second Reading Gal 4:4-5

or NT (Yrs 1 & 2 and 1-Yr) Gal 3:22 – 4:7

---

[17] Solemnity in the Personal Ordinariate of Our Lady of Walsingham.

[18] Judith 13 ends at verse 20 but the Vulgate adds verses 27-31.

SS Michael, Gabriel and Raphael
(29 September)
Morning Prayer
Matins Pss 97; 103; 148-150
First Reading Job 38:1-7
or Gen 28:12-13a
NT (Yrs 1 & 2 and 1-Yr) Rev 12:1-17
or Second Reading Rev 5:1-14
Evening Prayer
Vespers Pss 8; 138
First Reading Dan 12:1-3
or 2 Kings 6:8-17
or Dan 9:22-23
or Tob 12:11-22
Second Reading Rev 5:1-14
or NT (Yrs 1 & 2 and 1-Yr) Rev 12:1-17

St Luke the Evangelist (18 October)
Morning Prayer
Matins Pss 19:1-6; 64; 97; 148-150
First Reading Ezek 47:1-12
NT (Yrs 1 & 2 and 1-Yr) Acts 9:27-31; 11:19-26
or Second Reading 1 Cor 15:1-4
Evening Prayer
Vespers Pss 116; 126
First Reading Is 52:7-10
Second Reading Acts 1:1-8
or Col 1:3-12
or NT (Yrs 1 & 2 and 1-Yr) Acts 9:27-31; 11:19-26

Saint Simon and Jude, Apostles
(28 October)
Morning Prayer
Matins Pss 19:1-6; 64; 97; 148-150
First Reading Is 28:9-16
NT (Yrs 1 & 2 and 1-Yr) 1 Cor 1:18 – 2:5

or Second Reading Eph 2:19-22
Evening Prayer
Vespers Pss 116; 126
First Reading Is 4:2-6
Second Reading Eph 2:19-22
or NT (Yrs 1 & 2 and 1-Yr) 1 Cor 1:18 – 2:5

ALL SAINTS (1 November)
Evening Prayer I
Vespers I Pss 113; 147:12-20
First Reading Wis 3:1-9
Second Reading Heb 12:22-24a
or Gospel Mt 5:13-16
or Jn 15:1-8
or Jn 15:9-17
Morning Prayer
Matins Pss 8; 15; 16
Lauds Pss 63:1-9; 148-150
First Reading Wis 4:10-17
NT (Yrs 1 & 2 and 1-Yr) Rev 5:1-14
or Second Reading Rev 21:1-4, 22 – 22:5
or 2 Cor 6:16b – 7:1
Evening Prayer II
Vespers II Pss 110; 116
First Reading Wis 5:1-5, 14-16
Second Reading Rev 21:1-4, 22 – 22:5
or 2 Cor 6:16b – 7:1
or NT (Yrs 1 & 2 and 1-Yr) Rev 5:1-14

ALL SOULS' DAY (2 November)
Morning Prayer
Matins Pss 40; 42
Lauds Pss 51; 146 *or* 150
First Reading Is 25:6-10a
NT (Yrs 1 & 2 and 1-Yr) 1 Cor 15:12-34
or Second Reading 1 Cor 15:35-57

Evening Prayer
Vespers Pss 121; 130
First Reading Lam 3 17-26
Second Reading 1 Cor 15:35-57
or 2 Cor 4:16 – 5:10
or NT (Yrs 1 & 2 and 1-Yr) 1 Cor
15:12-34

Dedication of St John Lateran
(9 November)
Morning Prayer
Matins Pss 24; 84; 87
First Reading Is 49:1-6
or Is 56:7
NT (Yrs 1 & 2 and 1-Yr) 1 Pet 2:1-17
or Second Reading 1 Cor 3:9b-13, 16-
17
Evening Prayer
Vespers Pss 46; 122;
First Reading 1 Macc 4:52-59
Second Reading Rev 21:2-3, 22-27
or NT (Yrs 1 & 2 and 1-Yr) 1 Pet 2:1-
17

St Andrew (30 November)[19]
Morning Prayer
Matins Pss 19:1-6; 64; 97
First Reading Is 49:1-6
NT (Yrs 1 & 2 and 1-Yr) 1 Cor 1:18 –
2:5
or Second Reading Eph 4:11-16
Evening Prayer
Vespers Pss 116; 126
First Reading Is 55:1-5
Second Reading Eph 4:11-16
or NT (Yrs 1 & 2 and 1-Yr) 1 Cor 1:18
– 2:5

---

[19] Solemnity in Scotland

915

Commons

Common of the Dedication of a Church

Evening Prayer I
Vespers I Pss 147
First Reading 2 Chron 5:6-10 – 6:2
Second Reading Eph 2:11-22
or Gospel Reading *The Gospel from the Common read at Mass*

Morning Prayer
Matins Pss 24; 84; 87 Lauds *(Outside Lent)* Pss 63:1-9; 148-150 *(Lent)* Pss 63:1-9; 149
First Reading Is 49:1-6
or Is 56:7
NT (Yrs 1 & 2 and 1-Yr) Rev 21:9-27 *(Advent, Christmas, Eastertide)*
or NT (Yrs 1 & 2 and 1-Yr) 1 Kings 8:1-4, 10-13, 22-30 *(Lent)*
or NT (Yrs 1 & 2 and 1-Yr) 1 Pet 2:1-17 *(Time per annum)*
or Second Reading 1 Cor 3:9b-13, 16-17
or Rev 21:2-3, 22-27

Evening Prayer II
Vespers II Pss 46; 122
First Reading 1 Macc 4:52-59
Second Reading 1 Cor 3:9b-13, 16-17
or Rev 21:2-3, 22-27
or NT (Yrs 1 & 2 and 1-Yr) Rev 21:9-27 *(Advent, Christmas, Eastertide)*
or NT (Yrs 1 & 2 and 1-Yr) 1 Kings 8:1-4, 10-13, 22-30 *(Lent)*
or NT (Yrs 1 & 2 and 1-Yr) 1 Pet 2:1-17 *(Time per annum)*

Common of the Blessed Virgin Mary

Evening Prayer I[1]
Vespers I Pss 113; 147:12-20
First Reading Zeph 3:14-20
Second Reading Gal 3:22 – 4:7 *(Time per annum)*
or Gospel Reading *The Gospel from the Common read at Mass*

Morning Prayer
Matins Pss 24; 46; 87
Lauds *(Outside Lent)* Pss 63:1-9; 148-150 *(Lent)* Pss 63:1-9; 149
OT (Yrs 1 & 2 & 1-Yr) 1 Chron 17:1-15 *(Advent, Christmas, Lent)*
or OT (Yrs 1 & 2 & 1-Yr) Is 7:10-14; 8:10; 11:1-9 *(Time per annum)*
or First Reading Is 61:10-11
NT (Yrs 1 & 2 and 1-Yr) Rev 11:19 – 12:17 *(Eastertide)*
or NT (Yrs 1 & 2 and 1-Yr) Gal 3:22 – 4:7 *(Time per annum)*
or Second Reading Gal 4:4-5

Evening Prayer (II)
Vespers (II) Pss 122; 127
First Reading Judith 16:13-16
or Judith 13:31
or OT (Yrs 1 & 2 & 1-Yr) 1 Chron 17:1-15 *(Advent, Christmas, Lent)*
or OT (Yrs 1 & 2 & 1-Yr) Is 7:10-14; 8:10; 11:1-9 *(Time per annum)*
Second Reading Gal 4:4-5
or NT (Yrs 1 & 2 and 1-Yr) Rev 11:19 – 12:17 *(Eastertide)*

---

[1] EP I is used for Solemnities and certain Feasts which occur on Sundays.

or NT (Yrs 1 & 2 and 1-Yr) Gal 3:22 –
4:7 *(Time per annum)*

**Common of Apostles and
Evangelists**
Evening Prayer I
Vespers I Pss 116; 126
First Reading Ex 29:1-9
or Num 11:16-30
Second Reading Acts 2:37-47
or Gospel Mk 3:13-19
Morning Prayer *(see Propers)*
Evening Prayer (II) *(see Propers)*
Common of Martyrs
(i)   **Several Martyrs**
Evening Prayer I
Vespers I Ps 118
First Reading Wis 10:17-21
or OT (Yrs 1 & 2 & 1-Yr) Sir 51:1-12
Second Reading Rom 8:35-39 *(Advent,
Christmas, Lent, Time per annum)*
or Second Reading Rev 3:10-12
(Eastertide)
Morning Prayer
Matins Pss 2; 11; 17
Lauds *(Outside Lent)* Pss 63:1-9; 148-
150 *(Lent)* Pss 63:1-9; 149
OT (Yrs 1 & 2 & 1-Yr) Wis 3:1-15
(Advent, Christmas, Lent)
or First Reading Wis 3:1-9 *(Eastertide,
Time per annum)*
NT (Yrs 1 & 2 and 1-Yr) Rev 7:9-17
(Eastertide)

or NT (Yrs 1 & 2 and 1-Yr) Rom 8:18-
39 *(Time per annum)*
or Second Reading 2 Cor 1:3-5 *(Advent,
Christmas, Lent)*
or Second Reading 1 Jn 5:3-5
(Eastertide)
Evening Prayer (II)
Vespers (II) Pss 116
First Reading Wis 10:17-21
or OT (Yrs 1 & 2 & 1-Yr) Sir 51:1-12
Second Reading 1 Pet 4:13-14
or Rev 7:14-17 *(Eastertide)*
NT (Yrs 1 & 2 and 1-Yr) 2 Cor 4:7 –
5:8
(ii)   **One Martyr**
Evening Prayer I
Vespers I Ps 118
OT (Yrs 1 & 2 & 1-Yr) Sir 51:1-12
Second Reading Rom 8:35-39
Morning Prayer
Matins Pss 2; 11; 17
Lauds *(Outside Lent)* Pss 63:1-9; 148-
150 *(Lent)* Pss 63:1-9; 149
First Reading Wis 3:1-9
NT (Yrs 1 & 2 and 1-Yr) 2 Cor 4:7 –
5:8 *(Time per annum)*
or **Second Reading 2 Cor 1:3-5**
Evening Prayer (II)
Vespers (II) Pss 116
First Reading Wis 10:17-21
or OT (Yrs 1 & 2 & 1-Yr) Sir 51:1-12
Second Reading 1 Pet 4:13-14

---

[2] EP I is used for Solemnities and
certain Feasts which occur on
Sundays.
[3] EP I is used for Solemnities and
certain Feasts which occur on
Sundays.

---

[4] EP I is used for Solemnities and
certain Feasts which occur on
Sundays.

Common of Pastors
Evening Prayer I[5]
Vespers I Pss 113; 146;
First Reading Wis 5:1-16
Second Reading 1 Pet 5:1-4
Morning Prayer
Matins Pss 21:1-7, 13; 92
Lauds *(Outside Lent)* Pss 63:1-9; 148-150 *(Lent)* Pss 63:1-9; 149
OT (Yrs 1 & 2 & 1-Yr) *see below*
or First Reading Wis 5:15-16
NT (Yrs 1 & 2 and 1-Yr) *see below*
or Second Reading Heb 13:7-9a
Evening Prayer (II)
Vespers (II) Pss 15; 112
First Reading Wis 5:1-16
or OT (Yrs 1 & 2 & 1-Yr) *see below*
Second Reading 1 Pet 5:1-4, (5-11)
or NT (Yrs 1 & 2 and 1-Yr) *see below*

Major Readings for Morning or Evening Prayer:
Pope or Bishop (Advent and Christmas, Lent) NT (Yrs 1 & 2 and 1-Yr) 1 Thess 2:1-13, 19-20
Pope or Bishop (Eastertide)
NT (Yrs 1 & 2 and 1-Yr) Acts 20:17-36
Pope or Bishop (Time per annum)
NT (Yrs 1 & 2 and 1-Yr) Tit 1:7-11; 2:1-8
Priest or Missionary (Advent, Christmas, Lent, Eastertide) NT (Yrs 1 & 2 and 1-Yr) 1 Tim 5:17-22; 6:10-14
Priest or Missionary (Time per annum)
NT (Yrs 1 & 2 and 1-Yr) 1 Pet 5:1-11

Doctor (Advent, Christmas, Lent)
OT (Yrs 1 & 2 & 1-Yr)Wis 7:7-16, 22-30
Doctor (Eastertide)
NT (Yrs 1 & 2 and 1-Yr) 1 Cor 2:1-16
Doctor (Time per annum)
OT (Yrs 1 & 2 & 1-Yr) Sir 39:1-10

Common of Virgins
Evening Prayer I[6]
Vespers I Pss 113; 147:12-20
First Reading Wis 8:17-21a
Second Reading1 Cor 7:32-35
Morning Prayer
Matins Pss 19:1-6; 45
Lauds *(Outside Lent)* Pss 63:1-9; 148-150 *(Lent)* Pss 63:1-9; 149
First Reading Song 8:5-7
NT (Yrs 1 & 2 and 1-Yr) 1 Cor 7:25-40
or Second Reading Rev 19:6-8
Evening Prayer (II)
Vespers (II) Pss 122; 127
First Reading Wis 8:17-21a
Second Reading 1 Cor 7:32-35
or NT (Yrs 1 & 2 and 1-Yr) 1 Cor 7:25-40

Common of Saints
Evening Prayer I[7]
Vespers I Pss 113; 146;
First Reading Proverbs 8:1-11
or Sir 2:7-11

---

[5] EP I is used for Solemnities and certain Feasts which occur on Sundays.

[6] EP I is used for Solemnities and certain Feasts which occur on Sundays.

[7] EP I is used for Solemnities and certain Feasts which occur on Sundays.

or OT (Yrs 1 & 2 & 1-Yr) *see below*
Second Reading Phil 3:7-8a
or NT (Yrs 1 & 2 and 1-Yr) *see below*
Morning Prayer
Matins *(Men saints)* Pss 21:1-7, 13; 92
(Women saints) Pss 19:1-6; 45
Lauds *(Outside Lent)* Pss 63:1-9; 148-
150 *(Lent)* Pss 63:1-9; 149
OT (Yrs 1 & 2 & 1-Yr) *see below*
or First Reading Micah 6:6-8
NT (Yrs 1 & 2 and 1-Yr) *see below*
or Second Reading Rom 12:1-8
Evening Prayer (II)
Vespers (II) Pss 15; 112
First Reading Sir 2:7-11
or Proverbs 8:1-11
or OT (Yrs 1 & 2 & 1-Yr) *see below*
Second Reading Rom 8:28-30
or NT (Yrs 1 & 2 and 1-Yr) *see below*

**Major Readings for Morning or
Evening Prayer:**
General
OT (Yrs 1 & 2 & 1-Yr) Wis 5:1-16
(Advent, Christmas, Lent)
NT (Yrs 1 & 2 and 1-Yr) Phil 1:29 –
2:16 *(Advent, Christmas, Lent)*
NT (Yrs 1 & 2 and 1-Yr) Col 3:1-17
(Time per annum)
or Rom 12:1-21 *(Time per annum)*
NT (Yrs 1 & 2 and 1-Yr) Rev 14:1-5;
19:5-10 *(Eastertide)*

*Abbot, Abbess, Religious (Advent,
Christmas, Lent, Eastertide)*
NT (Yrs 1 & 2 and 1-Yr) Eph 4:1-24
Abbot, Abbess, Religious (Time per annum)
NT (Yrs 1 & 2 and 1-Yr) Phil 3:7 –
4:1, 4-9

*Noted for Works of Mercy (Advent,
Christmas, Lent, Eastertide)*
NT (Yrs 1 & 2 and 1-Yr) 1 Jn 4:7-21
*Noted for Works of Mercy (Time per
annum)*
NT (Yrs 1 & 2 and 1-Yr) 1 Cor 12:31
– 13:13
*Married man (Advent, Christmas, Lent,
Eastertide)*
NT (Yrs 1 & 2 and 1-Yr) 1 Pet 3:7-17
Married man (Time per annum)
NT (Yrs 1 & 2 and 1-Yr) Eph 5:21-32
Married woman
OT (Yrs 1 & 2 & 1-Yr) Prov 31:10-31
NT (Yrs 1 & 2 and 1-Yr) 1 Pet 3:1-6,
8-17

Office of the Dead
Morning Prayer
Matins Pss 40; 42
Lauds Pss 51; 146 *or* 150
First Reading Wis 1:12-15
NT (Yrs 1 & 2 and 1-Yr) 1 Cor 15:12-
34
or 1 Cor 15:35-57
or Second Reading 1 Thess 4:14-18
Evening Prayer
Vespers II Pss 121; 130;
First Reading Lam 3 17-26
or Job 19:25-27a
Second Reading 2 Cor 4:16 – 5:10
or 1 Cor 15:51-57

A Short Lectionary for Morning and Evening Prayer

Travellers may find the following Short Readings convenient for Morning and Evening Prayer. Other suitable readings for general use are as set for Prayer during the Day on pages 78-97. Short Readings for particular days and occasions can be found in **Times and Seasons.**

Sunday Evening Prayer I

Is 6:1-8

In the year that King Uzziah died I saw the Lord sitting upon a throne, high and lifted up; and his train filled the temple. Above him stood the seraphim; each had six wings: with two he covered his face, and with two he covered his feet, and with two he flew. And one called to another and said: Holy, holy, holy is the Lord of hosts; the whole earth is full of his glory. And the foundations of the thresholds shook at the voice of him who called, and the house was filled with smoke. And I said: Woe is me! For I am lost; for I am a man of unclean lips, and I dwell in the midst of a people of unclean lips; for my eyes have seen the King, the Lord of hosts! Then flew one of the seraphim to me, having in his hand a burning coal which he had taken with tongs from the altar. And he touched my mouth, and said: Behold, this has touched your lips; your guilt is taken away, and your sin forgiven. And I heard the voice of the Lord saying, Whom shall I send, and who will go for us? Then I said, Here am I! Send me.

Rom 11:33-36

O the depth of the riches and wisdom and knowledge of God! How unsearchable are his judgments and how inscrutable his ways! For who has known the mind of the Lord, or who has been his counsellor? Or who has given a gift to him that he might be repaid? For from him and through him and to him are all things. To him be glory for ever. Amen.

Sunday Morning Prayer

Ex 20:1-17

God spoke all these words, saying, I am the Lord your God, who brought you out of the land of Egypt, out of the house of bondage. You shall have no other gods before me. You shall not make for yourself a graven image, or any likeness of anything that is in heaven above, or that is in the earth beneath, or that is in the water under the earth; you shall not bow down to them or serve them; for I the Lord your God am a jealous God, visiting the iniquity of the fathers upon the children to the third and the fourth generation of those who hate me, but showing steadfast love to thousands of those who love me and keep my commandments. You shall not take the name of the Lord your God in vain; for the Lord will not hold him guiltless who takes his name in vain. Remember the Sabbath day, to keep it holy. Six days you shall labour, and do all your work; but the seventh day is a Sabbath to the Lord your God; in it you shall not do any work, you, or your son, or your daughter, your manservant, or your maidservant, or your cattle, or the sojourner who is within your gates; for in six days the Lord made heaven and earth, the sea, and all that is in them, and rested the seventh day; therefore the Lord blessed the Sabbath day and hallowed it. Honour your father and your mother, that your days may be long in the land which the Lord your God gives you. You shall not kill. You shall not commit adultery. You shall not steal. You shall not bear false witness against your neighbour. You shall not covet your neighbour's house; you shall not covet your neighbours wife, or his manservant, or his maidservant, or his ox, or his ass, or anything that is your neighbour's.

Rev 7:9-12

I looked, and behold, a great multitude which no man could number, from every nation, from all tribes and peoples and tongues, standing before the throne and before the Lamb, clothed in white robes, with palm branches in their hands, and crying out with a loud voice, Salvation belongs to our God who sits upon the throne, and to the Lamb! And all the angels stood round the throne and round the elders and the four living creatures, and they fell on their faces before the throne and worshipped God, saying, Amen! Blessing and glory and wisdom and thanksgiving and honour and power and might be to our God for ever and ever! Amen.

Sunday Evening Prayer II

Is 43:16-21

Thus says the Lord, who makes a way in the sea, a path in the mighty waters, who brings forth chariot and horse, army and warrior; they lie down, they cannot rise, they are extinguished, quenched like a wick: Remember not the former things, nor consider the things of old. Behold, I am doing a new thing; now it springs forth, do you not perceive it? I will make a way in the wilderness and rivers in the desert. The wild beasts will honour me, the jackals and the ostriches; for I give water in the wilderness, rivers in the desert, to give drink to my chosen people, the people whom I formed for myself that they might declare my praise.

2 Cor 1:3-7

Blessed be the God and Father of our Lord Jesus Christ, the Father of mercies and God of all comfort, who comforts us in all our affliction, so that we may be able to comfort those who are in any affliction, with the comfort with which we ourselves are comforted by God. For as we share abundantly in Christ's sufferings, so through Christ we share abundantly in comfort too. If we are afflicted, it is for your comfort and salvation; and if we are comforted, it is for your comfort, which you experience when you patiently endure the same

921

sufferings that we suffer. Our hope for you is unshaken; for we know that as you share in our sufferings, you will also share in our comfort.

Monday Morning Prayer

1 Chron 29:10-13

David blessed the Lord in the presence of all the assembly; and said: Blessed are you, O Lord, the God of Israel our father, for ever and ever. Yours, O Lord, is the greatness, and the power, and the glory, and the victory, and the majesty; for all that is in the heavens and in the earth is yours; yours is the kingdom, O Lord, and you are exalted as head above all. Both riches and honour come from you, and you rule over all. In your hand are power and might; and in your hand it is to make great and to give strength to all. And now we thank you, our God, and praise your glorious name.

2 Thess 3:6-13

Now we command you, brethren, in the name of our Lord Jesus Christ, that you keep away from any brother who is living in idleness and not in accord with the tradition that you received from us. For you yourselves know how you ought to imitate us; we were not idle when we were with you, we did not eat anyone's bread without paying, but with toil and labour we worked night and day, that we might not burden any of you. It was not because we have not that right, but to give you in our conduct an example to imitate. For even when we were with you, we gave you this command: If anyone will not work, let him not eat. For we hear that some of you are living in idleness, mere busybodies, not doing any work. Now such persons we command and exhort in the Lord Jesus Christ to do their work in quietness and to earn their own living. Brethren, do not be weary in well-doing.

Monday Evening Prayer

Jer 17:7-10

Blessed is the man who trusts in the Lord, whose trust is the Lord. He is like a tree planted by water, that sends out its roots by the stream, and does not fear when heat comes, for its leaves remain green, and is not anxious in the year of drought, for it does not cease to bear fruit. The heart is deceitful above all things, and desperately corrupt; who can understand it? I the Lord search the mind and try the heart, to give to every man according to his ways, according to the fruit of his doings.

Col 1:9b-14

We have not ceased to pray for you, asking that you may be filled with the knowledge of his will in all spiritual wisdom and understanding, to lead a life worthy of the Lord, fully pleasing to him, bearing fruit in every good work and increasing in the knowledge of God. May you be strengthened with all power, according to his glorious might, for all endurance and patience with joy, giving thanks to the Father, who has qualified us to share in the inheritance of the saints in light. He has delivered us from the dominion of darkness and transferred us to the kingdom of his beloved Son, in whom we have redemption, the forgiveness of sins.

Tuesday Morning Prayer

Tob 13:1b-8

Blessed is God who lives for ever, and blessed is his kingdom. For he afflicts, and he shows mercy; he leads down to Hades, and brings up again, and there is no one who can escape his hand. Acknowledge him before the nations, O sons of Israel; for he has scattered us among them. Make his greatness known there, and exalt him in the presence of all the living; because he is our Lord and God, he is our Father for ever. He will afflict us for our iniquities; and again he will show mercy, and will gather us from all the nations among whom you have been scattered. If you turn to him with all your heart and with all your soul, to do what is true before him, then he will turn to you and will not hide his face from you. But see what he will do with you; give thanks to him with your full voice. Praise the Lord of righteousness, and exalt the King of the ages. I give him thanks in the land of my captivity, and I show his power and majesty to a nation of sinners. Turn back, you sinners, and do right before him; who knows if he will accept you and have mercy on you? I exalt my God; my soul exalts the King of heaven, and will rejoice in his majesty. Let all men speak, and give him thanks in Jerusalem.

Rom 13:8-14

Owe no one anything, except to love one another; for he who loves his neighbour has fulfilled the law. The commandments, You shall not commit adultery, You shall not kill, You shall not steal, You shall not covet, and any other commandment, are summed up in this sentence, You shall love your neighbour as yourself. Love does no wrong to a neighbour; therefore love is the fulfilling of the law. Besides this you know what hour it is, how it is full time now for you to wake from sleep. For salvation is nearer to us now than when we first believed; the night is far gone, the day is at hand. Let us then cast off the works of darkness and put on the armour of light; let us conduct ourselves becomingly as in the day, not in revelling and drunkenness, not in debauchery and licentiousness, not in quarrelling and jealousy. But put on the Lord Jesus Christ, and make no provision for the flesh, to gratify its desires.

Tuesday Evening Prayer

Job 5:17-18

Behold, happy is the man whom God reproves; therefore despise not the chastening of the Almighty. For he wounds, but he binds up; he smites, but his hands heal.

1 Jn 3:1-3

See what love the Father has given us, that we should be called children of God; and so we are. The reason why the world does not know us is that it did not know him. Beloved, we are God's children now; it does not yet appear what we shall be, but we know that when he appears we shall be like him, for we shall see him as he is. And every one who thus hopes in him purifies himself as he is pure.

Wednesday Morning Prayer

Judith 16:2-3a

Begin a song to my God with tambourines, sing to my Lord with cymbals. Raise to him a new psalm; exalt him, and call upon his name. For God is the Lord who crushes wars. I will sing to my God a new song:. O Lord, you are great and glorious, wonderful in strength, invincible. Let all your creatures serve you, for you spoke, and they were made. You sent forth your Spirit, and it formed them; there is none that can resist your voice. For the mountains shall be shaken to their foundations with the waters; at your presence the rocks shall melt like wax, but to those who fear you you will continue to show mercy.

1 Pet 1:13-16

Therefore gird up your minds, be sober, set your hope fully upon the grace that is coming to you at the revelation of Jesus Christ. As obedient children, do not be conformed to the passions of your former ignorance, but as he who called you is holy, be holy yourselves in all your conduct; since it is written, You shall be holy, for I am holy.

Wednesday Evening Prayer

Tob 4:16-20

Give of your bread to the hungry, and of your clothing to the naked. Give all your surplus to charity, and do not let your eye begrudge the gift when you made it. Place your bread on the grave of the righteous, but give none to sinners. Seek advice from every wise man, and do not despise any useful counsel. Bless the Lord God on every occasion; ask him that your ways may be made straight and that all your paths and plans may prosper.

Be doers of the word, and not hearers only, deceiving yourselves. For if anyone is a hearer of the word and not a doer, he is like a man who observes his natural face in a mirror; for he observes himself and goes away and at once forgets what he was like. But he who looks into the perfect law, the law of liberty, and perseveres, being no hearer that forgets but a doer that acts, he shall be blessed in his doing.

Thursday Morning Prayer

Jer 31:10-14

Hear the word of the Lord, O nations, and declare it in the coastlands afar off; say, He who scattered Israel will gather him, and will keep him as a shepherd keeps his flock. For the Lord has ransomed Jacob, and has redeemed him from hands too strong for him. They shall come and sing aloud on the height of Zion, and they shall be radiant over the goodness of the Lord, over the grain, the wine, and the oil, and over the young of the flock and the herd; their life shall be like a watered garden, and they shall languish no more. Then shall the maidens rejoice in the dance, and the young men and the old shall be merry. I will turn their mourning into joy, I will comfort them, and give them gladness for sorrow. I will feast the soul of the priests with abundance, and my people shall be satisfied with my goodness, says the Lord.

Rom 2:14-16

When Gentiles who have not the law do by nature what the law requires, they are a law to themselves, even though they do not have the law. They show that what the law requires is written on their hearts, while their conscience also bears witness and their conflicting thoughts accuse or perhaps excuse them on that day when, according to my gospel, God judges the secrets of men by Christ Jesus.

Thursday Evening Prayer

Is 66:1-2

Thus says the Lord: Heaven is my throne and the earth is my footstool; what is the house which you would build for me, and what is the place of my rest? All these things my hand has made, and so all these things are mine, says the Lord. But this is the man to whom I will look, he that is humble and contrite in spirit, and trembles at my word.

1 Pet 1:6-9

In this you rejoice, though now for a little while you may have to suffer various trials, so that the genuineness of your faith, more precious than gold which though perishable is tested by fire, may redound to praise and glory and honour at the revelation of Jesus Christ. Without having seen him you love him; though you do not now see him you believe in him and rejoice with unutterable and exalted joy. As the outcome of your faith you obtain the salvation of your souls.

Friday Morning Prayer

Is 45:15-22

Truly, you are a God who hide yourself, O God of Israel, the Saviour. All of them are put to shame and confounded, the makers of idols go in confusion together. But Israel is saved by the Lord with everlasting salvation; you shall not be put to shame or confounded to all eternity. For thus says the Lord, who created the heavens (he is God!), who formed the earth and made it (he established it; he did not create it a chaos, he formed it to be inhabited!): I am the Lord, and there is no other. I did not speak in secret, in a land of darkness; I did not say to the offspring of Jacob, Seek me in chaos. I the Lord speak the truth, I declare what is right. Assemble yourselves and come, draw near together, you survivors of the nations! They have no knowledge who carry about their wooden idols, and keep on praying to a god that cannot save. Declare and present your case; let them take counsel together! Who told this long ago? Who declared it of old? Was it not I, the Lord? And there is no other god besides me, a righteous God and a Saviour; there is none besides me. Turn to me and be saved, all the ends of the earth! For I am God, and there is no other.

Eph 4:29-32

Let no evil talk come out of your mouths, but only such as is good for edifying, as fits the occasion, that it may impart grace to those who hear. And do not grieve the Holy Spirit of God, in whom you were sealed for the day of redemption. Let all bitterness and wrath and anger and clamour and slander be put away from you, with all malice, and be kind to one another, tender-hearted, forgiving one another, as God in Christ forgave you.

Friday Evening Prayer

Is 45:22-25

Turn to me and be saved, all the ends of the earth! For I am God, and there is no other. By myself I have sworn, from my mouth has gone forth in righteousness a word that shall not return: To me every knee shall bow, every tongue shall swear. Only in the Lord, it shall be said of me, are righteousness and strength; to him shall come and be ashamed, all who were incensed against him. In the Lord all the offspring of Israel shall triumph and glory.

Rom 15:1-3

We who are strong ought to bear with the failings of the weak, and not to please ourselves; let each of us please his neighbour for his good, to edify him.

For Christ did not please himself; but, as it is written, The reproaches of those who reproached you fell on me.

Saturday Morning Prayer

Ex 15:1-18

Then Moses and the sons of Israel sang this song to the Lord, saying: 'I will sing to the Lord, for he has triumphed gloriously; the horse and his rider he has thrown into the sea. The Lord is my strength and my song, and he has become my salvation; this is my God, and I will praise him, my father's God, and I will exalt him. The Lord is a man of war; the Lord is his name. Pharaoh's chariots and his host he cast into the sea; and his picked officers are sunk in the Red Sea. The floods cover them; they went down into the depths like a stone. Your right hand, O Lord, glorious in power, your right hand, O Lord, shatters the enemy. In the greatness of your majesty you overthrow your adversaries; you send forth your fury, it consumes them like stubble. At the blast of your nostrils the waters piled up, the floods stood up in a heap; the deeps congealed in the heart of the sea. The enemy said, I will pursue, I will overtake, I will divide the spoil, my desire shall have its fill of them. I will draw my sword, my hand shall destroy them. You blew with your wind, the sea covered them; they sank as lead in the mighty waters. Who is like you, O Lord, among the gods? Who is like you, majestic in holiness, terrible in glorious deeds, doing wonders? You stretched out your right hand, the earth swallowed them. You have led in your merciful love the people whom you redeemed, you have guided them by your strength to your holy abode. The peoples have heard, they tremble; pangs have seized on the inhabitants of Philistia. Now are the chiefs of Edom dismayed; the leaders of Moab, trembling seizes them; all the inhabitants of Canaan have melted away. Terror and dread fall upon them; because of the greatness of your arm, they are as still as a stone, till your people, O Lord, pass by, till the people pass by whom you have purchased. You will bring them in, and plant them on your own mountain, the place, O Lord, which you have made for your abode, the sanctuary, Lord, which your hands have established. The Lord will reign for ever and ever'.

2 Pet 1:5b-11

Make every effort to supplement your faith with virtue, and virtue with knowledge, and knowledge with self-control, and self-control with steadfastness, and steadfastness with godliness, and godliness with brotherly affection, and brotherly affection with love. For if these things are yours and abound, they keep you from being ineffective or unfruitful in the knowledge of our Lord Jesus Christ. For whoever lacks these things is blind and short-sighted and has forgotten that he was cleansed from his old sins. Therefore, brethren, be the more zealous to confirm your call and election, for if you do this you will never fall; so there will be richly provided for you an entrance into the eternal kingdom of our Lord and Saviour Jesus Christ.

Anthems to the Blessed Virgin,
Latin Plainsong

Alma Redemptoris Mater

Al - ma * Redemptó-ris Ma-ter, quæ pérvi- a cæ- li porta manes, Et stella

ma-ris, succúrre cadénti súrgere qui cu-rat pópu-lo: Tu quæ genu- ís-ti,

na-tú-ra mi-rante, tu-um sanctum Ge-ni-tó-rem: Virgo pri-us ac poster-i-us,

Gabri-é- lis ab o-re sumens illud Ave, pecca-tó-rum mi-se-ré- re.

Ave Regina cælorum

A- ve Re-gí-na cæ-ló- rum, * A-ve Dómi-na Ange-ló-rum: Salve ra-dix, sal-ve

porta, Ex qua mundo lux est orta: Gaude Virgo glo-ri- ó-sa, Su-per omnes

spe-ci-ó-sa: Va-le, o valde de-có- ra, Et pro no- bis Christum ex-ó- ra.

Re-gína cæ- li * lætá-re, al-le-lú- ia: Qui- a quem me-ru-ís-ti   portá-re,

al-le-lú- ia: Re-surré-xit, sic-ut di-xit, alle- lú- ia: O- ra pro no-bis De- um,

alle- lú- ia.

Salve Regina, Simple Tone

Salve Re-gí-na, * ma-ter mi-se-ri-córdi-æ, Vi-ta, dul- cé- do,   et spes nostra,

salve.   Ad te clamámus, éxsu-les, fí-li-i Hevæ. Ad te suspi-rámus, geméntes

et flen-tes in hac lacrimá-rum valle.   E-ia ergo, Advo-cá-ta nostra, illos tu-os

mi-se-ri-córdes ó-cu- los ad nos con-vér-te.   Et Je-sum, be-ne-díctum fructum

ventris tu- i, no-bis post hoc exsí- li- um ostén-de.   O   cle- mens:

O pi- a: O dulcis Virgo Ma- rí- a.

Salve Regina, Solemn Tone

Sal- ve, * Re- gí- na, ma-ter mi- se-ri-córdi- æ: Vi- ta, dulcé- do, et

spes nostra, sal- ve. Ad te clamá- mus, éxsu-les, fí- li- i He- væ.

Ad te suspi-rá- mus, geméntes et flentes in hac lacrimá- rum val- le.

E- ia ergo, Advo-cá- ta nostra, il-los tu- os mi-se- ri-cór-des ócu-los ad nos

convér- te. Et Je-sum, be- ne-dí- ctum fructum ventris tu-i, nobis post hoc

exsí-li- um osténde: O cle-mens: O pi- a: O dulcis * Virgo Marí-a.

ACKNOWLEDGEMENTS

The Editors and Publishers are grateful to the following for permission to reproduce copyright material:

John Blair, for extract from *Saint Frideswide, Patron of Oxford: The earliest texts*, ed. and trans. John Blair (Perpetua Press, 2nd ed., 2004).

Brepols, for extract from *Writing the Wilton Women. Goscelin's Legend of Edith and Liber confortatorius*, ed. Stephanie Hollis (Turnhout: Brepols, 2004), pp. 40-41

Continuum International Publishing Group, a Bloomsbury Company, for extracts from *The Shape of the Liturgy*, Gregory Dix, (London: Adam and Charles Black, 1982 [1945], 2nd edition), pp. 265-267; Monica Stephens (ed.), *Dialogue of Comfort against Tribulation by Thomas More*,1951, pp. 8-10; Dom Gerard Sitwell OSB (trans.) *The Scale of Perfection by Walter Hilton*,1953, pp. 248-250; C. H. Talbot, *The Anglo-Saxon Missionaries in Germany* 1954, pp. 6-8; *Butler's Lives of the Saints*: October, November, December, ed. Herbert Thurston S J and Donald Attwater IV, (London: Burns & Oates, 1956) pp. 635-636; Geoffrey Wenn ad Adrian Walker (ed. and trans.), *The Mirror of Charity: The Speculum Caritatis of St Ælred of Rievaulx*, 1962, pp. 1-2; Isaac of Stella, Sermons on the Christian Year v. 1, trans. Hugh McCaffrey, (Kalamazoo: MI: Cistercian Publications, 1977) pp. 73, 75-6, 77-8, 79; John of Ford: Sermons on the Song of Songs I, trans. Wendy Mary Beckett, (Kalamazoo: MI: Cistercian Publications, 1977) pp. 239-241; Gilbert of Hoyland: Sermons on the Song of Songs III, trans. Lawrence C. Braceland S J, (Kalamazoo: MI: Cistercian Publications, 1979) pp. 529-530; John of Ford: Sermons on the Song of Songs V, trans. Wendy Mary Beckett, (Kalamazoo: MI: Cistercian Publications, 1983) pp. 98-101, 204-206; The Works of Gilbert of Hoyand IV: Treatises, Epistles and Sermons, trans. Lawrence C. Braceland S J, (Kalamazoo: MI: Cistercian Publications, 1981) pp. 110-111

Darton, Longman & Todd, for extract from *The Blessed Virgin Mary. Essays by Anglican Writers*, ed. E.L. Mascall and H.S. Box (London: Darton, Longman, and Todd, 1963)

Faber & Faber, for extract from *Murder in the Cathedral*, T.S. Eliot (London: Faber & Faber, 1935)

The Friends of Hereford Cathedral, for extract from 'Saint Thomas Cantilupe, Bishop of Hereford. Essays in His Honour', ed. Meryl Jancey (Hereford: Friends of Hereford Cathedral, Publications Committee for the Dean and Chapter, 1982)

Oxford University Press, for extracts from M. Lapidge, *Winchester Studies 4: The Cult of St Swithun*, (Oxford: Clarendon Press, 2003) pp.637-9; *Magna Vita Sancti Hugonis: Volume I: Life of St.Hugh of Lincoln v.1*, ed. Decima L. Douie and D. H. Farmer (Oxford: Clarendon Press, 1985) pp.101-3; texts from the *English Hymnal*, by R.E. Roberts, *EH* 151; Gabriel Gillett *EH* 58; Robert Martin Pope, *EH* 54; Richard Ellis Roberts, *EH* 223; Laurence Housman, *EH* 234, 191; and Athelstan Riley, *EH* 213, 193

Peeters and Prof. R. W. Thomson, for extract from *The Armenian Adaptation of the Ecclesiastical History of Socrates Scholasticus*, trans. and commentary by Robert W. Thomson (Peeters: Leuven, 2001).

Peregrina Publishing, for extract from *Two Mediæval Lives of Saint Winefride*, trans. Robert Pepin and Hugh Feiss (Eugene, OR: Wipf and Stock, 2004 [2000])

Sussex Record Society, for extract from *St Richard of Chichester. The Sources for his Life*, ed. D. Jones (Lewes: Sussex Record Society, 1995)

Taylor & Francis Group, for extracts from *Nicholas Love's 'Mirror of the Blessed Life of Jesus Christ'*, ed. Michael G. Sargent, (New York and London: Garland, 1992)

Application has also been made to the relevant bodies for permission to publish extracts from the following:

The Life of Saint Anselm, Archbishop of Canterbury, by Eadmer, edited with introduction, notes and translation by R. W. Southern (Oxford: Clarendon Press, 1972); *Anselm of Canterbury. The Major Works*. Edited with an Introduction by Brian Davies and G. R. Evans (Oxford: Oxford University Press), 1998); R. Foreville and G. Keir, *The Book of Saint Gilbert* (Oxford: Clarendon Press, 1987); Bede *'Ecclesiastical History of the English People'* trans. Bertram Colgrave (Oxford: Oxford University Press, 2008 [1994]); *'English Works of John Fisher, Bishop of Rochester (1469-1535). Sermons and Other Writings, 1520-1535'*. Edited by Cecilia A. Hart (Oxford: Oxford University Press, 2002); *Adomnan's Life of Columba*, edited with translation and notes by the late Alan Orr Anderson (d.1958) and by Marjorie Ogilvie Anderson, revised by Marjorie Ogilvie Anderson (Oxford: Clarendon Press, 1991); *William of Malmesbury, Saints' Lives. Lives of Saints Wulfstan, Dunstan, Patrick, Benignus and Indract*, by M. Winterbottom and R. M. Thomson (Oxford: Clarendon Press, 2002); *Eadmer of Canterbury, Lives and Miracles of Saints Oda, Dunstan, and Oswald*, edited and translated by Andrew J. Turner and Bernard J. Muir (Oxford: Clarendon Press, 2006); Geoffrey Webb and Adrian Walker (translated and arranged), *The Mirror of Charity. The Speculum Caritatis of Saint Aelred of Rievaulx* (London: Mowbray, 1962); *Thomas More, Dialogue of Comfort against Tribulation, edited by Monica Stevens* (London: Sheed and

Ward, 1986 [1951]); *The Commentary on the Seven Catholic Epistles of Bede the Venerable'* trans. David Hurst (Kalamazoo, MI: Cistercian Publications, 1985); *Richard of St Victor, 'The Twelve Patriarchs. The Mystical Ark. Book Three of The Trinity',* trans. Grover A. Zinn (London: Society for the Promotion of Christian Knowledge, 1979); *'The Cloud of Unknowing'* ed. Clifton Wolters (Harmondsworth: Penguin, 1961) *Richard Rolle, 'The Fire of Love'* ed. Clifton Wolters (London: Penguin, 1988 [1972]); *The Age of Bede* ed. D. H. Farmer (London: Penguin, 2004 [1988]); J. F. Webb *Lives of the Saints* (Harmondsworth: Penguin, 1965) *The Letters of Gregory the Great v.3,* trans. John R. C. Martyn (Toronto: Pontifical Institute of Mediaeval Studies, 2004) *Aldhelm, The Prose Works* trans. Michael Lapidge & Michael Herren (Ipswich: Brewer, 1979); *Austin Farrer: The Essential Sermons,* (London: Society for the Promotion of Christian Knowledge, 1991); *Selected Works of Richard Rolle, Hermit,* ed. G. C. Heseltine (d.1980) (London: Longmans, Green 1930); *Abbo of Fleury's Life of Saint Edmund,* trans. Kenneth Cutler: http://www.fordham.edu/Halsall/source/870abbo-edmund.asp; *Julian of Norwich, Showings,* trans. Edmund Colledge and James Walsh (New York: Paulist, 1978); Arthur Michael Ramsey, *The Resurrection of Christ. A Study of the Event and its meaning for the Christian Faith* (London: Collins, 1965 [1961], 2nd edition); *The Prayers and Meditations of Saint Anselm with the Proslogion* trans. Sister Benedicta Ward (London: Penguin, 1988 [1973]); *Saint John Fisher: 'Exposition of the Seven Penitential Psalms'* ed. Anne Barbeau Gardiner (San Francisco: Ignatius Press 1998); *Thomas More, 'The Supplication of Souls...',* ed. Eileen Morris (London: Primary Publications 1970); *Matthew Paris: 'The Life of Saint Edmund',* trans. C.H. Lawrence (London: Sandpiper 1999); Francis Rice *'The Hermit of Finchale'* (Durham: Pentland Press 1994).

INDEX

INDEX OF CELEBRATIONS

The following index contains those celebrations and saints for which propers are provided in this Customary.

Alphabetical Index of the Feasts of Our Lord Jesus Christ

Annunciation, 25 March, 481
Ascension, 346
Baptism, 233
Body and Blood (Corpus Christi), 374
Easter Sunday, 317
Epiphany, 226
Exaltation of the Holy Cross (Holy Cross Day), 14 September, 527
Holy Family of Jesus, Mary, and Joseph, 202
Holy Name of Jesus, 3 January, 207
Kingship, 451
Presentation, 2 February, 236
Sacred Heart, 382
Transfiguration, 6 August, 511
Trinity Sunday, 371

Alphabetical Index of the Feasts of Our Lady

Assumption, 15 August, 517
Immaculate Conception, 8 December, 460
Holy Name, 12 September, 526
Mother of God, 1 January, 204
Nativity, 8 September, 524
Presentation, 21 November, 548
Visitation, 31 May, 491
Walsingham, 24 September, 621

Cyril and Methodius, 14 February, 476

David, 1 March, 563
Dedication of the Lateran Basilica 9 November, 389
Dominic, 8 August, 515
Dominic of the Mother of God, 26 August, 607
Dunstan, 19 May, 580

Edith of Wilton, 16 Sepember, 618
Edmund Campion, 1 December, 654
Edmund of Abingdon, 16 November, 644
Edmund the Martyr, 20 November, 651
Edward the Confessor, 13 October, 633
Elizabeth of Hungary, 18 November, 548
English Martyrs, 4 May, 577
Ethelburga, 11 October, 630
Etheldreda (Audrey), 23 June, 598

Francis de Sales, 24 January, 472
Francis of Assisi, 4 October, 535
Frideswide, 19 October, 634

George, 23 April, 573
Gilbert of Sempringham, 4 February, 561
Godric of Finchale, 21 May, 583
Gregory the Great, 3 September, 612

Helena, 21 May, 582
Hilary, 13 January, 470
Hilda, 17 November, 649
Holy Innocents, 28 December, 467
Hugh of Lincoln, 17 Novmber, 647

Ignatius, 17 October, 536
Irenaeus, 28 June, 499

James, 25 July, 507
John the Apostle, 27 December, 465
John the Apostle in Eastertide (*formerly St John ante Portam Latinam*), 6 May, 578
John Chrysostom, 13 September, 526

Index of Other Texts and Services